AF754780

The Emerald Handbook of Women and Entrepreneurship in Developing Economies

Since my original work in female entrepreneurship in the United States, one of the first academic articles on the topic, which was followed by numerous articles focusing on female entrepreneurs in various countries throughout the world and one book on the topic, I have concluded that the best outcomes occur when a strong, effective private sector of female entrepreneurs occurs. I commend the contributors of this work on women entrepreneurship in developing economies as they address an area that has not received the attention that has occurred in developed economies. After providing the reader with a conceptual understanding of the topic as well as gender differences and diversity, the book focuses on aspects of women entrepreneurs in specific countries (Latin America, Gulf Cooperation Council (GCC), and Kuwait, China, Kosovo, Modern Persian, Afghanistan, Iran, Turkey, the MENA and Nordic regions, and Pakistan). I know that as you read this book will appreciate and gain valuable insights on the role that over 163 million women entrepreneurs play in developing economies worldwide.

–Robert D. Hisrich, PhD
Bridgestone Professor of International Business,
Director of the Global Management Center
Kent State University (USA)

This is a definitive contribution to our understanding of gender and entrepreneurship. Rezaei and his collaborators offer the first comprehensive assessment of the role of women in self-employment and business formation in less developed countries. Of special interest is their focus on the relationship between women's economic activity and institutions. The book weaves a rich tapestry in which women come alive as agents of their own destiny, devising survival strategies but also ways to enhance businesses as they interact, often through contestation, with imperfect institutions. This is the best available portrayal of a subject as significant as it is timely.

–Patricia Fernández-Kelly, Professor of Sociology,
Princeton University

This book led by Shahamak Rezaei made an important contribution to the important research field of women entrepreneurship and emerging economies. The wide geographical coverage shows the prevailing issues and challenges that women entrepreneurs encounter in developing and growing their ventures. I highly recommend this book to students of entrepreneurship, international business, public policy, and organization studies.

–Prof. Dr. Yipeng Liu FAcSS
Professor in Management and Organisational Studies
Henley Business School
University of Reading, UK
Founding Director, China Management and Global Business

The Emerald Handbook of Women and Entrepreneurship in Developing Economies provides an insightful and complete review of all important aspects of female entrepreneurship in the setting of a developing country. The book investigates this increasingly important phenomenon from individual and institutional point of view. The reader will be able to grasp the motivation, main challenges, barriers, drivers, and opportunities for female entrepreneurs in certain developing economies of the Middle East and Northern Africa, Latin America, Europe, and Asia. Finally, the book provides significant review of the challenges imposed by COVID-19 pandemic on business activity of women entrepreneurs. Ultimately, the literature in this area gains valuable, multicultural, and contemporary contribution with this title.

–Dr. Vladimir Dzenopoljac
American University of the Middle East, Kuwait

Women's entrepreneurship is a rapidly growing phenomenon in developing economies. With the endless effort of the authors and editors during the COVID-19 pandemic, this book suggests a comprehensive analysis of the challenges and opportunities women entrepreneurs encounter in the process of entrepreneurship and, more importantly, how they emancipate in a dynamic environment full of uncertainties and gender disparities. Indeed, women entrepreneurs, experts, and policymakers can enjoy this research as it provides a foundation for understanding this phenomenon from multiple perspectives. This collection will be a valuable reference for students, educators, policymakers, and entrepreneurs.

–Dr. Ying Chen
School of Economics, Fujian Normal University, China

The Emerald Handbook of Women and Entrepreneurship in Developing Economies

EDITED BY

SHAHAMAK REZAEI

Roskilde University, Denmark

JIZHEN LI

Tsinghua University, China

SHAYEGHEH ASHOURIZADEH

Tsinghua University, China

VELAND RAMADANI

South East European University, North Macedonia

And

SHQIPE GËRGURI-RASHITI

American University of the Middle East, Kuwait

emerald PUBLISHING

United Kingdom – North America – Japan – India – Malaysia – China

Emerald Publishing Limited
Howard House, Wagon Lane, Bingley BD16 1WA, UK

First edition 2021

Copyright © 2021 by Emerald Publishing Limited

Reprints and permissions service
Contact: permissions@emeraldinsight.com

No part of this book may be reproduced, stored in a retrieval system, transmitted in any form or by any means electronic, mechanical, photocopying, recording or otherwise without either the prior written permission of the publisher or a licence permitting restricted copying issued in the UK by The Copyright Licensing Agency and in the USA by The Copyright Clearance Center. Any opinions expressed in the chapters are those of the authors. Whilst Emerald makes every effort to ensure the quality and accuracy of its content, Emerald makes no representation implied or otherwise, as to the chapters' suitability and application and disclaims any warranties, express or implied, to their use.

British Library Cataloguing in Publication Data
A catalogue record for this book is available from the British Library

ISBN: 978-1-80071-327-7 (Print)
ISBN: 978-1-80071-326-0 (Online)
ISBN: 978-1-80071-328-4 (Epub)

Printed and bound by CPI Group (UK) Ltd, Croydon, CR0 4YY

ISOQAR
REGISTERED
Certificate Number 1985
ISO 14001

ISOQAR certified Management System, awarded to Emerald for adherence to Environmental standard ISO 14001:2004.

INVESTOR IN PEOPLE

Contents

Part 2: Institutions, History, Culture as Catalysator or Blockage for Woman Entrepreneurship

About the Contributors

Nur İlkay Abacı is a PhD Research Assistant in the subdepartment of Agricultural Policy and Extension in the Department of Agricultural Economics, Faculty of Agriculture, Ondokuz Mayıs University, Samsun, Turkey. She got MSc about Rural Women Entrepreneurship from Tokat Gaziosmanpaşa University. She did her PhD from Agricultural Policy and Extension Department of Ondokuz Mayis University, Samsun. She PhD thesis was about "Farmers' Decision Making Process on Product Pattern: The Case of Vegetable Growers in Bafra District of Samsun Province of in Turkey." She has nine years professional experience and conducted research in rural women entrepreneurship, factors affecting microcredit adoption by rural women, organic agriculture, and good agriculture. She has also worked as a researcher in projects such as TUBITAK, BAP, DOKAP in Turkey. She is also an academic advisor in a student project.

Zeynab Aeeni holds a PhD in Entrepreneurship from University of Tehran, and currently, she is a Lecturer of Entrepreneurship at Kurdistan University, Iran. Zeynab is interested in researching entrepreneurship, institutions, gender, and sustainability. Zeynab formerly has published in *Journal of Entrepreneurship in Emerging Economies*, *MENA Journal of Cross-Cultural Management*, and *European Research on Management, Business and Economics.*

Abdulbari Ahmadzai is an Assistant Professor at Kabul University, Faculty of Economics. Previously, Assistant Professor at Jahan University, Faculty of Economics. In addition, from 2014 to 2016, he served as tax vocational trainer and audit general manager in the Ministry of finance. He optioned MA in Economics from Yamaguchi University, Japan and a Bachelor in Economics from Herat University, Afghanistan. His research interest is in macroeconomics, public finance, and entrepreneurship. He has researched in "Factors, which have impact on Households income in Paktia province" and "The impact of tax audit on tax compliance and revenue generation in Afghanistan."

Ahmet Akin received his PhD in Finance from Istanbul University, Turkey. He gained research experience as a visiting scholar in the School of Management at Syracuse University, US. He served at several universities in different countries. He most recently worked as an Associate Professor of Finance at the American University of the Middle East, Kuwait. He has published in leading business journals including *Emerging Markets Finance and Trade*, *International Business Review*, and *Journal of International Studies*. His research interests include firm performance, capital structure, corporate social responsibility, market risk assessment, bankruptcy estimation, and behaviors of investors.

Dr Huda Al Matroushi is a Member of the Abu Dhabi Business Women Council, Owner and Chairman of Ancestors Heritage Factory, and Partner in Food and Beverage (Saj Al Feerej, Chocolate Republic, Salad Boutique, and Baeet Omai) and the founder of the Emarat Al Mutakamela for retired people. She is a Doctoral Graduate of the College of Business, Abu Dhabi University (ADU).

José Ernesto Amorós is Professor and Doctoral Programs Director at EGADE Business School, Tecnológico de Monterrey, Mexico. Until December 2015, he was the Executive Director of the Entrepreneurship Institute at Universidad del Desarrollo, Chile. He holds a PhD in Management Sciences from ESADE Business School. He has a Bachelor's Degree in Business Administration and MSc in Marketing from Tecnológico de Monterrey, Mexico. He is a Member of several academic organizations and VP of Iberoamerican Academy of Management. His research interests are entrepreneurship and competitiveness, high growth new business, entrepreneurship, and gender and corporate entrepreneurship.

Zahra Arasti is an Associate Professor of Entrepreneurship at the University of Tehran. Her research and teaching span women's entrepreneurship, social entrepreneurship, and entrepreneurship education programs. She publishes in premier journals, in English, French, and Persian.

Shayegheh Ashourizadeh is a Research Fellow at the Research Center of Technological Innovation at Tsinghua University, China. She received her Postdoc in Entrepreneurship and Business in 2020 from the School of Economics and Management, Tsinghua University. She employs quantitative and qualitative research methodologies to scrutinize small business and entrepreneurship phenomena and better understand the economic decision-making, psychological and institutional underpinnings. She has presented her works at international conferences, including AoM, RENT, Babson, and Druid. Her recent works are published in international journals, including the *International Entrepreneurship and Management Journal, European Journal of International Management, International Journal of Business and Globalization, International Journal of Entrepreneurship and Small Business, and Gender in Management.*

Neda Bahmani graduated from the Faculty of Entrepreneurship, University of Tehran. Her research interest is women's entrepreneurship and entrepreneurship education programs. She designs entrepreneurship programs at Hormozgan Science and Technology Park (Iran).

Radoslav Baltezarevic is an Associate Professor in Marketing, Communication, and Media at the Cyprus International Institute of Management, Nicosia, Cyprus. He worked before that as a HOD and Professor in Marketing, Communication and Media at the College for Communications in Belgrade. Since 2018, he has been an Academic Member of Athens Institute for Education, and prior to that, he worked as an Associate Professor at the University College of Bahrain, Assistant Professor at the American University of the Middle East in

Kuwait, and Assistant Professor at the Faculty of Business Economy and Entrepreneurship in Belgrade. He is a well-rounded researcher with nearly 90 publications, published in national and international journals and scientific conferences.

Elda Barron is an Assistant Professor and Researcher of Entrepreneurship and Innovation at Universidad de Monterrey (Mexico). She holds a PhD in Business Administration from EGADE Business School, Tecnologico de Monterrey. Her research interests include Science-based Entrepreneurship and Entrepreneurship Education. Also, she is a Consultant and Entrepreneurship Mentor.

Nicia Raies Moreira de Souza is Social Scientist with master's and doctorate in Sociology from the Federal University of Minas Gerais, is a Researcher at João Pinheiro Foundation since 1994, has experience in research management households and data analysis, and works in the area of inequality and social stratification studies; labor market, youth, and gender.

Kürşat Demiryürek is a Professor in Ondokuz Mayıs University (OMU), Samsun, Turkey. He got BSc on Agricultural Economics and MSc on Rural Distance Education both from Ankara University, PhD from Agricultural Extension and Rural Development Department of Reading University, England. He has professional experiences in rural extension, innovation systems, social network analysis, organic agriculture, rural distance education, and entrepreneurships, and worked in several FAO, UNDP, WB, and EU projects. He is an Editor of *Journal of Agricultural Extension and Rural Development* and also established préincubation and informatics centers for entrepreneurship and coordinated entrepreneurship and innovation programmes at OMU. More info available at: https://personel.omu.edu.tr/en/kursatd, https://www.researchgate.net/profile/Kursat_Demiryurek

Dr Sherine Farouk joined the faculty of the College of Business at ADU in 2007. Before joining ADU, she was the Assistant Professor at the London School of Economics and Arab Academy for Science and Technology. Dr Sherine taught training courses in Accounting, Finance, and Management fields in many organizations worldwide. Sherine received the "Best Paper Award" in different international conferences for her research. She has a vibrant and high ranked intellectual contribution in the area of Accounting, Finance, Sustainability, and Innovation. Dr Sherine is also part of the editorial board of different Scientific Journals.

Amir Forouharfar received his Bachelor's Degree in English Language and Literature from Arak University. He graduated as an honor student both for a Master's Degree in Entrepreneurship Management and a PhD in Public Administration from University of Sistan and Baluchestan. His main areas of research are entrepreneurship, organization theory, public administration, and philosophy. His key areas of expertise include strategic entrepreneurship, organization theory development, and philosophical epistemology. Dr Forouharfar has over 30 fully refereed articles in prestigious journals, conferences, and books. Currently, he is coediting several book titles on strategic entrepreneurship and COVID-19 repercussions in state administration with Springer.

Shqipe Gërguri-Rashiti is an Associate Professor at the American University of the Middle East, Kuwait – currently serving as the Dean of the College of Business Administration. Shqipe has very diverse education background in different international institutions which can be a great asset for an academic, with excellent communication, decision-making, planning, and organizing skills with strong touch of personal and professional integrity. She has a unique experience in living and working in diverse cultural environments worldwide. Her research interests are on female entrepreneurship, innovation, technology, and strategic management based on which she has written and coauthored papers focused in these areas. She published research articles in journals such as *Strategic Change: Briefings in Entrepreneurial Finance* (UK), *European Journal of Social Sciences* (UK), and *International Bulletin of Business Administration* (UK).

Fauzia Jabeen is a Professor of Management at the College of Business at Abu Dhabi University, UAE. She has published in leading journals like *International Journal of Hospitality Management, Knowledge Management Research & Practice, Journal of Cleaner Production, Food Quality and Preferences, International Journal of Productivity and Performance Management, International Journal of Organizational Analysis, Gender in Management: An International Journal.* She has been honored with the "Outstanding Paper Award" and "Highly Commended Paper" in the 2018 and 2019 Emerald Literati Awards, Abu Dhabi University Research Fellow Award 2018. She can be reached at fauzia.jabeen@adu.ac.ae.

Ali Kahramanoğlu works as an Assistant Professor at Ondokuz Mayıs University, Bafra Faculty of Business Administration. He received his PhD in accounting and finance. He teaches undergraduate and graduate courses in the field of entrepreneurship. His main areas of expertise are accounting, finance, banking, and insurance, and he is engaged in academic studies in entrepreneurship and innovation.

Kaltrina Kajtazi holds the position of Lecturer in the Department of Business and Management at the Universum College in Prishtina, Kosovo. In terms of her education, she completed her Bachelor Studies at the University of Prishtina, in the Department of Management and Informatics, Faculty of Economics, with a maximum average, being selected the most distinguished student of the generation. She obtained a Master's Degree in Human Resource Management from City College, the International Faculty of the University of Sheffield, in Thessaloniki, Greece. She is currently pursuing a PhD in Business Administration at the South East European University in Tetovo, North Macedonia.

Hiroko Kawamorita is a Lecturer of Entrepreneurship, as well as creating and implementing international projects at Ondokuz Mayıs University. Her research interests include Entrepreneurial University, Media Entrepreneurship, and Rural Women Entrepreneurship. She holds a Master of Business Administration from Cardiff Metropolitan University, UK, studied and worked in different countries for over 20 years including Italy, Iran, Turkey, Jordan, Maldives, Tunisia, Malta, and Japan. She is the Editor in Chief for *International Journal of Economics &*

Strategic Management of Business Process, as well as the *International Journal of Business & Economic Strategy*. She was recently appointed as an academic coordinator at Global Education Career Center, UK.

Piotr Kwiatek is the Head of Marketing Department at American University of the Middle East (Kuwait) and a former member of the Faculty of Management at Poznan University of Economics and Business (Poland). He holds the Certified Management and Business Educator (Chartered ABS) qualification and graduated Artificial Intelligence and Machine Learning program at McCombs Business School (University of Texas at Austin). His research concentrates on customer relationship management, loyalty programs, and sales management. He authored over 50 articles in refereed journals, and recognized business outlets. Piotr is a cofounder of Global Sales Science Institute and Centrum B2B.

Jizhen Li is the Professor of Innovation and Entrepreneurship Management at Tsinghua University School of Economics and Management (SEM). He is also the Associate Dean of Tsinghua SEM. He holds a PhD (2002) in Management Science, a MA in Management Science, and BE (1997) both in Automobile Engineering and Industrial Engineering from the Tsinghua University. He visited MIT Sloan School of Management as an International Faculty Fellow for half a year in 2006. He teaches courses such as Management of Technological Innovation, Innovation Research Seminar, Technological Entrepreneurship, and Project Management. His research interests include management of technological innovation, strategic management, and project management. As Principal Investigator, he has finished or is working on many projects, including six research projects funded by the National Science Foundation (NSF) of China. His research has appeared in *Administrative Science Quarterly*, *Information and Management*, *Journal of Management*, *Research Policy*, *R&D Management*, and *Strategic Management Journal*.

Ziyu Long (PhD, Purdue University) is an Assistant Professor of Organizational Communication in the Department of Communication Studies at Colorado State University, US. Her research interests include career, entrepreneurship, work–life negotiation, and workplace resistance and resilience. Her work has appeared in such outlets as *Management Communication Quarterly*, *Journal of Applied Communication*, *Gender, Work & Organization*, *Journal of Business and Technical Communication*, *Journal of Business and Entrepreneurship*, as well as a number of edited books and conference proceedings.

Denise Helena França Marques is an economist, PhD in demography and Researcher at João Pinheiro Foundation (FJP), Brazil. She has experience in the areas of social indicators, human development, data analysis, components of demographic dynamics and labor market. She is currently Principal Research Coordinator of the Population Studies Center of Fundação João Pinheiro and member of the Brazilian Association of Population Studies.

Salman Bashir Memon, PhD, is Chairman of the Department of Business Administration at Shaheed Benazir Bhutto University, Shaheed Benazirabad. His current research interests include knowledge management, work–life balance, workplace diversity, work design, mixed-methods research, and structural equation models. He earned his doctoral degree in management science from Queen Margaret University in Musselburgh, Scotland.

Meisam Modarresi is an Assistant Professor of Entrepreneurship at University of Semnan. He received his PhD and Master's Degree in entrepreneurship from the University of Tehran. His research interests include Academic Entrepreneurship, Women Entrepreneurship, and Home Business. Dr Modarresi's research has been published in several peer-reviewed journals including *Gender in Management* and *International Journal of Gender and Entrepreneurship*. He also has several published books and book chapters in Persian.

Zabihullah Modaser is Associate Professor at Faculty of Economics, Kabul University since 2001. He obtained his Master's Degree of Art in Development Management from Ruhr University Bochum – Germany. His Bachelor's is in economics from Kabul University. Currently, he is working on his PhD in philosophy of accounting in International Islamic University of Malaysia. Beside academic tasks, Mr. Modaser has practical experience in management, accounting, and finance since he worked with international NGOs such as USAID. His some papers are published in academic magazine of economics faculty.

Dr Moza Tahnoon Al Nahyan is a Professor of Management at the College of Business at ADU, where she teaches management principles to business students. She has published her research works in international refereed journals and has received the "best paper award" in international conferences. She is also an entrepreneur and philanthropist and is known for her various charitable activities in the community.

Ahsanullah Mohsen is Assistant Professor at Kabul University, Faculty of Economics. Previously, he was Assistant Professor in Economics Department and head of research and publication committee at the faculty of Economics, Kardan University. Previously, he worked as academic vice chancellor at Jahan University, Kabul. He obtained Master of Science in Management and Economics from Ruhr University Bochum, Germany and a Bachelor in Business Management from Goa University, India. "Technical Efficiency of Fruit Production in Afghanistan" and Employee participation in decision-making and its effect on job satisfaction are his recent published article in IEE, Ruhr University Bochum, and *Asian Journal of Technology Management*, respectively. Furthermore, he is the coauthor of a book chapter "Entrepreneurship in Emerging Economies: A Contextualized Approach (Edward Elgar Publishing)."

Stavros Papakonstantinidis is an Associate Professor at the American University of the Middle East in Kuwait with more than 15 years of multicultural academic and professional experience in strategic communications, public relations, and advertising. He is a published author of two books in New York, multiple peer-reviewed journal papers and book chapters, and an appointed researcher and country expert for labor market studies conducted by Cedefop and Eurostat. He is a Doctor of Social Sciences from the University of Leicester, UK, specializing in Social Media Recruiting and Digital Natives. He holds an MSc in Strategic Communication from Ithaca College and a BA in Organizational Communication from the State University of New York, US.

Veland Ramadani is a Professor of Entrepreneurship and Family Business at the Faculty of Business and Economics, South East European University, North Macedonia. His research interests include entrepreneurship, small business management, and family businesses. He authored or coauthored around 140 research articles, 11 textbooks, and 18 edited books. He has published in *Journal of Business Research, International Entrepreneurship and Management Journal, International Journal of Entrepreneurial Behavior & Research, Technological Forecasting and Social Change*, among others. Dr Ramadani is Editor-in-Chief of the Journal of Enterprising Communities (JEC). He has received the Award for Excellence 2016 – Outstanding Paper by Emerald Group Publishing. In addition, Dr Ramadani was invited as a keynote speaker in several international conferences and as a guest lecturer by President University, Indonesia and Telkom University, Indonesia. In 2017, he was appointed as a member of the Supervisory Board of Development Bank of North Macedonia, where for ten months served as an acting Chief Operating Officer (COO) as well.

Shahamak Rezaei obtained his PhD in Business Administration, with focus on Network Theory and Entrepreneurship, from the University of Southern Denmark. He is currently Associate Professor at the Department of Social Sciences and Business, Roskilde University, Denmark. He consults Nordic Governments (Nordic Council of Ministers) and international organizations (OECD, EU REA). Further, he is affiliated with Sino-Danish Center (SDC) for Education and Research, which is the flagship in Science Diplomacy between the Danish government and the Chinese government. In his SDC activities, he focuses on "Innovation Management" research groups where he since 2010 has been conducting research and heading research teams between Chinese and Danish scholars. He is also affiliated as Non-Resident Research Associate at Princeton University, Office of Population Research (OPR), Center for Migration and Development (CMD), where he collaborates with colleagues at Princeton on STEM (Science, Technology, Engineering, and Math) – Migration and Global Talent Mobility. He is the winner of "Danske Bank" 2014 award in "Social Innovation & Social Entrepreneurship" (September 19, 2014). He has also been appointed as one of the most influential persons in immigration and integration issues in Denmark in the magazine *EUROMAN* (February 2006, p. 49). Dr Rezaei's research focuses on Transnational Knowledge Transfer, Migration, Global Entrepreneurship, Transnational Entrepreneurship, and Diaspora Entrepreneurship. He is Research Coordinator for the research project "DiasporaLink," financed by the European Commission (EU REA) under "Horizon 2020 – RISE Program."

Sareh Rotabi is an Executive Manager of Investor Relations and Development at Human Soft Holding Company in Kuwait. She is an experienced economist with a demonstrated history of working in Higher Education, management and financial services. She has participated in several international and domestic conferences as well as an academic student exchange program in France. Her research interests are Macroeconomics and Macroeconomic policies, Entrepreneurship, and Happiness.

Linda Elizabeth Ruiz is a Professor in the Business School at Tecnologico de Monterrey in Mexico. She holds a PhD in Business Administration. Her central area of study is oriented to the entrepreneurial and innovative behavior that occurs within established organizations. She has deepened to study the influence of external factors over the activity. She is particularly interested in the study of entrepreneurial behavior from a gender perspective. Moreover, she seeks to analyze the implications of the activity over the regions. She has collaborated with researchers in other areas like entrepreneurial education and regional development.

Mehrzad Saeedikiya is based at the Center of Future Enterprise (CFE) at Queensland University of Technology, Brisbane, Australia. Formerly, he has had some teaching and research positions at University of Tehran, University of Milan, and Tsinghua University. Mehrzad is interested in researching entrepreneurship and innovation in the context of institutions. He has published some piece of research in *European Journal of International Management*, *Journal of Entrepreneurship in Emerging Economies* and *MENA Journal of Cross-Cultural Management*.

Yashar Salamzadeh is a PhD scholar in Human Resources Management and is a Senior Lecturer in Graduate School of Business at Universiti Sains Malaysia. He has published more than 100 research articles in international and national journals and conferences. He has the experience of eleven years teaching in MBA and Master of management courses in five different universities. He has supervised more than 70 graduate students (On MBA and Master level) in their thesis and dissertation and is supervising 8 PhD and DBA students as well. He has developed many managerial workshops on leadership, social entrepreneurship, HRM, Business models in different countries such as Iran, Turkey, Russia, Malaysia, Hungary and UK. He has worked as a project management in many national and international research projects. He has the experience of five years management consultancy for different public and private organizations on Leadership, Organizational restructuring, EFQM, Culture, HRM systems, Organizational behavior. He also has cooperated in more than twenty international journals as an editorial board member and review board member. He is also an EFQM auditor. He has served GSB as Head of "Global Strategy and Organizational Behavior" research cluster since 2018. He is leading the micro-credential initiative of GSB as well. His fields of interest include entrepreneurship, Entrepreneurial Universities, Leadership and digital leadership, business models, strategic management, green business and CSR, HRM (HCM) and networked organizations. Yashar can be contacted using below emails: yashar@usm.my or yasharsalamzadeh@gmail.com.

Aidin Salamzadeh is an Assistant Professor at the Faculty of Management, University of Tehran. He has several publications in journals such as *Journal of Economic Psychology*, *Journal of Enterprising Communities*, *Journal of Enterprising Culture*, and *International Journal of Entrepreneurship and Small Business*. His main areas of interest are contextual entrepreneurship, start-ups, new venture creation, media entrepreneurship, and social entrepreneurship. He serves as an editor, a member of the editorial board of journals such as *The Bottom Line* (Emerald), and *SAGE Open* (Sage), as well as a reviewer in a series of distinguished international journals such as *Baltic Journal of Management*, *Journal of Small Business and Enterprise Development* (Emerald), *Journal of Cleaner Production* (Elsevier), *Canadian Journal of Administrative Sciences* (Wiley), and *Economic Research* (Taylor & Francis). He is also a member of the European SPES Forum (Belgium), the Asian Academy of Management (Malaysia), Institute of Economic Sciences (Serbia), and Ondokuz Mayis University (Turkey).

Dr Claire Seaman holds the Chair in Enterprise and Family Business at Queen Margaret University in Edinburgh, Scotland. She has published extensively in the field of family businesses research, in the UK, New Zealand, Canada, Asia, Jordan, and Latin America, and is a regular contributor to family business conferences worldwide. Her books include *Corporate Citizenship* and the *Family Business* (Greenleaf, an imprint of Routledge, forthcoming) and *The Modern Family Business*, published by Palgrave McMillan. Claire maintains close links with the business community and business organizations such as Family Business United Scotland and local economic development agencies. She is a frequent speaker at gatherings of family businesses and professional advisors. This interaction enables her to share insights from evidence-based research with practitioners, while ensuring that her research focuses on areas of importance to the family business and entrepreneurship communities. Her current research interests include work on family business, business start-up, and entrepreneurship in a variety of contexts and cultures, including work in Scotland, the Basque Region of Spain, Malaysia, Ghana, Jordan, Pakistan, Nepal, and Uzbekistan.

Mohamed M. Sraieb holds a PhD in Economics from the European Center for Advanced Research in Economics and Statistics (ECARES), Université libre de Bruxelles. Mohamed is currently Assistant Professor at American University of the Middle East, Kuwait. Formerly, he was Assistant Professor of Economics at University of Essex, UK. Mohamed is an applied economist. He carries out research at ECARES where he is an associate fellow. His research interests include macroeconomics, international trade, development economics, and quantitative methods. He is particularly interested in exploring the microfoundations of development strategies, trade policies, and environmental negotiations.

Noriyuki Takahashi is a Vice President at Musashi University, Tokyo, Japan. He is also the leader of the GEM Japan team. He obtained his Bachelor of Economics from Keio University, Tokyo, Japan, then a Master of Business Administration from Babson College, Wellesley, US. Besides, he has worked over 20 years at Japan Finance Corporation prior to his Professorship Appointment at the University.

Elnaz Tarzamni is an Independent Researcher in entrepreneurship from the Faculty of Entrepreneurship, University of Tehran, Iran. She is interested in research in the field of women's entrepreneurship.

Serdar Temiz is a Researcher and Lecturer at the Industrial Engineering and Management Division of Uppsala University, Sweden. His research and lectures focus on open innovation, business models, entrepreneurship, and new product development in different industries and contexts.

Hui Zhang is a PhD Candidate in the School of Economics and Management at Nanjing University of Science and Technology, and she was born in Anhui province, China. She has a one-year visiting scholar experience at University of Southern Denmark. Her research interests cover women entrepreneurship and entrepreneurial emotion. Her work has appeared in Chinese management studies and leading Chinese business journals. Moreover, her recent work is being reviewed by Entrepreneurship Theory and Practice.

Chuqing Zhang received her PhD degree from Tsinghua University, P.R. China. Now, she works in Economic Research Institute, Beijing Language and Culture University. Her research interests include project evaluation, technology innovation, and machine learning.

Xiaohu Zhou is a PhD and a Professor of Economics and Management of Nanjing University of Science and Technology, a Professor of Jiangsu Talent Research Institute, and a doctoral tutor. His research interests cover corporate strategic management, entrepreneurial management, and talent management. His works have been published by *Journal of Business Ethics, Chinese Management Studies, Frontiers in Psychology, International Journal of Social Behavior and Personality*. He also published his researches in top Chinese journals.

List of Contributors

Nur İlkay Abacı	Ondokuz Mayıs University, Turkey
Zeynab Aeeni	University of Kurdistan, Iran
Abdulbari Ahmadzai	Kabul University, Afghanistan
Ahmet Akin	American University of the Middle East, Kuwait
Huda Al Matroushi	Abu Dhabi University, UAE
José Ernesto Amorós	Tecnológico de Monterrey, Mexico
Zahra Arasti	University of Tehran, Iran
Shayegheh Ashourizadeh	Tsinghua University, China
Neda Bahmani	Hormozgan Science and Technology Park, Iran
Radoslav Baltezarevic	Cyprus International Institute of Management, Cyprus
Elda Barron	Universidad de Monterrey, Mexico
Nicia Raies Moreira de Souza	João Pinheiro Foundation, Brazil
Kürşat Demiryürek	Ondokuz Mayıs University (OMU), Turkey
Sherine Farouk	Abu Dhabi University, UAE
Amir Forouharfar	University of Sistan and Baluchestan, Iran
Shqipe Gërguri-Rashiti	American University of the Middle East, Kuwait
Benson Honig	McMaster University, Canada
Fauzia Jabeen	Abu Dhabi University, UAE
Ali Kahramanoğlu	Ondokuz Mayıs University, Turkey
Kaltrina Kajtazi	Universum College in Prishtina, Kosovo
Hiroko Kawamorita	Ondokuz Mayıs University, Turkey

Piotr Kwiatek	American University of the Middle East, Kuwait
Jizhen Li	Tsinghua University School of Economics and Management (SEM), China
Ziyu Long	Colorado State University, USA
Denise Helena França Marques	João Pinheiro Foundation (FJP), Brazil
Salman Bashir Memon	Shaheed Benazir Bhutto University, Shaheed Benazirabad, Pakistan
Meisam Modarresi	University of Semnan, Iran
Zabihullah Modaser	Kabul University, Afghanistan
Moza Tahnoon Al Nahyan	Abu Dhabi University, UAE
Ahsanullah Mohsen	Kabul University, Afghanistan
Stavros Papakonstantinidis	American University of the Middle East, Kuwait
Veland Ramadani	South East European University, North Macedonia
Shahamak Rezaei	Roskilde University, Denmark
Sareh Rotabi	Human Soft Holding Company, Kuwait
Linda Elizabeth Ruiz	Tecnológico de Monterrey, Mexico
Mehrzad Saeedikiya	Queensland University of Technology, Australia
Yashar Salamzadeh	Universiti Sains Malaysia, Malaysia
Aidin Salamzadeh	University of Tehran, Iran
Claire Seaman	Queen Margaret University, United Kingdom
Mohamed M. Sraieb	American University of the Middle East, Kuwait
Noriyuki Takahashi	Musashi University, Japan
Elnaz Tarzamni	University of Tehran, Iran
Serdar Temiz	Uppsala University, Sweden

Hui Zhang	Nanjing University of Science and Technology, China
Chuqing Zhang	Beijing Language and Culture University, China
Xiaohu Zhou	Nanjing University of Science and Technology, China

Foreword

This handbook makes a valuable contribution by uniquely combining three exciting and relevant arenas of research: (1) entrepreneurship promotion, (2) gender studies, and (3) emergent economies. It is highly relevant to scholars, policymakers, and practitioners, alike. While considerable work has examined these issues separately, the bulk of existing research focuses on advanced economies, and is often phenomenologically driven. This is problematic because institutional and cultural barriers to entrepreneurship, and particularly to women entrepreneurs, often tend to be more constrained in emergent economies. As well, this work arrives during an important time of transition – as the world experiences a global pandemic, the nature of work, as well as previously well-established cultural norms, expectations, and career trajectories are upturned and revised. These transitions present important opportunities for entrepreneurs, particularly more marginalized persons including women, to adapt to new constraints with ingenious and unexpected innovations.

As the work in this handbook illuminates, cultural variations may play a more extensive role in either facilitating or hampering women entrepreneurs than other factors often examined by entrepreneurship scholars, highlighting an important research gap often overlooked in the literature. As well, much scholarship continues to focus on the economic contributions that entrepreneurs make, frequently overlooking their social contributions, a characteristic that has been associated with gender and offers an important distinction when examining issues of community development.

Professor Rezaei and his colleagues have amassed an important contribution to the literature that firmly anchors their work in a reframing of the "entrepreneurship for economic development" narrative. They span multiple levels (e.g. individual and institutional/national) highlighting the need for contextual understanding of these phenomenons. Their focus includes not only life-cycle factors, but also historical, cultural, and regional specificities that provide important generalizable insight when we move outside the heavily research environments of Europe and North America.

Scholars who have worked in entrepreneurship over the past few decades fully recognize the importance of gender studies, including feminist perspectives on social change and development. From a relatively marginalized perspective, the field has grown with important scholarship, including its own prestigious international annual scholarly conference (the Diana International Research Conference, associated with the Diana Project). Much work continues to focus on inequality in advanced economies, including gender biases that impact venture capital and other financial support, industry location, leadership, limited growth and/or market capitalization, and a dearth of suitable role models, particularly in STEM or in fortune 500 companies. However, our knowledge of entrepreneurial pursuits in emergent economies is less complete.

I found the work in this handbook to be both unique and valuable, providing important insights into contexts and regions previously overlooked. How, for example, does entrepreneurship innovation intersect with gender roles? Little is known regarding female entrepreneurship in regions such as Iran, China, and Afghanistan, where exceptional cultural and institutional factors are likely to strongly impact entrepreneurial opportunities for women. This handbook provides an important collection of unique insights, handily collated into one significant volume. I'm certain to utilize this handbook in my own scholarly research as well as in the classroom, and I salute professor Rezaei and his colleagues for carefully providing this important addition to my library shelf. I'm sure you'll agree.

Benson Honig
Teresa Cascioli Chair in Entrepreneurial Leadership
DeGroote School of Business, McMaster University
Hamilton, Ontario, Canada
26, October 2020

Part 1
Conceptual Understanding of Woman Entrepreneurship in Developing Economies

Chapter 1

Women Entrepreneurship Footprints: Some Introductory Reflections from Emerging Economies Prospects

Shahamak Rezaei, Jizhen Li, Shayegheh Ashourizadeh, Veland Ramadani and Shqipe Gërguri-Rashiti

Abstract

Women Entrepreneurship has received increasing attention over the past decade. In particular, a new area dealing with women entrepreneurs in the developing societies. The aim of this study is how is women entrepreneurship in developing economies? More specifically, we are excavating various questions at the individual and institutional level. The results of this study contribute to understanding the importance of the context on women entrepreneurs' activities. Additionally, it systematically provides a comprehensive framework at multilevel analyses to cover all aspects of women entrepreneurship in developing countries. Ultimately, knowing women entrepreneurship in developing countries helps policymakers provide a firm ground for self-employment of women.

Keywords: women entrepreneurship; developing context; culture; entrepreneurship barriers; female entrepreneurial activities; analytical Levels

Introduction

Earlier twenty-first-century scholars have tapped on women entrepreneurship in the United States and Europe (Brush, 1992; De Bruin, Brush, & Welter, 2006; Hughes, Jennings, Brush, Carter, & Welter, 2012). In this regard, publications try to explore women entrepreneurship at the individual, organizational, and environmental levels (Brush, Carter, Gatewood, Greene, & Hart, 2006) and compared women entrepreneurs' resources, such as human and social capital, and their performance with their counterparts (Wadhera & Koreth, 2012). Studies have also investigated the propensity of women engagement in the entrepreneurial

The Emerald Handbook of Women and Entrepreneurship in Developing Economies, 3–12
Copyright © 2021 by Emerald Publishing Limited
All rights of reproduction in any form reserved
doi:10.1108/978-1-80071-326-020211001

process in different countries (Minniti & Nardone, 2007; Terjesen, 2004) and how they overcome barriers to entrepreneurial activities (Fielden & Davidson, 2005). During the last five years, frontiers in women entrepreneurship have noticed the stimulating effect of context and ecosystem on women's entrepreneurial activities (Manolova, Brush, Edelman, Robb, & Welter, 2017). Also, how it may enhance or impede their performance (for example, Guelich, Bullough, Manolova, & Schjoedt, 2021; Birkner, Ettl, Welter, & Ebbers, 2018; Blackburn, Hytti, & Welter, 2015) in developed countries like the United States.

Though the literature has advanced our knowledge in women entrepreneurship in developed countries, there is a paucity of research in developing countries (Yadav & Unni, 2016). There are 137 countries with a GNI of US $11,905 or less that are counted as developing countries and carrying 90%+ of the world's population, and half of this population consists of women. (Singhal & Khadilkar, 2014). Worldwide experience advocates that economic growth will happen through more substantial support for women to contribute to the economy. Thus, it is merit to investigating women entrepreneurship in developing countries for two reasons:

(1) Over 163 million women pursue entrepreneurial activities worldwide (Global Entrepreneurship Monitor, 2017), which shows women entrepreneurs' significant contribution to the economy. Recent reports on women's entrepreneurial endeavors (Global Entrepreneurship Monitor, 2017) have revealed that women's Total Entrepreneurial Activity (TEA) rate has increased in all 74 countries. The Global Entrepreneurship Monitor (GEM) has reported the highest rising-rate women's role in TEA in developing countries by 15.1% in 2017–18. Women have surpassed men's TEA in developing regions such as Asia (Philippines and Vietnam) and Latin America (Mexico and Brazil), where the gender gap is an institutional challenge.
(2) Developing countries are a matter of interest since their context includes traditional, incomplete, and unstable institutions (Gaur, Kumar, & Singh, 2014) that affect entrepreneurial activities and entrepreneurs' behaviors. However, prior research has not unveiled the impact of such institutions on especially women entrepreneurs and how they face various challenges that are different from developed countries (Coad & Tamvada, 2012; Manolova, Carter, Manev, & Gyoshev, 2007). For instance, how women entrepreneurs struggle with these institutions and construct new values and structure in those societies (Ahl, 2006) to achieve success is yet unknown.

However, very few studies have considered this category. One of the closest research studies is the book on Female Entrepreneurship in Transition Economies, edited by Ramadani, Gërguri-Rashiti, and Fayolle (2015). Other works are about solo-country cases; for instance, some scholars have come up to publish books about countries like India (Jamil, 2019), China (Sun & McLean, 2019), and Iran (Sarfaraz, 2017). Though studies have improved our understanding of women entrepreneurship in developing countries, it lacks comprehensive research to give insights into women's entrepreneurial behavior and understanding to policymakers to design and deliver initiatives that truly exploit women entrepreneurs' economic growth potentials.

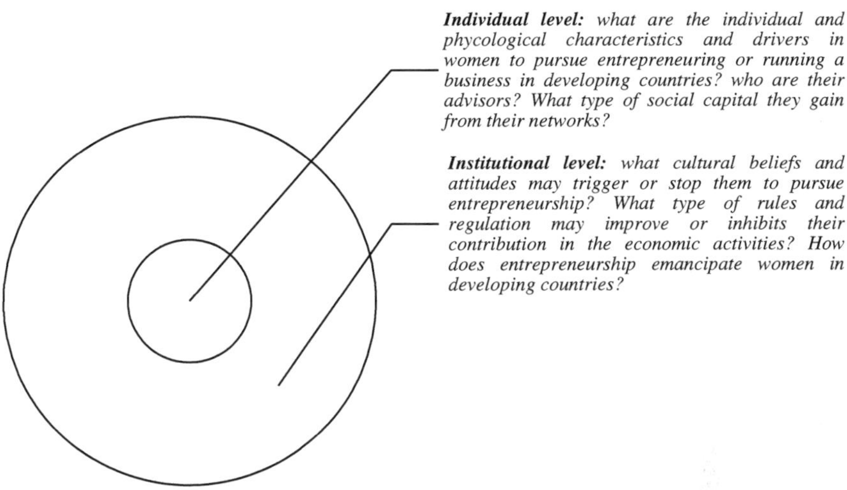

Fig. 1.1. Women Entrepreneurship in Multilevels of Analysis.

Thus, the purpose of this book is to investigate women entrepreneurship in a multilevel analysis. We are about to answer the general research question that *How is women entrepreneurship in developing economies?* More specifically, we are excavating various questions at the individual and institutional level. Fig. 1.1 illustrates some of the specific research questions at each level.

At the individual level, understanding the nature, aspirations, human and social capitals, psychological derivers, and barriers in such societies may help us to explain the high rate of entrepreneurial activities among women in developing countries.

At the institutional level, drawing upon the institutional view (North, 1990), which consists of formal and informal institutions, it is interesting to know how different policies, rules, and regulations in developing countries affect women entrepreneurs' outcomes and overcome difficulties hindering institutions.

We believe that working on women entrepreneurship in developing countries is an excellent opportunity to contribute to this field. First, it sheds light on women entrepreneurship in a new context that has been called for research by scholars in women entrepreneurship (e.g., Jennings, Jennings, & Sharifian, 2016; De Bruin et al., 2006). It also provides an opportunity to comprehensively study women entrepreneurship and enable scholars to compare and contrast among different countries and explain the psychological, sociological, and institutional mechanisms that enhance entrepreneurship among women in these societies.

Second, it systematically provides a comprehensive framework at multilevel analyses to cover all aspects of women entrepreneurship in developing countries. Such a framework provides a vivid picture of women entrepreneurship in developing countries, which can help prospective women entrepreneurship scholars position their research correctly in this area.

Last but not least, this research provides fruitful knowledge for policymakers and practitioners. Knowing women entrepreneurship in developing countries helps policymakers provide the ground for self-employment of women when the unemployment rate is higher for women than men (in 2017, the global unemployment was 6.2% women and 5.5% men) and in times of crises. It is specifically noticeable after the COVID-19 pandemic. Women-dominated industries like day cares, education, and other service industries have been some of the most disrupted, and many working mothers have found their work disrupted to stay home. This has led to an unprecedented shock to women's employment by severe uncertainties regarding when businesses might return to normal operations and whether those jobs and the income they imply might still be there.

Understanding women entrepreneurship in developing countries also assists policymakers both in developed and developing countries. In developing countries, they may become aware of the gender gap in the entrepreneurship ecosystem and introduce better policy practices from developed countries to solve these issues. In developed countries, policymakers may inspire women entrepreneurs in developing countries and find solutions to improve the entrepreneurship rate among women in these societies, declining in recent years (Global Entrepreneurship Monitor, 2017).

Structure of the Book

The Emerald Handbook of Women and Entrepreneurship in Developing Economies covers various topics in women entrepreneurship from the gender perspective and institutional view. It includes understanding women's emancipation and empowerment, gender roles, firm performance, digitalization, barriers, and challenges of existing institutions in developing countries. This book represents a comprehensive state-of-the-art picture of women entrepreneurship issues. It provides significant theoretical and empirical evidence that is likely to offer a brighter view of this area from the gender and institutional view.

This work is an outcome of all contributors' long-lasting effort during one of the rough times of human history (COVID-19 pandemic). It includes contributions of highly reputed authors and experts of developing economies. According to the levels of analyses, this book has been divided into four parts, namely: (1) Conceptual Understanding of Woman Entrepreneurship in Developing Countries; (2) Institutions, History, Culture as catalysator or blockage for Woman Entrepreneurship; (3) Entrepreneurial Ecosystem and Female Digital Entrepreneurship; and (4) Early-stage Female Entrepreneurship, Drivers, and Outcomes.

Part I – *Conceptual Understanding of Woman Entrepreneurship in Developing Countries* – is followed by a chapter about *Entrepreneurship and Innovation Emancipation among Women Entrepreneurs in Developing Countries* that has been prepared by Huda Al Matroushi, Fauzia Jabeen, Sherine Farouk, and MOZA BINT TAHNON BIN MOHAMED ALNAHYAN. It discusses encouraging innovation in Small and Medium Enterprises (SMEs), one of the government's main policy initiatives at the local, regional, and national levels in the United

Arab Emirates (UAE). This study's primary purpose is to explore the innovation characteristics, challenges, and factors influencing innovation in the Emirati female-owned nascent, start-up, and established SMEs. The analysis reveals that respondents believed in a strong vision, education, and risk-taking attitude as an innovative entrepreneur's essential characteristics. This study's findings will help policymakers and business women's councils identify the specific inhibitors and facilitators linked to innovation. The results will help develop various effective policies to promote innovation among Emirati women-owned SMEs.

The next chapter is entitled *Gender Roles in Developing Countries and Women Entrepreneurs' Intention/entry/Business Engagement and Performance* written by Hui Zhang and Xiaohu Zhou. They have conducted a systematic literature review on female entrepreneurship. The authors answer this question of how gender role works in developing countries and especially its influence on female entrepreneurs' intention/entry/business participation and performance. While women entrepreneurship is designated as the new economic growth engine in developing countries, prior research shows how men and women differ in starting a business. Women usually are facing more restrictions on entrepreneurial financing, entrepreneurial growth, and entrepreneurial performance. Gender roles have often explained this, yet there is still a lack of systematic understanding of how gender roles impact women's entrepreneurial processes in developing countries.

In *Gender Diversity, Environmental Performances and the Role of Countries' Development Status* by Mohamed M. Sraieb and Ahmet Akin, they investigate the relationship between gender diversity on corporate boards and firms' environmental performances. The central focus is the extent to which a country's economic status (developed, developing) can shape such a relationship. They found evidence that gender diversity is positively correlated to the environmental performances of firms. Interestingly, this correlation is stronger in developing countries and is also increasing in gender diversity. Such benefits can be a leverage for an efficient implementation of the United Nations Sustainable Development Goals (UN-SDGs), both as gender diversity stands as a goal by itself and facilitates achieving other environmental-related SDGs.

Part II is *Institutions, History, Culture as catalysator or blockage for Woman Entrepreneurship* that is opened up by a chapter about *Female Entrepreneurship in Latin America and the Key Role of Informal Institutions in the Reproduction of Gender Asymmetries* written by Shahamak Rezaei and Denise Helena França Marques. This chapter is a comprehensive overview of institutional factors in Latin America and how such institutions may constrain exploitation opportunities. The literature review showed how informal institutions, impregnated by patriarchal and macho culture, shape and determine gender relations in the world of work in the region, especially in women's business activities. Although the cases presented cannot be generalized to all Latin American countries, they provide a small sample of the obstacles, challenges, and limitations imposed on female entrepreneurs by the social structure and its repeated practices consolidated in Latin American society.

The following chapter, *Women Entrepreneurship in Developing Countries: With Focus on GCC and Kuwait* is contributed by Shqipe Gerguri-Rashiti and Sareh

Rotabi. This chapter defines women entrepreneurship's role in developing countries in general, emphasizing GCC countries. It also introduces trends and challenges women entrepreneurs face, incentives to start their businesses, the support mechanism provided for them, the common conditions for women entrepreneurship, and women entrepreneurs' profiles in the GCC and Kuwait. The chapter also covers the impacts of the COVID-19 crisis on entrepreneurship (SMEs) along with the country policy responses to mitigate these impacts and ends with sharing useful recommendations on what needs to be taken into consideration in the future for the development of women entrepreneurship in general and more specifically within GCC countries and Kuwait.

Ziyu Long authored *Exploring Contextual Influences on Women's Everyday Entrepreneuring: A Case from China*. This chapter uses women entrepreneurs' entrepreneurial experiences in urban China as an empirical case to discuss contextual influences on women's everyday entrepreneurial experience in developing countries. Based on thematic analysis of women's own accounts of their entrepreneurial experiences, four societal influences emerged: (1) pre-entrepreneurial work experience, (2) national entrepreneurial development, (3) cultural values, and (4) gendered work ideology. These influences shaped and were shaped by women's entrepreneurial identities, decisions, and actions in situated contexts.

Linda Elizabeth Ruiz, Elda Barron, and José Ernesto Amorós have studied *The Role of Gender and Institutional Factors for Entrepreneurs and Corporate Entrepreneurs in Latin-American Countries*. Applying the data from the GEM, the Heritage Foundation and the World Bank, the authors attempted to disclose the women entrepreneurs' characteristics and behaviors in 10 Latin American countries. The results show that antecedents of entrepreneurship activity differ by gender. Specifically, the effect is different when analyzing labor regulations. We also find different intensity depending on gender.

The chapter *Women Entrepreneurs and the Challenge of Work-Life Balance: Evidence from Kosovo* is authored by Kaltrina Kajtazi. This chapter aims to answer three fundamental questions: do women entrepreneurs face difficulties in work–life balancing? Do they involve other family members in business operations to help work–life balance? and Is their marital status a factor in work–life balance? Through a qualitative research method, the author has found that most women entrepreneurs face difficulties in work–life balance. However, to overcome this challenge, they engage their family members in business activities. Also, married women, especially those with more than one child, have more difficulties in this aspect than those unmarried.

Amir Forouharfar has contributed to the chapter titled *The Institutional History of Women Entrepreneurship in Modern Persia: A Socio-Historicism Approach*. Through a historical approach, the author explores the gender institutions in Persia. Thus, the chapter first sets the historical context in each period and then sheds light on each period's women's pivotal issues. The undergirding base of the discussions assumes the change in institutions as natural metamorphosis in the animate. Finally, the discussions contribute to the conceptualization of the Institutional Triangulation and in the case of Persia. A cultural-driven triangulation has paved the way to forming a stupendously hegemonic patriarchal and masculine sociopolitical economy in Persia, which has historically affected women's institutionalization, subjugation, subordination, marginalization, socialization, emancipation, and most recently, Islamization phases.

Female Entrepreneurship à Brasileira: Entrepreneurship by Choice or Entrepreneurship by Force? is authored by Denise Helena França Marques, Nicia Raies Moreira de Souza, and Shahamak Rezaei. While the contingent of nascent entrepreneurs was 11.1 million people and in just one year it grew to 390%, there is less attention to women entrepreneurs since in a country like Brazil, transformations brought by innovative thoughts, technological development, and expansion of education are not privileges of the entire population. Therefore, the objective of this work is to present the national reality of female entrepreneurship, contributing with the understanding of who are the Brazilian women entrepreneurs that correspond to *pure* concepts and, therefore, shed light on new studies and research that can contribute with more accurate diagnoses about these women.

Ahsanullah Mohsen, Abdulbari Ahamadzai, and Zabihullah Modaser contributed to *Women Entrepreneurship in Developing Countries: The Context of Afghanistan*. The study comprises and analyzes three levels – individual, societal, and institutional – of women entrepreneurship in Afghanistan. A total number of 104 women entrepreneurs are interviewed and filled questionnaires. The results show the desire for achievement, desire for wealth, and desire for independence are motivational factors for women entrepreneurs. Furthermore, the propensity to risk and locus of control are the psychological drives for women entrepreneurship in Afghanistan.

Meysam Modarresi and Zahra Arasti have elaborated on the *Cultural Challenges of Women Entrepreneurs in Iran*. While they admit numerous difficulties in starting and running a business for women compared to men, the authors emphasize that the cultural context in societies is a significant factor affecting the status of entrepreneurship among Iranian women. Therefore, the present research is an attempt to identify the challenges affecting entrepreneurship among Iranian women. The results obtained from 30 semi-structured interviews with women entrepreneurs and women with entrepreneurial roles showed that sociocultural challenges faced by women entrepreneurs are classified into: "the society's perception of entrepreneurship among women," "women's social security," and "common family norms governing a society."

The last chapter of part II, *Gendered Social Capital in Developing Countries: The Case of Turkey* has been authored by Hiroko Kawamorita, Yashar Salamzadeh, Ali Kahramanoğlu, Kürşat Demiryürek, Nur İlkay Abacı, and Noriyuki Takahashi. This chapter addresses the impact of gendered social capital in developing countries to understand women's entrepreneurship's barriers and opportunities with social capital development. It also examines factors influencing the development of social capital for women and how the identified factors benefit the creation of their entrepreneurial activities. A quantitative methodology shows that social capital strongly impacts women entrepreneurs' entrepreneurial activities in developing countries, especially in Turkey.

Part III – *Entrepreneurial Ecosystem and Female Digital Entrepreneurship* – opens up with a chapter *Digital Natives' Entrepreneurial Mindset: A Comparative*

Study in Emerging Markets by Piotr Kwiatek, Stavros Papakonstantinidis, and Radoslav Baltezarevic. Recent studies conducted in Europe and the Middle East found the growing interest of young entrepreneurs in using social media as a venue for business activities. The Digital Natives, young people who cannot recall their lives without the Internet and digital devices, are thought to be the most entrepreneurial generation so far. In this chapter, the authors take a closer look at the role of gender in entrepreneurship and provide more insights for effective policy-shaping with the Digital Natives in mind.

The following chapter, *Entrepreneurial Ecosystem and Female Digital Entrepreneurship – Lessons to Learn from an Iranian Case Study*, is authored by Aidin Salamzadeh and Veland Ramadani. This chapter provides a better understanding of Iran's multilayered entrepreneurial ecosystem and then elaborates on how female entrepreneurs are positioned in this ecosystem. Digital entrepreneurs are an integral part of this ecosystem, as most of the early achievements are the results of their proactive behaviors. Hopefully, the number of female digital entrepreneurs have increased, and their entrepreneurial activities have profoundly changed the competition scene. Here, six well-known award-winning female digital entrepreneurs are introduced, and their challenges are scrutinized accordingly through narrative research. Finally, the chapter concludes with some remarks and directions for future research.

The last chapter of this Part is *Networking Activity of Female Entrepreneurs Over Time: An Exploratory Case Study on Female Entrepreneurs from Early-Stage to Establishment* by Zahra Arasti, Elnaz Tarzamni, and Neda Bahmani. They have shed a light on the networking activities of female entrepreneurs since the ability to develop and maintain an effective network is an entrepreneurial competency. Thus, a qualitative study was conducted on a sample of Iranian female entrepreneurs. The results of data analysis of 10 semi-structured interviews show a considerable change in networking activity over time. Although the most important role of networking for women entrepreneurs in both early-stage and established businesses is to achieve opportunities, information, and resources. Also, the combination of female entrepreneurs' networks is most male-dominated.

Part IV is entitled *Early-stage Female Entrepreneurship, Drivers, and Outcomes*. It investigates the individual factors' impact on entrepreneurship behavior. The first chapter of the last part is authored by Shayegheh Ashourizadeh and Chuqing Zhang entitled *Lessons from Global Financial Crisis: Human Capital and Business Activities among Nascent Women Entrepreneurs in China*. This chapter investigates the influence of a crisis on women's entrepreneurial activities. Through a quantitative method, the authors answer the research questions that how the positive effects of the human capital (self-confidence, opportunity alertness, and risk-willingness) on start-up activities are changed after the global financial crisis.

Additionally, how knowing an entrepreneur boosts up these relationships. Results reveal a sharp drop in effect size of self-confidence and opportunity recognition upon women's entrepreneurial actions after the crisis. The global financial crisis nullified the effect of fear of failure on potential women entrepreneurs' business activities. Furthermore, knowing an entrepreneur has no significant moderating effect.

The next chapter, *Innovation Amplifies Growth Ambitions of Early-Stage Female Entrepreneurs: More in Nordics Less in MENA Region* has been authored by Mehrzad Saeedikiya, Zeynab Aeeni, Serdar Temiz, and Hiroko Kawamorita. This chapter investigates the regional differences in benefiting from innovation toward growth ambitions in a sample of female entrepreneurs in the MENA and Nordic regions. Preliminary results revealed that innovation benefits the growth ambitions of early-stage female entrepreneurs. Further analysis showed that regional differences affect the benefit of innovation in shaping growth ambitions. In the Nordic region, the early-stage female entrepreneurs expect more growth out of their innovation compared with their counterparts in the MENA region.

Salman Bashir Memon and Claire Seaman have presented the last, not the least chapter, *Empowering Women through Micro Finance Banks in Rural Areas of Pakistan*. The authors have explained the critical role of microfinance on women's financial, socioeconomic, and political empowerment. The sample was gathered from the customers of microfinance banks operating in the specific areas of Sukkur, PanoAqil, and Khairpur districts of Sindh province. Women's perception of the microfinance bank was positive as they give positive feedback about the banks. However, limited knowledge about business and financial matters makes it highly challenging for women entrepreneurs to start and run a business smoothly.

References

Ahl, H. (2006). Why research on women entrepreneurs needs new directions. *Entrepreneurship: Theory and Practice*, *30*(5), 595–621.

Birkner, S., Ettl, K., Welter, F., & Ebbers, I. (Eds.). (2018). *Women's entrepreneurship in Europe: Multidimensional research and case study insights*. Cham: Springer.

Blackburn, R., Hytti, U., & Welter, F. (Eds.). (2015). *Context, process and gender in entrepreneurship: Frontiers in European entrepreneurship research*. Cheltenham: Edward Elgar Publishing.

Brush, C. G. (1992). Research on women business owners: Past trends, a new perspective and future directions. *Entrepreneurship: Theory and Practice*, *16*(4), 5–30.

Brush, C. G., Carter, N. M., Gatewood, E. J., Greene, P. G., & Hart, M. M. (2006). *Women and entrepreneurship*. Cheltenham: Edward Elgar Publishing.

Coad, A., & Tamvada, J. P. (2012). Firm growth and barriers to growth among small firms in India. *Small Business Economics*, *39*, 383–400. doi:10.1007/s11187-011-9318-7

De Bruin, A., Brush, C. G., & Welter, F. (2006). Introduction to the special issue: Towards building cumulative knowledge on women's entrepreneurship. *Entrepreneurship: Theory and Practice*, *30*(5), 585–593.

Fielden, S. L., & Davidson, M. (Eds.). (2005). *International handbook of women and small business entrepreneurship*. Cheltenham: Edward Elgar Publishing.

Gaur, A. S., Kumar, V., & Singh, D. (2014). Institutions, resources, and internationalization of emerging economy firms. *Journal of World Business*, *49*(1), 12–20.

Global Entrepreneurship Monitor. (2017). Women's entrepreneurship report. Retrieved from https://gemconsortium.org/report/49860

Guelich, U., Bullough, A., Manolova, T. S., and Schjoedt, L. (Eds). (2021). *Women's entrepreneurship and culture: Socio-cultural context, traditional family roles and self-determination*. Cheltenham: Edward Elgar Publishing.

Hughes, K. D., Jennings, J. E., Brush, C., Carter, S., & Welter, F. (2012). Extending women's entrepreneurship research in new directions. *Entrepreneurship: Theory and Practice*, *36*(3), 429–442.

Jamil, G. (2019). *Muslim women speak: Of dreams and shackles*. New Delhi: Sage Publications.

Jennings, J. E., Jennings, P. D., & Sharifian, M. (2016). Living the dream? Assessing the "entrepreneurship as emancipation" perspective in a developed region. *Entrepreneurship: Theory and Practice*, *40*(1), 81–110.

Manolova, T. S., Brush, C. G., Edelman, L. F., Robb, A., & Welter, F. (Eds.). (2017). *Entrepreneurial ecosystems and growth of women's entrepreneurship: A comparative analysis*. Cheltenham: Edward Elgar Publishing.

Manolova, T. S., Carter, N. M., Manev, I. M., & Gyoshev, B. S. (2007). The differential effect of men and women entrepreneurs' human capital and networking on growth expectancies in Bulgaria. *Entrepreneurship: Theory and Practice*, *31*(3), 407–426.

Minniti, M., & Nardone, C. (2007). Being in someone else's shoes: The role of gender in nascent entrepreneurship. *Small Business Economics*, *28*(2–3), 223–238.

North, D. C. (1990). A transaction cost theory of politics. *Journal of Theoretical Politics*, *2*(4), 355–367.

Ramadani, V., Gërguri-Rashiti, S., & Fayolle, A. (Eds.). (2015). *Female entrepreneurship in transition economies: Trends and challenges*. Berlin: Springer.

Sarfaraz, L. (2017). *Women's entrepreneurship in Iran: Role models of growth-oriented Iranian women entrepreneurs*. Cham: Springer International Publishing.

Singhal, B. S., & Khadilkar, S. V. (2014). Neurology in the developing world. In J. Biller & J. M. Ferro (Eds.), *Handbook of clinical neurology* (Vol. *121*, pp. 1773–1782). San Diego, CA: Elsevier.

Sun, J. Y., & McLean, G. N. (2019). *Chinese women in leadership*. Cham: Palgrave Macmillan.

Terjesen, S. (2004). Female business owners: A review of the last decade of research. Paper presented at the Annual Academy of Management Meetings—Entrepreneurship Division, New Orleans, LA.

Wadhera, K., & Koreth, G. (2012). *Empowering rural women: Micro-enterprise through achievement motivation*. New Delhi: Sage Publications India Pvt Ltd.

Yadav, V., & Unni, J. (2016). Women entrepreneurship: Research review and future directions. *Journal of Global Entrepreneurship Research*, *6*(1), 12.

Chapter 2

Entrepreneurship and Innovation Emancipation among Women Entrepreneurs in Developing Countries

Huda Al Matroushi, Fauzia Jabeen, Sherine Farouk and Moza Tahnoon Al Nahyan

Abstract

Encouraging innovation in small and medium enterprises (SMEs) is one of the government's main policy initiatives at the local, regional, and national levels in the United Arab Emirates (UAE). This study's primary purpose is to explore the innovation characteristics, challenges, and factors influencing innovation in the Emirati female-owned nascent, start-up, and established SMEs. A semi-structured interview method was used to explore ten Emirati female entrepreneurs' experiences on innovation and adoption intent, and the data were analyzed using NVIVO software. The analysis reveals that respondents believed in a strong vision, education, and risk-taking attitude as an innovative entrepreneur's essential characteristics. Furthermore, new technology adoption, networking, implementation of new or improved products, processes, marketing, and organizational innovation are considered essential to help entrepreneurs commercialize their innovative business idea. This study's findings will help policymakers and business women's councils identify the specific inhibitors and facilitators linked to innovation. The results will help develop various effective policies to promote innovation among Emirati women-owned SMEs.

Keywords: Innovation; female entrepreneurs; Emirati; small and medium enterprises (SMEs); United Arab Emirates (UAE); empowerment

Introduction

To sustain the current volatile environment, entrepreneurial small and medium-sized enterprises (SMEs) embed innovation to leverage their business strategy

The Emerald Handbook of Women and Entrepreneurship in Developing Economies, 13–34
Copyright © 2021 by Emerald Publishing Limited
All rights of reproduction in any form reserved
doi:10.1108/978-1-80071-326-020211002

(Cenamor, Parida, & Wincent, 2019; Li, Liu, Belitski, Ghobadian, & O'Regan, 2016). Innovation has become one of the most crucial drivers of long-term development (Lederman, 2010) and needs to be encouraged, supported, and cultivated to the greatest possible extent (Perera & Wijeyaratnam, 2013). In the past, innovation was thought of as the territory of large corporations; however, recently, there has been a growing acceptance of the fact that any business can be innovative, regardless of size or sector (Mbizi, Hove, Thondhlana, & Kakava, 2013). SMEs play a crucial role in the United Arab Emirates' (UAE) economy as a whole, by creating job opportunities, exporting performance, and significantly contributing to the country's GDP. It contributes more than 60% of UAE's GDP (Al-Ansari, Xu, & Pervan, 2014). Women-owned SMEs in the UAE have also emerged as strong, competitive firms in almost all fields (Jabeen, Faisal, Al Matroushi, & Farouk, 2019). Women own more than 30% of all SMEs in the UAE, with most of these enterprises being on the forefront in providing practical solutions across the UAE (Dubai SME, 2015).

Globally, SMEs face challenges linked to innovation issues such as an inability to balance successful improvements to a broader universal market, inadequate financial support, complexity in creating disruptive and encouraging ideas, and the company's failure to recognize threats (Hadi, 2015). The determinants for small businesses' innovation also vary substantially across sectors and countries (Romero & Martínez-Román, 2012). Five innovation resources – education, finance, a skilled workforce, extension, and support services and partnership – are necessary for both male and female entrepreneurs. In developing countries like Brazil, Jordon, and Uganda, innovation is vision-led rather than market-led, and women and men entrepreneurs are less comfortable with risk because there are fewer support systems. The firm's probability to undertake innovation activities has been shown to enhance firm performance (Gërguri-Rashiti et al., 2017). Lack of training and education, cultural constraints, information and communications technology (ICT), and the Internet hinders innovation and success. There are gender differences in developing countries such as women being more active in using ICT and obtaining educational training whereas men get more patents than women (UNCTAD, 2013).

Prior researchers (Faisal, Jabeen, & Katsioloudes, 2017; Gutcher, 2013; Jabeen & Faisal, 2018; Jabeen, Katsioloudes, & Das, 2015; Jabeen, Faisal, & Katsioloudes, 2017; Naser, Mohammed, & Nuseibeh, 2009) have conducted several studies on female Emirati entrepreneurs motivations and challenges. However, very little research (Al Matroushi, Jabeen, & Abdel All, 2018) has been done to explore the factors inhibiting or facilitating innovation in Emirati women-owned SMEs. Therefore, to fill the existing gaps, the study will provide a better understanding of the pertinent issues affecting innovation in Emirati women-owned SMEs. Hence, this research aims to examine the development of innovation in women-owned SMEs in the UAE by identifying the types of innovation and the main obstacles the Emirati women entrepreneurs face while incorporating innovation into their businesses. Thereby, the current research attempts to answer the following questions:

RQ 1. What kind of innovation is brought by Emirati women entrepreneurs?

RQ 2. What are the factors influencing innovation in Emirati women-owned SMEs?

Literature Review

Women entrepreneurs offer society diverse, regularly innovative solutions to organizational and management issues (Fernandez & Ali, 2015). However, they are an essential untapped resource within the business sector (Ramadani, Dana, Gërguri-Rashiti, & Abazi-Alili, 2015). The opportunity for women to attain their potential as entrepreneurs is dependent on both women's role and status in society and the powers operating inside the society that influence entrepreneurship (Madichie & Gallant, 2012). Such aspects translate to institutional frameworks, market forces, political context, family policies, and the sustainability of specific individuals regarding qualifications and temperament to assume entrepreneurial roles (Rowland-Jones, 2013). Particular obstacles to higher entrepreneurship by women include lack of mentors, inadequate educational background, weak social standing, entrepreneurship gendering, limited contact with finance, and competing time demands, which are linked with family responsibilities (Naser et al., 2009; OECD, 2015; Perera & Wijeyaratnam, 2013). In the UAE, many women indicated that a lack of family support demoralizes them, causing them to refrain from starting businesses (Itani, Sidani, & Baalbaki, 2011). There are other issues such as the complexity of marketing their goods and inadequate demand that cause women not to enter into entrepreneurship in general (Gutcher, 2013) and innovative business ventures in particular.

In the MENA region, even with the wide gender gap, women entrepreneurs are more innovative than their counterparts and offer specialized and innovative products or services (GEM, 2012). Tunisia and Morocco have high R&D investments and innovation compared with other countries in the MENA region (UNCTAD, 2013). In Nigeria, innovation plays a vital role in survival, and there is a positive relationship between organizational and marketing design and business performance in female-owned businesses (Ajayi & Morton, 2015). Studies have shown that in other countries such as in Cambodia, marketing, innovation, and learning capabilities are positively related to SME performance. These capabilities also interact with one another to create great synergy in achieving SME performance (Sok, O'Cass, & Sok, 2013). In Finnish and Spanish SMEs, the degrees of innovation capability, research and development (R&D) investments, and profitability are associated with the diversity of developed innovation types such as product, process, management, and organizational innovation (Forsman & Annala, 2012; Hervas et al., 2014). Globally, product innovation is affected by three sets of factors: the extent of global engagement, information spillovers, and market structure (Lederman, 2010).

Innovation Topology in Female-owned SMEs

Despite the challenges women SMEs face, they have embraced a number of innovations to tap into opportunities (Madrid-Guijarro, Garcia-Perez-de-Lema, & Van Auken, 2013). There are various types of innovations in which entrepreneurs may engage, including product, process, marketing, and organizational innovations. Women entrepreneurs in the UAE bring multiple forms of innovation into industries. One such innovation is incremental. Incremental innovation is an innovation that refines and improves an existing design by making improvements to its components (Zain & Kassim, 2012). This type of innovation is related to product or process innovation that involves creating new products or the improvement of existing products based on changes in customer needs and market trends (Barringer & Ireland, 2012). Emirati women have been able to implement incremental innovations through advanced technology and improve product components. The main sectors that have experienced incremental innovations include the fashion and cosmetics industries. In other contextual studies, women entrepreneurs in Canada are more involved in facilitating processes that enhance innovative outcomes and may make peripheral contributions to innovation clusters (Crowden, 2003). Among Spanish women entrepreneurs, three factors affect innovation activities among the self-employed: the personal characteristics of the self-employed, such as their motivation, and their educational and professional background; firm size does not influence innovation.

Emirati women have also initiated radical innovations, especially in the service sector (Sahoo, 2015). They have also implemented new forms of architecture in manufacturing by overhauling the design of electronic devices, jewelry making, farming, handicrafts, and cosmetics (Zakaria, Abdul-Talib, & Osman, 2016). This innovation is related to organizational innovation, which is associated with the business structure innovations adopted to ensure that an organization maximizes its internal capacity to achieve maximum efficiency in its production and marketing activities (Aulet, 2013). Another unique form of innovation initiated by Emirati businesswomen is marketing innovation (Ajayi & Morton, 2015). Emirati women have improved marketing strategies by redesigning warehouses and showrooms to better view products for clients. SMEs in the fashion and cosmetics industries have created online showrooms that reach clients across the globe. Many SMEs have embraced market segmentation, producing goods suited to different markets depending on different markets' economic status (Zakaria et al., 2016). Those market innovations have allowed SMEs to secure and control huge markets and stay ahead of their peers.

Theoretical Framework

Resource-Based View (RBV) is relevant to innovation research because innovation adoption is potentially an element of competitive success. Based on an RBV, innovation does not occur only by observing the external environment in search of market opportunities and developing and building on core competencies from inside the firm. This indicates that the ability to innovate is related to the firm (Del Canto & Gonzalez, 1999). Thus, even if an innovation appears to be better than currently adopted ideas, a firm may not adopt the innovation if it does not have a mix of assets or capabilities required for it. Therefore, there is an essential relationship between a firm's resources and capabilities and its ability to adopt an innovation.

As per the institutional theory, the institutional environment can significantly affect how formal structures develop in an organization even more than market pressures. If a company has an innovative structure that leads to improved technical efficiency, then the company is legitimized in its environment. After some time, adopting these technologies reaches a critical level where a company that does not use them and is termed negligent or irrational. Besides, other companies continue to adopt these technologies even though they do not add value by increasing efficiency. According to Lasagni (2012), most of these institutional myths are ceremoniously accepted because organizations accepting them want to maintain or gain legitimacy within the institutional environment. For example, companies in the SME category might adopt some vocabularies of structure in the environment, such as specific procedures, job titles, and organizational roles to avoid losing legitimacy in their respective industries. This trend is notable within the technology industry. Such companies are likely to innovate or adopt a structural form that does not necessarily help increase efficiency.

Rogers's model of the innovation-decision process is one of the dominant theories on innovation adoption. During the knowledge stage, the decision-making unit is exposed to the innovation's existence and starts to understand how it operates (Rogers, 1995). Factors that affect this stage include previous practice, needs and problems, innovativeness of the social system's individual and norms. At the persuasion stage, the "individual becomes more psychologically involved with the innovation" and actively seeks information about the new idea. Perceived characteristics of the innovation, relative advantage, compatibility, complexity, trialability, and observability are important in helping the individual form an innovation attitude. The perceived attributes of innovation provide an important explanation of the innovation (Al Mourad & Hussain, 2014). In addition to these five perceived attributes, other factors such as the type of innovation-decision, nature of communication channels diffusing the innovation, nature of the social system also influence the rate of adoption of an innovation (Al Mourad & Hussain, 2014).

Research Methodology

Researchers should select a research method that serves the research problem (Noor, 2008). We, therefore, chose the case study methodology for this research. Creswell (2013) describes case study methodology as "a qualitative approach in which the investigator explores a bounded system (a case) or multiple bounded systems (cases) over time, through detailed, in-depth data collection involving multiple sources of information." The case study method helped us understand and explore the complex issues faced by women entrepreneurs. When a complex, in-depth investigation is required, this research method is very useful. Hence, the case study method helps us explore a specific context through close data examination. The case study method investigates a phenomenon from real life through the detailed analysis of a limited number of conditions or events and their relationships (Yin, 2013). This method is critical in researching topics that have not gained much attention in previous research (Vissak, 2010).

Understandably, a single case study is not enough for adequate research in this study. According to Creswell (2007), a collective case study (multiple cases) shows different perspectives on an issue and helps generalize the findings. As was the case in the research of Naser et al. (2009) and Al Hallami, Van Horne, and Huang (2013), there is no frame for recognizing innovative SMEs in the UAE. R&D can be used as a proxy to assess innovation performance in SMEs. Still, it cannot serve as an essential tool for measuring innovation because not all firms have R&D departments (Kleinknecht et al., 2002). Every country and region has its frame through which the innovativeness of SMEs is measured. Because there is no clear or generally accepted structure for identifying innovative SMEs, this chapter explores the characteristics of innovative SMEs in the UAE to provide a clearer understanding of the differences between innovative SMEs and ordinary SMEs. Table 2.1 summarizes the characteristics of innovative SMEs.

In this research, ten female-owned Emirati SMEs from different sectors deemed highly innovative were interviewed based on the innovation criteria mentioned in Table 2.1. These SMEs were chosen as per their business stage – nascent, start-up, or established as defined by Global Entrepreneurship Monitor (2013). They were also based on how they met the innovation criteria as per

Table 2.1. Characteristics of Innovative SMEs.

Characteristics	**Author**
Is observable and compatible	Rujirawanich, Addison, and Smallman (2011); Rese and Baier (2011)
Invests in training for employees	Laforet and Tann (2006)
Has leader with future-oriented, innovative vision	Krueger, Linan, and Nabi (2013)
Exhibits networking skills	Laforet and Tann (2006); Rujirawanich et al. (2011)
Adds value to customers and firm	Damanpour and Aravind (2012)
Takes risks	Blumentritt (2004)
Offers open, innovative environment	Bigliardi, Colacino, and Dormio (2011)
Invests in research and development activities	Al Hallami et al. (2013)
Invests in new technology	Data I.I. OSLO Manual (2005)
Has a leader with a strong education	Fernandez, Simo, and Sallan (2009)

Table 2.1. The respondents were selected from all the seven Emirates of UAE. The chosen entrepreneurs were from various business sectors, including service, manufacturing, F&B, construction, technology, health care, retail, and special needs therapy. Focusing on different sectors has helped the researchers to understand the challenges the entrepreneurs face in their respective fields. All the selected respondents have a product, process, marketing, and organizational innovations for their businesses. They have implemented radical innovation and have come up with novel developments in the UAE SME sector. The researcher interviewed each respondent separately at their business venture or a place convenient to the respondent. The researcher conducted face-to-face interviews over two months, making appointments in advance to prevent conflicts with the respondents' other engagements. Interviews averaged 30 minutes and were recorded using a voice recorder with the interviewees' consent. *NVIVO 10, a qualitative data analysis software package was used.* Because of the multiple cases in this study, the analytical techniques we will use are the cross-case and within-case analyses suggested by Creswell (2007). Table 2.2 provides the profile of businesses considered for the case study.

Findings and Discussion

Emirati women entrepreneurs demonstrated innovation characteristics such as the owner's innovative vision; educational background; new or improved IT adoption, product/process, marketing strategy/organizational process; R&D activities; networking; allocation of R&D funds; and risk-taking attitude. Factors such as

Table 2.2. Women-owned Businesses for the Study.

S. No.	Business Name	Year of Establishment	Type of Business	Location
1	SME1	2014	Service	Abu Dhabi
2	SME2	2005	Manufacturing	Abu Dhabi
3	SME3	2010	Special needs therapy	Dubai
4	SME4	2013	F&B	Sharjah
5	SME5	2012	Interior design	Abu Dhabi
6	SME6	2010	Technology	Abu Dhabi
7	SME7	2014	Fitness in health care	Dubai
8	SME8	2004	Graphic designing	Dubai
9	SME9	2012	F&B	Abu Dhabi
10	SME10	2012	Artisan soap retail	Dubai

government policies, R&D, innovation strategy, and skills development are among the main criteria influencing innovation and must be present in the preliminary stages of initiating a business. Family support is a core factor for an entrepreneur's success. All the respondents agree that practicing innovative culture, having strong social networks, allocating funds for R&D activities, and access to external finance will help Emirati women entrepreneurs be innovative and successful. The study results align with the previous research (Al Matroushi et al. 2018) which affirmed that opportunity recognition, finance, and motivation are the main criteria that promote innovation in Emirati women-owned SMEs in the UAE. Table 2.3 compares each respondent's views on innovation characteristics, perceptions on innovations, and the factors influencing innovation in their businesses.

Innovative Vision

All the respondents agree that an entrepreneur should be a visionary before starting a business. When an entrepreneur has a vision, she will develop a new business idea, and proactive behavior will help her identify market opportunities that will realize her ideas. One of the main qualities entrepreneurs should possess is patience; they should also inspire and communicate their visions to their colleagues and guide them (Shahnawaz, 2015).

Educational Background

All the entrepreneurs agree that education is vital for an entrepreneur but that where innovation is concerned, educational background is secondary. Education qualifications play a significant role in entrepreneurship, primarily if they are related to a venture or industry (Mulnix, Beede, & Mulnix, 2014; Romero & Martínez-Román, 2012). Entrepreneurial education is a lifelong process developed through experience and learning from mistakes (UNCTAD, 2013). Training and skills development is one entrepreneurial criterion and has more value for entrepreneurs than a higher education qualification. Training in financial accounting and bookkeeping is a must for women entrepreneurs (Jabeen et al., 2017). It will help them to take more responsibility in the business, reduce overhead expenses, and make them less dependent on their employees (Schilirò, 2015).

New or Improved IT Adoption

All respondents agreed that they had created new technology by introducing new products or processes in their respective fields. To maintain an advantage over their competitors and have a creative output, entrepreneurs must introduce new technology (Parrilli & Elola, 2011).

New or Improved Product and Process Innovation

All the respondents have initiated product and process innovation in their business. These respondents have introduced unique products; their main aim is to

Table 2.3. Analysis of Case Studies.

Innovation Characteristics	Respondents Views
Innovative vision	• All ten respondents agree that an entrepreneur should be a visionary. Leaders first need to envision venturing into new areas and developing them. Then, they should inspire and guide their staff in that direction. • According to respondents 1 and 3, an entrepreneur's innovation and visionary characteristics are inseparable. Respondents 1, 4, 5, and 9 believe that an innovative entrepreneur should always have 5-year, short-term and long-term plans. • Respondent 8 believes that there is no need to include "visionary" as a characteristic because she thinks it is almost apparent and argues that entrepreneurs are taught ways to develop realistic visions, missions, and objectives. However, according to respondents 2, 4, 5, and 7, a visionary without the passion for innovating will not be a successful entrepreneur. • Respondent 2 believes innovation and proactive behavior follow the vision. For example, "When an entrepreneur has a vision for his venture, innovative ideas are born, and an entrepreneur's proactive character brings innovative ideas into reality by recognizing the opportunity in the market." • According to respondents 10, 9, and 6, innovative entrepreneurs practice patience and revive their business from failure through positive attitude and visionary characteristics.
Education background	• Among respondents, opinions regarding educational requirements as characteristics of innovation were mixed. All the entrepreneurs agree that education is essential for an entrepreneur, but where innovation is concerned, educational background is secondary. • All respondents agree that entrepreneurial education is a lifelong process that one may gain through experience, learning from mistakes, etc. They also believe that education qualification or training in financial accounting and bookkeeping is a must for women entrepreneurs.

Table 2.3. *(Continued)*

Innovation Characteristics	**Respondents Views**
	• According to respondents 2, 3, 4, and 5, education qualifications play a significant role in entrepreneurship, primarily related to one's venture or industry. This will help the women entrepreneurs to take more responsibility in the business, reduce overhead expenses, and make them less dependent on their employees. • Respondent 1 has a different view on the ideal educational background for women entrepreneurs: "Basic education is good enough to be a successful entrepreneur, whereas to be a successful innovator, knowledge about trending markets, understanding client's requirements, and providing them with appropriate services is necessary." • Respondent 8 says, "Education qualification helps an entrepreneur gain skills and build character to succeed in your entrepreneurial venture."
New or improved technology adoption	• All respondents have initiated new technology either for producing new products or making new products successful.
New or improved product or process innovation	• All ten respondents have implemented product and process innovation in their businesses concerning their fields. • Respondents 1 and 3 are in the service industry, providing educational training for special needs students with dyslexia and deafness. They possess specialized teaching approaches, and an education plan is prepared according to students' capabilities and medical statuses. • Respondents 4 and 9 are from the F&B industry, but their products occupy different genres. Respondent 4 creates recipes that fuse American, European, and Emirati ingredients. Respondent 9 has introduced an Emirati food truck, a niche concept, and she prepares Emirati cuisine from her mother's and grandmother's recipe book.

Table 2.3. *(Continued)*

Innovation Characteristics	Respondents Views
	• Respondents 6 and 8 are from the technological sector, specializing in IT solutions and digital printing. Here, respondent 6 says, "We tailor make our products according to our clients' requirements." Respondent 8 says, "We upgrade the services and technology depending on the new market needs and trends at an affordable price." • Respondent 2 is from the jewelry-making industry. Innovation is her forte, and her products are unique. She has come up with innovative solutions such as going outside the country to find alternate production methods. • Respondent 5 is from the interior design sector. Innovation refers to new modern designs with an Arabic touch that she and her design team execute. The design team and the process innovation refer to the procedures implemented to complete the project in a limited time with limited cost. • Respondent 7 is from the health service industry; here, she has introduced a new concept, "Pilates training." Pilates already include set exercises, stretches, and breathing exercises; hence, the studio's trainers customize workout plans and combine them with diet and supplements for customers. • Respondent 10 is a handmade soap artisan who combines traditional and modern natural ingredients for her products, which are innovative. She is one of the first Emirati woman entrepreneurs to commercialize herbal healing through soaps and skin products.
New or improved marketing or organizational innovation	• All respondents agree that marketing and organizational innovation are significant characteristics of innovation. Most respondents have implemented marketing innovations, which are a necessity to sustain the business.

Table 2.3. *(Continued)*

Innovation Characteristics	Respondents Views
	• All the respondents agree that "word of mouth" and "social media" are active and robust marketing strategies. • Respondents 1 and 3 get their customers only through word of mouth from students' parents, whereas respondent 2 gets new customers through her satisfied customers, and her designs speak for her uniqueness. • The marketing and branding done for respondents 4, 9, and 10 are explicable; social media services such as Instagram and Facebook play a significant role in their businesses. They also have online purchase portals from their website. Customers use apps like Zomato for online delivery from respondents 4 and 9. • Respondents 5 and 7 use social media such as Facebook, Twitter, Instagram, and Whatsapp to market their ventures and advertise new services. • Respondents 6 and 8 use word of mouth and print media and have strong sales and marketing teams. When there are offers, this team will personally inform the client through face-to-face interactions or email. The usage of social media is lower than that of other respondents.
Research and Development (R&D)	• All the respondents agree that R&D plays a crucial role in innovation characteristics. All respondents agree that they initiate R&D to develop new or improve existing products or services.
Networking	• All respondents agree that networking is one of the main means to increase client lists, get to know one's competitors in the same field, and understand market trends. • Most of the respondents are registered under the Abu Dhabi business women council, Emirates business women council, and Sharjah business women council to network with other women entrepreneurs and understand the facilities these organizations provide.

Table 2.3. *(Continued)*

Innovation Characteristics	**Respondents Views**
	• Respondent 9 has frequent interaction with media through her articles, her success stories, and Pinterest interaction with famous international personalities that have kept her venture under constant review among the Emirati social groups. • Respondent 10 interacts with her customers and other viewers through videos on YouTube and her blog, informative for other women with unique skin conditions. • Respondent 7 actively participates in the media by giving interviews and hosting talks on health and adventure, promoting her business. • Majlis was developed by respondent 4 not only to educate the local community on socially essential matters but also to encourage them to take action to help make a difference. This process can be a combination of networking and giving back to society.
Allocation of R&D and training Fund	• All the respondents mentioned that they allocate some funds every year for R&D from their profits. Any of the entrepreneurs mentioned no set amount. R&D funds also include training for the employees in their respective fields, an added advantage for the respondent's businesses. • Respondents 1 and 3 spend on R&D every year by sponsoring research to come up with new methods to overcome dyslexia and pediatric speech, communication, and language disorders; new teaching methods for trainers, and many studies have been published in several well-regarded publications.
Risk-taking	• Risk-taking is one of the primary characteristics an entrepreneur should possess. Until and unless an entrepreneur takes risks, she cannot be innovative; she must believe in her passion and abilities. All the respondents interviewed for the case study are risk-takers and innovators.

Table 2.3. *(Continued)*

Innovation Characteristics	Respondents Views
	• Respondents 2, 4, 6, 7, and 9 believe that introducing a new concept in the market is a major risk of its acceptance among the people. • Respondents 1, 3, and 5 states that "risk-taking behavior is dependent on the motivation level received from the family and government." • Respondents 8 and 10 believe that women entrepreneurs will accept change when there is less credit financial pressure from the financial institutions and take risks to develop their venture.
Perception of innovation	• There are different perceptions of innovation; all the respondents have defined innovation from their experience and ventures point of view. • Respondent 1: "Innovation is the production of new technology, new knowledge, and new resources; continuous improvement in the organization and being different from the competitors or thinking out of the box." • Respondent 2: "Innovation means creating new pieces that use available materials in a never-created way." • Respondent 3: "Innovation is providing services above customer's expectations and outdoing competitors' services." • Respondent 4: "Creativity is thinking of a new idea, whereas innovation is implementing something new." • Respondent 5: "Innovation is creativity to stand out from one's competitors." • Respondent 6: "To turn new ideas into products, services which add value to the client's requirements and perspective." • Respondent 7: "Innovation is the creation of something new that improves the way we live." • Respondent 8: "Innovation is a commercialized invention." • Respondent 9: "Innovation converts ideas into numbers, introducing something new or different in your region."

Table 2.3. *(Continued)*

Innovation Characteristics	Respondents Views
	• Respondent 10: "Innovation means identifying the niche opportunity in the society, exploring them with individual ideas and coming up with innovative products, marketing strategies to commercialize and take over the market."
Influencing factors	• Respondents have selected some factors that influence innovation among Emirati women entrepreneurs. All the respondents have chosen family support as the main influential factor. Women are more sensitive to family issues, and lack of support from the family affects their creativity and confidence. • Respondents 1 and 9 mentioned that social and societal culture affects innovation among women. • Respondents 3, 4, and 5 believe that practicing innovative culture influences innovation in the venture. • Respondents 4, 5, 8, and 10 believe that innovation strategies such as feasibility studies, feedback from customers, and tracking competitor moves help entrepreneurs be more innovative. • Respondents 10, 3, and 7 mention that "recognizing the opportunity is the primary solution for innovation." • Respondents 2, 4, 7, and 10 agree that financial assistance from banks and venture capitalists will be a great help for development. • Respondents 2, 5, 6, and 8 believe that participating in social networks will help Emirati women entrepreneurs to connect with other entrepreneurs and competitors. • Respondents 4, 5, and 9 agree that entrepreneurial training and financial management training help entrepreneurs succeed, whereas respondent 1 believes training is not very important; relatively, on-the-job experience, strong vision, and confidence to take risks help women entrepreneurs to be innovative.

Table 2.3. *(Continued)*

Innovation Characteristics	Respondents Views
	• Respondents 2, 6, and 9 believe that lack of government support affects innovation. • According to respondent 6, networking with mentors and business consultants and encouraging competition in business women's councils will motivate Emirati women entrepreneurs to be innovative. • All the respondents have asked to include R&D as one of the criteria and allocate funds for R&D activities and to train their employees as subcriteria.

internationalize their products and gain global recognition and acceptance (Barringer & Ireland, 2012; Sahoo, 2015). This is because when women entrepreneurs are recognized internationally, they achieve visibility, credibility, and access to financial and other resources in their own countries (Alsos, Ljunggren, & Hytti, 2013).

New or Improved Marketing and Organizational Innovation

Most respondents have implemented marketing innovations, which are necessary to sustain their businesses (Sok et al., 2013). Emirati entrepreneurs have implemented some marketing innovations, including changes in business logos, attractive packaging, and advertising in new media, product promotion techniques, new pricing methods, and new sales channels (Ajayi & Morton, 2015). All the respondents agree that "word of mouth" and "social media" are strong and active applied marketing strategies (Hervas-Oliver, Sempere-Ripoll, & Boronat-Moll, 2014). Emirati women entrepreneurs prefer marketing through social media because it is less expensive and focuses only on the target audience. In contrast, advertising in newspapers or other media is costly and mainly for the public.

R&D and Allocation of Funds

All the respondents have initiated R&D in their businesses and invested a part of their profits in research for new products and improving existing products (Al-Ansari, Pervan, & Xu, 2013). Investing in training employees is also a part of R&D. Off-the-job training for employees played an essential role in employee growth and reducing turnover among SMEs post recession (Bryson & Forth, 2016).

Networking

According to the respondents, networking is one of the primary resources for increasing one's client list, getting to know one's competitors in the same field, and understanding market trends. A typical networking community, such as a business women's council, provides women entrepreneurs opportunities to showcase their products in exhibitions and organizes training sessions (CAWTAR, 2007; Gutcher, 2013; Mulnix et al., 2014). All respondents believe that radical innovation and networking are directly connected (Lee, Park, Yoon, & Park, 2010). Most respondents have their blogs, enabling them to continually interact with their clients and receive feedback on their products and services (Aulet, 2013). Involving corporate governance in their ventures by giving back to the society also is a form of positive networking.

Risk-taking Attitude

Risk-taking is one primary characteristic an entrepreneur should possess, and an entrepreneur's belief in her passion and abilities provides a basis for a risk-taking attitude (Majumdar & Varadarajan, 2013). The respondents believe risk-taking behavior depends on the support that family and government provide. Favorable policies for promoting the availability of risk capital during the initial stages of innovative SMEs help reduce the pressure on risk (Gackstatter, Kotzemir, & Meissner, 2014; OECD, 2015).

Implications of the Research

This research will be useful in future academic and entrepreneurial studies and will add to the existing literature linked to innovation decisions in the SME studies. In practical terms, the research includes interpretations and discussions that will help policymakers and related associations formulate and develop policies to empower Emirati female entrepreneurs and initiate significant innovation in their businesses. The UAE government-designated 2015 as the innovation year, directing all government entities to revise their policies to provide a nurturing environment for innovation (Gulf News, 2014). This study's findings will encourage various government bodies to take the first steps toward incorporating national policies supporting SMEs by establishing support centers and innovation councils and promoting entrepreneurial restructuring and development. Furthermore, the study stresses on continuous training and skill-building of staff. It also highlights the importance of strengthening one's business plan and business model and maintains a strong commitment to the business idea. In alignment with Piterou and Birch (2016), the research study suggests offering entrepreneurship courses as required components of lower- and intermediate-level student curricula to encourage and nurture the development of entrepreneurship and innovation among Emirati women.

The study proposes several recommendations to the business women's councils, including amendments to employment laws, simplification of registration paperwork, reduction in registration fees, establishment of an advisory board, and external financial support implementation. It is essential for business women's councils to initiate entrepreneurial, economic, and risk-management training to boost female entrepreneurs' self-confidence. Furthermore, business women's boards should also keep track of progress in nascent businesses for 3–4 years, guiding them with creative marketing strategies and introducing minimal advertising fees in popular magazines.

Limitations and Future Research Directions

Although this chapter has provided fruitful insights into factors promoting innovation in Emirati female-owned SMEs in the UAE, the study nonetheless has faced several limitations that need to be acknowledged. The research was conducted based on Emirati entrepreneurs in the UAE and cannot be generalized. Another limitation is in the case study method. The researcher has focused on one Emirati women entrepreneur from each sector; hence, each case study's findings cannot be generalized to that respective sector.

Future research should focus on other GCC/Arab countries to compare the factors affecting innovation and entrepreneurship among Emirati women entrepreneurs to local women entrepreneurs from other countries. Also, in-depth research studies need to be conducted in the technology, construction, and agriculture sectors to identify hindrances affecting Emirati women entrepreneurs' participation in these sectors. Hence future studies may also focus on one particular industry, which will help policymakers to understand sector-specific challenges.

References

Ajayi, O. M., & Morton, S. C. (2015). Exploring the enablers of organizational and marketing innovations in SMEs: Findings from South-Western Nigeria. *Sage Open*, *5*(1).

Al Hallami, M. O., Van Horne, C., & Huang, V. Z. (2013). Technological innovation in the United Arab Emirates: Process and challenges. *Transnational Corporations Review*, *5*(2), 46–59.

Al Matroushi, H., Jabeen, F., & Abdel All, S. (2018). Prioritising the factors promoting innovation in Emirati female-owned SMEs: AHP approach. *International Journal of Entrepreneurship and Innovation Management*, *22*(3), 220–250.

Al Mourad, M. B., & Hussain, M. (2014). The impact of cloud computing on ITIL service strategy processes. *International Journal of Computer and Communication Engineering*, *3*(5), 367–371.

Al-Ansari, Y., Pervan, S., & Xu, J. (2013). Innovation and business performance of SMEs: The case of Dubai. *Education, Business and Society: Contemporary Middle Eastern Issues*, *6*(3/4), 162–180.

Al-Ansari, Y., Xu, J., & Pervan, S. (2014). A study of organisational determinants and innovation practices in Dubai SMEs. *International Journal of Innovation Management*, *18*(1), 1–22.

Alsos, G. A., Ljunggren, E., & Hytti, U. (2013). Gender and innovation: State of the art and a research agenda. *International Journal of Gender and Entrepreneurship*, *5*(3), 236–256.

Aulet, B. (2013). *Disciplined entrepreneurship: 24 steps to a successful start-up*. New York, NY: Wiley.

Barringer, B. R., & Ireland, R. D. (2012). *Entrepreneurship: Successfully launching new ventures*. Harlow: Pearson.

Bigliardi, B., Colacino, P., & Dormio, A. I. (2011). Innovative characteristics of small and medium enterprises. *Journal of Technology Management & Innovation*, *6*(2), 83–93.

Blumentritt, T. (2004). Does small and mature have to mean dull? Defying the ho-hum at SMEs. *Journal of Business Strategy*, *25*(1), 27–33.

Bryson, A., & Forth, J. (2016). *What role did management practices play in SME growth post-recession?* IZA Discussion Paper No. 10042. Retrieved from https://www.iza.org/publications/dp/10042/what-role-did-management-practices-play-in-sme-growth-post-recession

CAWTAR. (2007). *Women entrepreneurs in the Middle East and North Africa: Characteristics, contributions and challenges*. Tunis: Centre of Arab Women for Training and Research. Retrieved from www.cawtar.org/Assets/ Documents/pdf/Women_Entrepreneurs_in_the_ME_Jun07.pdf

Cenamor, J., Parida, V., & Wincent, J. (2019). How entrepreneurial SMEs compete through digital platforms: The roles of digital platform capability, network capability and ambidexterity. *Journal of Business Research*, *100*, 196–206.

Creswell, J. W. (2007). *Qualitative inquiry and research design: Choosing among five approaches* (2nd ed.). London: SAGE Publications.

Creswell, J. W. (2013). *Qualitative inquiry and research design: Choosing among five approaches*. Thousand Oaks, CA: SAGE Publications.

Crowden, N. (2003). *Examining gender bias in studies of innovation*. MA Thesis. Simon Fraser University, Burnaby, BC.

Damanpour, F., & Aravind, D. (2012). Managerial innovation: Conceptions, processes and antecedents. *Management and Organization Review*, *8*(2), 423–454.

Data, I. I. (2005). *Oslo manual*. Paris and Luxembourg: OECD/Eurostat.

Del Canto, J. G., & Gonzalez, I. S. (1999). A resource-based analysis of the factors determining a firm's R&D activities. *Research Policy*, *28*(8), 891–905.

Dubai, S. M. E. (2015). The Dubai SME definition. Retrieved from http://www.sme.ae/en/aboutus/pages/sme-definition.aspx

Faisal, M. N., Jabeen, F., & Katsioloudes, M. I. (2017). Strategic interventions to improve women entrepreneurship in GCC countries: A relationship modeling approach. *Journal of Entrepreneurship in Emerging Economies*, *9*(2), 161–180.

Fernandez, R., & Ali, S. (2015). SME contributions for diversification and stability in emerging economies - An empirical study of the SME segment in the Qatar economy. *Journal of Contemporary Issues in Business and Government*, *21*(1), 23–45.

Fernandez, V., Simo, P., & Sallan, J. M. (2009). Podcasting: A new technological tool to facilitate good practice in higher education. *Computers & Education*, *53*(2), 385–392.

Forsman, H., & Annala, U. (2012). Small enterprises as innovators: Shift from a low performer to a high performer. *International Journal of Technology Management*, *56*(2/3/4), 154–171.

Gackstatter, S., Kotzemir, M., & Meissner, D. (2014). Building an innovation-driven economy - the case of BRIC and GCC countries. *Foresight*, *16*(4), 293–308.

Gërguri-Rashiti, S., Ramadani, V., Abazi-Alili, H., Dana, L. P., & Ratten, V. (2017). ICT, innovation and firm performance: The transition economies context. *Thunderbird International Business Review*, *59*(1), 93–102.

Gulf News. (2014). UAE cabinet approves 2015 as year of innovation. *Gulf News*. Retrieved from http://www.gulfbusiness.com/articles/industry/uae-cabinet-approves-2015-as-year-ofinnovation

Gutcher, L. (2013). Women in UAE SMEs told to look beyond cupcakes. *The National*. Retrieved from http://www.thenational.ae/business/economy/women-in-uae-smes-told-to-look-beyond-cupcakes

Hadi, Y. (2015). SMEs in the UAE's creative industries: Female employees and lax marketing efforts. *International Journal of Business and Management*, *10*(11), 122.

Hervas-Oliver, J.-L., Sempere-Ripoll, F., & Boronat-Moll, C. (2014). Process innovation strategy in SMEs, organizational innovation and performance: A misleading debate? *Small Business Economics*, *43*(4), 873–886.

Itani, H., Sidani, Y. M., & Baalbaki, I. (2011). United Arab Emirates female entrepreneurs: Motivations and frustrations. *Equality, Diversity, and Inclusion: An International Journal*, *30*(5), 409–424.

Jabeen, F., & Faisal, M. N. (2018). Imperatives for improving entrepreneurial behavior among females in the UAE: An empirical study and structural model. *Gender in Management: An International Journal*, *33*(3), 234–252.

Jabeen, F., Faisal, M. N., Al Matroushi, H., & Farouk, S. (2019). Determinants of innovation decisions among Emirati female-owned small and medium enterprises. *International Journal of Gender and Entrepreneurship*, *11*(4), 408–434.

Jabeen, F., Faisal, M. N., & Katsioloudes, M. I. (2017). Entrepreneurial mindset and the role of universities as strategic drivers of entrepreneurship: Evidence from the United Arab Emirates. *Journal of Small Business and Enterprise Development*, *24*(1), 136–157.

Jabeen, F., Katsioloudes, M. I., & Das, S. S. (2015). Is family the key? Exploring the motivation and success factors of female Emirati entrepreneurs. *International Journal of Entrepreneurship and Small Business*, *25*(4), 375–394.

Global Entrepreneurship Monitor. (2012). D. J. Kelley, C. G. Brush, P. G. Greene, & Y. Litovsky (Eds.), *Women's report*. Babson College, GERA.

Kleinknecht, A., Van Montfort, K., & Brouwer, E. (2002). The non-trivial choice between innovation indicators. *Economics of Innovation and New Technology*, *11*(2), 109–121.

Krueger, N., Linan, F., & Nabi, G. (2013). Cultural values and entrepreneurship. *Entrepreneurship & Regional Development*, *25*(9–10), 703–707.

Laforet, S., & Tann, J. (2006). Innovative characteristics of small manufacturing firms. *Journal of Small Business and Enterprise Development*, *13*(3), 363–380.

Lasagni, A. (2012). How can external relationships enhance innovation in SMEs? New evidence for Europe. *Journal of Small Business Management*, *50*(2), 310–339.

Lederman, D. (2010). An international multilevel analysis of product innovation. *Journal of International Business Studies*, *41*(4), 606–619.

Lee, S., Park, G., Yoon, B., & Park, J. (2010). Open innovation in SMEs - an intermediated network model. *Research Policy*, *39*(2), 290–300.

Li, W., Liu, K., Belitski, M., Ghobadian, A., & O'Regan, N. (2016). e-Leadership through strategic alignment: An empirical study of small-and medium-sized enterprises in the digital age. *Journal of Information Technology*, *31*(2), 185–206.
Madichie, N. O., & Gallant, M. (2012). Broken silence: A commentary on women's entrepreneurship in the United Arab Emirates. *The International Journal of Entrepreneurship and Innovation*, *13*(2), 81–92.
Madrid-Guijarro, A., Garcia-Perez-de-Lema, D., & Van Auken, H. (2013). An investigation of Spanish SME innovation during different economic conditions. *Journal of Small Business Management*, *51*(4), 578–601.
Majumdar, S., & Varadarajan, D. (2013). 'Students' attitude towards entrepreneurship: Does gender matter in the UAE? *Foresight: The Journal of Futures Studies, Strategic Thinking and Policy*, *15*(4), 278–293.
Mbizi, R., Hove, L., Thondhlana, A., & Kakava, N. (2013). Innovation in SMEs: A review of its role to organizational performance and SMEs operations sustainability. *Interdisciplinary Journal of Contemporary Research in Business*, *4*(11), 370–389.
Mulnix, M. W., Beede, P., & Mulnix, E. L. (2014). Emerging issues among women Emirati entrepreneurs: A research agenda. *European Scientific Journal*, *1*(3), 209–2016.
Naser, K., Mohammed, W. R., & Nuseibeh, R. (2009). Factors that affect women entrepreneurs: Evidence from an emerging economy. *International Journal of Organizational Analysis*, *17*(3), 225–247.
Noor, K. B. M. (2008). Case study: A strategic research methodology. *American Journal of Applied Sciences*, *5*(11), 1602–1604.
OECD. (2015). OECD Innovation Strategy 2015: An agenda for policy action. In *Meeting the OECD council at Ministerial level*. Paris: OECD.
Parrilli, M. D., & Elola, A. (2011). The strength of science and technology drivers for SME innovation. *Small Business Economics*, *39*(4), 897–907.
Perera, T., & Wijeyaratnam, I. P. W. (2013). Barriers of women entrepreneurship: SME sector in Sri Lanka. *Sri Lankan Journal of Management*, *18*(1–2), 51–81.
Piterou, A., & Birch, C. (2016). The role of higher education institutions in supporting innovation in SMEs: University-based incubators and student internships as knowledge transfer tools. *The Journal of Innovation Impact*, *7*(1), 72–79.
Ramadani, V., Dana, LP., Gërguri-Rashiti, S., & Abazi-Alili, H. (2015). The profile of female entrepreneurs in the Republic of Macedonia. In V. Ramadani, S. Gërguri-Rashiti, & A. Fayolle (Eds.), *Female entrepreneurship in transition economies*. London: Palgrave Macmillan. doi:10.1057/9781137444516_9
Rese, A., & Baier, D. (2011). Success factors for innovation management in networks of small and medium enterprises. *R&D Management*, *41*(2), 138–155.
Rogers, E. (1995). *Diffusion of innovations* (4th ed.). New York: NY: Free Press.
Romero, I., & Martínez-Román, J. A. (2012). Self-employment and innovation: Exploring the determinants of innovative behavior in small businesses. *Research Policy*, *41*(1), 178–189.
Rowland-Jones, R. (2013). A perspective on United Arab Emirates small and medium-sized enterprises management utilising the European Foundation for Quality Management concepts of excellence. *Total Quality Management & Business Excellence*, *24*(1/2), 210–224.

Rujirawanich, P., Addison, R., & Smallman, C. (2011). The effects of cultural factors on innovation in a Thai SME. *Management Research Review*, *34*(12), 1264–1279.

Sahoo, S. (2015). Female Emirati entrepreneurs taste of success. *The National*. Retrieved from http://www.thenational.ae/business/retail/female-emirati-entrepreneurs-taste-success

Schilirò, D. (2015). Innovation in small and medium enterprises in the United Arab Emirates. Retrieved from http://mpra.ub.uni-muenchen.de/64309/

Shahnawaz, M. R. (2015). Preliminary investigation of Emirati women's Entrepreneurship in the UAE: Motivating factors, challenges and government initiatives. *International Journal of Scientific & Technology Research*, *4*(8), 50–61.

Global Entrepreneurship Monitor. (2013). H. E. Sokari, C. V. Horne, V. Z. Huang, & M. M. Al Awad (Eds.), *Entrepreneurship an Emirati perspective*. Zayed University, Abu Dhabi.

Sok, P., O'Cass, A., & Sok, K. M. (2013). Achieving superior SME performance: Overarching role of marketing, innovation, and learning capabilities. *Australasian Marketing Journal*, *21*(3), 161–167.

UNCTAD. (2013). A survey on women entrepreneurship and innovation. *United Nations Conference on Trade and Development*. Retrieved from unctad.org/en/Publications Library/tdr2013_en.pdf

Vissak, T. (2010). Recommendations for using the case study method in international business research. *The Qualitative Report*, *15*(2), 370–388.

Yin, R. K. (2013). *Case study research: Design and methods*. Thousand Oaks, CA: SAGE Publications.

Zain, M., & Kassim, N. M. (2012). Strategies of family businesses in a newly globalized developing economy. *Journal of Family Business Management*, *2*(2), 147–165.

Zakaria, N., Abdul-Talib, A.-N., & Osman, N. (2016). *Handbook of research on impacts of international business and political affairs on the global economy*. Hershey, PA: IGI Global.

Chapter 3

Gender Roles in Developing Countries and Women Entrepreneurs' Intention/Entry/ Business Engagement and Performance*

Hui Zhang and Xiaohu Zhou

Abstract

Women entrepreneurship is designated as the new engines of economic growth in developing countries. Prior research shows how men and women differ in starting a business, with women normally facing more restrictions on entrepreneurial financing, entrepreneurial growth, and entrepreneurial performance. This has often been explained by gender role, yet we still lack a systematic understanding of how gender roles impact on women's entrepreneurial process in developing countries. In this chapter, we review literatures on female entrepreneurship in developing countries to show how gender role works in developing countries and especially its influence on the intention/entry/business participation and performance of female entrepreneurs.

Keywords: Women entrepreneurship; developing country; gender role; entrepreneurial intention; entrepreneurial entry; entrepreneurial performance

Introduction

Despite the unprecedented number of women choosing to enter into a professional workforce over the past 50 years, there has always been a lag compared to their male counterparts in the opportunities available (Acker, 2006). In order to avoid the disadvantages they may face in the workplace, many women set up new

*The classification standard for the designation of "developed" and "developing" countries or areas in the United Nations system is consistent with M49. Full details of the M49 standard can be found on the Statistics Division website at https://unstats.un.org/unsd/methodology/m49.

The Emerald Handbook of Women and Entrepreneurship in Developing Economies, 35–48
Copyright © 2021 by Emerald Publishing Limited
All rights of reproduction in any form reserved
doi:10.1108/978-1-80071-326-020211003

enterprises, giving them more personal control over their own career (Heilman & Chen, 2003; Thébaud, 2015). However, studies also find that there is a gender inequality in entrepreneurship, where male-led ventures generally are seen as more superior to female-led enterprises in terms of resource acquisition and several aspect of economic success (Jennings & Brush, 2013).

One of the reasons for this inequality is stereotypying of gender roles, which exist in people's minds and the pattern or expectations that men and women should (should not) traditionally follow. Given the differences in cultural and social background, educational system structure, and gender concepts between developing and developed countries, the stereotypes of gender role between developed and developing countries are different to some extent. Specifically, existing research has proved that gender role stereotypes play a particularly important role in developing countries than in developed countries (Williams & Best, 1990).

Studies on gender role issues in female entrepreneurship have proven its effectiveness in explaining women entrepreneurial cognition, entrepreneurial behavior, and entrepreneurial performance. However, those studies mainly paid their attention to developed countries (Eddleston, Ladge, Mitteness, & Balachandra, 2016; Kanze, Huang, Conley, & Higgins, 2018; Lee & Huang, 2018). It is also very important to study these issues under developing country circumstances as gender inequality is more pronounced in developing countries and has severely hindered the development of women entrepreneurship. Therefore, we have laid a foundation for explaining female entrepreneurship within developing countries, especially explaining the gender roles in developing countries and their influence on the intention/entry/business participation and performance of female entrepreneurs. We hope that our research can provide insights into the understanding of gender issues in the entrepreneurial field within developing countries. In the following sections, to highlight the role of gender in developing countries, we first compare two major gender equality indexes, Gender Development Index (GDI) and Gender Empowerment Measure (GEM), among developing and developed countries to describe the gender phenomenon. Then we discuss the link between gender role and women's entrepreneurial cognition, behavior, and performance in developing countries. Finally, we collate the literature on the solutions for women entrepreneurship in developing countries.

Gender Role in Developing Countries

Bird and Brush (2002) stated that the important premise of gender research in entrepreneurship is to distinguish biology (male VS. female) and socialization (masculine VS. feminine). The socialized gender role, and not biological gender, plays an important part in entrepreneurship. Gender roles include the common expectation of people's behavior based on gender identity, which helps people become members of a specific social category (Eagly & Karau, 2002). Literature on gender role in the field of gender stereotypes suggest that people possess differing beliefs about the typical characteristics of men and women (Eagly, Wood, & Diekman, 2000). Those beliefs about the sexes generally can be divided into two attributes, namely, communal and agentic. Communal attributes are typical characteristics of women, which reflect their concern for others' well-being, including emotion, kindness, sensitivity to interpersonal relationships, and cultivation. In contrast, agentic attributes are typical characteristic of men, which involve assertion, control, and confidence. Gender can play a role under specific career or life scenes by shared and reinforced gender stereotypes through wide social interactions (Borkenau, Mauer, Riemann, Spinath, & Angleitner, 2004; Solnick & Schweitzer, 1999). For example, in the workplace, people possess different expectations for males and females, even when they are employed in the same work situation (Eagly & Karau, 2002), thereby men, more than women, are considered to be self-confident, assertive, and a top manager.

However, an interesting question is whether gender stereotypes and perceived differences in psychological characteristics are consistent in different cultures. To address this issue, Williams and Best (1990) conducted a cross-cultural study including 25 countries within Europe, Asia, Africa, and the Americas. In this study, the participants from these 25 countries are required to rate each of 300 adjectives to evaluate their applicability to both men and women, and the results show that adjectives such as dominance, autonomy, aggression, and achievement related to men are stronger and more active than adjectives related to women in every culture, suggesting the existence of a pancultural stereotype – that is, a gender stereotype that commonly exists across different cultures. However, their additional analysis suggested that economic development can moderate gender differences, that gender stereotypes tended to be more severe among less developed countries (Smith, Dugan, & Trompenaars, 1997).

Two indices often used to measure gender equity are Gender Development Index (GDI) and Gender Empowerment Measure (GEM) constructed by UNDP. GDI comes from human development index (HDI) and mainly reflects gender inequality. GEM focus on the opportunities for men and women to participate in the economic and political life of a country. GDI and GEM attempt jointly to grasp the level of women's development and the extent to which women are not discriminated against in gaining access to resources and opportunities. Table 3.1 and Table 3.2 show the data of GDI and GEM index in 2019.

The two tables above show the scores and rankings of some countries in terms of GDI and GEM. The scores and rankings are used to measure regional gender equality. Although they are not exactly equal to the regional gender roles gap, it still could to a large extent reflect the gender attitudes embedded in the regional social norms. It can be seen from the tables that developed countries rank relatively high, while developing countries rank relatively low both in the GDI and GEM surveys. In particular, we presented several typical rankings of developing countries, such as the Russian Federation, China, Malaysia, India, and Egypt. According to the GDI survey, among 177 countries, the gender equality rankings of the above five countries are 49, 85, 61, 129, and 116 respectively. Furthermore, according to the GEM survey, among 177 countries, the gender equality rankings of the above five countries are 71, 57, 65, 88, and 91 respectively. It can be seen that gender equality in major developing countries is still at a medium or even below level.

Table 3.1. Part Data of GDI in 2019.[a]

Rank	Country	GDI Value	HDI Value	
			Female	Male
1	Norway	0.990	0.946	0.955
2	Switzerland	0.963	0.924	0.959
3	Ireland	0.975	0.929	0.953
15	United Kingdom	0.967	0.904	0.935
15	United States	0.991	0.915	0.923
49	Russian Federation	1.015	0.828	0.816
61	Malaysia	0.972	0.792	0.815
85	China	0.961	0.741	0.771
116	Egypt	0.878	0.643	0.732
129	India	0.829	0.574	0.692

[a]The full data of GDI in 2019, http://hdr.undp.org/en/content/table-4-gender-development-index.

Table 3.2. Part Data of GEM in 2019[a].

Rank	Country	GEM Value	Seats in Parliament Held by Women	Female Legislators, Senior Officials and Managers
1	Norway	0.910	37.9%	30%
2	Sweden	0.906	47.3%	30%
3	Finland	0.887	42.0%	30%
14	United Kingdom	0.783	19.3%	34%
15	United States	0.762	16.3%	42%
57	China	0.534	20.3%	17%
65	Malaysia	0.504	13.1%	23%
71	Russian Federation	0.489	8.0%	39%
91	Egypt	0.263	3.8%	9%
88	India	0.325	9.0%	12%

[a]The full data of GEM in 2019, https://www.rrojasdatabank.info/hdr20072008tab29.pdf.

Women Entrepreneurship

Entrepreneurship is defined as self-employment based on the concept that a person can be unemployed, self-employed, or in wage employment. In developing countries, entrepreneurship is an important issue related to economic development, especially women's entrepreneurship, which has been designated as the new engines of economic growth and a new start of prosperity and welfare. Governments, charities, and private companies all claim that women's entrepreneurship is crucial to growth and development. Some even argue that women entrepreneurs' contribution tends to be higher than that resulting from entrepreneurial activity of men (Minniti, 2010).

The development of women entrepreneurship in developing countries has great potential to empower women and transform the society; this potential is being brought into play in many countries, no matter whether the level of economic development is high or low.

Fig. 3.1 shows the female TEA (Total Entrepreneurial Activity Rate) (% women) divided by male TEA (% men) in 2019 from GEM (Global Entrepreneurship Monitor) data.[1] Data state that seven economies with a ratio of female to male early-stage entrepreneurial activity that is 0.9 or more, suggesting that women are at least nine-tenths as active as men in entrepreneurship. These countries are Madagascar, Saudi Arabia, and Qatar (Middle East and Africa), Mexico and Brazil (Latin America and the Caribbean), and Spain and the United States (Europe and North America). Most of those countries are developing countries, among which high female participation boosts overall entrepreneurial activities.

Although it is often stated in the literature that the degree of women entrepreneurship development is closely related to the degree of gender equity, which in developing countries is generally lower than that in developed countries (Williams & Best, 1990). The ratio of female entrepreneurship in developed and

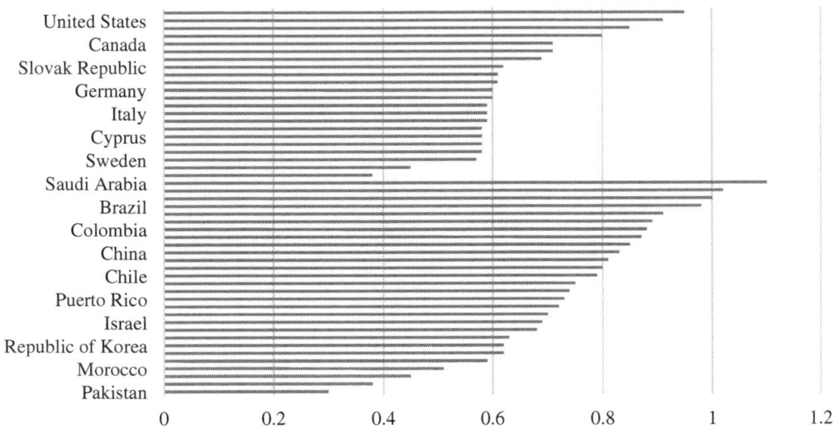

Fig. 3.1. The Relative Gender Gap: Female TEA (% Women) Divided by Male TEA (% Men).

Table 3.3. Categories of Women Entrepreneurs in Asian Developing Countries.

Category	Main Reason/Motivation
Chance entrepreneurs	• To keep busy • Was a hobby/special interest
Forced entrepreneurs	• Family/spouse had business • Financial/needed the money
Created or pulled entrepreneurs	• Control over time/flexibility • Challenge, try something on one's own • Show others I could do it • To be independent • Self-satisfaction • Example to children • Employment to others/do something worthwhile

developing countries does not show obvious gaps. Within the developing countries, the degree varies by country, depending on many factors, including level of economic development and social, cultural, and political factors.

However, we don't need to be pessimistic about this result as the entrepreneurial motivations of female are quite different from each other. Existing literature suggest that based on the motivations of starting businesses, there are three categories of women entrepreneurs in Asian developing country, that is, "chance," "forced," and "created" entrepreneurs (Das, 2000). Chance entrepreneurs refer to those who start a business without clear goals or plans, and who might be motivated by their hobbies. Forced entrepreneurs refer to those who start their own business due to economic difficulties and family factors. Created entrepreneurs refer to those who start their business motivated by entrepreneurial projects and higher achievements. Table 3.3 shows the characteristics of the different categories.

According to Das (2000), for female entrepreneurship in developing countries, only about one-fifth of women were drawn to entrepreneurship by "pull" factors, for instance, the need for a challenge, the urge to try something on their own and to be independent, and to show others that they are capable of doing well in business.

Gender Role and Women Entrepreneurship in Developing Countries

Gender roles represent the descriptively normative characteristics for the sexes, which is used to distinguish men from women. These descriptive norms set desirable and admirable behaviors for men and women (Cialdini & Trost, 1998), and therefore guide the behavior that may be more suitable in a particular situation, especially when a situation is ambiguous or confusing, such as in the context of entrepreneurship. For example, Lee and Huang (2018) indicate that evaluations of entrepreneurial programs are particularly prone to stereotype because the entrepreneurial environment itself is uncertain, and there is a lack of objective evidence of the quality of entrepreneurship. Therefore, when evaluating entrepreneurs, resource providers rely heavily on stereotypes to build the complex images of new enterprises as there is only limited information about objective founder and venture (Huang & Pearce, 2015). However, this kind of evaluation is bad for women and might lead to female entrepreneurs being viewed with skepticism because female gender stereotypes are incongruent with cultural images of entrepreneurship linked with stereotypically masculine characteristics (Vishal K Gupta & Turban, 2012). Obayelu and Ogunlade (2006) indicate that those kinds of challenges faced by women caused by gender roles is particularly obvious in developing countries, especially in rural areas, where social and cultural barriers for centuries have limited access to education and information that is conducive to the development of gender awareness. These challenges in turn result in women in these countries being highly underrepresented in entrepreneurial activities (Venkatesh, Shaw, Sykes, Macharia, & Wamba, 2017).

In all, women entrepreneurs are subject to barriers due to gender discrimination in various ways in developing countries, with many barriers not often experienced by men. In recent years, the general attention to women and entrepreneurship in developing countries are increasing and tried to explain why the gender gap in entrepreneurship persists from the perspective of gender role (Minniti & Naudé, 2010). However, those research studies are scattered in various entrepreneurial topics, such as entrepreneurial attitudes, entrepreneurial opportunities, entrepreneurial networks, and entrepreneurial performance. This dispersion prevents us from systematic understanding of female entrepreneurship within developing countries. In the following section, to clarify what the literature suggests to us about how gender roles affect women's entrepreneurship, we will discuss the link between gender role and women's entrepreneurial cognition, behavior, and performance in developing countries.

Gender Role and Entrepreneurial Cognition in Developing Countries

There are several studies that suggest women's entrepreneurial cognition is affected by gender roles, including entrepreneurial intention and entrepreneurial opportunity evaluation. It is found that gender stereotypes explain cognitive differences among entrepreneurs (Bird & Brush, 2002; Byrne & Fayolle, 2010), and these effects are even greater in underdeveloped regions or countries (Bertaux & Crable, 2007; Roomi & Parrott, 2008). These studies provide solid evidence that gender roles affect women's cognition of entrepreneurship in different developing countries.

For example, Vishal K Gupta, Turban, Wasti, and Sikdar (2009) examine the role of gender stereotypes in entrepreneurship and their impact on entrepreneurial intentions, the empirical results of which based on data from India and Turkey showed that those who perceived themselves as more similar to males had higher entrepreneurial intentions than those who have low male gender identification. In Turkey, Vishal K Gupta, Goktan, and Gunay (2014) conducted two experiments, the results of which show that men reported higher opportunity evaluation than women when no gender stereotypical information was presented, whereas men and women evaluated the business opportunity equally when entrepreneurs were under gender-neutral environments. The results imply that due to the existence of gender roles, activated stereotypes will impact women's opportunity assessment. Furthermore, Vishal K. Gupta, Turban, and Pareek (2013) based on the data from India indicate that gender stereotype activation can both boost and impede the role in women's entrepreneurial actions such as opportunity evaluation, depending on the way in which it is presented. Specifically, feminine stereotypical information presented to women entrepreneurs subtly can significantly alter opportunity evaluation, making their evaluation more negative. However, when the information is presented blatantly, this effect will disappear.

In China, Shinnar, Giacomin, and Janssen (2012) draw on gender role theory and examine how culture and gender shape entrepreneurial perceptions and intentions. The empirical results show that women possess low entrepreneurial intention as the existence of gender stereotypes in the business world show that women are expected to be more concerned with taking care of the home rather than achievements outside the home in general. Additionally, studies in various Arab Middle Eastern countries such as the United Arab Emirates (Erogul & McCrohan, 2008; Madichie & Gallant, 2012), Oman (Dechant & Lamky, 2005), and Lebanon (Jamali, 2009) highlight the negative impact of the sociocultural values on women entrepreneurship. They stress the interaction effect among sociocultural values, gender stereotypes, and Islam in explaining the underprivileged status of women in entrepreneurship.

Gender Role and Entrepreneurial Financing in Developing Countries

Access to finance is critical to launch a start-up and its subsequent performance when engaging in an entrepreneurial project. Research studies show consistent results about the gender gap in entrepreneurial financing. That is, women entrepreneurs have more difficulty in accessing financing resources, especially in developing countries (Sara & Peter, 1998). This situation is not due to lack of ability, but because of the more complex and multifaceted restrictions brought about by gender characteristics, which adds more obstacles to many women entrepreneurs (Marlow & Patton, 2005).

For example, based on the data from China, Zhang, Chen, and Zhou (2020) found the evidence that women faces huge constrains in formal and informal financing because their gender makes them regarded as a group with insufficient entrepreneurial competence by resource providers. In Pakistan, Roomi and Parrott (2008) found that women entrepreneurs receive little encouragement from some male family members, resulting in limited spatial mobility and a dearth of social capital and financing resource. Wu, Chen, Mei, and Liang (2017) stated that under the social construction of gender stereotype, there is conflict and inconsistency between the female default image and outstanding female innovators, which leads to their lack of identity legitimacy and role consistency when seeking funds for technology start-ups.

Additionally, previous studies have emphasized the positive role played by informal financing in economic development and boosting entrepreneurship in developing countries (Biggadike, 1989; Elston, Chen, & Weidinger, 2016). Different from formal financing, informal financing relies more on funding seekers' personal social network and social capital (Lorenz, 2000). However, the scale and diversity of female entrepreneurs' social network are normally built around families and thus women entrepreneurs are less likely to be familiar with fund providers in developing countries (Roomi & Parrott, 2008; Venkatesh et al., 2017; Zhang et al., 2020). For example, in India, inherent attitudes of patriarchal societies have created great challenges for women, which make them unable to play any other role except being housewives (Goyal & Parkash, 2011; Kaushik, 2013). These challenges include unfavorable social norms, limited capital and skills, and limited access to business networks (Malhotra, Kanesathasan, & Patel, 2012). Thus, women experience greater difficulties than men do in accessing the source of funding (Kuada, 2009).

Gender Role and Entrepreneurial Performance in Developing Countries

Women entrepreneurship plays a vital role in regional economic development, but some obstacles, such as poverty, unemployment, and social discrimination, prevent them from playing this role effectively, especially in developing countries (Watson, 2002). Previous literature on this gender gap in performance mainly focused on two interrelated factors. On the one hand, researchers found that one reason of the gender performance gap is based on structural factors, such as industry and start-up size. On the other hand, researchers also agree that the discrimination based on gender attitudes of entrepreneurs should be considered as an important reason for gender performance gap. Furthermore, existing research studies have proven that the entrepreneurial projects led by women do not perform well in terms of sales and profits even after controlling the demographic factors, suggesting that discrimination arising from gender plays an important role (Watson, 2002).

For example, Fischer, Reuber, and Dyke (1993) suggest that small and medium-sized enterprises (SMEs) run by women will exhibit poorer performance because women are obviously discriminated against by lenders. Venkatesh et al. (2017) address a grand entrepreneurial performance challenge faced by women, and the empirical results from a seven-year field quasi-experiment in 20 rural villages in India supports that the interplay of women's social networks (ties to family, to community, and to men in power), information and communication technology (ICT) use can effectively weaken the performance constraints faced by women entrepreneurs. In Nigeria, Ekpe, Mat, and Razak (2010) explored the multiple antecedents of female entrepreneurial performance by structured questionnaire and an in-depth interview and found that due to gender discrimination and women entrepreneurs' lack of social capital and education restrictions led to their poor performance in entrepreneurship, such as scale, net income, and venture capital. Lerner, Brush, and Hisrich (1997) found that compared to developed countries, in Israel, network affiliations more significantly influence women entrepreneurial performance, but the gender bias prevalent in the Israeli culture served to constrain women's networks.

Solutions for Women Entrepreneurship in Developing Countries

Numerous potential solutions are studied to promote empowerment of women and generate and support their entrepreneurial activities, such as providing education, training resources, providing advanced technical tools, and conducting gender identity management strategies.

Literature supports that previous business experience is crucial to the success of entrepreneurship. However, most women entrepreneurs in developing countries lack such experience because they suffer from poverty, low education levels, and other social discrimination (Porter & Nagarajan, 2005). In these special situations, education and training are very important for women entrepreneurs because it would provide the skills and experience needed by businesses (Garavan & Barra, 1994). Consistent with this notion, Harrison and Mason (2007) suggest that women need to study credit jointly with training on entrepreneurship performance in developing countries to deal with financial constraints. Additionally, modern technology can also help female entrepreneurs deal with gender disadvantages, such as information and communication technology (ICT) and Meerut Seva Samaj (MSS). For example, Best and Maier (2007) suggest that a promising way to eliminate the disadvantages of women entrepreneurs caused by gender issues is to provide information to women, especially rural women, by using ICTs. Women can speak to clients and suppliers, expand their markets, communicate to their mentors in their business networks, and even obtain skills and training to help build their entrepreneurial capacity through the ICTs (Malhotra et al., 2012) and thus alleviate the gender disadvantages. Venkatesh et al. (2017) provide the evidence that ICT intervention positively influences entrepreneurial profit and also plays a moderating role in the relationship between social networks and entrepreneurial activities and profit in rural India. Bertaux and Crable (2007) describe and assess the impact and effectiveness of their learning with a particular focus on their exposure to MSS, an economic development initiative concentrating on India rural women. The results show that MSS provides an effective technologic tool to India rural women to obtain resources and become successful entrepreneurs. Further, recent studies emphasize that the gender penalties for women entrepreneurs arising from incongruity between a stereotypical female figure and the role of a successful entrepreneur could be averted if they conduct the appropriate gender identity strategies (Lee & Huang, 2018; Zhang et al., 2020), such as performing CSR behavior and displaying both feminine and masculine characteristics (Schock, Gruber, Scherndl, & Ortner, 2019).

Conclusion

Nowadays, entrepreneurship is regarded as a related tool for economic development, and women all over the world have made important contributions to it. Over the years, attention has focused on analyzing the characteristics of women entrepreneurs in developed countries. Until recently, the role of women entrepreneurs in emerging economies has been studied. Drawing on gender role perspectives, we discussed how gender role plays an important part in women entrepreneurship in developing countries, especially in entrepreneurial cognition, entrepreneurial financing, and entrepreneurial performance. We also discussed potential solutions for women entrepreneurs to deal with gender disadvantages in developing countries.

Note

1. TAE is used to measure the relative amount of nascent entrepreneurs with specific countries or regions by the sum of those actively starting a new business, plus those already running a new business.

References

Acker, J. (2006). Inequality regimes: Gender, class, and race in organizations. *Gender & Society*, *20*(4), 441–464.

Bertaux, N., & Crable, E. (2007). Learning about women. Economic development, entrepreneurship and the environment in India: A case study. *Journal of Developmental Entrepreneurship*, *12*(04), 467–478.

Best, M. L., & Maier, S. (2007). Gender, culture and ICT use in rural south India. *Gender, Technology and Development*, *11*(2), 137–155.

Biggadike, R. (1989). The risky business of diversification. In D. Asch & C. Bowman (Eds.), *Readings in strategic management* (pp. 177–190). Cham: Springer.

Bird, B., & Brush, C. (2002). A gendered perspective on organizational creation. *Entrepreneurship: Theory and Practice*, *26*(3), 41–65.

Borkenau, P., Mauer, N., Riemann, R., Spinath, F. M., & Angleitner, A. (2004). Thin slices of behavior as cues of personality and intelligence. *Journal of Personality and Social Psychology*, *86*(4), 599.

Byrne, J., & Fayolle, A. (2010). A feminist inquiry into entrepreneurship training. In D. Smallbone, J. Leitao, M. Raposo, & F. Welter (Eds), *The theory and practice of entrepreneurship* (pp. 76–100). Northampton, MA: Edward Elgar Publishing.

Cialdini, R. B., & Trost, M. R. (1998). Social influence: Social norms, conformity and compliance. In D. T. Gilbert, S. T.Fiske, & G.Lindzey (Eds.), *The handbook of social psychology* (pp. 151–192). New York, NY: McGraw-Hill.

Das, M. (2000). Women entrepreneurs from India: Problems, motivations and success factors. *Journal of Small Business and Entrepreneurship*, *15*(4), 67–81.

Dechant, K., & Lamky, A. A. (2005). Toward an understanding of Arab women entrepreneurs in Bahrain and Oman. *Journal of Developmental Entrepreneurship*, *10*(02), 123–140.

Eagly, A. H., & Karau, S. J. (2002). Role congruity theory of prejudice toward female leaders. *Psychological Review*, *109*(3), 573.
Eagly, A. H., Wood, W., & Diekman, A. B. (2000). Social role theory of sex differences and similarities: A current appraisal. *The Developmental Social Psychology of Gender*, *12*, 174.
Eddleston, K. A., Ladge, J. J., Mitteness, C., & Balachandra, L. (2016). Do you see what I see? Signaling effects of gender and firm characteristics on financing entrepreneurial ventures. *Entrepreneurship: Theory and Practice*, *40*(3), 489–514.
Ekpe, I., Mat, N. B., & Razak, R. C. (2010). The effect of microfinance factors on women entrepreneurs' performance in Nigeria: A conceptual framework. *International Journal of Business and Social Science*, *1*(2), 255–263.
Elston, J. A., Chen, S., & Weidinger, A. (2016). The role of informal capital on new venture formation and growth in China. *Small Business Economics*, *46*(1), 79–91.
Erogul, M. S., & McCrohan, D. (2008). Preliminary investigation of Emirati women entrepreneurs in the UAE. *African Journal of Business Management*, *2*(10), 177–185.
Fischer, E. M., Reuber, A. R., & Dyke, L. S. (1993). A theoretical overview and extension of research on sex, gender, and entrepreneurship. *Journal of Business Venturing*, *8*(2), 151–168.
Garavan, T. N., & Barra, O. (1994). Entrepreneurship education and training programmes: A review and evaluation. *Journal of European Industrial Training*, *18*(8), 3–12.
Goyal, M., & Parkash, J. (2011). Women entrepreneurship in India-problems and prospects. *International Journal of Multidisciplinary Research*, *1*(5), 195–207.
Gupta, V. K., Goktan, A. B., & Gunay, G. (2014). Gender differences in evaluation of new business opportunity: A stereotype threat perspective. *Journal of Business Venturing*, *29*(2), 273–288.
Gupta, V. K., & Turban, D. B. (2012). Evaluation of new business ideas: Do gender stereotypes play a role?. *Journal of Managerial Issues*, *24*, 140–156.
Gupta, V. K., Turban, D. B., & Pareek, A. (2013). Differences between men and women in opportunity evaluation as a function of gender stereotypes and stereotype Activation. *Entrepreneurship: Theory and Practice*, *37*(4), 771–788.
Gupta, V. K., Turban, D. B., Wasti, S. A., & Sikdar, A. (2009). The role of gender stereotypes in perceptions of entrepreneurs and intentions to become an entrepreneur. *Entrepreneurship: Theory and Practice*, *33*(2), 397–417.
Harrison, R. T., & Mason, C. M. (2007). Does gender matter? Women business angels and the supply of entrepreneurial finance. *Entrepreneurship: Theory and Practice*, *31*(3), 445–472.
Heilman, M. E., & Chen, J. J. (2003). Entrepreneurship as a solution: The allure of self-employment for women and minorities. *Human Resource Management Review*, *13*(2), 347–364.
Huang, L., & Pearce, J. L. (2015). Managing the unknowable: The effectiveness of early-stage investor gut feel in entrepreneurial investment decisions. *Administrative Science Quarterly*, *60*(4), 634–670.
Jamali, D. (2009). Constraints and opportunities facing women entrepreneurs in developing countries. A relational perspective. *Gender in management: An International Journal*, *24*(4), 232–251.

Jennings, J. E., & Brush, C. G. (2013). Research on women entrepreneurs: Challenges to (and from) the broader entrepreneurship literature?. *The Academy of Management Annals*, *7*(1), 663–715.

Kanze, D., Huang, L., Conley, M. A., & Higgins, E. T. (2018). We ask men to win and women not to lose: Closing the gender gap in startup funding. *Academy of Management Journal*, *61*(2), 586–614.

Kaushik, S. (2013). Challenges faced by women entrepreneurs in India. *Education*, *35*(53), 53.

Kuada, J. (2009). Gender, social networks, and entrepreneurship in Ghana. *Journal of African Business*, *10*(1), 85–103.

Lee, M., & Huang, L. (2018). Gender bias, social impact framing, and evaluation of entrepreneurial ventures. *Organization Science*, *29*(1), 1–16.

Lerner, M., Brush, C., & Hisrich, R. (1997). Israeli women entrepreneurs: An examination of factors affecting performance. *Journal of Business Venturing*, *12*(4), 315–339.

Lorenz, E. H. (2000). Neither friends nor strangers: Informal networks of subcontracting in French industry. In D. Gambetta (Ed.), *Trust: Making and breaking cooperative relations* (Chapter 6, pp. 183–191), Electronic edition, Department of Sociology, University of Oxford.

Madichie, N. O., & Gallant, M. (2012). Broken silence: A commentary on women's entrepreneurship in the United Arab Emirates. *The International Journal of Entrepreneurship and Innovation*, *13*(2), 81–92.

Malhotra, A., Kanesathasan, A., & Patel, P. (2012). Connectivity how mobile phones. Computers and the Internet Can Catalyze Women's Entrepreneurship.

Marlow, S., & Patton, D. (2005). All credit to men? Entrepreneurship, finance, and gender. *Entrepreneurship: Theory and Practice*, *29*(6), 717–735.

Minniti, M. (2010). Female entrepreneurship and economic activity. *The European Journal of Development Research*, *22*(3), 294–312.

Minniti, M., & Naudé, W. (2010). What do we know about the patterns and determinants of female entrepreneurship across Countries?. *European Journal of Development Research*, *22*(3), 277–293.

Obayelu, A., & Ogunlade, I. (2006). Analysis of the uses of information communication technology (ICT) for gender empowerment and sustainable poverty alleviation in Nigeria. *International Journal of Education and Development using ICT*, *2*(3), 45–69.

Porter, E. G., & Nagarajan, K. (2005). Successful women entrepreneurs as pioneers: Results from a study conducted in Karaikudi, Tamil Nadu, India. *Journal of Small Business and Entrepreneurship*, *18*(1), 39–52.

Roomi, M. A., & Parrott, G. (2008). Barriers to development and progression of women entrepreneurs in Pakistan. *The Journal of Entrepreneurship*, *17*(1), 59–72.

Sara, C., & Peter, R. (1998). The financing of male–and female–owned businesses. *Entrepreneurship & Regional Development*, *10*(3), 225–242.

Schock, A.-K., Gruber, F. M., Scherndl, T., & Ortner, T. M. (2019). Tempering agency with communion increases women's leadership emergence in all-women groups: Evidence for role congruity theory in a field setting. *The Leadership Quarterly*, *30*(2), 189–198.

Shinnar, R. S., Giacomin, O., & Janssen, F. (2012). Entrepreneurial perceptions and intentions: The role of gender and culture. *Entrepreneurship: Theory and Practice*, *36*(3), 465–493.

Smith, P. B., Dugan, S., & Trompenaars, F. (1997). Locus of control and affectivity by gender and occupational status: A 14 nation study. *Sex Roles*, *36*(1), 51–77.

Solnick, S. J., & Schweitzer, M. E. (1999). The influence of physical attractiveness and gender on ultimatum game decisions. *Organizational Behavior and Human Decision Processes*, *79*(3), 199–215.

Thébaud, S. (2015). Business as plan B: Institutional foundations of gender inequality in entrepreneurship across 24 industrialized countries. *Administrative Science Quarterly*, *60*(4), 671–711.

Venkatesh, V., Shaw, J., Sykes, T., Macharia, M., & Wamba, S. F. (2017). Networks, technology, and entrepreneurship: A field quasi-experiment among women in rural India. *Academy of Management Journal*, *60*(5), 1709–1740.

Watson, J. (2002). Comparing the performance of male-and female-controlled businesses: Relating outputs to inputs. *Entrepreneurship: Theory and Practice*, *26*(3), 91–100.

Williams, J. E., & Best, D. L. (1990). *Measuring sex stereotypes: A multination study* (Rev. ed.). Newbury Park, CA: Sage Publications, Inc.

Wu, X., Chen, J., Mei, L., & Liang, L. (2017). Gender stereotype: The threat or opportunity for female innovators in technological innovation?. *Foreign Economics and Management*, *39*(11), 45–60.

Zhang, H., Chen, Y., & Zhou, X. (2020). Gender and financing in entrepreneurship: Research evidence from China. *Chinese Management Studies*, *14*(3), 677–694.

Chapter 4

Gender Diversity, Environmental Performances, and the Role of Countries' Development Status

Mohamed M. Sraieb and Ahmet Akin

Abstract

We investigate the relationship between gender diversity on corporate boards and environmental performances of firms. Our central focus is the extent to which a country's economic status (developed, developing) can shape such a relationship. We find evidence that gender diversity is positively correlated to environmental performances of firms. Interestingly, this correlation is not only stronger in developing countries but also increasing in gender diversity. These findings have considerable importance in terms of policy.

Promotion of gender diversity in developing countries, where abatement costs are the lowest, would improve global environmental quality in a cost-effective way. This is best achieved through building institutions and strengthening them. The benefits of such policy go beyond developing countries frontiers, particularly when global environmental problems (pollution, global warming, ozone layer depletion, loss of biodiversity, etc.) are concerned. These benefits can be a leverage for an efficient implementation of the United Nations Sustainable Development Goals (UN-SDGs) both as gender diversity stands as a goal by itself and also because it facilitates achieving other environmental-related SDGs.

Keywords: Gender diversity; board of directors; environmental performance; energy sector; endogeneity; dynamic panel data

JEL classification: G30; G34; J16; M14; Q40; Q56

Introduction

How important is gender diversity to firms' environmental performances and therefore to environmental quality? Recently, this question attracted increasing

The Emerald Handbook of Women and Entrepreneurship in Developing Economies, 49–69
Copyright © 2021 by Emerald Publishing Limited
All rights of reproduction in any form reserved
doi:10.1108/978-1-80071-326-020211004

interest. Surprisingly most studies focused on developed countries with markets characterized by consolidated institutions and well-functioning corporate governance systems (Boulouta, 2013; Glass, Cook, & Ingersoll, 2016; Kassinis, Panayiotou, Dimou, & Katsifaraki, 2016; Li et al., 2017; Lu & Herremans, 2019; Post, Rahman, & Rubow, 2011; Velte, 2016). This may be rationalized on the ground of data availability and length of coverage. Importantly, only a small but growing number of studies in the field is devoted to developing countries (Alazzani, Hassanein, and Aljanadi (2017) for Malaysia, Nguyen, Locke, and Reddy (2015) for Vietnam, etc.).

A stream of research has studied the relationship between economic development and environment (Koirala & Mysami, 2015; Lu et al., 2017). Yet, no study in the literature has investigated the role of countries' economic status in shaping the relationship between gender diversity and corporate social responsibility nor, a fortiori, environmental concerns. This is puzzling since firms' environmental performances depend heavily on the country's institutional development, the quality of the regulatory framework (Auffhammer & Kellogg, 2011; Campbell, 2007; Zhang, Zhu, & Fan, 2018; Zhao & Luo, 2017), and the rule of law. Obviously, these factors have different magnitude across countries. Specifically, they take different depth in developed and developing countries (Manrique & Martí-Ballester, 2017). Therefore, country economic status should be explicitly taken into account if the relationship between firm's environmental performance and gender diversity is to be modeled accurately. To the best of our knowledge, no attempt has been made to build a unified framework where the difference in economic development status between countries is exploited to shed light on the effect of gender diversity on environmental performance.

This is precisely the main purpose of this chapter. In terms of policy, this approach can be highly informative to policy-makers, managers, and investors. A public policy that encourages gender diversity as a leverage to environmental quality would be more efficient in regions where marginal benefits of gender diversity is high. Theoretically, this is more likely to be the case in developing countries. The reason is that these are countries for which environmental concerns are relatively more recent compared to their developed pairs. In addition, the legal framework tends be less coercive due to weaker institutions and dominance of economic priorities over ecological concerns. As such, their efficiency frontier is farther compared to developed countries and there is room for further efficiency gain by improving gender diversity. Yet, these are theoretical conjectures that may not be validated by observations. An empirical assessment is thus required.

On the econometric side, most of the literature is cast in a static framework making use of a fixed effects (FEs). An inherent limitation common to all studies in the field is the omitted variables concern. The problem is further exacerbated by the trigger of reverse causality since gender diversity may improve firms' (environmental) performance. Female managers, in turn, may self-select in well-performing firms and the causality goes in both directions. This is where instrumental variables approach intervenes in the literature.

Unfortunately, in our particular context, instrumental variables may not be of great help for at least two major reasons. The first is that finding a valid and reliable instrument for gender diversity can be drastically difficult. A "good" candidate must be correlated with gender diversity on board, but uncorrelated with environmental performance, except through control variables. Finding such a variable may turn impossible since all variables that determine environmental performance of firms must be already part of the regression. As such, they are not available as instruments (Adams & Ferreira, 2009).

The second limitation of the instrumental variable approach is its inability to address dynamic endogeneity. This type of endogeneity arises when the relationship between the independent variable and its determinants is dynamic in nature (Schultz, Tan, & Walsh, 2010; Wintoki, Linck, & Netter, 2012). Failure to identify and address dynamic endogeneity invalidates statistical inference.

Given these constraints, we follow Sila, Gonzalez, and Hagendorff (2016), Ngyuen et al. (2015), Deszö and Ross (2012), Adams and Ferreira (2009), Lu and Herremans (2019), Kassinis et al. (2016) and opt for a dynamic modeling approach to study the relationship between gender diversity and firms' environmental performances (Arellano-Bover 1995; Blundel-Bond 1998).

The System-GMM estimator makes use of internal instruments in the regression as opposed to external ones. This is a major advantage in our particular context given the lack of appropriate external instruments. Furthermore, System-GMM generates consistent estimates even in the presence of FEs in a dynamic panel data (DPD; see Arellano, 2003). This estimator is particularly suited to panels with large number of individuals and few time periods, which is the case for this chapter. Moreover, it accommodates situations where the independent variable changes slowly (Antoniou, Guney, & Paudyal, 2008).

Our chapter focuses on the extractive industry – oil, gas, and mining. Although, it represents a substantial source for financial revenues and economic growth for countries, this industry has a sizable adverse effect on the environment. Pollution, loss of biodiversity, soil erosion, water stress are some of the other threats that can affect the natural environment and resources. According to UNEP's Global Resources Outlook (2019), resource extraction along with processing causes 90% of biodiversity loss and water stress in the world and about half of global greenhouse gas emissions (Oberle et al., 2019).

Any improvement in the extractive industry's environmental impact would have a high marginal benefit. This is precisely how gender diversity may feed firms' transition toward better environmental impact. Women on board would be more inclined to adopt ethical-oriented business practices, including those pertaining to the environment (Lara, Osma, Mora, & Scapin, 2017). They tend to be more risk-averse then men and therefore would be more willing to "follow precautionary routes if science is unclear" (Lu & Herremans, 2019). Moreover, they tend to show more concern for environmental issues compared to men (Jones & Dunlap, 2010).

This chapter contributes to the literature in several ways. Most studies in the field focus on a particular country or group of countries. By contrast, we bring evidence, at the international level, on the impact of gender diversity on environmental performances of firms. Besides, we explicitly take into account the dynamic nature of the relationship under study and use a dynamic framework that models appropriately dynamic endogeneity. Most importantly, our chapter integrates the difference in development across countries as a contextual factor that shapes the relationship between gender diversity on boards and firms' environmental performances. We highlight the role of institution building and rule of law as a leverage for promoting environmental quality in developing countries.

On a macroeconomic level, empowering women in the corporate boards can be seen as a facilitator for an efficient implementation of the United Nations Sustainable Development Goals (UN-GDGs) both as gender diversity stands as a goal by itself (goal 5) and also because it helps achieving other environmental-related SDGs. Among these we find: taking urgent action to combat climate change and its impacts (goal 13), as well as protecting, restoring, and promoting sustainable use of ecosystems (goals 14 and 15).

Literature and Hypothesis Development

Previous literature found that gender diversity has several benefits to the organizations. A disproportionately large part of this literature has focused on firms' financial performance or more globally firms' corporate social responsibility (Adams & Ferreira, 2009; Byron & Post, 2016; Cabeza-García, Fernández-Gago, & Nieto, 2018; Dezsö & Ross, 2012; Galbreath, 2015; Hillman, 2015; Shaukat, Qiu, & Trojanowski, 2016). In these studies, the environmental dimension is either ignored or diluted in the overall composite corporate social responsibility score. Although the concern for the environment is among the different dimensions of corporate social responsibility, it is clear that it should be examined separately since desegregating social responsibility helps identifying the particular dimension along which firms can better improve performance. Considering the all-encompassing global score hides details and the specific relationship between gender diversity and environmental performance may be subject to dilution effects.

A number of influential studies have paved that path. Some investigated environmental policy in general (Li et al., 2017). Others specifically considered environmental performance (Boulouta, 2013; Galbreath, 2011; Lu & Herremans, 2019; Ortiz-de-Mandojana & Aragon-Correa, 2015; Post et al., 2011; Walls, Berrone, & Phan, 2012). Yet, other papers focused on the relationship between women on boards and environmental sustainability (Glass et al., 2016) or environmental disclosure (Ben Ammar, Chang, & McIlkenny, 2017; Rao, Tilt, & Lester, 2012).

The common denominator of all of these studies is that gender diversity on board enriches firms in terms of "professional experience, skills, and diverse perspectives" (Kassini et al., 2016). This, in turn, promotes innovative ideas and enhances group decision-making within the board (Post & Byron, 2015). Furthermore, women bring some ethical business-related values as they tend to be less willing to accept unethical practices (Lara et al., 2017). Moreover, women tend to exhibit less risk-taking behavior than men and therefore are more patient and more inclined to seek experts' advicee when uncertainty is involved (Liu,

2018). Prior research has also found that women tend to be more "emotionally engaged, empathetic, and show more concern about the environment than men" (Davidson & Freudenburg, 1996; Jones & Dunlap, 2010). With this strand of literature, the link between gender diversity and environmental performances of firms then started to take shape.

Interestingly, gender diversity in the boardroom is found to be more influential in industries that have stronger adverse environmental impact. Li et al. (2017) show that the beneficial impact of gender diversity on corporate environmental policy is stronger in those industries that are more likely to cause environmental pollution. Lu and Herremans (2019) found that gender diversity has a stronger effects on firms' environmental performance in more environmentally impacting industries. Therefore, we focus on firms in the extractive industry. The strength of its adverse effect on the environment is documented in UNEP's Global Resources Outlook (2019). Accordingly, we propose the following hypothesis:

Hypothesis 1: Gender diversity is positively associated with environmental performance in the extraction sector globally.

Our second hypothesis relates to the quality and intensity of the association between gender diversity on boards and environmental performance of firms. Previous studies have found that institutional quality of countries, environment awareness, and advances in the technology and innovation leads to reduction in environmental degradation (Sarkodie & Strezov, 2019). These factors witness the level of economic development of countries. It is very likely that the effect of gender diversity on the environment will be more salient in countries where improvement is less costly. Consequently, developing countries should be associated, on average, with a stronger impact. Therefore, we conjecture that the difference in development across countries is a contextual factor that shapes such a relationship. We exploit this dimension to highlight the role of institution building and rule of law as a leverage for promoting environmental quality in developing countries.

Hypothesis 2: The impact of gender diversity on board on environmental performance is, on average, more salient for firms in developing countries compared to their pairs in developed countries.

Data and Descriptive Analysis

Our sample consists of firms in the extractive industry – oil, gas, and mining. Data cover 448 firms across the world. The information collected concerns environmental and financial conditions of these firms for the period 2008–2018.

Data are obtained from Refinitive Eikon database (Eikon thereafter) – a comprehensive database providing environment, social, and governance (ESG) data.[1]

Our study relates firms' environmental performances to their past values (lagged value of environmental performances) and to a measure of gender diversity in firms' board of directors. A set of conventional firm-level control variables are included. These are firm size, asset tangibility, leverage, Tobin's q, profitability, board independence, and board size.

We also include unobserved firm FEs to account for unobserved firm-specific factors that do not change over time, as well as a set of year dummies to control for the effect of general changes over time unrelated to firms' performances. A description of the variables is presented in Table 4.1. Summary statistics are provided in Table 4.2, and correlation matrix is presented in Table 4.3.

The main focus of this study is the impact of extraction firms' operations on the environment. Table 4.2 shows that our sample firms are characterized by low emission scores and underrepresentation of female members in the corporate boards. Emission reduction scores for our sample range from 1.007 to 99.045 with a mean of 47.168 which is below mean emission reduction score reported by Ting, Azizan, Bhaskaran, and Sukumaran (2020) for all sectors in the developed and emerging markets.

The average percentage of female board members in our sample is 9.6%. Importantly, there are firms with only male board members. The highest value for the proportion of females on the boards of firms is 50%. Notice that the average score globally for all the sectors is 13.5% and 19.4% for 2014 and 2018, respectively (Refinitive, 2020). For the same years, our sample returns the scores of 9.63% and 15.03%, respectively. Scores that are well below the average for all sectors, but values that have steadily increased between the two years.

Table 4.3 shows that the Pearson's correlation between the emission reduction score (*Emis. Score*) and each of the other variables is statistically highly significant, including with our variable of interest percentage of female in firm's board (*Gender Div.*). The coefficient on the lagged dependent variable *LagEmis. Score* (0.915) further motivates our choice of a dynamic specification. The highest correlation coefficient across independent variables is observed between *Board Size* and *firm size* (0.659), which may point to a multicollinearity problem between the two variables.

However, the variance inflation factors (VIFs) for each of the variables and the mean VIF were found to be all less than 5. Thus, multicollinearity should not be a concern for our analysis.

Model Specification and Estimation Method

The environmental performance equation can be described by the following DPD model.

$$Emis.Scor_{it} = \alpha_i + \delta_t + \rho \ EmiScor_{it-1} + X^{'}_{it-1} \ \vartheta + \varepsilon_{it}; \quad i = 1,\ldots,448; \ t = 1,\ldots,8. \quad (4.1)$$

where $Emis.Scor_{it}$ is the emission score of firm i in year t. α_i represents unobserved firm FEs and δ_t represents time FEs. The dynamic nature of a problem imposes to integrate the lag of the dependent variable $Emis.Scor_{it-1}$ in the equation. The matrix X includes explanatory variables and a set of control representing firms' financial performances as well as board characteristics. These are gender diversity, firm size, leverage, Tobin-Q, profitability, board size, and independent board. Finally, ε_{it} is the error term assumed to be i.i.d with zero mean and constant variance.

Table 4.1. Variables Definition.

Emis. Score	The emission reduction score ranges from zero (lowest performance) to 100 (highest performance). The emission score measures a company's commitment and effectiveness toward reducing environmental emission in the production and operational processes. Emission concerns air pollutants, water discharges, solid and hazardous waste, wastes produced, accidental spills, etc (Refinitive, 2020). We follow Ellimäki, Gómez-Bolaños, Hurtado-Torres, and Aragón-Correa (2021), Gómez-Bolaños, Hurtado-Torres, and Delgado-Márquez (2020) and use this variable as our metric for environmental performance.
Gender Div.	Percentage of female board members (Adams & Ferreira, 2009; Glass et al., 2016; Kassinis et al., 2016; Liu, 2018; Velte, 2016). This is our proxy for gender diversity. We will also use the Blau index for robustness check (see definition in the section relative to robustness check.
Firm size	This is the log of total assets. We follow Kassinis et al. (2016), Li et al. (2017), Liu (2018), Dyck et al. (2019) and include firm size since larger firms may pollute more. Yet, they also have larger means for abatement or mitigation.
Leverage	This is the ratio of book value of total debt to book value of total assets ratio. This variable is used as previous studies showed that firms with higher leverage are associated with better environmental performances (Biswas, Mansi, & Pandey, 2018; Glass et al., 2016; Liu, 2018).
Tobin-Q	The ratio of the market value of a firm's assets to their replacement (Dyck et al., 2019; Kassinis et al., 2016; Liu, 2018)
Profitability	This is the ratio of operating profit to total assets. It controls for the fact that profitable firms tend more to afford environmental compliance costs (De Villiers, Naiker, & Van Staden, 2011; Lu & Herremans, 2019).
Tangibility	This is the net plant, property, and equipment to total assets ratio. It is used here to control for high processing cost and environmental damage (Hoogendoorn, Guerra, & Van der Zwan, 2015) and also for financial constraint (Dyck et al., 2019)

Table 4.1. *(Continued)*

Board Size	The number of board members. Previous studies showed that better environmental scores were associated with larger boards (Biswas et al., 2018; De Villiers et al., 2011; Galbreath, 2015; Liu, 2018; Lu & Herremans, 2019). We log the variable to reduce outliers and have better distributional properties.
Indep. Board	This is the percentage of independent board members. This variable controls for the fact that independent members in the board are likely to be more effective monitors including for firms' environmental management (Biswas et al., 2018; De Villiers et al., 2011; Liu, 2018).

We introduce a one-year lag for all explanatory variables. Intuitively, lagging variables allow to account for the delay necessary to the transmission mechanism. From an econometric perspective, the lag is justified by the need to avoid reverse causality. Furthermore, we take the natural log for the emission reduction score, Tobin-Q, and board size. This gives a less skewed distribution for these variables and the resulting log-log model would reduce outlier effects.

Eq. (4.1) is our baseline model. Its estimation may result in several econometric problems. The lagged dependent variable is correlated, by construction, to the country FE α_i. Within transformation leads to correlation between $EmiScor_{it-1}$ and the error term. The resulting bias in the estimate of ρ is not mitigated by increasing the number of individual units. In addition, some of the dependent variables are suspected of carrying simultaneity, since they can themselves be influenced by the dependent variable (the causality goes in both directions).

We use the Arellano and Bover (1995); Blundel and Bond (1998) System-GMM estimator. This is shown to have high finite sample properties.

The procedure consists in first-differencing Eq. (4.1) to remove unobserved time-invariant country-specific effects. Then, the right-hand-side variables in the equation in first-difference are instrumented using levels of the series lagged two periods or more. To increase efficiency, the equation in level is reintroduced to obtain a system of equations in both first-differences and levels. The instruments used in the equations in first-differences are variables lagged in levels and the instruments for the equation in levels are lagged first-differences of the series. These instruments are valid under restrictions on the initial conditions: changes in instrumenting variables (for the equation in levels) are uncorrelated with the FE. The system of equations obtained provides more moment conditions which will be exploited in a GMM framework to give efficient estimates of the parameters.

Interestingly, the use of System-GMM has major advantages as it generates consistent estimates even in the presence of FEs in a DPD (see Arellano, 2003).

Table 4.2. Summary Statistics.

	Min	Max	Mean	Median	St.Dev	Skewness	Kurtosis	N
Emis. Score	1.007	99.045	47.168	16.258	28.027	0.108	1.837	3,760
Env. Score	9.01	95.227	46.758	45.087	20.001	0.355	2.148	3,758
Res. Use Score	4.762	99.045	48.278	47.297	28.081	0.131	1.713	3,758
Gender Div.	0	0.5	0.096	0.083	0.11	1.008	3.43	3,753
Blau	0	0.5	0.15	0.153	0.156	0.464	1.881	3,753
Firm size	15.403	25.605	21.145	21.301	2.001	–0.273	2.865	4,963
Leverage	0	0.979	0.211	0.187	0.196	1.107	4.38	4,949
Tobin Q	0.457	11.094	1.597	1.245	1.182	3.335	18.418	4,623
Profitability	–1.126	0.119	0.036	0.046	0.148	–2.059	13.278	4,908
Tangibility	0	0.946	0.589	0.63	0.245	–0.561	2.483	4,891
Board Size	4	21	8.596	8	2.947	0.734	3.505	3,752
Indep. Board	0	1	0.63	0.667	0.226	–0.759	2.942	3,732

Note: These summary statistics relate to environmental and social scores for the energy sector ("Mining, Quarrying, and Oil and Gas Extraction" based on the NAICS classification). The data cover the period 2008–2018 and are obtained from ASSET4 ESG database. All variables are winsorized at the 1st and 99th percentiles.

Table 4.3. Correlations Matrix.

Variables	**(1)**	**(2)**	**(3)**	**(4)**	**(5)**	**(6)**	**(7)**	**(8)**	**(9)**	**(10)**
(1) Emis. Score	1.000									
(2) Gender Div.	0.278***	1.000								
(3) Firm Size	0.553***	0.231***	1.000							
(4) Leverage	0.097***	0.121***	0.290***	1.000						
(5) Tobin Q	–0.008***	–0.042**	–0.170***	–0.017***	1.000					
(6) Profitability	0.291***	0.046***	0.457***	0.049***	–0.126***	1.000				
(7) Tangibility	–0.094***	–0.049***	0.092***	0.160***	–0.210***	0.073***	1.000			
(8) Board Size	0.436***	0.21–3***	0.659***	0.168***	–0.082***	0.261***	–0.073***	1.000		
(9) Indep. Board	0.043***	0.072***	0.116***	0.050***	–0.074***	0.001	0.268***	–0.013	1.000	
(10) LagEmis. Score	0.915***	0.278***	0.541***	0.093***	–0.131***	0.277***	–0.098**	0.430***	0.030*	1.000

Notes: Asterisks indicate significance at 0.01 (***), 0.05 (**), and 0.10 (*) levels. Board size and Tobin-Q arc both log-ed. All variables are winsorized at the 1st and 99th percentiles.

Unfortunately, implementation of System-GMM is not exempt from risks. Given that the number of instruments is quadratic in the time dimension, the variance matrix of the moments can be very large.

Estimating its elements may be problematic in particular in a finite sample lacking the adequate amount of information. This finite sample bias could weaken Hansen *J*-test, overstating its *p*-value and therefore validating instruments where they should have failed. The problem is known as instruments proliferation (Roodman, 2009).

We run a two-step GMM regression and use robust standard errors (Windmeijer, 2005 finite sample corrected standard errors). We collapse the instrument matrix which prevents the model from being overfitted and allows to avoid bias and inconsistency due to instruments proliferation.

Notice that the econometric technique used is particularly suited to panels with large number of individuals and few time periods, which is the case for the chapter. Moreover, it has the advantage of accommodating situations where the independent variable changes slowly (Antoniou et al., 2008).

Empirical Results and Discussion

Main Findings

Eq. (4.1) is our base-line model. However, for reference and in order to compare with previous studies, we start by estimating a version of base-line model where $\rho = 0$. This is an FE regression whose results are reported in Model (1) of Table 4.4.

We find evidence that gender diversity affects positively firms' environmental performances. This relation is statistically significant at the 5% level. The coefficient of *gender diversity* means that a 1% increase in the percentage of females in the boardrooms is associated with a 0.56% increase, on average, in emission score, holding all other factors constant. A result providing support for a positive association between gender diversity on boardrooms and environmental performance of firms.

However, previous literature (Adams & Ferreira, 2009; Byron & Post, 2016; Lu & Herremans, 2019) challenged this result on the ground of simultaneity and dynamic simultaneity concerns in the estimation process.[2] Gender diversity may affect firms' environmental performances but it may also be the case that firms with higher environmental performances are likely to be more attractive for female directors. Causality may work in both directions. This is an inherent problem in gender diversity studies (Adams & Ferreira, 2009; Campbell & Minguez-Vera, 2008) which may lead to biased and inconsistent parameter estimates. To address the problem, instrumental variable approach has been proposed. However, the literature argues that finding a "good" instrument is itself a challenge since most variables that determine environmental performance of firms must be already part of the regression (Adams & Ferreira, 2009) and are not available for being used as instruments.

Table 4.4. Environmental Performance and Gender Diversity.

Variables	FE (1)	System G MM (2)	(3)
Emission Score		0.662*** (0.070)	0.650*** (0.071)
Gender Div.	0.560** (0.252)	0.715*** (0.235)	2.424** (1.068)
Dev (dummy)			0.199* (0.111)
Dev#Gen.Div.			–2.174** (1.075)
Firm Size	0.223*** (0.061)	0.055*** (0.014)	0.069*** (0.015)
Leverage	0.077 (0.190)	–0.116 (0.075)	–0.070 (0.078)
Tobin Q	0.043 (0.063)	–0.018 (0.029)	–0.026 (0.030)
Profitability	0.340* (0.179)	0.355** (0.145)	0.345** (0.155)
Tangibility	–0.026 (0.148)	–0.042 (0.054)	–0.090 (0.064)
Board Size	0.065 (0.116)	0.020 (0.048)	–0.007 (0.055)
Indep. Board	0.194* (0.111)	0.015 (0.054)	0.012 (0.057)
Constant	–1.647 (1.228)	0.015 (0.166)	–0.311 (0.201)
Time FE	Yes	Yes	Yes
Observations	3,083	3,083	3,083
R-squared	0.2527		
Instruments count		27	29
Firms count	448	448	448
AR(1)		[0.000]	[0.000]
AR(2)		[0.363]	[0.425]
Hansen *J*-test		[0.289]	[0.349]
Diff Hansen *J*-test		[0.385]	[0.461]

Note: The dependent variable is the natural log of emission score. Windmeijer finite sample corrected standard errors in parentheses. *p*-values in brackets. Instrument matrix collapsed to avoid instrument proliferation. Hansen *J*-test reported the *p*-values for the null that instruments are valid. The *p*-values reported for *AR(1)* and *AR(2)* are for first- and second-order autocorrelated disturbances in the first differences equations. We take the log of the lagged dependant variable, Tobin-Q and Board size. All models are run on data winsorized at the 1st and 99th percentiles. Asterisks indicate significance at 0.01 (***), 0.05 (**), and 0.10 (*) levels.

This is a major limitation for the analysis of the effects of gender diversity on firms' environmental performances. Consequently, we opt for a system-GMM estimator (Table 4.4, Model 2) that relies on internal instruments as opposed to external instruments (Roodman, 2009). Of central interest here are the advantages provided by the system-GMM approach. On the one hand, it addresses the endogeneity problems associated with the use of gender diversity as a covariate. On the other hand, it allows to deal with the dynamic nature of the relationship being examined (dynamic endogeneity).

Interestingly, we find evidence that gender diversity affects environmental score. This effect is positive and highly significant. A 1% change in gender diversity is associated, on average, with 0.715% change in emission score, ceteris paribus. It is worth noting that, given the conjunction of relatively small size of the boards and gender diversity ratios, the magnitude of the coefficient is economically large. For example, a firm's board of eight persons (the median value of board size for our data) with only one female member that substitutes a man for an additional female member would double firm's gender diversity (100% increase). Therefore, it would be associated with an increase in the emission reduction score by 71.5%.

The coefficient on the lagged dependent variable shows that the emission reduction score is highly persistent. If a firm puts in efforts in reducing emissions during a certain year, it will continue doing so in the following year, everything else equal. On average, a 1% increase in emission reduction score is associated with a 0.66% increase in the following year, ceteris paribus. This finding suggests that past performance captured some time unobserved heterogeneity. It strongly supports the argument that the relationship between gender diversity and environmental performance is dynamic, in essence, and should be studied using a dynamic framework.

As for control variables, we find that *firm size* is positively and significantly associated with emission reduction score across all models. This suggests that large firms may generate more pollutants, yet they tend to have, on average, more resources to reduce their emission into the natural environment. The result is in line with Lu and Herremans (2018). The same argument applies to the finding on *profitability* whose coefficient is positive and statistically significant. All other control variables are not statistically significant.[3]

Instruments count (27) and firms count (448) reported at the end of Table 4.4 suggest that instruments proliferation (Roodman, 2009) is not an issue. *AR(2)* test shows a *p*-value of (0.363). This implies that we cannot reject the null hypothesis of absence of second-order autocorrelation disturbances in the first difference equation. Furthermore, the *p*-value associated with the Hansen J-test (0.289) cannot reject the null hypothesis that instruments are valid as a group. Table 4.4 also reports on Difference in Hansen J-test, whose *p*-value (0.385) does not reject the null that the subsets of instruments are exogenous.

The Contextual Effect of Country Status

Obviously, environmental quality in a particular country would rely heavily on the quality of its institutions, as well as on the coerciveness of its regulations. It is also conditional on government and people's awareness and consciousness about the effect of environmental problems on their living conditions. Unfortunately, institutions strength and society awareness may be constrained by short-term concerns for better economic outcomes. Environmental quality may be then passed to a lower order importance in the scale of national priorities.

It is common knowledge that the effect of these contextual factors depends on the social and economic development of a society. Firms in developed country are more likely to face a more coercive environmental regulatory framework. They are also more likely to face strong well-established institutions. These include developed legal framework favoring rule of law, better organized implementing parties, more involved civil society, etc. In short, an institutional organization, which is the medium in which firms behave and interact, tends to differ between developed and developing countries. As such, the "economic" status of countries imposes different contextual factors to firms and tend to influence differently their behavior. This includes their environmental performances. Therefore, it is of first importance to integrate the economic status of countries as a contextual effect in the study of the relationship between gender diversity and firm's environmental performance.

To account for economic status of countries in our sample, a new variable *Dev* is introduced to the base-line model (Table 4.4, Model 3). This is a dummy obtained by coding the pairs country/year so as to have one for those pairs where the country is classified as developed and 0 otherwise. The coding is based on information from the classification system of the Department of Economic and Social Affairs of the United Nations Secretariat (UN-DESA).[4]

The dummy variable *Dev* is introduced in interaction with the *gender diversity* variable in order to assess whether the country economic status has an impact of the relationship between gender diversity and firms' environmental performances. Results in Model 3 show that the coefficient of the interaction term is negative and statistically significant (-2.174). This is the difference in slope between the developed and developing groups. The coefficient for gender diversity is 2.424, which is the slope of the regression line for firms in developing countries (i.e., Dev = 0). It follows that the slope for the developed countries' group is 0.25 (2.424–2.174). Therefore, for both country types the association between gender diversity and environmental performances tend to be positive and statistically significant. However, there is a strong and significant difference in effects.

To investigate further this finding, we examine, for different gender diversity levels, (i) the slope comparison between developed and developing countries and (ii) the marginal effect of economic status on firms' environmental performances. The results are reported in Fig. 4.1.

Fig. 4.1a confirms the finding on the difference between developed and developing countries in terms of the effect of gender diversity on environmental performances. This effect is positive regardless of the country economic status. However, the marginal effect of a percentage increase in gender diversity tends to cause, on average, a higher increase in environmental performances among firms in developing countries as compared to their pairs in developed countries.

The question then is whether the difference developed/developing countries is statistically significant for different values of gender diversity. Fig. 4.1b depicts the intensity of this difference between the two country types. It shows that the differences in effects is increasing in absolute terms and is significant at 95% for values of gender diversity above about 15%.

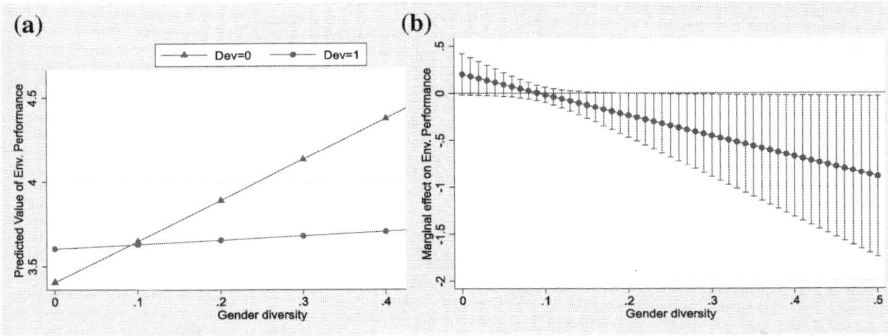

Fig. 4.1. Interaction Effects, (a) Slope Comparison of Gender Diversity among Developed and Developing Countries, (b) Marginal Effect of Country Economic Statute on Env. Performance across Gender Diversity Levels.

One potential explanation of this result finds ground in Adams and Ferreira (2009) argument that female directors are tougher monitors compared to men. Knowing that the marginal benefit of monitoring is negative for well-governed firms, this may affect negatively firms' financial performances. By contrast, Nguyen et al. (2015) find that, because firms in developing countries are generally poorly governed, the benefit from additional monitoring (marginal benefit of monitoring) may be positive.

For our analysis, the arguments above easily extend to firms' environmental performances. On the one hand, female board members are associated with tougher monitoring efforts. On the other hand, women have higher inclination for environmental quality (Davidson & Freudenburg, 1996; Jones & Dunlap, 2010). They have higher risk-aversion that leads them to avoid environmental violation more than men (Liu, 2018); They are more willing to wait until elucidation of uncertainty, particularly in situation with high uncertainty and tend more to seek experts advise in such situations (Liu, 2018).[5] Higher monitoring will then tend to extend to environmental issues and given the low records on firms' environmental performances, it would have a positive marginal benefit. Its magnitude would be even stronger in developing countries where firms have way more room to improve governance.

Robustness Analysis

Our variable of interest is *gender diversity*. In order to facilitate comparison, we report the results of the base-line model in Table 4.5 (Model 1). For robustness check, we first substitute the *Blau* index for the *gender diversity* variable. This index reflects the chances that two randomly selected group members belong to different categories (Harrison & Klein, 2007). Here, categories are the two genders, while the group is the firm's board of directors. The results are reported in

Table 4.5. Robustness Chocks.

Variables	Model (1)	Model (2)	Model (3)	Model (4)
Emission Score	0.662*** (0.070)	0.675*** (0.069)		
Res. Use Score			0.964*** (0.038)	
Env. Score				0.875*** (0.048)
Gender Div.	0.715*** (0.235)		0.331** (0.139)	0.202** (0.079)
Blau		0.505*** (0.185)		
Firm Size	0.055*** (0.014)	0.053*** (0.014)	0.010 (0.008)	0.016*** (0.006)
Leverage	–0.116 (0.075)	–0.122* (0.074)	–0.041 (0.035)	–0.043* (0.023)
Tobin Q	–0.018 (0.029)	–0.016 (0.028)	0.025** (0.012)	0.017** (0.007)
Profitability	0.355** (0.145)	0.359** (0.144)	0.078 (0.049)	0.058* (0.031)
Tangibility	–0.042 (0.054)	–0.046 (0.053)	0.008 (0.029)	–0.017 (0.019)
Board Size	0.020 (0.048)	0.006 (0.048)	–0.042* (0.023)	–0.008 (0.017)
Indep. Board	0.015 (0.054)	0.014 (0.054)	–0.007 (0.026)	–0.002 (0.017)
Constant	0.015 (0.166)	0.037 (0.166)	0.079 (0.074)	0.186*** (0.066)
Time FE	Yes	Yes	Yes	Yes
Observations	3,083	3,083	3,081	3,081
Instruments count	27	27	27	27
Firms count	448	448	448	448
AR(1)	[0.000]	[0.000]	[0.000]	[0.000]
AR(2)	[0.363]	[0.374]	[0.678]	[0.250]
Hansen J-test	[0.289]	[0.387]	[0.219]	[0.129]
Diff Hansen J-test	[0.385]	[0.502]	[0.213]	[0.553]

Note: Windmeijer finite sample corrected standard errors in parentheses. *p*-values in brackets. Instrument matrix collapsed to avoid instrument proliferation. Hansen *J*-test reports the *p*-values for the null that instruments are valid. The *p*-values reported for *AR(1)* and *AR(2)* are for first- and second-order autocorrelated disturbances in the first differences equations. We take the log of the lagged dependant variable, Tobin-Q and Board size. All models are run on data winsorized at the 1st and 99th percentiles. Asterisks indicate significance at 0.01 (***), 0.05 (**), and 0.10 (*) levels.

Table 4.5 (Model 2). The coefficient on *Blau* is positive (0.505) and statistically significant at the 1% level. Substituting *Blau* for *gender diversity* does not alter the magnitude nor the statistical significance of the remaining variables. This confirms earlier findings that gender diversity is positively associated with environmental performances, and the relationship is robust to the metric used.

So far, our proxy for firms' environmental performances is *Emission Score*. This score is a pillar for the measurement of environmental performances. Yet, other dimensions may consolidate the analysis. These includes resources use reduction which is of high importance to the extraction sector as highlighted in the introduction of this paper. Therefore, a firm that has a strong commitment toward emission is supposed to have aligned concerns for resources use and for the environment as a whole.

A second line of robustness analysis is to check whether firms' efforts in emissions reduction are in line with their performances in terms of reduction of resources use *Res.Use Score* (Model 3 of Table 4.5) as well as with its global environmental performances as measured by the aggregate environmental score *Env.Score* (Model 4 of Table 4.5).[6] Although both scores measure different dimensions of environmental efforts, they strongly signal firms' commitment toward a better environmental management. As such, improvements in these scores should witness better records in terms of emission reduction for firms.

Both Model (3) and Model (4) reveal that gender diversity, our variable on interest, is positive and highly significant (at the 1% level). Their magnitude is lower than the coefficient of Model (1) associated with emission reduction score, though. This is expected as the three scores are measuring different (but complementary) aspects of firm's environmental commitments. Our focus here is rather on the sign and the statistical significance of *gender diversity*. The finding comforts our previous result on emission reduction and suggests that it is in line with firms' environmental orientations.

Concluding Remarks

Environmental degradation is one of the most pressing challenges to countries today. Understanding the factors driving corporate environmental performance is crucial to protect the environment. Using a dynamic modeling, this study brings a global evidence on the positive effect of gender diversity on environmental performances of firms.

Importantly, we find that the intensity of this positive effect is shaped by the economic status of a country. The marginal effect of gender diversity on firms' environmental performances is found to be higher for firms in developing countries as compared to their pairs in developed countries. This status reflects superiority of developed economies in terms of strength of institutions, existence and quality of the regulatory framework, the consciousness and awareness about the environment, and involvement of the civil society in these matters.

One of the most salient implications of our finding is that given our focus on extractive firms with high level of CO_2 emissions, and given the public good nature of the environment, economic efficiency requires emission abatement where they are the less costly. As developing countries are further to their efficiency frontier compared to their developed pairs, abatement costs tend to be lower therein. As such, putting emphasis on promoting gender diversity in developing countries further improves efficiency gains globally and has a higher and less costly impact on the environment.

Interestingly, gender diversity has a feedback effect in the long term that is completely ignored in the literature. This effect is extremely important for policy design, particularly in developing countries. According to World Bank report (2009), the effect of gender diversity on the natural environment is felt differently between men and women. In lowest income countries, the report states that women bear most of the cost of environmental degradation. A better environmental quality means higher and easier access to resources including, water, firewood, food, etc – a task typically under women responsibility in these societies. Ensuring and facilitating access to resources reduces time to gather them and can improve their health condition and foster women and girls' abilities to go to school or do other tasks. In a long-term perspective this, in turn, enlarges the pool of talents firms can rely on. Gender diversity is actually a very effective solution to reduce the negative impact of environmental degradation and improve firms' conditions.

Notes

1. Eikeon covers 70% of the global capitalization (Refinitive, 2020). It is one of the most preferred databases for ESG research (Dyck, Lins, Roth, & Wagner, 2019; Velte, 2016).
2. Omitted variables problem is also an issue identified in the literature (Adams & Ferreira, 2009). Firm fixed effects has been used to address such problems.
3. The coefficient on *independent board* in Model 1 seems to be carried by spurious correlation, since it become statistically nonsignificant after we control for dynamic endogeneity
4. Data are collected from World Economic Situation and Prospects (WESP) report produced yearly by UN-DESA.
5. This includes greenhouse gas emissions and their effect on ozone layer.
6. The resource use score "reflects a company's performance and capacity to reduce the use of materials, energy or water, and to find more eco-efficient solutions by improving supply chain management." (Refinitive 2020)

References

Adams, R. B., & Ferreira, D. (2009). Women in the boardroom and their impact on governance and performance. *Journal of Financial Economics*, *94*(2), 291–309.

Alazzani, A., Hassanein, A., & Aljanadi, Y. (2017). Impact of gender diversity on social and environmental performance: Evidence from Malaysia. *Corporate Governance*, *17*(2), 266–283.

Antoniou, A., Guney, Y., & Paudyal, K. (2008). The determinants of capital structure: Capital market-oriented versus bank-oriented institutions. *Journal of Financial and Quantitative Analysis*, *43*(1), 59–92.

Arellano, M. (2003). *Panel data econometrics. Advanced Texts in Econometrics*. Oxford; New York, NY: Oxford University Press.

Arellano, M., & Bover, O. (1995). Another look at the instrumental variable estimation of error-components models. *Journal of Econometrics*, *68*(1), 29–51.

Auffhammer, M., & Kellogg, R. (2011). Clearing the air? The effects of gasoline content regulation on air quality. *The American Economic Review*, *101*(6), 2687–2722.

Ben Ammar, W., Chang, M., & McIlkenny, P. (2017). Board gender diversity and corporate response to sustainability initiatives: Evidence from the carbon disclosure project. *Journal of Business Ethics*, *142*(2), 369–383.

Biswas, P. K., Mansi, M., & Pandey, R. (2018). Board composition, sustainability committee and corporate social and environmental performance in Australia. *Pacific Accounting Review*, *30*(4), 517–540.

Blundell, R., & Bond, S. (1998). Initial conditions moment restrictions in dynamic panel data models. *Journal of Econometrics*, *87*(1), 115–143.

Boulouta, I. (2013). Hidden connections: The link between board gen-der diversity and corporate social performance. *Journal of Business Ethics*, *113*(2), 185–197.

Byron, K., & Post, C. (2016). Women on boards of directors and corporate social performance: A meta-analysis. *Corporate Governance: An International Review*, *24*(4), 428–442.

Cabeza-García, L., Fernández-Gago, R., & Nieto, M. (2018). Do board gender diversity and director typology impact CSR reporting? *European Management Review*, *15*(4), 559–575.

Campbell, J. L. (2007). Why would corporations behave in socially responsible ways? An institutional theory of corporate social responsibility. *Academy of Management Review*, *32*(3), 946–967.

Campbell, K., & Minguez-Vera, A. (2008). Gender diversity in the boardroom and firm financial performance. *Journal of Business Ethics*, *83*(3), 435–451.

Davidson, D. J., & Freudenburg, W. R. (1996). Gender and environ-mental risk concerns. *Environment and Behavior*, *28*(3), 302–339.

De Villiers, C., Naiker, V., & Van Staden, C. J. (2011). The effect of board characteristics on firm environmental performance. *Journal of Management*, *37*(6), 1636–1663.

Deszö, C. L., & Ross, D. G. (2012). Does female representation in top management improve firm performance? A panel data investigation. *Strategic Management Journal*, *33*(9), 1072–1089.

Dyck, A., Lins, K. V., Roth, L., & Wagner, H. F. (2019). Do institutional investors drive corporate social responsibility? International evidence. *Journal of Financial Economics*, *131*(3), 693–714.

Efttimie, A., Heller, K., & Stronman, J. World Bank Report. (2009). Mainstreaming gender into extractive industries project. Retrieved from http://hdl.handle.net/10986/18235

Ellimäki, P., Gómez-Bolaños, E., Hurtado-Torres, N., & Aragón-Correa, J. A. (2021). Do global firms increase their environmental disclosure and performance? Symbolic versus effective operations and the moderating role of liability of origin. Legitimation implications. *Industrial Marketing Management*, *92*, 354–363.

Galbreath, J. (2011). Are there gender-related influences on corporate sustainability? A study of women on boards of directors. *Journal of Management and Organization, 17*(1), 17–38.

Galbreath, J. (2015). A study of women in top business roles: The case of the wine industry. *International Journal of Wine Business Research, 27*(2), 143–158. (pp. 401–421).

Glass, C., Cook, A., & Ingersoll, A. R. (2016). Do women leaders promote sustainability? Analysing the effect of corporate governance composition on environmental performance. *Business Strategy and the Environment, 25*(7), 495–511.

Gómez-Bolaños, E., Hurtado-Torres, N., & Delgado-Márquez, B. L. (2020). Disentangling the influence of internationalization on sustain-ability development: Evidence from the energy sector. *Business Strategy and the Environment, 29*(1), 229–239.

Harrison, D. A., & Klein, K. J. (2007). What's the difference? Diversity constructs as separation, variety, or disparity in organizations. *Academy of Management Review, 32*, 1199–1228.

Hillman, A. J. (2015). Board diversity: Beginning to unpeel the onion. *Corporate Governance: An International Review, 23*(2), 104–107.

Hoogendoorn, B., Guerra, D., & Van der Zwan, P. (2015). What drives environmental practices of SMEs? *Small Business Economics, 44*(4), 759–781.

Jones, R. E., & Dunlap, R. E. (2010). The social bases of environmental concern: Have they changed over time? *Rural Sociology, 57*(1), 28–47.

Kassinis, G., Panayiotou, A., Dimou, A., & Katsifaraki, G. (2016). Gender and environmental sustainability: A longitudinal analysis. *Corporate Social Responsibility and Environmental Management, 23*(6), 399–412.

Koirala, B. S., & Mysami, R. C. (2015). Investigating the effect of forest per capita on explaining the EKC hypothesis for CO2 in the US. *Journal of Environmental Economics and Policy, 4*(3), 304–314.

Lara, J. M. G., Osma, B. G., Mora, A., & Scapin, M. (2017). The monitoring role of female directors over accounting quality. *Journal of Corporate Finance, 45*, 651–668.

Liu, C. (2018). Are women greener? Corporate gender diversity and environmental violations. *Journal of Corporate Finance, 52*, 118–142.

Li, J., Zhao, F., Chen, S., Jiang, W., Liu, T., & Shi, S. (2017). Gender diversity on boards and firms' environmental policy. *Business Strategy and the Environment, 26*(3), 306–315.

Lu, Z. N., Chen, H., Hao, Y., Wang, J., Song, X., & Mok, T. M. (2017). The dynamic relationship between environmental pollution, economic development and public health: Evidence from China. *Journal of Cleaner Production, 166*, 134–147.

Lu, J., & Herremans, I. M. (2019). Board gender diversity and environmental performance: An industries perspective. *Business Strategy and the Environment, 28*(7), 1449–1464.

Manrique, S., & Martí-Ballester, C. P. (2017). Analysing the effect of corporate environmental performance on corporate financial performance in developed and developing countries. *Sustainability, 9*(11), 1957.

Nguyen, T., Locke, S., & Reddy, K. (2015). Does boardroom gender diversity matter? Evidence from a transitional economy. *International Review of Economics & Finance, 37*, 184–202.

Oberle, B., Bringezu, S., Hatfield-Dodds, S., Hellweg, S., Schandl, H., & Clement, J., … et al. (2019). *Global resources Outlook 2019: Natural resources for the future we want.* A report of the international resource panel. United Nations Environment Programme, Nairobi, Kenya.

Ortiz-de-Mandojana, N., & Aragon-Correa, J. A. (2015). Boards and sustainability: The contingent influence of director interlocks on corporate environmental performance. *Business Strategy and the Environment*, *24*(6), 499–517.

Post, C., & Byron, K. (2015). Women on boards and firm financial performance: A meta-analysis. *Academy of Management Journal*, *58*(5), 1546–1571.

Post, C., Rahman, N., & Rubow, E. (2011). Green governance: Boards of directors' composition and environmental corporate social responsibility. *Business & Society*, *50*(1), 189–223.

Rao, K. K., Tilt, C. A., & Lester, L. H. (2012). Corporate governance and environmental reporting: An Australian study. *Corporate Governance*, *12*(2), 143–163.

Refinitive. (2020). Environmental, social and governance (ESG) scores. Retrieved from https://www.refinitiv.com

Roodman, D. (2009). A note on the theme of too many instruments. *Oxford Bulletin of Economics & Statistics*, *71*(1), 135–158.

Sarkodie, S. A., & Strezov, V. (2019). A review on environmental Kuznets curve hypothesis using bibliometric and meta-analysis. *The Science of the Total Environment*, *649*, 128–145.

Schultz, E. L., Tan, D. T., & Walsh, K. D. (2010). Endogeneity and the corporate governance–performance relation. *Australian Journal of Management*, *35*(2), 145–163.

Shaukat, A., Qiu, Y., & Trojanowski, G. (2016). Board attributes, corporate social responsibility strategy, and corporate environmental and social performance. *Journal of Business Ethics*, *135*(3), 569–585.

Sila, V., Gonzalez, A. & Hagendorff, J. (2016). Women on board: Does boardroom gender diversity affect firm risk? *Journal of Corporate Finance*, *36*, 26–53.

Ting, I. W. K., Azizan, N. A., Bhaskaran, R. K., & Sukumaran, S. K. (2020). Corporate social performance and firm performance: Comparative study among developed and emerging market firms. *Sustainability*, *12*(1), 26.

United Nations Department of Economic and Social Affairs; UN-DESA. (various years). World economic situation and Prospects report-WESP.

Velte, P. (2016). Women on management board and ESG performance. *Journal of Global Responsibility*, *7*(1), 98–109.

Walls, J. L., Berrone, P., & Phan, P. H. (2012). Corporate governance and environmental performance: Is there really a link? *Strategic Management Journal*, *33*(8), 885–913.

Windmeijer, F. (2005). A finite sample correction for the variance of linear efficient twostep GMM estimators. *Journal of Econometrics*, *126*(1), 25–51.

Wintoki, M. B., Linck, J. S., & Netter, J. M. (2012). Endogeneity and the dynamics of internal corporate governance. *Journal of Financial Economics*, *105*(3), 581–606.

Zhang, H., Zhu, Z., & Fan, Y. (2018). The impact of environmental regulation on the coordinated development of environment and economy in China. *Natural Hazards*, *91*(2), 473–489.

Zhao, X., & Luo, D. (2017). Driving force of rising renewable energy in China: Environment, regulation and employment. *Renewable and Sustainable Energy Reviews*, *68*, 48–56.

Part 2
Institutions, History, Culture as Catalysator or Blockage for Woman Entrepreneurship

Chapter 5

Female Entrepreneurship in Latin America and the Key Role of Informal Institutions in the Reproduction of Gender Asymmetries

Shahamak Rezaei and Denise Helena França Marques

Abstract

The aim of this chapter is to provide an overview of female entrepreneurship in Latin American countries and to show how the environment, through formal and especially informal institutions, influences the characteristics of the business and to some extent limits the exploitation of opportunities by women. Entrepreneurship addressed in the text consists of initiatives characterized by creativity, risks, use of available resources, and the ability to generate wealth and change economic and social contexts, especially at the micro level. The literature review showed how informal institutions, impregnated by patriarchal and macho culture, shape and determine gender relations in the world of work in the region, especially in business activities conducted by women. Although the cases presented cannot be generalized to all Latin American countries, they provide a small sample of the obstacles, challenges, and limitations imposed on female entrepreneurs by the social structure and its repeated practices consolidated in Latin American society.

Keywords: Latin America; female entrepreneurship; informal institutions; formal institutions; entrepreneurial talent; gender asymmetries

Introduction

The gender division of labor and the power relations imposed by it remain today as a latent characteristic of relations between men and women in Latin American countries. Although women are increasingly protagonists in the management and maintenance of families and households, inequalities in access, use, and control of production factors remain, on the one hand, as obstacles to income generation and business initiatives, and on the other hand, family responsibilities and the lack

The Emerald Handbook of Women and Entrepreneurship in Developing Economies, 73–90
Copyright © 2021 by Emerald Publishing Limited
All rights of reproduction in any form reserved
doi:10.1108/978-1-80071-326-020211005

of stimulation of the environment and the absence of policies and programs to support entrepreneurial activity (Heller, 2010; Rezaei & Marques, 2016). These factors together limit the autonomy of Latin American women and create barriers to creative work and innovation, important ingredients for the practice of entrepreneurship.

The data published by GEM-Brasil (2018) show that in 2018, for every 10 initial male entrepreneurs, there were eight women in the same situation in the region. Disaggregating the data by country, there are differentials between them, always with the predominance of men as initial entrepreneurs (TEA) in relation to women: ranging from 0.93 (Brazil) to 0.64 (Uruguay). In relation to opportunity as the main motivation for opening a new venture, women were also behind men, but in a more equal position: for every 10 men who pointed out the opportunity as the main driver for establishing a new business, there were 0.86 women. Peru was the only country that reported gender equality in this indicator. The lowest figure was for Argentina, with a ratio of 0.78.

The literature on entrepreneurship sets two main motivations for establishing a new business: opportunity and need (De la O & Urbano, 2020; Santander, Fernández, & Yáñez, 2016; Smith-Hunter & Leone, 2010; Terjesen & Amorós, 2010). It also analyzes the relationship between sociodemographic characteristics and entrepreneurial activity, as well as personality traits (willingness to take risks, willingness and ability to discover new niches, and access to credit conditions and favorable information) as important factors in decision-making (Thurik, Verheul, & Grilo, 2010). In fact, these elements are fundamental for the understanding of entrepreneurship, but they are insufficient if not contextualized (social, economic, cultural, spatial, and institutional contexts).

Some scientific studies have called attention to the theoretical weakness of entrepreneurship by presenting an idealized, generalist, and globalized view of practice, in which entrepreneurial people differ only from nonentrepreneurs when, in fact, we empirically observe differences of gender and race, social class and environment, the latter permeating socialization patterns and positions in the family, society, labor market, and companies (Santander et al., 2016).

Minniti and Nardone (2007), in attempting to demonstrate the universal effects of gender on decisions to start a business, showed that the probabilities of beginning among men and women with the same characteristics, under identical social and macroeconomic conditions, don't change. The same procedure adopted for the perception variables highlighted their importance in explaining the difference between genders in the behavior of undertaking, especially the perception of opportunity which, for the authors, is directly linked to feelings of security and self-esteem which, in turn, are associated with the cultural context and environmental/institutional conditions. Thus, to consider gender effects as universal, not considering their historical and social construction, is to incur mistakes. "*Hacer negocios es una práctica social y, en consecuencia, es 'hacer género,' reelaborar relaciones de género*" (Duque, 2014, p. 242).

The aim of this chapter is to provide an overview of female entrepreneurship in Latin American countries and show how informal institutions like cultural norms, maternity, and values influence women's decisions and characteristics of their business (North, 1990). To this end, bibliographic research was conducted on female entrepreneurial activity in different countries of the region from the perspective of current institutional structures, especially informal ones. It is important to point out that it is impossible to have a precise view on the subject due to the lack of data and incomplete information coming exclusively from case studies.

It is noteworthy that the entrepreneurship addressed by the authors is not the one established by Schumpeter (1947), in which innovation is the basic premise of business. The entrepreneurial activities dealt within this chapter are characterized by creativity, risks, use of available resources, and the ability to generate wealth and change economic and social micro contexts (Elizundia Cisneros, 2015).

The chapter is divided into four parts, besides this introduction. The second section reviews some of the main theoretical approaches to entrepreneurship, with emphasis on the influence of the environment, through institutions on entrepreneurial activities. The third part brings some elements to understand the insertion of women on the Latin American work market, and the fourth part presents some empirical works that show the interaction and influence of informal institutions on entrepreneurial practices.

Conceptual Framework

Interest in entrepreneurship has gained new followers around the world. Its ability to generate jobs and income through the creation of new businesses has long been recognized by economic theories as *a sine qua non* for the economic development of any region. In order for the entrepreneurial activity to exist, it is essential to have actors capable of adding value to goods and services and to manage the business efficiently and effectively.

Entrepreneurship is the process of creating new business ventures which require individuals have the ability to deliver valuable products and services under various mixed market risks. However, being an entrepreneur is hard and is not for everyone. It takes much more money, energy, time, and effort than being an employee (Rezaei, 2017).

The society and media promote entrepreneurship with a focus on successful entrepreneurial activities and, because of that, the public may think it is straightforward and profitable. But in fact, entrepreneurship is a complicated process that requires individuals have certain credentials and what the author calls competencies, like self-efficacy; opportunity-alertness; risk-propensity; role-modeling knowledge; skills; and experiences.

According to Baggio and Baggio (2014), there is no scientific consensus or absolute paradigm on what entrepreneurship is. For them, what exists is a field of study that recognizes entrepreneurial activities as a set of practices that generates wealth and is known to induce development. In fact, by exclusively considering entrepreneurship as defined by Shumpeter (1991), the literature and studies on the subject would be restricting the scope of analysis and, therefore, leaving aside countless initiatives that, although they do not cause "creative destruction," are steeped in creativity, risks, use of available resources, and the capacity to modify economic and social contexts. This is a basic premise to be considered when one wishes to study entrepreneurship, especially in less developed regions where the opening of new businesses is fundamental for the generation of jobs and income.

The theoretical approach to entrepreneurship has two main strands: the economic, focusing on innovation, and the behavioral. In the first case, the authors Richard Cantillon, Jean Baptiste Say, and Joseph Schumpeter stand out, establishing that the origin of entrepreneurship lies in the creation of new ways of using resources and in new combinations that create and institutionalize new practices, new products, and administrative structures, that is, the entrepreneurial practice is necessarily associated with innovation, with the alteration, in some way, of production functions. For Schumpeter (1991), entrepreneurship establishes a dynamic imbalance that is the vein of a healthy economy. The so-called "creative destruction process" causes the production of better quality goods and services and breaks with established market structures, generating development and competition through new technologies.

According to the author, the entrepreneur, inventor, capitalist, and manager are different actors, although they can coexist in the same person. The entrepreneur is the one who implements new ideas; the inventor is the one who produces new ideas; the capitalist provides the means for investment; and the manager performs the administrative functions. The entrepreneur has above-average motivation and willpower that go beyond that related to profit (Schumpeter, 1985). He is a rational person, but does not guide his actions purely by rationality. The entrepreneur is not part of any social class, unlike the capitalist, his social position is the result of achievements and the condition of innovator is not lasting, since there are few innovations capable of generating ruptures and, therefore, significant changes in the balance of the economy.

Institutions play a key role in the development of entrepreneurial activities, whether through the supply of credit and policies, making available and taxing capital, or through the opposition of the social environment to such activities, such as competitors, consumers themselves, beliefs and behaviors instituted by the collectivity (Schumpeter, 1985).

The behavioral or psychological approach emerged from the economic one and focused on the motivations and behavior of entrepreneurs. One of its main authors is David McClelland, who used theories of behavioral science to conduct empirical studies. Before McClelland, Weber (1958) was already interested in the behavior of businessmen and their capacity for innovation through rationalization. Hagen (1962) also contributed to the studies on the psychological traits of an enterprising individual and created the concept of creative personality. For this author, entrepreneurship was associated with the need for self-realization and autonomy.

According to McClelland (1961), the desire for achievement was seen as the driving force of entrepreneurship which, in turn, would be responsible for the progress and economic development of different societies. According to the author, achievement is related to intrinsic qualities of individuals, to something endogenous, and not only to prestige or social recognition. As for

Schumpeter (1985), McClelland (1961) recognizes differentiated psychological traits in entrepreneurs. They are audacious, ingenious, persistent, determined, and courageous to take risks. Such traits can be explained by some factors, such as the association between self-realization and positive feelings; encouragement of personal independence through education; the idea of rewarding success; and the willingness to pursue challenges (McClelland, 1961). The need for fulfillment is what stimulates people to undertake, and this need is rooted in a society's culture, beliefs, values, and norms. Different societies and cultures produce different stimuli for entrepreneurial activity.

Baggio and Baggio (2014) emphasize that behavioralist theory has not opposed economic theory, but has only broadened the range of analyses and, consequently, the understanding of businessmen in society and their contributions to economic development. Such approach considers the entrepreneur an individual actor, whose personality modifies society and vice versa.

Zarpellon (2010), Cordero and Pulido (2020), and Hansen (2019) associate Douglas North's institutional economic theory with entrepreneurship. While the first author does so in general, the two other works dive into the feminine universe and show how institutional theory proves adequate for the study of gender and entrepreneurship. For North (1990), institutions are the rules of the game, generally accepted by individuals who form a social group. They impose restrictions and frame the process of political, economic, and social interaction, since they function as "...guide to human action...institutions define and limit the set of choices of individuals... they evolve and are altered by human beings" (pp. 36–37). Institutions can be formal, such as laws, regulations, and government norms, or informal, such as ideas, beliefs, attitudes, values, and culture. Informal institutions precede formal ones, and shape and structure human relationships. According to Hansen (2019):

> ...when one considers one's behaviour in for instance a business transaction, our first instinct for action are informal institutions, governing our conduct, representing a guidebook or frames of reference for how we interpret and react to situations. (p. 51)

Individuals, each with their own mental model and their interactions, justify the existence of institutions. These, in turn, by organizing and coordinating divergent expectations, reduce uncertainties and, consequently, the transaction costs involved in human activities. Nevertheless, institutional structures are not identical in all societies, as is efficiency from the social point of view, which makes transaction costs, production, and access to information different. The historical trajectories of societies are associated with their institutional matrices, that is, the combination of formal and informal rules and norms that shape the set of choices of agents, in different contexts, and in a dynamic process of feedback, the institutions.

> Institutions are a creation of human beings. They evolve and are altered by human beings; hence our theory must begin with the individual. At the same time, the constraints that institutions impose

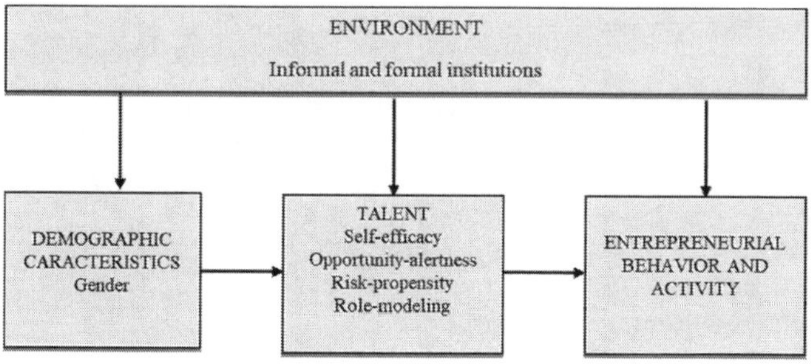

Fig. 5.1. Conceptual Model for Interaction between Environment, Gender, and Entrepreneurial Talent. *Source:* Self-elaboration.

> on individual choices are pervasive. Integrating individual choices with the constraints institutions impose on choice sets is a major step toward unifying social science research. (North, 1990, p. 5)

Fig. 5.1, inspired by Jensen, Rezaei, and Scott (2016), is a conceptual model that shows the interaction between environment, gender, entrepreneurial competencies/talent, and behavior and activity. In Fig. 5.1 the authors developed hypotheses of the impact of gender on entrepreneurial talent (self-efficacy, opportunity-alertness, risk-propensity, and role-modeling) and the moderating effect of environment (formal and informal institutions). Complementing Jensen, Rezaei, and Schøtt (2016)'s conceptual model and adding elements of Aboal and Veneri (2016)'s research, the authors developed a new conceptual structure where interaction between environment, gender and business talent, and behavioral variables and business activity occurs.

Comparing entrepreneurial activities of residence of a given country with diasporas of that country residing abroad, this typology could be used more widely to represent the interactions between the aspects mentioned above in a given country.

Jensen, Rezaei, & Schøtt (2016) define entrepreneurial competencies/talent as a set of cognitive skills that enables the capture and processing of information. Some of these are intrinsic to individuals, others can be acquired and developed under certain circumstances. In the field of entrepreneurship, the literature points to four main competencies: self-efficacy, opportunity-alertness, risk-propensity, and role-modeling.

Self-efficacy, according to the authors, would be related to people's self-perception about their organizational capabilities and the realization of actions necessary to achieve their goals. According to Bandura (1977, 1986) and Anton and Lawrence (2014), the self-efficacy of individuals changes according to their place of residence, since it is a consequence of people's experiences and feedback received from the public. In this sense, environments that provide positive feedback tend to improve the self-efficacy of individuals. *Opportunity-alertness* is the ability to perceive opportunities that have been neglected until then. Thus, individuals able to scan, evaluate, and transform information from various sources into new opportunities will probably become entrepreneurs (Tang, Kacmar, & Busenitz, 2012). *Risk propensity* is the ability to accept uncertainties because of perceived rewards. It is traditionally considered an important characteristic of entrepreneurs, since entrepreneurship is subject to consequences associated with failure. The risk propensity is impacted by the environment. Familiarity with government policies, with financing channels, and knowledge of markets and their peculiarities diminish, to some extent, the uncertainties and, therefore, dispose individuals to take more risks. *Role-modeling*, in turn, consists of social capital in the form of relationship networks. As Rezaei (2017) says, a model to be followed can become a source of know-how, tacit knowledge on how to start a business, especially for those who have no business experience. If people have a network of friends and family who are successful entrepreneurs, they will feel "inspired" to open their own business, especially in incomplete information environments and weak economic markets.

Gender has a strong influence on entrepreneurial talent. The specialized literature shows the relationship between the female gender and lower levels of self-efficacy and entrepreneurial intentions (Jensen, Rezaei, & Schøtt, 2016). The authors emphasize the historical role of women's disadvantage in relation to men and the determination of private sphere as the first place of women as possible determinants of their low confidence in their abilities. Furthermore, women are more averse to risk and have higher preferences for starting up low risk/return businesses. Aboal and Veneri (2016) also identified greater risk aversion of entrepreneurial women in relation to men, reinforcing the statement of the cited authors. In investigating the correlation of personality traits with the decision to become an entrepreneur in some Latin American countries, the authors highlight the greater presence of women in the group called self-employed, whose predominant characteristics were low to middle education, some experience and influence of parents in entrepreneurial activity (role-modeling) and medium-low and medium-high risk preference.

There is no consensus in the literature on the direction of gender association and the ability to discover opportunities. Some studies emphasize only the differentials between men and women, others believe in greater male capacity (Gonzalez-Alvarez & Solis-Rodriguez, 2011). According to Kirzner (1997), opportunities arise from information asymmetries and women's limited or incomplete access to information due to male dominance in certain niches, which means that they cannot identify opportunities for entrepreneurship.

Kuah-Pearce (2016) by examining the emergence of migrant women entrepreneurs in the garment industry in Guangzhou (Guangdong Province) shows the importance of role-modeling for the development and success of their business. Social networks operate in different ways for these women, whether through the initial financial support of parents, relatives, or friends to open the business; in the form of learning opportunities and familiarity with the garment industry acquired from previous work in the family business; or through the care of their children by grandparents or other extended family members who remain in the region of origin and function as important informal social structures. The author also demonstrates the interaction between the patriarchal context present in the place of residence and gender by explaining the need for these women to negotiate the time and energy between business and family. Besides the guilt of leaving their children in the home village under the care of relatives so that they can reside in Guangzhou, they still have to deal with the social obligation of a wife and the tensions and mistrust of infidelity due to the spatial separation of husbands who remain in the home village. In other words, despite their professional success, the female roles of mother and wife remain the same, plus the role of the one who supports the family.

The environment in the model reflects the impact of institutional structures on the entrepreneur's competencies/talent and, consequently, on entrepreneurial activities. In general, enterprises led by women belong to traditional sectors associated with the female image, mainly in the trade and services sectors and in segments that have greater familiarity (sale of clothing, accessories and footwear, beauty, food, and esthetics). In addition, they seek activities that guarantee them a source of income combined with greater flexibility to care for the family.

Countries and regions with different beliefs, values, and cultures institutionalize gender stereotypes of disparate forms and, therefore, influence formal institutions in distinct ways, in a mutual feedback process that is constantly changing. Decisions are based on learning and are guided by cultural patterns, in which the agents are inserted. In this sense, decisions related to the labor market, whether political or business, are influenced by transformations not only in the productive structure but also by gender relations.

Rezaei (2015), through a comparative analysis between Chinese entrepreneurs in China and entrepreneurs in the Chinese diaspora, empirically shows the relationship between gender and the behavior and talent of entrepreneurs under different institutional structures. Chinese women entrepreneurs in the diaspora, for example, are less likely to be self-efficient and alert to opportunities than those living in China, but are more willing to take risks. The author points out that this difference is not determined by gender but by formal and informal institutional practices and the discourse of society at home and in host countries. The results of the Rezaei study (2015) demonstrate how institutions can favor some individuals over others by assessing certain talents and providing opportunities for individuals to use and develop those talents. Whether an individual's talents unfold or are undervalued is in part a question of the extent to which the individual carries characteristics that within the institutional framework in question are associated with having such talents. In fact, talent is evaluated, valued, and nurtured based on distinct values and traditions in different institutional contexts. Institutional structures establish expectations about who plays certain roles in society and how those roles are played (Brinton, 1998).

For Zukin and DiMaggio (1990) all economic action and behavior is culturally embedded. People's responses to opportunities and challenges are not identical and automatic. They are associated with a cultural context where norms, values, and beliefs interact. In this sense, when analyzing female entrepreneurship in

Latin America, the important role of formal and, above all, informal institutions in the entire process can be seen. There is no doubt about the relevance of laws, policies, and incentive programs to female entrepreneurship in the region, but it is the stereotypes or images and, therefore, the positions that women occupy in society, in the family, in the labor market, and inside companies that weigh more on their economic behavior. The patriarchal context is strongly rooted in Latin American culture and has perpetuated rigid and traditional gender identities in public and private spaces until this day.

Women and the Labour Market in Latin America

The incorporation of women into the labor market has been pointed out by some authors as the most important silent social revolution of the twentieth century (Heller, 2010). The growing participation of women in public spaces and productive activities is observed all over the world, concomitantly with increases in educational levels and transformations in their private relations, specifically in relation to the care of the home and children.

Elizundia Cisneros (2015) lists some factors that have contributed to this phenomenon. These include women's access to formal education and increased participation in the labor market, factors that contribute to learning, experience, and training for new activities; growth in the service sector, which has few barriers to entry and is perhaps the sector that has traditionally sheltered women; the national and international economic context, which has demanded that more people from the same family or household enter the labor market and contribute a share of expenses; and changes in the structure of families, with an increase in the number of divorces and female-headed households.

For Heller (2010), one of the great difficulties for women in Latin America to participate in productive activities is related to their ability to reconcile private and public life in a strongly patriarchal context. Breaking this status quo means overcoming patriarchal cultural patterns in which women are responsible for domestic work and care of children and home. By way of illustration, the author points out that women in the region spend on average two-thirds of their time on domestic chores and one-third on paid work, while men spend the same proportion in the opposite way. Factors such as pregnancy, childcare or other dependents, domestic work, or the prohibition of household members are cited as the main obstacles to seeking paid work. This overload of domestic work acts as a barrier to women's full employment, reducing their participation in decision-making processes and hindering their careers, occupational possibilities, creative work, and innovation.

Of the total number of unpaid domestic workers in Latin America, 62.0% were women, and of the paid domestic workers, 93.8% were women. Among employers, employees, and self-employed, men predominate, with 70.0%, 61.9%, and 59.8%, respectively (United Nations, 2016). Many women perform paid activities to supplement their household income and not as a way of achieving economic autonomy. Even a large proportion of women employers, who accounted for 3.4% of the total employed in the region, operated microenterprises informally and did so much more out of necessity than opportunity.

Abramo (2004) recognizes three interrelated but distinct dimensions, in which the imaginary about Latin American women in the labor market impacts the way they are inserted. The first one is the *social* dimension, where the rationalized and structured visions of men and women about their places, roles and functions in society, work, home and family are found. In this case, the idea of the nuclear family imposes on women the role of being almost exclusively responsible for the private sphere, for caring for the home and the family, while for men the role of main provider is stipulated. Women become the main providers only when men are unable to perform their duties or when they are absent from the home/family, i.e. female labor is considered secondary until second order. This idea of secondary insertion is echoed in the *business* sphere, which has high costs (related to maternity and childcare) and certain limitations, such as the impossibility of working overtime, traveling frequently and performing night activities, given that women's centrality is the family. Finally, there is the imagination of *public agents and policymakers* who, in designing and implementing policies for employment, income generation, vocational training, access to property and agricultural credit, direct their efforts at men, who are mostly recognized as heads of the family and as primary labor.

Although the author was talking about the insertion of women in productive activities as a whole, her observations are corroborated by several case studies in the field of female entrepreneurship in Latin American countries and even by some theoretical approaches. Some entrepreneurship theories show how important is the institutions, especially informal ones, on decisions, development and the characteristics of businesses led by women (Grasmuk and Espinal, 2000; Amorós, Guerra, Pizarro & Leguina, 2009).

Entrepreneurship has proved to be an important alternative for women's participation in productive activities in Latin America. Entrepreneurial activities offer them possibilities of autonomy, empowerment, combating inequalities and, consequently, control of their lives. Furthermore, women's entrepreneurship impacts economic development and contributes to reducing the poverty of these women and their families. Heller (2010) estimates an impact between 5% and 7% of the Gross Domestic Product of developing countries and goes beyond emphasizing the importance of women's income for the education, health and well-being of their families.

The entrepreneurial activity developed by Latin American women has received increasing attention in recent years. Their importance as an inducer of economic development and overcoming poverty, especially among the most vulnerable groups, has given rise to stimulus policies. However, this importance has not been sufficient to situate the generalized and idealized discourse on entrepreneurship in the different national, political, social, cultural and gender contexts of the region. The theoretical framework of the issue also contributes to this situation, as the practice historically belongs to the symbolic universe of the male, which in turn has its roots in the gender division of labor that imposes on women the domestic space and the practice of family care (Santander et al., 2016).

The next section brings some case studies of female entrepreneurship in Latin America that show the influence of the current institutional structure on female entrepreneurship activities. Although the case studies presented refer to different countries of the region, there are very similar patterns of social organization in which the dominant images of gender prevail over female entrepreneurship.

Female Entrepreneurship in Latin America: Some Empirical Evidence

Although female entrepreneurship has emerged at the same time as an opportunity and alternative for women in Latin American countries, the relationship between new business and the female gender remains conflictive. Women are more sensitive to a wide variety of non-monetary issues related to the gender role imposed by the macho culture of the region. Whether they are workers or entrepreneurs, Latin American women face structural disadvantages in the labor market that make it difficult for them to access different types of capital (financial, human, technological, social and cultural). These difficulties come from the maintenance of the gender division of labor in the region and take different forms, such as wage differentials vis-à-vis men, the feminization of informality and poverty, and the predominance of women in subsistence production units (Duque, 2014).

De Bowman (2000) investigated the intersection between gender and class and how it affects female middle-class industrialists in Peru. According to the author, there is little literature on this type of entrepreneurial woman in developing countries, which makes them stereotyped in the broad group of bussiness women artisans who undertake to escape poverty. The women studied by De Bowman (2000), small scale industrialists (SSI), flee this stereotype. They are middle-class women, most of them mothers, who have become entrepreneurs with the primary objective of supplementing the family income and, especially, of paying for the education of their children. However, the maturation of their businesses has transformed them into self-sufficient and economically independent women. A large part of the sample of female entrepreneurs interviewed by the author was women with higher education, coming from families with a solid middle-class background, using modern technologies to standardize production, employing between 5 and 20 people, and having significant potential for capital accumulation and social mobility. Although concentrated in traditionally female sectors, they were also found in markets dominated by men, such as ceramics, chemicals, metal products and tool production.

This figure of entrepreneurial middle-class Peruvian women emerged in the country in the 1990s, when Peru was the scene of neoliberal economic programs that led to widespread unemployment. In this scenario, small-scale production emerged as an attractive alternative for maintaining the position in the middle social stratum of the population, expressed, among other things, through the type of school attended by the children (public or private). Thus, this group of women started to see SSI as an alternative to minimize the negative impacts of the economic crisis on their families' income level and, consequently, to maintain the standard of living, especially the financing of their children's education, pointed out as the motivation/core concern of the interviewees.

Despite the professional success of these women, the author draws attention to the family conflict between the roles of mother, wife, entrepreneur and the frequent negotiation of time for work and family. Factors that generate stress, anxiety and guilt, feelings that don't exist in the world of men's work. In addition, De Bowman (2000) highlights the inability of many husbands to deal with the financial and social independence of their wives, feeling diminished by patriarchal cultural patterns.

Martins et al. (2010), studying the professional performance of Brazilian women entrepreneurs in their markets, interviewed women entrepreneurs with a profile similar to those investigated by De Bowman (2000) in Peru. The women entrepreneurs worked in the service and industrial sectors with a high level of professionalism, had a high educational average, were mothers and most of them married. The difference is that all of them had worked before, but never as entrepreneurs. Moreover, only one was driven to undertake out of necessity, the others were for professional achievement or family inheritance. Despite the success of the business, the conflict between the public and private spheres was also present in the lives of these women, and the cultural context imposed on them the need to develop and reconcile the skills commonly associated with men (rationality, decision-making ability, aggressiveness in conducting business, leadership, etc.) with those historically linked to women (domestic care, raising children, understanding and caring for others).

Machado's work (2012) also carried out in Brazil complements the notes of Martins et al. (2010) by exposing, through the eyes of the women interviewed, the invisible barriers, imposed by gender, faced by them when leading with nascent business (with up to three years of existence) with innovation. Machado (2012) surveyed entrepreneurs in the jewelry and accessories, health/aesthetic/nutrition, design, audio and video, consulting, fashion and specialized services. Most of them were married, with college degree, dedicated more than 30 hours weekly to the business and some had children. The results of the work corroborate the strong influence of informal institutions on the activities by creating a less favorable environment for women entrepreneurs.

The author describes how the female gender is associated with entrepreneurship and entrepreneurial talent in the country. During the initial phase of the business, women are often viewed with skepticism in relation to commitment and purpose, especially when the branch of activity is viewed as male. Women continue in the imagery of society professionally associated with careers as elementary school teachers, librarians, nurses, psychologists, and social workers (Machado, 2012). The business, even though innovative, is considered a secondary activity and, in certain cases, a luxury and hobby. This idea and the very characteristic of the business and the profile of the professionals are pointed out by the literature as the main reason for the difficulties in raising funds from financial institutions and angel investors. Because women, in general, develop innovative activities in areas with little attractiveness for accelerated gains, such as trade and services, and present a behavioral profile different from the male, with appreciation of interpersonal relationships and more conservative attitude in the management of their business, they face certain distance from investors. Machado (2012) also identified conflicts between the entrepreneurial activity and family relationships transvested in the location of the business within their own residence, activities taken to be carried out in the residence, much concern and obligations with the company.

Although they are different contexts, the conclusions of Grasmuck and Espinal (2000) on the relationship between gender and entrepreneurship in the Dominican informal market reinforce De Bowman's (2000) notes on women's conflicts over the role of mother, wife, and entrepreneur. The authors conducted a survey of 201 informal microentrepreneurs in the city of Santiago, Dominican Republic, in different sectors of activity. The women in the sample focused on traditionally female activities, mainly in the clothing sector, generated fewer employment ties (1.5 jobs compared to 3.1 vacancies generated by businesses headed by men), were more likely to work in one-person establishments, and perform their activities at home. Even though they started the business with a similar amount of capital as men, their ventures accumulated fewer assets and generated lower monthly income, characteristics that can be explained by the strong influence of traditional gender norms imposed by the country's sexist and patriarchal culture, which relegate women to the primary responsibility for domestic and family care. Of the total number of women interviewed, between 88 and 97% indicated the parallel performance of professional and domestic activities as the main motivation for locating the microenterprise in their homes, which in a way drains the attention and time of their business. In fact, Dominican women were twice as likely as men to point out personal relationships as one of the main reasons for the failure of their business. Competition between personal and professional life in the same social space imposes considerable pressure on the lives of these women. Grasmuck and Espinal (2000) also noted the appropriation of many businesses, created by women, by their respective husbands, due to the maturing and expansion of the business and unemployment of the family's "main provider." In a strongly patriarchal context and under certain circumstances, attitudes of this kind are perfectly acceptable to society, since male incomes should be sufficient to cover household expenses and when there is income from female labor, the amount should be supplementary to the main income.

The relationship between gender and entrepreneurship in Colombia, specifically in the activities associated with beauty salons, was investigated by Duque (2014) who noted the importance of the sector in the country, especially among informal women workers who see in the segment of beauty and body care an alternative of self-employment, work, and business, given the few barriers to entry. The author, based on data from the Bogotá Chamber of Commerce for 2009, shows that the activities related to beauty salons represented 1/3 of the total number of microenterprises registered in the service sector in the city and that if one considers unregistered businesses, this number should be much higher. The household survey conducted in the country in 2008 revealed that the sector employed about 47,000 people in the country's capital, 82% of whom were women, whose average monthly income was around U$250.00, half the average income of the service sector, highlighting the precariousness of work in these activities and, consequently, the unfavorable situation of women. Duque (2014) shows that, on the one hand, the percentage difference between men and women who own beauty salons is small and, therefore, is not able to explain the income differential between them, as well as the total capital invested to set up the business: 42.0% of women against 46.0% of men with capital above 5 million pesos – a difference of only 4.0 percentage points. On the other hand, the predominance of men who own beauty salons in the highest income strata of the city and the difference between the total hours worked in the week of men and women are important aspects that must be considered to explain the income differential between the genders. Men spent an average of 67 hours per week on paid activities, while women worked 59 hours. As Duque (204) points out, this difference of eight hours less for them is justified by their dedication to unpaid domestic activities, reproducing in this group of entrepreneurs the traditional gender division of labor. The author's findings corroborate the results of the household survey, which showed that women have on average 31 hours a week devoted to unpaid work, while the male average is 12 hours. Another factor highlighted in the survey was the gender division of occupations, with men predominating in the highest paid activities and in higher positions in the hierarchy.

Espinosa and Stiepoviæ (2006) analyzed in an exploratory way some indicators of the entrepreneurial dynamics of Chilean women and show the absence of incentives to start a business and the unequal access to opportunities. Although in Chile women's entrepreneurial activity is diverse and covers almost all sectors of economic activity, there are important gender differences, especially in terms of motivation. Most women undertake business out of necessity and in sectors with low added value. According to the authors, a study by GEM in Chile showed that only 13.0% of female entrepreneurs believed in the growth of their business, reflecting a lack of confidence and fear of failure. Because the women in the sample had a higher level of education, were married, and had a higher average age than in other countries Espinosa and Stiepoviæ (2006) raised the hypothesis that their entrepreneurial activities are associated with family stability. As in many other Latin American countries, in Chile, in general, businesses run by women are seen as a supplementary activity, i.e., an extension of the family.

Conclusions

There is a vast literature on the interaction between entrepreneurship, institutions, and competence/traits of entrepreneurs, but little on entrepreneurship led by women, especially in Latin America. In fact, along the bibliographical research, it was observed the predominance of researches turned to the United States and European countries with an idealized, generalist, and globalized vision of entrepreneurism. Only a few works approached gender differences on entrepreneurship in developing countries, mainly in Latin America. It is also worth mentioning the scarcity of official government information and statistics about female entrepreneurial activity, making it impossible to analyze quantitatively the situation of female entrepreneurship in the countries of the region and to make robust comparisons.

Due to this lack of data and studies, the chapter presented was developed based on literature review and case studies. The literature surveyed revealed how tensions and interrelations between the public and private spheres remain latent in the twenty-first century and have a direct impact on the talents/competencies of Latin American women entrepreneurs. These skills, in turn, end up defining the quantity, nature, and qualities of the enterprises led by them.

In this sense, the first step to understand the Latin American labor market and, especially, the universe of female entrepreneurship in the region, is necessarily to understand the role of women in social order.

Despite all the female conquests in the world of work, they still run into a social system that reproduces stereotypes and maintains a gender division of work that relegates them to secondary participation in home decision-making. These factors are structural in Latin America and work as limitations to entrepreneurial activities.

References

Aboal, D., & Veneri, F. (2016). Entrepreneurs in Latin America. *Small Business Economics*, *46*, 503–525. Retrieved from https://link.springer.com/article/10.1007/s11187-015-9696-3. Accessed on August 2020.

Abramo, L. (2004). Inserción laboral de las mujeres en América Latina: una fuerza de trabajo secundaria. *Estudos Feministas*, *12*(2), 224–235. Retrieved from https://www.scielo.br/pdf/ref/v12n2/23969.pdf. Accessed on May 2020.

Amorós, J. E., Guerra, M., Pizarro, O., & Leguina, A. (2009). *Perfil de la mujer emprendedora en Chile*. Global Entrepreneurship Monitor.

Anton, C. E., & Lawrence, C. (2014). Home is where the heart is: The effect of place of residence on place attachment and community participation. *Journal of Environmental Psychology*, *40*, 451–461.

Baggio, A. F., & Baggio, D. K. (2014) Empreendedorismo: Conceitos e Definições. *Rev. de Empreendedorismo, Inovação e Tecnologia*, *1*(1), 25–38. Retrieved from https://seer.imed.edu.br/index.php/revistasi/article/viewFile/612/522. Accessed on August 2020.

Bandura, A. (1977). Self-efficacy: Toward a unifying theory of behavioral change. *Psychological Review*, *84*(2), 191–215. Retrieved from https://psycnet.apa.org/record/1977-25733-001. Accessed on May 2020.

Bandura, A. (1986). *Social foundations of thought and action: A social cognitive theory*. Englewood Cliffs, NJ: Prentice-Hall.

Brinton, M. C. (1998). The social-institutional base of gender stratification: Japan as an illustrative case. *American Journal of Sociology*, *94*(2), 300–334.

Cordero, D. O. & Pulido D. U. (2020). Actividad Empresarial Femenina en Latinoamérica: Una revisión de literatura bajo la perspectiva de la Teoría Institucional. *Revista Academia & Negocios*, *5*(2), 9–28. Retrieved from https://papers.ssrn.com/sol3/papers.cfm?abstract_id=3514120. Accessed on May 2020.

De Bowman, O. C. (2000). Peruvian female industrialists and the globalization project: Deindustrialization and women's independence. *Gender & Society*, *14*(4), 540–559. Retrieved from www.jstor.org/stable/190301. Accessed on May 2020.

De la O, D. & Urbano, D. (2020). Female entrepreneurial activity in Latin-America: A literature review within perspective of institutional theory. *RAN – Revista Academia & Negocios*, *5*(2). Retrieved from https://ssrn.com/abstract=3514120. Accessed on May 2020.

Duque, P. A. J. (2014). Empreendimento e gênero: o caso da indústria da beleza en Bogotá. *Sociedad y Economía*, (26), 239–270. Retrieved from http://www.scielo.org.co/pdf/soec/n26/n26a11.pdf. Accessed on May 2020.

Elizundia Cisneros, M. E. (2015). Desempeño de nuevos negocios: Perspectiva de género. *Contaduría y Administración*, *60*(2), 468–485. Retrieved from http://www.scielo.org.mx/scielo.php?script=sci_arttext&pid=S0186-10422015000200468&lng=es&nrm=iso. Accessed on May 2020.

Espinosa, J. E. A. & Stiepoviæ, O. P. (2006). Mujeres y dinámica emprendedora: unestudio exploratorio. *Revista Universidad & Empresa*, *8*(11), 15–32. Retrieved from https://revistas.urosario.edu.co/index.php/empresa/article/view/940. Accessed on May 2020.

GEM-Brasil. (2018). *Empreendedorismo no Brasil: relatórioexecutivo 2018*. Curitiba: IBPQ. Retrieved from http://materiais.cer.sebrae.com.br/relatorio-executivo-gem-2018. Accessed on May 2020.

Gonzalez-Alvarez, N., & Solis-Rodriguez, V. (2011). Discovery of entrepreneurial opportunities: A gender perspective. *Industrial Management & Data Systems*, *111*(5), 755–775.

Grasmuk, S. & Espinal R. (2000). Market success or female autonomy?: Income, Ideology, and Empowerment among Microentrepreneurs in the Dominican Republic. *Gender and Society*, *14*(2), 231–255. Retrieved from https://www.jstor.org/stable/190273?seq=1. Accessed on May 2020.

Hagen, E. E. (1962). *On the theory of social change*. Homwood, IL: Dorsey Press.

Hansen, B. (2019). The digital revolution – Digital entrepreneurship and transformation in Beijing. *Journal of Small Enterprise Research*, *26*(1), 36–54. doi: 10.1080/13215906.2019.1570321

Heller, L. (2010). *Mujeres emprendedoras en América Latina y el Caribe: Realidades, obstáculos y desafíos*. Santiago de Chile: División de Asuntos de Género, CEPAL. Retrieved from https://www.cepal.org/es/publicaciones/5818-mujeres-emprendedoras-america-latina-caribe-realidades-obstaculos-desafios. Accessed on May 2020.

Jensen, K., Rezaei, S., & Scott, T. (2016). Talent among Chinese entrepreneurs at home and abroad. In H. Wang & Y. Liu (Eds.), *Entrepreneur and talent management from a global perspective: Chinese returnees. New horizons in management series* (pp. 62–91). Cheltenham: Edward Elgar Publishing Limited.

Kirzner, I. M. (1997). Entrepreneurial discovery and the competitive market process: An Austrian approach. *Journal of Economic Literature*, *35*, 60–85.

Kuah-Pearce, K. E. (2016). Migrant women entrepreneurs in the garment industry in modern China: Embedding translocality and feminized guanxi networks. *International Journal of Business and Globalisation*, *16*(3), 335–349.

Machado, F. B. (2012). Dilemas de Mulheres Empreendedoras em Empresas Inovadoras Nascentes. In *36 Anais do Encontro da ANPAD, Rio de Janeiro*. Retrieved from http://www.anpad.org.br/diversos/down_zips/63/2012_GCT1184.pdf. Accessed September 2020.

Martins, C. B., Crnkovic, L. H., Pizzinatto, N. K., & Maccari, E. A. (2010). Empreendedorismo feminino: Características e perfil de gestão em pequenas e medias empresas. *Revista de Administração da Universidade Federal de Santa Maria*, *3*(2), 288–302. Retrieved from https://www.redalyc.org/pdf/2734/273420396010.pdf. Accessed on September 2020.

McClelland, D. C. (1961). Entrepreneurial behavior. In D. C. McClelland (Ed.), *The achieving society* (pp. 205–258). D Van Nostrand Company.

Minniti, M. & Nardone, C. (2007). Being in someone else's shoes: The role of gender in nascent entrepreneurship. *Small Business Economics*, *28*, 223–238. Retrieved from https://link.springer.com/article/10.1007/s11187-006-9017-y. Accessed on May 2020.

North, D. C. (1990). *Instituciones, cambio institucional y desempeño económico*. México: Fondo de Cultura Económica.

Rezaei, S. (2017). Entrepreneurial competencies benefiting, entrepreneurial intention: Iranian adults at home and in the diaspora. In S. Rezaei, L. P. Dana, & V. Ramadani (Eds.), *Iranian entrepreneurship. Deciphering the entrepreneurial ecosystem in Iran and in the Iranian diaspora*. New York, NY: Springer International Publishing.

Rezaei, S. & Marques, D. H. (2016). The role of family network in circular migration and formation of transnational communities: A Brazilian case study. *International Journal of Business and Globalisation*, *16*(3), 284–304.

Rezaei, S., Schøtt, T., & Jensen, W. K. (2016). People's human and social capital benefiting careers in entrepreneurship: Adults in China and in the Chinese diáspora. *International Journal of Business and Globalisation*, *16*(3), 378–400. Retrieved from https://www.inderscience.com/info/inarticle.php?artid=75737. Accessed on September 2020.

Santander, P., Fernández, C., & Yáñez, D. (2016). Motivaciones y condicionantes contextuales en el emprendimiento liderado por mujeres chilenas. *Revista de Ciencias Sociales*, *22*(2), 63–77.

Schumpeter, J. (1947). The creative response in economic history. *The Journal of Economic History*, *7*(2), 149–159. Retrieved from https://www.cambridge.org/core/journals/journal-of-economic history/article/abs/creative-response-in-economic-history/C657999B51A39841F82FBA14FA0CCF92. Accessed on May 2020.

Schumpeter, J. (1985). O Fenômeno Fundamental do Desenvolvimento Econômico. In *A Teoria do Desenvolvimento econômico*. Rio de Janeiro: Nova Cultural.

Schumpeter, J. A. (1991). Comments on a plan for the study of entrepreneurship. In R. Swedgerg (Ed.), *Joseph A. Schumpeter: The economics and sociology of capitalism* (pp. 406–428). Princeton, NJ: Princeton University Press.

Smith-Hunter, A. E., & Leone, J. (2010). Evidence on the characteristics of women entrepreneurs in Brazil: An empirical analysis, *International Journal of Management and Marketing Research*, *3*(1), 85–102. Retrieved from https://ssrn.com/abstract=1668889. Accessed August 2020.

Tang, J., Kacmar, K. M., & Busenitz, L. (2012). Entrepreneurial alertness in the pursuit of new opportunities. *Journal of Business Venturing*, *27*(1), 77–94.

Terjesen, S., & Amorós, J. E. (2010). Female entrepreneurship in Latin America and the Caribbean: Characteristics, drivers and relationship to economic development. *European Journal of Development Research*, *22*(3), 313–330. doi:10.1057/ejdr.2010.13

Thurik, R., Verheul, I., & Grilo, I. (2010). *Explaining preferences and actual involvement in self-employment: New insights into the role of gender*. Scales research reports H200803, EIM business and policy research.

United Nations. (2016). Economic Commission for Latin America and the Caribbean (ECLAC). Gende Equality Observatory for Latin America and the Caribbean. Retrieved from https://oig.cepal.org/en/indicators/total-work-time. Accessed on May 2020.

Weber, M. (1958). *The protestant ethic and the spirit of capitalism*. New York, NY: Charles Scribner's Son.

Zarpellon, S. C. (2010). O empreendedorismo e a teoria econômica institucional. *Revista Iberoamericana de Ciências Empresariais y Economia*, *1*(1), 47–55.

Zukin, S., & DiMaggio, P. (Eds.). (1990). *Introduction to structures of capital*. Cambridge: Cambridge University Press.

Chapter 6

Women Entrepreneurship in Developing Countries: With Focus on GCC and Kuwait

Shqipe Gërguri-Rashiti and Sareh Rotabi

Abstract

This chapter defines the role of women entrepreneurship in developing countries in general with more emphasis on Gulf Cooperation Council (GCC) countries. It also introduces trends and challenges faced by women entrepreneurs, incentives to start their own businesses, the support mechanism provided for them, the common conditions for women entrepreneurship, and profile of women entrepreneurs in the GCC and Kuwait. The chapter also covers the impacts of Covid-19 crisis on entrepreneurship (small and medium-sized enterprises (SMEs)) along with the country policy responses to mitigate these impacts and ends with sharing useful recommendations on what needs to be taken into consideration in the future for the development of women entrepreneurship in general and more specifically within GCC countries and Kuwait.

Keywords: Women entrepreneurship; government policies; GCC; Kuwait; entrepreneurial incentive; entrepreneurial trends and challenges

Introduction

Entrepreneurship is a process by which individuals – either on their own or within a firm – follow prospects (Stevenson & Jarillo, 1990, p. 23). It has recently been appealed that if managers and business owners of many of our firms were to implement entrepreneurial manners when developing their strategy, companies would be dealing with a much happier future than current insights recommended (Lee & Peterson, 2000).

According to Shane and Venkataraman, 2000, the function of entrepreneurial intent involves the finding, valuation, and utilization of prospects, which can be new goods, services, or processes, new plan, and new line of business for outputs and inputs that previously did not exist.

The Emerald Handbook of Women and Entrepreneurship in Developing Economies, 91–109
Copyright © 2021 by Emerald Publishing Limited
All rights of reproduction in any form reserved
doi:10.1108/978-1-80071-326-020211006

With regards to prospects, Alvarez and Busenitz, 2001, p. 756 opinions are that these prospects are there as different parties have different thoughts or ideas on the value of the resources and/or when the resources are converted from inputs to outputs. It is worth highlighting that the theory of the entrepreneur emphasizes on the heterogeneity of views about the worth of resources.

Taking to account that there is no market for prospects, the entrepreneur is required to find them; in another word, he or she should improve his or her capabilities to attain these resources and capture these prospects. The negative side of the market for prospects is that it is difficult to protect the ownership rights of the ideas that are not related to patents or copyrights of the different expectations ran by entrepreneurs and investors on the economic value of thoughts and business prospects, and of the entrepreneur's need to reserve information that may impact the worth of the project (Cuervo, Ribeiro, & Roig, 2007).

Entrepreneurial creativity, moreover, covers the thoughts of formation, adventurous, rebirth, or novelty inside or outside a current organization. Finally, the entrepreneurial essence focuses on examination, search, and creation, as opposed to the utilization of business prospects relating to managers. As per the GEM report 2019/2020, entrepreneurship is extremely crucial for societal health and wealth and the main driver of economic growth, which leads to exploiting new opportunities, promote productivity, and create employment.[1] Moreover, it helps addressing some of society's toughest challenges as stated by the United Nations Sustainable Development Goals (SDGs).

When it comes to gender and gender differences for starting and running a business, men have been seen traditionally more prone to start a new business. However, women entrepreneurship has been gaining a particular attention in the academic arena, and as per GEM global report 2019/2020, "female participation in entrepreneurship is an important policy objective in many countries." As seen in the figure below, women are becoming more active into entrepreneurial initiatives/activities, and as indicated on the GEM 2019/2020 global report, out of 49 economies surveyed by GEM in 2018, *six show equal TEA (Total early-stage Entrepreneurial Activity) rates between women and men. Two are in the East and South Asia region (Indonesia and Thailand), one is in Latin America (Panama), and three are in the Middle East and Africa region (Qatar, Madagascar, and Angola). These countries span all three income levels*", (See Fig. 6.1).

Women in Entrepreneurship

In general, women tend to be underrepresented among the population of entrepreneurs. As compared to men, women have a tendency to run smaller businesses and function in noncapital demanding sectors such as delicate services, which tend to have lower capability to generate a sustainable and high income. Also, women entrepreneurs tend to have different incentives and purposes in entrepreneurship as compared to men. For example, some of women entrepreneurs prefer to go into self-employment where they can better achieve their work–life balance. Even though it is important for individuals to have options in the labor market, women

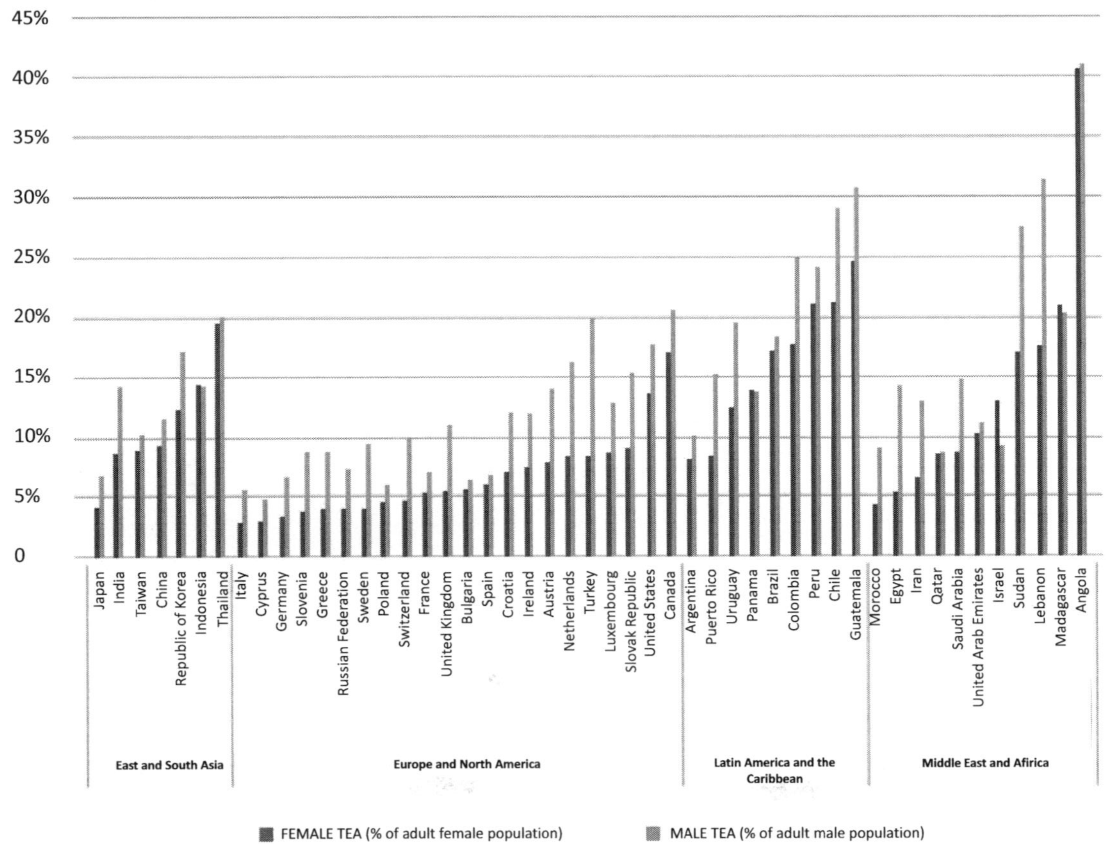

Fig. 6.1. Total Early-stage Entrepreneurial Activity (TEA) Rates by Gender among Adults (Ages 18–64) in 48 Economies, in Four Geographic Regions. *Source:* GEM REPORT 2019–2020.

on average have hidden entrepreneurial potential that is not fully comprehended. There have been several attempts by the policymakers aiming to unlock this potential, while distinguishing women as heterogeneous group with numerous variances in their incentives, purposes, and plans. Some of the difficulties that women find while establishing a business are unfavorable social and cultural approaches, less entrepreneurship abilities, higher challenges in terms of getting access to startup funds, and less active entrepreneurial networks and policy structures that demotivate women entrepreneurship. There have been several initiatives in this aspect, aiming to raise these constraints; however, they need to be expanded since they have not reached fully into the population yet (OECD/European Union, 2017). Women's entrepreneurship, particularly in developing countries, is an important driver for economic development as they are able to create new jobs for themselves and others by delivering different solutions for management, organizational, and business issues and constraints as well as the exploitation of business opportunities (Anggadwita, Luturlean, Ramadani, Ratten, 2017).

Women Entrepreneurs Trends and Challenges

According to Kavitha B. and Dr V. Basil Hans, women entrepreneurs are being recognized for their liberated roles. For example, in India, where some of the women are much disregarded, there are other women who have faced challenges and reached the top levels of entrepreneurs in their respective country. Their contributions have reflected in the economy of the country alongside with exposing the capabilities that a woman carries. On average, women contribute to about half of the total world population and have been overperforming among different sectors including academics, social, administration, politics etc. Previously, women used to focus on traditional activities, but nowadays as a result of education spread along with government support and policies favoring skill development, women over time have moved toward nontraditional activities including engineering, IT, and so on. Yet, the multirole of women continues to remain a challenge. And, entrepreneurship associated in providing women with the sense of satisfaction and accomplishment to represent their individuality in the community (Kavitha & Hans, 2018).

Women-owned businesses have experienced a rapid growth in the last decades; however, they still face significant challenges. According to Brush et al. (2019), women still lack access to important assets in order for them to launch and scale their business. Moreover, they are often expected to take on specific roles especially in private sphere, such as being mother, wife, and/or daughter. Therefore, women entrepreneurs are more often questioned about their competency of running a business and the types of businesses they can run (Wang, 2019).

Entrepreneurial Incentives

Profit is always considered as an important incentive that encourages entrepreneurs to take risks in developing new product and start new businesses, mainly they enjoy working for themselves, and accept challenges. Overall, the entrepreneurial incentive for women can be categorized in:

- Need-driven and prospect-driven entrepreneurship
- Individual characteristics, perceptions, and affiliations

Need-driven and Prospect-driven Entrepreneurship

On average, people around the globe are encouraged to start businesses mainly for two reasons: they are not employed or do not have an economic support; or they are chasing business prospects. Usually, the TEA rate tends to decline among higher level national income countries, and so as the possibility of those who are starting their businesses are doing it out of need. At the same time, among higher levels of national income countries, the prospect incentive raises. On an international level, around 27% of women entrepreneurs stated that they started their business due to need versus almost 22% of men. Furthermore, women entrepreneurs tend to state less prospect incentive as compared to men entrepreneurs. In a same study, about 68% of women entrepreneurs stated that they started their businesses to chase business prospects versus 74% of men entrepreneurs reporting for the same purpose (see Table 6.1).

Among countries with different national income level, what drives TEA rate for women tend to be the highest within low-income level countries (around 37%), whereas prospect-driven TEA rate for women are highest within low-income level countries. The result of these statistics shows that a need may be the engine drive for higher TEA rates among lower levels of national income countries, whereas less necessity for entrepreneurship results in less people to begin in high income level countries, considering few exemptions. Hence, differences in need and prospects are the main incentives in different countries. For example, mainly 9% of women entrepreneurs in North America started their businesses out of need versus 79% of women entrepreneurs started their business mainly to chase a business opportunity. As for sub-Saharan Africa, the trend is completely different. For instance, 42% of women entrepreneurs started their businesses out of need, and around 56% reported that the starting of their business were mainly due to prospect incentives (Fig. 6.2).

Table 6.1. Need-driven and Prospect-driven Entrepreneurship between Female and Male.

	Started Their Business due to Need	**Started Their Business Prospect Incentive**
Female	27%	68%
Male	22%	74%

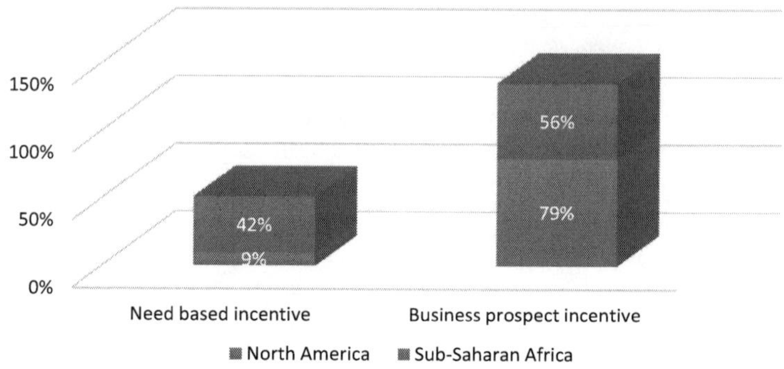

Fig. 6.2. Need-driven and Prospect-driven Entrepreneurship between North America and Sub-saharan Africa.

As for Asia and Europe, women entrepreneurs started their business mainly due to prospect incentive and are almost equal with men entrepreneurs. The peak of gender gap in the prospect incentive was spotted in sub-Saharan Africa where women entrepreneurs are less likely than men to state prospect incentive as the main incentive for starting their businesses. Moreover, the sub-Saharan Africa reflects the highest gender gap when it comes to necessity incentive, as women entrepreneurs were about 64% more likely to state necessity incentives as compared to men for starting a business. As for Latin America, women entrepreneurs are more likely to state necessity as the main incentive for starting their businesses. Moreover, women entrepreneurs in the respective region are less likely to state a necessity incentive as the main purpose to start their businesses. As for the United States and Canada, women entrepreneurs have noticeably a lower necessity-driven TEA rates as compared to men. The gender gap in Canada when it comes to necessity entrepreneurship is as large as 50% versus 10% in the United States. Furthermore, in Canada, women entrepreneurs are more likely to state prospect as an incentive to start their business as compared to men, meaning that on average, women entrepreneurs are supported well in Canada. As for the United States, women entrepreneurs are less likely to state prospect as an incentive to start their businesses as compared to men. The fact that these two countries are categorized more or less under the same income level and geographical location brings interesting queries from the entrepreneurial ecosystem perspective. After North America, Asia and Europe, the highest rates of prospect incentives for women entrepreneurs, possibly showing a line of support for women's entrepreneurship. Notably, 21 economies in this year's report reflected parity with men in prospect incentives, as compared to only 10 countries showing parity for necessity incentives. Eight of these countries are at parity for both sets of motives: China, Germany, Ireland, Italy, Lebanon, Peru, Taiwan, and the United Arab Emirates (UAE) (Global Entrepreneurship Monitor, 2019).

Individual Characteristics, Perceptions, and Affiliations

According to different reports across the globe, the age range of both women and men entrepreneurs are within 25–34. After this range, the second highest age range is within 34–44. The reports also reveal that the age range is more or less the same across the globe with an exception in sub-Saharan Africa and Latin America where it is higher within the age range of 25–34. It is worth highlighting that starting a business at an age range of 18–24 is the highest startup rate in sub-Saharan Africa. Further to this, the reports also show that on average, startup businesses are more common across younger women and men where they are more likely to get involved in businesses in low-income countries (Figs. 6.3 and 6.4).

Alongside with age, education level is also a potent factor among entrepreneurial incentives. Different studies across the globes show that less educated women are more likely willing to begin businesses regardless of the country's level of income, and when women are more educated, they are less likely willing to begin businesses except in low-income level countries. Moreover, when women are more educated and based in higher income level countries, they are more likely to find better job opportunities and then having less incentive to start their own businesses. In addition to age and education level, there are also other common incentive that triggers the entrepreneurial action and prospects. These are known to be opportunities, individual skills, and viewpoints about the possibility of failure in that particular business and lastly having an effective network (Global Entrepreneurship Monitor, 2019).

Support Mechanism. So far, there have been plenty of new policy emergences, which aim to encourage and support woman in entrepreneurship. For instance, many countries are checking the possibility of using public procurement to open up market prospects for women and offering more aid for growth-driven women entrepreneurs with dedicated business incubator and business accelerator platforms and building of a base for risk capital. Another factor that needs to be improved is the general institutional conditions including culture. It is worth mentioning that entrepreneurs are highly impacted by the social influences. Accordingly, it is important to support women entrepreneurs as role models and make sure that the education structure is free from any form of gender biases and does not demotivate women from exploring and studying STEM fields (i.e. science, technology, engineering, and mathematics). Lastly, more focused attempts can be taken to make sure that other policies including family, social, and tax are not biased toward entrepreneurship by women (OECD/European Union, 2017).

Conditions for Female Entrepreneurship. There are critical issues that have slowed down women entrepreneurs from operating competitive businesses. Some of these common issues are as follows:

- Conventional gender roles, gender segregation treatment from the community, loss of social support, lack of self-confidence across women entrepreneurs, cultural values, and so on.
- Lack of support from legal authoritarians – the legal base usually offers equal chances for both female and male; however, the practices of these laws are quite different.

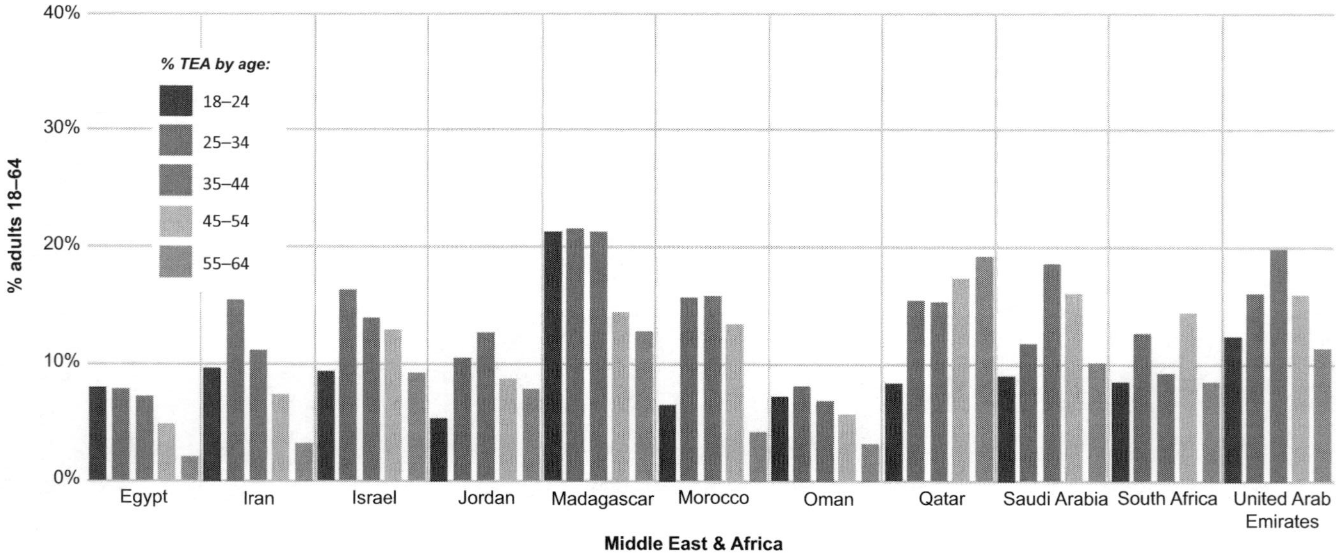

Fig. 6.3. Total early-stage Entrepreneurial Activity (TEA) by Age, Middle East and Africa. *Source:* GEM REPORT 2019–2020.

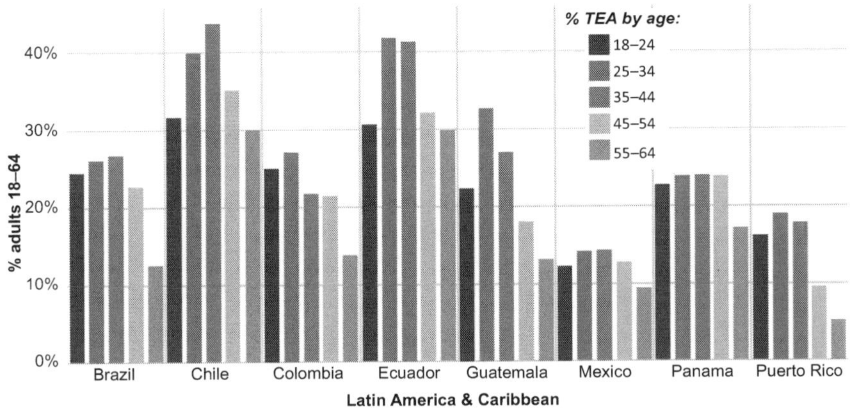

Fig. 6.4. Total early-stage Entrepreneurial Activity (TEA) by Age, Latin America and Caribbean. *Source:* GEM REPORT 2019–2020.

- Lack of managerial and technical skills needed to run a business – women entrepreneurs tend to lack these skills which result their dependence on intermediaries to run their businesses.
- Tough competition from larger and established units – women entrepreneurs in less developed countries may find it challenging to promote their products as compared to larger businesses.
- Lack of capital – women entrepreneurs usually have insufficient levels of financial assets/capital needed to start their businesses which enforce them to approach banks or other financial agencies to secure the capital needed to launch their businesses.

Profile of Women Entrepreneurs in GCC

The Gulf Cooperation Council (GCC) was established in 1981 and includes six countries: Saudi Arabia, UAE, Qatar, Kuwait, Oman, and Bahrain. According to Al Masah Capital Limited (2016), one of the main important economic growth factors in the Middle East and North Africa (MENA) region that has been noticeably increasing is the women's entrepreneurship role. It is worth highlighting that in the MENA region, percentage of the women entrepreneurs in small and medium-sized enterprises (SMEs) and the MENA reaches about 50%. The overall role of the women in the economic growth has also been noted in the GCC region which is supported by the increasing female population. On average, the population of the female has growth at a 10-year compound annual growth rate (CAGR) of 3.3 %. Simultaneously, the overall development and progresses in the education sector has contributed in the increase of the proportion of female in the labor force. In 2015, only in UAE, around 70% of the graduated students in the college were women, 60% of the governmental workforce were women, and one-third of them were in senior/high positions.

Overall, there is lack of research conducted on women's entrepreneurship in the context of GCC. However, as per the literature review, the challenges that affect women entrepreneurs' success in the Western countries are very much applicable in the context of the women entrepreneurs in the GCC.

According to a study conducted by Taqi (2016), among others, intellectual property; patronage and connections; and lengthy regulatory procedures were identified as the main challenges for women entrepreneurs in the GCC region. These challenges were the main reason for the low percentage (around 2%) of business activities attributable to women-owned enterprises in the GCC countries, in business activities in the GCC, and perhaps in other regions surrounding the GCC countries.

However, recently women are taking a stronger and more robust role in some economies, though they still lag significantly behind men in others. According to GEM 2019, there are three economies in which the *female rate exceeds the male rate (Saudi Arabia, Qatar, and Madagascar). The Saudi Arabia result is of particular note and may be the outcome of recent policy changes.*

According to Laffaz, some of the most influential GCC women entrepreneurs and their position in the respective company/country are as follows[2]:

- Amal Dokhan – CEO, Global Entrepreneurship Network, KSA;
- Dr Buthaina Al-Ansari – Founder and Chairperson, Qatariat T&D Holding Company, Qatar;
- Mona Ataya – Founder and CEO, Mumzworld, UAE;
- Areije Al Shakar – Director & Fund Manager, Al Waha Venture Capital Fund of Funds, Bahrain.

Motives for Starting a Business in GCC

There have been several studies examining the motives for starting a business by women entrepreneurs in the GCC countries. McElwee and Al-Riyami (2003) studied the factors that motivate women to become entrepreneurs in Oman using face-to-face meetings. The result of their study shows that most of the businesses that are conducted by Omani women entrepreneurs are focused in the services sector, and their businesses are usually small in size. The reasoning for starting a business by Omani women entrepreneurs are triggered by their past experiences gained either through their education or that particular business was initially their hobbies. Moreover, the result of the study indicates that majority of these women are happy in their field, and their happiness level overcomes profitability purposes. The result also reveals that these women do not have sufficient network level with other women in the same field where they can get relevant information and learn from one another.

Another study was conducted by Al-Sadi, Belwal, and Al-Badi (2012) examining the factors that limit women entrepreneur in the Al-Batina region of Oman. The result of the study shows that the lack of financial and industrial aids, knowledge to collaborate, access to technology, interaction with males, training or workshop chances, information about these chances, and the timing for the training are some of the constraints that influence women entrepreneurship in Oman.

As for Saudi Arabia, McKenna (2009) studied the problems which women entrepreneurs tend to face through open-ended interview. The result of the study shows that the barriers the Saudi women face are more or less the same as the problems which any women across the global would face; however, there are also additional barriers facing Saudi women entrepreneurs, which are domestic government regulations and religious traditions act. Moreover, the study reveals that the absence of support from other women is also another serious issue in Saudi Arabia. Another study was conducted by Sadi and Al-Ghazali (2010) to test the audacity, and it requires women in Saudi Arabia to do a business. The result of their study shows that self-accomplishment is the number one motivational reason for women entrepreneurs in Saudi Arabia. According to the same study, some of the operational constraints that these women face are the lack of coordination across governmental departments, absence of law protecting their investments and clients, and lack of support from community along with sociocultural limitations.

Another study conducted by Haan (2004) through survey examines the factors inhibiting UAE women from starting their own businesses. He found that one of the reasons of low contribution of women entrepreneurs in UAE is mainly because Emirati women are skeptical to start a business due to perceived risks, and they are less involved in networking as compared to male. Moreover, the social status of women, the predominant sociocultural reasons, and having less access to the capital as compared to man prevent them from starting a business. Itani, Sidani, and Baalbaki (2011) studied the characteristic of women entrepreneurs in UAE. The result of their study shows that the absence of support, community, traditions along with family, and personal reasons are the main constraints at the startup of their venture.

As for Kuwait, Alowaihan (2004) studied the performance of Kuwaiti small companies by focusing on gender as a differentiating factor. The result of the study revealed that women as compared to male counterparts had less experience in business, higher education levels, and they were older. Moreover, the businesses which were owned by women were lower in terms of financial performance and suffered from liability of newness. Another study conducted by Naser, Nuseibeh, and Al-Hussaina (2012) examined the factors that could potentially impact women in their decisions of becoming women entrepreneurs in Kuwait. The result of the study showed that factors such as religious obligations along with family responsibilities prevent women from becoming entrepreneurs. As for what can motivate women to start their own businesses, they found that their hobbies and interests along with their presence of business ideas encourage them to start their own businesses.

Profile of Women Entrepreneurs in Kuwait

Kuwait is a small open economy with a population of around 4.8 million where about 70% of the population is categorized as expats and the rest are Kuwaiti nationals. Across GCC countries, the country shares Islamic religion, Arabic language, and economic status, yet Kuwait stands out for its uniqueness in its cultural position through its political, cultural, and social views (Al Mutairi & Fayez, 2015).

Throughout past decades, women have played a dynamic role in the social and economic developments of the country, whereas Kuwaiti women have become doctors, ambassadors, leaders, government ministers, engineers, and educators at different levels (Tetreault, 2001). It is worth highlighting the fact that Kuwait government have made a tremendous progress in enhancing women status in the society and obtaining gender equality in various aspects including social, educational, legal, medical, and political professions.

Motives for Starting a Business in Kuwait

According to the study conducted by Al Mutairi and Fayez (2015), determining the factors motivating female entrepreneurs in Kuwait, the main constraints that inhibit females from becoming entrepreneurs are the role of women in the family along with high competition. However, it is worth mentioning that women entrepreneurship in Kuwait is emerging as owning a business is providing them with a freedom of making a decision. Kuwaiti women have also learned how to handle constraints related to cultural traditions and family structure. According to the same study, Kuwaiti women entrepreneurs are mainly into tailoring of traditional female clothing, catering, and women's beauty parlors and spas. The study also suggests the need for government support through policies that would aid in empowering women entrepreneurs in starting their own businesses, introducing a list of successful small business to women entrepreneurs along with decreasing the bureaucratic procedures for women entrepreneurs while starting their businesses. Moreover, conducting trainings and workshops are encouraged by the government for women entrepreneurs, and this is to improve their skills and business competences.

Entrepreneurship has witnessed a growth and more respect from Kuwait Society. The government has allocated tremendous efforts to influence the mindset of prospect entrepreneurs. These efforts are reflected in the government's attempts including a special allowance payment to the locals who work in the private sectors (World Economic Forum, 2011). However, Kuwait's entrepreneurship ecosystem is yet in the stage of getting developed. The overall regulations, bureaucracy, and other relevant issues slow down the growth of the country (O2one Labs, 2018).

In addition to the family businesses, Kuwait has shown its determination with respect to additional development of the entrepreneurship. For example, in 2013, an amount of USD 6.1 billion has been given to the SMEs innovation by the National Fund for Small and Medium Enterprise Development in the country. Yet, it is worth highlighting the lack of bureaucracy and the current monopoly in the country which is creating a huge obstacle in the development of SMEs and slows down the growth of entrepreneurship. The state has attempted to split it up in order to create a fair competition for all prospect entrepreneurs (Pupic, 2018).

Some of the main official public entities which play the role of the support mechanism for the prospect and the current entrepreneurs are: Industrial Bank of Kuwait and National Fund for the Development of SMEs. Furthermore, Kuwait Chamber of Commerce has been playing a crucial role for supporting SMEs through offering training and professional courses. Beside the public entities, some of the local private companies including Rataj has also been known for providing support for SMEs (Hertog, 2010, p. 32).

Innovation is a crucial aspect of entrepreneurship. Global Innovation Index (GII) offers a general report on innovation and highlights details of countries' capability for and succeeds in the innovation. According to this report and the overall index of GII, within GCC countries, following Qatar and UAE, Kuwait is still better off as compared to Saudi Arabia, Oman, and Bahrain. Kuwait government supports the growth of the SMEs and that is taking place through its public entities. The country has great opportunity to generate new entrepreneurial environment where its dependence on oil production decreases. According to the World Bank, the World Economic Forum and Global Entrepreneurship Monitor, in order to decrease the gap between its SMEs and the SMEs in Europe and North America, the government is required to improve many aspects. Furthermore, the country needs to invest in its education sector and provide training for its labor force and improve their skills, which all contribute in the development of its human capital. Skilled human capital will add value via innovation which will support the country's socio-economic development in the long run.

The Impact of Covid-19 Crisis on Entrepreneurship

During this period, it is imperative to talk about the impact of Covid-19 crisis, in particular, on entrepreneurship. In early 2020, the world faced a battle with the Covid-19 global health pandemic case along with its overall and social impacts.[3] The result of the pandemic showed that the world was not ready for such crisis and its subsequent consequences. However, as the next phase of the Covid-19 began in several countries, where the states and governments have a chance for recovery which they need to capture, such recovery is not limited to income and jobs, but also has general state of well-being goals, which integrate strong climate and biodiversity action and create resilience (OECD, 2020).

Due to Covid-19, the world is witnessing a fast, unexpected, and expansionary spread that has created one of a kind crisis. Some of the impacts are listed below:

- Worst global economic recession since great depression;
- Fast and unexpected growth in unemployment level;
- Uncertainty impact on consumers' confidence and businesses;
- Uncertainty regarding the duration and the depth of the crises and the expected time for recovery along with its economic and social impacts, as well as the probability of which the virus would return;

- The highest reduction in oil prices for over 20 years (double crisis at Kuwait level);
- Expected to lose 305 million jobs by the 2nd quarter of the year 2020;
- 3–5% expected reduction in the global gross domestic product (GDP).

It is worth highlighting that the governmental supports toward Covid-19 crisis at a global level have exceeded USD 11 trillion (15% of the global GDP) (Al Nahar, 2020).

Entrepreneurship, its role, and contribution to the economy are already well acknowledged as there are several global literatures that support this statement. As Covid-19 is transferring from public health pandemic to economic crisis, major trends under and after Covid-19 are being identified and aid in predicting how entrepreneurial initiatives around the globe will react. During this period, most of the enterprises have found difficulties in functioning, and the overall demand for goods and services have decreased. Accordingly, their abilities to manage costs have got impacted. Therefore, it is expected that many entrepreneurs will be affected and will go out of business during and after Covid-19 (OECD, 2020).

According to OECD-SME policy responses to Covid-19, there are many ways where the Covid-19 pandemic is influencing the economy and particularly on SMEs, both on the demand and supply side. From the supply side, the companies are being affected as their employees are either not feeling well or have to look after their families and other needs, since schools are closed and the overall movements of people are being limited. The measures used to control the spread of the virus including lockdown and quarantine have negatively impacted the capacity utilization, and, therefore, the overall supply chains are being disturbed, causing a shortage of intermediate goods and parts. As for the demand side, the unexpected and a drastic reduction in the demand and revenues for SMEs have noticeably impacted their ability to function, causing a shortage in their liquidity. Moreover, consumers went through loss of income, uncertainty, and the fear of contagion which all together negatively impacted their appetite to spend and consume (OECD, 2020).

As compared to larger firms, entrepreneurs may not have the same level of flexibility in handling the cost associated with such kind of shocks. Moreover, they might find it challenging to get information on methods that could stop the spread of the virus but also on potential strategies to manage the shock. Considering these challenges, difficulty of accessing capital, and the limited resources of entrepreneurs, the period that SMEs could survive from the shock is less as compared to large firms.

Country Policy Responses

While the first concern during Covid-19 crisis is the public health, several measures have been initiated by countries around the globe to reduce the economic impacts of the Covid-19 outbreak on businesses including SMEs. These policies are in different shapes as some of the countries have emphasized more on general policies that stimulate the economy as a whole. For example, in many countries, central banks have used their expansionary monetary policies and allowed commercial banks to offer more loans to entrepreneurs. This approach applies on US Federal Reserve and European Central bank. Some other countries initiated specific policy measures to support businesses including (OECD, 2020):

- Shortening the working time;
- Temporary layoff and sick leave;
- Government providing wage and income support for employees who went through temporarily layoff, or for companies to keep the employment.

To ease the liquidity constraints, several countries have initiated measures toward:

- Deferral of tax;
- Social security payments;
- Debt payments;
- Rent and utility payments;
- Providing grants and subsidies to SMEs;
- Extended or simplified the provision of loan guarantees, to enable commercial banks to expand lending to SMEs;
- In some cases, tax relief or a moratorium on debt repayments have been implemented;
- In some cases, countries have provided direct lending to SMEs through public entities;
- Gradually, more and more countries are allocating structural policies to support SMEs to implement new and more digitalized working approaches, and finding new markets and sales networks to keep operating under the predominant controlled measures.

In Kuwait, the supreme committee has identified specific goals across all of its economic sectors and made plans and objectives to achieve for the same. The main sectors are families, businesses, banking, and government. The focal elements in providing fast and effective financial support for the economic units are to provide:

- Enough liquidity for financing at the banking sector;
- Attractive interest rate for lenders and borrowers through monetary policy and support the cost of financing;
- Sharing in handling the credit risk to stimulate banks to increase their financings.

When it comes to entrepreneurs, one of the cabinet measures is to offer them loans with flexible conditions. The measure took place at an early stage of the crisis, taking to account the sensitivity of the crisis ramifications. Accordingly, through its prudential and monetary policy, Central Bank of Kuwait reduced the capital requirements in providing funds for SMEs (Al Nahar, 2020).

Recommendations for Developing Women Entrepreneurship

Considering the main obstacles that women entrepreneurs face in general and more specifically in the GCC and Kuwait, we recommend the followings:

- General:
    - Build a supportive regulatory environment;
    - Enhance the social network opportunities for women entrepreneurs;
    - Provide training and workshops specifically for women entrepreneurs in the field of information technology, managerial, and coaching skills;
    - Reduce government bureaucratic procedures needed for establishing a startup.
- GCC countries:
    - Reduce the overreliance of women in governmental job;
    - Launch a campaign to raise the awareness of the role of women entrepreneurs in economic development;
    - Educate women entrepreneurs about the importance of networking and how to become part of a network;
    - Reduce operational constraints across governmental departments;
    - Form a law that protect women investments and clients;
    - Increase the support from family and the community.

Conclusion

This chapter aimed to provide a better understanding of the women entrepreneurship in developing countries, in general, and more specifically in GCC and then Kuwait. It also introduced trends and challenges faced by women entrepreneurs, incentives to start their own businesses, the support mechanism provided for them, the common conditions for women entrepreneurship, and profile of women entrepreneurs in the GCC and Kuwait. The chapter also covers the impacts of Covid-19 crisis on entrepreneurship (SMEs) along with the country policy responses to mitigate these impacts. As for women entrepreneurs, the literatures illustrate that women around the globe are more or less facing similar challenges when starting their own businesses, and female in the GCC countries are not exempted from those challenges. In general, GCC women are reluctant to start a business due to perceived risks, and they are less involved in networking as compared to male. Moreover, the social status of women, the predominant sociocultural reasons, having less access to the capital as compared to man, and religious obligations along with family responsibilities are some of the additional reasons preventing women in this region from becoming entrepreneurs and starting their own businesses. Hence, there have been several new policy emergences, which aim to encourage and support woman in entrepreneurship. For instance, many countries are checking the possibility of using public procurement to open up market prospects for women and offering more aid for growth-driven women entrepreneurs with dedicated business incubator and business accelerator platforms and building of a base for risk capital. As for Kuwait, throughout past decades, women have played a dynamic role in the social and economic developments of the country, whereas Kuwaiti women have become doctors, ambassadors, leaders, government ministers, engineers, and educators at different levels, and the government has made a tremendous progress in enhancing their status in the society and obtaining gender equality in various aspects including social, educational, legal, medical, and political professions.

Notes

1. GEM Global Report 2019/2020 file:///Users/shqipe/Desktop/My%20paper%20/Women%20Entre.%20-Book%20chapter%20/gem-2019-2020-global-report-rev-280520-1590656414.pdf.
2. Laffaz is a digital tabloid of startup news, startup stories, and features concerning MENA (Middle East and North Africa) and have featured the most influential women entrepreneurs in the MENA region. The women selected and listed in the above table are from Gulf Cooperation Council (GCC) countries. *Source:* https://laffaz.com/influential-women-entrepreneurs-mena-2020/.
3. Covid-19 is a disease caused by a new strain of coronavirus. "CO" stands for corona, "VI" for virus, and "D" for disease. Formerly, this disease was referred to as "2019 novel coronavirus" or "2019-nCoV." The Covid-19 virus is a new virus linked to the same family of viruses as severe acute respiratory syndrome (SARS) and some types of common cold (*Source:* https://www.who.int/docs/default-source/coronaviruse/key-messages-and-actions-for-covid-19-prevention-and-control-in-schools-march-2020.pdf?sfvrsn=baf81d52_4).

References

Al Masah Capital Limited. (2016). GCC women – Entrepreneurs in a new economy report. Retrieved from. http://www.almasahcapital.com/

Al Mutairi, A., & Fayez, F. (2015). Factors motivating female entrepreneurs in Kuwait. *Journal of Applied Management and Entrepreneurship*, *20*(1).

Al Nahar. (2020). Kuwait balance path: Supreme committee for economic stimulation. *Al Nahar* (Arabic). Retrieved from https://nabd.com/s/73428996-3b6420/

Alowaihan, A. (2004). Gender and business performance of Kuwait small firms: A comparative approach. *International Journal of Commerce and Management*, *14*(3), 69–82.

Al-Sadi, R., Belwal, R., & Al-Badi, R. (2012). Woman entrepreneurship in the Al-Batinah region of Oman: An identification of the barriers. *Journal of International Women's Studies*, *12*(3), 58–75.

Alvarez, S. A., & Busenitz, L. W. (2001). The entrepreneurship of resource-based theory. *Journal of Management*, *27*, 755–775.

Anggadwita, G., Luturlean, B. S., Ramadani, V., & Ratten, V. (2017). Socio-cultural environments and emerging economy entrepreneurship: Women entrepreneurs. *Indonesia Journal of Entrepreneurship in Emerging Economies*, 2053–4604. ISSN.

Brush, C., Edelman, L. F., Manolova, T, & Welter, F. (2019, August). A gendered look at entrepreneurship ecosystems. *Small Business Economics*, *53*, 393–408.

Cuervo, Á., Ribeiro, D., & Roig, S. (2007). Entrepreneurship: Concepts, theory and perspective. Introduction. In Á. Cuervo, D. Ribeiro, & S. Roig (Eds.), *Entrepreneurship*. Berlin, Heidelberg: Springer.

Global Entrepreneurship Monitor. (2019). Women's entrepreneurship report. Retrieved from https://www.gemconsortium.org/report/gem-20182019-womens-entrepreneurship-report

Haan, H. (2004). Small enterprises: Women entrepreneurs in the UAE. Labour Market Study No. 19. Centre for Labour Market Research & Information (CLMRI). The National Human Resource Development. Retrieved from http://www.zu.ac.ae/infoasis/modules/mod8/Business/documents/SmallEnterpriseReport.pdf

Hertog, S. (2010). *Benchmarking SME policies in the GCC: A survey of challenges and opportunities*. Brussels: Eurochambres.

Itani, H., Sidani, Y., & Baalbaki, I. (2011). United Arab Emirates female entrepreneurs: Motivations and frustrations. *Equality, Diversity and Inclusion. An International Journal*, *30*(5), 409–424.

Kavitha, B., & Hans, V. (2018). Women entrepreneurs in modern era – Opportunities, trend and challenges. Retrieved from https://www.researchgate.net/publication/328333312_Women_Entrepreneurs_in_Modern_Era_-_Opportunities_Trends_and_Challenges

Lee, S. M., & Peterson, S. J. (2000). Culture, entrepreneurial orientation, and global competitiveness. *Journal of World Business*, *35*(4), 401–416. doi:10.1016/S1090-9516(00)00045-6

McElwee, G., & Al-Riyami, R. (2003). Women entrepreneurs in Oman: Some barriers to success. *Career Development International*, *8*(7), 339–346.

McKenna, D. (2009). Women entrepreneurs in Riyadh, Saudi Arabia. UMUC Working Paper Series– Number 2009, 002. University of Maryland University College, Adelphi, MD (pp. 1–14). Retrieved from http://ncys.ksu.edu.sa/sites/ncys.ksu. edu.sa/files/Saudi%20women%2014.pdf

Naser, K., Nuseibeh, R., & Al-Hussaina, A. (2012). Personal and external factors effect on women entrepreneurs: Evidence from Kuwait. *Journal of Development Entrepreneurship*, *17*(2), 1–23.

O2one Labs. (2018). Kuwait start-up ecosystem. Retrieved from https://o2one-labs.com/kuwait-startup-ecosystem/. Accessed on January 07, 2019.

OECD. (2020). OECD policy responses to coronavirus (COVID-19) - coronavirus (COVID-19): SME policy responses – OECD overview. Retrieved from https://www.oecd.org/coronavirus/en/. Accessed on May 19, 2020.

OECD/European Union. (2017). *Policy brief on woman's entrepreneurship*. Luxembourg: Publications Office of the European Union, 2016. Retrieved from http://www.oecd.org/cfe/leed/inclusive-entrepreneurship.htm

Pupic, T. (2018). A cultural shift: Changes in Kuwait's entrepreneurship discourse as seen at Nuqat's human capital Forum. Retrieved from https://www.entrepreneur.com/article/310279. Accessed on January 7, 2019.

Sadi, M., & Al-Ghazali, B. (2010). Doing business with impudence: A focus on women entrepreneurship in Saudi Arabia. *African Journal of Business Management*, *4*(1), 1–11.

Shane, S., & Venkataraman, S. (2000). The promise of entrepreneurship as a field of research. *Academy of Management Review*, *25*(1), 217–226.

Stevenson, H. H., & Jarillo, J. C. (1990). A paradigm of entrepreneurship: Entrepreneurial management. *Strategic Management Journal*, *11*, 17–27.

Taqi, N. (2016). Contributors: Özbilgin, M. Hamdan, A.the challenges facing women entrepreneurs: A study on Gulf cooperation Council (GCC) countries. Brunel University, 2016, Dissertation thesis.

Tetreault, M. (2001). A state of two minds: State cultures, women, and politics in Kuwait. *International Journal of Middle East Studies*, *33*(2), 203–220.

Wang, Q. (2019). Gender, race/ethnicity, and entrepreneurship: Women entrepreneurs in a US south city. *International Journal of Entrepreneurial Behavior & Research*, 1355–2554. ISSN.

World Economic Forum. (2011). *Accelerating entrepreneurship in the Arab world: A world economic Forum report*. Geneva; Abu Dhabi: World Economic Forum and Booz & Company.

Chapter 7

Exploring Contextual Influences on Women's Everyday Entrepreneuring: A Case from China

Ziyu Long

Abstract

This chapter uses the entrepreneurial experiences of women entrepreneurs in urban China as an empirical case to discuss contextual influences on women's everyday entrepreneurial experience in developing countries. Based on thematic analysis of women's own accounts of their entrepreneurial experiences, four contextual influences emerged: (1) preentrepreneurial work experience, (2) national entrepreneurial development, (3) cultural values, and (4) gendered work ideology. These influences shaped and were shaped by women's entrepreneurial identities, decisions, and actions in situated contexts. To further understand women's negotiations with these influences in developing countries, future research are called for to investigate how women resist dominant structures to carve out entrepreneurial agencies and enact resiliency to build sustainable businesses.

Keywords: Women's entrepreneurial experiences; entrepreneurial contexts; gender and cultural influences; resistance and resilience

Introduction

According to Global Entrepreneurship Monitor's report on women's entrepreneurship, an estimated 126 million women worldwide are starting or running new businesses in 67 economies around the world, with 98 million running established businesses (Amorós & Bosma, 2014). Corresponding with this growth, there are calls for research that explain, critique, and reconsider entrepreneurial discourses and career models to better understand how women do entrepreneurship, particularly in less studied contexts such as in developing economies and transitional societies. This chapter employs the entrepreneurial experiences of women entrepreneurs in

The Emerald Handbook of Women and Entrepreneurship in Developing Economies, 111–124
Copyright © 2021 by Emerald Publishing Limited
All rights of reproduction in any form reserved
doi:10.1108/978-1-80071-326-020211007

urban China as an empirical case to discuss contextual influences on women's everyday entrepreneurial experience in developing countries.

Fueled by Reform and Opening Up and subsequent national policies, China's entrepreneurship emerged from the country's transition from a centrally planned to a market-oriented economy (Yueh, 2008). After nearly four decades of sustained market transition, entrepreneurial organizations have become some of the most important driving forces behind China's rapid economic development. China has witnessed significant increases in women's entrepreneurship participation with more than a quarter of all entrepreneurs being women and 55% of new Internet companies in China owned by women (Yang, 2017). Nevertheless, recent reports suggest that women face gender biases/discriminations and pressures that constrain their venture development (Liu, 2017).

Little empirical research has privileged women's voices and their everyday entrepreneurial experiences in China. Everyday career experiences of entrepreneurship, whereby cultural and gendered power dynamics intersect with labor market and venture creation processes, remain understudied in developing countries. Using women's entrepreneurship in urban China as the empirical context, this chapter draws from women's own accounts to examine what and how various contextual influences play into women's constructions of their entrepreneurial identities and their entrepreneurial actions.

The remainder of this chapter will be organized as following. First, a brief background of women's entrepreneurship in China is discussed. Next, empirical findings are presented to illustrate four contextual influences that shape Chinese women's entrepreneurial choices and experiences, which can shed light to understanding societal factors' impacts to women's entrepreneurship in developing countries. Finally, a set of future directions are proposed to further understand women's negotiations of contextual influences.

Brief Background: Women's Entrepreneurship in China

Gender inequity is still largely a reality across the global entrepreneurial scene. This inequity is evident in the systemic differences in the size, industry, and growth rate of businesses owned by both women and men (Jennings & Brush, 2013), and the consistent lower participation rate of women in the entrepreneurial activities compared to that of men across different regions (Amorós & Bosma, 2014). Furthermore, the dominant entrepreneurial career model continues to be disproportionally associated with masculinity (Ahl, 2006), rendering women entrepreneurs' status as less legitimate to that of men's (Hughes, Jennings, Brush, Carter, & Welter, 2012).

China traditionally has been a patriarchal society with a clear demarcation of gender roles. Rooted in Confucius teachings, men are the providers and leaders of the family, and women are the subservient homemakers (Peng, Ngo, Shi, & Wong, 2008). Since the birth of People's Republic of China (PRC) in 1949, many economic and social policies were introduced to promote women's status and address the negative stereotypes about women. Although progress has been made, gender inequity was not eradicated. Recent research documented that Chinese working women suffer disadvantages in the workplace as the intensive market competition might have contributed to the resurgence of gendered work ideology that women were less efficient workers (Cai & Wu, 2006). Additionally, leadership stereotypes of women as less competent both physically and mentally are still quite prevalent (Peng et al., 2008).

China's entrepreneurship emerged from the country's transition from a centrally planned economy to a market-oriented one in early 1980s (Yueh, 2008). Entrepreneurship experienced tremendous growth in the 1990s with the dismantling of the employment system and massive layoffs as the state-owned enterprises restructured and governmental policies, such as the Small and Medium-Sized Enterprises Promotion Law, promoted key entrepreneurial initiatives. Domestic entrepreneurial organizations (i.e., private start-ups, township and collective enterprises, and transformed state-owned enterprises) have driven China's rapid economic development (Guo & Miller, 2010). Chinese entrepreneurs are navigating, changing institutional environment in China as a transitional society (Yueh, 2008). Research also highlighted the importance of fostering good *guanxi* (relational network) and entrepreneurs' social skills (i.e., proactive and elaborate social strategies and relational perseverance) to sustain and grow businesses in China (Guo & Miller, 2010).

Empirical Case: Key Contextual Influences in Women's Entrepreneurship

Privileging the lived experience of women entrepreneurs, this chapter draws from empirical data which consisted of 25 in-depth interviews with women entrepreneurs in urban China that the author collected to understand key contextual influences that shaped their entrepreneurial experiences. Among the group of women entrepreneurs, their businesses ranged from real estate, marketing, advertising, art, social networking, education, fashion, to healthcare. Their businesses were based in Beijing, Qingdao, Jinan, Shanghai, Hangzhou, and Shenzhen. Participants were all college educated, with an average age of 32 (ranging from 25 to 40). All belonged to Han majority ethnicity. Half were married, and two with children. Pseudonyms were used to protect participant's identity in the following findings.

Based on thematic analysis of women's own accounts of their entrepreneurial experience, four key contextual influences emerged: (1) preentrepreneurial work experience, (2) national entrepreneurial development, (3) cultural values, and (4) gendered work ideology.

Preentrepreneurial Work Experience

All women entrepreneurs interviewed had work experiences before they start their own business. For many, entrepreneurship was not their first choice but derived from their dissatisfactions of previous employment. For instance, Li shared that she started her own Public Relations practice because her previous workload was very heavy, and she did not have a sense of control of her work. In her own words:

> I had to work really hard, getting off work at 2 or 3 am was normal. The workload was heavy and I didn't have control over it. If my boss thinks the plan needs to be changed, I will have to make the changes. The numerous hours I devoted to rounds of revisions are to satisfy other's requirement, not to help me improve my skills...[after I start my own PR practice], I still work hard, but at least this time the hours that I put in will not go to waste.

After starting her own company, Li had more control of her work and felt that her time devoted to work can bring her values rather than simply "go[ing] to waste."

Feifei echoed the frustration of working for a large company. She further talked about how structures of the corporation and complex interpersonal relationships can lead to burnout. In her words:

> For big companies, the good thing is that it has established structure. Things are developed, you have the resource you need, you have a giant team, you can learn many things. But it also has its downsides, because of the established structure, you will have to obey, and try to find a balance of multiple and complex interests and relationships within its existing structure. I can be good at it, but I don't like it. I like to be simple and direct. I am pretty much a free spirit who does not like to be constrained.

Motivated to work in a less bureaucratic culture, Feifei decided to become a partner in a start-up company that can utilize her talents and experience, and had a flat organizational structure.

Different from Li and Feifei, Wanyu talked about how she was pushed into self-employment in the 1990s due to labor market restructuring:

> My *danwei* (单位, public/state-owned organization) encouraged us to "find job on one's own" (自谋职业). *Danwei* provided initial funding, and held shares of the company. I just seized the opportunity and submitted a business proposal to the leaders of *danwei*. It got approved, and I started a Laundromat.

Wanyu's case illustrated how national labor market changes can impact individual career choices and life trajectories. Different from Li and Feifei who chose to become entrepreneurs, entrepreneurship chose Wanyu as a way to survive the job loss during structural change of the economy and the labor market.

In addition, women shared that preentrepreneurial employment allowed them to accumulate work experience and skills, build clientele and *guanxi* network, and form relationship with coworkers who may become future business partners. One key aspect of how women's preentrepreneurial work experience paved the way for their entrepreneurial venture was the establishment of a *guanxi* network in the field. As illustrated by Juan:

> One of my former colleagues [at the e-commerce company] was an engineer, and we became cofounders for our start-up. Because we have worked together and known each other, we trust each other. Throughout the process, we have not argued over money. Many of my former colleagues and clients also introduced business to us, and some of them also provided financial support and useful information. I am very grateful for these people.

In Juan's case, her start-up company was in the same field as her former employment. Instead of working for the company, she now worked for herself. Her colleagues became her partners, and her former clients referred businesses. From this perspective, she was able to use her preentrepreneurial employment as the springboard to launch her business.

These empirical cases suggested that it is important to capture women's work experience before entrepreneurship to understand their motivation and decisions to start their own businesses. Specifically, women's preentrepreneurial work experience can reveal women's education, socioeconomic status, professional skills and expertise, social capital, and industry experiences, which are all important factors to holistically understand women's path to embark on the entrepreneurial journey.

National Entrepreneurial Development

Women entrepreneurs framed the national entrepreneurial development as an important backdrop that shaped how they perceived the viability and outlook of entrepreneurship. Jing described that China is going through "a golden time of entrepreneurship." In her words:

> The environment for entrepreneurship has not matured in China, but it works to entrepreneurs' advantage. In Shanghai, if you have an idea, the courage to give it a try, and seize the opportunity to start a business, you can be successful...The entrepreneurial vibes in Beijing and Shenzhen are pretty good too. The media are promoting entrepreneurship in the country with positive media stories...I think it is the golden time for entrepreneurship in China in the next 5–10 years. Everyone has a chance. It is a great time to be an entrepreneur.

Jing's narrative of "the golden time for entrepreneurship" suggested that everyone who's willing to take risks and work hard has a chance to be a successful entrepreneur. Similar to Jing, others expressed their optimism of the development of entrepreneurship in China due to the revolutionary technological advancement, active capital market, and governmental support.

In terms of technological advancement, women invoked mobile networks as an agent in promoting technology entrepreneurship in China. According to Feifei:

> The 4G and 5G network in China is developing even faster than that of the U.S.. China directly hopped on the second phase of mobile technology development. Therefore, you can develop even faster. You can use the latest technology directly, and it will transform how you do things. In China, the number of smart phone users skyrocketed, and people are open minded to try new things…there is a huge potential.

Comparing the development of mobile technology in China to that of the United States, Feifei framed China's late start in its technological advancement as an advantage as it allowed the country to build a mobile network infrastructure using the "second phase" mobile technology from its very beginning. In addition, technology afforded a cheaper and faster way to start one's own business and potentially make huge profit. According to Nini:

> Internet startup is different from traditional industries, you need to have capital and produce tangible product. The internet is "light." You need a team, engineers, designers, product managers, a group of 2–3 people can start a business. For me, it is NOT something that scares me.

Here, Nini contrasted traditional and Internet start-ups in terms of its influence on her entrepreneurial intention. The Internet was invoked as a facilitating force for her to start her own company as it allowed venture creation at a low cost.

In terms of capital market, women talked about the growing numbers of angel investors (i.e., affluent individuals who provide capital for business start-ups in exchange for convertible debt or ownership equity) and infusion of capital from home and abroad. Interestingly, while women talked about how infusion of investment could facilitate them in scaling up their business, they warned that one needs to be cautious in navigating the relationships with investors to avoid unnecessary loss. Mei talked about the danger to fall into an investor's scam:

> Many of them invest a small amount of money, and they still demand shares from the company. Now entrepreneurship is hot, everyone wants to invest. Investors take advantage of this need. My lawyer told me now many investors printed fake name cards, with titles such as CEO or VP. In reality they may not have such a high title. They lied about their title because they wanted to appear more credible, you know, I am the one who is in charge of my company's cash flow, you need to tell me how you are running the company. So you need to be really careful when you are interacting with investors.

Shuo also called attention to the unethical practices of investors affiliated with large companies:

> Many big companies, they have money, resource, and many talents working for them. If you have a good idea, they can quickly copy it, and turn it into something 100 times better and bigger than what you have. I know in these big companies, they have an investment department. People in that department buy good ideas, and use their resources to turn ideas into products. They can do it so fast that it kills small businesses instantly.

As noted by Mei and Shuo, women entrepreneurs were cautious as they approached potential investors. On one hand, investors could bring needed funding for the new start-ups. On the other hand, unethical conducts of some investors might "kill small businesses instantly."

Women entrepreneurs in China also noted how governmental support, policies related to entrepreneurship, and local incubators can facilitate their venture creation and development. Many were aware of national and local policies that aimed to alleviate the administrative procedures and financial burden of small and medium-sized business. For instance, Wanyu talked about the government funding opportunities:

> There has been more and more policies and grants. A few years ago, the economy went down, and many small businesses closed their doors. The state has been supporting small and medium sized businesses since then. These businesses helped the government in job creations. Individuals who lost their jobs can apply for start-up loans, and some start-ups, those related to the environment and innovative technology can apply for grant and gain financial support from the government.

Wanyu shared that she has not taken advantages of these opportunities. When asked why, Wanyu said she thought the chance for her to get a grant[1] was slim because of the nature of her business (she owned two laundromats and a restaurant).

As seen in this section, it is important to situate the development of individual businesses in the broader national trends of economic and technological development. The vibrant development of technology, active capital advancement, and government initiatives in China all facilitated women's participation in entrepreneurship and entrepreneurial development, in general. Women can take advantage of national entrepreneurial development if they can align their start-up with entrepreneurial trend and national initiatives.

Regional, Generational, and Familial Cultural Values

Women entrepreneurs interviewed also talked about how aspects of regional and generational culture played into how they construct their entrepreneurial identities. Jian, for instance, shared that she felt "really lucky to be living in Shanghai. The city has a unique *Hai Pai* [海派 , Shanghai Style] culture – very inclusive to different ideas and people." A couple of other women entrepreneurs in Shanghai also framed the megacity in China as "melting pot" and "hub for Chinese entrepreneurship." As a result, they situated their business in Shanghai, so that they could take advantage of Shanghai's proentrepreneurship culture to facilitate their entrepreneurial career development.

Women entrepreneurs also talked about how regional culture can be a constraining force for entrepreneurial development. For instance, according to Sheng, the culture notion of *Guan Ben Wei* (官本位 , culture with strong emphasis on authority and hierarchy) in northern China animated itself as a barrier for business growth:

> I think one of the common problems [for the development of start-up companies] is that the management structure does not develop as fast as the company does, as the company evolves from a small self-employed business to a full-fledged company with employees. Particular in the Northern China, usually one boss leads it, and the company highly relies on the boss... It can be problematic. The company needs to have its rules, and you need a structure to manage your team. 70% of the companies have this problem, and it can hurt the business.

Here, the regional cultural value was invoked by Sheng as a possible constraining force for entrepreneurs to achieve sustainable venture growth. As a Northerner herself who started her business in the North, Sheng observed the leadership practices that reinforced *Guan Ben Wei* culture in other small businesses and made the point to build and develop a different culture for the sustainable development of the organization.

Other than regional culture, participants reported negotiating with different generational understandings of work as they embark on the entrepreneurial career. Hui highlighted how her parents did not understand why she wanted to become an entrepreneur:

> Both of my parents were quite conservative. They try to hide it, but I can tell that they are extremely worried about me. They do not understand why you give up a stable, well-paid job and do this, what if you fail? They think I was in a better situation before, and starting my own company was not wise.

Indeed, generational cultural differences are prevalent in the global workforce but are especially salient in developing countries that are undergoing great social, economic, and cultural transformations, such as China (Long, Buzzanell, & Kuang, 2016). It is not surprising that women entrepreneurs and their parents hold different views of entrepreneurial careers. For their parents' generation, *wending* (stable) lifestyle with a corporate or government job was considered as ideal.

Cultural values such as familial piety further complicated how Chinese women entrepreneurs discussed their career choices with their families. For instance, many women entrepreneurs kept their parents in the dark as they quit their government or corporate jobs to start their companies. Others had to market their entrepreneurial career "as good as the corporate career" to reassure their parents. Instead of trying to change their parents' perceptions, women entrepreneurs used strategic disclosure (i.e., only sharing the positive aspects of their entrepreneurial career) and strategic ambiguity (i.e., not sharing the details of how they are running the company, its risks, struggles, and potential failures) as they discussed their entrepreneurial career choices.

As illustrated above, women's entrepreneurial experiences were embedded in the local contexts and their family and relational lives. While entrepreneurship research often conceptualizes culture as national culture, this chapter suggests the importance to nuance our understanding of how we conceptualize culture and its influences on women's entrepreneurial journey. First, as illustrated in the case, we need to consider regional culture's influence to entrepreneurship. This is particularly important when different regions of the country experience different levels of socioeconomic development and have their unique cultural heritage and tradition. Second, we need to understand generational differences when it comes to understanding work and entrepreneurship. In developing countries, different generations can have drastically different life experiences which can create generational gaps. In collectivist societies valuing family and community such as China, women needed to negotiate with different generational orientations to work in order to legitimize their entrepreneurial identity.

Gendered Ideology of Work

Finally, women entrepreneurs in China reported that they needed to deal with gender-based discriminations and microaggressions, defined as "brief and commonplace daily verbal, behavioral, or environmental indignities, whether intentional or unintentional, that communicate hostile, derogatory, or negative gender slights and insults" (Sue, 2010, p. 5). For instance, women reported challenges to recruit and retain skilled software engineers and seek funding in the male-dominated entrepreneurial field because they were perceived as emotional and incompetent technology leaders. Participants also told stories about being put down or not taking seriously during business negotiations. Hao shared her experience:

> When I go out to talk about business, there are men who unconsciously put you down and do not treat you equally. They have the natural tendency to teach me, or they say you are very inexperienced on this, let me show you how I do it. They just like to teach.

Like Hao, other Chinese women entrepreneurs found themselves being treated condescendingly. As another example, Yan shared a memorable episode of micro-aggression where her former students came to visit her when she started her own English language school with a couple of women founders:

> A former student came to me and said, do you know, you can go with travel groups to Europe and be their translators, you can earn more money [compared to starting her own company]. Of course, I know he means well, but I felt quite uncomfortable… They think you are just a group of girls, you want to make money, and you can speak English. Well then, you can just use your language skills to make money as a tour guide. But what they don't see is we are building an organization from scratch, we have ideas to realize, we have organizational structures, and we have great potential in generating profit and changing the ways that English language training is done in China…If I were a man, and I am starting a company, will he say the same thing, asking me to become a tour guide rather than opening up my own language training school. Do you think this will happen?

As noted by Yan, women's career ambition was closely monitored by community members. Gendered ideology such as appropriate work for women was present and can constrain women's entrepreneurial agency.

As women do not fit into the dominant leadership model, the Chinese women entrepreneurs interviewed explained how they had to work extra hard to gain trust and support from their employees. Huang talked about how she intentionally set her leadership image as *ping ming* (拼命, put one's life into work), strategically embodying passion, commitment, and strive for innovation that are important for a start-up culture:

> For new companies, leaders play a very important role in establishing the organizational culture, motivating employees, and building core teams. I show them the strong faith I have for our company, positive about our future, and I work extremely hard. I am always the last one to leave the company. Everyone see my hard work and perseverance, they are asking themselves "what should I do if the boss is ping ming [put life into work]?"

Indeed, leaders need to inspire to retain employees in start-up companies as employees usually work with lower salary, longer hours, and less sense of security compared to those who work in established businesses. Huang used herself to set an example for her employees.

As shared by the group of Chinese entrepreneurs, gender stereotypes and biases were daily encounters in their everyday doing of entrepreneurship. From networking and recruiting to business negotiations and daily management, women were aware of their marginalized status and sought for opportunities to resist the negative impacts of gender stereotypes.

A Call to Study Women's Entrepreneuring as Negotiations for Emancipation

In summary, four societal influences emerged from the data in shaping women's entrepreneurial experiences: (1) preentrepreneurial work experience, (2) national entrepreneurial development, (3) cultural values, and (4) gendered work ideology. Acknowledging that these insights derived from the experiences of a small group of women entrepreneurs, the chapter by no means aims to provide a comprehensive list of societal influences to women's entrepreneurship. Instead, the findings privilege women's voices and illustrate how various contextual influences play into women's entrepreneurial experiences on a daily basis. These four influences can be explored further in future entrepreneurship research.

Moving forward, scholars can dig deeper into how women negotiated with various contextual influences in their everyday doing of entrepreneurship. Women's entrepreneurial projects can be viewed as emancipatory endeavors, that is, as pursuits of liberation from perceived constraints in their situated context. Envisioning women's entrepreneurship as processes of emancipation raises important questions regarding the negotiations between women entrepreneurs and societal influences in the everyday doing of building a new business. Specifically, research can investigate how women resist dominant structures to carve out entrepreneurial agencies and how women enact resilience to build sustainable businesses.

Resistance is defined as

> an effort to engage in some form of praxis – individual or collective, routine or organized – in the context of 'established social patterns and structures' (including mechanisms of control), such that these patterns and structures are, at some level, deified and their 'identity logic' interrogated. (Mumby, 2005, p. 23)

Guided by an emancipation perspective, entrepreneurial actions can be understood as resistance practices as they challenge existing norms and practices. Stead (2017) summarized strategies that women employ to carve out a space in the male-dominated entrepreneurial community into four categories: (1) proxy, accessing entrepreneurship and entrepreneurial networks through male partners; (2) concealment, hiding femininity and/or their identity as an entrepreneur to be less visible; (3) modeling the norm, reproducing prevailing masculine norms of what constitutes an entrepreneur; and (4) tempered disruption, disrupting gendered expectations of what is an "entrepreneur" to stand out. However, most of the empirical studies used in the review were done in developed countries. This chapter calls for more entrepreneurship researchers to focus on women's entrepreneurship in developing/non-Western countries. Research can study how contextual factors empower or constrain women entrepreneurs in doing entrepreneurship in transitional economies (e.g., networking, recruiting, seeking funding, making business deals, etc) and how women engage in everyday actions of resistance in managing meanings and identities in developing countries (e.g., how women legitimize their career choice despite gendered career ideology, how women manage their identities as entrepreneur, partner, mother, and daughter).

Another fruitful line of research is look at how women entrepreneurs enact resilient mindset and actions as they continue to develop their business. Entrepreneurship scholars have explored how resilience is considered as an important trait or competency to facilitate entrepreneurs in overcoming challenges and extreme events (Bullough, Renko, & Myatt, 2014), collaborating with others to handle adversity (Blatt, 2009) and enabling the longitudinal success of the business (Ayala & Manzano, 2014). Research suggested that entrepreneurial resilience can be augmented by enhancing networking and forming a professional network of coaches and mentors, accepting that change is a part of life, and avoiding seeing crises as insurmountable (Davidson, 2000). Increasingly, scholars have begun to pay attention to external factors responsible for resilience including cultural norms, stages of economic development, and institutional context (Hedner, Abouzeedan, & Klofsten, 2011). Empirical research can continue to uncover how entrepreneurs develop and cultivate resiliency in the situated contexts. Specifically, the Communication Theory of Resilience (Buzzanell, 2018) can be helpful as this theory captures potential resilience strategies women entrepreneurs can enact. These strategies include: (1) crafting normalcy, that is, engaging in daily rituals to gain a sense of consistency and comfort, (2) affirming identity anchors, that is, holding onto certain identity anchors that help them confirm who they are and what roles to perform, (3) maintaining and using communication networks, that is, utilizing networks to engage in sensemaking and gain support, (4) emotion work to legitimize negative feelings while simultaneously foreground both positive emotions and productive action, and finally, (5) enacting alternative logics, whereby individuals use creative ways of reframe situations and find roundabout solutions.

To conclude, this chapter used empirical qualitative evidence to surface contextual influences to women's everyday doing of entrepreneurship. More research that focused on how women negotiate with these influences are called for as we continue to develop theories and practical insights to realize the emancipatory potentials of women's entrepreneurship in developing countries.

Note

1. The government programs that Wanyu references include the "Targeted funding support for small and medium sized company in Technology industry" (科技型中小企业创新发展专项扶持资金) and "Innovation grant for small and medium sized company in Shandong."

References

Ahl, H. (2006). Why research on women entrepreneurs needs new directions. *Entrepreneurship Theory and Practice*, *30*, 595–621. doi:10.1111/j.1540-6520.2006.00138.x

Amorós, J. E., & Bosma, N. (2014). *Global entrepreneurship monitor 2013 global report: Fifteen years of assessing entrepreneurship across the globe*. Retrieved from http://www.gemconsortium.org/docs/download/3106

Ayala, J. C., & Manzano, G. (2014). The resilience of the entrepreneur. Influence on the success of the business. A longitudinal analysis. *Journal of Economic Psychology*, *42*, 126–135. doi:10.1016/j.joep.2014.02.004

Blatt, R. (2009). Resilience in entrepreneurial teams: Developing the capacity to pull through. *Frontiers of Entrepreneurship Research*, *29*, 1–14. Retrieved from http://digitalknowledge.babson.edu/cgi/viewcontent.cgi?article=1564&context=fer

Bullough, A., Renko, M., & Myatt, T. (2014). Danger zone entrepreneurs: The importance of resilience and self-efficacy for entrepreneurial intentions. *Entrepreneurship: Theory and Practice*, *38*, 473–499. doi:10.1111/etap.12006

Buzzanell, P. M. (2018). Communication theory of resilience: Enacting adaptive-transformative processes when families experience loss and disruption. In D. Braithwaite, E. Suter, & K. Floyd (Eds.), *Engaging theories in family communication* (2nd ed., pp. 98–109). New York, NY: Routledge.

Cai, H., & Wu, X. P. (2006). Social changes and occupational gender inequality. *Chinese Sociology and Anthropology*, *28*, 37–53. doi:10.2753/CSA0009-4625380402

Davidson, R. J. (2000). Affective style, psychopathology and resilience: Brain mechanisms and plasticity. *American Psychologist*, *55*, 1196–1214. Retrieved from https://www.ncbi.nlm.nih.gov/pubmed/11280935

Guo, C., & Miller, J. K. (2010). Guanxi dynamics and entrepreneurial firm creation and development in China. *Management and Organization Review*, *6*, 267–291. doi: 10.1111/j.1740-8784.2010.00180.x

Hedner, T., Abouzeedan, A., & Klofsten, M. (2011). Entrepreneurial resilience. *Annals of Innovation & Entrepreneurship*, *2*, 7986. doi:10.3402/aie.v2i1.6002

Hughes, K. D., Jennings, J. E., Brush, C., Carter, S., & Welter, F. (2012). Extending women's entrepreneurship research in new directions. *Entrepreneurship: Theory and Practice*, *36*, 429–442. doi:10.1111/j.1540-6520.2012.00504.x

Jennings, J. E., & Brush, C. G. (2013). Research on women entrepreneurs: Challenges to (and from) the broader entrepreneurship literature?. *The Academy of Management Annals*, *7*, 663–715. doi:10.1080/19416520.2013.782190

Liu, M. (2017). Chinese women's entrepreneurship report. Chinese entrepreneurs & Mulanhui Fund. Retrieved from http://www.iceo.com.cn/com2013/2017/0420/302629.shtml

Long, Z., Buzzanell. P. M., & Kuang, K. (2016). Positioning work amid discontinuities and continuities: Chinese Post80s workers' dialogical constructions of meanings of work. *Management Communication Quarterly*, *30*, 532–556. doi: 10.1177/0893318916636237

Mumby, D. K. (2005). Theorizing resistance in organization studies: A dialectical approach. *Management Communication Quarterly*, *19*, 19–44. doi:10.1177/0893318905276558

Peng, K. Z., Ngo, H., Shi, J., & Wong, C. (2008). Gender differences in the work commitment of Chinese workers: An investigation of two alternative explanations. *Journal of World Business*, *44*, 323–335. doi:10.1016/j.jwb.2008.08.003

Stead, V. (2017). Belonging and women entrepreneurs: Women's navigation of gendered assumptions in entrepreneurial practice. *International Small Business Journal: Researching Entrepreneurship*, *35*, 61–77. doi:10.1177/0266242615594413

Sue, D. W. (2010). *Microaggressions in everyday life: Race, gender, and sexual orientation*. Hoboken, NJ: John Wiley & Sons, Inc.

Yang, V. (2017). Five ways China's women are closing the gender gap. *World Economic Forum*. Retrieved from https://www.weforum.org/agenda/2017/11/chinese-women-are-closing-the-gender-gap-heres-how/

Yueh, L. (2008). China's entrepreneurs. *Business Strategy Review*, *19*, 60–64. doi:10.1111/j.1467-8616.2008.00537.x

Chapter 8

The Role of Gender and Institutional Factors for Entrepreneurs and Corporate Entrepreneurs in Latin American Countries

Linda Elizabeth Ruiz, Elda Barron and José Ernesto Amorós

Abstract

Interest in the role and behavior of women entrepreneurs has increased in the last decades. This research study examines personal characteristics and labor and business regulations on entrepreneurship and corporate entrepreneurship. It also analyzes how gender differed in these forms of entrepreneurship across Latin American countries. We performed logistic regressions to different models with information from the Global Entrepreneurship Monitor (GEM) from 2016. We used a sample from 10 countries. We also used information from the Heritage Foundation and The World Bank. The results show that antecedents of entrepreneurship activity differ by gender. Specifically, the effect is different when analyzing labor regulations. We also find different intensities depending on gender. The study contributes to the literature about gender and different forms of entrepreneurship. We suggest developing policies in favor of women's entrepreneurial activity within the workplace and as independent entrepreneurs.

Keywords: Women entrepreneurship; Latin America; early-stage entrepreneurship; corporate entrepreneurship; Global Entrepreneurship Monitor; formal institutions; individual characteristics

Introduction

The role of women entrepreneurs has attracted the attention of different spheres. The OECD (2017) has described that countries in Latin American would impact their economy if women's participation in the working population increases as close as males' participation. Therefore, governments are making significant efforts to launch programs to increase the culture of participation in entrepreneurial

The Emerald Handbook of Women and Entrepreneurship in Developing Economies, 125–143
Copyright © 2021 by Emerald Publishing Limited
All rights of reproduction in any form reserved
doi:10.1108/978-1-80071-326-020211008

activities and promote women's participation in the workplace and public positions.

Hence, researchers around the world have dedicated significant efforts to try to understand the entrepreneurial activity from a gender perspective (e.g., Bernart et al., 2017; Brush, Ali, Kelley, & Greene, 2017), but just a few have studied the role of gender on corporate entrepreneurship activity (e.g., Adachi & Hisada, 2017), which is basically the activity that occurs within organizations. Corporate entrepreneurship is also an opportunity to engage in start-up activities and has been recognized as being similarly important as independent entrepreneurship.

Latin America has been identified as a region with a high rate of independent entrepreneurship in diverse countries (Bosma et al., 2020). However, entrepreneurship and innovation activities within established companies in the region lag significantly behind when compared with developed economies. This situation is problematic and needs further attention since the 2019/2020 report from the Global Entrepreneurship Monitor (GEM) describes employees' significant activity with their employer in starting new businesses. This situation leads to deduce a considerable increase in the activity in the following years.

Diverse factors contribute to let entrepreneurship flourish. Latin America has been affected by a turbulent worldwide environment. As this is the case, policymakers need to pay attention to the environment and develop policies to create a good business environment. Consequently, research studies have analyzed the impact of institutions in the behavior of entrepreneurs (Aparicio, Urbano, & Audretsch, 2016) and corporate entrepreneurs (Urbano & Turró, 2013). However, not many studies analyzed the role of gender in these two forms of entrepreneurship in Latin America. This situation represents a significant omission because the significance of women participation in economic and societal progress is recognized (Bullough, Renko, & Abdelzaher, 2017).

Adachi and Hisada (2017) dedicated efforts in comparing these two types of entrepreneurship from a gender perspective. In their study, authors compared employment characteristics such as working part-time and family-related factors such as having children. Results suggest that employment-related variables have a stronger effect on entrepreneurship forms than family-related variables. In this regard, the authors describe that women may be at a disadvantage in these two entrepreneurship forms. In another way, Welter (2011) suggests paying special attention to the context, and other researchers have called for an evaluation of the entrepreneurship activity from different perspectives. They recommend considering feminist theories (Calás, Smircich, & Bourne, 2009).

Pettersson, Ahl, Berglund, and Tillmar (2017) describe that liberal feminist theory suggests that women and men do not have any difference in engaging in entrepreneurship activities. Possible differences are due to contextual factors. Considering this perspective, we develop hypotheses consistent with this approach, claiming that any difference between men and women in the two types of entrepreneurial behavior (entrepreneurship and corporate entrepreneurship) is due to contextual factors. In this chapter, we explore the activity of independent and corporate entrepreneurship from a gender perspective. To do that, we considered individual variables as a form of human capital and institutional variables.

The chapter is structured in the following form. In the second section, we present a literature review on entrepreneurial activity and individual and contextual determinants. This section presents two sets of hypotheses: individual determinants and the role of regulations as institutional variables. We formulated each hypothesis from a gender perspective, taking into consideration the liberal feminist theory. Section three describes the methods used for the analysis. Section four presents the empirical results. Section five discusses the study's findings as well as the limitations of the research and future research directions.

Theoretical Development

Entrepreneurship brings diverse positive effects over a country; for example, it brings significant contribution to socioeconomic mobility; in this regard, their activity should be considered, especially of those developing regions like Latin America (Amorós, 2011). However, less developed countries like this region have been presenting a constant entrepreneurial activity growth (Fernández-Serrano & Liñán, 2014). This situation has attracted the attention of scholars because most of these countries struggle with diverse contextual factors that may harness the activity. Diverse scholars have dedicated their efforts to understanding the institutional settings around regions, agreeing that these settings substantially differed from nondeveloped and developed countries (e.g., He, Tian, & Chen, 2007). In this sense, the authors describe that emerging economies may struggle with environments with inadequate business regulations (Peng, 2000). Besides the environment as an important factor for developing forms of entrepreneurship, human capital has long been recognized as an essential element in developing the entrepreneurship activity because it is essential for discovering entrepreneurial opportunities (Alvarez & Barney, 2007). The following sections present relevant literature regarding human capital and institutional settings around entrepreneurship.

Individual Factors for Entrepreneurial Activity

Human Capital – Skills

Different authors have considered human capital resources when analyzing different forms of entrepreneurship (Klyver & Schenkel, 2013). These capabilities are considered necessary in nascent entrepreneurs (e.g., De Clercq & Arenius, 2006). Brush et al. (2017) analyzed the role of perceived capabilities over different types of entrepreneurship; they extend previous studies by emphasizing the essential role that this factor has in closing the gender gap on entrepreneurial activities. They describe that if genders have a similar perception of their capabilities, the likelihood of engaging in entrepreneurial activity will be similar. Previously, Martiarena (2013) analyzed entrepreneurial skills and other factors on different forms of entrepreneurship. The author suggests that skills are important, but those who work within established organizations seem to be less confident in their entrepreneurial skills than nascent entrepreneurs.

Guerrero and Peña-Legazkue (2013) analyzed the role of individual capabilities on the entrepreneurial activity that occurs within established organizations; the authors describe an "intrapreneurial experience" as a set of skills and knowledge that an individual acquires through their life and are considered important for creating new ventures within corporations. On the other side, different theories try to explain gender differences within the entrepreneurial activities. Liberal theory suggests that any variance between women and men is due to contextual forces. Barriers and lack of access to resources are causes for differences in entrepreneurial activity (Pettersson et al., 2017). Based on these arguments, we propose the following hypothesis:

H1. The perception of having the required skills to run a business will increase the probability of engaging in any type of entrepreneurial activity (Entrepreneurship and Corporate Entrepreneurship) in Latin American countries for both women and men. The effect will be stronger for men.

Human Capital – Perceived Opportunities

In certain regions, individuals may be more able to detect good environments to develop entrepreneurial activities. In this regard, the ability to perceive opportunities has long been recognized as an important skill for developing entrepreneurial opportunities (Ardichvili, Cardozo, & Ray, 2003). DeTienne and Chandler (2007) suggest that women and men have different stock of knowledge that they acquired through their experiences. They use this knowledge to detect entrepreneurial opportunities. Authors describe that either women or men may have differences because they take different processes to detect opportunities.

More recently, Gonzalez-Alvarez and Solis Rodriguez (2011) and Dahalan, Jaafar, and Rosdi (2013) support this finding, suggesting that there are gender differences in the process of discovering an entrepreneurial opportunity; the authors describe that men are the ones that are more likely to discover opportunities compared to women. In the form of corporate entrepreneurship, the authors (Turró, López, & Urbano, 2013) suggest that the ability to detect entrepreneurial opportunities will increase an employee's probability of engaging in corporate entrepreneurship activities.

However, we believe that those differences are due to contextual factors that individuals usually face. Gupta, Goktan, and Gunay (2014) suggest that the opportunity recognition may be gender biased. The usually masculine stereotype assigned to entrepreneurship activities may intensify the evaluation of business opportunities by men. The same thing may happen to women if the positive skills of women are emphasized. Based on these arguments and taking into consideration the liberal feminist perspective, we propose the following hypothesis.

H2. The perception of business opportunities in the Latin America region will increase the probability of engaging in any type of entrepreneurial activity for both women and men. The effect will be stronger for men.

Country-level Factors for the Entrepreneurial Activity

Labor Freedom and Entrepreneurship

The role of the environment has been the focus of research in recent years (e.g., Bjørnskov & Foss, 2016; Gimenez-Jimenez and Calabro, 2018). Several authors have dedicated their efforts to understand those country institutions that affect the entrepreneurial activity. In this regard, Kuckertz, Berger, and Mpeqa (2016) suggest paying special attention to economic development and institutions; authors suggest performing more in-depth analysis because of each country's different conditions. Analyzing either necessity or opportunity motivations to start a business, the authors suggest that economic freedom may better explain the necessity motivation of starting a business. Powell and Weber (2013) analyzed different economic freedom elements and their effect on entrepreneurship. In the breakdown of the economic freedom components the authors found that labor freedom is significant for the venture capital stage in entrepreneurship.

Concerned about the effect of economic freedom and its components over the regions, Angulo-Guerrero, Pérez-Moreno, and Abad-Guerrero (2017) followed a similar approach as Kuckertz et al. (2016). They analyzed economies that are members of the OECD. They suggest that those countries primarily driven by opportunity to entrepreneurship may benefit most from good legal environments, such as labor freedom. However, the relationship seems to be negative for necessity-driven countries. In this case, as are the most cases in Latin America, other factors such as trading internationally may affect entrepreneurial activity. Labor freedom is important for entrepreneurs and corporate entrepreneurs. In some regions, women may be at a disadvantage by a weak external labor market (Kuada, 2009). As this is the case, we would like to explore this effect from a gender perspective, so we propose the following hypothesis:

H3. The quality of a regulatory and legal framework of a country's labor market increases the likelihood of engaging in any type of entrepreneurial activity for both women and men in the Latin American region. The effect will be stronger for men.

Business Regulatory Environment and Entrepreneurship

Having a business legal environment is recognized as an essential element for developing new businesses and growing existing ones (e.g., Klapper, Laeven, & Rajan, 2006). In their research study, Panda and Dash (2014) reviewed the constraints faced by entrepreneurs in developing countries, finding that financial and infrastructure factors are the main constraints from an entrepreneur's perspective. Van Stel, Storey, and Thurik (2007) suggest that entrepreneurs would like to skip long procedures and engage in informal entrepreneurship activities without a strong business regulatory environment. In the same manner, Fonseca, Lopez-Garcia, and Pissarides (2001) reviewed different elements of the business environment, specifically the authors pointed out that higher costs in the opening of new businesses encourage the population to work in established organizations.

Similarly, Kaplan, Piedra, and Seira (2011) analyzed the Mexican context, confirming other related studies, so they describe that lowering the cost of procedures to start a business may encourage entrepreneurs to develop businesses. More recently, Canare (2018) analyzed the effect of doing business measurements from the World Bank, over regions, and again confirmed that having a good business environment will promote entrepreneurial activity. However, this situation may be different in nondeveloped and developing countries. Results suggest that governments should pay attention to the operating costs and overall procedures of established businesses and not only to start-up businesses.

The business environment also has important implications, especially for Latin American regions, where a significant business rate is considered informal. Having sufficient elements that promote a good business environment will enhance formal entrepreneurship and lower informal entrepreneurship (Thai & Turkina, 2014). Scholars have also analyzed the business environment and their effect on entrepreneurship from a gender perspective; they describe that different factors in the business environment affect in a greater manner women than men. Women may potentially have more barriers in developing their business (Carter & Williams, 2003), for example, by finding difficulties to access financial resources (Klapper & Parker, 2011; Marlow & Patton, 2005). We deduce that established organizations that want to expand their business by opening new business units will benefit from a proper business environment (Gómez-Haro, Aragón-Correa, & Cordón-Pozo, 2011. Based on these arguments, we propose the following hypothesis:

H4. The quality of a regulatory environment for starting a business in Latin America increases the likelihood of engaging in any type of entrepreneurial activity for both women and men. The effect will be stronger for men.

Methodology

Sample and Data Collection

The present study is primarily based on the GEM data from 2016. We also included in the study variables from the Heritage Foundation and the World Bank. We decided to use the GEM database since it allows us to have information from intrapreneurs and entrepreneurs and offer different variables that are well suited for this study. GEM has been used in research studies. It has been considered valuable because of the rich information that the organization collects each year. GEM also includes information from many countries around the world and includes data from Latin American countries – Argentina, Brazil, Chile, Colombia, Ecuador, Mexico, Panama, Peru, Uruguay, and Puerto Rico – that are analyzed in the present study.

The Heritage Foundation and the World Bank get information from the countries' context to promote public policies to support enterprises. Different studies (e.g., Powell & Weber, 2013) have used their indexes and their information to analyze different implications around companies. Since our goal is to analyze the context where new companies are arising and existing companies engage in entrepreneurship and innovative activities, we considered they are well suited for this study. The database considered 30,533 observations of individuals working within an established business and individuals that declared they are starting a business.

Measures

The dependent variables for this study use entrepreneurial employee activity and nascent entrepreneurs for both women and men. The first variable relates to the activity of employees that have been involved in the development of new projects for the last three years. This variable includes the participation of employees as leaders and supporters of new projects. The second independent variable includes information of women and men that have been involved in an early stage of entrepreneurial activity. Both are considered binary variables. The response is 1 if they are involved in the activity and 0 if they are not.

On the other hand, the independent variables considered for the study relate to the perception of having the opportunities to develop entrepreneurial activities in the participant's context. We also included the perception of having the skills to develop business opportunities. These characteristics are considered essential as individual attributes of entrepreneurs. Since our goal is also to analyze the environment's implication for both activities from a gender perspective, we decided to use the ease of doing business from the World Bank and labor freedom from the Heritage Foundation. The first variable relates basically to the environments of countries concerning economic factors. Ease of doing business emphasizes effective business regulations. The index includes dealing with construction permits, getting electricity, registering property, getting credits, protecting minority investors, paying taxes, trading across borders, enforcing contracts, and resolving insolvency and labor market regulation.

For control variables, we include education, age, and income household. From an institutional environment, we include GDP (ppp) and fertility rates. GDP is widely used in different research studies because different GDP levels may lead to different entrepreneurial activities. Since our focus is on exploring two different forms of entrepreneurship, we considered it essential to use it. The fertility rate is also significant to include since research studies have explored the implications of an entrepreneur having a family, so we use it as a proxy. Table 8.1 provides a summary of the variables included in the study.

Results

The means, standard deviations, and pairwise correlation coefficients for the variables are reported in Tables 8.2, 8.3, and 8.4. We can see that the rate of women employees involved in entrepreneurial activities is around 8.6% in Latin American countries against 12.02% of the involvement of their counterpart, the males. On the other hand, the rate of females involved in early-stage entrepreneurial activity is around 15.7%, and for males, the rate is around 20%. Figs. 8.1 and 8.2

Table 8.1. Description of Variables.

	Variable	Description	Source
Dependent variables	Entrepreneurial employee	In the last three years, have you been involved in the development of new activities for your main employer? (Yes/No)	GEM APS-2016
	Early stage of entrepreneurial activity	Involved in total entrepreneurial activity (Yes/No)	GEM APS-2016
Independent variables	Skills	Do you have the knowledge, skill, and experience required to start a new business? (Yes/No)	GEM APS-2016
	Opportunities	In the next six months, will there be good opportunities for starting a business in the area where you live? (Yes/No)	GEM APS-2016
	Labor Freedom index	Score in the index of Economic Freedom (0–100)	Heritage Foundation 2016
	Ease of doing business index	Overall score in the index of doing business (0–100)	World Bank 2016
Control variables	Age	Respondent's age at the time he/she was surveyed	GEM APS- 2016
	Education	Harmonized educational attainment (0 = None; 5 = Graduate experience)	GEM APS-2016
	Household income	Household income recoded into thirds (1 = Lowest 33% tile, 2 = Middle 33% tile, 3 = Highest 33% tile)	GEM APS-2016
	GDP(ppp)	Gross domestic product at purchasing power parity per capita (US dollars)	World Bank, 2016
	Fertility Rate	Number of children that would be born to a woman if she were to live to the end of her childbearing years and bear children in accordance with age-specific fertility rates of the specified year.	World Bank, 2016

Table 8.2. Means and Standard Deviation.

	Male				Female			
Variable	**Mean**	**Std. Dev**	**Min**	**Max**	**Mean**	**Std. Dev**	**Min**	**Max**
Corporate entrepreneurship	0.120	0.325	0	1	0.086	0.280	0	1
Entrepreneurship	0.199	0.399	0	1	0.157	0.364	0	1
Opportunity	0.437	0.496	0	1	0.437	0.496	0	1
Skills	0.559	0.496	0	1	0.560	0.496	0	1
Education	2.958	1.359	0	5	2.958	1.359	0	5
Age (log)	3.629	0.393	2.890	4.595	3.630	0.393	2.890	4.595
Household income	2.025	0.796	1	3	2.025	0.796	1.000	3
Labor Freedom	59.327	8.820	42.9	89	59.327	8.820	42.900	89
Ease of Doing Business	66.602	5.880	55.6	71.6	66.602	5.880	55.600	71.600
GDPppp (log)	26.905	1.123	24.983	28.709	26.905	1.123	24.983	28.709
Fertility Rate	1.972	0.343	1.243	2.514	1.972	0.343	1.243	2.514

show the rate of entrepreneurship and corporate entrepreneurship in Latin American countries. We ran two models for each activity, one for women and one for men, to see the effect of institutional factors on the activity. To verify for multicollinearity issues, we ran the Variance Inflation Factor (VIF); all scores are below 3.0, indicating that we do not have a problem in the analysis.

Tables 8.5 and 8.6 show the logistic regression results in the different models used in the analysis. It is important to mention that we do not use hierarchical analysis as we do not have the recommended number of groups to justify the analysis (Aguinis, Gottfredson, & Culpepper, 2013), so we proceeded with regular logistics regressions. The independent variables of skills remain significant in all the models. Opportunity recognition did not result significantly in the intrapreneurial models; however, results were significant for both women and men in the entrepreneurial models. Therefore, we confirmed hypothesis 1 and partially number 2 regarding human capital variables. In Figs. 8.3 and 8.4, we can see the marginal effect on entrepreneurial activity and intrapreneurial activity for low and high values on the perception of having the right skills to develop a business idea. We can visualize in figure one that perceiving having the right skills to develop a business has a greater effect on men than women. In addition, when quantifying the intensity of the perception of having the right skills on the corporate entrepreneurship activity (Fig. 8.4), we found that the effect is particularly intense for men. According to the findings of hypothesis 2, we also

Table 8.3. Corporate Entrepreneurship Correlation Variables.

	Corporate Entrepreneurship	Education	Skills	Opportunity	Age (Log)	Household Income	Labor Freedom	Ease of Doing Business	GDP (Log)	Fertility Rate
Corporate Entrepreneurship	1									
Education	0.039*	1								
Skills	0.104*	0.182*	1							
Opportunity	0.148*	0.026*	0.135*	1						
Age (Log)	0.013	−0.053*	0.018*	−0.158*	1					
Household income	0.134*	0.005	0.073*	0.322*	−0.021*	1				
Labor Freedom	0.0745*	0.054*	0.067*	0.206*	0.008	0.037*	1			
Ease of Doing business	0.057*	0.038*	−0.040*	0.145*	−0.014*	−0.010	0.588*	1		
GDP (Log)	0.022*	0.024*	−0.064*	−0.053*	−0.091*	−0.017*	0.006	0.134*	1	
Fertility rate	−0.081*	0.027*	−0.009	−0.249*	−0.086*	0.053*	−0.652*	−0.361*	0.069*	1

Note: * < 0.05.

Table 8.4. Total Entrepreneurial Activity Correlation Variables.

	Total Entrepreurial Activity	Education	Skills	Opportunity	Age (Log)	Household Income	Labor Freedom	Ease of Doing Business	GDP (Log)	Fertility Rate
Total entrepreneurial activity	1									
Education	0.143*	1								
Skills	0.269*	0.182*	1							
Opportunity	0.088*	0.026*	0.135*	1						
Age (Log)	−0.059*	−0.053*	0.018*	−0.158*	1					
Household income	0.049*	0.005	0.073*	0.322*	−0.021*	1				
Labor Freedom	0.063*	0.054*	0.067*	0.206*	0.008	0.037*	1			
Ease of Doing business	−0.014*	0.038*	−0.040*	0.145*	−0.014*	−0.010	0.588*	1		
GDP (Log)	−0.029*	0.024*	−0.064*	−0.053*	−0.091*	−0.017*	0.006	0.134*	1	
Fertility rate	−0.011	0.027*	−0.009	−0.249*	−0.086*	0.053*	−0.652*	−0.361*	0.069*	1

Note: * < 0.05.

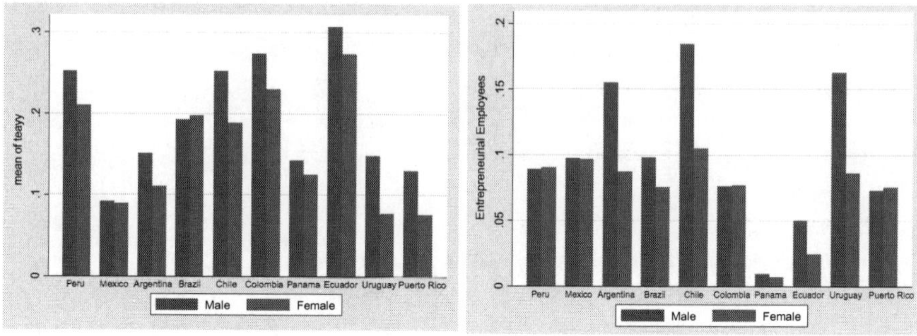

Figs. 8.1 and 8.2. Entrepreneurship and Corporate Entrepreneurship Rate Overview.

Table 8.5. Logistic Regressions for Corporate Entrepreneurship.

	Male		Female	
Variables	**B**	**SE**	**B**	**SE**
Opportunity	0.069	0.083	0.135	0.112
Skills	0.408***	0.091	0.609***	0.119
Education	0.267***	0.038	0.262***	0.052
Age (Log)	−0.023	0.125	−0.079	0.173
Household income	0.546***	0.066	0.555***	0.086
Labor Freedom	−0.019**	0.008	−0.004	0.010
Ease of doing business	0.021**	0.009	0.016	0.012
GDP (Log)	−0.005	0.045	0.177**	0.057
Fertility Rate	−1.655***	0.210	−0.568**	0.284
_cons	−1.272	1.665	−9.262***	2.102

Notes: *$p < 0.1$; **$p < 0.05$; ***$p < 0.01$.

quantified the marginal effects of opportunity recognition. In Figs. 8.5 and 8.6, we can visualize the magnitude of this effect, confirming that recognizing opportunities may have a greater effect on men than women.

The labor freedom institutional variable remains significant in the entrepreneurship models for both women and men. However, it did not result in significance in the intrapreneurial female model. It is shown that having a good labor regulatory environment will promote entrepreneurial behavior in Latin America. We partially confirmed hypothesis 3 since we could not have the same results in women's and men's corporate entrepreneurship models. Figs. 8.7 and 8.8 show that the effect is greater for men than women.

Table 8.6. Logistic Regressions for Total Entrepreneurship Activity.

	Male		Female	
Variables	**B**	**SE**	**B**	**SE**
Opportunity	0.489***	0.050	0.459***	0.052
Skills	1.454***	0.064	1.440***	0.067
Education	0.104***	0.021	0.076***	0.022
Age (Log)	−0.563***	0.066	−0.328***	0.070
Household income	0.110**	0.035	−0.021	0.036
Labor Freedom	0.013**	0.004	0.011**	0.004
Ease of doing business	−0.020***	0.005	−0.028***	0.005
GDP (Log)	−0.136***	0.026	−0.016	0.026
Fertility Rate	−0.267**	0.115	−0.290**	0.130
_cons	3.583***	0.971	0.426	1.013

Notes: *$p < 0.1$; **$p < 0.05$; ***$p < 0.01$.

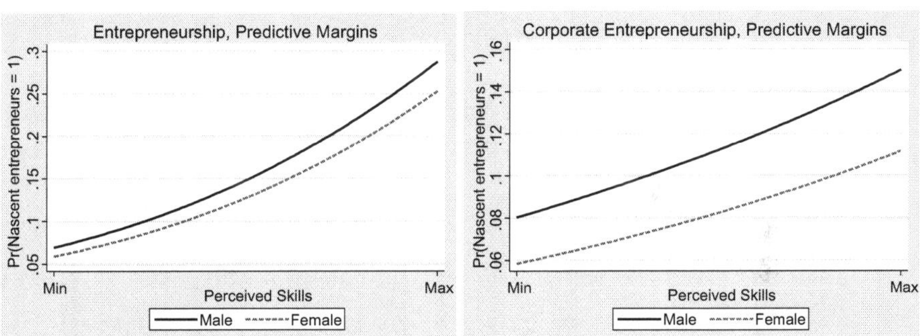

Figs. 8.3 and 8.4. Perceived Skills Predictive Margins on the Entrepreneurial Activity.

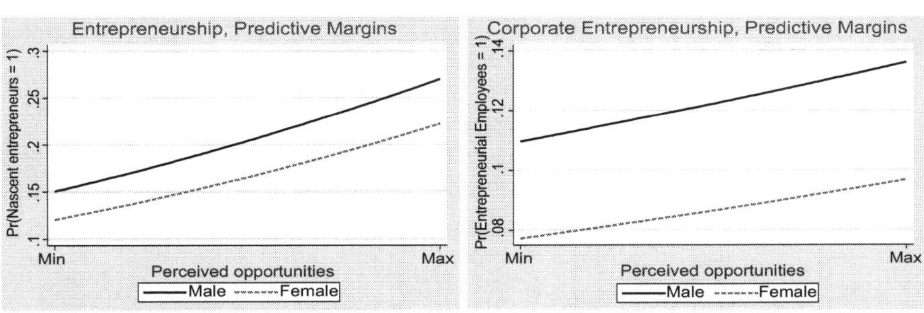

Figs. 8.5 and 8.6. Opportunity Recognition Predictive Margins on the Entrepreneurial Activity.

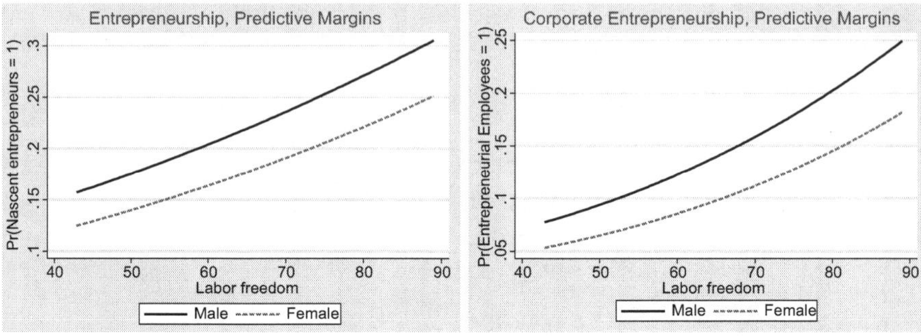

Figs. 8.7 and 8.8. Labor Freedom Predictive Margins on the Entrepreneurial Activity.

Additionally, the variable of ease of doing business became significant when analyzing the entrepreneurial models of women and men. Fig. 8.9 shows that the presence of unfavorable business environment will have a greater effect on women than men. We partially confirmed hypothesis 3 since we could not have the same results in women's and men's corporate entrepreneurship models. Figs. 8.9 and 8.10 show that the effect is greater for men than women.

Additionally, the variable of ease of doing business was significant when analyzing women and men's entrepreneurial models. Fig. 8.9 shows that an unfavorable business environment will have a greater effect on women than men. We partially confirmed hypothesis 4 since we did not find any statistical significance of ease of doing business in the women corporate entrepreneurship model. Fig. 8.10 shows the intensity of this variable on women and men. It is important to mention that the direction in the graphs is different from the one in independent entrepreneurship.

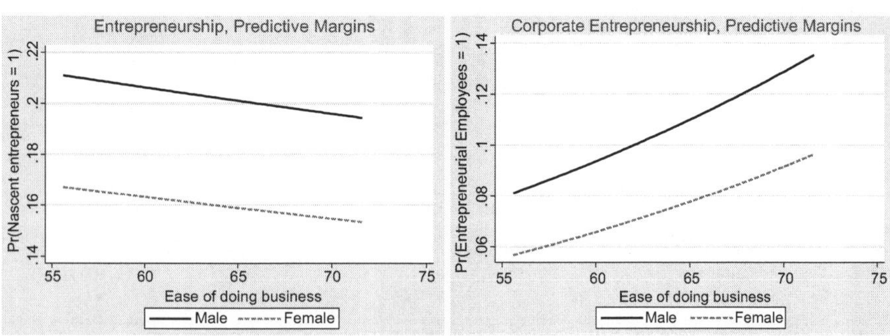

Figs. 8.9 and 8.10. Ease of Doing Business on the Entrepreneurial Activity.

Discussion

Different authors have inferred that individual factors and institutional factors substantially affect entrepreneurial activity (e.g., Klyver & Schenkel, 2013). This study used two forms of entrepreneurship: independent entrepreneurship and corporate entrepreneurship, and we analyzed them from a gender perspective. We examined information in the Latin American context since it is a region with a high rate in the intention to start a business (Global Entrepreneurship Monitor, 2020). However, the activity within organizations has not been fully explored. We took the approach of the liberal feminist theory to construct our hypotheses.

Results suggest capital human in the opportunity recognition and the perception of having the right skills to develop an entrepreneurial activity as a strong predictor for independent entrepreneurship. The perception of having the right business skills is also essential for developing the corporate entrepreneurship activity by women and men. However, the opportunity recognition may be influenced by other factors when analyzing corporate entrepreneurship, for example, the company's innovation culture or the current strategy that the organization is following. These factors may influence the entrepreneurial behavior of employees.

We also noticed that the effect is stronger in men than in women. We deduce these results are because Latin American societies may have different perceptions of men's and women's professional development (Estrin & Mickiewicz, 2011). Business skills may be associated with men and not women (Bamiatzi, Jones, Mitchelmore, & Nikolopoulos, 2015). We think that women and men in these regions follow a more traditional role, and for instance, they modify their entrepreneurial behavior. This situation could explain the disparity in the activity between genders; there are countries in these regions where the gender gap is evident. However, we also recognized there are countries with almost a parity in the forms of entrepreneurship. For example, Colombia, Puerto Rico, and Peru show signs of a more entrepreneurial activity within corporations by women.

The second set of hypotheses (3 and 4) deals with the environmental role in entrepreneurship forms. We also have mixed results in these models. The labor freedom variable impacts both women and men entrepreneurial models, so we agreed with Angulo-Guerrero et al. (2017) on the impact of labor freedom on the entrepreneurship activity. Organizations and institutions in this region should continue to develop labor policies. However, the influence of this variable only resulted in the men's corporate entrepreneurship model. We will need further analysis to investigate the reasons for this result since we expected that better labor freedom regulations would enhance women in the workplace. The men model's negative result may lead to think that the organizational culture plays a significant role.

The result of business environments was significant for the traditional entrepreneurial form; we agree with Van Stel et al. (2007) that structural factors are determinant for the entrepreneurial activity. In this regard, we also find that the effect is stronger in men than in women. The opposite direction in the marginal effects graph in the corporate entrepreneurship model leads us to think that when a person perceives an unfavorable business environment they will prefer to stay within the corporate umbrella. Besides, this person may engage in the development of corporate entrepreneurial activities. We deduce that benefits that organizations provide to employees during this time may be attractive to entrepreneurs.

This study contributes to gender and entrepreneurship literature by analyzing determinants into two forms of entrepreneurship. We also expand studies that take feminist theories to explain the phenomena (Pettersson et al., 2017). This study shows that antecedents of entrepreneurial activity may have different effects depending on gender in the Latin American context. So, women may face more barriers than men to develop these forms of entrepreneurship. Besides, the study contributes to the theories of human capital and institutions. From a practical implication, these results highlight the importance of developing entrepreneurial activities within organizations by promoting entrepreneurial skills and developing practices to recognize business opportunities. Education is a significant factor that organizations and governments need to continue developing. The significance in the business regulations variable encourages policymakers to continue developing policies to simplify the process for start-up businesses. Moreover, more equality regulations may close the gender gap in the activity.

The study is not free of limitations; we only included 10 Latin American countries. Further research may include more countries and different dependent variables since we rely on the ones described by the GEM. Secondly, we included binary variables as predictors; further research will also include different types of variables. Future studies may also include different types of institutional variables to analyze forms of entrepreneurship. Further research may include more countries and different dependent variables since we rely on the ones described by the GEM. Secondly, we included binary variables as predictors; further research will also include different types of variables. Future studies may also have different types of institutional variables to analyze forms of entrepreneurship. We also encourage other research studies to include organizational-level variables when studying corporate entrepreneurship; culture and innovation strategies may be some factors that explain the entrepreneurial behavior of employees.

References

Adachi, T., & Hisada, T. (2017). Gender differences in entrepreneurship and intrapreneurship: An empirical analysis. *Small Business Economics*, *48*(3), 447–486.

Aguinis, H., Gottfredson, R. K., & Culpepper, S. A. (2013). Best-practice recommendations for estimating cross-level interaction effects using multilevel modeling. *Journal of Management*, *39*(6), 1490–1528.

Alvarez, S. A., & Barney, J. B. (2007). Discovery and creation: Alternative theories of entrepreneurial action. *Strategic Entrepreneurship Journal*, *1*(1–2), 11–26.

Amorós, J. E. (2011). El Proyecto global entrepreneurship monitor (GEM): Una aproximación desde el contexto Latinoamericano. *Academia Revista Latinoamericana de Administración*, *46*, 1–15.

Angulo-Guerrero, M. J., Pérez-Moreno, S., & Abad-Guerrero, I. M. (2017). How economic freedom affects opportunity and necessity entrepreneurship in the OECD countries. *Journal of Business Research*, *73*, 30–37.

Aparicio, S., Urbano, D., & Audretsch, D. (2016). Institutional factors, opportunity entrepreneurship and economic growth: Panel data evidence. *Technological Forecasting and Social Change*, *102*, 45–61.

Ardichvili, A., Cardozo, R., & Ray, S. (2003). A theory of entrepreneurial opportunity identification and development. *Journal of Business Venturing*, *18*(1), 105–123.

Bamiatzi, V., Jones, S., Mitchelmore, S., & Nikolopoulos, K. (2015). The role of competencies in shaping the leadership style of female entrepreneurs: The case of North West of England, Yorkshire, and North Wales. *Journal of Small Business Management*, *53*(3), 627–644.

Bernat, L. F., Lambardi, G., & Palacios, P. (2017). Determinants of the entrepreneurial gender gap in Latin America. *Small Business Economics*, *48*(3), 727–752.

Bjørnskov, C., & Foss, N. J. (2016). Institutions, entrepreneurship, and economic growth: What do we know and what do we still need to know? *Academy of Management Perspectives*, *30*(3), 292–315.

Bosma, N., Hill, S., Ionescu-Somers, A., Kelley, D., Levie, J., & Tarnawa, A. (2020). Global entrepreneurship monitor 2018/2019 global report. Global Entrepreneurship Research Association (GERA). Retrieved from https://www.gemconsortium.org/file/open?fileId=50443

Brush, C., Ali, A., Kelley, D., & Greene, P. (2017). The influence of human capital factors and context on women's entrepreneurship: Which matters more? *Journal of Business Venturing Insights*, *8*, 105–113.

Bullough, A., Renko, M., & Abdelzaher, D. (2017). Women's business ownership: Operating within the context of institutional and in-group collectivism. *Journal of Management*, *43*(7), 2037–2064.

Calás, M. B., Smircich, L., & Bourne, K. A. (2009). Extending the boundaries: Reframing "entrepreneurship as social change" through feminist perspectives. *Academy of Management Review*, *34*(3), 552–569.

Canare, T. (2018). The effect of ease of doing business on firm creation. *Annals of Economics & Finance*, *19*(2), 555–584.

Carter, N. M., & Williams, M. L. (2003). Comparing social feminism and liberal feminism: The case of new firm growth. In J. Butler (Ed.), *New perspectives on women entrepreneurs* (pp 25–50). Charlotte, NC: Information Age Publishing.

Dahalan, N., Jaafar, M., & Rosdi, S. (2013). Local community readiness in entrepreneurship: Do gender differ in searching business opportunity. *Procedia-social and Behavioral Sciences*, *91*, 403–410.

De Clercq, D., & Arenius, P. (2006). The role of knowledge in business start-up activity. *International Small Business Journal*, *24*(4), 339–358.

DeTienne, D. R., & Chandler, G. N. (2007). The role of gender in opportunity identification. *Entrepreneurship: Theory and Practice*, *31*(3), 365–386.

Estrin, S., & Mickiewicz, T. (2011). Institutions and female entrepreneurship. *Small Business Economics*, *37*(4), 397.

Fernández-Serrano, J., & Liñán, F. (2014). Culture and entrepreneurship: The case of Latin America. *Innovar*, *24*, 169–180.

Fonseca, R., Lopez-Garcia, P., & Pissarides, C. A. (2001). Entrepreneurship, start-up costs and employment. *European Economic Review*, *45*(4–6), 692–705.

Giménez, D., & Calabrò, A. (2018). The salient role of institutions in women's entrepreneurship: A critical review and agenda for future research. *International Entrepreneurship and Management Journal*, *14*(4), 857–882.

Global Entrepreneurship Monitor. (2020). Global entrepreneurship monitor 2019/2010 global report. Global Entrepreneurship Monitor. Retrieved from https://www.gemconsortium.org/report/gem-2019-2020-global-report

Gómez-Haro, S., Aragón-Correa, J. A., & Cordón-Pozo, E. (2011). Differentiating the effects of the institutional environment on corporate entrepreneurship. *Management Decision*, *49*(10), 1677–1693.

Gonzalez-Alvarez, N., & Solis-Rodriguez, V. (2011). Discovery of entrepreneurial opportunities: A gender perspective. *Industrial Management & Data Systems*, *111*(5), 755–775.

Guerrero, M., & Peña-Legazkue, I. (2013). The effect of intrapreneurial experience on corporate venturing: Evidence from developed economies. *International Entrepreneurship and Management Journal*, *9*(3), 397–416.

Gupta, V. K., Goktan, A. B., & Gunay, G. (2014). Gender differences in evaluation of new business opportunity: A stereotype threat perspective. *Journal of Business Venturing*, *29*, 273–288.

He, Y., Tian, Z., & Chen, Y. (2007). Performance implications of nonmarket strategy in China. *Asia Pacific Journal of Management*, *24*(2), 151–169.

Kaplan, D. S., Piedra, E., & Seira, E. (2011). Entry regulation and business start-ups: Evidence from Mexico. *Journal of Public Economics*, *95*(11–12), 1501–1515.

Klapper, L., Laeven, L., & Rajan, R. (2006). Entry regulation as a barrier to entrepreneurship. *Journal of Financial Economics*, *82*(3), 591–629.

Klapper, L. F., & Parker, S. C. (2011). Gender and the business environment for new firm creation. *The World Bank Research Observer*, *26*(2), 237–257.

Klyver, K., & Schenkel, M. T. (2013). From resource access to use: Exploring the impact of resource combinations on nascent entrepreneurship. *Journal of Small Business Management*, *51*(4), 539–556.

Kuada, J. (2009). Gender, social networks, and entrepreneurship in Ghana. *Journal of African Business*, *10*(1), 85–103.

Kuckertz, A., Berger, E. S., & Mpeqa, A. (2016). The more the merrier? Economic freedom and entrepreneurial activity. *Journal of Business Research*, *69*(4), 1288–1293.

Marlow, S., & Patton, D. (2005). All credit to men? Entrepreneurship, finance, and gender. *Entrepreneurship: Theory and Practice*, *29*(6), 717–735.

Martiarena, A. (2013). What's so entrepreneurial about intrapreneurs? *Small Business Economics*, *40*(1), 27–39.

OECD. (2017). *Building an inclusive Mexico: Policies and good governance for gender equality*. Paris: OECD Publishing.

Panda, S., & Dash, S. (2014). Constraints faced by entrepreneurs in developing countries: A review and assessment. *World Review of Entrepreneurship, Management and Sustainable Development*, *10*(4), 405–421.

Peng, M. W. (2000). *Business strategies in transition economies*. Thousand Oaks, CA: SAGE Publications.

Pettersson, K., Ahl, H., Berglund, K., & Tillmar, M. (2017). In the name of women? Feminist readings of policies for women's entrepreneurship in Scandinavia. *Scandinavian Journal of Management*, *33*(1), 50–63.

Powell, B., & Weber, R. (2013). Economic freedom and entrepreneurship: A panel study of the United States. *American Journal of Entrepreneurship*, *6*(1), 67.

Thai, M. T. T., & Turkina, E. (2014). Macro-level determinants of formal entrepreneurship versus informal entrepreneurship. *Journal of Business Venturing*, *29*(4), 490–510.

Turró, A., López, L., & Urbano, D. (2013). Intrapreneurship conditioning factors from a resource-based theory. *European Journal of International Management*, *2*(7), 315–332.

Urbano, D., & Turró, A. (2013). Conditioning factors for corporate entrepreneurship: An in (ex) ternal approach. *The International Entrepreneurship and Management Journal*, *9*(3), 379–396.

Van Stel, A., Storey, D. J., & Thurik, A. R. (2007). The effect of business regulations on nascent and young business entrepreneurship. *Small Business Economics*, *28*(2–3), 171–186.

Welter, F. (2011). Contextualizing entrepreneurship—conceptual challenges and ways forward. *Entrepreneurship: Theory and Practice*, *35*(1), 165–184.

Chapter 9

Women Entrepreneurs and the Challenge of Work–Life Balance: Evidence from Kosovo

Kaltrina Kajtazi[a]

Abstract

This research aims to reveal the challenges faced by female entrepreneurs in Kosovo, emphasizing the challenge of work–life balance (WLB). As deliberated by many authors, concerning the term work–life balance, it is defined as the opportunity of balancing between personal life on the one hand and work on the other. The three research questions of this chapter were: do women entrepreneurs face difficulties on work–life balancing? do they involve other family members in business operations in order to help work–life balancing? and is their marital status a factor on WLB? This issue is more or less studied in the context of Kosovo. This is the reason why this research is conducted in Kosovo, with the sample of 24 female entrepreneurs. 21 questions of interviews are designed accordingly to the three research questions. The findings indicated that the majority of female entrepreneurs face difficulties on work–life balancing, but to overcome this challenge, they engage their family members on business activities and also, women who are married, especially those with more than one child have more difficulties on this aspect than those unmarried.

Fulfilling the gaps relied by previous studies and recommendations to female entrepreneurs in terms of better management of life and work simultaneously, it is considered the greatest contribution of this investigation.

Keywords: Entrepreneurship; females; work–life balance; challenges; Kosovo; family support

[a]*Note:* Females entrepreneurs in this chapter are fictionalized.

The Emerald Handbook of Women and Entrepreneurship in Developing Economies, 145–164
Copyright © 2021 by Emerald Publishing Limited
All rights of reproduction in any form reserved
doi:10.1108/978-1-80071-326-020211009

Introduction

Kosovo, as a new state, has recently begun to take the "wings" of economic development. These days, the phenomenon of women's inclusion in entrepreneurship has "broken" the long-standing barriers of the mindset of this country, where we now see female leading their business, even very successfully. Earlier studies conducted in Kosovo speak of many concerns facing female entrepreneurs in this country but also of their motive of starting their own business.

Therefore, this research aims to further analyze and elaborate the businesses led by females in Kosovo, taking into account the main challenges they face in developing their business, where one of the biggest challenges is thought to be the work–life balance (WLB). This indicator will have a special emphasis in this study, which will necessarily be related to the marital status of these women.

Based on the research conducted in this area, there are many contradictions between the authors related to WLB of female entrepreneurs. A study by Walker et al. (2008) in Western Australia have analyzed women entrepreneurs in relation to the WLB challenge, noting that the majority of women entrepreneurs choose to do business from home by enabling them to have more flexibility between life and work. Indeed, in general, women who choose to start their own business, compared to women who are employed in the company, have more time flexibility. The similar opinion is shared by the authors Rehman and Roomi (2012), where in their study conducted in Pakistan, they claimed that one of the most important motivators for starting a new business for women entrepreneurs is WLB, in order to perform religious obligations easier on time. Also, Agarwal and Lenka (2015) in their study they discussed the numerous contradictions between the authors regarding women entrepreneurs and the balance of life and work. A large number of authors agreed with the fact that women who work in different companies in executive positions find it more difficult to properly manage work and life, at the same time. This is one of the reasons why these women decide to start their own business.

In spite of this, other studies conducted in this field, but unlike the above-mentioned authors, oppose the idea of establishing a business by women in order for them to improve work-life balance. In a research by Ahmed et al. (2019) conducted in Qatar, one of the biggest cities in Pakistan, women entrepreneurs are studied in regards to the challenge of work-life balance that they face. Work-life balance in this study is determined by several influential factors and in conclusion, it turns out that women entrepreneurs in this country suffer from work–life imbalance that often causes stress and psychological disorder. Clercq et al. (2019) also argued that a very big challenge for women entrepreneurs is work–life imbalance by linking this factor to job dissatisfaction, accordingly affecting the overall performance of the business, which can easily lead to bankrupt. The work–life imbalance seems to be very crucial factor for enterprise's success, especially when it comes to women entrepreneurs.

However, there are still shortcomings in this regard as stated by the following authors, which are addressed by this research.

Authors	**Gaps Identification**
Ramadani, Dana, Sadiku-Dushi, Ratten, and Welsh (2017)	Since their research was conducted in Kosovo, Ferizaj was the only city from which women entrepreneurs have been interviewed. In accordance with the other questions, they were also asked about the challenges they face in performing daily business activities where, among others, the work–life balance (WLB) is emphasized. Consequently, from further studies in this field, it has been required to investigate cases in other cities of Kosovo.
Clercq and Brieger (2019)	The challenge of WLB or in particular the imbalance between work and life that face women entrepreneurs in their business leads to job dissatisfaction, and consequently, it affects the success of the firm. As suggested by the authors, further investigations are needed in order to elaborate further this issue and to fulfill this gap.
Bhatnagar et al. (2012)	India is the place where the examination of these authors was conducted. Their main purpose was to identify the incentives and motivating factors for female entrepreneurs, where one of the main encouraging factors was WLB. However, this factor is not motivating for women entrepreneurs in other countries, but rather a challenging factor. Therefore, it is suggested that future studies should be conducted in different countries.
Ahmed et al. (2019) Deery and Jago (2009) Ghalawat and Dahiya (2010)	Ahmed et al. (2019) conducted a research by interviewing women entrepreneurs in a large Pakistan city, Quetta, about factors influencing their WLB. Based on the literature review, they have identified several factors that affect the WLB of women entrepreneurs, among which are mentioned: family responsibilities, taking into account the support they have from husband and family, emotional distress, marital status, and the most influential factor was the level of religious engagement.

(Continued)

Authors	Gaps Identification
	However, they highlight that there are other factors that affect the WLB of women entrepreneurs, such as: the possibilities of stress and time management, framing and engagement of other family members in business operations by giving them different jobs as supported by the authors Deery and Jago (2009), the possibilities of executing work from home from time to time, then the factor of different presses from subordinates that directly affect the WLB of entrepreneurial women or even pressures from clients as mentioned by the authors Ghalawat and Dahiya (2010). So, considering the identification of these factors, future studies are expected to examine further some of these factors that have an impact on WLB of women entrepreneurs in different countries.

The main objective of this research is to analyze female entrepreneurs from different cities of Kosovo, emphasizing the importance of the challenge of WLB or more precisely how this phenomenon is perceived by female entrepreneurs and how they are dealing to solve this issue. Do women entrepreneurs face difficulties in work–life balancing? Do they involve other family members in business operations in order to help work–life balancing? Is their marital status a factor on WLB?

The findings of this research are expected to derive some recommendations for the best possible management of life and work simultaneously. This will be the most important contribution of this research because female entrepreneurs will have the opportunity to practice these recommendations in their daily business operations. Besides this, the research aims to fill the gaps that have arisen from previous researches, highlighted in the table above, and, thus, provides a significant academic contribution.

The structure of this investigation starts with the introduction part, where it included the background of research purpose, followed by theoretical background or the literature review, explaining the main concepts of this research. Then, the methodology will be analyzed accordingly with findings, discussions, and conclusions, by providing some recommendations derived by the findings, and at the end, limitations and areas for further research will be explained.

Theoretical Background

In this section, the main concepts of the literature related to the definition of entrepreneurship, the meaning of WLB, and its connection to female entrepreneurs, etc., will be analyzed and explained.

The Role of Women in Entrepreneurship

Firstly, starting by the concept of entrepreneurship, it has been deliberated by numerous authors throughout the years. An explicit study in this regard by Amabile (1988) pointed out the concept of entrepreneurship, which can be defined as a process that creates added value in the organization by synchronizing different resources, whether private or public, in order to make the best use of market conditions in a changing organizational environment. But earlier than Amabile, Kao and Stevenson (1985) attempted to give a definition of entrepreneurship, and they highlighted the characteristic of creating value within an organization by exploiting business opportunities as the most important feature of this term.

Many studies have been conducted to find important differences between genders in terms of entrepreneurship, although some observations show that women are no less successful than men in business operations (Jennings & Brush, 2013). Entrepreneurial women are the ones who start the business, lead it, and make important business decisions. Vijayakumar and Naresh (2013) stated that female entrepreneurs, although a small group in entrepreneurship, respectively, a minority compared to male entrepreneurs, nevertheless play an important role in the local economy. They are the creators of new jobs for people, not only for themselves, by significantly helping the economy, and also, making a special contribution to new ways of organizing and managing a business, while still suffer from gender bias.

Challenges Facing Female Entrepreneurs

Women entrepreneurs in their daily business operations seem to have significant differences compared to men entrepreneurs in regards to the challenges they face and how they overcome it. An investigation, where Nigerian female entrepreneurs participated, was conducted by Ukonu and Tafamel (2011) witnessing that the most important barriers the women entrepreneurs face by doing their business ranged from financial constraints, support by in-laws, conflict of the role, limitations of market accessibility, the barriers of implementing new technological equipment, resistant to change, etc. Nevertheless, taking more into account the factor of role conflict, meaning that women have many roles from home to work, such as the role of mother, a wife, a guider, a cooker, a cleaner, etc., on the one hand, and that of a business leader or a business owner, at the other. The performance of many roles simultaneously shows up how stressful the situation can be for women entrepreneurs (Ikram, Su, Fiaz, & Shabbir, 2016). They can be stress released only if they achieve simultaneously profitability for the business and the satisfaction of their family members.

Another study by Mahrous (2019) examines the challenges of women entrepreneurs in Egypt. The challenges that they face in their business operations vary by the lack of adequate education, lack of training opportunities, difficult access to finance, and various financial funds, where among other things that were mentioned, the biggest challenge was the inability to balance between life and work. In this case, work consumes the greater time of these entrepreneurs, especially for start-ups. Rahmatullah and Zaman (2014) analyzed the main challenges of women entrepreneurs in three regions of Bangladesh with particular emphasis on small businesses. They concluded that the challenges that entrepreneurial women face during the business entry phase are no different from other countries. Among the main challenges is the WLB issue, suggesting some important practices to better manage this problem.

Factors Affecting Work–Life Balance

WLB is an issue that has been much discussed in recent research. A definition of this term derives from the research of AlHazemi and Ali (2016) who claim that the WLB has the meaning of the best way of management between the role of personal life on the one hand and work on the other, where an improper management of this factor results in an imbalance between life and work. It is worth mentioning in this case that with the development of the way of people's life, it has been pointed out that there is a larger number of working women, who besides the financial benefits, also face problems in relation to proper management between personal life and work.

Numerous studies thoroughly deliberated the key factors that affect the WLB of employees in a company or self-employed. A study by Peter and Kavitha (2020) conducted in India examined the factors that influence the conflict between work and life, with particular emphasis on demographic data such as marital status, gender, age, and then the effect of nonsupporting families. A similar study also conducted in India by Mathew & Panchanatham (2011) shows the factors that determine or affect the balance between work and life, which according to the authors are the multiple roles at work and home simultaneously, improper time management, postponement of work until the deadline or too much procrastination, work overtime, many tasks for a short time, etc.

Methodology

The methodology of a paper presents the way in which the data of the paper have been collected and reviewed, from which the results are derived (Perry, 1998). The methodology approach of the research can be either quantitative or qualitative, or even both, which is known as the triangulation methodology. Researches that use qualitative approach of the methodology benefit by its main advantages such as the possibility to talk face to face with the respondents in order to eliminate the minor issues (Alase, 2017). The paper of this author, called "The Interpretative Phenomenological Analysis (IPA): A Guide to a Good Qualitative Research Approach," deliberates in depth the qualitative approach of methodology, indicating that it enables the researcher to "live" the experiences of the respondents, which is the reason behind choosing the qualitative methodology of this paper. As noted by the researcher, IPA, an approach of qualitative method, uses different techniques and tools of data collection in order to make it easier for researchers to collect qualitative data and analyze them.

The interview, as a research instrument, which is utilized to gather data for this research, is designed in such a way that it enables the researcher to extract qualitative data and give more explanatory results (Rubin & Rubin, 1995). A semistructured interview is considered the most appropriate design of this research interview, which is the most common qualitative design. The interviewer will be more able to comprehend important data through interviews by enabling the interviewees to express their opinions in the terms they understand (Kvale & Brinkmann, 2009).

Sampling

To conduct a study, researchers must obtain data from homogeneous samples. The sample represents a part or a smaller group of the population as a larger group, which have the same or similar characteristics (Sandelowski, 1995). The author also stated that there is no clear determination that regulate how large or small should be the sample, although it is relied on the research purposively. Firstly, the researcher decided to use purposive sample in order to collect easier data. Purposive sample, as noted by Tongco (2007), represents a nonrandom sample, where participants are selected based on their characteristics, as perceived by the researcher. Following by a well-known sampling technique for collecting data suggested by Geertz (1973), which is the snowballing strategy, whereas respondents, who have already agreed to participate in the research, suggest and encourage other respondents to participate, saying good words related to the research. This tool is very useful for researchers in case they did not reach the expected respondents for the research.

Relying on the aforementioned author's debate, it is indicated that the methodology of this study is based on qualitative approach as well as using purposive and snowball sampling as the well-known techniques for collecting qualitative data, where the female entrepreneurs have been interviewed. The main objective of this study is to find out the influence regarding the challenge of WLB among female entrepreneurs in Kosovo. In accordance to the research aim, the interview contained the following questions: What was the main reason for establishing your business? Where did you work before? What are the biggest challenges you face while doing business? How do you manage your work and personal life simultaneously? How long have you been running your business? Do you engage family members in your business activities in order to help you on work–life balancing? Do they have managerial positions or only outsiders? How many hours do you spend in your business daily? Do you ever work from home? What is your marital status? How many children do you have? Are your children interested in continuing your business? Is your education related to your business activity? Did your family encourage you to open the business? Did they help you to overcome difficulties?

Profile of female entrepreneurs

No.	Age	Education Level	City	Marital Status	Company Name	Business Operation
1	25	Bachelor	Vushtrri	Married	Daisy Bake and Cake	Cake bakery business
2	45	Master	Prishtina	Married	Melita and Partners	Financial consultancy based on QuickBooks
3	24	Bachelor	Mitrovica	Married	Gift Korniza	Photo frames with unique and personalized designs
4	30	Bachelor	Vushtrri	Married	M2-Real Estate	Real estate agency
5	34	Bachelor	Vushtrri	Married	M Kera	Muslim fashion tailor
6	23	Master	Vushtrri	Single	GetMeHome	An app that link people to bars and nearby events and ease them to go back home safely after an uncontrollable drink.
7	30	PhD cand.	Prishtina	Single	Anonymous	Nail salon
8	23	Bachelor	Fushe Kosove	Single	ORENDA studio	Architectural studio
9	30	Bachelor	Gjilan	Single	AMANA	Beauty, cosmetic, and personal care
10	27	Master	Istog	Married	KITCHEN OF DONA	Traditional food kitchen, many receipes through YouTube channel
11	49	High School Diploma	Podujeva	Married	Natural berry	Processing of natural juices from mountain fruits

12	23	Bachelor	Vushtrri	Married	For you-infinite designs	Personalized frames for gifts, ornaments for different events, business logos, and visit cards
13	27	Bachelor	Vushtrri	Married	Imrane Uka Fashion designer	Fashion designer, especially for famous people
14	45	Bachelor	Vushtrri	Married	Bleta Kindergarten	Kindergarten
15	22	Bachelor	Prishtina	Single	Anonymous	Design Company
16	24	Bachelor	Prishtina	Single	Vala Pupovci	Nutritionist
17	33	Master	Vushtrri	Married	KS Foods	Filo dough sheets for pie
18	31	Master	Vushtrri	Single	Driving school "BLINI"	Driving school
19	27	Master	Vushtrri–Prishtina	Single	Language Nest Academy	Foreign Languages Center
20	25	Bachelor	Vushtrri	Single	Glam Studio	Nail salon
21	22	High School Diploma	Vushtrri	Single	Liina Beauty	Beauty salon
22	43	High School Diploma	Vushtrri	Married	Beauty salon "Hava"	Beauty salon
23	40	Master	Prishtina	Married	Anonymous	Pharmacy
24	27	Bachelor	Vushtrri	Married	Studio Medina	Beauty salon

Data Collection

Although the time when the research took place was very inconvenient due to pandemic Covid-19, the collection of data as a result of this has had many barriers. Local government decisions blocked many businesses, depriving them of their activities for weeks. Also, as a result, female entrepreneurs stopped their activities due to health security concerns. Interviewing them face to face has been very difficult, often impossible. 24 female entrepreneurs participated in this research. Although, the researcher was forced to do some of the interviews through the phone (9 of them), some via email (10 of them), and a small number of participants were interviewed face to face (5 of them), mostly at the location where the researcher lives.

However, firstly are interviewed female entrepreneurs that the researcher knew, then following the recommendations of those who have already been interviewed, other women entrepreneurs participated in this survey. These female entrepreneurs, as indicated in the table above, operate in different business areas, but mostly are oriented on online entrepreneurship, which is a better choice to manage life and work successfully.

Participants were initially given an introduction to what research is all about, what the main topic is, and what the researcher is trying to achieve. Above all, they have been assured that their data will remain confidential and will only be used for this research. Some of them agreed to make their names and business names public, three of them allowed only the business name to be used, while two of them required to remain completely anonymous. Two face-to-face interviews were recorded, so as not to forget any details mentioned by them, while others did not agree to be recorded, although, after the interview was held, the answers were immediately written in detail. Also, the same answer transcription procedure was performed through the phone interviews.

All the interviews are conducted during May–June 2020, which have lasted from 8 minutes – the shortest to 20 minutes – the longest. The female entrepreneurs were from different cities of Kosovo, and accordingly, the interview was held in Albanian Language, since their mother language is Albanian, and then the answers are translated to English.

Findings

Based on previous discussions, the most appropriate method of data collection for this research is considered to be a qualitative method due to the fact that it enables the researcher to obtain detailed information from the respondents. Furthermore, the data were collected in accordance to the research questions.

- *RQ1:* Do women entrepreneurs face difficulties in work–life balancing?
  The interview, in addition to the demographic data that the respondents were asked at the beginning of the interview, regarding age, education, then the name of the company, it continued with the specific questions related to the topic. In this case, they answered related to the first research question. The first research question included questions about why female entrepreneurs established their

own business, where did they work before or it is the first job in their business, then what are the biggest challenges these women face while doing business, and with a special emphasis on how they manage work and personal life at the same time.

M.Y, the owner of M&P Company, regarding the question of the main reason for establishing her business and where did she work before, she has stated like this:

> Among the main reasons that motivated me to start my own business is the passion for accounting and finance since a long time ago, based on my previous experiences, as well as the need for an independence in finance, being able to generate my own income, without depending on anyone else.

I.U., a fashion designer and the owner of her atelier, told her motive to start the business and the actual situation of her studio:

> Firstly, after I finished some sewing courses, I noticed that I loved this job and I did it willingly. Afterward, I was hired by a well-known fashion designer to the Kosovar public, where my creativity and motivation for work are more highlighted. There, I met many famous people of politics, music and art. Then, because of the desire and willingness I had to do that job, I decided to open my own studio, making a good name in the market for a short time. Now my brand is liked and promoted by many local VIPs. Recently, I have designed a wedding dress for a famous model and a singer's wife.

A.M., the owner of Natural Fruit Juices Company, stated:

> The business has been operating since 2015, the idea came from previous work experience in Croatia 12 years with fruits and vegetables. While, now we have entered the processing of natural juices from mountain fruits, where we cover the Kosovo market with the aim of export.

Meanwhile, L.F., the owner of the Driving School, pointed out that she inherited the business by her father before he died. Although, regarding the reason that she wanted to own the business, she said:

> My father was the one who founded the business, but 10 years ago, before my father died, the business passed into my ownership. The reason I continued with the business was because of the desire I had to teach others to drive and generate extra income. My father began to grow old and he could not teach others to drive anymore, which was an additional reason why I owned the business.

Another entrepreneur, J. Sh., the owner of the firm about filo dough sheets for pie, explained why she started her own business, highlighting:

> After over 10 years of experience in the brand management and daily work on different cities, where I visited every retail in Kosovo, I noticed that there was a lack of a product that would help women, especially those employed, in shortening the time for cooking pies, which was exactly the pie sheets. There were some sheets for pie imported from other countries, but a product without additives and other unhealthy chemicals was missing. This is the main reason why I decided to open my own business.

As for the question of where they had worked before, most of these entrepreneurs indicated that they had worked in similar jobs, where they learned the job and then started their own business. Some of them said that working in their business was their first job. For example, Lendita, the owner of Driving School, said that the business was her first job, while the owner of KS Foods said that she has worked as a Brand Manager for 10 years and is currently using her experience in daily business operations. Meanwhile, the owner of a pharmacy in Prishtina, who asked to remain anonymous, said:

> My faculty education required me to work in pharmacies, to gain experience, and before I opened my pharmacy, I had previous experience in another pharmacy in Prishtina.

Regarding the question of what are the biggest difficulties that women entrepreneurs face while doing business, below are some of their statements:

> The business is profitable only in the summer season and during the other months it is difficult to ensure the survival of the business. In addition, another major difficulty is managing multiple roles simultaneously. Because in addition to business management, I am also a primary school teacher and at the same time I am the mother of a 2-year-old girl, who requires great dedication and suffers from this aspect. (Beauty salon M.)

> Among the main challenges encountered while doing business are competitive market prices, quality of services and transparency with customers. Also, it is worth mentioning here the challenge of balancing work and life at the same time. (Beauty salon H.)

> I face the challenge of being female. Clients very often do not take me seriously and that is why I always have to go to their property with my husband. Another very big challenge is the incorrectness of customers. While, with the balance of life and work I have no

> problem, work is without schedule and business is organized as desired. (Real Estate – G&A)

The majority of female entrepreneurs mentioned WLB as one of the main daily challenges in business. However, some who have chosen to do business online do not face much of this challenge. Thus, regarding the question of how these females manage their work and personal life at the same time, they answered:

> I run my business from home, it means online, this allows me to organize and manage the day easily. After praying the Fajr, I usually continue to work, in order to finish the work by noon and to have more free time in the afternoon. (D., Graphic design online company)
>
> I have more than one job at the same time, which is a bit challenging despite higher incomes. However, I try to organize my time a little better and I think that my status as a single makes it a little easier for me to have this flexibility. (Anonymous)
>
> Since the two children have already grown up, the daughter is married, so it's easier for me to manage my work and life at the same time, where I give more priority to business. (P.I., Kindergarten)
>
> I always manage my work and life at the same time, with the help of others. (L.S., KITCHEN OF D)

- *RQ2:* Do they involve other family members in business operations in order to help work–life balancing?
  The second research question includes several interview questions with which respondents were asked, starting from the time when female entrepreneurs started their business, then do they engage family members in business operations in order to help them in WLB, do they have managerial or just external positions, how many hours do they spend every day in business, and do they ever work from home.
  In regards to the time when did female entrepreneurs established their own business, some of them indicated that they established the business very long time ago. For instance, Dita, the owner of Driving School, stated that her father established the business since 1993, and the business ownership passed to her 10 years ago. Melita, the owner of M&P Company, said that she established the business with the help of her husband 10 years ago. Another entrepreneur, M. K. B., the owner of Kera Atelier, who is a designer for Islamic women's clothing (e.g. hijab, jilbab, abaya, etc.), said that she opened her own business 7 years ago.
  But, do these entrepreneurs engage their family members in business operations in order to help them in work–life balancing, and if yes, what positions do they have, do they have managerial positions or only help them in any business activity? Below are provided some of these entrepreneurs' answers:

> Yes, I engage my husband in business activities, who has a managerial position. Since we are a real estate business, we must definitely go to visit customers at their property, and in this part, my husband is fully engaged. (Real Estate – G&A)

> Yes, it is a business where the whole family, husband and children are engaged on managerial positions. The help is great because together we are committed to work with shared tasks and responsibilities. (A.M., Natural fruit juices Company)

> Yes, of course. I engage my family members on business activities only when I need them. (Q.M., Foreign Language Academy)

> When I started the business, we committed together with my husband, and even my husband's business activity is more related to his profession. He deals with the product design and marketing. He helps me a lot and normally, we share the profit together. (Korniza)

> Of course. My daughter is engaged in many business activities, playing a managerial role within the enterprise. (H.I., Beauty salon H.)

Related to how many hours do they spend in business daily and do they ever work from home are received the following answers:

> I spend more than 10 hours in business every day and I work often from home. (M.Y., M&P Company)

> I usually spend 10-12 hours per day in the business. Unfortunately, I do not have the benefit to work from home, since I have nail salon and it requires face-to-face meeting with the clients…by default. (S.M., Nail salon)

> 8 hours definitely. But...sometimes even more. Some tasks I perform through home, such as ordering the supply, business marketing, etc. (Anonymous)

> I spend approximately 10 hours a day in my business. There are times when I spend more than 10 hours, especially during the summer season, where there is a greater influx of migrants. (M.G., Beauty salon M.)

> Since I do all the business online, I work from home, by spending 3 to 4 hours daily on business activities. (R. B., "Get me home")

- *RQ3:* Is their marital status a factor on WLB?
  The interview questions that the respondents are asked as a part of the third research question were regarding the marital status of these entrepreneurs, how many children do they have, and are them or any family member interested to continue the business? Is the education of these females related to the business

activity? Also, are the entrepreneurs encouraged by their families to open their business and did they help them to overcome initial difficulties?
In regards to their marital status, 14 of them declared that they are married, and the rest are not married yet or single. M. Y. (M&P), as a mother of three children, explained if her children or any other family member is interested to continue the business:

> I have three children, but… none of them is interested to continue the business.

The owner of Natural Fruit Juices Company, A. M., who is a mother of three children, pointed out if they are willing to continue the business:

> As I mentioned earlier, together with my husband and my children, all together, we have shared the tasks and responsibilities and everyone is fully committed. They like the business and aim to continue and develop it.

While, the owner of Kindergarten, P. I., stated:

> My two children, a married daughter and a son, have different occupations that are not related to the business. Perhaps, this is why they are not interested in business and its development.

Also, Beauty Salon H. has three children, and she explained if they are interested to continue the business:

> Only the youngest son is interested to continue the business. He is interesting on business activities and perceives it as a profitable business.

> I don't have children, but I opened the business with the help of my sister. She always works together with me in business, we cook cakes together, share creative ideas together, etc. She likes the business and she is willing to continue it. – said Zana, the owner of Bake and Cake Company.

Another question, if their education is related to the business activity, they answered like this:

> Yes, I am a nutritionist and I graduated from the Faculty of Dietetics in Athens, Greece. (V.P., nutritionist)

> Yes, I have finished the Faculty of Architecture and that's why I have established my own business, an architecture studio. (E.H., ORENDA)

> I graduated from the Faculty of Architecture, but the business activity is more or less related to my education, since there is more design. (D., Graphic design – online Company)

> No, because I'm studying for a PhD in Pharmacy and nail salon just started as a hobby. (Anonymous)

But, did their family encourage these female entrepreneurs to establish their own business and did the family help them to overcome difficulties? The majority of the respondents are answered positively, and only some of them declared that the encouragement was built within their minds; however, the family always helped them to overcome challenges, as per the description below:

> I always liked to decorate my nails. Despite the profession that was not related to this part at all, this was just a hobby and my parents were the ones who encouraged me to open the salon. (Anonymous)

> My family encouraged me to open the business as well as they always helped me overcoming initial barriers. (H.I., Beauty salon H.)

> The idea was mine! So, my family did not encourage me to open the business but of course they always supported me. (J. Sh., Filo Dough Sheets for pie Company)

Discussions

The main reason for conducting this research is to find out how difficult is for female entrepreneurs to manage many roles at the same time, or balancing life and work, simultaneously. Concerns observed included the query if female entrepreneurs face difficulties in work–life balancing, are their family engaged to business activities in order to help these females in work–life balancing, and also, is their marital status a factor on WLB. Regarding the challenge of WLB and do these women face this challenge, based on the responses, which are analyzed in the previous section, the study revealed that most of the respondents replied that they face the challenge of balancing between life and work. However, they stated that they try to share equal time for family and work within a day, which often sacrifices rest and relaxation. Some of them stated that their business activity gives them more time flexibility, but some showed that the summer season requires a lot of dedication, where even the whole day is not enough for business requirements.

In other words, not all women entrepreneurs face the same intensity with this challenge. The business activity they carry out has a great impact here. Those who have chosen to work online have much more time flexibility than those who are in the office and away from home, but this kind of businesses are fewer in number. In addition to this, a study conducted by Ramadani, Hisrich, and Gërguri-Rashiti (2015), where women entrepreneurs in Albanian-speaking countries or ALMAKOS (Albania, Macedonia, and Kosovo) were surveyed in relation to the challenges they face, 61% of women interviewed stated that the biggest challenge of all other challenges is to establish a balance between family obligations and work commitments. From the respondents of the three countries, the female entrepreneurs from Kosovo were the ones who stated that they are mostly challenged by this problem, compared to two other countries.

Similarly, in another study by Ramadani (2015), where women entrepreneurs from Albania have been part of the research, analyzing the biggest problems they have, the biggest problem that has been put in the spotlight by 51% of respondents has been the balance of life and work. Also, Despotović et al. (2018) in the study followed in Montenegro, where 50 women entrepreneurs participated in the survey, it was concluded that the biggest challenge they face is the conflict of multiple roles or WLB.

As the easiest way to overcome this obstacle, female entrepreneurs in Kosovo, most of them, engage family members in business activities in order to help them better balance work and life. To support this fact, Alsos, Carter, Ljunggren, and Jørstad (2016), in their study, showed that women entrepreneurs to overcome the challenge of multiple roles engage family members in business activities. They also suggest better management of day-to-day business operations in order to have free time in the afternoon and evening.

Meanwhile, is their marital status a factor of WLB, based on the responses received by surveyed females in Kosovo, can be concluded that this variable is strongly related to WLB. For some of them, who spend more than 10 hours in business and having a small kid that requires special dedication, in the same time, this kind of occurrence is very stressful and challenging. According to a study by Telraja (2017), it has been determined that women who are married, especially those who have more than one child, have more difficulties on work–life balancing. This is also supported by Annik et al. (2016), who after researching women entrepreneurs across Europe pointed out that their marital status is a very influential factor in the WLB.

Conclusion

The aim of this chapter was to analyze female entrepreneurs across Kosovo and challenge of WLB that they face. Some previous investigations have debated about female entrepreneurs, where one group of authors supported the fact that starting a business by female entrepreneurs allows them to have more flexibility in time because they organize the work as desired. Meanwhile, the other group of authors opposed this fact and supported the aspect that women who work in a company have better WLB.

To address this issue, this research was conducted in Kosovo, taking as a sample of 24 female entrepreneurs, operating in various sectors. The methodology of this study was qualitative approach, and the interview as a research tool. The research contained three questions, where the first one trying to find out if women entrepreneurs face the challenge of WLB, do their families help them in order to work–life balancing, and also, is marital status a factor on WLB. The interview questions are designed based on research questions. Respondents' answers showed that most of them face the challenge of balancing between life and work, which is also supported by the similar studies conducted in Kosovo. In order to help work–life balancing, they are helped by their families, husband, or in-laws, which is considered the easier way to overcome this challenge. However, those women that are married face more difficulties on WLB than those that are not.

The most important contribution of this research lies in the fact that through the answers of the interviewees, different ways are highlighted of how work and life should be better managed, in order to achieve a better balance, showing that the better work organization, the better work–life balancing.

Limitations and Areas for Further Research

This research was conducted in a difficult time of global pandemic Covid-19, which among other things has caused many barriers, especially in achieving a reliable sample number and proper differentiation between women with married status and those unmarried, where this has indicated as the first limitation of this research. Also, most of the interviews had to be done face to face, but the current situation caused most of the interviews to be conducted by phone and email.

Some of women entrepreneurs did not agree to participate in the study, since their business is not registered on Business Registration Agency of Kosovo and they were afraid if this will cause them any problem. Also, another limitation which is worth mentioning here is that research respondents were mostly young females and only few of them are older than 40.

In this regard, further studies are needed to be conducted on female entrepreneurs who have more than one child and operate in the business since long time ago. A comparison study between female and male entrepreneurs and the challenge of WLB they face are needed to be part of future investigation. Also, the same study is recommended to be conducted on North Macedonia and Albania in order to find out the differences between female entrepreneurs and the challenge of WLB in these three countries as well as in the other countries of Western Balkans.

References

Agarwal, S., & Lenka, U. (2015). Study on work-life balance of women entrepreneurs–review and research agenda. *Industrial & Commercial Training*, *47*(7), 356–362.

Ahmed, J., Saleem, N., & Fatima, K. (2019). Factors influencing work life balance of women entrepreneurs: A case of Quetta (Pakistan). *Dialogue*, *14*(3), 93–103.

Alase, A. (2017). The interpretative phenomenological analysis (IPA): A Guide to a good qualitative research approach. *International Journal of Education and Literacy Studies*, *5*(2), 9–19.

AlHazemi, A. A., & Ali, W. (2016). The notion of work life balance, determining factors, antecedents and consequences: A comprehensive literature survey. *International Journal of Academic Research and Reflection*, *4*(8), 74–85.

Alsos, G. A., Carter, S., Ljunggren, E., & Jørstad, M. O. (2016). Women, family and entrepreneurship: Strategies for managing work-life balance challenges. *Academy of Management Proceedings*, *16*(1), 78–99.
Amabile, T. M. (1988). A model of creativity and innovation in organizations. *Research in Organizational Behavior*, *10*(1), 123–167.
Annink, A., Den Dulk, L., & Steijn, B. (2016). Work–family conflict among employees and the self-employed across Europe. *Social Indicators Research*, *126*(2), 571–593.
Bhatnagar, A., Bhardwaj, B. R., & Gandhi, S. (2012). Problems and Challenges faced by Women Entrepreneur in India. *International Journal of Management*, *2*(1), 1–8.
De Clercq, D. D., Brieger, S. A., & Welzel, C. (2019). Leveraging the macro-level environment to balance work and life: An analysis of female entrepreneurs' job satisfaction. *Small Business Economics*, *1*(24), 1–35.
Deery, M., & Jago, L. (2009). A framework for work-life balance practices: Addressing the needs of the tourism industry. *Tourism and Hospitality Research*, *9*(2), 97–108.
Despotović, A., Joksimović, M., Jovanović, M., & Maletić, R. (2018). Female entrepreneurship in Montenegro: Motives and barriers. *Agriculture & Forestry/Poljoprivreda i Sumarstvo*, *64*(4), 195–218.
Geertz, C. (1973). *The interpretation of cultures*. New York, NY: Basic Books.
Ghalawat, S., & Dahiya, P. (2010). Work-life balance and organization practices- A study of selected bank in Sirsa. *KAIM Journal of Management and Research*, *3*(1), 94–101.
Ikram, A., Su, Q., Fiaz, M., & Shabbir, M. W. (2016). Cultural diversity and challenges for female entrepreneurs: Empirical Study of an emerging economy. *World Academy of Science, Engineering and Technology, International Journal of Social, Behavioral, Educational, Economic, Business and Industrial Engineering*, *10*(10), 3375–3378.
Jennings, J. E., & Brush, C. G. (2013). Research on women entrepreneurs: Challenges to (and from) the broader entrepreneurship literature. *The Academy of Management Annals*, *7*(1), 663–715.
Kao, J. J., & Stevenson, H. H. (1985). *Entrepreneurship, what it is and how to teach it: A collection of working papers based on a colloquium held at Harvard Business School*. Boston, MI: The School.
Kvale, S., & Brinkmann, S. (2009). *InterViews: Learning the craft of qualitative research interviewing*, Los Angeles, CA: SAGE Publications.
Mahrous, A. A. (2019). Female entrepreneurship in Egypt: New theoretical and public policy implications. *Marketing and Management of Innovations*, *1*, 151–160.
Mathew, R. V., & Panchanatham, N. (2011). An exploratory study on the work-life balance of women entrepreneurs in South India. *Asia Academy of Management Journal*, *16*(2), 77–105.
Perry, C. (1998). Processes of a case study methodology for postgraduate research in marketing. *European Journal of Marketing*, *32*(9/10), 785–802.
Peter, M., & Kavitha, D. S. F. (2020). A study on the impact of work life balance on the well being of employees at Quantum Software Solutions PVT LTD. *International Journal of Advanced Research in Engineering and Technology (IJARET)*, *11*(3), 120–127.
Rahmatullah, M. & Zaman, F. (2014). Female entrepreneurship in Bangladesh: Constraints, motivation and success. *Bangladesh E-Journal of Sociology*, *11*(2), 65–77.

Ramadani, V. (2015). The woman entrepreneur in Albania: An exploratory study on motivation, problems and success factors. *Journal of Balkan and Near Eastern Studies*, *17*(2), 204–221.

Ramadani, V., Dana, L. P., Sadiku-Dushi, N., Ratten, V., & Welsh, D. H. (2017). Decision-making challenges of women entrepreneurship in family business succession process. *Journal of Enterprising Culture*, *25*(4), 411–439.

Ramadani, V., Hisrich, R. D., & Gërguri-Rashiti, S. (2015). Female entrepreneurs in transition economies: Insights from Albania, Macedonia and Kosovo. *World Review of Entrepreneurship Management and Sustainable Development*, *11*(4), 391–413.

Rehman, S., & Roomi, M. A. (2012). Gender and work-life balance: A phenomenological study of women entrepreneurs in Pakistan. *Journal of Small Business and Enterprise Development*, *19*(2), 209–228.

Rubin, H. J., & Rubin, I. S. (1995). *Qualitative interviewing: The art of hearing data*. Thousand Oaks, CA: SAGE Publications.

Sandelowski, M. (1995). Sample size in qualitative research. *Research in Nursing & Health*, *18*(2), 179–183.

Talreja, M. (2017). Women entrepreneurship and work life balance. *Global Journal of Human-Social Science: H Interdisciplinary*, *17*(6), 1–13.

Tongco, M. D. C. (2007). Purposive sampling as a tool for informant selection. *Ethnobotany Research and Applications*, *5*(2), 147–158.

Ukonu, O. I., & Tafamel, A. E. (2011). Problems, challenges and prospects of female entrepreneurs in Gwagwalada, Abuja. *An International Multi-Disciplinary Journal, Ethiopia*, *5*(3), 226–246.

Walker, E., Wang, C., & Redmond, J. (2008). Women and work-life balance: is home-based business ownership the solution? *Equal Opportunities International*, *27*(3), 258–275.

Vijayakumar, T., & Naresh, B. (2013). Women entrepreneurship in India - role of women in small and medium enterprises. *Asian Journal of Marketing & Management Research*, *2*(7), 13–25.

Chapter 10

The Institutional History of Women Entrepreneurship in Modern Persia: A Socio-historicism Approach

Amir Forouharfar

Abstract

Institutional changes, in a historical context, through simultaneous evolutionary and metamorphic processes either deform or reform long-enduring institutions. The chapter delves into the Persian history from the early days of the reign of Nāṣer al-Dīn Shāh-e Qājār in 1848 to the recent years and traces Persian institutions' historical transformations, which culminated to the Persian women entrepreneurship. Thus, the chapter first sets the historical context in each period and then sheds light on the pivotal issues of each period's women. The undergirding base of the discussions is the assumption of the change in institutions as natural metamorphosis in the animate. Finally, the discussions contribute to the conceptualization of the *Institutional Triangulation* and in the case of Persia, a *cultural-driven triangulation*, which has paved the way to the formation of a stupendously hegemonic patriarchal and masculine sociopolitical economy in Persia, that has historically affected women's *institutionalization*, *subjugation*, *subordination*, *marginalization*, *socialization*, *emancipation*, and most recently *Islamization* phases.

Keywords: Persian women; women entrepreneurship; institutional change; historicism; institutionalization; Modern Persia

Introduction

Persia (Iran) is one of the ancient states with more than 2,500 years of establishment located on the north of the Persian Gulf.[1] Thus, the social history of its women dates back to antiquity and fades away to the prehistoric periods of this land of *One Thousand and One Nights*. Women have had a prominent impact on

The Emerald Handbook of Women and Entrepreneurship in Developing Economies, 165–189
Copyright © 2021 by Emerald Publishing Limited
All rights of reproduction in any form reserved
doi:10.1108/978-1-80071-326-020211010

Persian history, culture, literature, and mythology. From *Gordāfarid*, the Persian female legendary border keeper, to *Roudābeh*, the mother of *Rostam* who is the emblem of Persian national heroism of the antiquity. With the Arab conquest of Persia in AD 642 and the start of the deconstruction process of most pre-Islamic Persian national institutions, such as former religion and ideology (Zoroastrianism) and the collapse of the *Sassanid Empire* in AD 651, which also endangered even the existence of the Persian language, Persians after more than a millennium of world supremacy under three Empires of *Achaemenid* (550 BC–330 BC), *Parthian* (247 BC–224 AD), and *Sassanid* (224 AD–651 AD) found themselves in a country without borders and barriers. The conquerors' culture was fiercely forbidding and prohibiting the pre-Islamic Persian life manifested itself through rituals, traditions, music, dances, paintings, sculptures, etc. Women were at the center of these imposed restrictions and historical marginalization. Later by the *Mongols* conquest of the *Khwarezmid Empire* from 1219 to 1221 and its massive-scale massacres and burning of the cities and its repercussions which led to a widespread cataclysmic chaos and poverty, the Persians fell into an abysmal historical predicament. These historically imposed fiascos with their biting consequences in the deformation of Persian society's institutions and dissemination of chaos in every walk of their lives forced them to internalize their culture, beliefs, customs, rituals, ideas, and whatever their conquerors forbade. Hence, an *internal life* (at home and among confidants) beside an *external life* (in society especially among the foreigners, invaders, and their servants) emerged and felt required and later widely adopted, socialized, and finally erupted as a cultural institution, *Riyā* (Hypocrisy) which still persists. Such massive internalization of Persian identity and mentality was a response to a borderless country with foreigners as cruel governors. The plethora of language convolutions, figurative twists, and far-fetched ironies in Persian poetry and literature is a reflection of this unrevealing propensity in the Persian mind throughout history. For example, Persian poets usually speaks of *Mey* (Wine), *Zolf* (hair), *Abroo* (eyebrow), *Meykadeh* (Wine Bar), but a Persian listener knows that they must read between the lines. The poem of *Shams-al-Din Moḥammad, of Shirāz* (Known as *Hāfez*), who inspired *Johann Wolfgang von Goethe* to say *West–Östlicher Divan* (*West–Eastern Diwan*), is the pinnacle of such language convolutions, to say something and expect a listener to grasp a reality deep down. However, the historical insecurity of Persia beside the imposed cultural norms drove Persians to adopt a dualistic approach in life. Thus, they were acting in obedience to the cultural and religious norms of their conquerors outdoors and they had their own mannerism of life indoors. Such dualism was also penetrated into Persian architecture. The separation of Persian houses into *Andarūnī* (women's quarters) and *Bīrūnī* (men's quarters) was originated from the Persian's pragmatic adoption of "when in Rome do as the Romans do" and when you are at home "rule the roost."

On the other hand, Persian men in order to save their daughters and women from any harassment of the conquerors in an insecure lawless society tried to limit their women's social presence day in day out. Such a hypocritical insecure society, which was also fundamentally religious, imposed numerous marginalization forces against Persian women. Later, this social intention metamorphosed into a new shape. The prevalent religio-conservative male-dominant culture aggravated the condition and tried to exclude women from social arenas under the labels of *Qeyrat* (Male Zeal) and *Nāmoos* (Male Honor) and laid the preliminary foundations of women marginalization that did not change until thousands years up to the modern Persia.

Studying the institutional history of women generally and the Persian women specifically is a painstaking endeavor. Since first, history suffers from a ubiquitous male-dominancy tone and it is not only restricted to the historical condition of the Persian women. Thus, Sheila Rowbotham (1974) "asked why women were 'hidden from history' – and helped to found the field of women's history" (Moghadam, 2000, p. 377). Moghadam believes, "…there is a paucity of studies on working-class women" as well as "dearth of data on women workers" in the major literature on the economic, social, and political history (Moghadam, 2000). Nevertheless, we have to explore the voices of working women from the fugitive literature and gray literature. Second, this paucity of studies in Persian women's history is so severe although recent scholars of Women's Studies are trying to shed light on the dark corners of the Persian women. Third, the problem is more exacerbated in the case of special studies on the history of the Persian women (hence, the Persian women entrepreneurship). However, the life of the Persian women could not be detached from the historically social, political, and economic contexts of Persia, and an insightful comprehension of them could help a researcher to compensate for this literature paucity. Therefore, starting with the sociopolitical incidents of this unpredictable and mostly ill-comprehended state could be a possible entrance to the institutional history of women entrepreneurship in Persia. The following subheadings illuminate the chapter's roadmap in brief:

1848–1896 – The reign of *Nāṣer al-Dīn Shāh-e Qājār*: Incubation of revolutionary will and women
1896–1907 – The reign of *Moẓaffar-al-Din Shāh -e Qājār*: Constitutional revolution and women
1907–1909 – The reign of *Moḥammad-ʿAli Shāh -e Qājār*: Chaotic absolutism, women and the restoration of constitutionalism
1909–1925 – The reign of *Aḥmad Shāh -e Qājār*: Old institutions in transition
1925–1941 – The reign of *Reżā Shāh -e Pahlavi*: Women, state, and the modernization policies
1941–1979 – The reign of *Moḥammad Reżā Shāh -e Pahlavi*: Women in a modern state
1979–until now – The incumbent *Islamic Republic*: Islamizing women's institutions

Literature Review

Institution could sociologically be defined, "not only as enduring and recurring patterns of human activity, but also as characterizing and determining social frameworks, which give social entities special character and guide them toward special evolutionary path" (Forouharfar, 2020). Institutions are "the more enduring features of social life" (Giddens, 1984, p. 24). Moreover, institutions are "patterns of behavior" which are "stable," "valued," and "recurring" (Huntington, 1968, p. 12). To put it simply, institutions are *patterns*, but "relatively stable patterns of human activity" (Turner, 1997, p. 6). According to North (1991, p. 97), institutions are "the humanly devised constraints that structure political, economic and social interaction." Thus, "based on his definition we could consider institutions first as 'constraints'. These 'constraints' are 'humanly devised' which show they are fabricated by the human entity within society. Then, the 'constraints' (or institutions) have shaping capabilities, i.e. they shape or 'structure' human 'interaction'" (Forouharfar, 2020). Moreover, North (1991, p. 97) divided institutions into "informal constraints" and "formal rules." He believed that the *informal constraints* consisted of "sanctions, taboos, customs, traditions, and codes of conduct" and the *formal rules* embraced "constitutions, laws, [and] property rights." Finally, he viewed institutional change in the historical context as an evolution. He believed, institutions, "evolve incrementally, connecting the past with the present and the future; history in consequence is largely a story of institutional evolution in which the historical performance of economies can only be understood as a part of a sequential story" (North, 1991, p. 97). Therefore, the chapter has adopted an incremental approach; first, it unfolded the general Persian historical context and then embedded the Persian women issues that incrementally culminated to the Persian women entrepreneurship within.

Discussions

In the early periods from 1848, the beginning of *Nāṣer al-Dīn Shāh*'s succession to the throne, up to the end of the *Qājār Dynasty* in 1924 and the succession of *Reżā Shāh Pahlavi* to the Persian throne it is very hard to find instances of Persian women entrepreneurship. However, the study of the last four *Qājār* kings and their sociopolitical periods illuminate the subsequent evolutionary institutional changes and their impacts on the history of Persian women entrepreneurship. The following discussions shed light on the improbability of the flourishing of women entrepreneurship within the ecological arenas of a traditional society. Hence, we observe the first signs of women entrepreneurship and large-scale employment in Persia simultaneously with the modernization policies of the first *Pahlavi* king.

1848–1896, The Reign of Nāṣer al-Dīn Shāh-e Qājār: Incubation of Revolutionary Will and Women

The debate between two books of the *Nāṣeri* period illuminates the social stream under the superficial ice of the society. The anonymous *Ta'dib al-Neswān/Ta'dib al-Nesā'* (*The Education of Women*) and *Ma'āyeb al-Rejāl* (*The Vices of Men*) reflect the social quest of Persian women of the age for their violated rights. *The Education of Women* was presumably written by a man of *Qājār* aristocracy class with a didactical male-dominant tone. Through the book, he frequently mentions the vices of the Persian women of his age and then he presents solutions and substituting courteous behaviors. *Bibi Ḵānom Estarābādi/Astarābādi* wrote *The Vices of Men* in 1894 not only to respond to the attributed vices to women in *The Education of Women* but also to provide the economic, social, and cultural reasons originated from the Persian society and men that had led to the so-called attributes. Her style of writing and diction reveals that she is from an educated middle class. *The Education of Women*, which could be written between 1882–1885, implicitly reflects a society that its women did not like anymore to admit an *absolute obedience* of its men. The first chapter *Of Women's Character and Conduct* in the book (*The Education of Women*) reflects such an intention among at least some women of the society. Thus, female culture as a sociological institution was under a pivotal metamorphosis at least among some women of the *Nāṣeri* period. The Persian women were illuminating each other against a sexist and double-standard society, which had tried to marginalize women as much as possible. The Persian women's *public spheres* – to borrow the term from the philosopher *Jürgen Habermas* – was andarūnī for affluent families and women public baths for middle and low walks of society.[2] *Bibi Ḵānom Astarābādi* mentioned that he learnt about *The Education of Women* from the women of one of these andarūnī gatherings who had insisted she write a treatise in response to the book's attributed fallacies and vices (such as *Nāqesolaql, Ḵafifolaql* [*deficient-minded*] and *Zaēfolqalb* [*weak-hearted*]) to women.

The prevailing view to women in this age is *sexist* or viewing women as less intelligent, weak, and less important than men with numerous cases of polygamous men. However, women had had supporting roles to the main movements in decades before the *Nāṣeri* age from the *Bābi Movement*[3] with *Qorrat-al-ʿAyn Ṭāhera* as a key figure in the movement, a poet and one of the early women's rights activists to the killing of *Alexander Sergeevich Griboedov,* the Russian ambassador plenipotentiary (*wazir-e moḵtār*) in Persia on February 11, 1829 who,

> He and his staff insulted Muslims in the bāzār and took a number of Christian women, who had converted to Islam, to the [Russian] Mission. Their actions caused a riot in Tehran during which a mob attacked the Mission and killed *Griboedov* and some members of his staff. (Bournoutian, 2012, p. 363)

Women also had an influential support of the protest against the *Tobacco Régie* in 1891–1892.[4]

The entire cultural zeitgeist of the *Nāṣeri* period was against the idea of women working outside the home. *Bāzār* the main center for trade and business in large cities of Persia was completely filled and run by men (and still the case, in 2020, persists). *Bāzār*, "a unified, self-contained building complex of shops, passageways, and caravanserais, interspersed with squares (*meydān*), religious buildings, bathhouses (*ḥammām*), and other public institutions" (Bonine, 2000, p. 21), was one of the main places for the gathering of men, or male *public spheres*, and it has frequently played a major role in the Persian sociopolitical events.

Generally, the main social role of the women in *Nāṣeri* period was their supportive roles in the period's movements as well as their mainly traditional roles of housekeeping and child breeding at home. The male-dominant society expected them to be good and obedient homemakers than to be an impetus for social movements.

Nevertheless, the structural reforms of *Mīrzā Taqī Khān of Farāhān*, known as *Amīr Kabir* and *Amīr-e Neẓām* who was the chief minister to *Nāṣer-al-Dīn Shāh* in the early four years of his monarchy, which was unprecedented in whole the *Qājār* period, led to the enlightenment of the subsequent Persian generations. As one of the most capable and reputable figures in *Qājār* dynasty, he founded *Dār al-Fonūn* (a modern Western-like training institution) in Tehran as well as a state official newspaper *Rūz-nāma-ye waqāye'-e ettefāqīya.*

Dār al-Fonūn was a true example of the saying, "mighty oaks from little acorns grow." Mostly later Persian intelligentsias were educated in *Dār al-Fonūn.* According to Algar (2012, p. 962):

> The initial purpose of the institution was to train officers and civil servants to pursue the regeneration of the state that Amīr Kabīr had begun, but as the first educational institution giving instruction in modern learning, it had far wider impact. Among the subjects taught were medicine, surgery, pharmacology, natural history, mathematics, geology, and natural science. The instructors were for the most part Austrians...

Moreover, he also tried to reinforce Persian economy via encouraging state-sponsored entrepreneurship in mass-producing the products that could fulfill the needs of the public. As well as making encouraging financial policies under a *protectionism* policy for the newly established factories beside fiscal policies such as tax exemption in the mining sector of the economy:

> Factories were established with state patronage for the manufacture of items as diverse as carriages, stoves and samovars, crystal and ceramics, rope, silk and broadcloth, and sugar. Craftsmen were sent to Moscow and St. Petersburg to learn various industrial techniques, and others to Istanbul to study silk weaving. Tariffs were raised to discourage the import of foreign goods and to promote the products of the newly founded industries. Efforts were made to prevent the export of gold and silver from Iran, and a decree issued in 1267/1851 stipulated that any Iranian subject might freely engage in the mining of minerals and precious stones, having once obtained the permission of the government, and that his operations would be exempt from taxation for the first five years. A certain number of foreign

> geologists were also recruited to aid in the extraction of Iran's mineral wealth. (Algar, 2012, p. 962)

During the *Nāṣeri* period, numerous modern schools for educating women were established by foreigners especially by French and later by Americans in *Tabriz, Rasht, Hamedān, Isfāhān, Mashahd,* and *Urumieh.* The foreign teachers in these schools had one of the preliminary enlightenment effects on the Persian women who were educating in these schools. However, *Hāji-Mirzā Hassan Roshdieh* was one of the pioneering figures of Persian educational entrepreneurship. His first school in Persia was founded in *Tabriz* in 1887. Nevertheless, the religious strata of society were fiercely against these schools and even ransacked some of these schools under the allegations of blasphemy (his conversion to *Bābism*) and resemblance of the school bells to the church bells. In some cases, even some of the students were killed amid the ransack of the *Avām (illiterate religio-commons*) to the schools and *Roshdieh* broke his hand.

However, long after the execution of *Amīr Kabir*, the overwhelming social discontent, the mainly corrupt *Qājār* aristocracy, widespread poverty, and the cruelty of governors accompanied with the news disseminated via the Persian newspapers in Diaspora, especially in Istanbul and London, were fomenting one of the unprecedented revolutionary turning points in Persian history. For example, *Mīrzā Malkom Khan (1833-1908*) a Persian reformist journalist:

> …in his newspaper *Qānūn* (Constitution), published in London in the early 1890s, … blended advocacy of reform with an uninhibited critique of tyranny and political corruption. In the decade before the Constitutional Revolution the hazy notion of a parliamentary system with a constitution (*konsṭeṭūsīon, qānūn-e asāsī*), division of powers, and popular representation put forward in *Qānūn* was central to the emerging revolutionary ferment. (Amanat, 2011, p. 164)

The other illuminating newspapers of the age, which were publishing outside Persia, were *Akhtar* (in Istanbul), *Habl al-Matin* (in Calcutta), *Sorayā*, and *Parvaresh* (in Egypt).

Nāṣer al-Dīn Shāh's daughter, Princess Tāj-al-Salṭana's life and his numerous forced remarriages reflect dark conditions of the Persian women in the court and *andarūnī*. Her *Ḳāṭerāt* (*Memoirs*) is reflecting the gloomy prearranged marriages of the royal women. "When she was writing her memoirs in 1914, she had attempted suicide three times" (Najmabadi, 2009, para. 10). She wrote:

> … Look at the corners of Persia and see that in the houses that their walls are as high as 3 to 5 *Zer*, hand- and head-broken creatures, some of them are pale, some of them are hungry, some of them are bare, some of them are waiting all-night and weeping … all in the chains of captivity.[5] Are they women? The Persian women's lives are either black or white. Either they [have

> to] wear a black curtain and turn into a scary grieving physique or wear a white shroud and leave the world… against this black life, death is our whitest day.[6] (Adamiyat & Nateq, 1978, p. 157)

The prevailing sociopolitical discontent culminated to the assassination of the king, *Nāṣer al-Dīn Shāh,* on May 1, 1896 who was getting ready to hold his 50th commemoration of his imperial reign. *Mirzā Reżā of Kermān* who was deeply afflicted by the system and after long years of torture and imprisonment and had substantially been inspired by the ideas of *Jamāl-al-Din Afḡāni* and *Shaikh Hādi Najmābādi* assassinated the king. It is very hard to present a final judgment on *Nāṣer al-Dīn Shāh*'s character. However, in respect to the state administration he implemented some reforms such as the establishment of ministries for the first time in Persian state administration history. Nevertheless, his bureaucratic supervisory measures over the deeds of his appointees in cities were weak, dull, and frequently with reluctance. According to Yarshater (2012, p. 239):

> *Naser-al-Din Shāh* was a well-meaning king as long as his purse and pleasure were not involved. He attempted some reforms with limited success, including at one point establishment of a court of justice *(ʿedālat-ḵāna)*, and supported the sending of the graduates of *Dār-al-Fonun* to study abroad. His harem was only slightly smaller than that of his great grandfather, *Fatḥ-ʿAli Shāh*. He was keen on hunting and on French wine.

The first modern textile factory in Persia was founded in the 1850s (Floor, 1984). Nonetheless, the industry was mainly traditional and "spinning wool and cotton at home and in the new factories was a largely female working-class occupation" (Moghadam, 2000, p. 380). Women were the main workforce for producing silk and cotton. The silk and cotton which were mainly produced by women were sold in the markets of *Māzandarān, Gilān, Kāshān, Isfāhān*, and *Yazd* (Seyf, 2001).

1896–1907 The Reign of Moẓaffar-al-Din Shāh -e Qājār: Constitutional Revolution and Women

The succession of a new monarch in the Persian history was usually accompanied with the advent of a new era. If the monarch was reform-minded, the state affairs could be developed, reformed, and ultimately improved; if in contrary, he was a pleasure-seeking plain-minded monarch reluctant to the administration of the state, the state affairs would be disintegrated and subsequently corruption disseminated. "*Moẓaffar-al-Din Shāh* (r. 1896–1907) was a weak, pleasure-loving, simple-minded, and considerate king" (Yarshater, 2012, p. 239). However, he signed the *Constitutional Charter* on December 30, 1906, 10 days before his death. The *Constitutional Charter*, which included the first Persian *Constitutional Law* (*Qānun-e Asāsi*), was a giant leap forward by the Persians.

Balvāy-e Nān (*Bread Revolt*) had happened several times in the *Nāṣeri* period. Tabriz was one of the major conflicted cities especially in 1895. However, in 1898, nearly two years after the ascension of *Moẓaffar-al-Din Shāh-e Qājār* and eight years before signing the *Constitutional Charter*, a new *Bread Revolt* took place across the country. Women had a pivotal role in the revolt. *Zeynab Pāshā* accompanied with a group of *Tabrizi* women attacked *Nāzem-al Ulamā*'s house, who hoarded tons of wheat amid a severe famine.

Bībī Ḵānom, wife of *Mosā Ḵān-e Mirpanj,* not to be mistaken for *Bibi Ḵānom Astarābādi* the writer of *The Vices of Men*, was the pioneering figure of women educational entrepreneurship in Persia in the *Moẓaffari* period. *Madres-e Doushizegān (Doushizegān School)*, a modern school for the Persian girls, was founded by her in 1906. However, the foundation of a school for the Persian girls was not without fierce religious objection. For example, *Shaikh Fażl-Allāh Nuri*, the prominent Islamic jurist of the age, declared, "Establishment of girl schools is against Sharia of Islam" (Malekzadeh, 1956, p. 218) and *Seyed Ali Shoushtari*, sought *bast* and presumed the school establishment as an act of blasphemy and mentioned, "Alas! We should grieve to the condition of a country that a school for girls was established in" (Qavimi, 1973, p. 132).[7]

The king died in 1907; yet the Constitutional Revolution had not been finished. The Persian women of the era, especially among the middle classes, were questing in two arenas, first for achieving their equal rights with men and second for showing their zest for the constitutional spirit of the age.

1907–1909 The Reign of Moḥammad-ʿAli Shāh -e Qājār: Chaotic Absolutism, Women, and the Restoration of Constitutionalism

The 1900s saw the institutionalization of constitutional reform in Persian politics.

Mohammad Ali Shāh who ascended the throne in 1907 although take an oath to preserve the constitution did not accept the de jure results of the revolution and mainly because of his resistance against the proconstitutionalists and his order for the bombardment of the newly established political institution of *Majlis* was deposed by the constitutionalists. According to Forouharfar (2020):

> The 1900s in Iran's history is a prominent era for the metamorphosis of the dominant political institution from a monarchical absolutism with secretive and inherently central decision-making; albeit myriad of decision-making domains around the country that was due to the diminishing de facto power of the *Qājār* monarchs, to a semi-consultative and parliamentary political institution under a constitution.

Bibi Maryam Bakhtiārāi (1874–1937) a constitutionalist and a female military commander, who accompanied, "*Ḥājī ʿAlīqolī Khan Sardār Asʿad*, one of two military commanders who marched on Tehran, deposed Moḥammad-ʿAlī Shāh, and revived the aborted movement for constitutional government in Iran" (Saʿīdī

Sīrjānī., Digard & Navā';ī, 1988, p. 543) fought alongside *Sardār As'ad*'s forces in Tehran. Then he achieved the honorary title of *Sardār* (Commander) for her deeds, bravery, and military skills.

Constitutionalism shook Persian society dramatically and later pursuing women's rights was feverishly followed by some constitutionalists. For example, Moghadam (2000, p. 386), citing Afary (1996, p. 133) mentioned, "Muhammad Ali Shah's collaborator Sad al-Dawla devised several strategies to disgrace the Majlis and attack the advocates of women's rights, who were being accused of promoting immorality and prostitution. In one such action, he orchestrated a demonstration by a group of prostitutes who marched unveiled in the streets of Tehran chanting, 'The constitution has given us freedom to abandon our religious obligations and live as we wish'" (Afary, 1996, p. 133; see also Delrish, 1357, pp. 56–57; Bayat-Philipp, 1978, pp. 301–302).

1909–1925 The Reign of Aḥmad Shāh-e Qājār: Old Institutions in Transition

The nearly 11-year-old son of *Moḥammad-'Ali Shāh* and the last *Qājār* monarch, *Ahmad Shāh,* ascended the throne by the permission of *Majlis* in 1909. During his reign *World War I* occurred, and the Russian and British imperialist measures within the country expanded enormously. For example he was being coaxed and cajoled to give his consent to the *Anglo-Persian Agreement of 1919* which completely violated the entire national sovereignty of the Persians over their country and Britain was going to be considered as Persia's guardian and protector. Sheikh-ol-Islami (2011, p. 658) clearly sketches the Persian condition on the ground:

> [A] major crisis facing the country and the young shah at the end of the war was caused by the presence on Iranian territory of foreign troops, including the British forces that controlled much of the country. The British-commanded South Persia Rifles were in the south, the Dunsterforce (later known as the North Persia Force, or Norperforce) occupied the Qaṣr-e Šīrīn-Kermānšāh-Hamādān-Qazvīn line, and other British contingents were based in Mašhad. On 18 May 1920, the Soviets landed troops at the port of Anzalī (later Bandar Pahlavī) and proceeded to occupy the province of Gīlān, announcing they would remain until British forces were withdrawn. Iran took its case to the newly established League of Nations; but that august body proved ineffective.

After the evacuation of the forces by Britain, *Ahmad Shāh* presumed that the *Bolsheviks* will intend to occupy Tehran, although they promised to evacuate their forces after Britain. *Aḥmad Shāh*'s "thoughts and deeds were centered on one single object: to save himself and his fortune before Tehran fell to the Bolsheviks, whose advance on the capital seemed imminent. He continued to press Norman, the British minister in Tehran, to acquiesce to his departure for Europe, ostensibly for reasons of health. But it was clear to Norman that the *Shāh* was motivated by fear, and that he intended to wait out the crisis abroad, returning to Iran if it passed, but remaining in Europe if the Bolsheviks took over (*Documents* XIII, p. 678, cited in Sheikh-ol-Islami, 2011, p. 658).

The king's cowardice, the chaotic scene of Iran, the tribal widespread revolt, the imminent invasion of Persia by the foreign forces, the imperialist intentions of Russia mainly on the North and Britain mainly in the South and the East of the country, and amid a complete social and public insecurity, *Reżā Khān*, the commander of a division of the Persian *Cossack* brigade, marched from *Qazvīn* to *Tehran* and occupied the capital. The incident took place on March 20, 1921. The *Coup* happened exactly 40 days before the evacuation of the British forces and the disseminated news that after the British evacuation Russian *Bolshevik* forces intended to occupy *Tehran*. *Reżā Khān* appointed as *Sardār-e Sepah* (*the Commander-in-Chief*) of the Persian forces and

> The Soviet government hastened to reach an understanding with Reżā Khan and agreed to withdraw their support from the Gīlān rebels under Mīrzā Kūček Khan. Reżā Khan shortly thereafter invaded Gīlān and defeated Mīrzā Kūček Khan's forces. (Sheikh-ol-Islami, 2011, p. 657)

Ahmad Shāh's frequent travel to *Farang* (*Europe*) and his reluctance and indecisiveness in running the states' affairs beside the charismatic, tough, and military character of *Reżā Khān* led to the abrogation of the *Qājār* monarch by the *Majlis*. Thus,

> On 31 October 1925, the *Majlis* approved a bill deposing the *Qājārs* and entrusting the provisional government to *Reżā Khan*. Eighty deputies voted in favor of the bill, twenty abstained, and only five opposed it. On December 12, a special constituent assembly modified articles 36, 37, 38, and 40 of the constitution and by a vote of 257 to 3 conferred the crown on *Reżā Shāh* and his male heirs (Sheikh-ol-Islami, 2011, p. 660).

The scene of the Persian chess was so chaotic and the state was so close to complete destruction that Persia and its people were thriving for existence. Therefore, the scene was not suitable for any type of entrepreneurship by the Persians, male or female, although the oil facilities of Ā*bādān*, as a foreign state-sponsored oil enterprise, under the British managers were exploiting the Persian oil.

In the late *Qājār* period, a metamorphic transition was underneath the skin of the Persian society. According to Issawi (1971), Persia was changing from a mainly feudal society and economy toward a state with capitalistic characteristics. However, this behavior should be a *proto-capitalistic* behavior and at an emerging stage since the number of industries and enterprises were not many. However, women mainly in the rural regions of Persia had major contribution to the state's economy. Moghadam (2000, p. 380), citing Delrish (1996) and Poya (1999), mentions:

> In rural areas they were [Persian women] largely unpaid workers, though they produced rice, butter, dried fruits, and tea, and had an important role in the production of wheat, barley, tobacco, cotton, hides, skins, raw and manufactured silk, drugs, dyes, wool, and cotton.

Moreover,

> ...prior to the discovery and production of oil in 1911-14, Iran's main exports were agricultural products and handicrafts, and thus women's products were sold in national and international markets...Thus women's labor contributed significantly to Iran's export trade (Moghadam, 2000, p. 381).

The workforce in the Persian carpet industry, which Persia is historically known for, was mainly on the burden of women and children. For example, carpet weaving in *Azarbāijān*, the northwestern region of Persia, "was done exclusively by women, at home" (Issawi, 1971, p. 297). Nomad Persian women were usually preparing and dyeing the threads. On the other hand, Persian rice was mainly produced in *Gilān*, on Persia's north, mainly by the labor of *Gilaki* women (Delrish, 1996).

In sum, the state had catastrophic irregularities in respect with the women's work and according to Delrsih (1996, p. 48), "It was not difficult to exploit female labor, considering the absence of state regulation."

1925–1941 The Reign of Reżā Shāh-e Pahlavi: Women, State, and the Modernization Policies

The era witnessed some of the most significant Persian historical institutional changes, which also embraced the most considerable changes in the lives of women in Persia. For example, "for the first time, some women entered into modern sectors of the economy, family laws were modified, unveiling was enforced, and public co-educational primary schools were established in 1936" (Sedghi, 2012, p. 492). *Reżā Shāh* built a modern and secular but authoritative state. He was the first Persian king without royal *harem* and concubines and was against *andarūnī* culture and thus women segregation. The core state policy in his era was modernization policy of the state. Under these policies, some of the main features of the Persian economy changed. For example,

> ...in Persia, especially before the First World War we could see an extremely dominant bazaar-like economy. Then during *Reżā Shāh*'s reign and before the end of the Second World War we

could witness the first economic indications in Iran for an industry-based economy (Forouharfar, 2020).

Through this period, women's education was supported incessantly by the state. Especially, *Reżā Shāh* himself was advocating women's entrance and participation in the society and economy. However, he felt that for promoting women's participation in the state's social, economic, political, and cultural affairs he should change two sociocultural issues. The first was the historical propensity of veiling women and the second was widespread illiteracy among the Persian women. The propensity of veiling women and keeping them in *andarūnīs* was the main reason of women illiteracy according to him. Thus:

> *Reẓā Shah* formulated his policy of banning the veil (*čādor*, q.v.) after his state visit to Turkey in the Summer of 1934. A year later, *ʿAlī-Aṣḡar Ḥekmat*, the minister of education (*wazīr-e maʿāref*), called on his own initiative a number of leading women educators, veterans of the women's movement from the 1920s and 1930s, to form the Ladies' Center on 14 October 1935. *Ḥājar Tarbīat* was appointed as its director, and such women's rights activists as *Afšār, Dawlatābādī, Pārsā, Arḡūn, Parvīn Eʿteṣāmī* (q.v.), *Aḵtar Kāmbaḵš, Tāj-al-Molūk Ḥekmat, Eṣmat-al-Molūk Dawlatdād, Šams-al-Molūk Jawāher-kalām, Faḵr-al-Zamān Ḡaffārī Bāyandor, Parī Ḥosām Šahīdī, and Badr-al-Molūk Bāmdād* served as its board members. The Center campaigned against "the black shroud" (*kafan-e sīāh*, a pejorative reference to the *čādor*) and encouraged all participants to attend its meetings unveiled. Four months later *Reżā Shah* proclaimed the measures against the veil at the Tehran Teachers College (*Dānešsarā-ye Tehrān*) on 17 Dey 1314 Š./7 January 1936. (Sedghi, 2012, p. 492)

On January 7, 1936, *Reżā Shāh* made a lucid and concise speech for the women who were present at *Dānešsarā-ye Tehrān* (*Tehran Teachers College)*. In his several-minute-length speech, he accentuated the Persian word *Kār* (*work*) five times:

> I am very happy that I see women are acquainted with their own conditions as the results of wisdom and insight and they enlightened about their own rights and benefits. As *Ms. Tarbīat* mentioned the women of this country could not fulfill their own aptitudes and merits … and now they are going to benefit from the other capabilities of society beside their outstanding privilege of motherhood… We should not forget that half of our country's population were not counted that means half of the state's workable strength was idle [and unemployed]. Never did the state take the women's census as if women were different and they could not be counted in the Persia's population. It is a deep

> pity there was only one instance and that was when there had been a scarcity of food, thus they enumerated [women] to provide food…. (Rāzi, 1968, pp. 697–698)[8]

Nevertheless, from the early 1930s, the government promoted the state policies for gender equity. For example from 27 November to December 2, 1932, encouraged *Dovvomīn Kongera-ye zanān-e šarq* (*The Second Congress of Eastern Women*) in *Tehran* with the participation of women from around the world:

> There were … representatives from Afghanistan, Australia, China, Egypt, Greece, India, Indonesia, Iraq, Japan, Lebanon, Persia, Syria, Tunisia, Turkey, and Zanzibar. The participants discussed their movements and condemned the backward situation of Persian and Arab women, including female illiteracy and the tyrannical domination of husbands over their wives and the abuse of women in general. The Congress passed a resolution with 22 articles concerning, inter alia, women's suffrage, equal opportunity in education, occupation and wages, reform in family law, and abolition of polygamy and prostitution. (Sedghi, 2012, p. 492)

Whereas the masses remained attached to the veil, mostly the educated urban women and many middle-class women welcomed unveiling (Bāmdād I, 1968, pp. 88–91). This date was recognized by the researchers on Persian women as a pivotal turning point in the history (Amin, 2002). The event made the first evident bipolarization of the state between those with the conservative propensities of the past and those who are supporting modernization and change. Thus, this bipolar and paradoxical view to the question of Persian women revealed itself in the subsequent historical events of Persia. However, the state promoted its intention for publicizing active social life by women as well as socializing more Persian women and whenever it felt fierce endeavors for the reinstatement of previous home-confining intensions reacted with coercive measures. It was the embedded historical struggle of *andarūnī* versus *bīrūnī* metaphor in the history of modern Persian women.

In sum, the 1930s is a decade of "big leap forward" (Agah, 1958, p. 209; Floor, 1984, p. 20, Hakimian, 2011) not only in women's issues but also in the formation of a Persian modern state:

> It embraces the establishment of a modern nation-state, state-induced definition of Iranian nationalism, bureaucratic centralization, population growth and urbanization, fast industrialization, empowerment of the national economy, formation of modern Iranian army and its military forces, establishment of new official institutions in the administrative and judiciary branches, foundation of modern educational institutes, such as *Tehran University*, etc.

> Therefore ... the 1930s should be studied as state-induced and -promoted *Institutional Revolution* in modern Iran. (Forouharfar, 2020)

This decade should be also studied as the solidification of the cultural and social bedrock of future entrepreneurial will by the Persian women. *Culture* affects entrepreneurial orientation (EO) (Lee, Lim, & Pathak, 2011) and later in the Persian history, we observe EOs among women of modern social classes.

Furthermore, in this period the first, although meager, traces of transition from *feudalism* to *capitalism* emerged. *Industrialization* of the Persian economy not only pushed the economy toward capitalist structures of power and its side effects but also created a female working class in modern Persia. The final brick for the completion of the capitalist wall although planned with good and emancipating intentions of releasing vassals from the cruelty of the *Khāns* (*Landowners*) with its catastrophic ripples took place in *Moḥammad Reżā Shāh*'s *Enqelāb-e Sefīd* (*White Revolution*) which spread discontent among numerous classes of society.

One of the major effects of state-sponsored modernization and industrialization policies was the *Proletarianization* of the workforce and emergence of modern industrial and bureaucratic working class, which includes modern women's working class too. Agriculture, textile, carpet, and cotton spinning mills were among the main industries of the age, which also employed women workers. For example, according to Floor (1984, p. 60) only in *Kermān*,

> ...about 7,000 workers were employed in the carpet industry of which seventy-five percent were children between six and twelve years and women. The remaining twenty-five percent were almost exclusively composed of adolescents of fifteen to eighteen years.

Moreover, approximately 40% of the government revenues were from the agricultural sector (Poya, 1999), which provided the most job opportunities for women. However, the working conditions were not satisfactory.

1941–1979 The Reign of Moḥammad Reżā Shāh-e Pahlavi: Women in a Modern State

On August 25, 1941, the *Anglo-Soviet Invasion* violated the official neutrality *of Persia* in World War II. Persian oil, Persia's geopolitics, and the preemptive measure to block *Nazi* accessing *Khuzestān* oil wells were among the undeclared motives for the invasion. The invaders forced *Reżā Shāh* to resign and the propaganda machine of the BBC broadcast a series of radio programs against him. The crown prince, *Moḥammad Reżā*, acceded the throne in 1941. He ruled the country for the next 37 years up to the *1979/Islamic Revolution.*

The major incidents of the period were Persian oil *nationalization* on April 28, 1951, *Dr. Moṣaddeq's*, the democratically elected prime minister, deposition via the *Coup D'état of 28 Mordād 1332* (August 19, 1953), the *White Revolution*

(*Enqelāb-e Sefīd*), and the *1979 Revolution* which culminated to the establishment of an Islamic theocracy in Persia. According to Forouharfar (2020), the *Constitutional Revolution*; the *Institutional Revolution*; the *White Revolution*; and the *1979/Islamic Revolution* are major institution-making revolutions in modern Persia.[9]

Persian women had active roles in and affected by all the mentioned revolutions. The *Constitutional Revolution* later paved the way for new laws and regulations for women. The *Institutional Revolution* officially empowered Persian women to get out of the historical *andarūnī* and move toward the metaphorical *bīrūnī* and hence play more active roles in the Persian politics, economy, society, and culture. The White Revolution:

> Embraced a large domain from land distribution among peasants to enfranchisement of women. It was the second wave of comprehensive modernization program of the state. The first wave was ardently pursued by the first *Pahlavi* Monarch, *Reżā Shāh*. Under the second program literacy corps were sent to far corners of the state to teach the illiterate rudimentary of reading and writing, pastures, water resources and forests are nationalized, the profit of factories were also distributed among their workers, privatization of state industries was commenced, health corps were formed, educational reforms were started, policy of price stabilization was pursued, compulsory and free education for all the classes of the nation was promoted, free nutrition programs for poor mothers and infants – funded by the state budget – were set up, controlling land prices with the intention for public facilitation of home ownership, and the policy of fighting against bureaucratic corruption were followed. (Forouharfar, 2020)

In sum, "the *White Revolution* was an initial *deinstitutionalization* and subsequent *re-institutionalization* program. It tried to undo the traditional pluralistic feudal power structures and substitute them with a centralized state power" (ibid.). However, the results fell short and it united four social strata (feudal landowners mostly the tribal *Khāns* (chieftains); the *Bāzāries* (Iranian traditional merchants mostly dwelling in down town oriental bazaars); immigrated peasants from the villages; and the Islamic religious leaders). All had religious propensities and the *1979/Islamic Revolution* took place.

Persia has had the most flourishing economy and entrepreneurship increase in the period. According to Pesaran (2011, p. 143):

> The period between 1963 and the start of the revolutionary upheavals in 1978 undoubtedly represents the longest period of sustained growth in per capita real income the Persian economy has experienced… Persia's per capita income (in current prices) rose from $170 in 1963 to $2,060 in 1977… The production of

> cars, television sets, refrigerators, and other household durables increased manifold….

Thorough this period, women were enfranchised and they could be sent to diplomatic missions, appointed as judges, entered the government cabinets, the parliament and the police and the army forces, and were extensively educated at universities. The final stage of a modern state was successfully accomplished. On the other hand, solid private entrepreneurial establishments such as *Iran Nātionāl Company* (founded by *Khayāmi* brothers in 1962), *ARJ Company* (founded by *Khalil Ardjomand* in 1937), *Kafsh-e Melli Company* (founded by *Mohammad Taqi Iravāni* in 1957), *Azmāyesh Company* (founded by *Mohsen Azmāyesh* in 1959), etc flourished in this period. However, approximately all the main entrepreneurial establishments were founded by men. Moreover, nearly all the major entrepreneurial establishments were confiscated after the *1979 Revolution* and the private sector entrepreneurship was extremely vanished for nearly two decades.

1979–Until Now, The Incumbent Islamic Republic: Islamizing Women's Institutions

After the *1979 Revolution*, the constitution of the *Constitutional Revolution* was abrogated and a new constitution under *Islamic Shari'a* was formed. Moreover, major Islamizing programs were pursued by the state to reinstate the Islamic rules especially for women. In the early decades, large private entrepreneurial establishments were propagated as a taboo and *Tāqout* (*Paganism*). However, later after a major increase in the unemployment rate; first, the establishment of the cooperatives was encouraged and in the subsequent years, the state tried to ardently encourage entrepreneurship and spirit of entrepreneurism among the youth. Therefore, numerous industrial towns were established in the major cities' suburbs and multiple free trade zones were demarcated near the Persia's boarders and some Persian Gulf islands (e.g., *Kish* and *Qeshm* islands). The unprecedented literacy and population boom occurred and public programs were funded by the state for providing nearly all the populated villages of Persia with public utilities. Moreover, from the 1990s, the population of unemployed university graduates – also consisting female graduates – were increased dramatically; and hence Persia currently has one of the largest unemployed youth in the Middle East:

> According to the 2015 World Economic Forum report, Iran is among the countries with a high gender gap in economy ranking 141 in terms of women's economic participation among the 145 countries. In the other hand, women's entrepreneurship does not seem to be enjoying an appropriate status in Iran and despite increased entrepreneurial activities by women, the ratio of businesses run by women to business run by their male counterparts are 2–10. (Arasti & Bahmani, 2017, p. 109)

In general, entrepreneurship in current Persia has a meager and delicate system. The entrepreneurial ecosystem embracing government regulations and the economic status of the state with unprecedented international sanctions accompanied with major stagflations prevents successful establishment, growth, and flourishing of entrepreneurial efforts. Women's entrepreneurship is also in a declining trend.

On the other hand, Persia, after the *1979 Revolution*, has had multiple major waves of immigration abroad. However, three major waves are more distinguishable. The first wave took place exactly some months before, during, and some months after the revolution and embraces some of the wealthiest families, intelligentsias, and major Persian entrepreneurs. The second took place during the Iran–Iraq War (1980–1988), "While the earlier exiles fled the Revolution, the later ones included draft-age men escaping the Iran-Iraq war" (Boyce et al., 2011, p. 370). The third wave happened after the large and widespread unemployment among the educated youth, both male and female, after the 1990s and which still sporadically continues. These waves of immigrations among Persians, which were unprecedented in Persian history, have created a large Persian diaspora especially in the United States and western European countries. The Persians in the United States are among the most successful social strata:

> The statistical profile of Iranian immigrants in the United States shows them to be even more educated, skilled, and entrepreneurial than Americans, as well as most other foreign-born groups in the United States. According to the 1990 U.S. census, Iranian-born persons ranked third in educational achievement after Indians and Taiwanese among major immigrant groups in the United States. Reflecting this high level of education, Iranians once again ranked third after Indians and Taiwanese in holding the top occupations of managers and professionals. By comparison, only 20 percent of the native-born population of the United States had a bachelor's degree or higher, and only 27 percent were employed in these two top occupations. The median household income of Iranians ($36,000) ranked fifth in the United States, and was higher than that of the native-born ($30,000). (Boyce et al., 2011, p. 370)

Thus, we could observe the main major entrepreneurial establishments and enterprises among the Persian women diaspora, which could mainly be related to their EOs, education, family background, and by far the suitable entrepreneurial ecosystem in respect to Persia. The Persian women entrepreneurs in these countries live in communities with lower male-dominancy propensities and less preventative cultures for nurturing their entrepreneurial behaviors.

Some of these successful Persian women entrepreneur diaspora, as a few examples, are *Sahar Hāshemi* (cofounder of *Coffee Republic*, a coffee bar chain), *Shahrzād Rafati* (Founder and CEO of *BroadbandTV Corp*), *Roxānne Varzā* (Director of *STATION F*, one of the world's biggest start-up campuses based in Paris), *Cymā Zarghāmi* (President at *Nickelodeon Networks Group*), *Anousheh*

Ansāri (CEO at *XPRIZE* and the first Persian astronaut), *Parisā Tabriz* (Google's "Security Princess" as named by the *New York Times* (Conger, 2019, p. 1), and *Sorayā Dārābi* (founder of *Trail Mix Ventures* (TMV), an early-stage venture firm investing in the future of living well).

Theorization

Historical institutions could be discussed at least in three levels: (1) Macro-level institutions (e.g., the governments and their bodies, state, religion, dominant culture, etc.), (2) Mezzo-level institutions (e.g., city, town, tribal or ethnic culture, or role models, etc.), and (3) Micro-level institutions (e.g., family, relatives, cultural backgrounds, role models, etc.). However, the institutions could be discussed as either formal (e.g., government institutions) or informal (e.g., cultural institutions). Assuming all the abovementioned taxonomies of sociological institutions, in respect to the Persian institutions at any levels and with any degree of formality or informality, we could evidently observe the ubiquity of *Patriarchism* in mainly all the Persian sociological institutions. In other words, we could see a patriarchal organization of the Persian society and its institutions. The prevalence of absolutism in the Persian political history to the dominant role of fathers, especially in traditional Persian families, reflects the depth of such *patriarchism*. *Culture* and its offspring, *religion*, are a determining factor in sociological and economic studies. Max Weber's *Die protestantische Ethik und der Geist des Kapitalismus* (*The Protestant Ethic and the Spirit of Capitalism*) is a reflection of such mentality. Persian culture in a broad meaning of the term historically suffers from an excessive *patriarchism*. This cultural perspective (or *patriarchal cultural hegemony*) has penetrated to the Persian worlds of politics, society, economy, family, and nearly all Persian existence and it persists. Women have been and are the first victims of this perspective. This perspective is even observable at the micro-level institutions of Persian society. According to Moghadam (2000, p. 379):

> Women have worked throughout history and in all kinds of productive systems. And yet, at certain times in history, an ideology of domesticity has emerged, tying women to family roles and defining productive labor as exclusively masculine.

She has defined this relationship as the "patriarchal gender contract" (Moghadam, 1998) which is so evident in Persian society. The idea of women *domesticity* was another manifestation of such *patriarchal cultural hegemony* discussed above which is not only limited to the Persian society but different societies in respect to their stage of development could experience it. For example:

> British historians have noted the rise of an ideology of domesticity with the development of capitalism in England. Bradley explains that in the Victorian era, women were seen as essentially pure, but

> easily led astray; if they went out to work they were considered to risk moral corruption and sexual seduction. (Moghadam, 2000, p. 379)

Sex division of labor is the other prevailing manifestation of the *patriarchal cultural hegemony* in Persia that assumes only specific jobs for women and barricades some official, technical, judiciary jobs against women entrance.

Legal status of women and governmental empowerment of women in some periods of Persian history benefited the Persian women to push this *patriarchal cultural hegemony* back, at least for temporary periods, and could be more socially and economically active.

Women entrepreneurship as an institution itself and in any country could be affected by the major interplay of at least three factors: (1) the state politics, (2) the prevailing economic atmosphere, and (3) the state's dominant culture (Fig. 10.1).

The embedded historically cultural perspective in Persia has led to an *Institutional Triangulation* with a patriarchal sociopolitical economy, which does not bear the economic and entrepreneurial activities of the Persian women, and thus always women working in the *Bazaar economy* of Persia was culturally and socially forbidden and considered as a taboo. However, by a change in this culture or its nonexistence (e.g., by immigration) the major factor for the Persian women entrepreneurial ecosystem was agreeable and has led to more women's social and economic activism and hence entrepreneurship by the Persian women diaspora.

In Fig. 10.2, three possible scenarios of the formation of sociopolitical economy were unfolded. (a) In the first scenario, state's politics has hegemonic effects on the state's economy and people's culture. (b) In the second scenario, state's economy and its requisites demand a special adaptation on the side of the state's politics and its people's culture. Finally, (c) in the third scenario people's culture affects the state's politics and economy.

In respect to Persia, the third scenario (*Cultural-Driven Triangulation*) explains the institutional-driven status of women entrepreneurship. As discussed above, the Persian society's prevalent patriarchal and male-dominant characteristics, beside an embedded women-restricting religious propensities especially among the

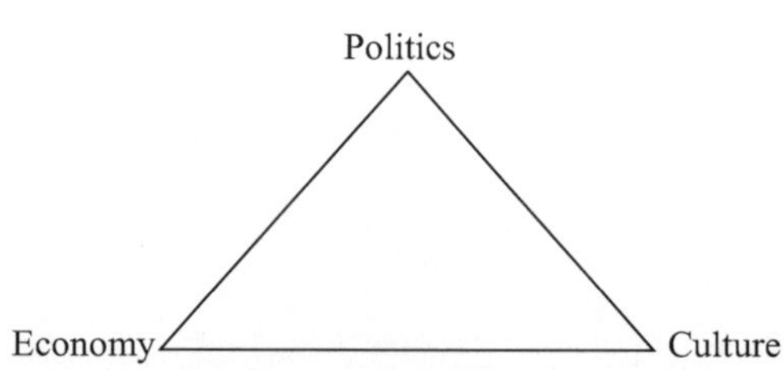

Fig. 10.1. Institutional Triangulation: The Emergence of Sociopolitical Economy. *Source:* Author's own theory.

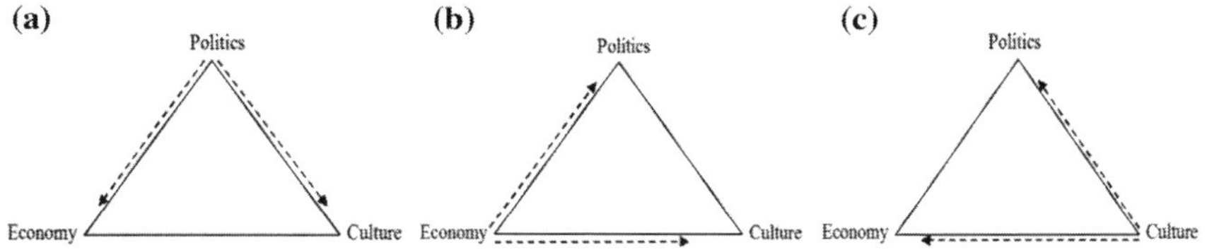

Fig. 10.2. Emergence of Sociopolitical Economy Through Triangulation Processes: (a) Political-driven Triangulation, (b) Economic-driven Triangulation, (c) Cultural-driven Triangulation. *Source:* Author's own work.

traditional strata of Persia, have culminated to the establishment of the political and economic institutions with the same characteristics. Thus, the laggard Persian women entrepreneurship inside Persia and its status among other ecosystemic factors should be first and foremost attributed to the cultural dimensions of this society. However, once people's cultures shape its similar characteristics in the state politics and economy they have reciprocal symbiotic relations and they reinforce each other and lead to a triangular iron cage. In other words, in a social constructionist view, people construct their cultural, political, and economic realities, that is, people make their sociocultural surrounding and it reciprocally makes them (Berger & Luckman, 1966; Burr, 2003; Crotty, 1998; Gergen, 1999, 2001; Hacking, 1999; Harre, 1986; Latour & Woolgar, 1979; Potter, Wetherell, Gill, & Edwards, 1990; Shotter, 1993; Fairhurst & Grant, 2010).

Conclusion

Persian women entrepreneurship is historically a cultural issue. The solidification of the Persian politics and economy via Persian culture, which itself embraces numerous ethnic subcultures, was culminated to a sociopolitical economy that overshadows the entrepreneurial endeavors by the Persian women. In other words, Persian culture historically and metamorphically has shaped its political and economic institutions that in turn reciprocally affected the cultural institutions which have already formed them.

Studying the Persian women's modern history reveals the metamorphic phases of early *feminist institutionalization* (e.g., through the debate among works such as *Bibi Ḵānom Astarābādi*'s *Maʿāyeb al-Rejāl* (*The Vices of Men*) in response to the *Taʾdib al-Neswān*/*Taʾdib al-Nesāʾ* (*The Education of Women*) in the *Nāṣeri* period. This debate and its hidden underlying social discontent among many Persian women through the *Qājār* period was due to the long history of Persian women's *subjugation* and *subordination* which led to their *institutional marginalization* up to end of *Qājār* period with the abdication of *Aḥmad Shāh*, the last *Qājār* king. *Reżā Shāh*, the new monarch under his large-scale modernization policies, planned the Persian women's *socialization* programs that culminated to the historical *emancipation* of the Persian women especially in the middle and upper-middle social strata. *Moḥammad Reżā Shāh*'s reign, the second *Pahlavi* monarch, coincided with quick, vast, and nationwide educational and employment programs for inducing women's historically and mainly culturally suppressed potentials. Later after the collapse of the *Pahlavi Dynasty*, the new regime pursued the *Islamization* of women's institutions which persists.

The interplay of each state's politics, economy, and culture leads to a sociopolitical economy that could be envisaged via a triangular relationship. The dynamism among the institutional components of this triangle makes an *institutional triangulation* process, which forms and dynamically affects the underlying sociopolitical economy of a state. In respect to Persia, the *patriarchal* and *male-dominant* culture, which historically led to the male supremacy through a *cultural-driven triangulation*, has shaped the Persian society's historically absolute politics as well as male-centered and *Bāzāri* (masculine bazaar-like) economy. The effect of the Persian masculine culture on the state's politics and economy was later bounced and echoed again toward the culture, which previously had generated them. This cultural reinforcement through the state's politics and economy especially from the early 1980s onward has made a *hegemonic masculinity* in the sociopolitical economy of Persia, which justifies women's subordination, subjugation, and marginalization via reestablishment of traditional cultural institutions, which have passed their metamorphic stage due to the Persian historical requisites, and now they are not existent anymore. Thus, scarcely could we find large-scale women entrepreneurship within this entrepreneurial ecosystem. However, the mentioned historical incidents especially from late 1970s has either forced or motivated some families with entrepreneurial-minded women to pursue their entrepreneurial intentions in a different cultural context with a different entrepreneurial ecosystem. Hence, nearly all major entrepreneurial establishments and enterprises by the Persian women in recent years could be found out of Persia and by the Persian women diaspora.

Acknowledgments

To the memory of the late Dr. Ehsan Yarshater, (1920–2018) an eminent scholar of Iranian Studies, and founder and Editor-in-Chief of the Encyclopædia Iranica, who dedicated more than forty years of his valuable life for the accomplishment of this comprehensive project of *Iranian Studies.*

Notes

1. On 21 March 1935 with the advent of the first day of Iranian New Year – *Nowruz* – and suggestion of three Persian scholars *Prof. Saeed Nafisi*, *Mohammad Ali Forouqi*, and *Seyed Hasssan Taqizadeh* the name of *Iran* was officially substituted for *Persia*. However, the term *Iran* was always used by Iranians from the horizons of history which dates back to the thousands-years-old Zoroastrian scriptures which Aryans call their country as *Airyana Waējah* (*The Lands of Aryans*) and thus the substitution of the name was not new for the Persian Farsi speakers in the state.

2. Öffentlichkeit: The places in society where people usually gather and discuss issues which culminate in political actions.
3. A nineteenth-century religious movement under the leadership of *Sayyed ʿAlī-Moḥammad Shīrāzī*, the *Bāb*, a movement first within *Shīʿite Islam* but later established as a new religious system.
4. A monopolistic concession [*emtīāz*] in 1890 transferred not only the production but also the sale and export of Persia's entire tobacco crop for 50 years to British Major *G. F. Talbot* that led to the *Tobacco Protest* [*Nehzat-e Tanbāku*] under the mutual cooperation of the public and *Shīʿite Islam* religious leaders which set the initial embryonic phase for their future intervention in subsequent social events.
5. 1.04 meter.
6. Original text is in Persian, translated by the chapter's author from Persian into English.
7. *Bast-nešīnī*, i.e., "(sanctuary, asylum), the designation of certain sanctuaries in Iran that are considered inviolable and were often used by people seeking refuge (bast nešastan, bast-nešīnī) from prosecution (even common criminals), called bastīs" (Calmard, 1988, p. 856).
8. Original text is in Persian, translated by the chapter's author from Persian into English.
9. *Institutional Revolution* was coined by the chapter's author to refer to the first stupendous reformist modernization policies, established modern institutions, and institutional reforms during the reign of *Rezā Shāh* (1925–1941).

References

Adamiyat, F., & Nateq, H. (1978). *Afkar-e Ejtemaē va Siyasē va Eqtesadē dar Asar-e Montashr Nashod-e Doran-e Qājār*. Unpublished Social and Political and Economic Works in Qājār Period, Tehran, Iran.

Afary, J. (1996). *The Iranian constitutional revolution, 1906–1911: Grassroots democracy, social democracy, & the origins of feminism*. New York, NY: Columbia University Press.

Agah, M. (1958). *Some aspects of economic development of Modern Iran*. Ph.D. dissertation, Oxford University.

Algar, H. (2012) Amīr Kabīr, Mīrzā Taqī Khan. In E. Yarshater (Ed.), *Encyclopædia Iranica* (I/9, pp. 959–963). Retrieved from https://iranicaonline.org/articles/amir-e-kabir-mirza-taqi-khan

Amanat, A. (2011) Constitutional revolution: Intellectual background. In E. Yarshater (Ed.), *Encyclopædia Iranica* (Vol. VI, Fasc. 2, pp. 163–176). Retrieved from https://iranicaonline.org/articles/constitutional-revolution-i

Amin, C. M. (2002). *The making of the modern Iranian woman: Gender, state policy, and popular culture, 1865–1946* (1st ed.). Gainesville, FL: University Press of Florida.

Arasti, Z., & Bahmani, N. (2017). Women's entrepreneurship in Iran. In S. Rezaei, LP. Dana, & V. Ramadani (Eds.), *Iranian entrepreneurship* (pp. 109–137). Cham: Springer. doi:10.1007/978-3-319-50639-5_7

Bayat-Philipp, M. (1978). Women and revolution in Iran, 1905–1911. In L. Beck & N. Keddie (Eds.), *Women in the Muslim world* (pp. 295–308). Cambridge, MA: Harvard University Press.

Berger, P., & Luckman, T. L. (1966). *The social construction of knowledge: A treatise on the sociology of knowledge*. Garden City, NY: Doubleday.

Bonine, M. E. (2000) Bāzār. In E. Yarshater (Ed.), *Encyclopædia Iranica* (Vol. IV, Fasc. 1, pp. 21–25). Retrieved from https://iranicaonline.org/articles/bazar-i

Bournoutian, G. (2012) Griboedov, alexander Sergeevich. In E. Yarshater (Ed.), *Encyclopædia Iranica* (Vol. XI, Fasc. 4, pp. 363–364). Retrieved from https://iranicaonline.org/articles/griboedov-alexander-sergeevich

Boyce, M., Zarrinbaf-Shahr, F., Hakimian, H., Nakash, Y., Mojtahed-Zadeh, P., Bozorgmehr, M., … Pahlavān, Č. (2011). Diaspora. In E. Yarshater (Ed.), *Encyclopædia Iranica* (Vol. VII, Fasc. 4, pp. 370–387). Retrieved from https://iranicaonline.org/articles/diaspora#pt.8

Burr, V. (2003). *Social constructionism* (2nd ed.). London: Routledge.

Bāmdād, B. (1968). *Zan-e Īrānī az enqelāb-e mašrūta tā enqelāb-e safīd, 2 vols.*, Tehran. tr. and ed. F. R. C. Bagley, *From darkness into light: Women's emancipation in Iran*, Smithtown, NY, 1971.

Calmard, J. (1988) Bast. In E. Yarshater (Ed.), *Encyclopædia Iranica* (Vol. III, Fasc. 8, pp. 856–858). Retrieved from https://iranicaonline.org/articles/bast-sanctuary-asylum

Conger, K. (2019). The work diary of Parisa Tabriz, Google's 'Security princess. *New York Times*, September 5. Retrieved from https://www.nytimes.com/2019/09/05/business/parisa-tabriz-google-work-diary.html

Crotty, M. (1998). *The foundations of social research: Meaning and perspective in the research process*. Sydney: Allen & Unwin.

Delrish, B. (1357/1996). Woman in the Qajar Era (Tehran: Office of studies and research). (In Persian.)

Fairhurst, G. T., & Grant, D. (2010). The social construction of leadership: A sailing guide. *Management Communication Quarterly*, *24*(2), 171–210.

Floor, W. (1984). Industrialization in Iran: 1900–1941, University of Durham, Centre for Middle Eastern and Islamic Studies, Occasional Paper, no. 23.

Forouharfar, A. (2020). De Jure and De Facto power of Oil and Institutional change in Modern Iran: A critical historicism analysis (1900–1979). In N. Faghih & A. M. Samadi (Eds.), *Dynamics of institutional change in emerging market economies*. Cham: Contributions to Management Science. Springer.

Gergen, K. (1999). *An invitation to social construction*. London: SAGE Publications.

Gergen, K. (2001). *Social construction in context*. London: SAGE Publications.

Giddens, A. (1984). *The constitution of society: Outline of the theory of structuration*. Cambridge: Polity Press.

Hacking, I. (1999). *The social construction of what?* Cambridge, MA: Harvard University Press.

Hakimian, H. (2011). Economy in the Qajar period. In E. Yarshater (Ed.), *Encyclopædia Iranica* (Vol. VIII, Fasc. 2, pp. 138–143). Retrieved from http://www.iranicaonline.org/articles/economy-viii-in-the-qajar-period

Harre, R. E. (1986). *The social construction of emotions*. Oxford: Blackwell.

Huntington, S. P. (1968). *Political order in changing societies*. New Haven: Yale University Press.

C. Issawi (Ed.) (1971)., *The economic history of Iran, 1800–1940*. Chicago, IL: The University of Chicago Press.

Latour, B., & Woolgar, S. (1979). *Laboratory Life: The social construction of scientific facts*. London: SAGE Publications.
Lee, S. M., Lim, S. B., & Pathak, R. D. (2011). Culture and entrepreneurial orientation: A multi-country study. *The International Entrepreneurship and Management Journal*, *7*(1), 1–15.
Malekzadeh, M. (1956). *Tārikh-e Enqelāb-e Mashroutiat-e Iran* [*Iranian constitutional revolution history*] in Persain (Vol. 4). Tehran: Ibn-e Sina.
Moghadam, V. M. (1998). *Women, work and economic reform in the Middle East and North Africa*. Boulder, CO: Lynne Rienner Publishers.
Moghadam, V. M. (2000). Hidden from history? Women workers in modern Iran. *Iranian Studies*, *33*(3–4), 377–401.
Najmabadi, A. (2009). Tāj-al-Salṭana. In E. Yarshater (Ed.), *Encyclopædia Iranica*. Retrieved from https://iranicaonline.org/articles/taj-al-saltana
North, D. C. (1991). Institutions. *The Journal of Economic Perspectives*, *5*(1), 97–112.
Pesaran, M. H. (2011) Economy in the Pahlavi period. In Prof. E. Yarshater (Ed.), *Encyclopædia Iranica* (Vol. VIII, Fasc. 2, pp, 143–156). Retrieved from http://www.iranicaonline.org/articles/economy-ix
Potter, J., Wetherell, M., Gill, R., & Edwards, D. (1990). Discourse: Noun, verb or social practice?. *Philosophical Psychology*, *3*, 205–217.
Poya, M. (1999). *Women, work and Islamism*. London: Zed Books.
Qavimi, F. (1973). *Kārnām-e Zanān-e Mashhour-e Iran*, (A report on famous Iranian women). in Persian, Tehran, Iran.
Rowbotham, S. (1974). *Hidden from history: Rediscovering women in history from the 17th century to the present*. New York, NY: Pantheon Books.
Rāzi, A. (1968). *Tārikh-e Kāmel-e Irān* [*The complete history of Iran*] in Persain. Teharn: Eqbāl Publication.
Sa'īdī Sīrjānī, A., Digard, J. P. & Navā'ī, A. Ḥ. (1988) Baḵtīārī. In E. Yarshater (Ed.), *Encyclopædia Iranica* (Vol. III, Fasc. 5, pp. 543–551). Retrieved from https://iranicaonline.org/articles/baktiari-1-nesba-of-a-number-of-baktiari-chiefs
Sedghi, H. (2012) Feminist movements in the Pahlavi period. In E. Yarshater (Ed.) *Encyclopædia Iranica* (Vol. IX, Fasc. 5, pp. 492–498). Retrieved from https://iranicaonline.org/articles/feminist-movements-iii
Seyf, A. (2001). Iranian textile handicrafts in the nineteenth century: A note. *Middle Eastern Studies*, *37*(3), 49–58.
Sheikh-ol-Islami, M. J. (2011) Ahmad Shah Qājār. In E. Yarshater (Ed.) *Encyclopædia Iranica* (Vol. I, Fasc. 6, pp. 657–660). Retrieved from https://iranicaonline.org/articles/ahmad-shah-qajar-1909-1925-the-seventh-and-last-ruler-of-the-qajar-dynasty
Shotter, J. (1993). *Conversational realities: Constructing life through language*. London: SAGE Publications.
Turner, J. (1997). *The institutional order*. New York, NY: Longman.
Yarshater, E. (2012) Islamic period: The Qajar dynasty. In E. Yarshater (Ed.), *Encyclopædia Iranica* (Vol. XIII, Fasc. 3, pp. 238–241). Retrieved from https://iranicaonline.org/articles/iran-ii2-islamic-period-page-5

Chapter 11

Female Entrepreneurship *à Brasileira*: Entrepreneurship by Choice or Entrepreneurship by Force?

Denise Helena França Marques, Nicia Raies Moreira de Souza and Shahamak Rezaei

Abstract

In 2019, Brazil had approximately 53.4 million entrepreneurs, of which 60.2% were start-ups. The contingent of nascent entrepreneurs was 11.1 million people and in just one year it grew 390%, a fact that can be explained, on the one hand, by the beginning of the economic recovery of the country which, although timid, began arousing with the gross domestic product closing the year 2019 with growth of 1.1%, and on the other hand, by the slow cooling of the national unemployment rate that reached 11.0% in the last quarter of 2019 (IBGE, 2019). Women have been occupying an important space in the country's entrepreneurial activities, with an initial specific rate of entrepreneurship (total early-stage entrepreneurial activity (TEA)) of 23.1%, similar to that of men, and established specific rates of entrepreneurship (total establishing entrepreneurial activity (TEE)) of 13.9% (GEM, 2019). Despite the enthusiasm brought by the numbers, it is necessary to pay attention to what are the entrepreneurial activities performed by these women, since in a country like Brazil, transformations brought by innovative thoughts, technological development, and expansion of education are not privileges of the entire population. Besides the differences between genders, even among women, the impact of changes in society occurs in different ways, and the "pure" concept of entrepreneurship, associated with innovation and the creation of new products and services, is valid for only a portion of them, leaving to others the broader concept related to creativity, risk, use of available resources, and economic sustainability in a context where individual characteristics and unfavorable structural conditions are intertwined (Haas, 2013). In this sense, the objective of this work is to present the national reality of female entrepreneurship, contributing with the

The Emerald Handbook of Women and Entrepreneurship in Developing Economies, 191–211
Copyright © 2021 by Emerald Publishing Limited.
All rights of reproduction in any form reserved
doi:10.1108/978-1-80071-326-020211011

understanding of who are the Brazilian women entrepreneurs that correspond to these "pure" and broad concepts and, therefore, shed light on new studies and research that can contribute with more accurate diagnoses about these women.

Keywords: Female entrepreneurship; Brazil; entrepreneurs by choice; entrepreneurs by force; self-employment; Brazilian necessity entrepreneurship; entrepreneurial opportunity structures

Introduction

References to entrepreneurship have become a commonplace. The word has often been used by the media, public and private institutions, academics, and the general public to highlight the benefits of the activity, either by generating jobs and income; stimulating competition; solving problems that demand innovation; economic development, especially when enterprises are technologically based; or the opportunity to work with what one likes, to develop skills and competencies, to be self-employed, and to achieve the much dreamed independence. Entrepreneurship contributes in various ways to the economic growth of a region and country and has increasingly become a key to economic autonomy, social emancipation, and human development.

In Brazil, in 2019, there were around 53.4 million entrepreneurs, of which 60.2% were initial – an increase of 2.8% and 31.5%, respectively, in the period of one year. The nascent entrepreneurs represented a contingent of 2.2 million people in 2018, and in 2019, reached the volume of 11.1 million, an extraordinary growth of 39.0% in 12 months (GEM, 2019). This increase can be explained, on the one hand, by the beginning of the economic recovery of the country which, although modest, began to show signs of life with the gross domestic product (GDP) reaching the end of 2019 with growth of 1.1%, and on the other hand, by the slow reduction of the national unemployment rate which reached 11.0% in the last quarter of 2019, representing a contingent of 12.6 million unemployed (IBGE, 2019).

Women have been occupying an important space in the country's entrepreneurial activities. Although the difference between them and men in the comparison of the total establishing entrepreneurial activity (TEE) remains, the data for 2019 reveal the maintenance of the balance between total early-stage entrepreneurial activity (TEA), with a differential of only 0.4 p.p. between the genders: 23.1% for women against 23.5% for men (GEM, 2016, 2019).

Despite the enthusiasm brought by the numbers, it is necessary to pay attention to what are the entrepreneurial activities performed by these women, since in a country like Brazil, transformations brought by innovative thinking, technological development, and the expansion of education are not privileges of the entire population. Besides the differences between genders, even among women, the impact of changes in society occurs in a different way, and the classic concept of entrepreneurship, associated with innovation and the creation of new products and services, is applicable to only a portion of them, leaving the strict concept related to creativity, risk, use of available resources, and economic sustainability to others in a context where individual characteristics and unfavorable environment are intertwined (Haas, 2013).

The definition of entrepreneurship relies on the contribution of different areas of study such as economics, psychology, and sociology, and perhaps due to its multidisciplinary nature, the definition is imprecise. It can be said that entrepreneurship is a condition, a state of economic creativity. Anderson, Dodd, and Jack (2012) emphasizes that entrepreneurship is not fixed in time and space and that entrepreneurial activity is reflected in the multiple social constructions where individual and collective forces interact, "When we talk of entrepreneurship, we usually mean the process of becoming, thinking, planning, conspiring, doing the things that may lead to entrepreneurship" (Anderson & Starnawska, 2008, p. 4).

The concept of entrepreneurship considered in this work is that inspired by the work of Bulgacov et al. (2011) which presupposes a subject and an intentionality focused on the object, immersed in an economic, political, cultural, historical, and institutional environment. In this sense, one can think of the subject as the Brazilian women who, according to the National Continuous Household Sample Survey (PNADc), conducted by the Brazilian Institute for Geography and Statistics (IBGE) in 2019, were inserted in some entrepreneurial activity in the country. The objective of this work is to present the national reality of entrepreneurship of these women, in other words, *à brasileira*, contributing with the understanding of who are the Brazilian women that correspond to the classical and strict concepts of entrepreneurship and, therefore, to throw light on new studies and researches that can contribute with more precise diagnoses about these women. The empirical analysis will follow the typologies proposed in Haas' (2013) analytical model, which unfolds the need motivation in two aspects: absolute and relative.

Entrepreneurship by Necessity versus Opportunity

For some authors, entrepreneurship is closely related to the personality traits of individuals, which in turn are associated with their "need for fulfillment" (Mcclelland, 1972). For others, the behavioral approach is more elucidative in proposing the individual as a reactive and, in a way, passive subject when influenced by the external environment. The two theoretical aspects are not mutually exclusive; on the contrary, they complement each other to the extent that entrepreneurship necessarily implies a subject and an intentionality aimed at the development of entrepreneurial activity, and this subject is embedded in an inseparable historical, economic, political, and cultural context.

Despite the divergent theoretical approaches, the studies on the theme are almost unanimous in recognizing two of the main motivations for its realization: the necessity and the opportunity. The basic distinction between them lies in the fact that some entrepreneurs create businesses by identifying opportunities, with the objective of maximizing their utility, while others are forced to undertake out of necessity, due to the lack of alternatives for economic sustainability (Fairlie & Fossen, 2018). Bulgacov et al. (2011, p. 699) enrich the authors' concept by defining entrepreneurs by necessity as "the symbol character of the neoliberal ideology, which, in its apology for the advantages it takes advantage of, covers up the precariousness that, in general, characterizes it." In fact, for most small entrepreneurs by necessity, especially those living in less developed regions of the globe, entrepreneurship operates as a buffer against unemployment and is a reflection of the structural changes that have occurred in labor relations.

This dichotomic opportunity versus necessity analysis has grown in strength in recent years as a result of research conducted by Global Entrepreneurship Monitor (GEM) which, until 2019, restricted the response options to these two categories. From that year on, the research expanded the number of alternatives to four in order to encompass other motivations: (1) "to earn a living because jobs are scarce"; (2) "to make a difference in the world"; (3) "to build great wealth or a very high income"; and (4) "to continue a family tradition" (GEM, 2019).

Despite the efforts of GEM to better understand the motivations that lead people to engage in entrepreneurship, the predominance of the alternative "to earn a living because jobs are scarce" among 90% of Brazilian entrepreneurs at an early stage reveals, on the one hand, the prevalence of entrepreneurship by necessity in the country but, on the other hand, unifies this necessity in a country permeated by different contexts. According to Haas (2013), there is a lack of theoretical consensus on what entrepreneurship by necessity is. Traditional theory points out a range of individual and circumstantial characteristics associated with entrepreneurial activities, whether by opportunity or by necessity, and generalizes these two dimensions. The author argues that there is a differentiation inside the category of entrepreneurship by necessity which, when not considered, is inconsistent with empirical evidence. This distinction originates from conjunctural and structural circumstances:

> Depending on the environmental circumstances we distinguish between an absolute form of necessity entrepreneurship, describing those in a state of need due to poor environmental conditions, and a relative form of necessity entrepreneurship, referring to those living in more developed locations, yet still affected by negative external circumstances. (Haas, 2013, p. 19).

In this sense, the author proposes four typologies of entrepreneur according to the conjuncture and environmental influences in which the entrepreneurs are embedded (Fig. 11.1).

Haas (2013) calls situational or conjunctural circumstances the combination and/or occurrence of events in people's lives, at a given moment, that differentiate them from one another and are inserted in the same structural conditions. The circumstances or structural conditions refer to the environment; business context including industry and market conditions; institutional and cultural context including politics, justice, religion, and corruption; spatial context such as geographical location, and distance to markets; social context such as networks

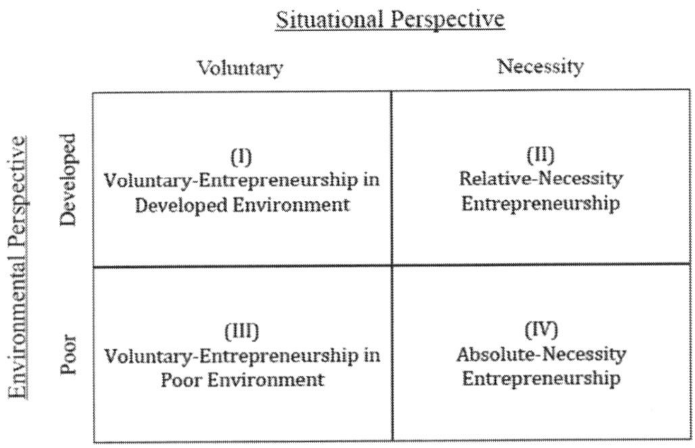

Fig. 11.1. Four Types of Entrepreneurs. *Source:* Haas (2013, p. 20).

and family characteristics; and economic context, such as level of development, innovation, and economic (Aboal & Veneri, 2016). They operate independently of individual life circumstances and impact the lives of a group of people.

Typology I – Voluntary Entrepreneurs in Developed Environment – is the classic case approached by literature, whose entrepreneurial behavior is almost exclusively related to demographic characteristics and personality traits such as self-efficacy, opportunity alertness, risk propensity, and role modeling, since environmental conditions are favorable to any professional decision (Jensen, Rezaei, Schøtt, 2015; Rezaei, 2017; Tang, Kacmar, & Busenitz, 2012). The choice to undertake is freely chosen and based on maximizing its utility.

Typology II – Relative Necessity Entrepreneurs – is that entrepreneur who finds himself in a favorable environment, but under negative conditions that restrict his freedom of choice. These conditions can be divorce, illness, unemployment, etc. In spite of this, due to the positive environment in which one lives, this individual enjoys a minimum standard of living that protects him/her from basic needs. Haas (2013) points out that the perception of relative need varies according to some aspects, such as demographic characteristics and the educational level of people. This group of entrepreneurs by necessity predominates in developed countries, especially in Western Europe and North America.

Typology III – Voluntary Entrepreneurs in Poor Environment – consists of the entrepreneur who, unlike typology I, is inserted in a structurally unfavorable environment (macroeconomic instability, high unemployment rates, social inequality and poverty, legal insecurity, and complex tax system), but who enjoys positive living conditions that allow them to combine and use a series of scarce resources to develop entrepreneurial activity. In general, they are creative and persistent people, with an acute sense of self-efficacy, opportunity alertness, risk propensity, and role modeling, but being inserted in another context, the range of business opportunities of this group is different from that.

Finally, Typology IV – Absolute Necessity Entrepreneurs – refers to entrepreneurs negatively affected by environmental and conjunctural conditions. In general, they are people who find in entrepreneurship a precarious alternative to exclusion. They have low educational level, little professional experience, limited income, and perform activities of low productivity. Unlike Relative Necessity Entrepreneurs, this type of entrepreneur is predominantly found in developing countries. According to Heller (2010), in poor regions and countries with high social inequality, a significant portion of the population is unable to access formal education and basic resources to implement an entrepreneurial activity that guarantees their personal fulfillment, restricting themselves only to ensuring reproduction.

The Fig. 11.2 shows the interaction of these dimensions and the typology of the entrepreneur according to the intersections. The three rectangles portray the universe of individuals affected by negative situational circumstances (A); individuals affected by negative environmental circumstances (B); and individuals engaging in entrepreneurial activity (C). The intersections between them form the typologies of entrepreneurship proposed by Haas (2013), and these are described above. The overlapping of the rectangles (A), (B), and (C) represents typology IV (Absolute Necessity Entrepreneurs); the overlapping of (A) and (C) typology II (Voluntary Entrepreneurs in Poor Environment); and the intersection of (A) and (B), the third typology (Voluntary Entrepreneurs in Poor Environment). Typology I is in rectangle C and does not cross with any of the other two rectangles. The ellipses represented in different sizes and shades of gray represent the selectivity and capacity of inclusion of entrepreneurs in the samples investigated by the researchers.

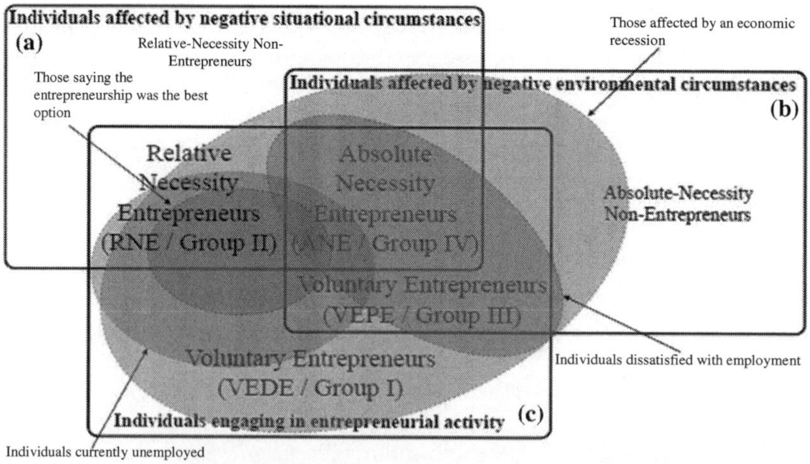

Fig. 11.2. Different Types of Entrepreneurs According to the Intersections of Approaches and Conjunctures. *Source:* Haas (2013, p. 30).

The findings of Williams and Youssef (2014), when investigating the motivations of Brazilian entrepreneurs inserted in the country's informal labor market, corroborate Haas (2013)'s suggestion about the caution of researchers when selecting a sample for the study of the phenomenon. Unlike several other surveys that employed case studies, the authors used the survey of the urban informal sector (Pesquisa Economia Informal Urbana, ECINF) conducted in Brazil, in 2003, by IBGE, and show the importance of the household survey to capture the activity, since 27.3% of informal entrepreneurs operated their businesses directly from their homes and 27.5% from client homes. These percentages show the strength of the household survey to capture the specific subject investigated by them, in relation to a business survey that would leave out an important share of informal entrepreneurs.

Women's Historical Journey in the Brazilian Labor Market

In the case of women, entrepreneurship has important nuances resulting from gender relations and the gender division of labor. In Brazil, as elsewhere, women have never been absent from the world of work. Apart from unpaid domestic work, poor Brazilian women, especially black women, have always worked either in invisible jobs in rural areas or in occupations in small businesses and services in urban areas. However, it is since the 1970s that there has been a significant entry of women into the labor market, including the middle strata of society. In 1940, 19.0% of the occupied labor force were women; 40 years later, they were 38.4%, according to the demographic census (Machado, 1986), and in 2019, they were 43.7% (IBGE, 2020).

The contours of women's participation in the labor sphere follow the structure of inequality characteristic of the country, which is intertwined with gender relations in the construction of specific places for men and women in the public and private spheres. In the first decade of the twenty-first century, indicators of income inequality in the country improved. The Gini coefficient, for example, fell by more than 10% between 2001 and 2011, as did poverty rates (12 p.p.) and extreme poverty (4 p.p.). Between 2012 and 2018, however, there is a reversal of this trajectory and the Gini increased by 0.8% reaching 0.545 (Barbosa, Souza & Soares, 2020). The economic contraction that began in 2014 partially reversed the distributional and welfare gains of the poorest, while for the richest, there was a rapid recovery that began as early as 2015 (Barbosa et al., 2020; IBGE, 2020).

There are several transformations in gender relations in this period, with the expansion of the education system, improvement in health indicators, with efforts to institutionalize public policies for women between 2000 and 2014, and increased political participation. Over time, more women reach positions of higher prestige, status, and income, but at the same time, they are still majority in the poor population, in the most precarious, unstable, and low-paid jobs (Brushini & Lombardi, 1999; Leta, 2014; Lima, 2013; Melo & Oliveira, 2006). The niches of women's work, in domestic employment, teaching, and nursing, for example, continue to occupy a significant part of them (Brushini, 2007; Oliveira &

Miranda-Ribeiro, 1998). In this sense, there is an inequality of occupational insertion and income not only between men and women but also between women from different social strata.

In this respect, the Brazilian labor market expresses and reproduces the deep social inequalities of the country. The bases of its configuration date back to its origins with the constitution of the Brazilian state and the slave society that served as its support. In the country, a degree of wage earning incorporating the majority of the population was never reached, and the economy always had a broad informal sector that was quite heterogeneous. Today, it can be said that this segment includes the self-employed, as well as small-scale activities organized in small production units, as well as unregulated and unpaid wage earners (Theodoro, 2009).

According to GEM-Brasil (2007), in Brazil, there is no culture that stimulates the creation of own businesses; but what is stimulated is formal education with the purpose of getting employment in a large company, private or public. However, the Brazilian is considered creative because of the need to avoid economic instabilities. It is this "creative" and "adaptation" capacity that can be seen in the different forms of insertion in the labor market.

The high heterogeneity of the Brazilian labor market can also be seen in the group called entrepreneurs, where the concept of entrepreneurship has taken on different connotations depending on the social strata. Thus, it is sought to demonstrate in this work that coexist in the entrepreneurial group both the dimension of the opportunity for personal and economic fulfillment as well as that of necessity, following the tradition of more recent studies (Williams & Youssef, 2014). But, it is also believed that structural dimensions are important even for the motivation and "choice" of paths to follow in the labor market (Bourdieu & Passeron, 1975), which is especially valid for the most vulnerable population groups.

The creation of own businesses, with or without employees, can be formalized or informal. Their degree of formalization is also an indicator of the degree of structuring, organization, and stability of the business. As previously mentioned, in Brazil, the informality of labor relations is not a recent phenomenon. The informal sector until the 1980s was very much linked to a reproduction mechanism of poverty and social exclusion – despite economic modernization. In the decade of 1990 and in the initial years of Twenty-first century, it is verified a deepening of the dissemination process of a new technological pattern, which imposed deep transformations in the production structure, in the markets organization, in the conditions of the work process, and in the management forms of the companies. In a first moment, the dynamism of occupation generation is diminished, raising the levels of unemployment, which together with the productive reorganization, is based on the high levels of labor outsourcing, within a panorama of incorporation of new technologies, and innovative organizational methods have raised the heterogeneity of occupational situations. In a second moment, job generation accelerates, but it is not able to incorporate the contingent that starts to enter the job market. The unemployment rate of women is permanently higher than that of men, especially black women.

The concept of the informal economy was first elaborated in the global south from a series of studies on the urban labor market in Africa. The theories developed in that period were very valuable, defining it almost as synonymous with poverty or underemployment. Thus, it was characterized by: (1) a small entry barrier in terms of skills, capital, or organization; (2) family businesses; (3) small-scale operation; (4) labor-intensive production and use of outdated technology; (5) competitive and deregulated markets (Portes, 1994).[1]

A large number of studies started to build functional classifications of informal activities according to their objectives. Such activities may address the issue of the survival of the individual or his/her household through subsistence production or by selling products and services on the market; they may be oriented toward a flexibility of labor relations and a decrease in labor costs of companies in the formal sector (for example, through subcontracting); and they may be organized for the accumulation of small companies through the mobilization of their solidarity relations, greater flexibility, and lower costs.

The informal economy is not a group of activities carried out by those on the margins of society. Several studies have shown that both in central and underdeveloped countries there is an economic dynamism in these activities that can even provide high levels of income, sometimes above the levels of workers in the formal sector. There is also strong evidence of systematic articulation between formal and informal sectors, following the requirements of profitability. The informal economy is, thus, not an individual condition but a process of income generation characterized by a central aspect: "it is unregulated by the institutions of society, in a legal and social environment in which similar activities are regulated" (Portes & Castells, 1989, p. 12).

The absence of institutional regulation in the informal economy can affect several elements of the work process, since each situation defines very different types of activities, for example, the status of work, working conditions, and the management of enterprises.

Female Entrepreneurship in Brazil

In the first place, the notion of classic entrepreneurship, associated with some skills such as innovation, creativity, inclination to risk, does not contemplate the stereotypes built about the "feminine." These stereotypes are important because they are transposed to the labor market generating spaces more or less affectionate to women's work. The gender division of labor makes it possible to understand the symbols and meanings that would represent the feminine and masculine gender. In the case of women, images are constructed that make their position in the labor market an extension of their work in the domestic space. Without wanting to advance in this discussion, the result is the segregation of women in certain occupations consistent with this notion. As an example, one can cite the one about the representation of women in careers in education (especially the teachers of small children), nursing, domestic service, and personal care services.

Secondly, the literature that discusses gender and the labor market is almost unanimous in highlighting the importance of the articulation – or conflict – between the reproductive and productive space as the great challenge for the insertion (and the way this insertion occurs) of women in the labor market (Abramo, 2004; Bruschini, 2007; OIT, 2013). The fact that reproductive work is unequally distributed in society generates several constraints to the performance of paid work by women. This applies not only to Brazil, but there is a deficiency in the provision of services by the State, as well as regulations capable of reducing access inequalities and gender segregation and discrimination in the labor market. Thus, the time women spend on reproductive work – caring for the home, children, the elderly, relatives – is much higher than that of men. The work of entrepreneurs, company owners, is structured in a whole of a "male" career model that implies full-time work commitments, high working hours, competition, geographic mobility, etc.

Thus, if self-employment and informality have always been present in the lives of poor women in the country, the entrepreneurial work of more structured, larger, better positioned businesses in the market is of difficult access for women. In other words, women candymakers, washerwomen, seamstresses, on their own, have always been present in the history of Brazil. What changes is that today there is a greater proportion of women from the medium and high strata running larger, more structured and formalized businesses.

In addition to the discussion of entrepreneurship by necessity or opportunity, the following is a portrait of the heterogeneity of the work held as an entrepreneur in Brazil. By the database that will be used, it will not be possible to see the motivation to create the business. Although some studies have shown the association between the motivation and the degree of success of the enterprise, it is intended here to explore another dimension, which although not new, is important to portray the different conditions of "choice" that vary according to social strata.

Results and Discussion

In accordance with the world trend, female entrepreneurship in Brazil has grown at an accelerated pace, especially businesses led by women who are at an early stage. To have an idea of the magnitude of this growth, in 2012 there were around 9.0 million women entrepreneurs in the country on initial stage and 8.0 million on stage established. In 2019, these numbers reached 16.1 million and 9.7 million, respectively – an increase of 78.8% and 21.2%, in that order, in seven years.

Although very discrepant in relation to the GEM estimates (2019), due to the methodological[2] difference, the PNADc data signal the increase of entrepreneurship (employers and self-employed) in general in the country, as shown in Fig. 11.3. It is observed oscillations in the total employment rate over the seven years considered and a continued growth of the contingent of employers and self-employed workers. In 2012, these two categories represented 3.9% and 22.8%, respectively, of the occupied population in Brazil, and in 2019, reached the

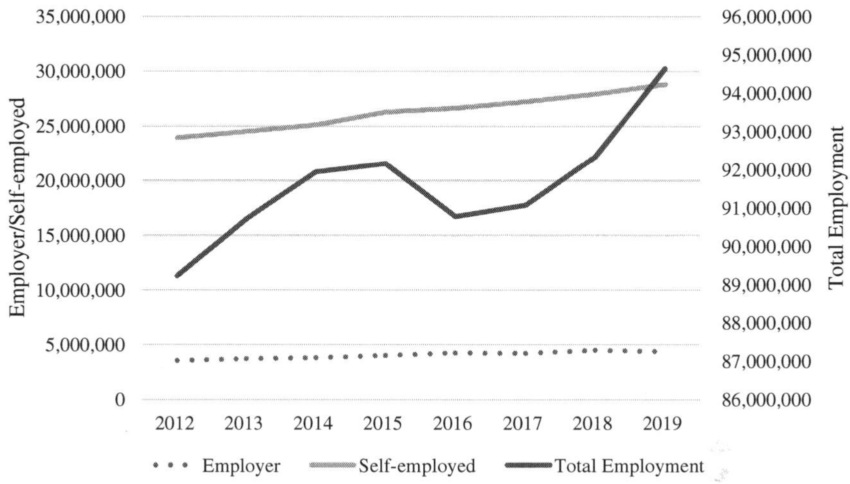

Fig. 11.3. Brazil: Evolution of the Occupied Population, Employers and Self-employed – 2012 to 2019. *Source:* IBGE. PNADc (2019).

percentages of 4.6% and 25.7%, in that order. In the average of the period, the number of entrepreneurs grew much more than the total occupied population: 20.3% against 6.0%. It should be noted that the increase in the number of entrepreneurs was due much more to the increase in the number of self-employed than employers, which even showed negative variations between 2016 and 2017 and between 2018 and 2019.

It is interesting to note that the greatest positive variations of the two categories of entrepreneurs occurred between 2015 and 2016, when the volume of occupied population contracted around 1.4 million people, suggesting transfer of occupations and what Bulgacov et al. (2011) calls the "desaguadouro" of unemployment. According to Barbosa Filho (2017), since the second quarter of 2014, the Brazilian economy has been in recession. Between 2014 and 2016, the GDP per capita declined by around 9%, and this retraction affected the various sectors of the economy differently. The industrial sector was the most impacted in terms of production retraction and formal job cuts. In 2015, the country registered the largest contingent of unemployed, reaching the level of 10 million Brazilians.

In fact, a portion of the unemployed may have recognized entrepreneurial activity as a single alternative for economic sustainability, and this outlook was not universal, given the differences in the context in which each one is inserted, the situation and demographic characteristics and personality among them. In this sense, one can think of entrepreneurs by relative necessity and absolute necessity (Haas, 2013). Even in an unfavorable environment, such as the Brazilian one, the probability of becoming an entrepreneur will differ greatly among individuals, even among those who face negative episodes in their daily lives (Banerjee & Newman, 1993; Bulgacov et al., 2011; Fairlie & Fossen, 2018).

According to Banerjee and Duflo (2007), there is an apparent lack of opportunity perception on the part of poor people that is associated not with psychological commitment but rather with the unavailability of energy and time to perceive other activities, especially among women, whose opportunity cost to look for opportunities to earn money outside the traditional activities in which they are accustomed is very high. Another important aspect is that for subsistence-level households, taking risks to exploit opportunities is unacceptable, and any cost arising from some loss during the process will certainly outweigh the benefits.

The differences in insertion between men and women in entrepreneurial activities in Brazil are shown in Fig. 11.4. There is a predominance of the proportion of men over women and small but continued increase in female participation.

However, Fig. 11.5 shows the difference in the patterns of relative variation in the volume of entrepreneurial men and women, especially from 2015 when women's rates far exceeded those of men and showed variations of more than 4.0% per year. In 2019, the level of employment for men was 3.5% higher than in the first year of the series; and for women, 9.6%. In the case of employers, there was an increase of 18.4% for men and 36.6% for women; and for the self-employed, the increase in occupation was 15.0% and 29.7%, respectively. Thus, although men are the majority among Brazilian entrepreneurs, women have entered into entrepreneurial activities, corroborating the international literature (De Bowman, 2000; GEM, 2019; Grasmuck & Rosario, 2000; Heller, 2010; Minniti & Naudé, 2010).

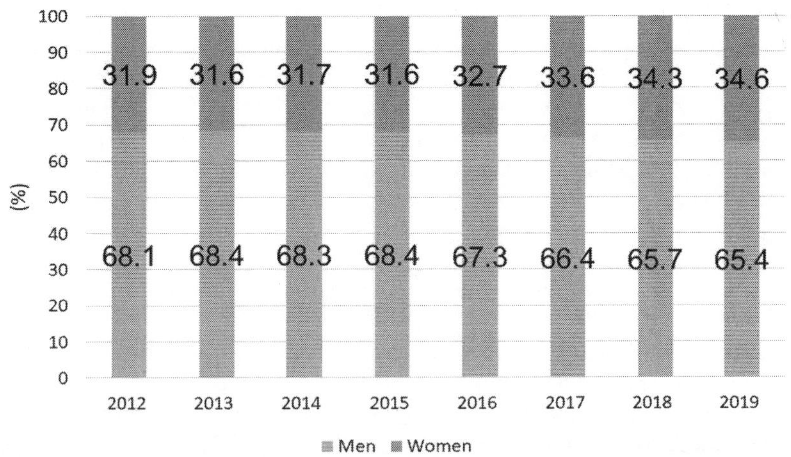

Fig. 11.4. Brazil: Relative Distribution of Men and Women Entrepreneurs – 2012 to 2019. *Source:* Self-elaborated by the authors based on public data: IBGE. PNADc (2019).

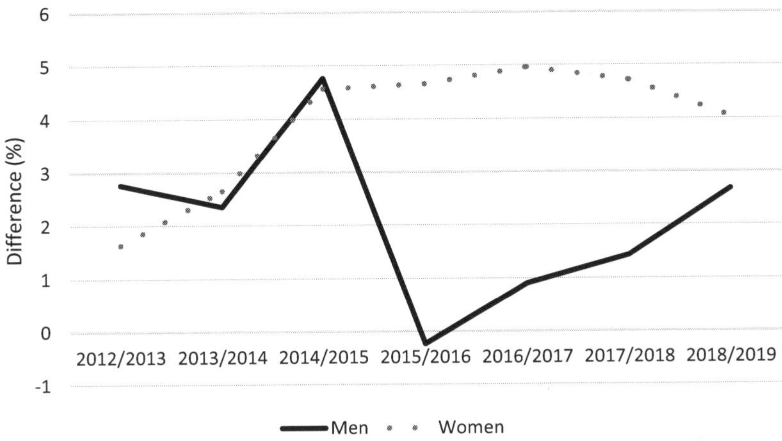

Fig. 11.5. Brazil: Relative Variation of Entrepreneurial Men and Women – 2012 to 2019. *Source:* Self-elaborated by the authors based on public data: IBGE. PNADc (2019).

The data also reveal that between 2015 and 2016, the number of women entrepreneurs grew 4.6%, while that of men decreased 0.2%. It is noteworthy that men were the most impacted by the Brazilian economic crisis, representing 85.6% of the total number of people who lost their jobs in the interval considered. Nevertheless, it was women who ventured into entrepreneurship, revealing that Brazil's unfavorable context affected the genders differently.

An exclusive and detailed look at the recent period provides more evidence about the kind of female entrepreneurship that is developed in the country. From the total of 9.9 million female entrepreneurs, in 2019, 86.5% were self-employed and the others were employers. With the exception of domestic work, the average years of study of women who worked on their own were less than the other conditions in the occupation: 10.7 years. Employers, on the other hand, studied an average of 13.2 years – behind only those in the public sector (Table 11.1).

Most female entrepreneurs, in both categories, were between 25 and 39 years of age. The second most representative age group among both employers and self-employed was 18–24 years old. The percentage of self-employed between 14 and 17 years of age is 7.5%, which may reflect the flexibilization of the labor market and its impacts on social relations. According to Bulgacov et al. (2011), one of the policy guidelines adopted by developed countries is to increase the training time of young people and delay their entry into the labor market. In developing countries, such as Brazil, young people are forced to work to support themselves, help their families, and pay for their education, which means that many of them are forced to become entrepreneurs due to absolute necessity. For the authors, these young entrepreneurs face a strong barrier associated with low educational level and lack of experience in business planning, reflecting in short life expectancy for their companies.

Table 11.1. Brazil: Sociodemographic Characteristics of Female Entrepreneurs – 2019.

Variables	Category	
	Employer	**Self-employed**
Average Years of Study	13.1	10.6
Age group		
14–17 years old	2.9	7.5
18–24 years old	34.1	35.8
25–39 years old	52.2	44.1
40–59 years old	10.7	11.9
60 and more	0.1	0.7
Education level		
Incomplete primary	7.8	25.8
Complete elementary school and incomplete high school	10.6	15.5
Complete high school and incomplete college degree	36.6	39.6
College degree	44,9	19.1
Average Family Size	3.26	3.28
Family		
Unipersonal	4.9	7.0
Nuclear	77.8	70.2
Extended	15,5	21,1
More than one family	1.9	1.7
Position in the Household		
Responsible	30.09	32,83
Others position	69.91	67.17

Source: Self-elaborated by the authors based on public data: IBGE. PNADc (2019).

Regarding the formation of entrepreneurs, it can be observed that, on average, 44.9% of the employers had completed higher education, 36.6% secondary school, and 10.6% elementary school. Among the self-employed, these percentages were 19.1%, 39.6%, and 15.5%. A quarter of this category had not completed primary education, against 7.8% of employers. The low level of schooling of self-employed women acts as an important limit to their personal and business growth. According to Minniti and Naudé (2010), in developing countries, entrepreneurship is a key variable in an individual's decision to become an entrepreneur and, consequently, in the success of the company. In general, such capacity is closely related to the formal level of education and professional training. Experience is also an important variable, and in some cases, can compensate for the low level of education, as Nafziger and Terrell (1996) show in a study developed in India and Naudé and Rossouw (2010) in China.

The average size of families was practically the same, and the nuclear family was predominant in both categories of entrepreneurs, especially among female employers. Among self-employed women, 21.1% belonged to extended families and 7.0% were unipersonal. For female entrepreneurs, these percentages were 15.1% and 4.9%, respectively. In relation to household position, data show that more than one-third of women in both categories were responsible for the household, mainly among the self-employed with a 32.8% share of the total group.

In Brazil, recurring economic crises and the context of unemployment have increasingly placed the family as a center of economic provision and well-being. The transition from a family model with men as the sole provider to a family model with multiple incomes has pushed many women into precarious employment and, among them, some types of entrepreneurship, especially those in charge of the household who, because they are women, carry an extra burden in relation to the others by having to deal with double insertion in the spheres of production and reproduction.

Among female employers, 74.3% were small business owners, with up to five employees. Great part of the companies of these women had two years or more of life, as well as the self-employed. The latter also stood out as very recent business owners: 15.1% from one month to less than one year and 9.1% from one year to less than two years (Table 11.2).

The location where the business operates is also an indication of the degree of organization and development of the enterprise. The business of 90.9% of women employers operated in stores, offices, and warehouses, and only 6.4% had no establishment. In contrast to employers, more than half of the women self-employed carried out their activities without an established location and only 36.5% in stores, offices, and warehouses. This difference may explain the discrepancy of 12 hours between the average weekly hours dedicated to enterprises between the two categories. The data corroborate the work of De Bowman (2000), Grasmuck and Espinal (2020), and Duque (2014) who in their research on women's entrepreneurship in Latin America show how the location of the business led by women in their homes is important to reconcile professional life with domestic work and child care, especially in a patriarchal society like Latin America. And it is exactly this location that divides women's time between domestic and professional activities. Moreover, the data reinforce the points made by Haas (2013) and Williams and Youssef (2014) about the selectivity of the sample and the importance of household surveys in capturing entrepreneurs who perform their home-based activities.

Regarding the economic activity sector, there is a predominance of female entrepreneurs, both employers and self-employed, in the trade sector characterized, in general, by low productivity and little demand for qualification and experience. Employers also stood out in the accommodation and food sector (16.0%) and information and communication (12.6%), while self-employed stood

Table 11.2. Brazil: Characteristics of Business Activity of Female Entrepreneurs – 2019.

Variables	Category	
	Employer	Self-employed
Average Hours	43.8	31.5
Sectors of the Economy		
Agriculture, livestock	2.6	6.9
General industry	9.1	15.6
Construction	1.1	0.7
Trading	36.6	27.4
Transport and storage	1.2	1.2
Accommodation and food	16.0	12.7
Information and communication	12.5	8.6
Education, health	11.6	6.1
Other services	8.9	20.3
Occupation		
Directors and managers	29.0	1.0
Science and intellectual professionals	17.5	11.3
Technicians and professionals – high school	2.9	4.5
Administrative support workers	0.1	0.1
Service workers, trade sellers, and markets	39.4	52.8
Skilled workers in agriculture, forestry, hunting, and fishing	2.3	6.3
Skilled workers, construction workers, and artisans, mechanical and other crafts	5.3	16.4
Plant and machine operators and assemblers	1.9	3.2
Elementary occupations	1.1	4.1
*Average Income**		
Directors and managers	1,417.2	934.1
Science and intellectual professionals	2,242.0	887.7
Technicians and professionals – high school	1,501.3	640.2
Administrative support workers	504.8	426.9
Service workers, trade sellers, and markets	847.3	279.9
Skilled workers in agriculture, forestry, hunting, and fishing	1,957.6	219.0
Skilled workers, construction workers, and artisans, mechanical and other crafts	832,1	232.5

Table 11.2. *(Continued)*

Variables	Category	
	Employer	Self-employed
Plant and machine operators and assemblers	552.1	338,2
Elementary occupations	415.3	187.5
Total	1,292.4	358.3
Age of Business		
Less than a year	0.3	2.2
From one month to less than one year	6.3	15.1
From one year to less than two years	5.7	9.1
Two years or more	87.5	73.5
Social Security		
Contributor	76.2	30.1
Formalization		
Percentage of formalization	85.8	21.8
Business Location		
Store, office, shed	90.9	36.5
Farms and ranches	2.5	6.2
No establishment	6.4	57.2

Note: Exchange December 30, 2019: US$ 1,00 = R$ 4,013.
Source: Self-elaborated by the authors based on public data: IBGE. PNADc (2019).

out in other services (20.3%) and general industry (15.6%). Despite the heterogeneous distribution, Brazil does not escape the rule regarding the concentration of women in activities traditionally associated with women (De Bowman, 2000).

In relation to occupational groups, one can see the difference in position in the social stratification system of employers and self-employed women. While there is a significant share of them in the best positioned groups in terms of income, career, status, and prestige among employers, self-employed women are in middle-level occupations, especially in services and trade. This difference is reflected in the average income differential between the two groups: US$ 934.1 between the average income of employers and self-employed, with the largest and smallest discrepancies in the occupations of "skilled workers in agriculture, forestry, hunting, and fishing" and "administrative support workers."

In Brazil, the CNPJ, the acronym for National Register of Legal Entities, indicates the formalization of the business or company. While 85.8% of women entrepreneurs had CNPJ, in 2019, only 21.8% of women self-employed were formalized. Moreover, not all workers in the country have social protection. Social security contributions are a prerequisite for various protection mechanisms such as unemployment insurance, retirement, healthcare, among others. Most employers have access to this system, but only 30.1% of self-employed women have it.

In summary, Brazil follows the worldwide trend of increasing entrepreneurial activities, especially those led by women. The changes brought about by new technological standards and the transformations in the productive structure, in the organization of markets, in working conditions, and in the forms of management of companies have propitiated women to participate more and more in the public sphere. However, this participation remains very unequal in relation to men and is not uniform among them. For many, working conditions are precarious and remuneration is very low, as are opportunities for entry into more qualified positions and diversified sectors of activity.

This is a reality that affects both salaried female workers and entrepreneurial women who, by receiving the single denomination, end up hiding the internal disparities of the group and giving the wrong idea of professional achievement and success. In this sense, the study presented shows how delicate such a denomination is, especially when considering the motivations for entrepreneurship.

The data revealed that the entrepreneurship *à brasileira* concentrates much more on self-employed women than on employers, and the analysis of their socioeconomic attributes, although it is not isolatedly the most appropriate way to capture the motivations that lead women to entrepreneurship, suggests that there are many more entrepreneurs out of absolute necessity than relative necessity.

The low schooling, the high representativeness of young women between 14 and 17 years old, the importance of the sectors of commerce and other services, the low formalization and contribution to social security, as well as the average income and the absence of a permanent place for the performance of the work are some of the symptoms of the vulnerability of women entrepreneurs and, once again, suggest the option for the entrepreneurial activity much more as a precarious alternative to exclusion than a means of professional accomplishment.

Notes

1. Keith Hart, who first used the term, postulated a dual model that expressed the differences in opportunity to measure income between salaried employees (formal) and self-employed – self-employment (informal). Hart emphasized the dynamism and diversity of these activities. But, this dynamic characterization was lost, and the concept that gained strength was almost synonymous of poverty (this concept that was institutionalized in international organizations such as the International Labor Office (ILO)?).
2. The Global Entrepreneurship Monitor (GEM) survey consists of a household survey with a representative sample of people between 18 and 64 years of age in Brazil (in 2019, there were 2,000 people interviewed). The National Continuous Household Sample Survey (PNADc) adopts a rotating panel scheme. This means that households are subsequently interviewed up to five quarters. In each quarter, about 211,000 households in approximately 16,000 census sectors in 3,500 municipalities are investigated.

References

Aboal, D., & Veneri, F. (2016). Entrepreneurs in Latin America. *Small Business Economics*, *46*, 503–525. Retrieved from https://link.springer.com/article/10.1007/s11187-015-9696-3. Accessed on August 2020.

Abramo, L. (2004). Women's participation in the labor market in Latin America: a secondary work force? *Revista Estudos Feministas*, *12*(2), 224–235. Retrieved from https://www.scielo.br/pdf/ref/v12n2/23969.pdf. Accessed on November 2020.

Anderson, A. R., & Starnawska, M., (2008). Research practices in entrepreneurship: Problems of definition, description and meaning. *The International Journal of Entrepreneurship and Innovation*, *9*(4), 221–230. Retrieved from https://journals.sagepub.com/doi/10.5367/000000008786208731. Accessed on November 2020.

Anderson, A. R., Dodd, S. D., & Jack, S. L. (2012). Entrepreneurship as connecting: Some implications for theorising and practice. *Management Decision*, *50*(5), 958–971. Retrieved from https://www.researchgate.net/publication/235290875_Entrepreneurship_as_Connecting_Some_Implications_for_Theorising_and_Practice. Accessed on May 2020.

Banerjee, A., & Duflo, E. (2007) The economic lives of the poor. *The Journal of Economic Perspectives*, *21*(1), 141–167. Retrieved from https://www.aeaweb.org/articles?id=10.1257/jep.21.1.141. Accessed on November 2020.

Banerjee, A., & Newman, A. (1993) Occupational choice and the process of development. *Journal of Political Economy*, *101*(2), 274–298. Retrieved from https://www.econ.nyu.edu/user/debraj/Courses/Readings/BanerjeeNewman.pdf?config=jstor&frame=frame&userID=807aabc3@nyu.edu/018dd5531e005041d63a&dpi=3. Accessed on November 2020.

Barbosa Filho, F. H. (2017). A crise econômica de 2014/2017. *Estud. av. [online]*, *31*(89), 51–60. Retrieved from http://www.scielo.br/scielo.php?script=sci_arttext&pid=S0103-40142017000100051&lng=en&nrm=iso. Accessed on November 2020.

Barbosa, R. J., Souza, P. H. G. F., & Soares, S. S. D. (2020). Uma Década Perdida para Desigualdade e Pobreza. *Texto para Discussão*. Rio de Janeiro, n. 2610. Retrieved from https://www.ipea.gov.br/portal/images/stories/PDFs/TDs/201106_td_2610_web.pdf. Accessed on November 2020.

Bourdieu, P., & Passeron, J. C. (1975). *A reprodução: elementos para uma teoria do sistema de ensino*. Rio de Janeiro: Francisco Alves.

Bruschini, C. (2007). Trabalho e gênero no Brasil nos últimos dez anos. *Cadernos de Pesquisa. Fundação Carlos Chagas. Set./dez.*, *37*(132). Campinas, Autores Associados.

Bruschini, C., & Lombardi, M. R. (1999). Médicas, arquitetas, advogadas e engenheiras: mulheres em carreiras profissionais de prestígio. *Revista Estudos Feministas*, *7*(1), 9–24, n. 1 and 2. Retrieved from https://periodicos.ufsc.br/index.php/ref/article/view/11950/11217. Accessed on November 2020.

Bulgacov, Y. L. M., Cunha, S. K., Camargo, D., Meza, M. L., & Bulgacov, S. (2011). Jovem empreendedor no Brasil: A busca do espaço da realização ou a fuga da exclusão? *Revista de Administração Pública*, *45*(3), 695–720. Retrieved from https://www.scielo.br/pdf/rap/v45n3/07.pdf. Accessed on October 2020.

De Bowman, O. C. (2000). Peruvian female industrialists and the globalization project: Deindustrialization and women's independence. *Gender & Society*, *14*(4), 540–559. Retrieved from www.jstor.org/stable/190301. Accessed on May 2020.

Duque, P. A. J. (2014). Empreendimento e gênero: o caso da indústria da beleza en Bogotá. *Sociedad y Economía*, *26*, 239–270. Retrieved from http://www.scielo.org.co/pdf/soec/n26/n26a11.pdf. Accessed on May 2020.

Fairlie, R. W., & Fossen, F. M. (2018). Opportunity versus necessity entrepreneurship: Two components of business creation. IZA Discussion Paper 11258. IZA Institute of Labor Economics. Retrieved from https://papers.ssrn.com/sol3/papers.cfm?abstract_id=3140340. Accessed on November 2020.

GEM-Brasil. (2007). *Empreendedorismo no Brasil: relatório executivo 2006*. Curitiba: IBPQ. Retrieved from https://ibqp.org.br/wp-content/uploads/2016/10/Empreendedorismo-no-Brasil-2006.pdf. Accessed on November 2020.

GLOBAL ENTREPRENEURSHIP MONITOR (GEM). Empreendedorismo no Brasil: 2016. Retrieved from http://www.ibqp.org.br/gem/download/. Accessed on November 2020.

GLOBAL ENTREPRENEURSHIP MONITOR (GEM). Empreendedorismo no Brasil: 2019. Retrieved from http://www.ibqp.org.br/gem/download/. Accessed on November 2020.

Grasmuck, S., & Espinal R. (2020). Market success or female autonomy? Income, ideology, and empowerment among microentrepreneurs in the Dominican Republic. *Gender and Society*, *14*(2), 231–255. Retrieved from www.jstor.org/stable/190273. Accessed on May 2020.

Grasmuck, S., & Rosario, E. (2000). Market success or female autonomy? Income, ideology, and empowerment among microentrepreneurs in the Dominican republic. *Gender & Society*, *14*(2), 231–255. Retrieved from www.jstor.org/stable/190273. Accessed on May 2020.

Haas, M. (2013). Necessity entrepreneurship: Individual, environmental and public policy-related factors influencing the process of opportunity exploitation under unfavorable circumstances. Dissertation Nr. 5830, École Polychnique Fédérale de Lausanne. Retrieved from https://core.ac.uk/download/pdf/147996882.pdf. Accessed on November 2020.

HELLER, L. (2010). *Mujeres emprendedoras en América Latina y el Caribe: Realidades, obstáculos y desafíos*. Santiago de Chile: División de Asuntos de Género, CEPAL. Retrieved from https://www.cepal.org/es/publicaciones/5818-mujeres-emprendedoras-america-latina-caribe-realidades-obstaculos-desafios. Accessed on May 2020.

INSTITUTO BRASILEIRO DE GEOGRAFIA E ESTATISTICA. (2019). *Pesquisa Nacional por Amostra de Domicílios Contínua*. Rio de Janeiro: IBGE.

INSTITUTO BRASILEIRO DE GEOGRAFIA E ESTATÍSTICA (IBGE). (2020). *Síntese de indicadores sociais: uma análise das condições de vida da população brasileira: 2020/IBGE, Coordenação de População e Indicadores Sociais*. Rio de Janeiro: IBGE.

Jensen, K. W., Rezaei, S., & Schøtt, T. (2015). Talent among Chinese entrepreneurs at home and abroad. In Y. Liu & H. Wang (Eds.), *Entrepreneurship and talent management from a global perspective*: Chinese returnees (pp. 62–91). Cheltenham; Northampton, MA: Edward Elgar Publishing.

Leta, J. (2014). Mulheres na ciência brasileira: desempenho inferior? *Revista Feminismos, Salvador*, *2*(3), 139–151. Retrieved from https://periodicos.ufba.br/index.php/feminismos/article/view/30039. Accessed on November 2020.

Lima, B. S. (2013). O labirinto de cristal: as trajetórias das cientistas na Física. *Revista Estudos Feministas, Florianópolis*, *21*(3), 883–903. Retrieved from https://www.scielo.br/scielo.php?script=sci_arttext&pid=S0104026X2013000300007&lng=pt&tlng=pt. Accessed on November 2020.

Machado, M. H. (1986). Participação da mulher no setor de saúde no Brasil 1970/1980. *Cadernos de Saúde Pública*. Rio de Janeiro, *2*(4), 449–465.

Mcclelland, D. C. (1972). *A sociedade competitiva: realização e progresso social.* Rio de Janeiro: Expressão e Cultura.

Melo, H. P., & Oliveira, A. B. (2006). A produção científica brasileira no feminino. *Cadernos Pagu*, [online], *27*, 301–331. Retrieved from https://www.scielo.br/scielo.php?pid=S0104-83332006000200012&script=sci_abstract&tlng=pt. Accessed on November 2020.

Minniti, M., & Naudé, W. (2010) What do we know about the patterns and determinants of female entrepreneurship across countries? *European Journal of Development Research*, *22*(3), 277–293. Retrieved from https://link.springer.com/article/10.1057/ejdr.2010.17. Accessed on November 2020.

Nafziger, E. W., & Terrell, D. (1996) Entrepreneurial human capital and the long-run survival of firms in India. *World Development*, *24*(4), 689–696. Retrieved from https://www.sciencedirect.com/science/article/abs/pii/0305750X95001615. Accessed on November 2020.

Naudé, W. A., & Rossouw, S. (2010). Early international entrepreneurship in China: Extent and determinants. *Journal of International Entrepreneurship*, *8*(1), 87–111. Retrieved from https://link.springer.com/article/10.1007/s10843-010-0049-7. Accessed on October 2020.

OIT. (2013). Domestic workers across the world: Global and regional statistics and the extent of legal protection. Retrieved from https://www.ilo.org/wcmsp5/groups/public/—dgreports/—dcomm/—publ/documents/publication/wcms_173363.pdf. Accessed on November 2020.

Oliveira, A. M. H. C., & Miranda-Ribeiro, P. (1998). *Diferenciais ocupacionais por raça e gênero no mercado de trabalho metropolitano no Brasil. XI Encontro Nacional de Estudos Populacionais da ABEP*, 9. Anais (pp. 2687–2717). Caxambu: ABEP. Retrieved from http://www.abep.org.br/publicacoes/index.php/anais/article/view/946/911. Accessed on October, 2020.

Portes, A. (1994). The Informal economy and its pardoxes. In N. Smelser & R. Sweberg (Eds.), *The handbook of economic sociology*. Princeton, NJ: Princeton University Prees.

Portes, A., & Castells, M. (1989). World underneath: The origins, dynamics, and effects of the informal economy. In Portes, A., Castells, M., & Benton, L. (Eds.), *The informal economy: Studies in advanced and less developed countries*. Baltimore: Johns Hopkins University Press.

Rezaei, S. (2017). Entrepreneurial competencies benefiting, entrepreneurial intention: Iranian adults at home and in the diaspora. In S. Rezaei, L. P. Dana, & V. Ramadani (Eds.), *Iranian entrepreneurship. Deciphering the entrepreneurial ecosystem in Iran and in the Iranian diaspora*. Cham: Springer International Publishing.

Tang, J., Kacmar, K. M., & Busenitz, L. (2012). Entrepreneurial alertness in the pursuit of new opportunities, *Journal of Business Venturing*, *27*(1), 77–94.

Theodoro, M. (2009). As características do mercado de trabalho e as origens do informal no Brasil. In: SILVA, Frederico Barbosa et al (Eds.), *Questão Social e Políticas Sociais no Brasil Contemporâneo*. Brasília: IPEA.

Williams, C. C., & Youssef, Y. A. (2014). Is informal sector entrepreneurship necessity- or opportunity-driven? Some lessons from urban Brazil. *Business and Management Research*, *3*(1), 41–53. Retrieved from http://www.sciedu.ca/journal/index.php/bmr/article/view/4302/0. Accessed on November 2020.

Chapter 12

Women Entrepreneurship in Developing Countries: The Context of Afghanistan

Ahsanullah Mohsen, Abdulbari Ahmadzai and Zabihullah Modaser

Abstract

The main purpose of this chapter is to analyze the women entrepreneurhip status in Afghanistan. The study comprises and analyzes three levels, namely, individual, societal, and institutional. All zones in Afghanistan are covered under this study. A total number of 104 women entrepreneurs are interviewed and filled out questionnaires. To ensure the appropriateness of data and accuracy of the model the authors used the required test. Reliability statistics, KMO and Bartlett's Test of Sphericity, and goodness of fit tests are applied. Factor analysis and structural equation modeling are used as econometric models to obtain the results. Two processes are applied, i.e., for motivational and psychological factors. Motivational factors and psychological factors are the latent variables where every latent variable has four and three observed variables, respectively. Factor loadings for observed variables were well above 0.5 and hence significant. The results show desire for achievement, desire for wealth, and desire for independence are motivational factors for women entrepreneurs. Furthermore, propensity to risk and locus of control are found to be the psychological drivers for women entrepreneurship in Afghanistan. The Government of Afghanistan needs to provide an environment for women entrepreneurs where they feel safe and undisturbed. Additionally, education, technical know-how, and financial support require serious government and institutional attention.

Keywords: Women entrepreneurship; factor analysis; entrepreneurs motivation; Afghanistan; challenges for entrepreneurs; psychological drivers

Introduction

Several research findings show the existence of the relationship between economic growth of a nation and entrepreneurship. Entrepreneurship also helps in bringing

The Emerald Handbook of Women and Entrepreneurship in Developing Economies, 213–228
Copyright © 2021 by Emerald Publishing Limited
All rights of reproduction in any form reserved
doi:10.1108/978-1-80071-326-020211012

about new innovations and fresh products/services which in their turn aid economics progress. Additionally, the entrepreneurship will create a large number of employments in developed and developing states (Venkataraman, 1997). Therefore, entrepreneurship endeavors are essential in developing as well as in developed countries.

Based on the World Bank data, globally women own a smaller number of businesses compared to men. Only one-third of businesses' ownerships belong to female entrepreneurs. Globally, only 34% small, medium, and large firms are owned by women. The women entrepreneurship share is relatively higher in advanced countries compared to developing nations. South Asia claims only 18% of businesses possessed by women (Halim, 2020).

Afghanistan is a developing country with a poor economy. The gross domestic product of the country is roughly $19.1 billion (World Bank, 2020). The entrepreneurship endeavors will extensively aid in Afghanistan's rapid economic growth. However, entrepreneurship is tied to several challenges and hurdles which makes this activity discouraged. Nevertheless, entrepreneurship has had some growth during the last two decades.

Out of the total the population, i.e., 32.2 million, 49% (15.8 million people) are female. From the women population 19.9% are aged between 15 and 24 years and 50.1% are aged between 15 and 64 years (NSIA, 2020). The aforementioned figures clearly indicate that the Afghan women population is young and has a huge number of working-age women. Hence, this equally means that Afghan women are in the appropriate condition from an age perspective to start their own businesses and firms. However, the appropriate age is not the only factor which helps women entrepreneurs to start their business, but there are several other preventive elements.

The business environment and organizational culture are usually under the shadow of societal culture. Businesses in Afghanistan are highly influenced by culture and tradition for the workforce comes from the heart of society. Afghanistan is a traditional country where women entrepreneurship can have several unique challenges. The overall condition of women in the country is different compared especially to European and Western countries. Furthermore, insecurity, war, and conflicts even make the situation worse. According to TrustLaw (2011), international business analysts and experts perceive Afghanistan as one of the top unsafe countries in the world.

Fig. 12.1 shows the photo of a restaurant which is managed by a woman entrepreneur. Restaurants and cafés are among the major famous businesses run by Afghan businesswomen. It is safe and has less risk compared to the technical and manufacturing businesses. These businesses require little technical know-how and expertise and have adequate demand in the market especially in recent years.

Theoretical Framework

There are several theories for women entrepreneurship in the literature. Some of them are discussed in the following section of this title. Two factors are known to be highly influential for entrepreneurial intentions. Firstly, the motivational factors and secondly, the psychological factors were found more relevant in this study.

Fig. 12.1. A Restaurant Owned by a Woman Entrepreneur. *Source:* Authors' work.

Motivational Factors

A study conducted by Nor & Yufizada (2004) shows that motivation is one of the prime reasons influencing the entrepreneurs' attitude and endeavors. The authors determined motivational factors to be desire for achievement, desire for independence, desire for wealth, and self-discovery. The desire for achievement influences businesspersons to take responsibility and being succeeded in the task which are even troublesome (Baum, Frese, & Baron, 2007). Desire for independence is another significant element which helps entrepreneurs in decision-making and planning (Collins & Moore, 1970). Additionally, the entrepreneurs' ultimate aim is desire for wealth (Cassar, 2007). A study indicates that self-discovery and job satisfaction encourage the people to think about entrepreneurship and starting their own businesses (Shapero & Sokol, 1982).

Psychological Factors

Personal characteristics of individuals are also determinants of several qualities of entrepreneurship (Shaver & Scott, 1991). A well-known theory, namely, trait theory, enlists personal traits as a need for achievement and the ability of entrepreneurs for taking risk. Furthermore, the locus of control is also considered as a vital characteristic of entrepreneurs. It determines the level of control that an individual has over life and event (Millet, 2005).

Methods

In this study the authors conducted a comprehensive study regarding various factors related to women entrepreneurship in Afghanistan. The first part explains the individual level followed by societal and institutional level elements for businesswomen in the country. For an in-depth analysis, 104 women entrepreneurs are considered for the interview. The data are collected from all zones of Afghanistan. These zones include Kabul the capital city, Herat, Balkh, Nangrahar, Qandahar, Bamayan, Khost, and others. The questionnaire is comprised of personal details, psychological and motivational factors, network influence, and family influence of women entrepreneurs. Analysis includes the descriptive statistics and statistical model, namely, confirmatory factor analysis. We used the Likert scale for measuring variables, 1 to 5 where it is from strongly disagree to strongly agree.

For achieving the objective, authors have developed a well-structured questionnaire from various sections. The questionnaires are thoroughly prepared and tested for accuracy and reliability. The questionnaire has various sections such as motivational and psychological factors. Every factor has three to four questions to measure the latent variable. Motivational and psychological factors are considered as latent variables which are measured through observed variable.

Descriptive Statistics

Types of businesses conducted by women entrepreneurs in Afghanistan are included but not limited to handicraft, online sales, jewelry, Afghani cloths, banking, restaurant, café, private schools, poultry products, tailor, export and import, tilers, and so on.

As Table 12.1 indicates, the majority of women entrepreneurs in this study are young women aged between 20 and 30 years. This category comprises 60% which are 62 women. The second category is aged between 31 and 40 years which includes 14 respondents. The third group is aged between 41 and 50 years which comprises 16 people. Only 12 women are aged 51–60 and none of them are above 60 years.

The marital status of respondents shows that the majority is single which includes 49 women and 47% of the total. This is followed by the married category (38%) and those engaged (9%). The number of widows is 9 women.

The frequency statistics of respondents show an absolute majority of Bachelors. 70 out of 104 women possess a Bachelor's degree and four a Master's degree. Four women were illiterate and 16 of them had only a basic preliminary education.

The family background of 52 women out of 104 were neither entrepreneur nor service provider. However, 33% of the interviewed women indicated that they have an entrepreneurial background.

According to the Table 12.2 the Cronbach's alpha is 0.85 which is well above 0.70 and shows the consistency of the responses and indicates the reliability of the

Table 12.1. Details of Respondent.

Variables	Frequency	Percentage
Age		
20–30	62	60
31–40	14	13
41–50	16	15
51–60	12	12
60+	0	0
Total	104	100
Marital Status		
Single	49	47
Married	40	38
Engaged	6	9
Widow	9	6
Total	104	100
Education		
Basic Preliminary Education	16	16
Baccalaureate 12 Grade	10	9
Bachelor's	70	67
Master's	4	4
Illiterate	4	4
Total	104	100
Family Background		
Entrepreneur	34	33
Service Sector	18	17
Other	52	50
Total	104	100

Source: Own data.

questionnaire. Additionally, the Kaiser–Meyer–Olkin (KMO) and Bartlette's tests are run to show the sample adequacy (Table 12.3). The value of sample adequacy test is 0.86 which is also above 0.7, and it is significant.

Fig. 12.2 illustrates the structural framework for psychological factors. The psychological factor is a latent variable. Need for achievement, propensity to risk, and locus of control are observed variables.

Fig. 12.3 indicates the motivational factor. Desire for achievement, desire for independence, desire for wealth, and self-discovery and job satisfaction are measured variables. Motivation is a latent or unobserved variable.

Table 12.2. Reliability Test.

Cronbach's Alpha	N of Items
0.850	7

Source: Own computation.

Table 12.3. KMO and Bartlett's Test.

Kaiser–Meyer–Olkin Measure of Sampling Adequacy.		0.860
Bartlett's test of Sphericity	Approx. Chi-Square	315.423
	Df	21
	Sig.	0.000

Source: Own computation.

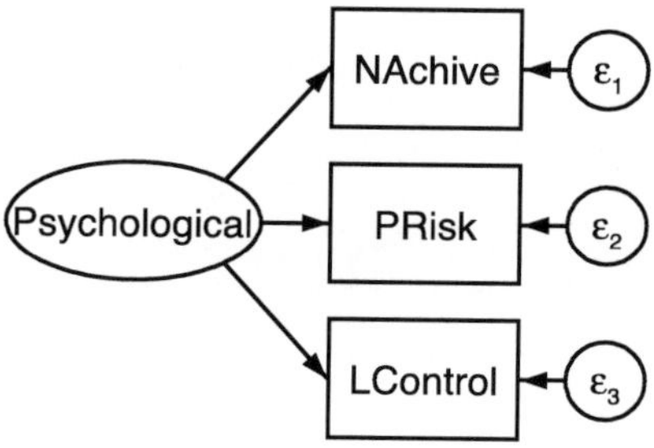

Fig. 12.2. Psychological Factors. *Source:* Own computation.

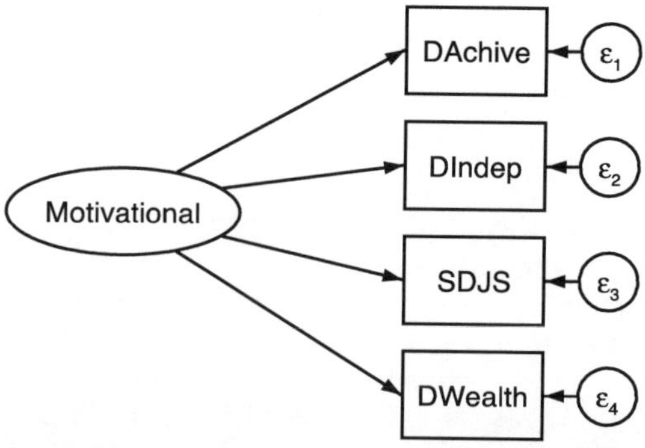

Fig. 12.3. Motivational Factors. *Source:* Own computation.

PART I: Individual Level

Description of Data and Variables

In order to make data convenient the authors have considered some modifications in the name of variables. There are four observed variables for motivational factors. Name of the variables and their descriptions are available in Table 12.4.

Table 12.5 shows the factor loadings of motivational factors. All factor loadings are above 0.5, therefore significant. The factor loading for desire for achievement is 0.8. Desire for independence has a value of 0.82. Desire for wealth indicates a value of 0.71. Finally, self-discovery and job satisfaction show 0.81 factor loadings. Therefore, the mentioned factors are confirmed to be the motivational factors for Afghan women entrepreneurs. Desire for independence has larger influence motivating women entrepreneurs in Afghanistan. This is due to the fact that economic and financial dependence in women results in several problems in families and society as a whole.

The fear of failure in Afghan women is considerably high since the support from institutions and society is inadequate. This also influences the risk-willingness negatively. Additionally, if there are opportunities, only a few people can avail the information.

Afghanistan is a male-dominated country, so the role of women in decision-making in the leadership is insignificant.

Table 12.6 indicates the factor loadings for psychological factors. In this case also all the measured or observed variables are significant and the loadings are well above the required level of 0.5. Only propensity to risk has just above 0.5 loadings and is still significant. This means that Afghan women have the psychological drives which lead them to start their own businesses. Among the factors, the locus of control is a strong psychological factor. Therefore, the Afghan

Table 12.4. Description of Variables.

Name of the Variables	**Description of Variables**
Motivational Factors:	
D-Achievement	Desire for achievement
D-Indep	Desire for independence
D-Wealth	Desire for wealth
SD-JS	Self-discovery and job satisfaction
Psychological Factors:	
N-Achive	Need for achievement
P-Risk	Propensity to risk
L-Control	Locus of control

Source: Authors.

Table 12.5. Factor Loadings for Motivation.

Structural equation model					Number of obs = 104	
Estimation method = ml						
Log likelihood = −434.73881						
(1) [Desire for achievement] Motivational = 1						
Standardized			OIM			
	Coef.	Std. Err.	z	P>|z|	[95% Conf. Interval]	
Measurement						
D-Achievement <-						
Motivational	0.8021648	0.0463017	17.32	0.000	0.7114152	0.8929145
_cons	5.24574	0.3767127	13.93	0.000	4.507397	5.984083
D-Indep <-						
Motivational	0.8240231	0.0433383	19.01	0.000	0.7390815	0.9089647
_cons	4.808658	0.3475408	13.84	0.000	4.127491	5.489826
D-Wealth <-						
Motivational	0.7109651	0.0575064	12.36	0.000	0.5982546	0.8236757
_cons	4.797396	0.3467917	13.83	0.000	4.117697	5.477096
SDSJ <-						
Motivational	0.8148134	0.044079	18.49	0.000	0.7284201	0.9012066
_cons	5.553624	0.3973635	13.98	0.000	4.774806	6.332442
var(e. D-Achievement)	0.3565316	0.0742832			0.2370012	0.5363465
var(e. D-Indep).	0.320986	0.0714236			0.2075308	0.496466
var(e. D-Wealth)	0.4945286	0.0817702			0.3576395	0.683813
var(e. SDSJ)	0.3360792	0.0718323			0.2210594	0.5109452
(Motivational)	1					
LR test of model versus saturated: chi2(2) = 2.21, Prob > chi2 = 0.3318						

Source: Own computati

Table 12.6. Factor Loadings for Psychology.

Structural equation model — Number of obs = 104
Estimation method = ml
Log likelihood = −394.84189
(1) [NAchievement]Psychological = 1

Standardized	Coef.	OIM Std. Err.	z	P>|z|	[95% Conf.	Interval]
Measurement						
NAchievement <-						
Psychological	0.6519536	0.0946147	6.89	0.000	0.4665123	0.8373949
_cons	4.268954	0.3118183	13.69	0.000	3.657802	4.880107
Propensity to Risk <-						
Psychological	0.5589255	0.0937518	5.96	0.000	0.3751754	0.7426756
_cons	3.629223	0.2700717	13.44	0.000	3.099892	4.158554
Locus of control <-						
Psychological	0.7554541	0.0975906	7.74	0.000	0.5641801	0.9467282
_cons	5.430373	0.3890877	13.96	0.000	4.667776	6.192971
var(e. Need for Achievement)	0.5749565	0.1233687			0.3775655	0.8755436
var(e. Propensity to Risk)	0.6876023	0.1048005			0.5100373	0.926985
var(e. Locus of control)	0.4292891	0.1474504			0.218969	0.8416219
var(L1)	1					

LR test of model versus saturated: chi2 (0) = 0.00, Prob > chi2 =.

Source: Own computation.

women entrepreneurs want to have control over their lives and events through having independent businesses. Another important psychological factor for the respondents is the need for achievement, where the Afghan women want to have achievements in their lives. The need for achievement is a psychological drive for women in Afghanistan to start their own businesses and experience success in their business field.

Table 12.7 explains the goodness of fit for the model applied in this study. Looking to root mean squared error of approximation (RMSEA) is significant. This is because the fit statistics value is 0.032 which makes it significant. Hence, the confirmatory factor analysis is the right model to use for this study.

In response to the question about the entrepreneur traits, 49% chose opportunity alertness. On the other hand, 40% opted for risk-willingness. Only 10% selected fear of failure. Therefore, the Afghan women entrepreneurs are having the characteristics of opportunity alertness. Additionally, they will take the calculated risk for the success of businesses (Table 12.8).

Table 12.7. Goodness of Fit.

Fit Statistic	Value	Description
Likelihood ratio		
chi2_ms(2)	2.207	Model versus saturated
p > chi2	0.332	
chi2_bs(6)	199.092	Baseline versus saturated
p > chi2	0.000	
Population error		
RMSEA	0.032	Root mean squared error of approximation
90% CI, lower bound	0.000	
Upper bound	0.200	
Pclose	0.422	Probability RMSEA <= 0.05
Information criteria		
AIC	893.478	Akaike's information criterion
BIC	925.210	Bayesian information criterion
Baseline comparison		
CFI	0.999	Comparative fit index
TLI	0.997	Tucker–Lewis index
Size of residuals		
SRMR	0.015	Standardized root mean squared residual
CD	0.874	Coefficient of determination

Source: Own computation.

Table 12.8. Entrepreneurial Traits.

Entrepreneurial Traits/Personality	Freq.	Percent	Cum.
Fear of failure	10	10	10
Opportunity alertness	51	49	59
Risk-willingness	43	41	100
Total	104	100.00	

Source: Own computation.

Fig. 12.4 is a photo of women entrepreneurs in a handcraft store. Handcraft has a deep root in the business culture of Afghanistan. It is formal and sometimes informal business for several people in Afghanistan. The main reason for the growth of this business is that it requires only basic machinery or equipment and is easy to learn. Additionally, the handcraft has reliable national and international demand.

PART II: Societal Level

Based on cultural factors Afghan society is highly male-dominated. Women are perceived as honorable and valuable in this culture. Being an honor of their family as well as of nation, it is perceived very vital to control and oversee the activities of women in the society where they are controlled by male members of their family or even relatives and society members. Most women are engaged in chores, agriculture, gardening, and other similar activities. Only 16% (NSIA, 2020) of women are employed in the formal economic sector.

Due to culture sensitivity and insecurity of women, it is very challenging for women to work outside their home or territory they feel safe. Women insecurity and lack of family support even further strengthens the challenges of women

Fig. 12.4. Women Working in Their Store. *Source:* Authors' work.

entrepreneurship in the country. Several family incidents which lead to conflict, fighting, and sometimes injuries are because of financial and economic dependency of female members on their families, where they are not even involved in decision-making.

In Islam, women have the right to receive their inheritance (a specific portion of their father's wealth after he dies). If the family is wealthy and a female member receives the inheritance, it can greatly help her to achieve financial independency and look for business opportunities. However, the prominent culture is that either women themselves or their brothers don't want to distribute wealth among all brothers and sisters. The brothers argue for married sisters that they have a husband and they are financially supported. On the other hand, some sisters simply don't want to get the portion of father's wealth as it is perceived negatively by society. In general, the culture is to perceive the family's shared wealth only belongs to male members. There are only an insignificant number of cases where both the male and female members distribute the inherited wealth.

Another social challenge for women is a limited access to education. Afghans are Muslims, and in Islam women have the right to education, freedom of choice, and business.[1] Nonetheless, in certain cases the culture overtakes the religion. Families argue that the required security and condition for women to go outside is not provided by government and hence, they prevent their female children from going to schools and universities. Statistics show only 30% of female adults (female ages 15 years and above) are literate. However, in the case of male adults it is above 55% and adult total literacy rate is 43% (World Bank, Literacy Rate of Afghanistan, 2018).

Fig. 12.5 illustrates the result of the question related to the business network. The results indicate that 54% of respondents strongly agreed that the business network has an influence on business performance among women entrepreneurs. Merely, 6% of respondents stated disagreement on the issue. Thus, the business network aids entrepreneurs to find new opportunities and develop partnerships and strategic alliances in the community with other businesses and intuitions. As a woman entrepreneur in a developing country, it is perceived vital to stay

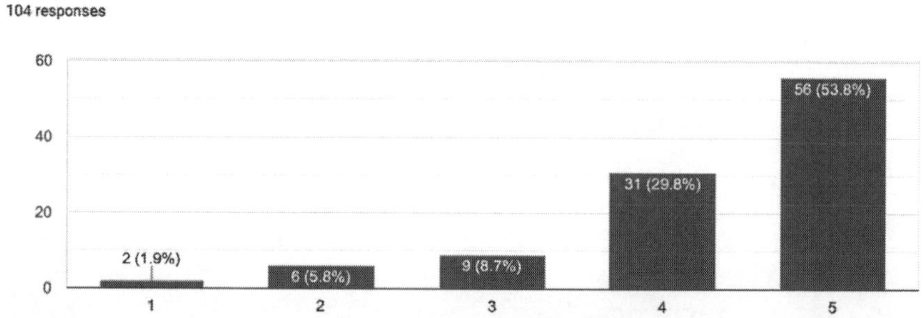

Fig. 12.5. Impact of Business Network on Performance. *Source:* Own computation.

connected with other peers and to utilize every opportunity for the success and sustainability of her business.

Fig. 12.6 is a photo showing a woman entrepreneur in her jewelry store. Afghans are traditionally connected with wearing and using jewellery. There are several precious stone mines in different areas of Afghanistan, especially in Badakhshan, Panjshir, and Nooristan provinces.

PART III: Institutional Level

Entrepreneurship has an important role in economic growth and development globally. Though entrepreneurship is typically thought of as a male-dominated activity, recently it is emphasized how important the contribution of women in today's developing countries is (Luisa De Vita, 2014). More importantly, men and women entrepreneurs face inherently different constraints involving institutional, psychological, and social factors.

In this section, it will be elaborated further how institutions play a significant role in the enhancement of women entrepreneurship. Additionally, we will explain the constraints women entrepreneurs face in developing countries like Afghanistan.

Institutions' Impact on Women Entrepreneurship in Developing Countries

Institutions built up through entrepreneurs adapt their activities and strategies molding them to fit the opportunities and limitations provided through the official and unofficial institutional framework (North, 1990).

Fig. 12.6. Women's Jewelry Store. *Source:* Authors' work.

Entrepreneurial activities could take productive, nonproductive, and even destructive forms, depending on the institutional context (Baumol, 1990).

The lack of a precise and well-organized system of recording, keeping, and trading of property rights may be the crucial problem that keeps entrepreneurs from applying and uniting potentially dynamic assets and turning them into the actual capital; this issue occurred mainly in developing nations (Mickiewicz, 2012).

In the last two decades, institutions have played a key role in women entrepreneurship in Afghanistan; before 2001, there was almost zero percent role of women entrepreneurship in the macroeconomics level. They didn't have permission to work outside of their homes. Girls were not allowed to go to schools and universities. The portion of women and men entrepreneurship was almost zero and almost all businesses, productions, and entrepreneurship were managed by men. Both national and global institutions in Afghanistan recognize that the empowerment of women is one of the big subjects of our time.

The people who care and think about the future of Afghanistan support women's empowerment as the base for economic growth, development, peace, and prosperity.

In the past 15 years' investment in women, the sector has been one of the top priorities of foreign assistance goals for the US Government, the European Union, and other international donors in Afghanistan. One of the key tasks of the USAID portfolio is to provide opportunities for women in Afghanistan. Health, education, agriculture, business, governance, economic growth, and other developmental programs have always addressed women and is still doing on.

Afghan women have made remarkable gains due to the partnership of the Afghan government with the US and other international communities:

- Since 2001 more than 3 million girls have been enrolled in primary and secondary schools.
- The life expectancy of women has been improved from the early 40s to 64 years.
- More Afghan women have access to the Basic Package of Health Services (BPHS).
- More than 62,000 women are enrolled in public universities (Promote, 2020).

In addition to international institutions in Afghanistan, public institutions also have been working in various fields to support women entrepreneurship and empowerment in Afghanistan. The Ministry of Rural Rehabilitation and Development (MRRD) has been playing a major role in women entrepreneurship and development in rural areas. The mentioned ministry has been providing opportunities for women in different aspects such as the Women Economic Empowerment Rural Development program (WEE-RDP). WEE-RDP is a program which assists and supports women to build on their economic security through participation in savings groups, the enterprise development, village-level savings groups (VSLAs), small and medium enterprises, and so on. The objective of the WEE-RDP is to increase the economic and social empowerment of poor rural women in designated communities of Afghanistan. The overall goal of WEE-RDP is to promote the economic empowerment of Afghan women through strong financially sustainable and self-managed community institutions, sustainable enterprises, enhanced income, and increasing access to finance and market. By the implementation of the mentioned program, the following results are achieved:

- Women from poor and extremely poor households have been mobilized into savings groups.
- Savings groups connected to both formal and informal financial institutions.
- The number of savings groups who have livelihood enterprises have been increased (MRRD, 2019).

Afghanistan women chamber of commerce and industry (AWCCI) was also established in 2002 to support women business and entrepreneurship in Afghanistan. The organization is working to represent, advance, and secure Afghan women's economic interests, domestically and globally. AWCCI is supplying services in the following fields: academic and policy-related research, sale support, investment support, advocacy and raising awareness, capacity building for both existing and aspiring Afghan businesswomen (AWCCI, 2020).

Finally, to conclude, women are crucial to the economic development of third world countries. In Afghanistan both national and international institutions have been working closely to support women entrepreneurship through policies such as greater access to educational opportunities, financial, and technical support. However, there are still cultural, social, and institutional challenges for Afghan women to be an entrepreneur and they are definitely influenced because of being women. The Government of Afghanistan needs to provide an environment for women entrepreneurs where they feel safe and undisturbed.

Concluding Thoughts

Results show several challenges in business for women entrepreneurs in Afghanistan. The challenges range from insecurity to lack of education, societal disturbance, and lack of structured government support. On an individual level, women entrepreneurs are ready to commence businesses if there is government and institutional support. There is considerable progress, especially in the last two decades, but there is still a long way to go and reach the level of other similar developing countries. The government should increase public awareness among women in order to inform them about their rights and the facilities they can use. Furthermore, especial measures, such as specific workplace and extra security personnel, are necessary to provide an environment for women entrepreneurs where they feel secure and undisturbed. Financial assistance and technical know-how are also important factors which need serious institutional attention.

Notes

1. Bibi Khadija, the Prophet Mohammad's wife, was a businesswoman. The Prophet Mohammad was her business representative before marriage.

References

AWCCI. (2020, August 28). From Afghanistan women chamber of commerce and industry. Retrieved from https://awcci.af/en/

Baum, J., Frese, M., & Baron, R. (2007). *The Psychology of entrepreneurship*. Mahwah, NJ: Lawrence Erlbaum Publishers.

Baumol, W. (1990). Entrepreneurship: Producitve, unproductive, and destrucitve. *Journal of Political Economy*, *98*(5), 893–921.

Cassar, G. (2007). Money, money, money? A longitudinal investigation of entrepreneur career reasons, growth preferences and achieved growth. *Entrepreneurship & Regional Development*, *19*(1), 89–107.

Collins, O., & Moore, D. (1970). *The organization makers: A behavioral study of independent entrepreneurs*. New York, NY: Appleton-Century-Crofts (Meredith Corporation).

Halim, D. (2020, March). Women entrepreneurs needed—stat! World Bank Blogs. Retrieved from https://blogs.worldbank.org/opendata/women-entrepreneurs-needed-stat. Accessed on August, 2020.

Luisa De Vita, M. M. (2014). Women entrepreneurs in and from developing countires: Evidences from the literature. *European Management Journal*, *33*(3), 451–460.

Mickiewicz, S. E. (2012). Shadow economy and entrepreneurial entry. *Review of Development Economics*, *16*(4), 559–578.

Millet, P. (2005). *Locus of control and its relation to working life: Studies from the fields of vocational rehabilitation and small firms in Sweden*. Doctoral Thesis, Luleå University of Technology Sweden.

MRRD. (2019, February 4). From Minsitry of Rural rehabilitaion and development. Retrieved from https://mrrd.gov.af

Nor, A., & Yufizada, M. (2004). Emographics and personal characteristics of urban Malaysian entrepreneurs: an ethnic comparison. Proceedings of the 3rd International Conference on SMEs in a Global Economy. Kuala Lumpur, Malaysia: University Technology Mara.

North, D. (1990). *Instituations, instititutional change and economic performance*. New York, NY: Cambrige University Press.

NSIA. (2020). *Afghanistan statistical yearbook* (Vol. 41). Kabul, Kabul, Afghanistan: National Statistics and Information Authority.

Promote. (2020, Aug). From USAID. Retrieved from https://www.usaid.gov/afghanistan/promote

Shapero, A., & Sokol, L. (1982). Social dimensions of entrepreneurship. In D. Sexton, C. Kent, & K.H. Vesper (Eds.), *The encyclopedia of entrepreneurship* (pp. 72–90). Englewood Cliffs, NJ: Prentice-Hall.

Shaver, K., & Scott, L. (1991). Person, process, choice: The psychology of new venture creation. *Entrepreneurship: Theory and Practice*, *16*(2), 23–45.

TrustLaw. (2011). *The world's five most dangerous countries for women*. TrustLaw Poll: Thomson Reuters Foundation.

Venkataraman, S. (1997). The distinctive domain of entrepreneurship research: An editor's perspective. In J. Katz & R. Brockhaus (Eds.), *Advances in entrepreneurship, firm emergence, and growth* (Vol. 3). Greenwich, CT: JAI Press.

World Bank. (2018). Literacy rate of Afghanistan. Retrieved from https://data.worldbank.org/indicator/SE.ADT.LITR.ZS?locations=AF. Accessed on August, 2020.

World Bank. (2020, April). Retrieved from https://www.worldbank.org/en/country/afghanistan/overview. Accessed on August, 2020.

Chapter 13

Cultural Challenges of Women Entrepreneurs in Iran

Meisam Modarresi and Zahra Arasti

Abstract

Despite the expansion of women's entrepreneurial activities and its positive effects on the economic development of societies, women still face numerous difficulties in starting and running a business compared to men, especially in developing countries because of gender discrimination in the field. The cultural context in societies is a significant factor affecting the status of entrepreneurship among the Iranian women. Therefore, the present research is an attempt to identify the challenges affecting entrepreneurship among Iranian women. The results obtained from 30 semi-structured interviews with women entrepreneurs and women with entrepreneurial roles showed that sociocultural challenges faced by women entrepreneurs are classified into: "the society's perception of entrepreneurship among women," "women's social security," and "common family norms governing a society."

Keywords: Context; cultural context; cultural factors; entrepreneurship among women; Iran

Introduction

Traditionally, the likelihood of starting up a business is more in men than women. In most countries, the level of entrepreneurial activity in men is more than women. However, encouraging the participation of women in entrepreneurial activities is a major political goal in numerous countries (GEM, 2020). Women's participation in entrepreneurial activities enhances the family income and plays a key role in society's economic development and social welfare (Sajjad, Kaleem, Chani, & Ahmed, 2020). According to the Global Entrepreneurship Monitor (GEM), the potential for starting a business for women entrepreneurs around the globe (Africa, Latin America, European countries with an efficiency-based economy and Asia-Pacific countries with factor-based and efficiency-based economies) is higher than

The Emerald Handbook of Women and Entrepreneurship in Developing Economies, 229–245
Copyright © 2021 by Emerald Publishing Limited
All rights of reproduction in any form reserved
doi:10.1108/978-1-80071-326-020211013

men (Kelley et al., 2015). The growth of women's businesses will lead to growth in employment. Despite effective incentive policies in most countries, the entrepreneurial activities of women entrepreneurs are less than men. According to a GEM report, in most countries men have a higher share of the nascent entrepreneurship rate compared to women. Only in the three countries of Qatar, Saudi Arabia, and Madagascar the nascent entrepreneurship rate is lower for women. Despite the significant development of women-owned businesses in the past two decades, the women entrepreneurs' status quo does not seem very favorable, while the established business ownership for Iranian women is 6.1%, for men it is 14.2% (GEM, 2020). Moreover, women's economic participation and unemployment rate is not favorable. Statistical Center of Iran reported in 2020 that men's economic participation rate is 67.9%, while it is 14.10 for women. The unemployment rate is 9% for men and 13.7% for women. The unemployment rate for male unemployed graduates is around 10% and for females, it is double the rate for men at approximately 20% (Statistical Center of Iran, 2020). Women's low economic participation and high unemployment rate prove that half the Iranian population with significant educational and training face countless difficulties for economic and entrepreneurial participation. Although women's participation rate has witnessed an increasing growth trend in recent years, the rate has always been under 17% in recent decades, which is significantly lower compared to the global average and even similar countries. This low level of participation has been mainly due to cultural barriers and challenges and to some extent legal barriers. In recent decades, the cultural context has mainly been a restrictive factor for women intending to participate in economic activities. Deep gender gaps continue to hold women back from men, increasing women's unemployment rate many times higher. As stated in previous studies, gender inequalities in Iranian society have roots in social and cultural aspects and reduce women's entrepreneurial capacity (Javaheri & Ghozati, 2004). In general, cultural and structural restrictions have a significant negative impact on Iranian women's business and investment activities (Gelard, 2007).

In general, financial sanctions have negatively affected businesses in Iran, including women entrepreneurs. However, sociocultural circumstances unique to Iran have made the situation more difficult. Cultural conditions of women have been a significant issue as confirmed in the literature on Iranian women entrepreneurs (Arasti, 2006; Arasti & Akbari Jokar, 2009; Arasti, Rezayee, Zarei, & Shariat Panahi, 2012; Gelard, 2007; Modarresi, Arasti, Talebi, & Farasatkhah, 2017; Saber, 2002). Therefore, studying the country's context seems necessary when analyzing the factors affecting women entrepreneurship. On the one hand, identifying the cultural challenges affecting entrepreneurship among women could help to better understand the issue to curb the negative cultural barriers. To this end, this research aims at identifying the cultural challenges affecting entrepreneurship among Iranian women living in a developing Islamic country.

Theoretical Backgrounds

Challenges Facing Women's Entrepreneurship

The literature on women entrepreneurship indicates that, compared to men, women are less involved in various forms of entrepreneurial activity (such as starting, owning/managing, financializing a business, etc.). They start a business mostly with limited capital, their business is small, and they are not willing to grow their businesses rapidly (Jennings & Brush, 2013). Small women-owned businesses are less successful than their male peers because they invest less and have less human capital (normally generated in previous entrepreneurial efforts) and less experience in family businesses. In addition, women have shorter working hours and different preferences for business-related goals (Fairlie & Robb, 2009).

Experimental studies show that small and medium-sized enterprises owned by women grow more slowly than those owned by men. While the difference may be partly due to the situation of women's small and medium-sized enterprises, which often operate in low-growth sectors, women still show less growth if the position factor is controlled (Nichter & Goldmark, 2009). In obtaining capital, women face numerous difficulties (Derera, Chitakunye, & O'Neill, 2014). Due to the cultural and socioeconomic contexts in which women work, and in terms of work experience and personal contexts, there is inequal access to diverse entrepreneurial forms of capital for women (Carter, Shaw, Wilson, & Lam, 2006). Because of these limitations, they participate in small ventures (Roomi, 2013) and want to stay small (Fleck, Hegarty, & Neergaard, 2011). They often lack the economic power and social structure and family support to grow their businesses (Brush, Carter, Gatewood, Greene, & Hart, 2004).

In addition, gender differences in social capital, which are themselves the result of dominating gender roles, affect both the decision to start and the decision to expand a business, as well as its survival and success (Elam & Brush, 2010). For example, poor links and lower resource levels in women's social networks negatively affect their business performance (Kim & Sherraden, 2014). Women also have lower entrepreneurial self-efficacy than men, which can be due to less entrepreneurial experience, less inclination to entrepreneurship, and a greater likelihood of receiving failure feedback (Dempsey & Jennings, 2014). Women have lower expectations of their businesses than men. They expect lower profits and fewer employees because they are less motivated to start a business and more inclined to achieve other business goals (Brush, 1992). Moreover, from the traditional view toward women's roles, balancing work and family can be one of the reasons for the low employment rate of women all around the world (Adam et al., 2017). However, this is especially important for women entrepreneurs, as they are responsible for the success of their businesses, on the one hand, and their capital and the capital of their employees on the other. For women entrepreneurs, business success means individual success in their family and career. This overshadows the negative impacts of work–family conflict, occupational and marital success, and life satisfaction of women entrepreneurs (Kim & Ling, 2001).

Different theories have been proposed on barriers to entrepreneurship among women and why they lag behind their male counterparts. The liberal feminist theory argues that gender discrimination limits women in their capabilities and growth. Social feminists contend that women's objectives and priorities differ based on their social values. This is a barrier to the growth's perspective among women. The institutional theory focuses on the boundaries set on entrepreneurship among women through law, policies, institutions, norms, and culture and argues that entrepreneurship among women is affected by the status quo of formal and informal institutions governing a society (Welter, Brush, & De Bruin, 2014). Adopting an institutional approach, this research investigates the effect of culture, as an informal institution, on entrepreneurship.

The Effect of the Cultural Context on Entrepreneurship among Women

Context is a key factor affecting business growth among women (Brush, Carter, Gatewood, Greene, & Hart, 2006, pp. 3–22). It includes circumstances, situations, or environments existing outside a phenomenon and either reinforcing or limiting it (Welter, 2011). Emphasizing the importance of an entrepreneurial context in the literature, De Bruin, Brush, and Welter (2007) note that the literature has a gap on entrepreneurship among women in the context of different countries. The role played by social values and cultural traditions in growth in women's businesses remains to be studied (Roomi, 2013). Perhaps the most important environmental factors affecting entrepreneurial activities among women are cultural norms or informal institutions governing a society. The reason is that those norms define sex roles in a society and dictate masculine or feminine behaviors (Ahl, 2006) and, thus, affect desirability of entrepreneurship for women, its nature, and dimensions. Regardless of how developed a country is, it has been argued that the more the norms of a society support women, the more involved the women will be in their entrepreneurial activities (Baughn, Chua, & Neupert, 2006). Women are in an unequal situation in acquiring business resources compared to men. The cultural context in which a woman is active plays a key role here (Carter et al., 2006). In fact, patriarchal societies and male-dominated labor markets hinder women's ambitions in an entrepreneurial environment (Karatas-Ozkan, Inal, & Ozbilgin, 2010). For example, women in Islamic societies are often more discriminated against than men. Because of sociocultural and religious issues women are generally dominated by men (Roomi & Harrison, 2008). Moreover, the role of gender stereotypes as a part of culture on women's entrepreneurship is highly important. These stereotypes ruin the success of many women-owned businesses and because of these stereotypes many women entrepreneurs feel uncertain to enter unknown sectors and larger businesses with greater interest (Adom & Anambane, 2019).

Overall, the cultural context has a significant impact on women's participation in entrepreneurial activities (Aldrich, Reese, & Dubini, 1989). The reason is, it can affect how women are welcome in economic activities and, thus, empower them to start and run a business successfully. In fact, culture can both create opportunities and limitations. For example, women's entrepreneurship participation rate in Western countries with less cultural barriers is significantly higher than in countries (such as the Middle Eastern countries) with limiting cultures. Women living in developing countries face traditions and sociocultural issues, aggravating their self-esteem, negatively affecting their decisions to start and finance a business and banks to fund their projects (Nilufer, 2001).

Women Entrepreneurship Status Quo in Iran

Half the Iranian population is comprised of women. However, their economic participation and employment rate is not favorable. Statistical Center of Iran reported in 2020 that men's economic participation rate is 67.9%, while it is 14.10 for women. Employment rate for men is 9%, meanwhile, for women it is 13.7 (Statistical Center of Iran, 2020). According to a World Economic Forum report (2020), Iran is among the countries with a high gender gap in the economic dimension. With respect to gender gap, Iran ranked 148 out of 153 countries in 2020, weakened by 6 steps compared to its 2018 ranking (among 149 countries). Among the Middle Eastern and North African countries, Iran ranks below the 10 top countries in terms of gender equality. According to the World Economic Forum, Iran is ranked 16th before Syria, Iraq, and Yemen (WEF, 2020). On the other hand, the overall level of entrepreneurial activity in Iran has declined in recent years, and the rate of start-up entrepreneurship, which was relatively high at the beginning of the last decade, has recently declined. In the National Entrepreneurship Context Index (NECI), Iran ranks lowest among 54 countries, while the appropriate environmental conditions for entrepreneurial activities can facilitate business growth and move start-ups to established businesses (GEM, 2020). Consequently, the mentioned conditions have affected the level of women's entrepreneurial activities more than men. The established entrepreneurship rate in Iran is 6.1% for women and 14.2% for men (GEM, 2020). Iranian women play an ever-growing and key role in businesses. In recent years, the role played by women in private and public businesses has witnessed a growing trend. However, like in other developing countries, the Iranian women's employment condition is not favorable and cultural barriers are one of the most important barriers to women's entrepreneurship in Iran. In fact, cultural barriers are more important to women entrepreneurs than any other challenge, and the common cultural values and beliefs in society have a direct impact on this issue. Due to their gender-driven perspective, the prevailing authoritarian culture has always promoted traditional beliefs and gender stereotypes in the field of women's entrepreneurship and has led to less social and job opportunities for women regardless of their qualifications. Currently, the dominant approach is to prefer working with men. Employers consider men to bring home the bacon, and if they are to make a choice between a male and a female with similar qualifications, they choose the male. In addition, some employers still believe that women do not possess the power and skill to work. All these problems together have led women to start to enter entrepreneurship and self-employed jobs. Meanwhile, according to the GEM, entrepreneurship among women is not favorable at all (2020).

The main reason for this is the sociocultural structures in Iran that do not encourage entrepreneurial activities among Iranian women. Numerous negative beliefs and values are therefore related to employment and entrepreneurship among women, including a woman's employment not being justified if her family is wealthy, belief in weakening the male authority and reducing female dependence in case of female employment, the common belief in society that housekeeping is a woman's first duty, not accepting women in some professions and occupations, not accepting women in a masculine workplace, not taking women seriously as managers, lack of public belief in women's abilities at management levels, and social insecurity for women (Arasti, 2006). These beliefs are reinforced in families through over-dependence of girls on their mothers, discrimination in letting girls live alone, and giving more freedom to boys compared to girls. In the educational system, this is intensified through gender inequalities such as demarcation between the sexes and gender segregation favoring male superiority in educational resources. Overall, this leads to the inappropriate formation of women's gender identity, which affects women's psychological and personality structure and the way women look and behave entrepreneurially (Javaheri & Ghozati, 2004).

With unique cultural parameters particularly for women, the Iranian context can affect women-owned businesses in different ways. For example, Iranian women entrepreneurs are highly conservative. According to a study, nearly 88% of graduate women entrepreneurs have chosen a nongrowth strategy deliberately, although some have run businesses with an acceptable growth (Arasti & Akbari Jokar, 2009). However, Arasti's research (2006) showed that after passing the early stages of starting up their business and showing an acceptable performance, some women have succeeded to change their families' viewpoint toward their entrepreneurial activities and get their satisfaction and support.

Having roots in family structure, educational system, role expectation mismatch, cliché roles imposed from community and relations ruling organizations, gender inequalities are among the restrictive cultural factors affecting entrepreneurship among Iranian women (Javaheri & Ghozati, 2004).

Research Method

The current research aims at identifying the cultural challenges of entrepreneurship among the women in Iran, a developing country with a unique cultural context. Conducted using qualitative research and the deep-interview technique, this study allows the researcher to attain a better understanding of the underlying logic behind women entrepreneurship and to yield and contextualize its findings (Zahra, 2011). The research participants included two groups of women: Women entrepreneurs with years of experience in launching and managing a business, and women with management roles associated with women entrepreneurship in public sector organizations. This way, this research draws on both women entrepreneurs' personal experience of challenges on the way to business success and on the perspective of women with management roles associated with women entrepreneurship in public organizations. Purposeful sampling based on information richness helps improve the internal validity of a qualitative research (Rao & Perry, 2003). Therefore, a list of women entrepreneurs was obtained from the public organizations and people with more experience, who were able to provide the research with valuable information, were selected from the list. A list was obtained from women with entrepreneurship roles in departments affiliated with the Ministry of Cooperatives, Labor, and Social Welfare. Snowball sampling was used to filter and select women in this group for the interview. From the selected population, the researcher started the interview with participants who gave consent for the interview. The interview was carried out with open-ended and semi-structured items, and the interviewees were asked about sociocultural challenges they face to succeed on the way to entrepreneurship in Iran. The interview was conducted until the analysis process reached theoretical saturation. Overall, 30 interviews were carried out. To analyze findings, the researcher used the thematic analysis method (Miles & Huberman, 1994). Data were simultaneously collected with data analysis. Each interview was compared to previous interviews. After paraphrasing each interview through a back-and-forth method between the data and literature (Strauss & Corbin, 1998), the researcher open-coded the interviews. In the next step, in axial coding or the second-level coding, similar levels were merged in bigger classes drawing upon the semantic relationship between the classes. Three classes of sociocultural challenges with 10 subclasses faced by women entrepreneurs were identified.

Results

After classifying the similar codes, secondary themes and then axial coding, sociocultural challenges faced by women entrepreneurs were categorized into: "the society's perception of women's entrepreneurial activities," "women's social security," and "common family norms in society."

The Society's Perception of Women's Entrepreneurial Activities

A society's perception of women's entrepreneurial activities is a key issue, having roots in cultural values and norms of that society. For example, a masculine culture might reduce the possibility of accepting women as entrepreneurs (Barrett, 2006). Unfortunately, there are various negative beliefs and norms related to women entrepreneurship in Iran that place women in an unequal occupational position regarding men and that affect their business success rate. This study categorized and examined society's perception of women's entrepreneurial activities as three secondary themes: the acceptance of women's business activities, being taken seriously in masculine business environments, and the nature of men's occupational interactions with women.

The Acceptability of Women's Business Activities

Social acceptance in women entrepreneurship and female-owned businesses has a key role to play in improving women's business (Jiang, Zimmerman, & Guo, 2012). Not having a positive perspective toward women in open markets is among the sociocultural limitations to women entrepreneurs (Jamshidi, Jamini, & Nazari, 2014). However, according to the women entrepreneurs interviewed in this study (especially those with more experience in the market), the perspective of Iranian men with respect to women's business activities has witnessed a rising trend and, currently, the entrepreneurial activities of Iranian women is reasonably acceptable.

As Gelard (2007) predicted, the changes in the traits of Iranian women, their education level, experiences, and skills have to some extent changed the society's perspective toward their capabilities. This, in turn, has minimized cultural limitations faced by women entering the realm of entrepreneurship.

Being Taken Seriously in Masculine Business Environments

Not being taken seriously in masculine environments is considered a significant challenge to business growth (Jamali, 2009; Mordi, Simpson, Singh, & Okafor, 2010). Women in this study face the same problem to some extent. Some witnessed negligence by men active in the market and believe that the market atmosphere does not count so much on women. Another problem faced by women entrepreneurs is not being trusted by men; some men even avoid trading with women. Overall, not believing in women's business capabilities and entrepreneurial activities is a cultural limitation to women entrepreneurs. This causes men not taking them seriously which, in turn, affects women's professional performance negatively through bringing about a discriminative atmosphere against women.

Men' Manipulative Behaviors with Women in Business Interactions

In many societies, women suffer the consequences of gender discrimination (Cliff, 1998). In societies with Islamic background, the discrimination is greater (Dzisi, 2008; Roomi & Harrison, 2008). Negative beliefs and old clichés are stronger in Iran than some other nations, to the extent that the business world has become a masculine world. According to women entrepreneurs in the study group, being a woman alone results in men allowing themselves to be manipulative and deceiving. A high number of women interviewed in the study complained about a masculine business atmosphere in Iran. They believe that negative clichés about women at work, particularly in a male-dominated environment, have led men to allow themselves to treat women unequally, to manipulate women, and to swindle them.

Women's Social Security

Social insecurity for women is an old common cliché in Iran (Arasti, 2006) and is often experienced at work. Recent inflation and higher living expenses have led women to cooperate in the economic activities of the family and have an active presence in society. However, it has come with consequences such as women's insecurity, particularly at work. Concerns about sexual harassment at work, feeling of being in ever-present danger, and the like are all issues playing a role in women's social insecurity (Ahmadi & Kaldi, 2012). This has affected women's entrepreneurial activities. In fact, women's social insecurity at market and in society is considered as a limitation for the Iranian women entrepreneurs. To procure equipment and material, do marketing and sales, promote business, and/or boost production, women entrepreneurs must be present at public and sometimes masculine places, making them prone to social insecurity. This research considers women's social security as three secondary themes: the necessity of not working alone in a masculine workplace, limitations related to women's social security, and sexual harassment. These are discussed below.

The Necessity of Not Working Alone in a Masculine Workplace

In many Islamic countries it is not that common for a woman to be present in a male-dominated atmosphere. Often a male family member accompanies them in such environments (Erogul & McCrohan, 2008). Such is the case in Iran, too; this is the result of social insecurity, posing limitations on women. For example, to attend an exhibition, if a male family member cannot accompany them, they are unable to attend. Some women, however, have made peace with the situation and believe that due to the current social insecurities, it is necessary for them to go to male-dominated workplaces with a male family member. In some cases, shops are male-dominated and are visited mostly by men. Therefore, a male family member is inevitable to accompany them to that place.

Limitations Related to Women's Social Security

Common in all countries and stronger in countries with a more traditional perspective toward genders are social limitations for women. These include, but are not limited to, late-night commutes, the first and last stops in public transportation routes, using city center parking spaces at night, particularly vertical parking, driving at night, open spaces, suburbs, underpasses, and dead ends (Bell, 1998). Iranian women should follow the traditional dress codes, arrival time, duration of staying out, and control their behavior in public places or they would be harassed or presumed guilty, deserving to receive such harassments. These restrictions are, therefore, totally binding and must be observed by Iranian women. A significant example of these is the restriction to choose a business workshop. Most women and their families prefer workshops to be located at a crowded place close to the city center. Meanwhile, this reduces their chances and stops them from more spatial and social mobility. Yet another limitation for the women in this study, set by their families, was the time they had to get back home. This is a common limitation for the Iranian women. It is worth mentioning that fear and safety and security at night is a crucial issue reducing women's late-night presence compared to men. Among other limitations mentioned by the women are commuting between cities at different hours of the day. While the above limitations improve the Iranian women entrepreneurs' social security to a great extent, they affect women's entrepreneurial activities negatively.

Sexual Harassment

An issue less dealt with by academia is sexual harassment at work and in social contexts. Sexual harassment could include a wide range of behaviors, from sexual comments about a person's clothing, anatomy, or looks and voyeurism to attempted rape and forcing someone into a sexual relationship. Unfortunately, this is prevalent in Iran; in defense against sexual harassment, most women take refuge in silence, toleration, and leaving the place. These, in most cases, do not stop sexual harassment and leave women with more problems (Sadeghi Fasaei & Rajab Larijani, 2011). Having an active presence in social contexts to accomplish occupational activities, women entrepreneurs are no exception. Mordi et al. (2010) name sexual harassment as a cultural limitation for entrepreneurship among Nigerian women. Most women in the current study complained about harassment and experienced problems such as staring, verbal conducts of sexual nature, and often getting sexual requests from men for doing a business procedure.

Common Family Norms in Society

While the current family norms in Iran are meant to protect women's privacy, they affect women more than men and impose limitations on them. According to the World Bank (2014), married women face more limitations compared to men. These include taking the responsibility of a family, choosing where to live, applying for a passport, choosing a job, going out of home, and traveling abroad. In addition to cultural norms related to acceptance of women entrepreneurship and their social security, some themes extracted from the interviews in this study were related to family and interfamily issues affecting entrepreneurship among women. Therefore, the researcher labeled them as "Common family norms in society." Common family norms include four secondary themes: the presumption that providing for the family is of masculine nature; men's sensitivity; women's work at home; husbands' consent for working outside.

The Presumption That Providing for the Family Is of Masculine Nature

As a social norm in Iran as a semitraditional society, men are responsible for providing for the family. Therefore, self-employed women might get humiliated. Sometimes these common social norms might cause women to be prohibited from working by their spouses (Jamshidi et al., 2014). This holds mostly true for women whose husbands believe that manhood is compromised if his wife works outside (Arasti, 2006). In some societies, the financial independence of single women is a violation of women's modesty and they face problems with their parents who are worried about their daughters' future (marriage prediction) (Mordi et al., 2010). However, the results of the present study show that despite the prevalence of the stereotype of family livelihood by men, this issue not only does not cause opposition and disrupt the business process of women, but most women have the support of their family in business.

Men's Sensitivity

A significant issue negatively affecting the business growth of female-owned businesses in Islamic countries is being allowed to go out and meet other men freely (Roomi,

2013). Another widespread norm related to family life is men's sensitivity to how women in the family interact with other men. This is believed to be out of sympathy to ensure their security. It is, however, a barrier to a woman's business growth. The sensitivity and rigidity have diminished in recent years due to the normalization of women's participation in economic and social activities and the role of women's income in helping the family economy, and in the present study, very few women mentioned this issue.

Women's Responsibility at Home

The old cliché about a woman's place being in the home and not doing entrepreneurial activities causes women to receive less social support (Jamali, 2009). In Iran, heavy family responsibilities as a sociocultural limitation is a limiting factor for Iranian women entrepreneurs (Jamshidi et al., 2014). Like many other communities, women shoulder the family responsibilities and men seldom cooperate with women in activities like cooking, cleaning, or looking after the children. Some of the women believed that housework is a barrier to business growth. These various roles and responsibilities bring about concerns and stress and limit the time required for managing a business. Heavy responsibilities on women also create a conflict between roles at home and at work.

The Necessity to Get Husband's Consent to Work

The Iranian cultural norms expect women to get permission from their husbands before making decisions or taking important actions. These are believed to help women be aligned with their spouses in doing their responsibilities and use their experience, opinion, and support. However, when couples do not share the same priorities, this could be a barrier (Javaheri & Ghozati, 2004). The abovementioned issue is followed by Iranian families as a cultural norm. However, it is also backed by the law: according to the Article 1117 of the civil law of the Islamic Republic of Iran, a man has the right to oppose his wife's employment, and without his consent, a woman is banned from work.

Conclusion

Today, women play an increasingly significant role in the economic development of societies. In the Middle Eastern countries, policy-makers are focusing on this issue more than ever (Basaffar, Niehm, & Bosselman, 2018). While the Persian Gulf states face various sociocultural barriers, women-owned businesses in recent years, particularly in the GCC countries, have experienced a significant growth. The reason is that these businesses are supported both by international institutions and both by technical training and commercial tools (Mathew, 2019). In Iran, the growth of women's entrepreneurial activities in recent decades has been significant (Modarresi et al., 2017) and compared to neighboring countries in the Persian Gulf, has experienced a significant decline. For example, the nascent entrepreneurship rate is the same for women in Qatar and Saudi Arabia.

However, for the Iranian women it is %8 compared to men which is %13 (GEM, 2020). A key factor affecting women's activities is cultural context of the Iranian society which is a big barrier to entrepreneurship among women. Therefore, the present research is an attempt at identifying this cultural context and the cultural challenges for entrepreneurship among the Iranian women. The results show that a wide range of cultural issues negatively affect women-owned businesses, the most significant of which are the norms governing a society that affect women's presence in entrepreneurship activities. Norms that are basically barriers to entrepreneurship activities among women even emerge as mistreating women in masculine environments. Even social insecurity for women, regardless of its importance to women's entrepreneurial activity, is a social stereotype (Arasti, 2006) and thus, has a double effect on their activity because it is accepted by society and inevitably has imposed limitations on women. Some of the factors that disrupt women's entrepreneurial activity have roots in common cultural norms in families. For example, the presumption that providing for the family is of masculine nature, women's responsibility at home, and sensitivity to controlling women. It seems that the idea that women are responsible for housework and childcare is a universal phenomenon, and that married women are still responsible for everything at home, despite business and income generation. Of course, the level of family support varies in different cultural contexts. This has been studied in developing countries such as Sri Lanka, and the important point has been the lack of cooperation and interaction of Sri Lankan men (Kailasapathy & Metz, 2012). However, this is the case even in the developed countries of Nordic Europe, and although men and women play an equal role in income generation, the burden of household responsibilities rests with women (Hagqvist, Gadin, & Nordenmark, 2016). Women are in a similar situation in the Middle East. Research by Itani, Sidani, and Baalbaki (2011) showed that women, as the primary caregivers of children, are pressured to fulfill their "feminine" responsibilities and, as such, are a "good" housewife in the life of patriarchal ideals. Women can work in the UAE, but leave work if their jobs interfere with their traditional roles at home (Itani et al., 2011). In Lebanon, balancing business and family life as well as negative social attitudes are among the most important obstacles for women entrepreneurs, and Lebanese women entrepreneurs face the challenge of opposing their families (Jamali, 2009). What is remarkable about the Islamic countries in the Middle East is the significant progress made by Qatar and Saudi Arabia in the field of women entrepreneurship. In recent years, the Saudi government has seen women entrepreneurship as a way to strengthen the family and the economy, and has developed programs to encourage more women to start businesses (Basaffar et al., 2018). Even though women make up half of Iran's population, economic and development programs in the country have not been given enough attention to the issue of women's entrepreneurship, and it has not been considered by policymakers in Iran as an independent and important sector. Therefore, it seems significant for improvement of women entrepreneurship indicators in Saudi Arabia and Qatar compared to Iran, in adopting specific support policies for women entrepreneurs and practical and applied measures in this field. Giving more freedom to women can be one of the reasons for the significant improvement of the nascent entrepreneurship rate. These include allowing women to travel without the permission of male relatives, to start their own businesses and using e-government services without having to prove their husbands' consent, and ensuring equal treatment of women in the environment; in Qatar, the joint initiative of the Qatar Non-Profit Institute and the University of Qatar to bridge the gender gap in the country to support the involvement of Qatari women in entrepreneurial activities is one of the most effective measures in this field (GEM, 2020). This comparison shows the importance of the role played by formal institutions and their potential effect on formal institutions and cultural norms dominating a society, as Islamic countries in the Middle East share culture as regards women. However, passive policy-making regarding women's economic activities and adopting plans supporting women in some countries, such as Iran, has led to decline in entrepreneurial activities among women. The seriousness and efforts of government programs to encourage women in entrepreneurial activities by reducing gender discrimination and neutralizing the norms of women's economic inactivity have led to the growth of women's entrepreneurship in countries such as Qatar and Saudi Arabia. Therefore, through adopting a special supportive approach for women, governments should make every effort to reduce the negative effects of male-centered cultural norms and to promote the growth of women's businesses. In this way, governments can gradually strengthen a culture favoring the presence, empowerment, and serious participation of women in entrepreneurial activities. Given the role played by the interaction of formal and informal institutions on women's entrepreneurship performance, it is worthwhile for future research to address the issue of the impact of formal institutions affecting women entrepreneurship in Iran.

References

Adom, K., & Anambane, G. (2019). Understanding the role of culture and gender stereotypes in women entrepreneurship through the lens of the stereotype threat theory. *Journal of Entrepreneurship in Emerging Economies*, *12*(1), 100–124.

Adom, K., Asare-Yeboa, I. T., & Quaye, D. M. (2017). A critical assessment of work and family life of female entrepreneurs in Sub-Saharan Africa. *Journal of Small Business and Enterprise Development*, *25*(3), 405–427.

Ahl, H. (2006). Why research on women entrepreneurs needs new directions. *Entrepreneurship: Theory and Practice*, *30*(5), 595–623.

Ahmadi, M., & Kaldi, A. (2012). Study of the feeling of social security of women in Sanandaj city and social factors affecting on it. *Quarterly Journal of Women and Society*, *3*(12), 1–20. (in Persian).

Aldrich, H., Reese, P. R., & Dubini, P. (1989). Women on the verge of a breakthrough: Networking among entrepreneurs in the United States and Italy. *Entrepreneurship & Regional Development*, *1*(4), 339–356.

Arasti, A. (2006). Iranian women entrepreneurs; socio-cultural factors in starting business. *Women Studies*, *4*(1–2), 93–119. (in Persian).

Arasti, Z., & Akbari Jokar, M. R. (2009). The research on the characteristics of Iranian educated women's business and their problems in start-up process. *Daneshvar, Special Issue on Management*, *15*(32), 37–46. (11) (in Persian).

Arasti, Z., Rezayee, S. O., Zarei, B., & Shariat Panahi, S. (2012). A qualitative study on environmental factors affecting Iranian women entrepreneurs' growth orientation. *Journal of Management and Strategy*, *3*(2), 39.

Barrett, M. (2006). Women's entrepreneurship in Australia: Present and their future. In C. G. Brush, N. M. Carter, E. J. Gatewood, P. G. Greene, & M. M. Hart (Eds.), *Growth oriented women entrepreneurs and their businesses: A global research perspective* (pp. 23–52). Cheltenham: Edward Elgar.

Basaffar, A. A., Niehm, L. S. & Bosselman, R. (2018). Saudi Arabian women in entrepreneurship: Challenges, opportunities and potential. *Journal of Developmental Entrepreneurship*, *23*(2), 1–20.

Baughn, C. C., Chua, B. L., & Neupert, K. E. (2006). The normative context for women's participation in entrepreneurship: A multicountry study. *Entrepreneurship Theory and Practice*, *30*(5), 687–708.

Bell, W. (1998). *Women and community safety* (Vol. 32, pp. 1–26). South Australia: Bell Planning Associates.

Brush, C. G. (1992). Research on women business owners; past trends, a new perspective and future directions. *Entrepreneurship Theory and Practice*, *16*(4), 5–30.

Brush, C. G., Carter, N. M., Gatewood, E. J., Greene, P. G., & Hart, M. M. (2004). *Clearing the hurdles: Women building high growth businesses*. Englewood, NJ: Prentice Hall.

Brush, C. G., Carter, N. M., Gatewood, E. J., Greene, P. G., & Hart, M. M. (2006). Introduction: The Diana project international. In *Growth-oriented women entrepreneurs and their businesses: A global research perspective* (pp. 3–22). Cheltenham: Edward Elgar.

Carter, S., Shaw, E., Wilson, F., & Lam, W. (2006). Gender, entrepreneurship and business finance: Investigating the relationship between banks and entrepreneurs in the UK. In C. G. Brush, N. M. Carter, E. J. Gatewood, P. G. Greene, & M. M. Hart (Eds.), *Growth oriented women entrepreneurs and their businesses: A global research perspective* (pp. 373–392). Cheltenham: Edward Elgar.

Cliff, J. E. (1998). Does one size fit all? Exploring the relationship between attitudes towards growth, gender, and business size. *Journal of Business Venturing*, *13*(6), 523–542.

De Bruin, A., Brush, C. G., & Welter, F. (2007). Advancing a framework for coherent research on women's entrepreneurship. *Entrepreneurship: Theory and Practice*, *31*(3), 323–339.

Dempsey, D., & Jennings, J. (2014). Gender and entrepreneurial self-efficacy: A learning perspective. *International Journal of Gender and Entrepreneurship*, *6*(1), 28–49.

Derera, E., Chitakunye, P., & O'Neill, C. (2014). The impact of gender on start-up capital: A case of women entrepreneurs in South Africa. *The Journal of Entrepreneurship*, *23*(1), 95–114.

Dzisi, S. (2008). Entrepreneurial activities of indigenous African women: A case of Ghana. *Journal of Enterprising Communities: People and Places in the Global Economy*, *2*(3), 254–264.

Elam, A., & Brush, C. G. (2010). Women, entrepreneurship and social capital: A dialogue and construction. *Organization Studies*, *31*(2), 245–249.

Erogul, M. S., & McCrohan, D. (2008). Preliminary investigation of Emirati women entrepreneurs in the UAE. *African Journal of Business Management*, *2*(10), 177–185.

Fairlie, R. W., & Robb, A. M. (2009). Gender differences in business performance: Evidence from the characteristics of business owners survey. *Small Business Economics*, *33*(4), 375–395.

Fleck, E., Hegarty, C., & Neergaard, H. (2011). The politics of gendered growth. *International Journal of Gender and Entrepreneurship*, *3*(2), 164–173.

Gelard, P. (2007). Productivity Iranian women entrepreneurs. *Journal of Commerce*, *12*(46), 179–209. (in Persian).

GEM. (2020). GEM 2019/2020 global report. Retrieved from https://www.gem consortium.org/

Hagqvist, E., Gadin, G. K., & Nordenmark, M. (2016). Work – family conflict and well-being across Europe: The role of gender context. *Social Indicator Research*. doi:10.1007/s11205-016-1301-x

Itani, H., Sidani, Y. M., & Baalbaki, I. (2011). United Arab Emirates female entrepreneurs: Motivations and frustrations. *Equality, Diversity and Inclusion: An International Journal*, *30*(5), 409–424.

Jamali, D. (2009). Constraints and opportunities facing women entrepreneurs in developing countries: A relational perspective. *Gender in Management: An International Journal*, *24*(4), 232–251.

Jamshidi, A., Jamini, D., & Nazari, H. (2014). Studying driving forces and hampering factors affecting development of rural women's entrepreneurship in Miankoh district, Ardal township. *Quarterly Journal of Women and Society*, *5*(17), 75–94. (in Persian).

Javaheri, F., & Ghozati, S. (2004). Women entrepreneurship barriers: The effect of gender discriminations on women entrepreneurs. *Iran Sociology Journal*, *18*(2), 161–178. (in Persian).

Jennings, J. A., & Brush, C. G. (2013). Research on women entrepreneurs: Challenges to (and from) the broader entrepreneurship literature? *The Academy of Management Annals*, *7*(1), 661–713.

Jiang, C., Zimmerman, M. A., & Guo, c. (2012). Growth of women-owned businesses: The effects of intangible resources and social competence. *Journal of Business Diversity*, *12*(1), 47–71.

Kailasapathy, P., & Metz, I. (2012). Work-family conflict in Sri Lanka: Negotiations of exchange relationships in family and at work. *Journal of Social Issues*, *68*(4), 790–813.

Karatas-Ozkan, M., Inal, G., & Ozbilgin, M. (2010). Turkey. In S. Fielden, & M. Davidson (Eds.), *International handbook of successful women entrepreneurs* (pp. 175–188). Cheltenham and New York, NY: Edward Elgar Press.

Kelley, D. J., Brush, C. G., Greene, P. G., Herrington, M., Ali, A., & Kew, P. (2015). Special report women's entrepreneurship. Global Entrepreneurship Monitor. Retrieved from https://www.gemconsortium.org/

Kim, J., & Ling, C. (2001). Work-family conflict of women entrepreneurs in Singapore. *Women in Management Review*, *16*(5), 204–221.

Kim, S. M., & Sherraden, M. (2014). The impact of gender and social networks on microenterprise business performance. *Journal of Sociology & Social Welfare*, *41*(3), 49–69.

Mathew, V. (2019). Women entrepreneurship in Gulf region: Challenges and strategies in GCC. *International Journal of Asian Business and Information Management (IJABIM), IGI Global, 10*(1), 94–108.

Miles, M. B., & Huberman, A. M. (1994). *Qualitative data analysis: An expanded sourcebook* (2nd ed.). Thousand Oaks, CA: SAGE Publications.

Modarresi, M., Arasti, Z., Talebi, K., & Farasatkhah, M. (2017). Growth barriers of women-owned home-based businesses in Iran: An exploratory study. *Gender in Management, 32*(4), 244–267.

Mordi, C., Simpson, R., Singh, S., & Okafor, C. (2010). The role of cultural values in understanding the challenges faced by female entrepreneurs in Nigeria. *Gender in Management: An International Journal, 25*(1), 5–21.

Nichter, S., & Goldmark, L. (2009). Small firm growth in developing countries. *World Development, 37*(9), 1453–1464.

Nilufer, A. (2001). *Jobs, gender and small enterprises in Bangladesh: Factors affecting women entrepreneurs in small and cottage industries in Bangladesh*. SEED working paper. (14). Retrieved from https://www.ilo.org/empent/Publications/WCMS_113774/lang–en/index.htm

Rao, S., & Perry, C. (2003). Convergent interviewing to build a theory in under-researched areas: Principles and an example investigation of internet usage in inter-firm relationships. *Qualitative Market Research: An International Journal, 6*(4), 236–247.

Roomi, M. A. (2013). Entrepreneurial capital, social values and Islamic traditions: Exploring the growth of women-owned enterprises in Pakistan. *International Small Business Journal, 31*(2), 175–191.

Roomi, M. A., & Harrison, P. (2008). Impact of women-only entrepreneurship training in Islamic Society. In I. Aaltio, E. Sundin, & P. Kyrö (Eds.), *The dialogue of woman entrepreneurship and social capital* (pp. 225–252). Copenhagen: Copenhagen Business School Press.

Saber, F. (2002). *Women's entrepreneurship development*. Tehran: Roshangaran Publication. (in Persian).

Sadeghi Fasaei, S., & Rajab Larijani, M. (2011). Strategies to empower women against sexual harassment in the workplace. *The Journal of Women's Studies (Journal of Scientific and Research on Women's Studies), 5*(3), 71–98. (in Persian).

Sajjad, M., Kaleem, N., Chani, M. I., & Ahmed, M. (2020). Worldwide role of women entrepreneurs in economic development. *Asia Pacific Journal of Innovation and Entrepreneurship*. Vol. ahead-of-print No. ahead-of-print. doi:10.1108/APJIE-06-2019-0041

Statistical Centre of Iran. (2020). A selection of labour force survey results: Spring 2020. Retrieved from https://amar.org.ir/gozideamari/ArticleType/ArticleView/ArticleID/12992

Strauss, A., & Corbin, J. (1998). *Basics of qualitative research: Grounded theory procedures and techniques* (2nd ed.). Thousand Oaks, CA: SAGE Publications.

Welter, F. (2011). Contextualizing entrepreneurship-conceptual challenges and ways forward. *Entrepreneurship Theory and Practice, 35*(1), 165–184.

Welter, F., Brush, C. G., & De Bruin, A. (2014). *The gendering of entrepreneurship context*. Institut für Mittelstandsforschung Bonn (Hrsg.): Working Paper, Bonn, SSRN. Retrieved from http://ssrn.com/abstract=2557272

World Bank. (2014). Women, business and the law 2014, removing restrictions to enhance gender equality. Retrieved from www.worldbank.org

World Economic Forum. (2020). The global gender gap report. Retrieved from www.weforum.org

Zahra, S. A. (2011). Doing research in the New Middle East. *Academy of Management Perspectives*, *25*(4), 6–21.

Chapter 14

Gendered Social Capital in Developing Countries: The Case of Turkey

Hiroko Kawamorita, Yashar Salamzadeh, Ali Kahramanoğlu, Kürşat Demiryürek, Nur İlkay Abacı and Noriyuki Takahashi

Abstract

This chapter addresses the impact of gendered social capital in developing countries to understand the barriers and opportunities to women's entrepreneurship with social capital development and also to examine factors influencing the development of social capital for women and how the identified factors benefit the creation of their entrepreneurial activities. This study follows a systemic literature review to achieve the purpose of the research by examining the selected articles in both English and Turkish, followed by factor comparison between developing, developed countries, and world datasets obtained from Global Entrepreneurship Monitor (GEM) database. The finding shows that social capital strongly impacts the entrepreneurial activities among women entrepreneurs in developing countries, especially in Turkey. Although the academic and practical studies on this field were started about two decades ago in Turkey, it has faced a radical increase in last 5 years and many practitioners and scholars working on these concepts. The clusters in English and Turkish resources are almost the same; however, the density and number of key terms are much lower in Turkish literature which shows a gap for Turkish researchers to publish more in this field to examine variables for better view about women entrepreneurship and social capital related to it.

Keywords: Female entrepreneurs; social network; social capital; developing countries; cultural norms; meso level

Introduction

Women entrepreneurs are considered as an important asset for economic development worldwide, contributing significantly to society. Gender equality is at the

The Emerald Handbook of Women and Entrepreneurship in Developing Economies, 247–292
Copyright © 2021 by Emerald Publishing Limited
All rights of reproduction in any form reserved
doi:10.1108/978-1-80071-326-020211014

forefront of the global humanitarian agenda in the twenty-first century where the business environment is changing rapidly. Social capital is a key component of entrepreneurship without which a business cannot be established (Dastourian, Kawamorita Kesim, Seyyed Amiri, & Moradi, 2017). Despite the increase in the number of women entrepreneurs and their high potential to boost the world economic development success, especially in low- and middle-income countries, they are still considered to be a largely untapped and undervalued resource (Allen, Langowitz, & Minniti, 2007). Henry, Foss, and Ahl (2015) criticized the work of Jennings and Brush (2013) that only 11 full research papers were published in academic journals among 30 selected papers studies between 1986 and 2012. Then, only 5 of them were adopting a systematic approach. Henry et al. (2015) argued in their conclusion that studies of gender in the entrepreneurship field are far behind compared to other disciplines, and narratives are rarely published. Social capital development became the crucial aspect in enhancing the performance of any businesses as many factors (such as trust, shared norms, principles, and values) through social networks contribute to the long-term success and stability of organizations and open up new opportunities for entrepreneurship (Dastourian et al., 2017).

The concept of social capital has been studied for over 30 to explain a wide range of social phenomena such as organizational dynamics, socioeconomic performance, entrepreneurial growth, democracy, and competitive advantages by recognizing the importance of interpersonal relationships (Roomi, 2009). He noted that social capital theory is complex with different dimensions, levels, and definitions (Bourdieu, 1986; Coleman, 1988; Putnam, 1993). Many studies were conducted on challenges and opportunities for women entrepreneurs to access resources (Abaci, Demiryurek, Emir, & Yildirim, 2015; Khan, 2020; Dastourian et al., 2017; Welter, Brush, & de Bruin, 2014). Similarly, some researchers investigated gender differences in the distribution of resources. For example, Brush et al. (2001) defined social capital as a facilitator of resource exchanges, particularly knowledge, within and between firms, and as a catalyst for value creation. The authors concluded that barriers such as less equity capital for women is determined by both institutional or network as well as the lack of human capital. In addition, the number of obtained access to finance is far less among female leaders. In 2008, a book called "Women Entrepreneurship and Social Capital: A Dialogue and Construction" was published by the Copenhagen Business School. Unlike gender studies, the authors highlighted that most previous studies exclude social status and cultural definitions of legitimacy. The book focused on examines the dimensions of social capital of enterprises for a better understanding of the gendered aspects of entrepreneurship.

Similar studies have been presented by many authors, highlighting the role of women's networks in how they use their agency to develop networks for gaining access to the marketplace (Khan, 2020; Lindvert, Patel, & Wincent, 2017; Roomi, 2011; Yetim, 2008). Yetim (2008) emphasized that there is evidence to the effect that women are better at establishing communication and convincing others (Ufuk & Özgen, 2001). This proves that women deal better when it comes to problem-solving using their interpersonal skills. By utilizing these skills, social capital can enhance and facilitate women's entrepreneurial activity by identifying potential market opportunities and attracting customers, suppliers, investors, and reducing transaction costs (Roomi, 2011). Social capital comprises different types of relationships, networks, and institutions that allow people to build trust and cooperation, and such networks have a very important function in determining policies for developing rural areas (Meinzen-Dick et al., 2014; Demiryürek, 2014).

Fewer studies focused on the impact of gendered social capital in developing countries. Therefore, to address this limitation, this chapter attempts to better understand the major barriers and opportunities to women's entrepreneurship, especially with social capital development, by focusing on developing countries and especially in the Turkish context. This research aims to further examine factors influencing the development of social capital for women and how the identified factors benefit the creation of their entrepreneurial activities by applying a systemic literature review to achieve the purpose of the study.

Theoretical Framework

Women Entrepreneurship

Female entrepreneur, working alone or with other persons employed in an out-of-home place, in a workplace has established on her behalf, and/or in partnership as the owner of the business, carrying out activities related to the production of any good or service, distribution, marketing, and sales of this good or service. The person who makes/has the work done establishes relations with the person, organization, institution, or organization on his/her behalf, decides on the organization of the business process, the planning of the production of goods and services, the operation, closure or development of the workplace, and the investment, and it is the woman who has a say on the areas of use (Ecevit, 1993, pp. 19–20).

Although women's entrepreneurship offers significant benefits and opportunities to economic and social life, it creates a leverage power with potential entrepreneurial activities in developing the country's economy (Öztürk & Arslan, 2016, p. 38). In other words, women entrepreneurs constitute an important source of economic development and growth. Therefore, women have an important effect on the fight against poverty by reshaping the workplaces, business networks, financial institutions, and other social and cultural values in society. Women entrepreneurs tend to increase in recent years with an increase in state support and good examples (İlter, 2010, p. 82).

Factors Propel Women to Entrepreneurship

Among the reasons that push women to become entrepreneurs, firstly need, and then opportunity motivation is effective. As people's intention to become an entrepreneur increases, the reason behind this increase arises primarily from need.

Tekin (2005) lists the main factors that generally lead women to become entrepreneurs as follows: women's self-sufficiency desire, purpose of realizing a business idea or dreams, women's need and motive to succeed, women's desire to work independently, having a workplace or business inherited from the family or in any other way, women wishing to work independently in their workplace or business with professional knowledge or diploma, as a result of only one person working in the family (difficulty living on a single income), lack of paid employment opportunities for women or lack of other options for employment, giving priority to men in some business lines due to personal prejudices, wrong attitudes, and behaviors, reasons such as excessive traditional domestic responsibilities and inadequacy of childcare homes lead women to home entrepreneurship (textiles, handicrafts, carpets, etc.), having flexible working hours, and providing additional income for the family, desire for a better life, and high social status, etc.

Women's affairs non-economic dimensions in the foreground want to establish is less than men. Based on this, there are studies (Soysal, 2010; Yetim, 2002) that reveal that women entrepreneurs attach importance to social reputation and social status rather than profit. Therefore, it is sufficient for most women entrepreneurs to earn a valid income for themselves and their families rather than earning high financial earnings (Keskin, 2017, p. 69).

Problems of Women Entrepreneurs

It is a known that entrepreneurs face many problems during their entrepreneurship life. However, it is obvious that women face certain difficulties due to some important differences between female and male entrepreneurs. These differences, decision-making styles, risk tolerance, goals for business, business financing, management styles, networking capabilities, and motivations are shaped in the frame (Karaturhan, Ünsal, Issabek, & Guler, 2017).

It is vital for a strong entrepreneurship sector that women start and develop businesses, remove barriers, and create a level playing field for women business owners. According to the results of the studies examining women entrepreneurs since the 1980s, in most developed and developing countries, women, in addition to the problems generally encountered by entrepreneurs, have different problems than men because they are women (Onay, 2013, p. 42). These problems may arise from some deficiencies or social prejudices stemming from the women themselves or their environment, as well as problems related to the state, sector, laws, or policies. These problems are: lack of experience, lack of trust, lack of knowledge/low education level, not being included in social network/lack of communication, role conflict, social pressure, and gender-based discrimination, glass ceiling syndrome, capital supply, bureaucratic barriers, market situation, and organization problem.

Although women, who constitute half of the world's population, have an important role in participating in economic life and creating value, and consequently in providing economic development, their share of benefiting from economic development is less than men. Due to gender discrimination, which originates from the male-dominated culture, women remain in the background in economic and social terms. The role of women as an influence, domestic with tasks limited and allows them to be perceived as the second role of women in working life (Karaman & Ay, 2017).

Solution Offers for Women Entrepreneurs

A woman who wants to start a business needs finance and wants to apply for a loan first. However, the fact that women cannot find the collateral requested by financial institutions since real estates are mostly registered on men and the lack of experience and knowledge of women entrepreneurs in relations with financial institutions pose a significant problem in capital supply. Alternative solutions are the fact that financial institutions keep the loan rates low by improving the collateral and loan conditions, alleviate the collateral conditions, and do not limit the areas to be lent (Sarvan & Tömen, 2015).

The fact that the current education system in Turkey is less capable of developing and strengthening women's entrepreneurship skills causes women to receive less formal education than men and face difficulties in terms of competition in business life (Şekerler, 2006, p. 123). Formal and nonformal education programs should be prepared to complete the training deficiencies for women entrepreneurs, and entrepreneurship training should be expanded and short-term programs should be organized.

Women entrepreneurs have problems in finding suitable personnel for the right job. These problems may arise from the inability of women entrepreneurs to hire suitable staff for the job, as well as the employee's lack of trust in the female boss (Çabuk et al., 2015). Qualified personnel can be obtained by obtaining support from various consultancy companies.

Bureaucratic difficulties that entrepreneurs face when starting the name of the company operations, according to the appropriate personnel and material supply of crucial importance in the rankings as problems, are encountered. The fact that women entrepreneurs are less experienced in intensive, and complex bureaucratic procedures compared to male entrepreneurs and lack of knowledge causes bureaucratic procedures to be an important problem. It is thought that providing consultancy support to women entrepreneurs who are in the process of establishing a company by the state and related organizations and organizing training about company establishment will help women entrepreneurs gain knowledge about bureaucratic procedures and prevent this process from being an important problem. The problem of providing suitable personnel is of vital importance in the establishment and successful execution of the company, and training personnel according to their areas of expertise should be encouraged through vocational high schools and universities (Yirik & Yıldırım, 2014).

Women entrepreneurs should be encouraged to export to grow their businesses and become economically stronger. To do so, the policy makers are supporting female entrepreneurs by introducing favorable policies and regulations such as providing tax breaks, exemption from customs duties, export consultant appointment. Financial supports are offered by the government for those female entrepreneurs to participate in trade fairs aboard annually. It will contribute to economic development by increasing women's knowledge and self-confidence (Uluköy & Bayraktaroğlu, 2014).

Social Capital

Today, with the increasing importance of knowledge, the social transformation experienced has brought the human element to the fore in organizations and caused the concept of social capital to come to the agenda. Social capital is defined as "the totality of the existing or potential resources arising from the social relations that individuals or groups have" (Nahapiet & Ghoshal, 1998).

According to Fukuyama, social capital is

> ...a capability arising from the prevalence of trust in a society or parts of it. The acquisition of social capital requires the adoption of the moral norms of a community and the acquisition of virtues such as loyalty and honesty, and the interdependence of individuals. Social capital is not gained by individuals acting on their own. It is based on the dominance of social values rather than individual values. (Fukuyama, 2005)

Social capital refers to all the real and potential resources that an entrepreneur has acquired through the network of relationships he has as an individual (Nahapiet & Ghoshal, 1998, p. 243). Social capital brings entrepreneurs face to face with new and different ideas in the entrepreneurship process; it provides them with a supportive and nurturing broad reference framework on potential opportunities (Aldrich & Zimmer, 1986).

Today, social capital is accepted as a factor that has positive effects not only on the entrepreneurship process but also in the labor market. While job seekers in the labor market try to find a job using their human capital and social capital, that is, their social connections, employees in a job try to increase their job success in the workplace by using their social capital (Aşkın & Barış, 2016, p. 66). In this way, the developing communication network, institutions, and rules determine the quantity, quality, and form of social relations, and healthy relationships with colleagues and superiors in the workplace increase job performance and positively affect their career.

Gendered Social Capital

Urban (2011) noted in his studies about gender perspectives on entrepreneurship that the theoretical framework of social feminism highlights that there are fundamental gender differences in human capital in the ways of viewing the world (DeTienne & Chandler, 2007; Fischer, Reuber, & Dyke, 1993). DeTienne and Chandler (2007) were the first authors who researched gender differences in opportunity identification. According to their findings, both women and men utilize their human capital to identify opportunities, but they have a fundamentally different way of processing it. Similarly, gender differences in a network (structures and behavior) were presented by authors such as Manolova, Carter, Manev, and Gyoshev (2007), Manolova, Gyoshev, and Manev (2007), and Surangi (2018). Gendered implications on social capital are the emerging concepts, studied by many authors (Addis & Joxhe, 2017; Badura, Grijalva, Newman, Yan, & Jeon, 2018; Urban, 2011).

Social Capital and Women Entrepreneurs in the Turkish Context

Social capital is a very effective tool to interpret women's position in society. Social capital, which harbors opportunities that lead women to success, helps them to understand and solve the barriers to them. Networks, one of the basic components of social capital, reflect social relations and are governed by gender-based social divisions that affect the ways of accessing resources such as time, money, and status in the entrepreneurship process (Aşkın & Barış, 2016, p. 66).

The sources of social capital that women have can create positive changes in reducing poverty, inequality, and injustice in working life and help overcome the gender discrimination that women are subjected to (Fidan & Nam, 2012).

For women entrepreneurs, social capital can be defined as the scope and effectiveness of social and social relations that have a level of trust to facilitate the gathering and use of resources. The concept of social capital contributes to a better understanding of the difficulties and opportunities faced by women entrepreneurs (Fidan & Nam, 2012).

The role of social capital in overcoming the difficulties faced by women entrepreneurs, especially in markets with imperfect competition, is the links established with important actors in strategic or hierarchical positions, and it helps to access information about the opportunities available in the market that cannot be achieved in thc absence of these links (Lin, 1999). Another function of social capital is to influence decision-making mechanisms in matters concerning the actor with the power of social ties. Especially at this point, some actors can have more influence on decision-making mechanisms depending on their strategic positions and status, and they can help reach more valuable resources (Okan, Sarı, & Peker, 2016).

Women prefer to consult with the ties in their immediate environment, especially family members, partners, and spouses, on problems they encounter within the scope of entrepreneurship activities. This situation is explained by the fact that women consult with women or conclude within themselves when making decisions. Therefore, with this feature, women are overly open to informal connections but relatively close to formal connections. If entrepreneurs have "family," it has a positive impact on the production of social capital relationships (Bozoğlu & Inel, 2015).

On the other hand, some women attribute their success to formal or informal channels such as their spouses, families, or customers within the scope of entrepreneurship activities, while some women attribute it to themselves. They accept to be burdened by believing in their success, especially because of the feelings of independence and obligation of women who are not married or who feel lonely (Bozoğlu & İnel, 2015).

The country introduced national action plans and policies toward gender equality. Turkey is also making progress to ease the women lead initiatives. The first National Action Plan on Gender Equality was introduced in 1996, specifically addressing the problems of rural women. Strategy Paper and Action Plan for Women's Empowerment (2018–2023) is the third action plan providing information about the challenges for rural women such as the lack of access to education, health services, and social security. Then besides, "The National Action Plan on the Empowerment of Rural Women (2012–2016)" was introduced within the framework mentioned including improving the status of rural women and promoting the gender sensitivity of the agricultural sector. The Rural Women Unit is also allocated at the Ministry of Agriculture and Forestry (MAF), which provides information about agricultural production methods, home economics, and handicraft courses for rural women, as well as organizing and implementing in-service training for all ministry staff. MAF implements projects to strengthen the national extension system to be able to provide efficient advisory support to farmers and rural communities, to contribute to increased productivity and food security of rural communities. Although this supporting mechanism is in place, just like in any other country, less women are engaging in entrepreneurial activities in Turkey. Female entrepreneurship in Turkey is highly influenced by the structural adaptation policies offered by international financial institutes such as the International Monetary Fund and the World Bank which brought new policies favorable for women. Yetim (2008) stressed that working in own business is considered to be a more appropriate option for women who want to work but cannot find a paid job due to the lack of education and skills. Kawamorita et al. (2020) noted that Turkey is in a different stage of development compare to developed countries, such as Japan. They emphasized that education and training are the keys to capacity building in Turkey, as well as the importance of utilizing social capital among rural women entrepreneurs.

Research Methodology

The research method is divided into two phases to answer three main research questions: "What factors influencing the development of social capital for women in developing countries?", "How the identified factors benefit the creation of women's entrepreneurial activities in developing countries?" and "What are the impacts of gendered social capital in developing countries?".

In the first phase, all previously known factors relevant to gendered social capital in developing countries at the societal level are extracted from the theoretical framework of a systematic literature review (content-analysis) by following the PRISMA diagram and checklist. The authors used major databases such as Academic Search Elite (EBSCO), JSTOR, and ABI/INFORM (Proquest), Scopus, and Web of Science in various fields including multidisciplinary and social sciences to obtain validated knowledge from popular and high impacted peer reviewed journals. In addition, Google Scholar and other academic search engines were used as a supplementary source. A quantitative analysis approach and knowledge mapping technique were performed to identify the topic for this research in both English and Turkish languages. The articles with keywords such as "Women Entrepreneurship" and "Social Capital" were all examined in topic related literature between the year 2010 to 2020, and the number of relevant articles was 152. Finally, the most relevant 40 papers including reports and articles published in English and Turkish languages were summarized and reviewed. Extracted key terms were grouped in clusters by utilizing VOS reviewer visual maps. Then, the analytical framework organizing the findings of the literature review is presented accordingly. This analysis aims at identifying patterns and trends from the result. Walliman (2010) presented that content analysis, data mining, and meta-analysis are the most suitable methods for secondary data, and among them, content analysis is applied in this study. White and Marsh (2006) noted that content analysis is a flexible research method, and it has been widely used in studies with different research goals and objectives by applying various analytical techniques to put the findings into context. This method was developed in the mid-1900s to achieve the generalizability and the development of theories. Content analysis is characterized as a systematic approach to serve the purposes of both quantitative research and qualitative research. To do so, the most important part is to select the data which are useful to test answering research questions. Coding is the key to achieve a high level of objectivity, reliability, and generalizability, especially for theory development.

In the second phase, factor analysis was performed to compare the Turkish data with other developing/developed and world data. The Global Entrepreneurship Monitor (GEM) datasets were utilized for this comparative study. Middle-income countries from Europe and Central Asia from the GEM report on Women Entrepreneurship 2018–2019 were selected as the sample of developing countries. Available data (entrepreneurial behavior and attitudes and entrepreneurial framework conditions) for Bulgaria, Kazakhstan, the Russian Federation, and Turkey with the latest year (2015–2018) were used from the GEM database. Then, the datasets for developing countries are compared with selected developed countries and the world on average.

Findings

Phase One – Systematic Literature Review (Content Analysis)

The list of the most relevant studies conducted in English and Turkish are summarized in Tables 14.1 and 14.2. More specifically, Table 14.1 is the list of literature in English from different developing countries (including Turkey), as well as, one's study on migrants from a developing country. Then, visual maps are created for both tables by extracted key terms only to demonstrate the list of literature. Findings from the study indicate growing interests in this research area in developing/emerging countries including Pakistan, Ghana, Turkey, Bangladesh, etc. Most of the studies are published by authors from the United States and United

Table 14.1. Literature Written in English (Gendered Social Capital in Developing Countries).

	Authors/Year	Data Collection and Analysis Method	Sample Size and Characteristics	Research Purpose	Key Findings	Keywords
1	Yetim (2008)	The face-to-face questionnaire survey, correlational analysis, ANOVA, and logistic regression analysis	304 migrant status female entrepreneurs in Mersin, Turkey.	(1) To describe female entrepreneurship based on entrepreneurial personality characteristics. (2) To demonstrate the differences between migrant and nonmigrant female entrepreneurship. (3) To predict high and low levels of social capital.	The higher social capital (age, professional training, and work experience) is predicted by migrant status from stronger personal contacts and the sociocultural properties of their respective communities. In contrast, lower social capital was discovered among nonmigrant status.	Social Capital, Entrepreneurial Personality Characteristics, Properties of Sociocultural Entrepreneurship, Gender Roles, Pull Factors, Push Factors.
2	Ali and Yousuf (2019)	A survey questionnaire, simple random sampling technique through randomization progress	325 respondents from the rural community (93% answered) in Gilgit-Baltistan, Pakistan.	(1) To investigate the influence of social capital on entrepreneurial intentions in the rural area of Pakistan. (2) To	Social capital has a significant positive impact on entrepreneurial intentions by forming perceived desirability,	Rural Community, Local Economic Development, Entrepreneurial Behavior.

				examine the influence of social capital on individuals' intentions in entrepreneurship. (3) To make policy recommendations to facilitate the entrepreneurs.	perceived self-efficacy, and perceived social norms toward entrepreneurship.	
3	Baranik, Gorman, and Wales (2018)	OLS regression analyses	84 female entrepreneurs participating in entrepreneurship training programs across Tunisia.	To explain the entrepreneurial success among Muslim women living in a democratic Tunisia.	Social capital is a critical asset for Muslim women entrepreneurs. Religiosity, on the other hand, had no statistically significant relationship with entrepreneurial performance.	Entrepreneur, Self-Employment, Tunisia, Islam, Arab, Muslim, Middle East, and North Africa (MENA) capital, Marital status, Wasta.
4	Kalafatoglu and Mendoza (2017)	A multiple research case study (qualitative, three-stage	25 women in Turkey and in four countries of the Middle East and North African	(1) To examine how gender and culture affect business creation, how women	Women entrepreneurs in a highly patriarchal society face important barriers	Gender, Turkey, Culture, Networking, MENA Region,

Table 14.1. *(Continued)*

	Authors/Year	Data Collection and Analysis Method	Sample Size and Characteristics	Research Purpose	Key Findings	Keywords
		interview-based methodology)	(MENA) region (Egypt, Saudi Arabia, Lebanon, and Morocco).	perceive social capital, and how important their personal networks are for their businesses, in chosen societies.	due to culture and social norms. Networking is the key factor to overcome barriers in male-dominated industries.	Women's Entrepreneurship.
5	Khan (2020)	Random walk methods (an exploratory survey)	Random sampling in Pakistan.	To contribute to the literature on the social capital of female entrepreneurs from a critical perspective of women's entrepreneurship and entrepreneurial networks.	Women's social capital play a crucial role in the survival and expansion of their business activities by facilitating access to the men's trading sphere of the marketplace, developing crossgender economic networks in a challenged environment (social norms).	Gender Inequality, Business, Dynamics, Impact.

6	Lindvert, Patel, and Wincent (2017)	Semistructured interview, a combination of serendipitous and snowball sampling	21 interviews with women entrepreneurs in microenterprises (fewer than 10 employees) operating in the service and retailing sectors in Lahore, Pakistan.	(1) To understand how the degree and type of social restrictions transmitted through social capital, hinder, or slow down women entrepreneurs' venturing efforts. (2) To understand how they deal with constraints and acquire resources for their enterprise by managing complex social restrictions.	Social capital puts high restrictions on women microentrepreneurs. Although women do get some selective access to resources from family members, they are restricted by limited access to social capital outside of family members.	Women Entrepreneurs; Social Capital; Context; Resource Acquisition; Developing Countries; Pakistan.
7	Muniady, Mamun, Rosli Mohamad, Yukthamarani Permarupan, and Binti Zainol (2015)	A cross-sectional approach, and quantitative through structured interviews	417 microentrepreneurs from Malaysia.	To examine the effect of relational and cognitive social capital on structural social capital and the effect of structural social capital on the performance of	Cognitive social capital has a positive effect on structural social capital, and structural social capital has a significant positive effect on microenterprise	Social Capital, Cognitive, Relational, Structural, Microenterprise, Performance, Women Entrepreneurs.

Table 14.1. *(Continued)*

	Authors/Year	Data Collection and Analysis Method	Sample Size and Characteristics	Research Purpose	Key Findings	Keywords
				microenterprises owned and managed by women in Peninsular Malaysia.	performance. Relational social capital has a positive but insignificant effect on structural social capital.	
8	Poon, Thai, and Naybor (2012)	Surveying and Interviewing	160 participants from 42 NGOs run microcredit programs in Vietnam.	(1) To examine the role of social capital on female entrepreneurship (measured by self-employment) in two distressed regions in Northern Vietnam.	Family social capital increases the women's probability of becoming entrepreneurs but institutional social capital has the opposite effect. The Women's Union is overly embedded, resulting in negative effect on network.	Social Capital, Entrepreneurship, Geographic Scale, Market Access, Family, Para-institution, Vietnam.
9	Yeroz (2019)	Life story narratives	17 women entrepreneurs from Turkey who have	To conduct an intersectional analysis on migrant women's	Policies addressing the aspirations and capital endowments of different groups	Immigrants, Identity, Human Capital, Women Entrepreneurs,

			migrated to Sweden in the late 1960.	cultural capital development processes on the basis of not only gender and ethnicity but also class relations.	would be helpful in tackling with the dominant focus on ethnicity and cultural traits of those groups.	Ethnic Entrepreneurship, Immigrant Entrepreneurs, Mixed Embeddedness, Identity Work, Gender, Forms, Swedish, Intersectionality, Integration, Relevance.
10	Yusuff, Abu Bakar, and Ahmad (2018)	A quantitative survey (random sampling)	184 women microentrepreneurs in Malaysia.	To examine the role of social capital as a mediator of the relationship between financial capital and the business performances of women entrepreneurs.	Social capital is about norms and groups; trusts and networking; economic equality; and volunteerism. Microcredit had a significant effect on business performance while volunteerism was a mediator in the social capital business performance relationship.	Financial Capital, Microcredit, Social Capital, Women Entrepreneurs, Business Performance.

Table 14.1. *(Continued)*

	Authors/Year	Data Collection and Analysis Method	Sample Size and Characteristics	Research Purpose	Key Findings	Keywords
11	Osei and Zhuang (2020)	The structural equation modeling (SEM) technique through SmartPLS software version 3.0	333 women entrepreneurs in the agribusiness sector from the Sekyere South District in Ghana.	To identify the impact and causative mechanisms through which social capital, women entrepreneurship growth, and social innovation contribute to poverty alleviation.	The transformative potential of rural women entrepreneurs who utilize social capital from both formal and informal social networks toward rural poverty alleviation. The impacts of social innovation and relational social capital on showed positive.	Social Capital, Women Entrepreneurship, Rural Poverty Alleviation, Ghana.
12	Wafeq et al. (2019)	Primary data collection via telephone	248 women business owners in Afghanistan.	To investigate the relationship between one aspect of entrepreneurial psychological capital – optimism regarding enterprise success	There is a significant relevance for economic development policymakers, nongovernmental organizations, and entrepreneurs throughout the	Female Entrepreneurs, Psychological Capital, Marketing Management, Afghanistan, Self-Efficacy, Opportunity

				of Afghan female entrepreneurs – and aspects of the marketing function.	developing world. What drives the psychological capital of these entrepreneurs under these extreme conditions should be of interest of the entrepreneurship literature and policymakers.	Recognition, Venture Performance, Mediating Role.
13	Ferdousi and Mahmud (2019)	Four key informant interviews	28 women Nobin Udyokta (new entrepreneurs) in Bangladesh.	This study attempted to analyze the role of social business for developing women entrepreneurship.	Social business fund plays an important role toward women entrepreneurship development through providing financial, human, and social capital (network) to the women entrepreneurs.	Gender Equality, Trust, Social Business Fund, Sustainable Development Goals, Women Empowerment, Women Entrepreneurship.
14	Solano and Rooks (2018)	Large-scale survey followed by face-to-face interviews/ multilevel logistic	608 female entrepreneurs in Uganda, 294 in the urban area (Kampala), and 314	To compare female and male entrepreneurs in terms of both the benefits they can	There are gender differences associated with access to, and requests for,	Developing countries, Gender, Personal Networks, Access to Resources,

Table 14.1. *(Continued)*

	Authors/Year	Data Collection and Analysis Method	Sample Size and Characteristics	Research Purpose	Key Findings	Keywords
		regression model logistic regressions	in the rural area (Nakaseke), average age 34 with 9 years of education.	get from their contacts (access to resources), and the claims they might receive from these contacts (social capital) focusing on financial resources.	financial resources. Requesting money from their husbands or their male relatives seems the only option for women entrepreneurs who wish to obtain financial support.	Social Capital, Small Businesses.
15	Pham and Talavera (2018)	Heckman sample-correction methodology/ Heckman regressions	Our dataset is from the 2011, 2013, and 2015 results of the Micro, Small, and Medium Enterprise Survey in Viet Nam.	Examines the relationship among gender, social capital, and access to finance of micro, small, and medium enterprises in the manufacturing sector in Viet Nam.	Firms with closer relationship with government officials and other business people can get loans of longer duration. Due to information asymmetry, banks tend to seek additional information via firms' social networks. Better social ties facilitate	Entrepreneurship, Financial Constraints, Gender, Discrimination, Women Entrepreneurs, Informal Credit, Gender, Access, Networks.

					loans, better social capital assist entrepreneurial activities.	
16	Kebede (2018)	Face-to-face survey questionnaire, multistage sampling procedure/social network analyses	254 Street entrepreneurs in Addis Ababa, Ethiopia.	To investigate the effect of Burt's structural holes theory of social capital in the context of the Ethiopian informal economy.	Entrepreneurs' dense network structure, which lacks structural holes, has a significant negative effect on entrepreneurial outcome. ++	Social Capital, Social Network Analysis, Entrepreneurs, Entrepreneurial Outcomes, Ethiopia.
17	Costa and Galina (2015)	Multiple cases (direct semistructured interviews) followed by email and phone data collection	Six cases of rural tourism in three different regions in Brazil to obtain different characteristics for the largest possible variation.	To understand the relationship between social networks, resources accessed, and social capital in the creation and development of rural tourism business.	The structural dimensions of social capital verify similarities in the creation of new business. The complexity seems to increase with business development. Both relational and cognitive dimensions are relevant at different stages of the business.	Entrepreneurship, Social Networks, Social Capital, Rural Tourism, Case Study.

Table 14.1. *(Continued)*

	Authors/Year	Data Collection and Analysis Method	Sample Size and Characteristics	Research Purpose	Key Findings	Keywords
18	Atmadja, Su, and Sharma (2014)	Questionnaires/ statistical analysis (multinomial probit model)	131 microbusiness owners in City of Surabaya, Indonesia, in the context of microfinance program.	(1) To investigate how microfinance might have played a role in helping Indonesian women's microenterprises (WMEs) performance. (2) To provide an adequate understanding of the role of microfinance in the WMEs' performance in urban area of Indonesia.	Microcredit has a negative relationship with the profit. With regard to human and social capitals, better formal education and family involvement are more likely to increase the chance of getting better business performance. Microfinance alone is not a perfect tool to improve the WMEs performance. It should be supported with human and social capitals.	Microfinance, Business Performance, Indonesia.

19	Surangi (2018)	In-depth narrative interviews and observations/ narrative analysis (NVivo 10)	14 female entrepreneurs in Sri Lanka.	To examine the important influences on these female entrepreneurs' networking behavior within small businesses in the tourism sector.	Culture and societal expectations, running home-based business and building trust were found as main influences on female entrepreneurial networking behaviors. The majority revealed stressful times trying to combine the business with multiple roles and societal expectations.	Gender, Networking, Social Constructionism, Narratives, Female Entrepreneurship.
20	Dastourian, Kawamorita, Seyyed Amiri, and Moradi, (2017)	Self-administered questionnaire/the structural equation modeling in LISREL software.	30 women entrepreneurs in Iran.	To investigates the mediatory role of innovation concerning the effect of social capital on entrepreneurship.	Social capital and innovation had a positive and significant effect on entrepreneurship. However, the impact of social capital on innovation was not confirmed.	Women Entrepreneurship, Social Capital, Innovation, Market Knowledge, Ilam Province.

Table 14.1. *(Continued)*

	Authors/Year	Data Collection and Analysis Method	Sample Size and Characteristics	Research Purpose	Key Findings	Keywords
21	Mozumdar et al. (2019)	Survey questionnaire/in-depth analysis/ multiple regression models	292 women entrepreneurs engaged in handicraft businesses in Bangladesh.	To analyze in what ways network embeddedness may influence the business performance of women entrepreneurs working in a socially constrained context.	A small network is positively related, while medium-sized and large networks are negatively related, to performance. The networks of many women entrepreneurs may be overembedded, due to extensive connections (family, friends).	Network (over-) embeddedness, Business Performance, Women Entrepreneurs, Socially Constrained Context.
22	Kawamorita, Takahashi, and Demiryurek (2020)	Bibliographic analysis and case studies	Literature between 2010 and 2020 and rural women entrepreneurs in Japan and Turkey.	To address the economic aspect of media literacy by studying how media literacy impacts entrepreneurial activities among rural women.	The appropriate use of media is one of the key elements for better economic performance by connecting entrepreneurs with broader networks.	Media/Female/ Rural Entrepreneurship, Media Literacy, Information Asymmetry, Capacity Building.

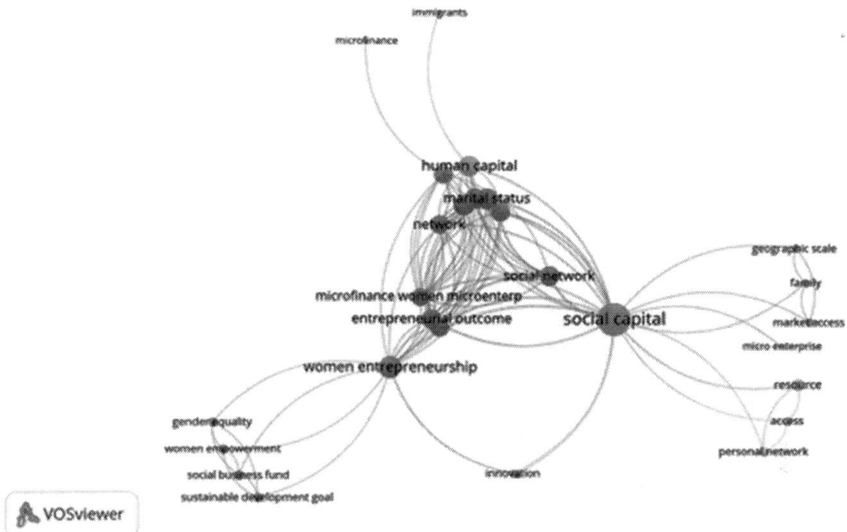

Fig. 14.1. Network Visualization Co-occurrence Map Based on Keywords Extracted from English Literature.

Kingdom with a higher number in citations. Figs. 14.1 and 14.2 are the Network Visualization co-occurrence map based on keywords extracted from English (22 articles) and Turkish Literature (18 articles). Table 14.1 is the cluster

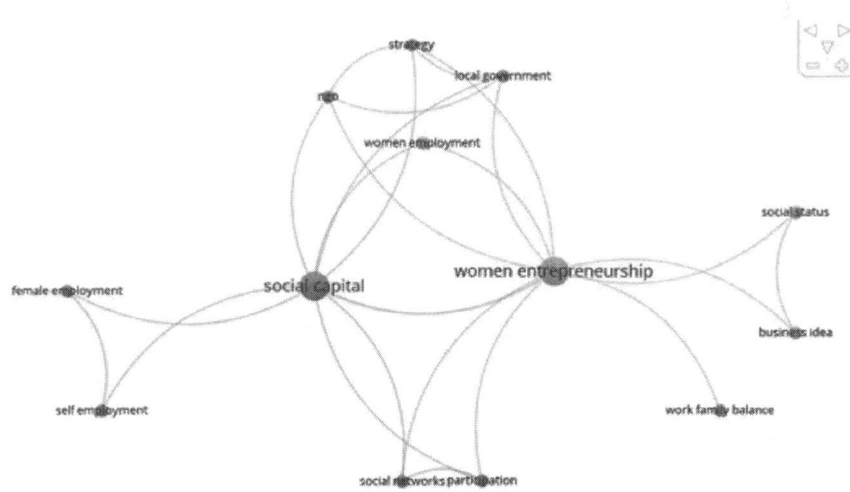

Fig. 14.2. Network Visualization Co-occurrence Map Based on Keywords Extracted from Turkish Literature.

comparison table between English and Turkish Literature (Figs. 14.1 and 14.2), and similar findings are presented. Cluster 1 and 2 are the most mentioned and studied variables in developing countries, namely "Networks and Norm" as such variable, for example. "Culture" is important in establishing a relationship and its network formation. Norm (cultural social capital) strongly affects the creation of networks (team, social networks, networking among women entrepreneurs, family connections, business network, relationships) to gain reciprocity trust, being engaged, and creating value for common goals.

For example, Kalafatoglu and Mendoza (2017) and Yeroz (2019) both emphasized on how culture influences the business creation and capital development processes. Women entrepreneurs are facing barriers due to cultural and social norms, and many authors highlighted that networking is the key factor to overcome these challenges (Ali & Yousuf, 2019; Kalafatoglu & Mendoza, 2017; Khan, 2020; Yusuff, Abu Bakar, & Ahmad, 2018). Similarly, the higher level of social capital among migrant women in developing country/from developing country shows a strong connection with cultural trails as well as class relations (Yeroz, 2019; Yetim, 2008). Baranik, Gorman, and Wales (2018) investigated the entrepreneurial success among Muslim women in Tunisia by applying ordinary least squares regression analyses. They concluded that social capital was a critical asset; however, no statistical evidence was found in relation with the entrepreneurial performance. Kebede (2018) conducted a research to investigate the effect of the social capital structural holes theory (Burt, 1992) in Ethiopia. The result demonstrated that dense network structure which lacks structural holes had a negative effect on entrepreneurial outcome. This finding confirmed the Burt's theory (structural holes = gap) that entrepreneurs with less dense networks have a greater diversity of information and greater freedom to act. Thus, the brokerage is a source of alternative ways of thinking and behaving.

Table 14.2 is the list of Turkish Literature and all research conducted within the country. When the articles are examined, except for the study of Çetin et al. (2016) which uses multivariate statistical methods, it is seen that all of them were carried out with primary data. Sampling methods and/or data collection methods are shown in Table. In these articles generally, semistructured interviews, frequency analysis, face-to-face survey, and interview methods were used. In these studies; the characteristics and motivations of women entrepreneurs, starting a business, business ownership, finance, gender, and social networks, performance, and growth issues were examined. Participants were asked to explain their point of view to the questions/problems on related issues, thus demonstrating the perspective of the participants toward women entrepreneurs. According to the findings of the research, women entrepreneurs were stylish and kind who are able to complement men, operate in sectors suitable for their social roles, prioritize their family, and have compassion, ready to sacrifice themselves for their children. Research findings indicate that women entrepreneurs primarily encounter social role pressure.

Most of the studies conducted abroad on women's entrepreneurship evaluate women entrepreneurs through a male-dominated discourse by comparing female and male entrepreneurs. In the literature of Turkey had a difference like research studies as local and were seen as focusing on "woman." For this reason,

Table 14.2. In Turkish Context.

	Authors/Year	Data Collection and Analysis Method	Sample Size and Characteristics	Research Purpose	Key Findings	Keywords
1	Yetim (2002)	Face-to-face survey, frequency analysis, T-test, chi-square analysis	224 women entrepreneurs in Mersin province.	To determine the qualifications and competencies of women entrepreneurs as social capital.	Women entrepreneurs mobilize different social capital resources at both the stages of starting a business and maintaining it and integrate them with their entrepreneurial qualities. Women's ability to use institutional information channels in particular supports the organization by increasing solidarity.	Entrepreneurship, Women Entrepreneurship, Social Capital, Rural Women Entrepreneurship, Civil Society.
2	Özkaya (2009)	Face-to-face survey, focus group analysis	All of the 25 women entrepreneurs who are members of the "Women Entrepreneurs Board" established under the leadership of TOBB in Manisa and affiliated with the Chamber of Commerce and Industry.	The research has three main objectives. (1) To determine the qualifications and competencies of women entrepreneurs, defined as "social capital," (2) To define the problems faced by women entrepreneurs, (3) To compare the methods developed by women entrepreneurs with the	The development and dissemination of women's entrepreneurship is, first of all, a "state policy"; all institutions in local governments (Municipality, Professional Chambers, Banks, Organized Area	Women Entrepreneurship, Strategy, Local Governments, Social Capital, Local Governments.

Table 14.2. *(Continued)*

	Authors/Year	Data Collection and Analysis Method	Sample Size and Characteristics	Research Purpose	Key Findings	Keywords
				policies and strategies developed based on both local governments, institutions, and the country.	Directorates, Associations, Press and Media organs, Directorate of National Education).	
3	Aşkın and Barış (2016)	Face-to-face interview, survey	In the research, 43 female members registered to Tokat Chamber of Industry and Commerce in Tokat city center and districts.	The purpose of the study is to examine and reveal the effect of social capital on women's entrepreneurship, which is an important way of expanding women's employment opportunities, and within this framework, to make suggestions for effective use of social capital in increasing employment through women entrepreneurship in the labor market.	The social capital factor, such as strong ties of their families, relatives, and friends, is effective in the participation of women in employment as entrepreneurs, in the stages of starting and maintaining a business, but it provides greater opportunities for women entrepreneurs to obtain resources and be successful than strong ties. Their weak ties	Social Capital, Women's Employment, Women's Entrepreneurship, Gender, Entrepreneur Civil Society.

					with public institutions and organizations in the sector are insufficient. The low level of education and responsibilities stemming from the gender-based division of labor cause women's social networks to be more limited.	
4	Toprakcı Alp and Aksoy (2019)	Semistructured interview technique	20 women entrepreneurs operating in Antalya.	Social capital and women's entrepreneurship have been examined using qualitative research methods. Women entrepreneurship perception of women and society, who were interviewed with the financial support, social supports, difficulties they face, and life satisfaction of women entrepreneurs, were evaluated within the scope of their social capital levels.	While women entrepreneurs' close relations such as spouse, family, or friends are generally effective in obtaining financial capital, active participation in nongovernmental organizations also strengthens the social capital levels of women.	Entrepreneurship, Woman Entrepreneur, Social Capital, Social Networks, Civil Society.
5	Özen (2008)	Semistructured interview technique	Operates around Sakarya and Kocaeli 80 women	Execution of their businesses, their personality traits, and the driving and attractive	When establishing their enterprises, women entrepreneurs	Entrepreneurship, Woman Entrepreneur,

Table 14.2. *(Continued)*

	Authors/Year	Data Collection and Analysis Method	Sample Size and Characteristics	Research Purpose	Key Findings	Keywords
			entrepreneurs identified.	factors that are effective in starting and maintaining their enterprises were investigated, also determined how much they benefit from the social capital phenomenon in the economy.	mostly resort to informal resources and therefore primarily consider family and friend support. They are less interested in formal resources such as bank loans. The most important factors driving them to start a business are economic imperatives and family orientation. One of the main factors that attract women entrepreneurs to entrepreneurship is the desire to be independent and to produce something.	Social Capital, Equal Opportunity, Social Justice.
6	Bozoğlu Batı and İnel (2015)	In-depth interview, questionnaire	15 women entrepreneurs registered with the Women	Examining the conflict that women entrepreneurs experience in the context of work–family and family–work	Those aged between 1 and 5 years of the enterprise experience more work–family	Entrepreneurship, Women Entrepreneurship, Work–Family Balance;

			Entrepreneurs Board of the Chamber of Commerce and Industry in Yalova.	with the dimensions of time, tension, behavior, and energy; Investigation of the characteristics of the enterprise and its relationship with the entrepreneur profile's self-confidence, risk-taking, and innovative features.	conflict when all dimensions (time, tension, behavior, and energy) are taken into account. It has been determined that women entrepreneurs with high time adequacy experience less family–business conflicts.	Nonparametric Tests, Social Capital.
7	Çetin et al. (2016)	Secondary data, frequency analysis, multivariate logistic regression	European and World Values survey-4 cross-sectional dataset.	The impact of formal and informal social capital on women's entrepreneurship in Europe.	Women are more likely to become entrepreneurs in the early years of business life. Marriage and informal social capital entrepreneurship affect women entrepreneurship positively and children negatively affect them. Women entrepreneurs benefit more from formal social capital than men.	Entrepreneurship, Women's Employment, Self-Employment, Social Capital, Meta-Analysis.

Table 14.2. *(Continued)*

	Authors/Year	Data Collection and Analysis Method	Sample Size and Characteristics	Research Purpose	Key Findings	Keywords
8	Kayalar and Ömürbek (2007)	Face-to-face survey, frequency analysis, T-test, chi-square analysis	Süleyman Demirel University Faculty of Economics and Administrative Sciences, 69 senior year students.	The impact of gender on risk-taking among college students seen as potential entrepreneurs.	Students are not the strong propensity to take risks, different they think about female students to take risks than male students, which play an important role of gender differences in choosing entrepreneurship in the thinking stage was detected.	Entrepreneurship, Risk-Taking, Gender, Equal Opportunity, Civil Society.
9	Çalıyurt (2011)	Face-to-face interview, semistructured interview form, frequency analysis	9 women entrepreneurs who are members of the Edirne Chamber of Industry and Commerce, Women Entrepreneurs Board, and have small and medium-sized enterprises (SMEs).	Measuring the financial knowledge of women entrepreneurs in SMEs managed by women.	It was stated that women entrepreneurs do not face gender discrimination, but their financial knowledge level is insufficient.	Women, Entrepreneurship, Financial Management, Turkey, SMEs, Education.
10	Fidan and Nam (2012)	Face-to-face interview, in-depth interview (semi-structured	50 women entrepreneurs who turned their homes into a tourism business in	The place and activity of women in rural tourism, women; the ability of their fields of activity and working	Women start businesses for incentives and obligations. Being withdrawn due to	Rural Tourism, Rural Development, Entrepreneurship,

		interview technique), and on-site observation	Sakarya's Taraklı district.	styles to use their knowledge and experience as an element of tourism and their contribution to the development of the region.	shyness and lack of education and low income are among the priority problems. The woman entrepreneur has gained self-confidence in the family and social field.	Woman Entrepreneur, Equal Opportunity.
11	Uluköy & Bayraktaroğlu (2014)	Easy? sampling, survey, frequency analysis, reliability analysis, ANOVA	84 women entrepreneurs in Adıyaman and Balıkesir.	How male entrepreneurs welcome women's entry into business life and what kind of pressure is exerted on women entrepreneurs.	Women entrepreneurs start businesses with their funds instead of loans. There is no significant difference in terms of the difficulties women entrepreneurs face according to their demographic characteristics.	Patriarchy, Gender, Entrepreneurship, Woman Entrepreneur, Entrepreneurship Pressure.
12	Yirik and Yıldırım (2014)	Random sample, questionnaire, frequency analysis, reliability analysis, Kruskal–Wallis, Mann–Whitney U	138 women entrepreneurs operating in Antalya.	Examination of the individual values of women entrepreneurs in the tourism sector in terms of their demographic characteristics.	While there is no difference in the success values of women entrepreneurs according to their education, entrepreneurship ages, and hedonism values, a difference was found in all	Entrepreneurship, Individual Values, Woman in Tourism, Woman Entrepreneur, Social Entrepreneurship.

Table 14.2. *(Continued)*

	Authors/Year	Data Collection and Analysis Method	Sample Size and Characteristics	Research Purpose	Key Findings	Keywords
					values according to the size of the enterprise.	
13	Çabuk, Südaş and Araç (2015)	Easy sampling, face-to-face interview, survey, frequency analysis	100 women entrepreneurs operating in Adana.	Difficulties faced by women entrepreneurs in the process of starting and running a business, in which areas they need training and support, what financial support they benefit from and identifying branding efforts.	Women entrepreneurs due to financial needs, start a business with personal earnings and loans from family members. Most of them work full-time after school life and before starting a business, stated that their work experience increased their knowledge, experience, professionalism, and self-confidence.	Women Entrepreneurs, Barriers, and Opportunities in Women Entrepreneurship, Level of Interest in Branding.
14	Tömen and Sarvan (2015)	Easy sampling, face-to-face interview method, survey, frequency analysis	Turkey Grameen Microfinance Program (GT) and 67 women entrepreneurs receiving	To what extent microfinance programs	They live with their families between the hunger line and the poverty line, usually live in a rented house, have difficulty	Entrepreneurship, Regional Development, Microfinance, Entrepreneurship, Women Entrepreneur.

			loans from the Antalya branch.	achieve their goals.	in purchasing basic food items, produce handicraft products at home with microcredit or sell ready-made products, and the use of microcredit is not yet sufficient to rid these women from poverty or make them entrepreneurs.	
15	Arıkan (2016)	Random sampling, online survey, frequency analysis, reliability, factor analysis, logistic regression	90 women who own a firm employing at least two people in Bursa.	To determine the current activities of women entrepreneurs in Bursa, to determine the reasons for becoming entrepreneurs, to reveal the factors that affect their success or failure.	Institutional barriers, inability to access the necessary financing, lack of capital are significant and affective variables that reduce success, while institutional support and entrepreneurial characteristics increase success.	Entrepreneurship, Success, Women Entrepreneurship, Women Entrepreneurs, Gender.
16	Karaturhan, Ünsal, Issabek and Güler (2017)	Stratified sampling, face-to-face survey, frequency analysis	65 women (30 entrepreneurs +35 nonentrepreneurs) living in the rural	To reveal the factors that affect the decision of women living in the rural areas of Izmir Aliağa district to become entrepreneurs, to identify	They mostly met their founding capital with their savings, mostly in the commercial sector, middle-age group, and	Entrepreneurship, Women Entrepreneurship, Rural Area, Rural Women Entrepreneurship.

Table 14.2. *(Continued)*

	Authors/Year	Data Collection and Analysis Method	Sample Size and Characteristics	Research Purpose	Key Findings	Keywords
			area of Aliağa district of Izmir province.	existing entrepreneurial activities, to identify obstacles to entrepreneurship.	almost half of them had their education at the primary school level, and the most important problem was the capital supply and lack of skills to use tools and equipment.	
17	Akyol (2017)	Full count, structured interview method and questionnaire, frequency analysis	41 entrepreneur women in Artvin city center and districts.	Describing what entrepreneur women have experienced in their working lives and what kind of struggle they have struggled for.	The problems faced by entrepreneur women in Artvin in their business life are listed as a family and environmental pressure, difficulty in finding capital, lack of self-confidence, and prejudice.	Woman, Entrepreneur Woman, Regional Development, Artvin.
18	Mert (2017)	Easy sampling, in-depth interview, semistructured interview, frequency analysis	128 housewives	How housewives will create a business plan for possible entrepreneurial activities.	Most of the housewives consider being entrepreneurs in home cooking and apparel.	Entrepreneurship, Women Entrepreneurship, Housewives, Business idea, Gaziantep.

descriptive statistics were used in 62% of the articles. Although there were expressions of "relationship" and "effect" among the purposes of some studies in terms of method, it was seen that descriptive statistics were used when analyzing methods. Studies on female entrepreneurs have generally been carried out with primary data and only one study (Çetin et al., 2016) with secondary data. Generally, the sample sizes of the studies range from 8 to 100. When the articles are examined by the unit of analysis, it is seen that the "entrepreneur woman" is the focal point. In none of the reviewed articles, women's entrepreneurship was discussed on a group basis, and the dynamics of women's entrepreneurship and/or management were not discussed.

Table 14.3 is the combined list of key terms obtained from both English and Turkish Literature by utilizing the VOS reviewer as presented in Figs. 14.1 and 14.2. The visual maps show the similarities found such as "Networks and Norm" are one of the key clusters identified in this study. The main differences between these clusters are that in the Turkish literature, entrepreneurs need support such as local governments or nongovernmental organizations. As the income of the countries increases, the need for external support decreases to implement new ideas and to engage in entrepreneurship activities. In addition, these clusters reveal that immigration, innovation, and performance are important in related fields in English literature. However, in the review of Turkish literature, it is seen that the family structure and microsupports aim to quickly earn an income. In Turkish literature, cost reduction, capital support, and short-term solutions are dominant rather than innovation and networking.

Phase Two

Factor analysis was performed by comparing similarities and differences in "Entrepreneurial Behavior And Attitudes" and "Entrepreneurial Framework Conditions" between developing countries, selected developed and world regional average. Based on the 2018/2019 GEM Women's Entrepreneurship Report, we distinguished developing countries (middle income) and developed countries (high income) based on their income levels. Europe and Central Asia region was selected as the sample region. We initially tried to include the world data for comparison; however, due to the high volume of available data on individual countries, the regional average was used to demonstrate simple and clear visualization images (Chart 14.1,14.2,14.3,14.4,14.5,14.6). We followed the groups of six geographic regions (East and South Asia and the Pacific, Europe and Central Asia, Latin America and the Caribbean, Middle East and North Africa, North America, and sub-Saharan Africa as in GEM Women's Entrepreneurship Report 2018/2019).

Entrepreneurial Behavior and Attitudes (Chart 14.1,14.2,14.3)

Based on our findings from the systematic literature review (Phase 1), the most priority indicators for social capital and women entrepreneurship were extracted from the GEM database. GEM Adult Population Survey (APS) is focusing on

Table 14.3. Cluster Comparison Table between English and Turkish Literature.

English	**Cluster 1**	**Cluster 2**	**Cluster 3**	**Cluster 4**	**Cluster 5**	**Cluster 6**	**Cluster 7**
	Networks and Norm	Access	Engagement and Reciprocity	Social Capital Resources	Trust	Knowledge Capital	Value Creation
	Entrepreneurial	**Family**	Gender Equality	Access	Business	Human	Innovation
	Outcomes	Geographic	Social Business	Personal	Performance	Capital	Market
	Marital Status	Scale	Fund	Network	Microfinance	Immigrants	Knowledge
	Microfinance	Market Access	Sustainable	Resource			
	Network	Microenterprise	Development				
	Self-Employment	Social Capital	Women				
	Social Network		Empowerment				
	Spirituality		Women				
			Entrepreneurship				
Turkish	**Cluster 1**	**Cluster 2**	**Cluster 3**				
	Networks	Norm	Engagement and Reciprocity				
	Female	Business Idea	Local Government				
	Employment	**Social Status**	NGO				
	Participation	Women	Strategy				
	Self-Employment	Employment					
	Social Capital	Women					
	Social Networks	Entrepreneurship					
		Work–Family					
		Balance					

entrepreneurial behavior and attitudes which are considered as entrepreneurial characteristics, motivations, and ambitions for business startups, as well as social attitudes toward entrepreneurship. The selected five indicators are: (1) Perceived Opportunities, (2) Perceived Capabilities, (3) Female/Male total early-stage entrepreneurial activity (TEA), (4) Female/Male Opportunity-Driven TEA, and (5) High Status to Successful Entrepreneurs.

The value of the sum of female and male opportunity is driven TEA and the sum of female/male TEA are below 1. Therefore, to avoid presenting unclear (line) figures, the Chart 1, 2, and 3 are divided into two parts to demonstrate the clear differences of value below 1, and both indicators are very similar. Unlike other developing countries, Turkey shows a steady growth in female/male opportunity-driven TEA between 2016 and 2018. In contrast, the female/male TEA scored below 0.5, and it has been declining every year. The remaining three indicator present similar movements, and Kazakhstan scored the highest value for "status," which means that population from this country agree that successful entrepreneurs receive high status.

Except for Sweden, the variable for high status to successful entrepreneurs was in better condition than others just like in developing countries. There is a considerable gap in value between high status and perceived capabilities in developing countries in this region; however, only Spain shows a close value among these variables just like in developing countries. On the other hand, Italy has the largest gap which means that population in this country believes they are lacking required skills and knowledge for business creation. Therefore, they believe that those entrepreneurs who overcome challenges to be successful receive high status as a reward. France, Netherland, and Spain show close value in their

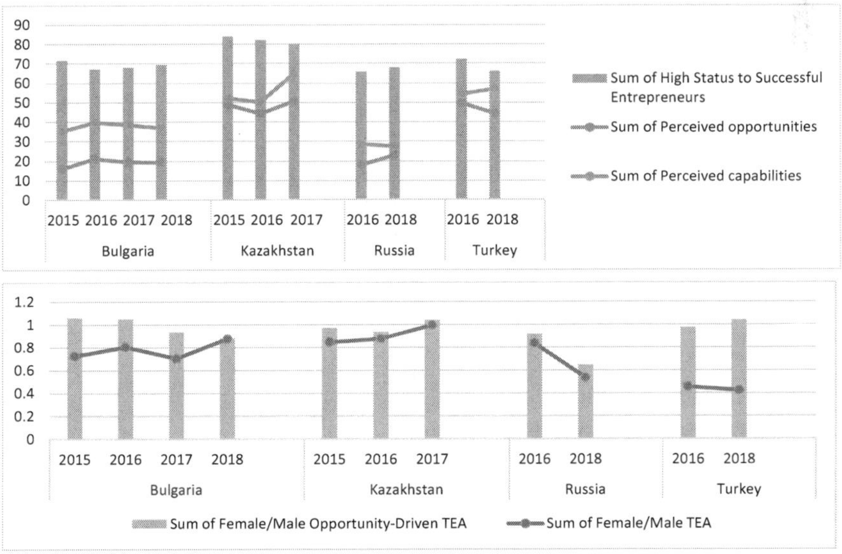

Chart 1. Developing Countries' Behavior and Attitudes.

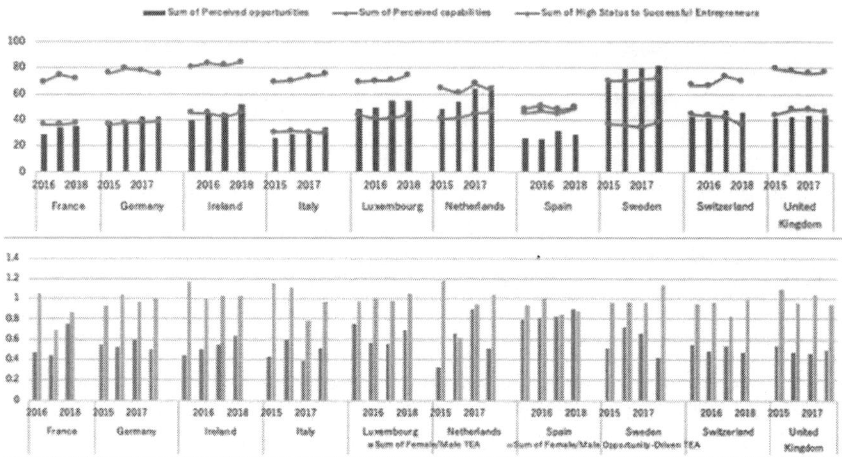

Chart 2. Selected Developing Countries' Behavior and Attitudes.

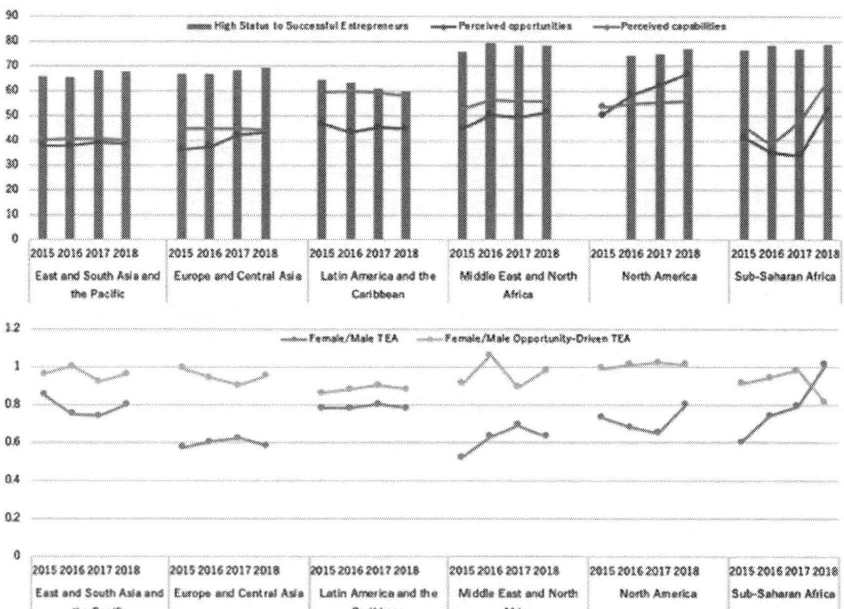

Chart 3. World Regional Average Behavior and Attitudes.

TEA and opportunity-driven TEA. Whereas Ireland and the United Kingdom are in a better position for opportunity-driven TEA which indicate the main driver in opportunity is to be independent or increasing their income.

As presented in Chart 1 and 2, the world regional average also indicates that status is in the best position among the chosen variables. This clearly confirms that entrepreneurial behavior and attitudes are seen as a positive impact on the social status as a result of successful entrepreneurial activities. Latin America and the Caribbean region relatively scored lower in the status, but the perceived capabilities are almost equaled with the status. This means that the population in this region believes their level of capabilities to pursue entrepreneurial activities equals with the success of entrepreneurs which has the same weight as the status. Among the six divided regions of the world, North America is in the best position in most of the variables except male/female TEA. Sub-Saharan Africa was the only region witnessed the decline in opportunity-driven TEA while TEA increased in contrast. The same result was also seen in Turkey.

Entrepreneurial Framework Conditions (Chart 4,5,6)

GEM National Expert Survey (NES) aims at identifying factors to determine the level of startups in the national context. Four indicators (taxes and bureaucracy, basic school entrepreneurial education and training, physical and services infrastructure, and cultural and social norms) were selected as the most priorities relevant to this study. Then, the same approach was performed to understand the position of each variable in developing and developed country groups and in the world regional average.

Physical and services infrastructure was the indicator with the highest value in developing countries, except in Bulgaria in 2018 with a sharp decline. Despite the low value for basic school entrepreneurial education and training, and taxes and bureaucracy, female entrepreneurs in Turkey are highly influenced by the cultural and social norms compared to Bulgaria, Kazakhstan, and Russia. The same result was found in phase 1 that this variable highly affects actions leading to entrepreneurial activities to increase personal income by encouragement and allowance among their network (social capital), which is linked to the level of accessible resources.

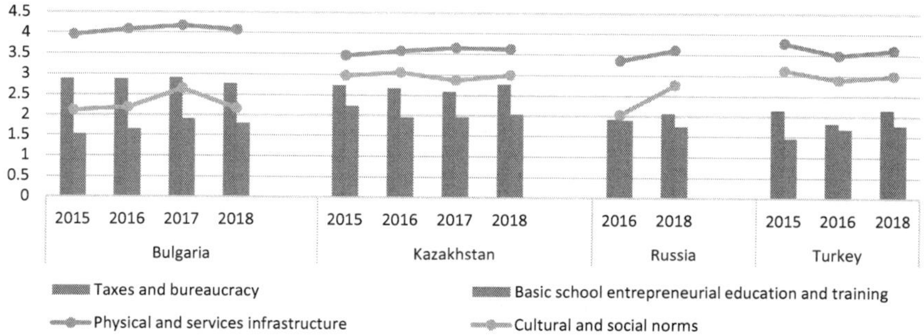

Chart 4. Developing Countries' Framework Conditions.

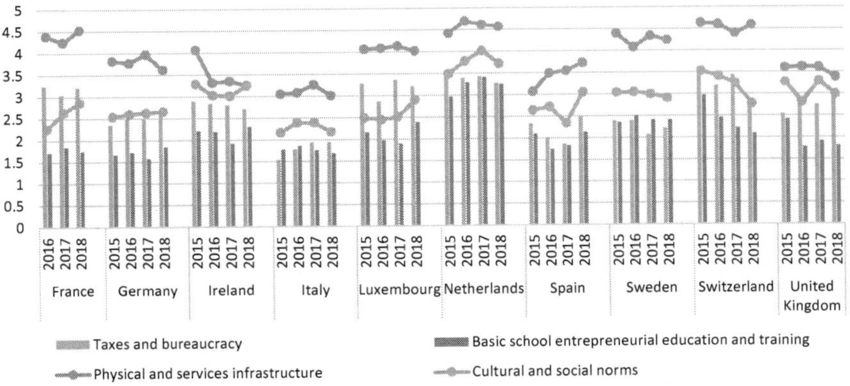

Chart 5. Selected Developed Countries' Framework Conditions.

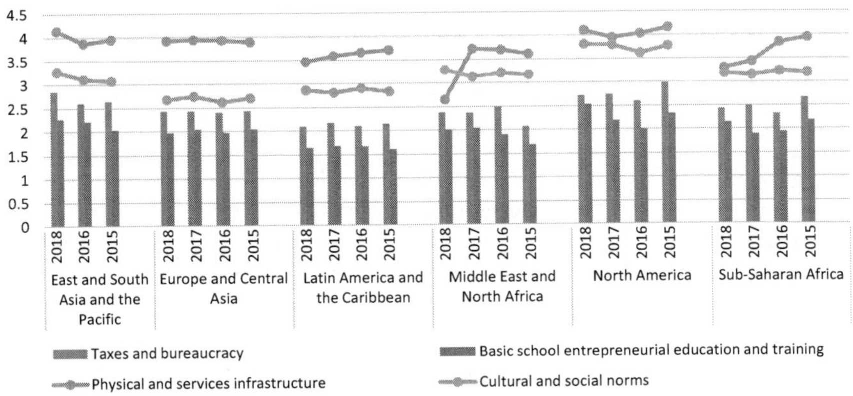

Chart 6. World Regional Average Framework Conditions.

Netherland is positioned in a better place considering all four variables, followed by Switzerland and Luxemburg. Population in Italy believes that they have fewer infrastructures compared to other developing countries. All variables in this country show stable movements over the years. The overall values are increasing in France, Germany, Luxemburg, and Spain. However, despite the ease in bureaucracy, the position of the United Kingdom is declining every year.

The world regional average for entrepreneurial framework and conditions shows similar positions for all four variables in all regions. Despite, the Middle East and North Africa region show a decline in its infrastructure against an increase in other variables such as culture and social norms. North America is again presented as the highest valued region, especially for culture and social norms, in contrast with developing countries such as Turkey. The word average shows a similar value for public policies supporting entrepreneurial activities. Basic school and entrepreneurial education and training are in the least valued position which needs improvements.

Discussion

The first goal of current study was to enlight on the current status of women entrepreneurs from social capital perspective in turkey. In order to answer to this question, we followed two steps. On the first step, by in-depth literature review, we extracted the main critical success factors for women entrepreneurs in Turkey from an academic perspective. Later by adding the analysis on GEM data and comparing the practical data in this field, the big picture about women entrepreneurship from social capital perspective became clearer.

The systematic approach of this research, including the content analysis, co-occurrence network analysis, and comparison of available real data, makes this research useable both for academicians and practitioners who work or make policies in this field.

As it is clear from the key term co-occurrence networks we had in previous sections that in Turkish language context not only the number of clusters is less but also the links between the key terms is not as strong as the English language literature, and it means that the number and depth of studies in Turkish language in this field needs improvements. Only in this way, Turkish speaking readers can get exposed to new academic findings both for policymaking and for practice. The main gap recognized by our study is that in Turkish language academic reports about women entrepreneurship with focus on social capital, some very vital factors such as social capital resources, trust, knowledge capital, and value creation are missing. We expect that including these concepts in researches in Turkish language can increase the impact of academia on business field.

Finally, the main finding of this research from the comparison charts shows that, Turkey not only has a good status in chosen criteria of women entrepreneurship from social capital perspective among chosen developing countries, but also if we consider the region that Turkey is located in, we can see the stability which can be counted as a positive symptom. It is clear that Turkey has a very small fluctuation both in behavior and attitude dimension and framework conditions. It is a good opportunity for policymakers, decision-makers, and practitioners to plan for a longer term, and it helps them to reach to better outputs from their planning and practices.

Limitations of the Study and Suggestions for Future Studies

A more in-depth literature review on this field might result in more adequate results as we needed to define limitation on our samples chosen for study. Also, more statistical analysis on similar studies can end in some other new outputs. In current research, we did the comparison analysis using GEM data for developed/ developing countries and regions. Future researchers can cluster the countries using some other criteria to add some other new novel findings. Doing a meta-analysis in this field can also be a new direction for future researchers, which is not defined in our research's scope. Our study was only on social capital perspective, but as women entrepreneurship can also be defined from other capital perspectives such as intellectual capital or human capital, we suggest future researchers to do investigations from these perspectives as well. In defining our research scope, we excluded the analysis on theories related to women entrepreneurship from social capital perspective, but future researchers can do some additional analysis on related theories and contribute more in this field.

References

Abaci, N. I., Demiryurek, K., Emir, M., & Yildirim, Ç. (2015). Factors affecting the use of microcredit among women entrepreneurs in the Samsun Province of Turkey. *Anthropologist, 20*(3), 397–406.

Addis, E., & Joxhe, M. (2017). Gender gaps in social capital: A theoretical interpretation of evidence from Italy. *Feminist Economics*. doi:10.1080/13545701.2016.1227463

Akyol, C. (2017). Girişimci Kadınların Bölge Kalkınmasına Katkıları; Artvin Örneği. *Karadeniz Sosyal Bilimler Dergisi, 9*(9), 443–464.

Aldrich, H. E., & Zimmer, C. (1986). Entrepreneurship through social networks. The University of Illinois at Urbana-Champaign's Academy for Entrepreneurial Leadership Historical Research Reference in Entrepreneurship. Retrieved from https://www.academia.edu/3793234/Entrepreneurship_through_social_networks

Ali, A., & Yousuf, S. (2019). Social capital and entrepreneurial intention: Empirical evidence from rural community of Pakistan. *Journal of Global Entrepreneurship Research, 9*(1). doi:10.1186/s40497-019-0193-z

Allen, E. I., Langowitz, N., & Minniti, M. (2007). *Global entrepreneurship monitor: 2006 report on women and entrepreneurship*. Global Entrepreneurship Monitor. Babson College and London Business School, Massachusetts, USA.

Arıkan, C. (2016). Kadin Girişimcilikte Başarı ve Başarıyı Etkileyen Faktörler: Bursa Örneği. *Yönetim ve Ekonomi Araştırmaları Dergisi, 14*(3), 138–156.

Aşkın, E., & Barış, S. (2016). Tokat Yerel İşgücü Piyasasında Kadın Girişimciler İstihdama Katılım Özellikleri Ve Sorunları. *Ömer Halisdemir Üniversitesi İktisadi ve İdari Bilimler Fakültesi Dergisi, 9*(4), 1–20.

Atmadja, A. S., Su, J. J., & Sharma, P. (2014). Financial, human, and social capital: What matters more for women's microenterprises? A case study of Indonesia. Proceedings of the 12th Eurasia Business and Economics Society (Ebes) Conference, 101–123. Retrieved from internal-pdf://254.2.105.98/SSRN-id2667312.pdf

Badura, K. L., Grijalva, E., Newman, D. A., Yan, T. T., & Jeon, G. (2018). Gender and leadership emergence: A meta-analysis and explanatory model. *Personnel Psychology, 71*(3), 335–367. doi:10.1111/peps.12266

Baranik, L. E., Gorman, B., & Wales, W. J. (2018). What makes Muslim women entrepreneurs successful? A field study examining religiosity and social capital in Tunisia. *Sex Roles, 78*(3–4), 208–219. doi:10.1007/s11199-017-0790-7

Bourdieu, P. (1986). The forms of capital. In J. Richardson (Ed.), *Handbook of theory and research for the sociology of education* (pp. 241–258). Westport, CT: Greenwood.

Bozoğlu Batı, G., & İnel, M. (2015). Kadın Girişimcilerin Profili Bağlamında Çatışma Düzeyleri Ve Yatırım Tercihleri Yalova İli Üzerine İnceleme. *Öneri Dergisi*, *11*(44), 101–119.

Brush, C., Greene, P. G., Hart, M. M., & Haller, H. S. (2001). From initial idea to unique advantage: The entrepreneurial challenge of constructing a resource base [and executive commentary]. *The Academy of Management Executive (1993–2005)*, *15*(1), 64–80. Retrieved from http://www.jstor.org/stable/4165711. Accessed on March 11, 2021.

Burt, R. S. (1992). *Structural holes: The social structure of competition*. Cambridge MA: Harvard University Press.

Çabuk, S., Südaş, H. D., & Araç, S. K. (2015). Kadin girişimcilerin iş yaşam süreçlerinin incelenmesi: Adana ilindeki girişimciler üzerinde bir uygulama. *Mustafa Kemal Üniversitesi Sosyal Bilimler Enstitüsü Dergisi*, *12*(31), 423–441.

Çalıyurt, K. T. (2011). Kadınlar tarafından yönetilen orta ve küçük ölçekli işletmelerde finansal bilginin önemi. *Trakya University Journal of Social Science*, *13*(2), 327–254.

Çetin, D., Fernandez-Zubieta, A., & Mulatero, F. (2016). Avrupa'da Erkek ve Kadın Girişimciliğinin Belirleyicisi Olarak Resmi ve Gayriresmi Sosyal Sermaye. *Çankırı Karatekin Üniversitesi İİBF Dergisi*, *6*(1), 723–748.

Coleman, J. S. (1988). Social capital in the creation of human capital. *The American Journal of Sociology*, 94, S95–S120. doi:10.1086/228943

Costa, T., & Galina, S. (2015). Networks and social capital: Multiple cases in rural tourism in Brazil. *E-Review of Tourism Research*, *12*(5–6), 241–262.

Dastourian, B., Kawamorita Kesim, H., Seyyed Amiri, N., & Moradi, S. (2017). Women entrepreneurship: Effect of social capital, innovation and market knowledge. *AD-Minister*. (June), 115–130. doi:10.17230/ad-minister.30.6

Demiryürek, K. (2014). *Agricultural knowledge and innovation and social communication network*. Agricultural Extension and Consultancy, 2. Publication of Gaziosmanpaşa University.

DeTienne, D. R., & Chandler, G. N. (2007). The role of gender in opportunity identification. *Entrepreneurship: Theory and Practice*. doi:10.1111/j.1540-6520.2007.00178.x

Ecevit, Y. (1993). *Kadını Girişimciliğe Özendirme ve Destekleme Paneli, Bildiriler ve Tartışmalar*. Devlet Bakanlığı Kadın ve Sosyal Hizmetler Müsteşarlığı Kadın Statüsü ve Sorunları Genel Müdürlüğü, Eğitim Serisi. Ankara. Yayın, (74).

Ferdousi, F., & Mahmud, P. (2019). Role of social business in women entrepreneurship development in Bangladesh: Perspectives from Nobin Udyokta projects of Grameen Telecom trust. *Journal of Global Entrepreneurship Research*, *9*(1). doi: 10.1186/s40497-019-0184-0

Fidan, F., & Nam, D. (2012). Kırsal turizmde yeni dinamikler: Kadın girişimcilertaraklı örneği. *Karamanoğlu Mehmetbey Üniversitesi Sosyal ve Ekonomik Araştırmalar Dergisi*, *14*(23), 51–57.

Fischer, E. M., Reuber, A. R., & Dyke, L. S. (1993). A theoretical overview and extension of research on sex, gender, and entrepreneurship. *Journal of Business Venturing*. doi:10.1016/0883-9026(93)90017-Y

Fukuyama, F. (2005). In A.Buğdaycı (çev.). *Güven: Sosyal Erdemler ve Refahın Yaratılması*. İstanbul: Türkiye İş Bankası Kültür Yayınları.

Henry, C., Foss, L., & Ahl, H. (2015). Gender and entrepreneurship research: A review of methodological approaches. *International Small Business Journal: Researching Entrepreneurship*, *34*(3), 217–241. doi:10.1177/0266242614549779

İlter, B. (2010). *Girişimcilik Sürecinde Kadın Girişimcilerin Karşılaştıkları Sorunların Analizi: KAGİDER Örneği*. Ankara: Adalet Yayınevi.
Jennings, J. E., & Brush, C. G. (2013). Research on women entrepreneurs: Challenges to (and from) the broader entrepreneurship literature. *Academy of Management Annals*, *7*, 663–715.
Kalafatoglu, T., & Mendoza, X. (2017). The impact of gender and culture on networking and venture creation an exploratory study in Turkey and MENA region. *Cross Cultural & Strategic Management*, *24*(2), 332–349. doi:10.1108/Ccsm-04-2016-0090
Karaman, D. E., & Ay, A. (2017). Kadın Girişimcilerin Sektöre Tutunma Çabaları: Merzifon Örneği. *Karadeniz Sosyal Bilimler Dergisi*, *9*(Kadın Özel Sayısı), 517–527.
Karaturhan, B., Ünsal, G., Issabek, B., & Guler, D. (2017). İzmir İlinde Kırsal Kadın Girişimciliği ve Bunu Etkileyen Faktörler. *Tarım Ekonomisi Dergisi*, *23*, 85–85.
Kawamorita, H., Takahashi, N., & Demiryurek, K. (2020). Media literacy and rural women entrepreneurship: Experience from Japan and Turkey. *Nordic Journal of Media Management*, *1*(3). doi:10.5278/njmm.2597-0445.5898
Kayalar, M., & Ömürbek, N. (2007). Girişimci Adaylarının risk Almaya Yatkınlık Özelliğinin Cinsiyet Bağlamında İncelenmesi. *Atatürk Üniversitesi İktisadi Ve İdari Bilimler Fakültesi Dergisi*. *21*(1), 185–200.
Kebede, G. F. (2018). Social capital and entrepreneurial outcomes: Evidence from informal sector entrepreneurs in Ethiopia. *Journal of Entrepreneurship*, *27*(2), 209–242. doi:10.1177/0971355718781250
Keskin, S. (2017). *Kadın ve Erkek girişimciler Arasındaki Farklılıklar*. *Mersin Üniversitesi Sosyal Bilimler Enstitüsü E-Dergi*, *1*(1), 64–76.
Khan, M. S. (2020). Women's entrepreneurship and social capital: Exploring the link between the domestic sphere and the marketplace in Pakistan. *Strategic Change-Briefings in Entrepreneurial Finance*, *29*(3), 375–387. doi:10.1002/jsc.2336
Lin, N. (1999). Social networks and status Attainment. *Annual Review of Sociology*, *25*, 467–487.
Lindvert, M., Patel, P. C., & Wincent, J. (2017). Struggling with social capital: Pakistani women micro entrepreneurs' challenges in acquiring resources. *Entrepreneurship & Regional Development*, *29*(7–8), 759–790. doi:10.1080/08985626.2017.1349190
Manolova, T. S., Carter, N. M., Manev, I. M., & Gyoshev, B. S. (2007). The differential effect of men and women entrepreneurs' human capital and networking on growth expectancies in Bulgaria. *Entrepreneurship: Theory and practice*. doi: 10.1111/j.1540-6520.2007.00180.x
Manolova, T. S., Gyoshev, B. S., & Manev, I. M. (2007). The role of interpersonal trust for entrepreneurial exchange in a transition economy. *International Journal of Emerging Markets*. doi:10.1108/17468800710739207
Meinzen-Dick, R., Johnson, N., Quisumbing, A. R., Njuki, J., Behrman, J. A., Rubin, D., & Waithanji, E. (2014). The gender asset gap and its implications for agricultural and rural development. In A. Quisumbing, R. Meinzen-Dick, T. Raney, A. Croppenstedt, J. Behrman, & A. Peterman (Eds.), *Gender in agriculture*. Dordrecht: Springer. doi:10.1007/978-94-017-8616-4_5
Mert, İ. S. (2017). Ev hanımlarinin girişimciliği: Gaziantep ilinde nitel bir araştırma. *Bingöl Üniversitesi Sosyal Bilimler Enstitüsü Dergisi*, *7*(İktisat Özel Sayısı), 63–78.
Mozumdar, L., Hagelaar, G., Materia, V. C., Omta, S. W. F., Islam, M. A., & van der Velde, G. (2019). Embeddedness or over-Embeddedness? Women entrepreneurs' networks and their influence on business performance. *European Journal of Development Research*. doi:10.1057/s41287-019-00217-3

Muniady, R. Al, Mamun, A. Al, Rosli Mohamad, M., Yukthamarani Permarupan, P., & Binti Zainol, N. R. (2015). The effect of cognitive and relational social capital on structural social capital and micro-enterprise performance. *SAGE Open*, *5*(4). doi:10.1177/2158244015611187

Nahapiet, J., & Ghoshal, S. (1998). Social capital, intellectual capital, and the organizational advantage. *Academy of Management Review*, *23*, 242–266.

Okan, T., Sarı, S., & Peker, İ. (2016). Girişimcilik Başarı Faktörü Olarak Sosyal Sermaye Kriterlerinin Analitik Hiyerarşi Süreci (AHS) İle Ağırlıklandırılması ve Bir Ölçek Önerisi. *Ekonomik ve Sosyal Araştırmalar Dergisi*, *12*. Yıl 12, Sayı 1.

Onay, Ü. G. (2013). *Kadın Girişimciliğini Etkileyen Sosyo Kültürel Faktörler: Isparta KOSGEB Girişimcilik Destekleri Üzerine Bir Araştırma*. Süleyman Demirel Üniversitesi İşletme Anabilimdalı Yüksek Lisans Tezi.

Önder, N. (2013). Türkiye'de Kadın İşgücünün Görünümü. *ÇSGB Çalışma Dünyası Dergisi, Cilt: 1, Sayı: 1*, 35–61.

Osei, C. D., & Zhuang, J. (2020). Rural poverty alleviation Strategies and social capital link: The mediation role of women entrepreneurship and social innovation. *SAGE Open*, *10*(2). doi:10.1177/2158244020925504

Özen, K. R. (2008). Girişimci ve Yönetici Kadınların Profilleri Farklı Mıdır? *Afyon Kocatepe Üniversitesi İ.İ.B.F. Dergisi*, *8*(2), 139–153.

Özkaya, M. (2009). Kadın Girişimcilere Yönelik "Strateji Geliştirmede" Yerel Yönetimlerle İşbirliği. İçinde Olmak Mümkün Mü? *Yönetim ve Ekonomi Araştırmaları Dergisi*, *7*(11), 56–72.

Öztürk, M. D. & Arslan, İ. K. (2016). *Türkiye'de Kadın Girişimcilik: Kadınları Girişimciliğe Yönelten Faktörler, Karşılaştıkları Sorunlar ve Çözüm Önerileri* (pp. 17–41). Istanbul: İstanbul Ticaret Üniversitesi Tartışma Metinleri, WPS NO/21/2016-05.

Pham, T., & Talavera, O. (2018). Discrimination, social capital, and financial constraints: The case of Viet Nam. *World Development*, *102*, 228–242. doi:10.1016/j.worlddev.2017.10.005

Poon, J. P. H., Thai, D. T., & Naybor, D. (2012). Social capital and female entrepreneurship in rural regions: Evidence from Vietnam. *Applied Geography*, *35*(1–2), 308–315. doi:10.1016/j.apgeog.2012.08.002

Putnam, R. (1993). The prosperous community: Social capital and public life. *The American Prospect*, 4, 35–42. Retrieved from http://faculty.washington.edu/matsueda/courses/590/Readings/Putham%201993%20Am%20Prospect.pdf

Roomi, M. A. (2009). Impact of social capital development and use in the growth process of women-owned firms. *Journal of Enterprising Culture*, *17*(4), 473–495. doi:10.1142/s0218495809000436

Roomi, M. A. (2011). Entrepreneurial capital, social values and Islamic traditions: Exploring the growth of women-owned enterprises in Pakistan. *The International Small Business Journal*, *31*(2), 175–191. doi:10.1142/s0218495809000436

Sarvan, F., & Tömen, G. (2015). Mikrofinans Programlarının Kadın Yoksulluğu ve Girişimciliği Üzerine Etkileri: Bir Araştırma ve Bir İşbirliği Modeli Önerisi. *Mediterranean Journal of Humanities*, *5*, 343–343.

Şekerler, H. (2006). *Kadın girişimciler, Karşılaştıkları Sorunlar ve Bu Sorunlara Yönelik Çözüm Önerileri*. Dumlupınar Üniversitesi Sosyal Bilimler Enstitüsü İşletme Ana Bilim Dalı. Yüksek Lisans Tezi, Kütahya.

Solano, G., & Rooks, G. (2018). Social capital of entrepreneurs in a developing country: The effect of gender on access to and requests for resources. *Social Networks, 54*, 279–290. doi:10.1016/j.socnet.2018.03.003

Soysal, A. (2010). *Kadın Girişimcilerin Özellikleri, Karşılaştıkları Sorunlar ve İş Kuracak Kadınlara Öneriler: Kahramanmaraş İlinde Bir Araştırma*. Nisan. Eskişehir Osmangazi Üniversitesi. İİBF Dergisi.

Surangi, H. A. K. N. S. (2018). What influences the networking behaviours of female entrepreneurs?. *International Journal of Gender and Entrepreneurship*. doi:10.1108/ijge-08-2017-0049

Tekin, M. (2005). Hayallerin Gerçeğe Dönüşümü: Girişimcilik. 4. Baskı, Günay Ofset.

Toprakcı Alp, G., & Aksoy, B. (2019). Kadın Girişimciliği Ve Sosyal Sermaye: NitelBir Araştırma - Women entrepreneurship and social capital: A qualitative research. *Mehmet Akif Ersoy Üniversitesi Sosyal Bilimler Enstitüsü Dergisi, 11*(27), 127–148.

Ufuk, H., & Özgen, Ö. (2001). Interaction between the business and family lives of women entrepreneurs in Turkey. *Journal of Business Ethics*. doi:10.1023/A:1010712023858

Uluköy, M., & Bayraktaroğlu, S. (2014). A field research about oppression incurred of woman entrepreneurs in patriarchal societies. *Yönetim ve Ekonomi Araştırmaları Dergisi, 24*, 356–369.

Urban, B. (2011). Gender perspectives on entrepreneurship and self-efficacy: Evidence from an emerging economy. *Journal of Humanities*.

Wafeq, M., Al Serhan, O., Catherine Gleason, K., Dasanayaka, S. W. S. B., Houjeir, R., & Al Sakka, M. (2019). Marketing management and optimism of Afghan female entrepreneurs. *Journal of Entrepreneurship in Emerging Economies*. doi:10.1108/JEEE-02-2018-0020

Walliman, N. (2010). *Research methods: The basics: 2nd edition* (1st ed.). London: Routledge. doi:10.4324/9780203836071

Welter, F., Brush, C., & de Bruin, A. (2014). The gendering of entrepreneurship context. *SSRN Electronic Journal*. doi:10.2139/ssrn.2557272

White, M. D., & Marsh, E. E. (2006). Content analysis: A flexible methodology. *Library Trends*. doi:10.1353/lib.2006.0053

Yeroz, H. (2019). Manifestations of social class and agency in cultural capital development processes an empirical study of Turkish migrant women entrepreneurs in Sweden. *International Journal of Entrepreneurial Behavior & Research, 25*(5), 900–918. doi:10.1108/Ijebr-03-2018-0146

Yetim, N. (2002). Sosyal Sermaye Olarak Kadin Girisimciler: Mersin Örneği. *Ege Akademik Bakış Dergisi, 2*(2), 79–92.

Yetim, N. (2008). Social capital in female entrepreneurship. *International Sociology, 23*(6), 864–885. doi:10.1177/0268580908095913

Yirik, Ş, & Yıldırım, B. I. (2014). Turizm sektöründeki kadin girişimcilerin bireysel değerlerinin demografik özellikleri açısından incelenmesi: Antalya ili örneği. *Mustafa Kemal Üniversitesi Sosyal Bilimler Enstitüsü Dergisi, 11*(26), 361–378.

Yusuff, Y. Z., Abu Bakar, A., & Ahmad, S. (2018). Relationship between financial capital, social capital and women entrepreneurs' business performance. *Advanced Science Letters, 24*(1), 202–204. doi:10.1166/asl.2018.11959

Part 3
Entrepreneurial Ecosystem and Female Digital Entrepreneurship

Chapter 15

Digital Natives' Entrepreneurial Mindset: A Comparative Study in Emerging Markets

Piotr Kwiatek, Stavros Papakonstantinidis and Radoslav Baltezarevic

Abstract

Recent studies conducted in Europe and in the Middle East found growing interest of young entrepreneurs in using social media as a venue for business activities. The Digital Natives (DNs), young people who cannot recall their lives without the Internet and digital devices, are thought to be the most entrepreneurial generation so far.

In this chapter, the authors take a closer look at the role of gender in entrepreneurship and provide more insights for effective policy-shaping with the DNs in mind.

This study adopts a quantitative approach to compare the entrepreneurial mindset (EM) of DNs from two frontier markets, Serbia, and Kuwait and examines the gender differences in entrepreneurial intention (EI) and entrepreneurial capacity.

The study shows that female respondents demonstrate a positive attitude toward using social media for entrepreneurial activities. Although technology drives EI, female DNs should receive more guidance and encouragement to feel more confident to start a business. Extending previous studies, the authors discuss the prominent role of social approvals and expert guidance in driving the EM.

Keywords: Digital natives; gender differences; social media; entrepreneurial mindset; Kuwait; Serbia

Introduction

Digital Natives (DNs) are the native speakers of the new digital age, children who grew up in a social environment defined by technology (Prensky, 2001). These

The Emerald Handbook of Women and Entrepreneurship in Developing Economies, 295–315
Copyright © 2021 by Emerald Publishing Limited
All rights of reproduction in any form reserved
doi:10.1108/978-1-80071-326-020211015

young people cannot recall their lives without the Internet or using a digital device. Born in the last two decades of the twentieth century, DNs are the product of an emerging culture of online learners, smartphone users, online gamers, content streamers, and recently social media entrepreneurs (Bennett, Maton, & Kervin, 2008). DNs learn and communicate differently than their parents, Digital Immigrants who migrated to the new technological era, demonstrating an exciting generation gap worth further investigation. This study investigates DNs' entrepreneurial mindset (EM) in two MSCI classified frontier markets, Serbia and Kuwait, which demonstrate distinct socioeconomical differences. In this regard, authors take a closer look at the role of gender in entrepreneurship and provide more insights for effective policy-shaping with the DNs in mind.

The MSCI Index is based on the Global Investable Market Indexes (GIMI) Methodology, which offers insights and cross-country comparisons across markets. MSCI rates and classifies markets to Developed, Emerging, and Frontier based on their liquidity, equity investment opportunity, and easiness to replicate their model in other countries. According to the 2020 MSCI Index, Serbia and Kuwait are classified as Frontier Markets, showing sufficient financial strengths and offering growth opportunities while being more volatile than the emerging economies ("Market classification – MSCI," 2020). Other frontier markets from the Middle East and Southeast Europe are Bahrain, Jordan, Lebanon, Oman, Croatia, Estonia, Lithuania, Romania, and Slovenia. It has been emphasized that frontier markets should encourage the youth population to develop an inclusive, growing, and sustainable business environment through entrepreneurship and innovation (Christensen, Ojomo, & Dillon, 2019). With an example of the National Fund for Small and Medium Enterprise (SME) Development in Kuwait, indeed, frontier markets offer growing support to entrepreneurship, at least in terms of covering needs of capital. However, tech-savvy youth might need different means of entrepreneurial support.

The proportion of the young population who use the new technologies is much higher than the older population (Cheong, 2008); still, there are enormous differences in why and how effectively young people use these new technologies (Hargittai & Hinnant, 2008). Technologies such as social media, open-source software, 3D printing, crowdfunding, online reputation assessment, digital imaging, and big data enable potential entrepreneurs to reduce the barriers between innovation and the creation of a new company (Steiniger, 2019). The use of digital platforms and tools is favoring the emergence of this new type of job. (Hull, Hung, Hair, Perotti, & DeMartino, 2007). However, the question is whether this type of business should be considered a new phenomenon or rather a "reconciliation of traditional entrepreneurship with the new way of creating and doing business in the digital era" (Le Dinh, Vu, & Ayayi, 2018, p. 1).

Tata Consultancy Services, an IT consulting and business solutions firm, conducted an online study in 2015 among 5,024 young (18–29 years old) adults in 15 European countries, including Serbia ("Social media is serious business: A view from European youth," 2015). The Tata study indicates how social media enables young entrepreneurs and shows that 33% of young Europeans utilize social media daily, ranging from hiring and networking to client communication, collaboration, and skill development. Six out of ten young entrepreneurs state that social media helps them find freelance employees, 41% stay in touch with clients via social media daily, and 62% use social media to grow a business network.

Similarly, the DNs living in the Middle East and North Africa (MENA) region present a unique generation of consumers, learners, and citizens, disrupting the status quo and adopting new lifestyles, following trends, and ideologies ("MENA's Millennials Decoded," 2018). Ipsos Group, a market research, and consulting firm, calls MENA's DNs as trendsetters who shape a generation without borders. More than half (57%) of MENA's DNs are eager to learn about other cultures, want to stay updated with global affairs (55%), and, not surprisingly, consider themselves global citizens (47%). The young people in MENA are online savvy as 97% report using the Internet, 94% having at least one social media account, and 56% are always looking for ways to increase the use of technology in their lives.[1]

Both studies, Tata in Europe and Ipsos in the Middle East, point out that social media has become a primary aspect of growing and sustaining a business for young (i.e., DN) entrepreneurs. Social media presents an excellent opportunity for young entrepreneurs to continue finding creative and effective ways to build their brands, serve their clients, cultivate relationships with their consumers and colleagues, and finally discover new business possibilities. All this implicates that the current generation of DNs could be the most entrepreneurial of all we have seen so far (Kuhl, 2016).

In line with the discussion, this study adopts a quantitative approach to compare the EM of DNs living in two frontier markets, Serbia, and Kuwait. Our study examines the gender differences in two countries in terms of DNs entrepreneurial intention (EI) and entrepreneurial capacity (EC) to start their business through social media. The main question that this study aims to answer is to what extent women DNs living in Serbia and Kuwait are willing (i.e., EI) and confident enough (i.e., EC) to accepting technology for entrepreneurial reasons. Through a systematic exploration, the objective of this study is to answer a set of research subquestions:

- What is the attitude of the DNs in Serbia and Kuwait toward technology?
- Which factors affect DNs' EI and EC?

This study contributes to DNs and entrepreneurship literature by suggesting a research model to explore the relationship between EI and EC. We also offer suggestions to empower women entrepreneurs in both frontier markets to overcome their doubts and achieve their entrepreneurial aspirations.

Literature Review

Entrepreneurship and Social Media

The field of entrepreneurship has been extensively researched, and the probable cause could be its contribution to public policy goals, such as economic growth, innovation in technology, job creation, increased productivity, and structural realignments (Eckhardt & Shane, 2003). An entrepreneur is a "person who owns, launches, and assumes the risk of an economic venture" (Gartner, Shaver, Gatewood, & Katz, 1994, p. 6). The term entrepreneur also refers to people who have bought an existing business (Gartner et al. 1994). An entrepreneur introduces new technologies/products/services, innovates in an existing, or creates a new market while increasing efficiency and productivity. To some extent, an entrepreneur could be a catalyst for economic, national, and global change (Deakins & Freel, 2012). Other traits that encourage entrepreneurial behavior can be seeking and utilizing opportunity, being responsible for taking calculative risks, and ownership of things (Bridge & O'Neill, 2013).

Entrepreneurship is defined

> …as an activity that involves the discovery, evaluation, and exploitation of opportunities to introduce new goals and services, ways of governing markets, processes, and raw materials through organizing efforts that previously had not existed. (Shane & Venkataraman, 2007, p. 218)

Entrepreneurship is also a process where individuals "use organized efforts and means to pursue opportunities to create value and grow by fulfilling wants and needs through innovation and uniqueness, no matter what resources are currently controlled" (Kobia & Sikalieh, 2010, p. 110). With the term entrepreneurial mindset, scholars explain people's intentions and capacity to acquire skills that will strengthen their employability, create occupational opportunities, and build their socioeconomic status (Bridge & O'Neill, 2013). Lastly, technology-oriented entrepreneurship is an answer to a country's increasing unemployment rates, job redundancy, and workforce dissatisfaction (Mueller & Thomas, 2001).

In the field of information technologies, innovations are being introduced through social networking sites (SNSs). SNSs such as LinkedIn, Facebook, Twitter, Instagram, etc. are providing new social interaction patterns of communication (Sapountzi & Psannis, 2018). Carr and Hayes (2015, p. 49) define social media as "internet-based, disdained, and persistent channels of mass personal communication, facilitating perceptions of interactions among users, deriving value primarily from user-generated content." Social media is a set of information technologies that facilitates interaction and networking. Social media offers a space for entrepreneurial growth, business transactions, cause awareness, information exchange, human connectivity through interests, and expression of ideas through virtual communities (Kapoor et al. 2017; Nielsen, 2017).

Social media mediates the creation of networks and communities by encouraging the interest and participation of users. This term is used for Internet tools and websites that offer an opportunity for their users to interact with one another through information, interest, opinion, and sharing. The most significant motive for people to be active on social media is the need to consume and share content with other online users (Ellison & Boyd, 2013). Studies have shown that people visit SNSs to receive information about specific brands and their promotional campaigns (Mangold & Faulds, 2009). The ability of social media to segment the market is one of the biggest reasons why SNSs are preferred for marketers to promote their brands. Also, the advent of SNSs allows marketing professionals to reach a considerable number of new opportunities (Wright, Khanfar, Harrington, & Kizer, 2016). With the use of social media, people have the power to influence brand awareness and loyalty, increase sales, and expand to global markets (Kapoor et al. 2017).

The Internet plays a role in business growth and online entrepreneurship using various social media tools such as Facebook, Twitter, etc. SNSs increased social contacts, strengthened customer relationships with entrepreneurs, accelerated business operations, and supported the hiring of competent intellectuals (Jagongo & Kinyua, 2013). SMEs use social media to develop tools for creating and attaining a sustainable competitive advantage since most of the consumer activity becomes virtual (Heller Baird & Parasnis, 2011). Social media relations are seen as a component of the establishment phase of any business or enterprise (Greve & Salaff, 2003), making it an essential tool for young entrepreneurs to start their business (Hull et al. 2007).

Social entrepreneurs seek profitable opportunities through social media. These entrepreneurs sell products or services on social media platforms, but also make money through the content they produce. We can distinguish this type of entrepreneur from other people through their ability to spot lucrative opportunities in an environment where millions of people spend their time daily, as well as their ability to transform innovative ideas into profit (Cicek, 2018). One of the most attractive motives for entering social media is low entry barriers. Social media offers an encouraging environment for entrepreneurial activities due to lower costs, fewer regulations, and unexplored market opportunities (Khajeheian, 2012). Social media entrepreneurship seems less risky than other types of entrepreneurship as entrepreneurs could start and promote their business with minimum resources (Cicek, 2018).

The innovative entrepreneur uses the advantage of social media in scanning, searching, and connecting information in the markets (Park, Sung, & Im, 2017). Social media can be useful and effective in a variety of ways, as evidenced by a large number of previous research studies (Taylor & Kent, 2010). Günther, Krasnova, Riehle, and Schoendienst (2009) argue that social media helps young entrepreneurs build their community through that medium for seamless interaction with their partners. Social media helps entrepreneurs create new opportunities by enabling them to more easily assess market changes and identify potential entrepreneurial opportunities (Yun, 2015). However, the use of social media in strategic decisions related to entrepreneurial opportunities remains uncertain. The lack of information and the rapid development of technology may result in entrepreneurs not understanding enough the strategic use of social media in the entrepreneurial process (DiStaso, McCorkindale, & Wright, 2011). For this reason, it is crucial to understand to what extent entrepreneurs should trust the information found on social media platforms (Park et al., 2017).

Entrepreneurs use social media as a marketing tool, which is vital for business growth because, in this way, they can quickly build a network of supporters (followers). Their supporters have the power to bring customers to small businesses, passing on company information to others (Yun, 2015). Also, social media helps to establish a long-term relationship between businesses and customers. However, the main problem that entrepreneurs face relates to the implementation of social media in business because there is a lack of consensus on how to obtain different activities and use them in business (Shabbir, Mohd Shariff, Salman, & Shabbir, 2017). The rapid proliferation of SNSs and other cutting-edge technologies creates an unclear environment as to what idea will last and appeal to a broad audience. Entrepreneurs generally opt for an experimental approach to achieve a better result. Every year, a large number of entrepreneurs join social media, but the cases of those who maintain their online presence effectively are relatively low. This is because many of the social entrepreneurs launch a social media campaign without clear strategic goals (Shabbir et al., 2017).

Thanks to the technological progress, we moved from the solely brick and mortar organizations to virtual organizations and virtual work teams (Salmela & Juvonen, 2016). This business shift has disrupted entrepreneurship on a global scale. In Serbia, entrepreneurship is recognized as one of the critical factors of economic growth, employment development, and a way out of the financial recession (Anicic, Laketa, Laketa, Anicic, & Lukic, 2014). However, social entrepreneurship in Serbia currently only exists in the shape of individual initiatives, in which the problems of social exclusion and unemployment are addressed in individual cases. In Serbia, the labor market is still undeveloped and not able to take on the role of the crucial factor of social integration (Damnjanovic, Ristic, & Danilovic, 2017). In contrast, local news reports that the State of Kuwait encourages entrepreneurship, fulfilling one of the 2035 New Kuwait Plan's strategic goals. Kuwait started the National Fund for Small and Medium Enterprise Development (NFSMED), of a KD2 billion (approx. 5.5 billion Euro), to motivate the nation's youth to start their SMEs, create right-size employment in the public sector, and combat unemployment (Pinto, 2019).

Gender Gap in Entrepreneurship

According to the World Economic Forum (2015), there are significant differences in access to financial resources for men and women who own and run their businesses in developing countries (World Economic Forum: Insight report global gender gap report, 2020). As a result, many entrepreneurs rely on family or friend loans, short-term loans, or their savings to start their businesses. However, short-term loan maturity and insufficient amounts of financial assets, usually do not allow female entrepreneur funds for long-term investments in their own business. An analysis by the World Bank indicates that only in 38 out of 141 countries, women have the same rights as men in crucial business areas, such as getting a job without her husband's permission, opening a bank account, and owning property. Therefore, the World Bank report emphasizes that the legal and institutional environment is essential for the growth of female entrepreneurship (World Bank: Female entrepreneurship resource point – Why gender matters, 2015).

Female entrepreneurship attracts attention in the literature, as there is a growing body of concrete evidence of the importance of opening new businesses for economic growth and development (Langowitz & Minniti, 2007). Women's entrepreneurship contributes to economic growth and job creation and recognizes an opportunity to improve the diversity of entrepreneurship in any economic system (Verheul, Stel, & Thurik, 2006). It is crucial to provide opportunities for women entrepreneurs to express themselves and potentially realize their business (Eddleston & Powell, 2008). Unfortunately, the talent and potential of women's entrepreneurship are largely untapped in most cases (Baughn, Chua, & Neupert, 2006). Gender differences have indeed been documented at a micro level concerning self-perception (Anna, Chandler, Jansen, & Mero, 2000), decision-making styles (Baker & Nelson, 2005), opportunity recognition (Eckhardt & Shane, 2003), and networking behavior (McManus, 2001).

Gender differences in opportunity identification relate to differences involving work experience and education. As a rule, men have a significantly higher level of previous industrial or entrepreneurial experience, as well as experience in managing employees compared to women (Fairlie & Robb, 2009). DeTienne and Chandler (2007) argue that the evidence generally suggests that women have less human capital for self-employment, which in turn hurts their ability to identify their opportunity and exploit the potential. Women-owned businesses tend to be smaller, less profitable, and slower growing than those owned by men (Greene, Hart, Gatewood, Brush, & Carter, 2003).

Gender inequality is a push factor to female entrepreneurship in developing as well as in developed economies (Aidis, Welter, Smallbone, & Isakova, 2007). Many women entrepreneurs have little choice of opportunities for self-employment in the labor market. Usually, women face discrimination or may have various problems if they want to advance in their careers. Often women perceive self-employment as a survival strategy or a means of providing flexibility in work scheduling (Baughn et al., 2006). When it comes to pulling factors, they are also important because they relate to opportunities for independence, initiative, and challenge, as well as success and satisfaction caused by entrepreneurship (Baughn et al., 2006). Past research suggests different sets of career satisfaction for male and female entrepreneurs. For men, they relate to the achievement of status, and for women, to social relationships and the achievement of goals (Eddleston & Powell, 2008).

In frontier markets, compared to their male counterparts, women entrepreneurs have a higher level of innovation as well as higher rates of reinvestment in human resources, contributing to household incomes as well as national economies through investment in health, education, and nutrition (Allen, Elam, Langowitz, & Dean, 2007). Women choose to become entrepreneurs, mainly because of the need for survival, health care, nutrition, or for educational reasons. When it comes to developing countries, where the situation is generally stable, as a basic need of an entrepreneurial woman to start her own business is the lack of opportunities in the labor market (Aidis et al., 2007). Performance in the context of women's entrepreneurship is recognized as a complex construct, influenced by various factors such as the nature and extent of family support, family obligations, but also general role expectations (Jamali, 2009).

The Kauffman Foundation conducted a study about the intrinsic motivators of women entrepreneurs. The study reveals that women who decided to become entrepreneurs were motivated primarily by financial and psychological factors, like building wealth, the desire to be independent, or to be company owners (Cohoon, Wadhwa, & Mitchell, 2010). Hasan and Almubarak (2016) argue that in small-business development initiatives, groups of women entrepreneurs with low levels of influence and power are often ignored. Starting and developing businesses is difficult for women, mainly because of expected cultural practices and traditional views that restrict female voices and other non–family-related responsibilities.

The lack of social and human capital makes female entrepreneurship uncertain, resulting in a reduction of their willingness to start their businesses (Roomi, 2013). Longman, Daniels, Bray, and Liddell (2018) state that women are either unconsciously or consciously rejected in a business environment in which men dominate. Companies owned by women may be considered riskier by banks because of the structural differences that exist between companies owned by women and men (Cole & Mehran, 2009). These differences are reflected in the size of the company, the area of economic activity, and legal status, as well as the age of the company, which can further affect the creditworthiness of the business owner. On average, women's enterprises are younger and smaller than male-owned enterprises. They are also less growth-oriented and more concentrated in the trade and services sectors. Finally, Cole and Mehran (2009) argue that women's businesses are mostly organized as sole proprietors, rarely as corporations.

The discussion provided thus far indicates a profound need for a better understanding of the needs of women DN entrepreneurs in the emerging markets. In the next sections, we take a closer look at DNs in Serbia and Kuwait and investigate the factors which affect their EI and EC.

Methodology and Results

In order to answer our research questions, we developed an online survey to gather the data in both countries. The questionnaire was developed in English and tested with a small (n = 10) convenience sample for proper comprehension. The English version was used to gather the data in Kuwait, while for Serbia, we translated and back-translated the questionnaire to verify the consistency in wording and content comprehension. The questionnaire consisted of 18 questions with constructs from the Technology Acceptance Model, an EM, as well as demographic descriptors.

To capture the EM of DNs in Kuwait and Serbia, we adopted the scales from the Entrepreneurial Intention Questionnaire (EIQ) (Liñán & Chen, 2009): EC and EI. The EC was measured through 5 items on a 7-point Likert-type scale anchored from "totally disagree" to "totally agree," and EI was measured through 4 items on an analogous type of a scale. The measures of TAM constructs (self-efficacy, anxiety, perceived usefulness, ease of use, and attitude toward social media) were adopted from Blut, Wang, and Schoefer (2016). The TAM constructs were measured trough a 5-point Likert-type (from "strongly disagree" to "strongly agree"). We collected the data with snowball convenience sampling. Due to COVID-19 restrictions, we invited participants through SNS. The survey was available for 10 days in both of the countries and allowed us to gather 394 responses. We used SPSS 24 (IBM Corp. Released, 2016) to analyze the data.

Sample Characteristic and Social Media Usage

The sample included 180 millennial participants from Kuwait and 214 from Serbia and consisted of 219 female and 175 male respondents (Table 15.1). Three-quarters of respondents (76.9%) reported a bachelor's degree, while one in nine (11.4%) a higher degree. Two-thirds had a "student" or "private sector employee" status (33.5% and 32.2%, respectively), and 15.4% registered as unemployed (Table 15.1).

In both countries, the millennials prefer visual channels (YouTube and Instagram). In Kuwait, these channels are equally distributed, while in Serbia, two-thirds are taken by Instagram (Fig. 15.1).

Table 15.1. Demographic Profile of Respondents.

	Kuwait (n = 180)		**Serbia (n = 214)**	
Demographic	N	%	n	%
Gender				
Male	95	52.8	80	37.4
Female	85	47.2	134	62.6
Age				
18–25	115	63.9	98	45.8
26–35	65	36.1	116	54.2
Education				
Secondary school	5	2.8	31	14.5
Vocational education	5	2.8	5	2.3
Bachelor	155	86.1	148	69.2
Masters and above	15	8.3	30	14
Occupation				
Student	40	22.2	92	43.0
Private sector employee	60	33.3	67	31.3
Self-employed	10	5.6	5	2.3
Government employee	25	13.9	28	13.1
Other	10	5.6		0.0
Unemployed	35	19.4	22	10.3

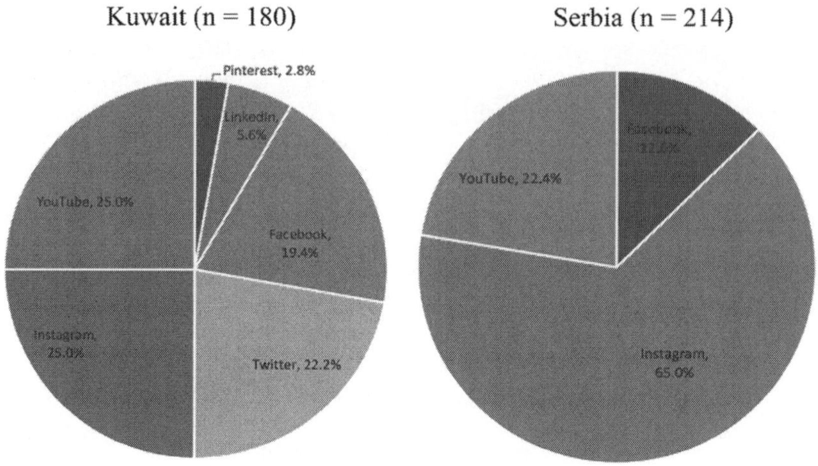

Fig. 15.1. Favorite Social Media.

Digital Natives in Kuwait and Serbia under the Microscope

The comparison between genders provides exciting results (Figs. 15.2 and 15.3). In Kuwait, male respondents use social media to contact family and friends more (M = 2.8) than female respondents (M = 2.0), whereas females use social media for entertainment more (M = 3.5) than males (M = 2.8).

In Serbia, it is also men who use social media to contact family and friends more (M = 3.1) than women (M = 2.7), though the difference is smaller than in Kuwait. On the other hand, Serbian women are more engaged in finding and sharing brand-related information (M = 2.6 for men and M = 3.3 for women). We note that irrespective of gender, social media is used much less for entertainment in Serbia.

The Entrepreneurial Mindset of Digital Natives

We investigated EC and EI from the perspective of adopting social media as a venue for entrepreneurial activity. In both country samples, EI outscores EC, though, the discrepancy is lower in Serbia (Table 15.2). Since both countries are comparable in terms of Hofstede's cultural dimensions (Kwiatek, Morgan, & Baltezarevic, 2018), the difference can be explained by higher diversity in Kuwait's population.

The normality assumption is violated with the Kolmogorov–Smirnoff test yielding significant results ($p < 0.01$). Thus, we test the group differences with Mann–Whitney's U test. We note no difference in EC between males (M = 4.42, SE = 0.10) and female respondents (M = 4.32, SE = 0.09, p = 0.46). However, women reported higher EI (M = 5.58, SE = 0.11) than men (M = 5.11, SE = 0.10). The difference is significant at $p < 0.01$ (pairwise comparison with Bonferroni adjustment).

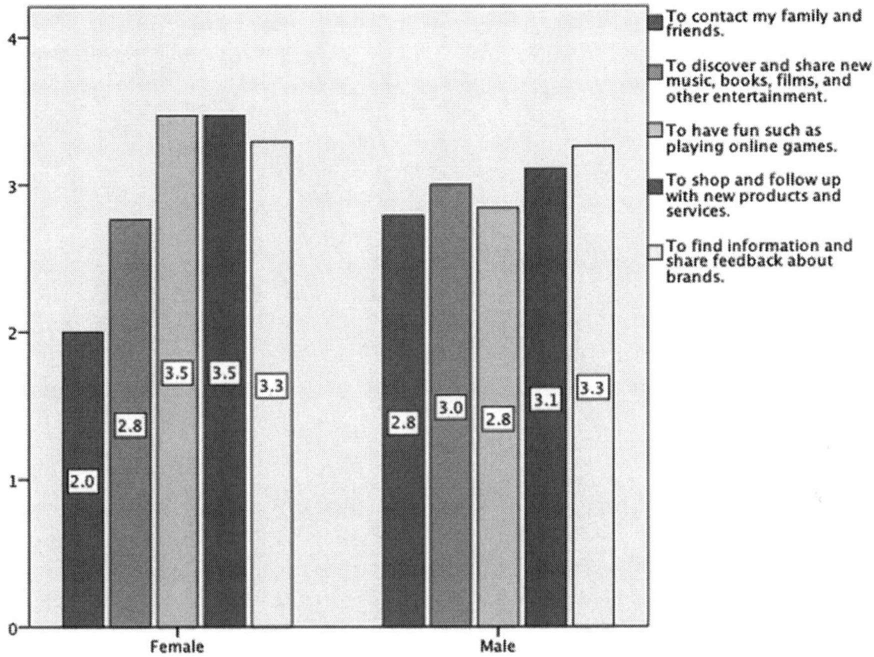

Fig. 15.2. Reasons to Engage in Social Media by Gender (Kuwait).

In the Kuwaiti sample, female respondents reported higher entrepreneurial intent ($M = 5.66$) than male ($M = 5.12$) respondents ($U = 4.075$, $Z = -2.78$, $p < 0.01$, $r = 0.31$). On the contrary, as shown in Fig. 15.4, Serbian men report higher EI than women ($U = 7.743$, $Z = 5.488$, $p < 0.01$, $\eta 2 = 0.17$). The essential component of EI is searching for external approval/support by young entrepreneurs (Fig. 15.5). We note that approvals are important for all respondents (over 4 on a 7-point scale of importance). Female respondents tend to look for approval from experts, more male respondents in both countries.

Entrepreneurial Mindset – A Closer Look

The two building blocks of the EM, EI and capacity, are positively correlated in both countries. In Kuwait, the attitude toward using social media in the entrepreneurial activity of female respondents is correlated negatively with EC ($r = -0.22$, $p < 0.05$) and positively with EI ($r = 0.36$, $p < 0.01$) as shown in Table 15.3. For male respondents, the correlations are not significant ($r = 0.18$ and $r = 0.08$, $p > 0.05$, respectively). Self-efficacy correlates positively with an EI for females ($r = 0.62$, $p < 0.01$) while there is no correlation in the male group ($r = 0.07$, $p > 0.05$).

Detailed results for the Serbian sample are provided in Table 15.4. On the contrary to Kuwait, it is men whose attitude toward using social media correlates

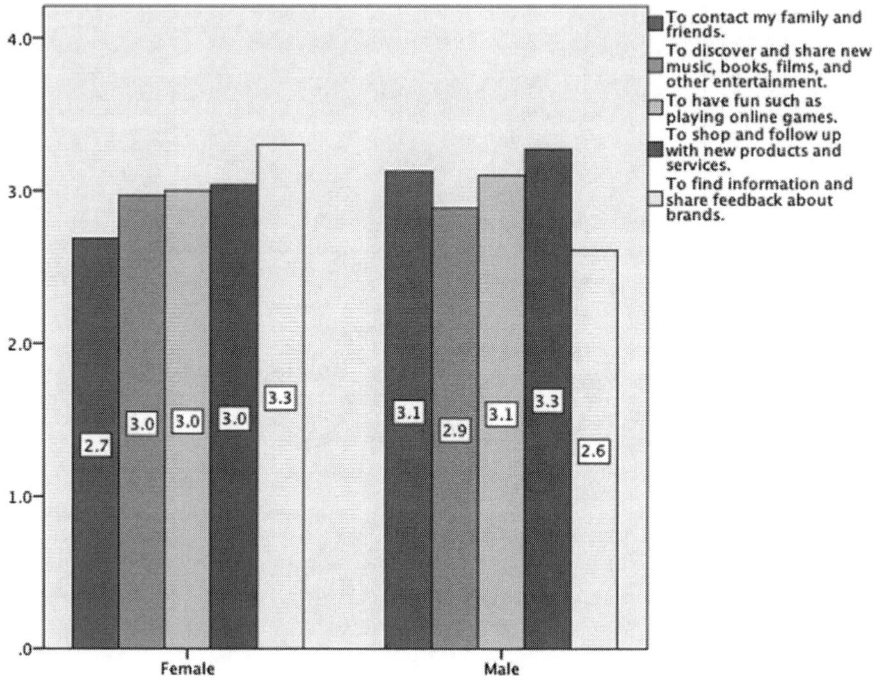

Fig. 15.3. Reasons to Engage in Social Media by Gender (Serbia).

Table 15.2. Entrepreneurial Intention and Capacity.

		Kuwait	Serbia
EI			
	M	5.37	5.11
	SD	1.39	1.76
EC			
	M	4.13	4.62
	SD	1.39	1.28

negatively with EC ($r = -0.43, p < 0.05$). For female respondents, the correlation is rather low, yet significant ($r = 0.22, p < 0.01$). In the female subsample, we note a considerable correlation of self-efficacy with both EC and EI ($r = 0.50$, $p < 0.01$). However, similarly to Kuwait, we do not find support for the correlation in the male subsample.

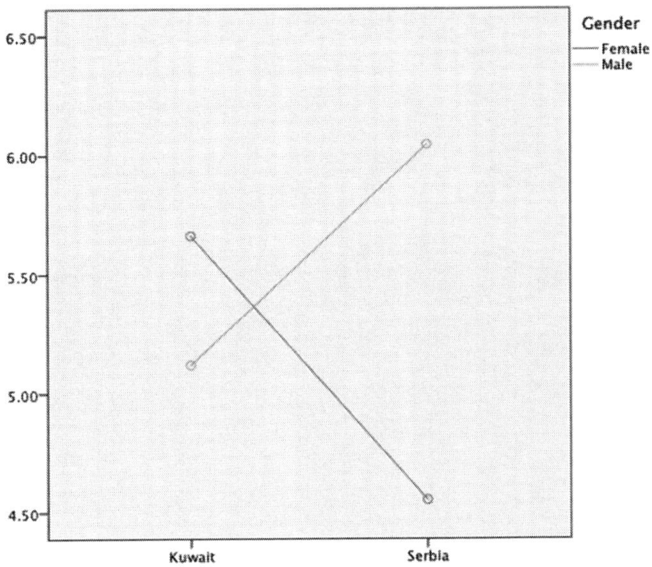

Fig. 15.4. Entrepreneurial Intention: Gender and Country.

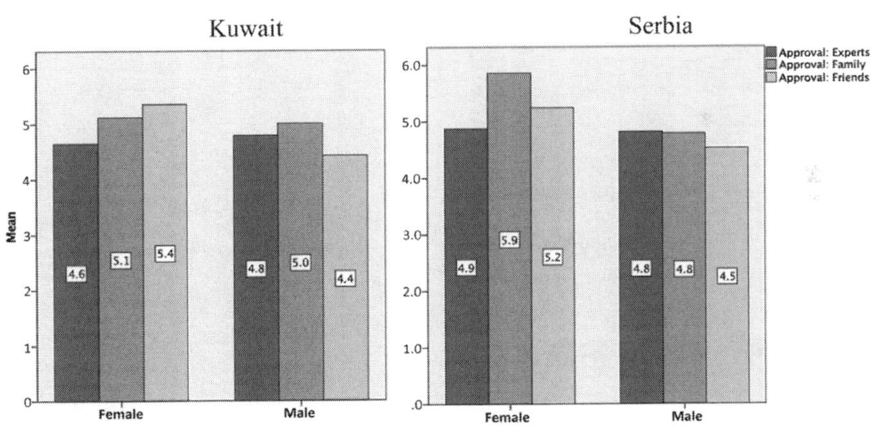

Fig. 15.5. Seeking Entrepreneurial Approval by Gender.

Discussions

"Want to do" versus "Can do"

Both Digital Natives in Kuwait (DNK) and Serbia (DNS) show their preference for social media entrepreneurship. Although DNS use social media much less for entertainment purposes than DNK, the young millennials demonstrate a

Table 15.3. Construct Correlations (Gender Split: Kuwait).

	EC	EI	SM_PU	SM_AT	Anxiety
EI	0.529**				
SM_PU	−0.225*	0.104			
SM_AT	−0.218*	0.361**	0.749**		
Anxiety	−0.167	−0.468**	−0.282**	−0.337**	
Self-efficacy	−0.033	0.621**	0.303**	0.406**	−0.436**
Male					
EI	0.692**				
SM_PU	0.073	−0.115			
SM_AT	0.182	0.082	0.790**		
Anxiety	−0.599**	−0.704**	0.087	0.031	
Self-efficacy	0.054	0.066	0.191	−0.064	0.244*

Note: EI = entrepreneurial intention; EC = entrepreneurial capacity; SM_PU = social media perceived usefulness; SM_AT = attitude toward social media; $^{**}p < 0.01$ (2-tailed); $^{*}p < 0.05$ (2-tailed).

Table 15.4. Construct Correlations (Gender Split: Serbia).

	EC	EI	SM_PU	SM_AT	Anxiety
Female					
EI	0.675**				
SM_PU	−0.158	0.023			
SM_AT	0.036	0.223**	0.839**		
Anxiety	−0.203*	−0.281**	−0.008	−0.020	
Self-efficacy	0.498**	0.503**	0.059	0.144	0.087
Male					
EI	0.158				
SM_PU	−0.042	−0.276*			
SM_AT	−0.429**	−0.203	0.621**		
Anxiety	−0.343**	−0.438**	−0.128	0.137	
Self-efficacy	−0.086	−0.063	−0.139	−0.061	−0.010

Note: EI = entrepreneurial intention; EC = entrepreneurial capacity; SM_PU = social media perceived usefulness; SM_AT = attitude toward social media; $^{**}p < 0.01$ (2-tailed); $^{*}p < 0.05$ (2-tailed).

"want-to-do" attitude to use social media and technology at large to start a business. The rapid proliferation of smart devices and the development of faster Internet connections create a new ecosystem where young millennials are eager to explore (Park et al., 2017). The study shows that YouTube and Instagram are the two dominant platforms among DNK, while Facebook and Twitter are also popular. For DNS, Instagram is the dominant platform, along with YouTube and Facebook. Instagram is an excellent platform for entrepreneurs (Post, 2019), offering marketing opportunities for collaboration and personal branding.

The study shows that male respondents in both counties use social media to communicate with family and friends. In contrast to Eddleston and Powell (2008), who argue that women use SNSs for social communication, our study shows that females in Serbia and Kuwait use social media for brand information and entertainment. In line with news stories and reports arguing that women prefer Instagram and Pinterest as their platform for entrepreneurial reasons (Seligson, 2016), our study confirms that women in Kuwait and Serbia see Instagram as a safe and more manageable platform to start a business (Cicek, 2018).

An interesting finding of this study is that Kuwaiti women showed higher EI than men, while in Serbia, the male respondents had a higher intention to do business online. Although DNK and DNS demonstrate a positive intention to use social media for entrepreneurial reasons, the study shows that both groups are uncertain as they feel they lack the capacity to set clear strategic goals (Shabbir et al., 2017). In other words, there is low self-efficacy, a "can't do" mentality among the women DNK and DNS, which hampers EI (Roomi, 2013) and reduces their confidence levels to start their businesses.

Factors Affecting the Entrepreneurial Mindset

Self-efficacy refers to people's belief that they can accomplish specific goals (Bandura, 1997). The study shows that self-efficacy correlates positively with both EI and EC for DNK and DNS females, while there is no correlation in the male groups. This means that the female respondents with low self-efficacy feel less confident to start a business, regardless of their financial status or social support. What women entrepreneurs seem to need is the tools to strengthen their EC. Such tools could be mastering the language, communicating publicly, collaborating in teams, and adapting to market changes. Similar to past research (Baughn et al., 2006), the current study reveals women's uncertainty to become social entrepreneurs.

DNs in Kuwait and Serbia may see the language as a barrier to attract a larger audience that extends beyond their countries' borders. English remains the dominant language on the Internet, and it could hinder a non-English native speaker from appealing globally. DNs will feel ready to embrace a fully online and social media-based lifestyle once they master the English language. Nevertheless, both Arabic and Serbian are languages that are widely spoken in certain parts of the world, creating opportunities for niche markets.

The study shows that an essential component of triggering the EM is the level of approval and support by family, friends, and experts. Although all respondents argue that approvals and encouragement play a vital role in their entrepreneurial endeavors, female respondents in both Kuwait and Serbia seek experts' approval as well. At the same time, men do not see experts are necessary to start their business. Women DNs in Kuwait and Serbia need more vital mass communication skills, which will allow them to be more extraverted and confident with using social media.

The study shows that female respondents demonstrate a positive attitude toward using social media for entrepreneurial activities. In line with Park et al. (2017), we argue that women DNK and DNS should be equipped with the right education and guidance by all approval factors (family, friends, experts) to ignite their EM. Seeking experts' advice to decide to start a business seems to be the last resort for DNK. The female respondents seem more open to accepting an expert's opinion than the male respondents do. Overall, the chapter argues that the development of an entrepreneurial culture with an emphasis on entrepreneurship workshops, a new start-up business ecosystem, and empowerment would increase women's EM in both Kuwait and Serbia.

Closing Thoughts

In conclusion, our study shows that although technology drives EI, female DNK and DNS should receive more guidance and encouragement to feel more confident to start a business. Social media is the right platform to affect DN's EM in both countries, regardless of their gender. The survey took place during the COVID-19 pandemic, which could affect its results. The respondents might have felt less confident to start a business during the uncertain times caused by COVID-19.

Nevertheless, the national plans for youth entrepreneurship should focus on social recognition and empowerment of business through social media in line with Kuwait's 2035 strategic vision ("Kuwait Vision, 2035 'New Kuwait' – Ministry of Foreign Affairs", 2020) and Serbia's start-up ecosystem (Bizinger, 2020). Entrepreneurship should be a crucial factor for desirable changes in both counties Kuwait and Serbia, which will allow offering more opportunities for employment outside the public sector. Entrepreneurship could lead to an improvement of goods and services' quality, an increase of labor productivity and exports, strengthening competitiveness, better use of existing capacities, and higher employment (DiStaso et al., 2011). Entrepreneurship could bring the desirable socioeconomic changes to increase people's self-confidence and improve the quality of life.

Note

1. https://www.ipsos.com/sites/default/files/ct/publication/documents/2018-09/MENAs_Millennials_Decoded.pdf

References

Aidis, R., Welter, F., Smallbone, D., & Isakova, N. (2007). Female entrepreneurship in transition economies: The case of Lithuania and Ukraine. *Feminist Economics, 13*(2), 157–183. doi:10.1080/13545700601184831

Allen, I. E., Elam, A., Langowitz, N., & Dean, M. (2007). *GEM global 2007 report on women and entrepreneurship*. Global Entrepreneurship Research Association, Babson College, Babson Park, MA.

Anicic, J., Laketa, M., Laketa, L., Anicic, D., & Lukic, S. (2014). Entrepreneurship development in Serbia: The chance for a way out of economic crisis. *UTMS Journal of Economics, 5*(2), 189–198. Retrieved from https://ideas.repec.org/a/ris/utmsje/0112.html

Anna, A. L., Chandler, G. N., Jansen, E., & Mero, N. P. (2000). Women business owners in traditional and non-traditional industries. *Journal of Business Venturing, 15*(3), 279–303. doi:10.1016/s0883-9026(98)00012-3

Baker, T., & Nelson, R. E. (2005). Creating something from nothing: Resource construction through entrepreneurial bricolage. *Administrative Science Quarterly, 50*(3), 329–366. doi:10.2189/asqu.2005.50.3.329

Bandura, A. (1997). *Self-efficacy: The exercise of control*. New York, NY: Freeman, Circa.

Baughn, C. C., Chua, B.-L., & Neupert, K. E. (2006). The normative context for women's participation in entrepreneurship: A multi-country study. *Entrepreneurship Theory and Practice, 30*(5), 687–708. doi:10.1111/j.1540-6520.2006.00142.x

Bennett, S., Maton, K., & Kervin, L. (2008). The 'digital natives' debate: A critical review of the evidence. *British Journal of Educational Technology, 39*(5), 775–786. doi:10.1111/j.1467-8535.2007.00793.x

Bizinger, D. (2020, May 19). Serbia's start-up ecosystem at a glance. Retrieved from EU-Startups website https://www.eu-startups.com/2020/05/serbias-startup-ecosystem-at-a-glance/. Accessed on August 27, 2020.

Blut, M., Wang, C., & Schoefer, K. (2016). Factors influencing the acceptance of self-service technologies. *Journal of Service Research, 19*(4), 396–416. doi:10.1177/1094670516662352

Bridge, S., & O'Neill, K. (2013). *Understanding enterprise: Entrepreneurship and small business*. Basingstoke: Palgrave Macmillan.

Carr, C. T., & Hayes, R. A. (2015). Social media: Defining, developing, and divining. *Atlantic Journal of Communication, 23*(1), 46–65. doi:10.1080/15456870.2015.972282

Cheong, P. H. (2008). The young and techless? Investigating internet use and problem-solving behaviors of young adults in Singapore. *New Media & Society, 10*(5), 771–791. doi:10.1177/1461444808094356

Christensen, C. M., Ojomo, E., & Dillon, K. (2019). Cracking frontier markets. Retrieved from https://hbr.org/2019/01/cracking-frontier-markets. Accessed on August 17, 2020.

Çiçek, B. (2018). Social media entrepreneurship [sosyal medya girişimciliği.]. *İçtimaiyat, 2*(1), 10–17. doi:10.33709/ictimaiyat.417271

Cohoon, J. M., Wadhwa, V., & Mitchell, L. (2010). Are successful women entrepreneurs different from men? *SSRN Electronic Journal*. doi:10.2139/ssrn.1604653

Cole, R. A., & Mehran, H. (2009). *Gender and the availability of credit to privately held firms: Evidence from the surveys of small business finances*. Federal Reserve Bank of New York. Staff Reports. doi:10.2139/ssrn.1799649

Damnjanovic, D., Ristic, Z., & Danilovic, N. (2017). Social entrepreneurship in Serbia: The entrepreneurial spirit leading to social changes. *21st International Scientific Conference on Economic and Social Development*, *21*, 304–313.

Deakins, D., & Freel, M. (2012). *Entrepreneurship and small firms*. London: Mcgraw-Hill Higher Education.

DeTienne, D. R., & Chandler, G. N. (2007). The role of gender in opportunity identification. *Entrepreneurship Theory and Practice*, *31*(3), 365–386. doi:10.1111/j.1540-6520.2007.00178.x

DiStaso, M. W., McCorkindale, T., & Wright, D. K. (2011). How public relations executives perceive and measure the impact of social media in their organizations. *Public Relations Review*, *37*(3), 325–328. doi:10.1016/j.pubrev.2011.06.005

Eckhardt, J. T., & Shane, S. A. (2003). Opportunities and entrepreneurship. *Journal of Management*, *29*(3), 333–349. doi:10.1177/014920630302900304

Eddleston, K. A., & Powell, G. N. (2008). The role of gender identity in explaining sex differences in business owners' career satisfier preferences. *Journal of Business Venturing*, *23*(2), 244–256. doi:10.1016/j.jbusvent.2006.11.002

Ellison, N. B., & Boyd, D. M. (2013). Sociality through social network sites. In W. H. Dutton (Ed.), *Oxford handbooks online*. doi:10.1093/oxfordhb/9780199589074.013.0008

Fairlie, R. W., & Robb, A. M. (2009). Gender differences in business performance: Evidence from the characteristics of business owners survey. *Small Business Economics*, *33*(4), 375–395. doi:10.1007/s11187-009-9207-5

Gartner, W. B., Shaver, K. G., Gatewood, E., & Katz, J. A. (1994). Finding the entrepreneur in entrepreneurship. *Entrepreneurship Theory and Practice*, *18*(3), 5–9. doi:10.1177/104225879401800301

Greene, P. G., Hart, M. M., Gatewood, E. J., Brush, C. G., & Carter, N. M. (2003). Women entrepreneurs: Moving front and center: An overview of research and theory.

Greve, A., & Salaff, J. W. (2003). Social networks and entrepreneurship. *Entrepreneurship Theory and Practice*, *28*(1), 1–22. doi:10.1111/1540-8520.00029

Günther, O., Krasnova, H., Riehle, D., & Schoendienst, V. (2009). Modeling microblogging adoption in the enterprise. AMCIS 2009 Proceedings. Retrieved from https://aisel.aisnet.org/amcis2009/544

Hargittai, E., & Hinnant, A. (2008). Digital inequality differences in young adults' use of the internet. *Communication Research*, *35*(5), 602–621. doi:10.1177/0093650208321782

Hasan, F. S. M. A., & Almubarak, M. M. S. (2016). Factors influencing women entrepreneurs' performance in SMEs. *World Journal of Entrepreneurship, Management and Sustainable Development*, *12*(2), 82–101. doi:10.1108/wjemsd-09-2015-0037

Heller Baird, C., & Parasnis, G. (2011). From social media to social customer relationship management. *Strategy & Leadership*, *39*(5), 30–37. doi:10.1108/10878571111161507

Hull, C. E., Hung, Y. T. C., Hair, N., Perotti, V., & DeMartino, R. (2007). Taking advantage of digital opportunities: A typology of digital entrepreneurship. *International Journal of Networking and Virtual Organisations*, *4*(3), 290. doi:10.1504/ijnvo.2007.015166

IBM Corp. Released. (2016). *IBM SPSS statistics for Windows, version 24.0*. Armonk, NY: IBM Corp.

Jagongo, A. O., & Kinyua, C. (2013). The social media and entrepreneurship growth (A new business communication paradigm among SMEs in Nairobi). *International Journal of Humanities and Social Science*, *3*(10). Retrieved from https://pdfs.semanticscholar.org/2c31/e9e5cddc63c01c73c3602dd895c4a7dddb52.pdf?_ga=2.91332314.1111441561.1597671142-2049322712.1594632157

Jamali, D. (2009). Constraints and opportunities facing women entrepreneurs in developing countries. *Gender in Management: An International Journal*, *24*(4), 232–251. doi:10.1108/17542410910961532

Kapoor, K. K., Tamilmani, K., Rana, N. P., Patil, P., Dwivedi, Y. K., & Nerur, S. (2017). Advances in social media research: Past, present and future. *Information Systems Frontiers*, *20*(3), 531–558. doi:10.1007/s10796-017-9810-y

Khajeheian, D. (2012). New venture creation in social media platform; Towards a framework for media entrepreneurship. In M. Friedrichsen, & W. Mühl-Benninghaus (Eds.), *Handbook of social media management. Media business and innovation* (pp. 125–142). Berlin, Heidelberg: Springer. doi:10.1007/978-3-642-28897-5_8

Kobia, M., & Sikalieh, D. (2010). Towards a search for the meaning of entrepreneurship. *Journal of European Industrial Training*, *34*(2), 110–127. doi:10.1108/03090591011023970

Kuhl, J. S. (2016, November 15). Social media is making young people more entrepreneurial than ever. Retrieved from https://digitalempowers.com/social-media-making-young-people-entrepreneurial-ever/. Accessed on August 17, 2020.

Kuwait Vision 2035 "New Kuwait" - Ministry of Foreign Affairs. (2020). Retrieved from https://www.mofa.gov.kw/en/kuwait-state/kuwait-vision-2035/. Accessed on July 6, 2020.

Kwiatek, P., Morgan, Z., & Baltezarevic, R. (2018). Actions speak louder than words: Understanding the meaning of loyalty program building blocks. *Economics & Sociology*, *11*(2), 305–319. doi:10.14254/2071-789x.2018/11-2/21

Langowitz, N., & Minniti, M. (2007). The entrepreneurial propensity of women. *Entrepreneurship Theory and Practice*, *31*(3), 341–364. doi:10.1111/j.1540-6520.2007.00177.x

Le Dinh, T., Vu, M. C., & Ayayi, A. (2018). Towards a living lab for promoting the digital entrepreneurship process. *International Journal of Entrepreneurship*, *22*(1), 1–17.

Liñán, F., & Chen, Y.-W. (2009). Development and cross-cultural application of a specific instrument to measure entrepreneurial intentions. *Entrepreneurship Theory and Practice*, *33*(3), 593–617. doi:10.1111/j.1540-6520.2009.00318.x

Longman, K., Daniels, J., Bray, D. L., & Liddell, W. (2018). How organizational culture shapes women's leadership experiences. *Administrative Sciences*, *8*(2), 8. doi:10.3390/admsci8020008

Mangold, W. G., & Faulds, D. J. (2009). Social media: The new hybrid element of the promotion mix. *Business Horizons*, *52*(4), 357–365. doi:10.1016/j.bushor.2009.03.002

Market classification – MSCI. (2020). Retrieved August 17, 2020, from Msci.com website https://www.msci.com/market-classification

McManus, P. A. (2001). Women's participation in self-employment in western industrialized nations. *International Journal of Sociology*, *31*(2), 70–97. doi:10.1080/15579336.2001.11770229

MENA's millennials decoded. (2018). in Ipsos.com. Retrieved from https://www.ipsos.com/sites/default/files/ct/publication/documents/2018-09/MENAs_Millennials_Decoded.pdf

Mueller, S. L., & Thomas, A. S. (2001). Culture and entrepreneurial potential: A nine country study of locus of control and innovativeness. *Journal of Business Venturing*, *16*(1), 51–75. doi:10.1016/s0883-9026(99)00039-7

Nielsen, M. I. S. W. (2017). Computer-mediated communication and self-awareness: A selective review. *Computers in Human Behavior*, *76*, 554–560. doi:10.1016/j.chb.2017.08.015

Park, J., Sung, C., & Im, I. (2017). Does social media use influence entrepreneurial opportunity? A review of its moderating role. *Sustainability*, *9*(9), 1593. doi:10.3390/su9091593

Pinto, C. (2019, April 3). Encouraging Kuwait's entrepreneurial ecosystem. Retrieved from https://www.timeskuwait.com/news/encouraging-kuwaits-entrepreneurial-ecosystem/. Accessed on August 19, 2020.

Post, J. (2019, December 4). 10 best business Instagram accounts for entrepreneurs. Retrieved from https://www.businessnewsdaily.com/11054-instagram-accounts-for-entrepreneurs.html. Accessed on August 27, 2020.

Prensky, M. (2001). Digital natives, digital immigrants part 1. *On the Horizon*, *9*(5), 1–6. doi:10.1108/10748120110424816

Roomi, M. (2013). The role of social capital and human capital in the growth of women-owned enterprises in the United Kingdom. Retrieved from Royal Holloway University of London Thesis website https://pure.royalholloway.ac.uk/portal/files/17823949/m._a._roomi_fs_10_10_13.pdf

Salmela, E., & Juvonen, P. (2016). Differences in motivational mindset affecting collaboration of virtual research organisation. *International Journal of Networking and Virtual Organisations*, *16*(3), 298. doi:10.1504/ijnvo.2016.079182

Sapountzi, A., & Psannis, K. E. (2018). Social networking data analysis tools & challenges. *Future Generation Computer Systems*, *86*, 893–913. doi:10.1016/j.future.2016.10.019

Seligson, H. (2016, June 7). Why are more women than men on Instagram? Retrieved from The Atlantic website https://www.theatlantic.com/technology/archive/2016/06/why-are-more-women-than-men-on-instagram/485993/. Accessed on August 27, 2020.

Shabbir, M. S., Mohd Shariff, M. N., Salman, R., & Shabbir, M. F. (2017). Exploring the link between entrepreneurial skills and entrepreneurial intentions: Proposing a hypothesized model for future. *Paradigms*, *11*(1), 72–77. doi:10.24312/paradigms110112

Shane, S., & Venkataraman, S. (2007). The promise of entrepreneurship as a field of research. In Á. Cuervo, D. Ribeiro, & S. Roig (Eds.), *Entrepreneurship* (pp. 171–184). doi:10.1007/978-3-540-48543-8_8

Social media is a serious business: A view from European youth #generationdirect. (2015). In Tata consultancy services. Retrieved from https://www.criticaleye.com/insights-servfile.cfm?id=4643

Steininger, D. M. (2019). Linking information systems and entrepreneurship: A review and agenda for IT associated and digital entrepreneurship research. *Information Systems Journal*, *29*(2), 363–407. doi:10.1111/isj.12206

Taylor, M., & Kent, M. L. (2010). Anticipatory socialization in the use of social media in public relations: A content analysis of PRSA's public relations tactics. *Public Relations Review*, *36*(3), 207–214. doi:10.1016/j.pubrev.2010.04.012

Verheul, I., Stel, A. V., & Thurik, R. (2006). Explaining female and male entrepreneurship at the country level. *Entrepreneurship & Regional Development*, *18*(2), 151–183. doi:10.1080/08985620500532053

World Bank: Female entrepreneurship resource point - Why gender matters. (2015). Retrieved from https://www.worldbank.org/en/topic/gender/publication/female-entrepreneurship-resource-point-introduction-and-module-1-why-gender-matters. Accessed on August 19, 2020.

World Economic Forum: Insight report global gender gap report 2020. (2020). World economic Forum. Retrieved from http://www3.weforum.org/docs/WEF_GGGR_2020.pdf

Wright, E., Khanfar, N. M., Harrington, C., & Kizer, L. E. (2016). The lasting effects of social media trends on advertising. *Journal of Business & Economics Research*, *14*(3), 75–82. doi:10.19030/jber.v14i3.9747

Yun, J. J. (2015). How do we conquer the growth limits of capitalism? Schumpeterian dynamics of open innovation. *Journal of Open Innovation: Technology, Market, and Complexity*, *1*(1). doi:10.1186/s40852-015-0019-3

Chapter 16

Entrepreneurial Ecosystem and Female Digital Entrepreneurship – Lessons to Learn from an Iranian Case Study

Aidin Salamzadeh and Veland Ramadani

Abstract

The Iranian entrepreneurial ecosystem has grown dramatically during the past decade. Several improvements have been made at different levels, and, therefore, one could witness its unique achievements. Digital entrepreneurs are an integral part of this ecosystem, as most of the early achievements are the results of their proactive behaviors. Hopefully, the number of female digital entrepreneurs has increased, and their entrepreneurial activities have profoundly changed the competition scene. Therefore, this chapter provides a better understanding of the multilayered entrepreneurial ecosystem of Iran and then elaborates how female entrepreneurs are positioned in this ecosystem. Moreover, six well-known award-winning female digital entrepreneurs are introduced, and their challenges are scrutinized accordingly through narrative research. Finally, the chapter concludes with some remarks and directions for future research.

Keywords: Challenges; digital entrepreneurs; entrepreneurial ecosystem; female entrepreneurs; Iran; start-up

Introduction

The entrepreneurial ecosystem of Iran has profoundly changed in the last two decades, as it experienced critical issues such as the emergence of entrepreneurship programs (Guerrero, Urbano, & Salamzadeh, 2014), the establishment of support mechanisms [such as venture capital (VC) funds, start-up accelerators, hatcheries, as well as angel investor firms] (Salamzadeh & Kawamorita, 2017), and the highlighted role of women entrepreneurs who actively involved in the business environment (Sarfaraz, 2017). Among the trending issues which contributed to

The Emerald Handbook of Women and Entrepreneurship in Developing Economies, 317–334
Copyright © 2021 by Emerald Publishing Limited
All rights of reproduction in any form reserved
doi:10.1108/978-1-80071-326-020211016

the fundamental developments of the enterprising ecosystem of the country, the role of women entrepreneurs was inevitable. Despite the challenges to advancement in a masculine society with rules facilitated for male rather than female entrepreneurs (Ratten, Dana, & Ramadani, 2017), they highlighted their role by using their creative mental capabilities as well as distinct personality traits, and prior experiences (Ratten & Dana, 2017; Sarfaraz, Mian, Karadeniz, Zali, & Qureshi, 2018, pp. 649–657). Nevertheless, they still face a glass ceiling which hopefully has many cracks on it now, primarily through the active engagement of young women digital entrepreneurs who have initiated entrepreneurial activities in leading Iranian start-ups (Salamzadeh, Arasti, & Elyasi, 2017).

This fact makes the story more interesting, as one might ask if these emerging groups of female digital entrepreneurs have facilitated the process of entrepreneurial activities for the previously frustrated and marginalized group of entrepreneurs in Iran? (Modarresi, Arasti, Talebi, & Farasatkhah, 2017). If the answer is yes, what has changed and what is still making the glass ceiling robust and impervious? (Ramadani, Gërguri, Dana, & Tašaminova, 2013; Lathabhavan & Balasubramanian, 2017). What has mainly changed? Is the context more appropriate for intended female digital entrepreneurs? (Dana, 2007). What are the main challenges which could be hopefully addressed soon? (Golzard, 2019). Several questions have remained unanswered. Thus, this chapter sheds light on several aspects of the above-mentioned questions by depicting the existing entrepreneurial ecosystem of Iran, which is classified in different levels and makes it more understandable for the readers. In addition to this, female digital entrepreneurs – as an influential type of women entrepreneurs – their position, and challenges are defined and scrutinized in this ecosystem.

In a nutshell, in this chapter, the author will first explain the state of the entrepreneurial ecosystem in Iran in a multilayered approach, which is unique. Then, it is elaborated on how women entrepreneurs are positioned in this ecosystem, considering different levels of it. Then, six cases of female digital entrepreneurs are introduced, and their challenges in this ecosystem are scrutinized by considering their narratives and thick descriptions. Finally, the chapter concludes with some remarks mainly on the questions mentioned above.

The Entrepreneurial Ecosystem in Iran

The entrepreneurial ecosystem of Iran has become more mature in the last decade. Several players are acting in this ecosystem. The previous research in this domain has profoundly contributed to the extant literature on the entrepreneurial ecosystem of Iran (Entezari, 2015; Rezaei, Dana, & Ramadani, 2017; Salamzadeh & Kawamorita, 2017); however, an integrated view is rarely presented by former scholars (Entezari, 2019). Therefore, in this section, the author provides an integrated multilevel approach toward the entrepreneurial ecosystem in Iran (Salamzadeh & Arbatani, 2020; Salamzadeh & Dana, 2020). According to this approach, the key players are acting at international, national, industrial, firm, team, and individual levels.

The following figure shows the big picture of the Iranian entrepreneurial ecosystem as well as the major players (Fig. 16.1).

At the individual level, university undergraduates, graduates, and high school students are the most targeted groups; however, there are initiatives like KASHEF (A national program for the identification and promotion of students with entrepreneurial potential) which pay attention to primary school students and try to find talented students who could be future entrepreneurs. Freelancers

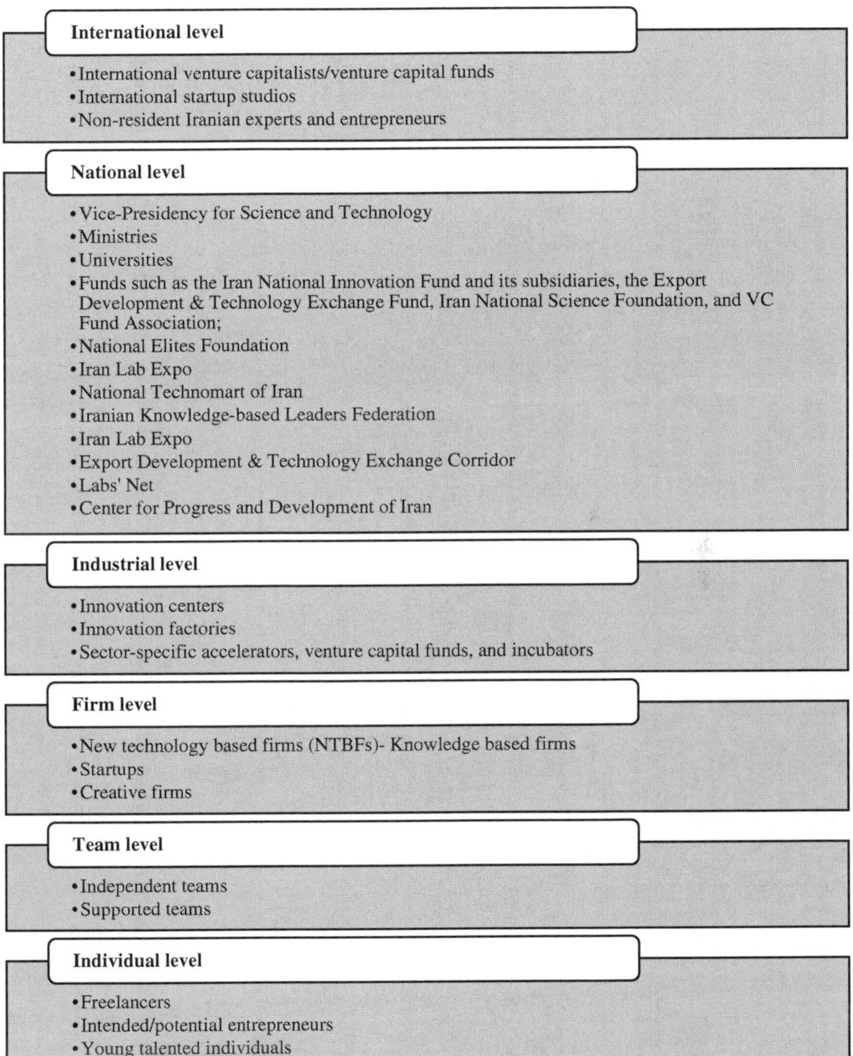

Fig. 16.1. The Major Players in the Iranian Entrepreneurial Ecosystem.

are also playing an essential role in this ecosystem as they take the burden of software development and are handling specialized issues at a lower price than the hired staff for individuals, start-ups, and new technology-based firms (NTBFs).

Teams are also an integral part of the ecosystem. It is noteworthy that most of the mentioned start-ups are not officially registered, and, therefore, they are acting as teams in coworking spaces, shared offices, or small areas in science parks, for instance. Nevertheless, they are the fuel which makes the engine of the ecosystem work. Thus, the whole ecosystem puts a considerable amount of attention to their existence and improvements, which is evident as there are nonstop events, gatherings, and competitions to make them motivated.

At the industrial and firm levels, different industries are taking advantage of the signs of progress and developments made by start-ups, creative, and knowledge-based firms, and generally speaking the NTBFs. Also, there are several firms and support mechanisms such as innovation factories, VC firms, start-up accelerators, incubators, hatcheries, science parks, technology transfer firms, and coworking spaces which are proactively searching for new opportunities in the ecosystem. Incidents like the establishment of joint VC funds and new collaborative platforms make the ecosystem more agile at the firm level. As of May 2020, there are 118 innovation centers, 4,457 registered knowledge-based firms or NTBFs, 411 creative firms, and 5,600 start-ups.

In addition to this, at the national level, several players are actively collaborating to help the ecosystem develop more appropriately. These entities include, but are not limited to the followings: the Vice-Presidency for Science and Technology, which is the linking pin of the ecosystem; the ministries; universities; funds such as the Iran National Innovation Fund and its subsidiaries, the Export Development and Technology Exchange Fund, Iran National Science Foundation, and VC Fund Association; the National Elites Foundation; Iran Lab Expo; the National Technomart of Iran; the Iranian Knowledge-based Leaders Federation; the Export Development and Technology Exchange Corridor; the Labs' Net; and the Center for Progress and Development of Iran.

At the international level, a series of joint ventures, limited partnerships, and multinational organizations are connecting the players to the international players beyond the boundaries of the country. Even a series of entities have established some international companies in countries like Turkey, Canada, and Germany, to help the ecosystem grow more actively. These entities were mostly created after the Joint Plan of Action was signed. It was an agreement signed between Iran and the P5+1 countries which helped the entrepreneurial ecosystem to flourish extensively. Moreover, some programs like the established system for collaboration with nonresident Iranian experts and entrepreneurs accelerated the growth rate of the ecosystem.

Women Entrepreneurs in the Iranian Ecosystem

The entrepreneurial ecosystem of Iran and its key players are described in the previous section, but the question remains that to what extent women entrepreneurs are playing roles in this ecosystem? Although females constitute a significant part of this ecosystem, still their positions, challenges, and problems need to be clarified, as the studies have already shown their distinct approaches and achievements in such ecosystems. Hechavarría and Ingram (2019) argue that when there are low barriers to entry in an entrepreneurial ecosystem and the government supports entrepreneurial activities, commercial and legal infrastructures are ready, the culture is supportive, and the prevalence in entrepreneurship will be higher for women. Such studies have shown that women entrepreneurs are prone to engage in entrepreneurial activities if they feel that the ecosystem is less hindering and more supportive. According to the studies conducted in the Middle East, most of the Arab, as well as traditional countries, suffer from lack of such an ecosystem (Ali, Ali, & Badghish, 2019; Pauceanu, Alpenidze, Edu, & Zaharia, 2019), although the Iranian entrepreneurial ecosystem is quite different, as it has a long history of entrepreneurial activities in which women were actively involved (Salamzadeh, Azimi, & Kirby, 2013).

Nevertheless, as most of the countries in this region are male-dominated, there are still several glass ceilings in front of the women entrepreneurs (Faghih & Zali, 2018; Hasan, Almubarak, & Ahmed, 2016). Female entrepreneurs face several challenges in these countries. For instance, as mentioned by Hasan et al. (2016), lack of access to financial and human resources, as well as lower profit margins, and the balance between work and personal life are among the essential impeding factors. Al-Dajani, Akbar, Carter, and Shaw (2019) also argue that "although entrepreneurial practices and processes are evolving and changing globally, models of entrepreneurship remain masculinised." In their research, they point out several pieces of evidence in this regard. Bastian, Sidani, and El Amine (2018) propose a general point of view regarding how women entrepreneurs are studied in the extant literature. They believe that issues such as the lack of sound theoretical frameworks for studying female entrepreneurship, overemphasis on macrolevel factors, and lack of investigations that investigate women entrepreneurs within ethnic groups are remained overlooked.

Taking all the regional factors into account, investigating the context of Iranian entrepreneurial ecosystem and its relevance to women entrepreneurs is of paramount importance. As Rezaei-Moghaddam, Karami, and Fatemi (2019) mention, only 11.7% of the Iranian women were active economically in 2000; however, some ratios increased in 2016, and we witness that the ratio of active female to active male individuals increased to almost 25% according to the report issued by the Statistical Center of Iran. Nevertheless, this ratio is still low. One should consider that only a small portion of these women are entrepreneurs. Hopefully, in recent years, some scholars have studied these entrepreneurs. For instance, Sarfaraz (2017) investigated seven award-winning female entrepreneurs who were mainly involved in culturally male-dominated economic fields. Their entrepreneurial journeys unwrapped several dark sides and also hopeful aspects of their entrepreneurial lives. Bahramitash and Esfahani (2016) also studied the gender-related issues on entrepreneurship in the Iranian entrepreneurial ecosystem. Their study resulted in a series of interesting findings. For example, female entrepreneurs are mostly active in larger firms. They are particularly active in the service sector and have fewer complaints regarding the business issues, and they are less prone to make complaints about the imposed sanctions against the country, as they are mostly running new and technology-based firms. As Sarfaraz et al. (2018) argue, due to the sanctions, Iranian female entrepreneurs were less able to export their products compared to their Pakistani and Turkish counterparts. Surprisingly, the percentage of female entrepreneurs who had 1–25% of foreign customers was higher than the male entrepreneurs. This is a sign of their high capacity to make substantial changes in the Iranian entrepreneurial ecosystem, especially at the international level, which is more challenging due to the economic sanctions against Iran than the other levels.

The role of women entrepreneurship at some levels of the Iranian entrepreneurial ecosystem is overlooked in the literature. At the international level, mostly Global Entrepreneurship Monitor (GEM)–based research manuscripts have pointed out the status of female entrepreneurs in Iran and have mostly used comparative analysis research designs to compare them with their foreign peers (e.g. see Javadian & Singh, 2012; Mian, Karadeniz, & Sarfaraz, 2013; Sarfaraz et al., 2018). At the national level, also GEM-based data were used to analyze different aspects of their entrepreneurial activities, as well as their challenges (e.g. see Farashah, 2013; Bahramitash, 2013; Modarresi et al., 2017). The lower levels, including industrial and firm-level research works, pay more attention to the achievements, challenges, and key success factors. Most of the research projects conducted at these levels are done based on [multiple] case study research design (e.g. see, Hosseini & McElwee, 2011; Arasti, Panahi, Zarei, & Rezaee, 2012; Dastourian, Kawamorita Kesim, Seyyed Amiri, & Moradi, 2017). Nevertheless, at the team and individual levels, the published research is minimal. At these levels of analysis, there is a lot to be investigated, as most of the emerging female technological entrepreneurs, who are becoming the change agents of the Iranian entrepreneurial ecosystem, are marginalized by researchers. Instead, the emphasis is mainly put on the traditional women entrepreneurs in the fields like arts and local products (e.g. see Modarresi, Arasti, Talebi, & Farasatkhah, 2016).

Research Methods

As it is mentioned earlier, a few research projects have focused on the teams and individual female entrepreneurs. Despite the impact of these women entrepreneurs, as the role models of the young generations, and the change agents of the masculine societies, unfortunately, the academic approach toward studying them is neglected to a great extent (Wang, Li, & Long, 2019). Therefore, in this qualitative research, we study the stories and challenges of six selected award-winning women entrepreneurs in Iran. Three types of risks – i.e. risks of abstract actors or beings of reason, circularity, and equifinality – are managed in this research by considering relevant requirements. Thus, respectively, the scope and unit of analysis are determined, and data are interpreted relatively independent of theory and considering different possibilities (Dana & Dumez, 2015). The purposeful sampling technique was used. According to this approach, the selected entrepreneur should have established a digital start-up, which is cash flow positive and profitable, and have been selected at least in one national or international event as an award-winning entrepreneur. The data were collected from both primary resources such as observations, interviews, and a focus group session, as well as secondary sources such as websites, press releases, reports, and online databases. The narrative research method is used to identify the main challenges (Groenland & Dana, 2020). Thus, their narrations and thick descriptions are analyzed to *learn directly from the research subject* which provides policymakers and researcher with a better understanding of their lived experiences (Dana & Dana, 2005).

Findings

Digital entrepreneurs are changing the competitive environment of emerging economies, and, thus, their impact is more evident. There are various Iranian start-ups founded by women entrepreneurs (Salamzadeh et al., 2017); however, the following table shows six well-known Iranian female digital entrepreneurs among them who were selected based on purposeful sampling technique (Table 16.1).

Case 1: Aseyeh Hatami

Aseyeh Hatami is the founder and chief executive officer of the leading Iranian recruitment website named IranTalent, which have profoundly changed the recruitment market. As a pioneer in this challenging market in Iran, she has navigated the growth of her venture through intense socioeconomic conditions of the Iranian recruitment market, which dealt with a lack of knowledge about demand and supply sides, as well as information asymmetry before such players come into existence (Hadavi & Zarifi, 2009). Her business is currently the leading recruitment online platform which offers several distinguished services to both recruiters and job seekers, as well as new innovative services which are designed and rendered creatively, including the introduction of Iran's first comprehensive salary survey, followed by the launch of IranSalary. IranSalary is essential for both employees and employers and sets the minimum payments required to hire a specific expert, and paved the way for handling the challenges which would emerge according to the equity theory (Keramati & Salehi, 2013). As a serial entrepreneur, she did not stop her hard work and founded TalentCoach, which seeks to address the highly inefficient graduate recruitment space and connects employers with higher education institutions and their graduates. She received an engineering degree from the Amirkabir University of Technology. After graduation and a period of working in Iran Khodro, she was recruited in a software company to manage a project titled "Iran Jobs." She had to convince foreign companies to recruit new employees. After a period of interviewing candidates, she started to write a cover letter for employees about candidates' qualifications. She had some conflicts with the software company and left it to start her entrepreneurial journey.

Table 16.1. Well-Known Iranian Female Digital Entrepreneurs.

Entrepreneur	Age	Educational Background	Start-Up	Domain	Year of Establishment
Aseyeh Hatami	41	Engineering	IranTalent	A leading job site and online recruitment service for professionals	2003
Nazanin Daneshvar	37	Information technology and business	Takhfifan	A leading online retail start-up like Groupon	2011
Narges Shayegh	38	Arts	Aranick	An online platform for selling handicrafts	2013
Tabassom Latifi	34	Engineering and business	MamanPaz	A network of [housewife] chefs at home	2014
Lena Vafaey	32	Engineering	Peeyade	A location-based media application	2015
Nikoo Niknam	36	Engineering	NikPrint	An online platform for designing and printing orders	2015

Case 2: Nazanin Daneshvar

She is an Iranian Internet entrepreneur who is the founder and directing manager of the Groupon of Iran, i.e. Takhfifan, which offers discounts on a range of products and services, as the first and foremost famous firm in its kind. The venture is operating in several cities of Iran, and most of its users are young generations who want the best deals, especially as a group (Sarrafzadeh & Esmaeili, 2016). Takhfifan offers substantial discounts to potential customers and later passes on discounts offered by the sellers (Golzard, 2019). Nazanin studied computer engineering at the University of Science and Culture and also gained a masters degree in information technology. While studying for her bachelor's degree, she used to work as a private tutor. Afterward, she started working in a software company, where she became an expert software developer. She moved to London as a representative of the company. After going back to Iran, she established an online supermarket named Meydoonak. The project was failed, but she did not stop trying and established Varchin. She received an offer from a German company who used to run a Groupon-like business in 30 countries, where she learnt a lot about this business. She turned back to Iran and established Takhfifan. In 2019, she was listed as one of the United Nations Conference on Trade and Development's (UNCTAD's) "eTrade for Women Advocates" from the developing economies.

Case 3: Narges Shayegh

Narges Shayegh is the founder and the managing director of Aranick, which is an online platform for selling handicrafts (Keshavarz & Javadi, 2020). She earned a bachelors degree in arts from the Shahrekord University, as well as a masters degree in arts (handicrafts) from the Soore University. After graduation, she started working as a research expert in the Iranian Academy of Arts. She started traveling with her family to rural areas around the country. She intended to write an encyclopedia of rural handicrafts. During her journeys, she became more aware of the challenges that poor and vulnerable artists – who made handicrafts in rural areas – faced. Then, she decided to establish an online platform to help them sell their products and earn money to expand their business and become more self-sufficient. In the next years, she added the artist from urban areas as well, to focus on a broader market. The business has grown and sold the products to international customers, mainly from China, France, Germany, Australia, and Canada. Based on her estimations, more than 70 percent of the suppliers are women. Therefore, besides being a role model, she has already increased the number of active women in the handicrafts industries, which is considered as a substantial social impact.

Case 4: Tabassom Latifi

Tabassom Latifi is the founder and chief executive officer of a leading start-up named MamanPaz which has shaped a network of chefs at home, most of whom are housewives who cook at their own home and sell it through this platform. As of May 2020, more than 1005 hundred housewives are cooking and selling their products on this platform. Tabassom earned a bachelors degree in electrical engineering as well as a masters degree of business administration from the Sharif University of Technology. She grew up in Khorramabad and left her city to continue her education. Before establishing MamanPaz, she used to work in a corporate bank. Nevertheless, working for an organization was not her dream job, and she was not satisfied with such positions. After getting her masters degree in business administration, she decided to run her own business. At a very early stage, she took care of the whole business. After a while, she recruited some team members to grow her business faster than before. While there are ome other competitors in the market, her unique business model made her business a specific choice for several customers who do not want to eat fast food or the food cooked in the restaurants, and instead, they want to taste the unique flavor of the traditional home-cooked dish. The business is growing, and she is also changing her business model to some extent. Based on several requests from male chefs who were willing to cook and sell their products on this platform, she started to open a new line of business which is based on male chefs who cook in restaurants. This reveals the high impact of Iranian female entrepreneurs who are vigorously following their dreams in a masculine society.

Case 5: Lena Vafaey

Lena Vafaey is the founder and the chief executive officer of Peeyade. Lena was born in Tehran and lived in London for three years while she was a child. She moved back to Tehran until she finished high school. As Lena has not dedicated enough time to her studies, she was not able to study in good universities in Iran. She moved to Canada and earned her bachelor's degree in geotechnical engineering from the University of British Columbia. Then, Lena moved to New York to continue her studies in an architecture program and Columbia University. She moved back to Tehran and worked in a studio for one year. As Lena was interested in exploring cities, she started to think about a business in this domain. Therefore, she concentrated on a project which led to the establishment of Peeyade. Peeyade is an online social media platform which provides people with location-based information of the cultural and recreational places and activities of people living in Tehran. It also highlights the city lights and attractions of Tehran.

Case 6: Nikoo Niknam

Nikoo Niknam is the founder and managing director of a leading start-up in printing industries, named NikPrint that is an online service platform for designing and printing orders, which is supported by a delivery system. She earned her bachelor's degree in chemical engineering from the Islamic Azad University in Tehran. She worked as a freelancer for several years and gained a whale of experience in graphic designing and printing in several companies, before establishing her own business. Nikoo noticed an imbalance between significant supply and demand. She tried to make graphic designing and printing services more affordable for potential customers and also thought about how to increase the income of graphic designers who are mostly working as freelancers. While the idea seemed to be simple and many people have challenged it, she stayed motivated and turned her dream to a successful business.

Challenges of the Iranian Female Digital Entrepreneurs

There are several barriers in front of female entrepreneurs in realizing their entrepreneurial dreams (Aidis, 2018). Even in more developed countries, glass ceilings are hindering their valuable efforts. The situation is more complicated in the masculine (Al-Kwifi, Tien Khoa, Ongsakul, & Ahmed, 2020) than the feminine societies (Anlesinya, Adepoju, & Richter, 2019). Several studies have previously investigated the challenges of women entrepreneurs in such societies (Sarfaraz, 2017). Nevertheless, there is limited evidence about the challenges of female digital entrepreneurs in such societies (Haghighi, Hajihoseini, Nargesi, & Bijani, 2018; McAdam, Crowley, & Harrison, 2019). McAdam, Crowley, and Harrison (2020) coined the word *digital girl* for considering this type of entrepreneurs. Therefore, in this section, we would like to elaborate on the main challenges that female entrepreneurs would face in the Iranian entrepreneurial ecosystem. The followings are the main challenges of Iranian female digital entrepreneurs.

Facing Social Expectations, Customs, and Beliefs

In masculine societies, females are expected to be less involved in business activities, and, therefore, female entrepreneurs are less likely to live an entrepreneurial life, or in better words, an entrepreneurial life similar to their male counterparts (Aghazamani, Kerstetter, & Allison, 2020; Muhammad, Robinson, & Nisar, 2019; Ribeiro, Rezaei, & Dana, 2012). Some of the female entrepreneurs have highlighted this issue. For instance, one of them says, *still, society adheres to this belief that women should mostly deal with family issues or work in a safe place... even other women do not support us when we are trying to survive... however, to be honest, we hear good things from them after we succeed, but not before.* Generally, society marginalizes these female entrepreneurs by lowering the height of such glass ceilings. Another woman entrepreneur mentioned that, *I was completely alone while running the pioneer business model of my start-up... even the family was thinking that I am just trying to make something interesting, but not a serious business...The younger generations in society and family have hopefully changed, which means a lot for us.* Most of them believed that by the advent of digital technologies, it became much easier for them to overcome the societal barriers, as people are facing online platforms. As one of them argued that, *one of my achievements was that I saw several male service providers are requesting to join my business, knowing that the founder is a woman... this shows the societal factors that are hopefully changing and make it easier for us to run a venture.*

Lack of Enough Access to Funding

The second main challenge is to access funding. Despite the availability of various financial resources in the Iranian entrepreneurial ecosystem, especially in the past decade (Salamzadeh & Kawamorita, 2017), female entrepreneurs have difficulties in financing their ventures (Modarresi et al., 2017). According to the existing literature, women entrepreneurs are less likely to receive funding due to their characteristics, such as lower rates of risk-taking, being more realistic about their projections, and higher levels of fear of failure (Zali, Faghih, Gelard, & Molaei, 2018). According to one of them, *I was so realistic about the goals of my start-up, and that is why I reckon that I raised less money for my business... but, I saw several less qualified start-ups which raised more money by exaggerating about their projections*. Another founder mentioned that, *I made a serious mistake by negotiating as an independent woman with the first venture capital fund... I was so close to signing a bad contract, and hopefully, by adding a male co-founder to my start-up, I was able to get a better deal... Although this seems not to be fair, I will find my way, anyway*. Finally, according to the interviews, it became evident that some of the women digital entrepreneurs are considering new ways of funding, such as crowdfunding and initial coin offerings (ICOs) as an alternative.

Improving the Work–Life Balance

Due to the structure of the families in most of the countries, especially in a country like Iran, women have several responsibilities regarding their families, spouses, and children (Gherardi, 2015). Simultaneously, female entrepreneurs have to deal with several professional commitments and responsibilities (Cullen, 2019). These two would make it hard for them to make a balance between their works and personal lives, particularly if they lack enough skills to manage both, and also if they lack sufficient social support (Erogul & Quagrainie, 2017; Hundera, Duysters, Naudé, & Dijkhuizen, 2019). The family expects them to be a perfect wife and mom, and the business needs more attention to flourish and grow. One of the female entrepreneurs mentioned that, *It was really a challenge for me to make my family happy, as I was mostly focused on the business at its early stages... but hopefully, my family understood my seriousness and let me keep the imbalance until I became able to make the balance after some three years*. While another one said that, *no one understood me rather than my father who supported me all the time... after some years I became serious about handling this challenge, but to be honest, still, I face a lot of unplanned events*. Despite all these issues, it is evident that digital technologies help them make a better balance to some extent. As one of them have mentioned, *I use team management software such as Trello, Asana, and Slack to handle daily issues, even from home*.

Lack of Enough Support Networks in the Business Environment

Generally, entrepreneurs highly rely on their support networks in their entrepreneurial journeys (Ashourizadeh & Schøtt, 2013; Doshmanli, Salamzadeh, & Salamzadeh, 2018; Salamzadeh, 2018). In fact, this depends on their potential to create such networks, and also the readiness of the business environment (Bastian, 2017; Neneh, 2017). In the case of female entrepreneurs, on the one hand, the situation is more critical, as they are less prone to expand their support networks in masculine societies. On the other hand, such business environments provide fewer opportunities for them to grow. As one of the women entrepreneurs mentioned, *I was not able to expand my networks as there were a series of problems... some men did not like to connect, and some misunderstood me*. Another one argued that, *I was selected in some national events among the best Iranian entrepreneurs, but the male juries did not like it, and they removed me from the list*. They also made some other arguments. One of them mentioned that, *Female entrepreneurs look at the details and mostly find better solutions for existing problems... by the way, we have some advantages compared with the traditional female entrepreneur. For example, as the manager of online platforms, we do our best to render high-quality services and products, and customers do not care about our gender. Even most of them do not know us!.. It is sad but true.*

Gender Inequality and Fear of Failure

Last but not least are gender inequalities and fear of failure, which could be considered as a by-product of it (Simmons, Wiklund, Levie, Bradley, & Sunny, 2019). Gender gaps are more substantial in religious and masculine countries than the others (Ashourizadeh, Chavoushi, & Schøtt, 2014; Hailemariam, Kroon, Van Engen, & Van Veldhoven, 2019; Wang et al., 2019). According to their argument, *it is not simple to live in male-dominated societies where you are marginalised... however, we are happy to see more women entrepreneurs in the last decade*. Another female entrepreneur mentioned that, *maybe our fear of failure is because we think that people will judge us with more criteria than men... when we fail, the society would consider it as proof to our disability and no other issues*. As Kamberidou (2020) argued, fear of failure *would lead to family disputes and marital problems*. This makes the situation more painful for them. Nevertheless, due to the nature of digital entrepreneurship, women entrepreneurs are less prone to be judged by society than their traditional peers.

Conclusion

This chapter paid attention to the specifications of the Iranian entrepreneurial ecosystem and the state of female entrepreneurs in this ecosystem. First, the Iranian entrepreneurial ecosystem is illustrated in a multilevel approach, and then, it is argued that how women entrepreneurs act in this ecosystem. The main focus of the chapter is on female digital entrepreneurs. Therefore, six award-winning women entrepreneurs are introduced, and five main challenges of these entrepreneurs – i.e. facing social expectations, customs and beliefs; lack of enough access to funding; improving the work–life balance; lack of enough support networks in the business environment; and gender inequality and fear of failure – are elaborated. The main challenges could be considered by government officials, especially in masculine and religious countries in order to devise relevant policies.

Directions for Future Research

Future researchers could measure the extent to which these challenges affect the success or failure of female digital entrepreneurs. Conducting quantitative research projects could also be useful to improve the impact of women entrepreneurs who are a significant part of the entrepreneurial ecosystems around the globe. As a qualitative research, the findings of this research are less generalizable; therefore, in order to increase the generalizability of the findings, future researchers could test a series of hypotheses in a larger population of women entrepreneurs.

Limitations

A limitation of such research projects is that the researcher must consider the possibility of self-censorship by participants, as they feel the glass ceiling as well as the social pressures (DeCoursey, 2017). In addition, this study is primarily focused on digital entrepreneurs in the service sector. Therefore, other types of sectors could be included in future studies.

References

Aghazamani, Y., Kerstetter, D., & Allison, P. (2020, March). Women's perceptions of empowerment in Ramsar, a tourism destination in northern Iran. *Studies International Forum*, *79*, 102340.

Aidis, R. (2018). Hitting the top: Is there a glass ceiling for high-growth women entrepreneurs?. In *Women entrepreneurs and the myth of 'underperformance'*. Cheltenham: Edward Elgar Publishing.

Al-Dajani, H., Akbar, H., Carter, S., & Shaw, E. (2019). Defying contextual embeddedness: Evidence from displaced women entrepreneurs in Jordan. *Entrepreneurship & Regional Development*, *31*(3–4), 198–212.

Al-Kwifi, O. S., Tien Khoa, T., Ongsakul, V., & Ahmed, Z. U. (2020). Determinants of female entrepreneurship success across Saudi Arabia. *Journal of Transnational Management*, *25*(1), 3–29.

Ali, I., Ali, M., & Badghish, S. (2019). Symmetric and asymmetric modeling of entrepreneurial ecosystem in developing entrepreneurial intentions among female university students in Saudi Arabia. *International Journal of Gender and Entrepreneurship*, *11*(4), 435–458.

Anlesinya, A., Adepoju, O. A., & Richter, U. H. (2019). Cultural orientation, perceived support and participation of female students in formal entrepreneurship in the sub-Saharan economy of Ghana. *International Journal of Gender and Entrepreneurship*, *11*(3), 299–322.

Arasti, Z., Panahi, S. M. S., Zarei, B., & Rezaee, S. O. (2012). A qualitative study on individual factors affecting Iranian women entrepreneurs' growth orientation. *International Business Research*, *5*(3), 81–90.

Ashourizadeh, S., Chavoushi, Z. H., & Schøtt, T. (2014). People's confidence in innovation: A component of the entrepreneurial mindset, embedded in gender and culture, affecting entrepreneurial intention. *International Journal of Entrepreneurship and Small Business*, *23*(1–2), 235–251.

Ashourizadeh, S., & Schøtt, T. (2013). Entrepreneurs' gender, age and education affecting their networks in private and public spheres: Denmark, Middle East and North Africa. *International Journal of Business and Globalisation*, *11*(4), 380–398.

Bahramitash, R. (2013). Women's employment in Iran. In *Gender and entrepreneurship in Iran* (pp. 73–100). New York, NY: Palgrave Macmillan.

Bahramitash, R., & Esfahani, H. S. (2016). Gender and entrepreneurship in Iran. In N. Chamlou & M. Karshenas (Eds.), *Women, work and welfare in the Middle East and North Africa: The role of socio-demographics, entrepreneurship and public policies* (pp. 291–319). Singapore: World Scientific Publishing Co. Pte. Ltd.

Bastian, B. L. (2017). Empowerment against all odds: Women entrepreneurs in the Middle East and North Africa. In P. W. Zgheib (Ed.), *Entrepreneurship: Concepts, methodologies, tools, and Applications* (pp. 1975–1987). Hershey, PA: IGI Global.

Bastian, B. L., Sidani, Y. M., & El Amine, Y. (2018). Women entrepreneurship in the Middle East and North Africa. *Gender in Management: An International Journal, 33*(1), 14–29.

Cullen, U. (2019). Sociocultural factors as determinants of female entrepreneurs' business strategies. *Journal of Entrepreneurship in Emerging Economies, 12*(1), 144–167.

Dana, L. P. (2007). *Handbook of research on ethnic minority entrepreneurship: A co-evolutionary view on resource management*. Cheltenham: Edward Elgar Publishing.

Dana, L. P., & Dana, T. E. (2005). Expanding the scope of methodologies used in entrepreneurship research. *International Journal of Entrepreneurship and Small Business, 2*(1), 79–88.

Dana, L. P., & Dumez, H. (2015). Qualitative research revisited: Epistemology of a comprehensive approach. *International Journal of Entrepreneurship and Small Business, 26*(2), 154–170.

Dastourian, B., Kawamorita Kesim, H., Seyyed Amiri, N., & Moradi, S. (2017). Women entrepreneurship: Effect of social capital, innovation and market knowledge. *AD-minister, 30*, 115–130.

DeCoursey, C. A. (2017). Attitudes of professional Muslim women in Saudi Arabia regarding wearing the abaya. *Asian Culture and History, 9*(2), 16–28.

Doshmanli, M., Salamzadeh, Y., & Salamzadeh, A. (2018). Development of SMEs in an emerging economy: Does corporate social responsibility matter?. *International Journal of Management and Enterprise Development, 17*(2), 168–191.

Entezari, Y. (2015). Building knowledge-based entrepreneurship ecosystems: Case of Iran. *Procedia – Social and Behavioral Sciences, 195*, 1206–1215.

Entezari, Y. (2019). Modelling the national knowledge ecosystem: Policy implications for Iran. *Procedia Computer Science, 158*, 826–835.

Erogul, M. S., & Quagrainie, F. A. (2017). Motivation, networking and business growth: Perspectives of Ghanaian female entrepreneurs. *Journal of Enterprising Culture, 25*(3), 297–316.

Faghih, N., & Zali, M. R. (2018). *Entrepreneurship ecosystem in the Middle East and North Africa (MENA)*. Cham: Springer.

Farashah, A. D. (2013). The process of impact of entrepreneurship education and training on entrepreneurship perception and intention: Study of educational system of Iran. *Education + Training, 55*(8–9), 868–885.

Gherardi, S. (2015). Authoring the female entrepreneur while talking the discourse of work–family life balance. *International Small Business Journal, 33*(6), 649–666.

Golzard, V. (2019). Economic empowerment of Iranian women through the internet. *Gender in Management: An International Journal, 35*(1), 1–18.

Groenland, E., & Dana, L. P. (2020). *Qualitative methodologies and data collection methods: Toward increased rigour in management research* (Vol. 1). Hackensack, NJ: World Scientific.

Guerrero, M., Urbano, D., & Salamzadeh, A. (2014). Evolving entrepreneurial universities: Experiences and challenges in the Middle Eastern context. In A. Fayolle & D. T. Redford (Eds.), *Handbook of research in entrepreneurship education: Entrepreneurial university handbook* (Vol. 4). Cambridge: Edward Elgar Publishing.

Hadavi, F., & Zarifi, A. (2009). Talent identification and development model in Iranian athletics. *World Journal of Sport Sciences*, *2*(4), 248–253.

Haghighi, N. F., Hajihoseini, H., Nargesi, G. R., & Bijani, M. (2018). Gap analysis of current and desired states of entrepreneurship development components in the field of ICTs in Iran. *Technology in Society*, *54*, 101–110.

Hailemariam, A. T., Kroon, B., Van Engen, M., & Van Veldhoven, M. (2019). Dreams and reality: Autonomy support for women entrepreneurs in Ethiopia. *Equality, Diversity and Inclusion: An International Journal*, *38*(7), 727–742.

Hasan, F. S., Almubarak, M. M. S., & Ahmed, A. (2016). Factors influencing women entrepreneurs' performance in SMEs. *World Journal of Entrepreneurship, Management and Sustainable Development*, *12*(2), 82–101.

Hechavarría, D. M., & Ingram, A. E. (2019). Entrepreneurial ecosystem conditions and gendered national-level entrepreneurial activity: A 14-year panel study of GEM. *Small Business Economics*, *53*(2), 431–458.

Hosseini, S. J. F., & McElwee, G. (2011). Improving the entrepreneurial potential of rural women entrepreneurs in Northern Iran. *International Journal of Entrepreneurship and Small Business*, *12*(1), 15–27.

Hundera, M., Duysters, G., Naudé, W., & Dijkhuizen, J. (2019). How do female entrepreneurs in developing countries cope with role conflict?. *International Journal of Gender and Entrepreneurship*, *11*(2), 120–145.

Javadian, G., & Singh, R. P. (2012). Examining successful Iranian women entrepreneurs: An exploratory study. *Gender in management: An International Journal*, *27*(3), 148–164.

Kamberidou, I. (2020). "Distinguished" women entrepreneurs in the digital economy and the multitasking whirlpool. *Journal of Innovation and Entrepreneurship*, *9*(1), 3.

Keramati, A., & Salehi, M. (2013). Website success comparison in the context of e-recruitment: An analytic network process (ANP) approach. *Applied Soft Computing*, *13*(1), 173–180.

Keshavarz, G., & Javadi, S. (2020). Symbolic abstraction in the aesthetics of Balochistan art, a case study of Baluchi People's needlework. *Bagh-e Nazar*, *16*(79), 5–14.

Lathabhavan, R., & Balasubramanian, S. A. (2017). Glass ceiling and women employees in Asian organisations: A tri-decadal review. *Asia-Pacific Journal of Business Administration*, *9*(3), 232–246.

McAdam, M., Crowley, C., & Harrison, R. T. (2019). "To boldly go where no [man] has gone before"–Institutional voids and the development of women's digital entrepreneurship. *Technological Forecasting and Social Change*, *146*, 912–922.

McAdam, M., Crowley, C., & Harrison, R. T. (2020). Digital girl: Cyberfeminism and the emancipatory potential of digital entrepreneurship in emerging economies. *Small Business Economics*, *55*, 349–362.

Mian, S., Karadeniz, E., & Sarfaraz, L. (2013, October 17–19). Entrepreneurship policy challenges in the Eco Region: Gender disparities facing women entrepreneurs in Iran, Pakistan and Turkey, Pakistan and Turkey. ICSB-GWU, Washington, DC.

Modarresi, M., Arasti, Z., Talebi, K., & Farasatkhah, M. (2016). Women's entrepreneurship in Iran. *International Journal of Gender and Entrepreneurship*, *8*(4), 446–470.

Modarresi, M., Arasti, Z., Talebi, K., & Farasatkhah, M. (2017). Growth barriers of women-owned home-based businesses in Iran: An exploratory study. *Gender in Management: An International Journal*, *32*(4), 244–267.

Muhammad, N., Robinson, D., & Nisar, M. (2019). The influence of Muslim marriages on entrepreneurial intentions of women entrepreneurs. *International Journal of Entrepreneurial Behavior & Research*, *25*(7), 1389–1409.

Neneh, B. N. (2017). Family support and performance of women-owned enterprises: The mediating effect of family-to-work enrichment. *The Journal of Entrepreneurship*, *26*(2), 196–219.

Pauceanu, A. M., Alpenidze, O., Edu, T., & Zaharia, R. M. (2019). What determinants influence students to start their own business? Empirical evidence from United Arab Emirates Universities. *Sustainability*, *11*(1), 92.

Ramadani, V., Gërguri, S., Dana, L. P., & Tašaminova, T. (2013). Women entrepreneurs in the Republic of Macedonia: Waiting for directions. *International Journal of Entrepreneurship and Small Business*, *19*(1), 95–121.

Ratten, V., & Dana, L. P. (2017). Gendered perspective of indigenous entrepreneurship. *Small Enterprise Research*, *24*(1), 62–72.

Ratten, V., Dana, L. P., & Ramadani, V. (2017). *Women entrepreneurship in family business*. London: Routledge.

Rezaei-Moghaddam, K., Karami, O., & Fatemi, M. (2019). The comparative analysis of marketing activities among rural women entrepreneurs in Fars province, Iran. *Journal of Global Entrepreneurship Research*, *9*(1), 65.

Rezaei, S., Dana, L. P., & Ramadani, V. (2017). *Iranian entrepreneurship: Deciphering the entrepreneurial ecosystem in Iran and in the Iranian diaspora*. Cham: Springer.

Ribeiro, A., Rezaei, S., & Dana, L. P. (2012). Gender and family in transnational entrepreneurship. *International Journal of Business and Globalisation*, *8*(3), 409–420.

Salamzadeh, A. (2018). Start-up boom in an emerging market: A niche market approach. In D. Khajeheian, M. Friedrichsen, & W. Mödinger (Eds.), *Competitiveness in emerging markets* (pp. 233–243). Cham: Springer.

Salamzadeh, A., Arasti, Z., & Elyasi, G. M. (2017). Creation of ICT-based social start-ups in Iran: A multiple case study. *Journal of Enterprising Culture*, *25*(1), 97–122.

Salamzadeh, A., & Arbatani, T. R. (2020). Developing a framework for understanding how media entrepreneurs act: An actor-network perspective. In I. Williams (Ed.), *Contemporary applications of actor network theory* (pp. 77–98). Singapore: Palgrave Macmillan.

Salamzadeh, A., Azimi, M. A., & Kirby, D. A. (2013). Social entrepreneurship education in higher education: Insights from a developing country. *International Journal of Entrepreneurship and Small Business*, *20*(1), 17–34.

Salamzadeh, A., & Dana, L. P. (2020). The coronavirus (COVID-19) pandemic: Challenges among Iranian startups. *Journal of Small Business and Entrepreneurship*, 1–24. doi:10.1080/08276331.2020.1821158

Salamzadeh, A., & Kawamorita, H. (2017). The enterprising communities and start-up ecosystem in Iran. *Journal of Enterprising Communities*, *11*(4), 456–479.

Sarfaraz, L. (2017). *Women's entrepreneurship in Iran*. Cham: Springer.
Sarfaraz, L., Mian, S. A., Karadeniz, E. E., Zali, M. R., & Qureshi, M. S. (2018). Women entrepreneurship in Iran, Pakistan, and Turkey, based on GEM data. In N. Faghih & M. R. Zali (Eds.), *Entrepreneurship ecosystem in the Middle East and North Africa (MENA)* (pp. 649–657). Cham: Springer.
Sarrafzadeh, O., & Esmaeili, N. (2016). iBridge Berlin 2015, city cube convention center, Berlin, Germany, 4–6 June 2015. *Journal of Medical Signals and Sensors*, *6*(1), 64–65.
Simmons, S. A., Wiklund, J., Levie, J., Bradley, S. W., & Sunny, S. A. (2019). Gender gaps and reentry into entrepreneurial ecosystems after business failure. *Small Business Economics*, *53*(2), 517–531.
Wang, J., Li, Y., & Long, D. (2019). Gender gap in entrepreneurial growth ambition. *International Journal of Entrepreneurial Behavior & Research*, *25*(6), 1283–1307.
Zali, M. R., Faghih, N., Gelard, P., & Molaei, R. (2018). The impact of age and entrepreneurial age-based self-image on entrepreneurial competencies of male and female: Evidence of GEM-Iran 2016 data. In N. Faghih & M. Zali (Eds.), *Entrepreneurship ecosystem in the Middle East and North Africa (MENA)* (pp. 399–418). Cham: Springer.

Chapter 17

Networking Activity of Female Entrepreneurs Over Time: An Exploratory Case Study on Female Entrepreneurs from Early-Stage to Establishment

Zahra Arasti, Elnaz Tarzamni and Neda Bahmani

Abstract

The ability to develop and maintain an effective network is an entrepreneurial competency. There are differences in female social networks' features as well as in the way of expanding it comparing to men's. But, there is little attention to female entrepreneurs' networks. This chapter focuses on the dynamics of female entrepreneurs' networks at different stages of the business life cycle. A qualitative study was conducted on a sample of Iranian female entrepreneurs in the trade sector situated in Tehran. The results of data analysis of 10 semi-structured interviews show a considerable change in networking activity over time. Although the most important role of networking for women entrepreneurs in both early-stage and established businesses is to achieve opportunities, information, and resources. Also, the combination of female entrepreneurs' networks is most male-dominated. And the main challenge of networking in the early-stage is being female, while it becomes rather an advantage for established ones. Finally, Iranian female entrepreneurs become more aware of networking benefits over time.

Keywords: Female entrepreneurs; female networks; networking; early-stage; establishment; Iran

Introduction

Women's entrepreneurship is viewed as a potential source of economic and social development (Kelley, Brush, Greene, & Majbouri, 2017). However, based on the report by GEM (2019), the rate of female entrepreneurship is much lower

The Emerald Handbook of Women and Entrepreneurship in Developing Economies, 335–352
Copyright © 2021 by Emerald Publishing Limited
All rights of reproduction in any form reserved
doi:10.1108/978-1-80071-326-020211017

than that of men in most countries. For instance, the rate of entrepreneurship for women and men is, respectively, 8% and 14% in the Middle East and North Africa, 6% and 9% in European and Central Asia, and 15% and 18% in the North America (Elam, Brush, Greene, Baumer, & Heavlow, 2019). Furthermore, in factor-efficiency transition economics such as Iran, the number of women starting a business is much higher than those running current businesses (Kelley et al., 2017), which indicates women have more problem in continuing their entrepreneurial practices. One of its main reasons is related to their networks (Hampton, McGowan, & Cooper, 2011; Hampton, Cooper, & Mcgowan, 2009). Women mostly rely on their families for networking and, as a result, their networks are characterized with less variety in comparison with men (Kelley, Bosma, & Amoros, 2011; Arregle et al., 2015). So, it leads to a reduction in useful information they receive. In fact, although the presence of relatives and acquaintances in social networks provides emotional and spiritual support, but the financial support cannot be realized in this manner (Arregle et al., 2015; Klyver, Grant, & Hindle, 2007; Renzulli, Aldrich, & Moody, 2000; Rutashobya, Allan, & Nilsson, 2009; Rutashobya et al., 2009, 2009). A neglected point in previous studies is not to consider entrepreneur's network as a dynamic entity (Fayolle, Jack, Lamine, & Chabaud 2016; Hampton et al., 2011). Most studies in this regard have considered the entrepreneur's network as static at a specific point of time (Klyver et al., 2007). However, investigating entrepreneur networks in different time lapses has revealed their needs in various stages of business and is an essential strategy for business development (Hampton et al., 2011; Jack, Moult, Anderson, & Dodd, 2010; Anderson and Jack, 2002). Moreover, some studies investigate on comparison of female entrepreneur's networks with men's. Only a limited number of studies have distinctively analyzed female entrepreneur's networks especially in a male-dominated sector. While, women have different priorities in building their networks compared to the men (Hampton et al., 2011; Jack et al., 2010). Even more limited is the number of studies specifically investigating female networks in various phases of their entrepreneurship, or in other words, during their business life cycle (Fayolle et al., 2016; Hampton et al., 2009, 2011). Also, it is important to understand how they build and develop their networks as they will be more matured and experienced over time (Kwapisz & Hechavarría, 2018). Furthermore, it is helpful to understand how the female entrepreneurs build their networks when they face challenges in each stages of their businesses (Hampton et al., 2011). In other words, studying the dynamics networks helps us to have a deeper sight into understanding of the networking behaviors of entrepreneurs across time (Chabaud, Alain, Jack, & Lamine, 2012).

Meanwhile, the majority of these studies are in developed countries. While, McKeever et al. (2015) explain that entrepreneurs are embedded in their social context and cultural, industrial and entrepreneurial characteristics are key factors which affect entrepreneurial networks (Brown, Mawson, Lee, & Peterson, 2019; Jack et al., 2010; Parveen & Junaid, 2019). So, this study aims to provide insights into how female entrepreneurs' networking activities change from early-stage to establishment. This study in the context of Iran with different social settings will have a considerable contribution in both women's entrepreneurship and entrepreneurial networking.

Theoretical Backgrounds

In this chapter, we apply social network theory to deepen our understanding about networking activities of female entrepreneurs over time. Networks are formed based on relationships (Aldrich & Zimmer, 1986; Leskinen, 2017; Rho & Lee, 2018) and facilitate people's access to social support and resources (Achchi, Nadee, & Surangi, 2018; Xie & Lv, 2016; Durbin, 2011; Jack et al., 2010; Roomi, 2009). Based on the theory of social networks, individuals are interdependent; an individual is a social entity, which can cause changes in or be changed by other individuals. The aim of this theory is to show the nature and the effects of the interactions among individuals (Jack et al., 2010; Lee et al., 2011; Leskinen, 2017; Xie & Lv, 2016). The network studies can include a wide range of subjects such as network size, structure, interactions, effects, and behaviors (Jack, 2010). Networks facilitate access to information, knowledge, capital, and also other networks (Achchi et al., 2018; Durbin, 2011; Jack et al., 2010; Leskinen, 2017; Martinez & Aldrich, 2011; McAdam, Harrison, & Leitch, 2019; Neumeyer, Santos, Caetano, & Kalbfleisch, 2019; Xie & Lv, 2016). Nowadays, the networks not only affect individuals but also affect management, development, and maintenance of the organizations (Achchi et al., 2018; Durbin, 2011). They are changing the form of global trade architecture (Jack et al., 2010).

Social Networks in Women's Entrepreneurship

In respect with entrepreneurship, a network consists of a set of members and the relationships which make them related (Leskinen, 2017). Networks accelerate entrepreneurial practices (Stam, 2014) through the information and resources they provide. Social networks refer to the ability of an individual to obtain social resources from a social structure (Lee, Sohn & Ju, 2011). Entrepreneurs use social networks to access knowledge, information, and financial aids through them, which provide essential sources for new ventures (Xie & Lv, 2016). Social networks are also essential for reducing potential threats in changing environments and act as intangible assets (Širec, 2009). Women join networks. As the key role of the networks, women entrepreneurs use networks to develop their skills which could help them in the career of their ventures (Durbin, 2011). This is crucial for a female since they access fewer resources and face more obstacles in acquiring resources compare with men counterparts (Carter, Brush, Greene, Gatewood, & Hart, 2003).

Men and women have various views in building networks (Kwapisz & Hechavarría, 2018). While, female networks include family, friends, and people with similar viewpoints, men's networks with various members are as a source of advice (Hampton et al., 2009). In fact, men and women have different priorities while forming networks; while women are seeking social relations, men are seeking personal benefits (Durbin, 2011; Hampton et al., 2011). Moreover, women's networking practices are usually centered over those individuals with whom they have a sense of identification or those whom they trust considerably (Arregle et al., 2015; Hampton et al., 2011).

There is some evidence indicating that female entrepreneurs use methods to develop their networks, which are different from men's methods, and that their networks have different characteristics from male entrepreneurs' networks (Hampton et al., 2009; Klyver & Terjessen, 2007; Rutashobya et al., 2009). Based on research in Africa, female networks mostly consist of relatives, while there are fewer relatives in men's networks (Rutashobya et al., 2009). In fact, in similar social situations, women tend to have more homogenous networks, in comparison with men (Arregle et al., 2015; Hampton et al., 2011; Neumeyer et al., 2019). Such combination brings damage to the business (Arregle et al., 2015). Moreover, they prefer to interact with individuals similar to themselves. Therefore, they refused to be in male-dominant groups, as they have less legitimacy and influence which lead to limited access to information and resources (McAdam et al., 2019; Durbin, 2011). Therefore, they generally do not enter men's networks due to reasons such as lack of self-confidence, concerns with discrepancy, lack of competitive feelings, and worrying about the time and efforts necessary to succeed in such networks (Hampton et al., 2009). Meanwhile, women do not, as much as men, try to identify entrepreneur individuals as predictors of entrepreneurial practices. This is while in case of identifying entrepreneur individuals, men and women will take effect from them equally. From this, one can conclude that female entrepreneurs are less successful in their networks because they lack role models and individuals who provide entrepreneurial resources (Klyver et al., 2007). According to Hampton et al. (2011), women's social networks are weak in terms of size, density, and variety, which directly affect the network quality and, subsequently, their business development (Durbin, 2011; Hampton et al., 2011). Women's weakness in networking has limited their access to new resources and potential business opportunities (Verheul & Thurik, 2001).

Women have less social capital than men (Eagly et al., 2007), and female entrepreneurs face serious problems in networks in that they do not or cannot invest in building their social capital (McAdam et al., 2019). It seems women may not be as skilled as men in building their networks (McAdam et al., 2019; Durbin, 2011; Kelley et al., 2011). Even Frederick and Foley (2008) believe that women understand the importance of social networking in their business, but they are deprived of it because they face gender and racism discrimination.

Women generally find it more difficult to access potential benefits of networks due to the time and costs required for effective networking (Blisson & Rana, 2001; Wharton & Brunetto, 2007). They are generally pressured by the community to take certain roles at home (in the family), which interrupts their business trend, disrupts their past relations, and reduces their power to create new relationships and networks as potential entrepreneurial resources (Hampton et al., 2009). As a result, a female entrepreneur is faced with future challenges and obstacles as she tries to acquire knowledge or to access limited resources and workforce. They will affect the potential success of any given business (Hampton et al., 2011).

Social Networks in Female's Businesses at Different Stages

Networks change as a response to changing entrepreneurial needs, so social network ties are activated by these needs (Hampton et al., 2011; Jack et al., 2010). For example, over time, businesses need various contacts and resources. A consequence of this view is that we should see the networks as a bundle of dynamics relationships, changing and process driven (Anderson & Jack, 2002).

Surveys of female entrepreneurs show that women networking are various due to different stages. Hampton et al. (2011) stated that the role of networks helps women in preventing isolation and providing necessary support in the initial phases of their business. Women in the early stages of start-up development form their social networks in order to have advice, emotional support, inspiration, encouragement, helping to establish the validity of the business idea and increasing self-confidence (Kwapisz & Hechavarría, 2018; Arregle et al., 2015; Hampton et al., 2011; Roomi, 2009). Connecting with other women entrepreneurs through personal contacts such as family and friends is a reason to make social networks; they are of great significance in female entrepreneurs' social networks (Kwapisz & Hechavarría, 2018; Arregle et al., 2015; Durbin, 2011; Hampton et al., 2009, 2011). Moreover, the social structure of networks for entrepreneurs are men; this vast gender differences will be vanishing in later stages (Klyver & Terjessen, 2007; Mitra & Basit, 2019).

Women who are owners of established companies stress the importance of joining formal and informal networks as the growth is more vital for these women (Roomi, 2009; Kwapisz & Hechavarría, 2018). Roomi (2009) stated that females in this phase use networks to find more clients, suppliers, distributors, potential employees, partners, training, professional business advisors, and access to financial resources. During the time, women are capable of developing their networks with diversity (Durbin, 2011; Hampton et al., 2011). Hampton et al. (2011) believe that during the time that more business is established, men and women become more similar in expanding and operating their networks. In other words, in posterior phases, men and women form similar social networks to meet similar needs (Hampton et al., 2011; Foss, 2010; Klyver et al., 2007). As the benefits of social networks, in all phases, female networks have a significant role in saving time via providing information required for decision-making and confirmation of the decisions already made (Hampton et al., 2009).

Context

Cultural and social factors affect the entrepreneurial process (Parveen & Junaid, 2019). Understanding context has crucial importance to have a deeper understanding of entrepreneurship (Welter, 2011). In order to develop insight into networks and networking of entrepreneurs, it is important to understand social and cultural context (McKeever, Jack, & nderson, 2015). Recent studies revealed that geographical and cultural factors are reflected in the nature of entrepreneur's networks (Batjargal, Webb, Carolina, Carolina, & Hitt, 2019; Mitra & Basit, 2019).

Women represent 49.3% of the 79 million people of Iran; but only 16.1% of women are economically active, resulting in total women's unemployment rate of 18.9% (www.amar.org.ir, 2018). According to Women GEM report (2019), the total entrepreneurship activity (TEA) for women was 8.2% which ranks 26th among 59 GEM member countries (Elam et al. 2019; Bosma et al., 2020).

Research on women's entrepreneurship is very limited in the Iranian context (Arasti & Bahmani, 2017; Modarresi, Arasti, Talebi, & Farasatkhah, 2016, 2017). Iranian women entrepreneurs, like other women entrepreneurs especially in developing countries, face many difficulties including access to finance (Arasti & Kanani, 2011), networking, work–family balance, and gender discrimination (Arasti & Bahmani, 2017).

In relation to networking activity of Iranian female entrepreneurs, studies show that the women's immediate families (spouses, children, parents) are their most important supporters. In other words, the most important individuals from whom female entrepreneurs receive support include, respectively, spouse and children (for married women), parents (for single women), friends, colleagues, consultants, and potential customers. In literature, the most important effects of networks for female entrepreneurs include motivation (emotional support), consulting (managerial and executive support), and access to opportunities, information and resources (introducing to valuable people). This is true for Iranian female entrepreneurs' networking activities too. However, the other important role of networks that is presentation of role models was not observed in Iranian female entrepreneurs' networks (Arasti & Bahmani, 2017).

It has been seen that business environment in Iran is not proper for female and despite increased entrepreneurial activities by women, the ratio of businesses run by women to businesses run by their male counterparts are 2–10. This is while the ratio is 50 to 50 in countries such as Nigeria, Ethiopia, South Africa, and Thailand (Kelley, Singer, & Herrington 2012). In addition, Iranian female entrepreneurs are too cautious. One of the main reasons for this can be traced in the sociocultural structures of Iran, which are not encouraging at all for women's entrepreneurial activities. Iranian women entrepreneurs face some barriers related to their access to financial and nonfinancial resources, social value about women's abilities in management, network and networking, lack of role model in the society, and finally diversity of their responsibilities, which cause difficulty in work–family balance (Arasti & Bahmani, 2017).

Iranian Businesswomen Association stated that the total exports of Iranian female entrepreneurs only to the three countries were $17 dollar (http://www.tccim.ir, 2018) and the rank of internationalization among Iranian women entrepreneurs in GEM (2019) report was 40th among 59 countries (Bosma & Kelley, 2019). Although the networks are as a bundle of dynamics relationships, changing and process driven (Anderson & Jack, 2002), no study has yet attempted to investigate female entrepreneurs' networks throughout the business life cycle in Iran. This research aimed at investigating the formation and development of female networks during the business life cycle dynamically.

Methodology

Research Approach

In this research, we need to develop insight about the changes in women's social network during their business life cycle. In entrepreneurial research, one should adopt a more careful approach toward qualitative methodologies such as biographies, case studies, and discourse analysis. So, a qualitative methodology was adopted based on in-depth interviews.

Sample and Data Collection

The study sample consists of females who own/manage established businesses (above 42 months as specified by GEM, 2018) in the trade sector in Tehran, the capital of Iran. We used purposeful sampling in the two database of Tehran Business women association and Iran Chamber of commerce, industries, and mines. In total, we conducted 10 semi-structured face-to-face interviews and each interview lasted about two hours. We undertook purposeful sampling, prolonged engagement, as well as disciplined subjectivity strategies to evaluate the validity of the research. We formulated interview questions based on the 5W1H technique about the change in networking activities over time. This technique helps us to cover all aspects of networking activities of women entrepreneurs. The main questions were: "What: What happened and what are its dimensions?", "Where: Where did the event take placc?", "When: When did the event take place?", "Who: Who was involved in creating this event?", "Why: What were the reasons or purposes for the phenomenon?" and "How: How and under what circumstances did this event occur?" (Ikeda, Okumura, & Muraki, 1998).

We revised the initial questions after two pretest interviews by two experts in women's entrepreneurship. However, we also included additional questions after the preliminary data analysis. Next, we transcribed and analyzed all the interviews. We used the same protocols for each interview to assess the reliability requirements, hence development of a unified database. Table 1 illustrates the demographic information of the participants.

Data Analysis

In this research, we conducted a thematic analysis, which is a method for identifying, analyzing, organizing, describing, and reporting themes found within a dataset (Braun & Clarke, 2006). According to Nowell et al. (2017), it is a linear, six-phased method, and it is in fact an iterative and reflective process that develops over time and involves a constant moving back and forth between phases. The analytic process can consist of six phases (Braun & Clarke, 2006), including familiarization with the data, generating succinct codes, generating initial themes, reviewing themes, defining and naming themes, and contextualizing the analysis in relation to existing literature.

Table 1. Demographic Characteristics of the Female Entrepreneurs in the Study.

Name	Business Activity	Age of Business	Age	Marital Status	Education
A	Commodity sleep	9	66	M	Diploma
B	Commerce	6	47	S	Bachelor
C	Minerals	8	37	M	Bachelor
D	Petrochemical	21	55	M	Master
E	Technical service	9	48	M	Bachelor
F	Trade	17	67	M	Diploma
G	Transport	27	54	M	Master
H	Technical services	17	44	M	Bachelor
I	Electricity and telecommunications	8	38	S	Bachelor
J	Oil and petrochemical derivatives	13	40	M	Master

Research Findings

This section demonstrates the research findings of the changes in the networking activity of female entrepreneurs over time from early-stage to establishment. The findings from this study presented in four dimensions elaborated by Hampton et al. (2009) which were "role of network," "network composition," "network challenges," and "perceived advantages of network development."

Role of Networks

Regarding the role of networks, four themes involved including "Supporting and motivating," "special professional guidance," "Accessing opportunities, information, and resources," and "Role model."

The results of analyses revealed networking was a crucial factor to how these women entrepreneurs did business throughout the various stages of the business life cycle. While in the early-stage, women entrepreneurs highlighted networking as a valuable means of supporting and motivating to run the business; they remember the supporting role of networks in the establishment stage that helps them in consulting and decision-making. Maryam's comment reflected this view:

> I strongly argue that I did not receive any help. However, my husband supported me mentally…
>
> I had gone abroad for installation of some machinery and I got familiar with a lady there. She asked me why I didn't attempt to do that by myself. Later, she became a board member and a stakeholder of this company…

Moreover, women entrepreneurs emphasize on the role of special professional guidance during business life cycle. Both in early-stage and establishment phase, women entrepreneurs state that academic comments and expertise opinions help them in saving time and energy. In this regards, Fatemeh's comment was typical:

> The presence of advisors was very important. In many cases, probable damage was prevented, and in other cases affairs were accelerated...

They also indicated that networking helps them to gain information about customers and resources. A typical comment to reflect this came from Elham's interview:

> I was in charge of relations with truck owners in the company where I was working. This helped me create various relationships with them. As a result, when I established my own company, drivers informed each other, and the number of truck owners increased among my customers.

Women claimed that presence of appropriate role models and relationships with them have a positive effect on learning business tactics in establishment phase. Fatemeh illustrated the need for learning strategy of business from role model:

> ...Mr. J is one of the best strategist man in Iran and he is a good role model for me in facing business problems and managing its challenges .... .

Network Composition

About network composition, we identified two themes including "male-dominated composition of network" and "diversity of members." For both early-stage and establishment phase, the study revealed that women's networks are more dominated by males. Nasrin's comment supported this view:

> Most of my business relations have been formed with men. Indeed, this sector is masculine... After my husband, my colleagues (those working in the same sector) helped me a lot, who were mostly men...

While within some both early-stage and established, anyone who could contribute to decision-making or providing information based on knowledge and expertise, regardless of gender would be welcome. This comment by Fatemeh characterizes this particular view:

> My husband is an influential person in my whole life. He supports me in all stages of my work. Also my sister-in law has a knowledge about this work because she graduated in this field

Another point about women networking is that women prefer to involve diverse people in their networks in different stages. For example, in the early-stage, women's networking is mainly through personal contacts and in informal form. These people include known persons to female entrepreneurs with knowledge of the relevant industry sector. Primarily, personal networks composed of family and friends, who female entrepreneurs relied upon to provide much needed mental support in the start-up phase. The following statements of Sara confirm this finding:

> My mother and sister were good advisors, while I also had the assistance of three men as financial, legal and technical advisors

Whereas, in establishment phase, they highlighted using both informal and formal networks. Indeed, in establishment stage, the building of relationships and networking with both family members and friends as well as professional advisors has critical importance, as Zohreh stated:

> ...Now I can afford to pay for expert advice if I need it, for all aspects of my business

Networking Challenges

This study shows that women entrepreneurs are affected by a number of networking challenges. Women entrepreneurs revealed that being a woman is the most challenging in networking activities especially in early-stage phase. Restrictions to communicate with women for men is another related challenge that is mentioned by these women. As Tahereh noted:

> The main challenge was my gender. When I went to receive my business license, no one even noticed my greetings! They were always making excuses and obstacles

Another challenge for some female entrepreneurs was that in early-stage phase, they do not know enough about business communication. While in establishment phase, they have restrictive attitude to communicate with others. The following statement by Maryam confirms the claim:

> ... I never asked others to do me a favor outside the legal order... I've always relied on myself in solving problems. Whenever I got stuck in an organization, I solved the problem via my persistence...

In the establishment phase, the networking challenges are more related to persons. Many female entrepreneurs are not motivated enough to communicate with others that are sources of ideas and could help them to identify useful people. Only in one case, the interviewee confessed the use of relationship for indentifyng useful people. As commented by Masumeh:

> There are a lot whom I can call to pave the way for me. It's called favoritism or something like this! But I never do illegal things! Sometimes, they accelerate the process; sometimes they help solve a dilemma…

Perceived Advantages of Network Development

The results revealed that female entrepreneurs at early-stage phase are not aware of advantages of networking development. They are Carter, Brush, Greene, Gatewood, andandHart (2003) (www.amar.org.ir, 2018) who just joined groups whose membership was essential to continue the process. As Fatemeh stated:

> We were only members of the Supreme Informatics Council and Computer Organization of the country… we referred to the informatics council once a year solely to extend our license… as our business activity depends on this license

While the business grows more, female owner-manager of established firms had actually more sophisticated and effective networks. They spent more time to build and extend their networks over a long period of time. Consequently, they joined various councils and entrepreneurial societies during the establishment phase. They also developed their relations, particularly international relations, and made contacts with universities and academic centers. These kinds of networks had brought opportunities to gain better and more current business information/guidance whenever they needed. The following comment from Najmeh reflected this trend:

> Although I have experienced in this field, I prefer to aware of other technical expertise to be sure in decision making…

Discussion

This study explores this question: How do female entrepreneurs' networks change over time from early-stage to establishment. This study investigated the Iranian context, a context which is rarely examined through the lens of social networks. Findings are shown in four dimensions: role of network, composition of network, challenges of networking, and benefits of the network development.

At the role of networks, we talked about the supporting and motivating role, which are important for women entrepreneurs at the early-stage, but over time they become more mature and, they do not need it as much as in the early-stage. Findings of Kwapisz and Hechavarría (2018), Durbin (2011), Hampton et al. (2009), and Roomi (2009) confirm this claim. Also, Iranian female entrepreneurs provide especial professional guidance from their networks in the establishment phase but this is not significantly different compared with the early-stage, as they may not have enough experience in the early-stage to understand its worth. Moreover, in the establishment phase, women entrepreneurs claim the wonderful opportunities that social networks create for them to find new customers and new partners. The study by Kwapisz and Hechavarría (2018), Hampton et al. (2009), Roomi (2009) has drawn a similar conclusion.

Interestingly, the benefit of networks as role models appears in the establishment stage. The main reason for it may refer to the few successful female entrepreneurs present in Iranian society. Findings are in line with the results of Klyver et al. (2007) and Arasti and Akbari Jokar (2006).

In the composition of the networks, in both early-stage and establishment phases, the members of Iranian female entrepreneurs' networks were mostly men. It may be rooted in Iranian society values which women grow up with it. They rarely can trust other women, as they believe that the other women do not have sufficient ability to be active especially in male sectors. Results of this present study concerning the gender of the members of social networks are in contrast with findings of previous studies. Mitra and Basit (2019), Hampton et al. (2009) and Renzulli et al. (2000) revealed more women members in female networks.

In addition, we mentioned diversity in the female networks, which is more in the establishment rather than the early-stage. During the establishment phase, women entrepreneurs' relationships with international companies, scientific centers and universities, and academic councils and entrepreneurial societies significantly increase. This finding is in line with the studies of Širec (2009), and Martinez and Aldrich (2011) on female entrepreneurs in Slovenia.

The major challenges in networking for Iranian female entrepreneurs at the early-stage of business is the lack of positive view about women that prevent them to connect with men's networks. In addition, it seems that they have no adequate knowledge about business communication that shows although Iranian women are educated they are not trained enough for business. This finding is in line with the findings of Frederick and Foley (2008), Batani and Salehi (2007), and Hampton et al. (2009). Interestingly this present study shows the modifications in attitude about women that affect their networking activity at the establishment phase. At the establishment stage, the networking challenges are more related to the person, which prevent them to communicate with useful people. The women in our study contended there is a restricted attitude to have relationships with their men counterparts and they were not enough motivated to have business relations especially with men. The main reason for it that is in the Islamic context women, especially married ones, have a restricted relation with the opposite gender.

The advantage of networking is revealed for women in the establishment stage of business. Women develop their social networks and social contacts over time. As their networks mature they understand the benefits of that and extend it to their advantage. This finding is in line with the studies by Frederick and Foley (2008) and Hampton et al. (2009), although Frederick and Foley (2008) have not stated whether awareness of the importance network development has existed from the beginning of their business or has been acquired through time and experience. Unlike Hampton et al. (2009), it cannot be stated that all female entrepreneurs have achieved this perception in early-stage. Fig. 17.1 shows the changes in women entrepreneurs networking activity over time from early-stage to establishment phase of business.

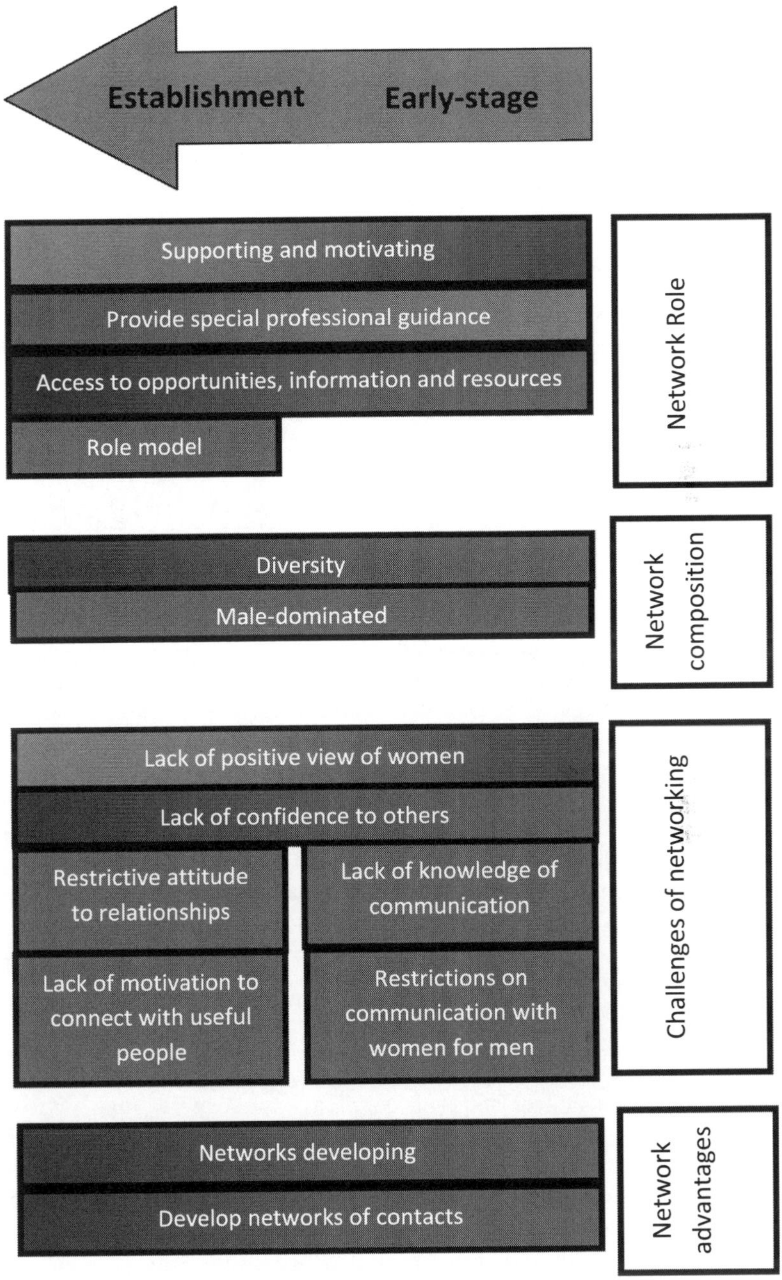

Fig. 17.1. Women Entrepreneurs' Networking Activity in Different Stages of Business.

This research investigating on women entrepreneur's networks in different time lapses has revealed their needs in various stages of business and help us to understand how they build and develop their networks, as they will be more mature and experienced over time.

In addition, we studied women entrepreneurs' networking activity in the trade sector which is a male-dominated that shows different priorities of women in building their networks.

Considering the embeddedness of entrepreneurs in their social context and culture, this study conducted in a different social setting of Iran could contribute to both women's entrepreneurship and entrepreneurship network studies.

In this research, we held interviews with women whose businesses were at the establishment stage and we asked a question about both early-stage and establishment. This is a threat to the data analysis and the validity of the data, for which, future research could investigate this subject by triangulation of data. Another limitation of this research is the small size of our sample. Future studies could investigate by a qualitative study on a larger sample in different sectors and from various geographic areas to allow generalizing the findings.

Conclusion

This research investigated the networking activity of Iranian female entrepreneurs over time by conducting a qualitative study with a sample of 10 women entrepreneurs engaged in the trade sector in Tehran, Iran. We presented the results through the roles of social networks. In the role of the networks, the results showed that for the Iranian female entrepreneurs networking clearly plays a crucial role in accessing opportunities, information, and resources, and this role is generally more emphasized in the establishment phase than in the early-stage of business, whereas the motivated and supporting role of the network is more highlighted at the early start-up. For women in our study, there is no difference in their role in terms of providing expert consulting in both business stages. Finally, unlike the businesses in the early-stage, the role of the network in providing role models for the established business is significant.

Other findings of this research about the combination of women entrepreneurs' networks showed that the men accounted for the majority of members of these networks at both business stages and the roles of family and relatives were reduced at the establishment stage; in contrast, more experts enter networks of women entrepreneurs.

The challenges networking challenges of Iranian entrepreneurs at the early start-up were more caused by environmental-driven challenges with a gender discriminative outlook. For Iranian women entrepreneurs there were a lack of positive attitude toward women, absence of credit for them, and the difficult nature of the relationship with women entrepreneurs by men. For the female entrepreneurs at this stage, there will appear some barriers such as lack of motivation to communicate and difficulties in identifying expert people. Moreover, they deal with some individual challenges such as "lack of communicating skills" and "lack of trust in others" at both stages; "time limit" becomes more challenging at the establishment stage.

Finally, the findings of our exploratory study on the importance of networking for women entrepreneurs revealed that Iranian women entrepreneurs realized the crucial role of networking development for their businesses along time. Trying to have more internal and external relationships and communication from the early start-up to establishment stages could explain this finding. Also, women entrepreneurs' networks became more formal at the establishment stage compared with the early-stage of business.

References

Achchi, H., Nadee, K., & Surangi, S. (2018). What influences the networking behaviours of female entrepreneurs?: A case for the small business tourism sector in Sri Lanka. *International Journal of Gender and Entrepreneurship*, 10(2), 116–133. doi:10.1108/IJGE-08-2017-0049.

Aldrich, H., & Zimmer, C. (1986). *Entrepreneurship through social networks*. University of Illinois at Urbana- Champaign's Academy for Entrepreneurial Leadership Historical Research Reference in Entrepreneurship.

Anderson, A. R., & Jack, S. L. (2002). The articulation of social capital in entrepreneurial networks: A glue or a lubricant? *Entrepreneurship & regional development*, 14(3), 193–210.

Arasti, Z., & Akbari Jokar, M. R. (2006). Impact of networking on Iranian women entrepreneurs to set up businesses. *Women Stud*, 4(3), 5–22.

Arasti, Z., & Bahmani, N. (2017). Women's entrepreneurship in Iran. In S. Rezaei, L.-P. Dana, & V. Ramadani (Eds.), *Iranian entrepreneurship* (pp. 109–137). Cham: Springer.

Arasti, Z., & Kanani, A. (2011). Barriers to business financing by women entrepreneurs in Iran. *The NIEW Journal*, 3, 91–101.

Arregle, J. L., Batjargal, B., Hitt, M. A., Webb, J. W., Miller, T., & Tsui, A. S. (2015). Family ties in entrepreneurs' social networks and new venture growth. *Entrepreneurship: Theory and Practice*, 39(2), 313–344. doi:10.1111/etap.12044

Batani, S., & Salehi, M. (2007). Social Capital, Network and gender: Investigation of structural, interactive and functional characteristics of women and men social network in Tehran. *Journal of Social Science*, 30(2), 62–95.

Batjargal, B., Webb, J. W., Carolina, N., Carolina, N., & Hitt, M. A. (2019). The moderating influence of national culture on female and male entrepreneurs' social network size and new venture growth. *Cross Cultural & Strategic Management*, 26(4), 490–521. doi:10.1108/CCSM-04-2018-0057

Blisson, D., & Rana, B. K. (2001). The role of entrepreneurial networks: The influence of gender and ethnicity in British SMEs. In *46th ICSB World Conference, Taipei, Taiwan*.

Bosma, N. S. A. D. J., Hill, S., Ionescu, A., Kelley, D., Levie, J., & Tarnawa, A. (2020). *Global Entrepreneurship Monitor 2019/2020 Global Report*. Global Entrepreneurship Research Association.

Braun, V., & Clarke, V. (2006). Using thematic analysis in psychology. *Qualitative Research in Psychology*, 3(2), 77–101.

Brown, R., Mawson, S., Lee, N., & Peterson, L. (2019). Start-up factories, transnational entrepreneurs and entrepreneurial ecosystems: Unpacking the lure of start-up accelerator programmes. *European Planning Studies*, 27(5), 885–904. doi: 10.1080/09654313.2019.1588858

Carter, N., Brush, C., Greene, P., Gatewood, E., & Hart, M. (2003). Women entrepreneurs who break through to equity financing: The influence of human, social and financial capital. *Venture Capital: An International Journal of Entrepreneurial Finance*, 5, 1–28.

Chabaud, D., Alain, F., Jack, S., & Lamine, W. (2012). Topic: Entrepreneurial process and social networks: A dynamic perspective. *Entrepreneurship & Regional Development*, 24, 729–732. doi:10.1080/08985626.2012.726508

Durbin, S. (2011). Creating knowledge through networks: A gender perspective. *Gender, Work and Organization*, 18(1), 90–112. doi:10.1111/j.1468-0432.2010.00536.x

Eagly, A. H., Eagly, L. L. C. A. H., Carli, L. L., & Carli, L. L. (2007). *Through the labyrinth: The truth about how women become leaders*. Harvard Business Press.

Elam, A., Brush, C., Greene, P., Baumer, B., & Heavlow, R. (2019). *Global entrepreneurship monitor 2018/2019 women's entrepreneurship report*. London: Global Entrepreneurship Research Association, London Business School.

Fayolle, A., Jack, S. L., Lamine, W., & Chabaud, D. (Eds.). (2016). *Entrepreneurial process and social networks: A dynamic perspective*. Edward Elgar Publishing.

Frederick, H., & Foley, D. (2008). Does culture and social capital impact on the networking attributes of indigenous entrepreneurs? *Journal of Enterprising Communities: People and Places in the Global Economy*.

GEM. (2018). *2019 Women's Entrepreneurship Report*. Global Entrepreneurship Research Association. London Business School.

Hampton, A., Cooper, S., & Mcgowan, P. (2009). Female entrepreneurial networks and networking activity in technology-based ventures: An exploratory study. *International Small Business Journal*, 27(2), 193–214. doi:10.1177/0266242608100490

Hampton, A., McGowan, P., & Cooper, S. (2011). Developing quality in female high-technology entrepreneurs' networks. *International Journal of Entrepreneurial Behaviour & Research*, 17(6), 588–606. doi:10.1108/13552551111174684

Ikeda, T., Okumura, A., & Muraki, K. (1998). Information classification and navigation based on 5W1H of the target information. In *Proceedings of the 17th international conference on Computational linguistics-Volume 1* (pp. 571–577).

Jack, S. L. (2010). Approaches to studying networks: Implications and outcomes. *Journal of Business Venturing*, 25(1), 120–137.

Jack, S., Moult, S., Anderson, A. R., & Dodd, S. (2010). An entrepreneurial network evolving: Patterns of change. *International Small Business Journal*, 28(4), 315–337. doi:10.1177/0266242610363525

Kelley, D. J., Bosma, N., & Amoros, J. E. (2011). *Global Entrepreneurship Monitor 2010 Global Report*. Global Entrepreneurship Research Association.

Kelley, D. J., Singer, S., & Herrington, M. (2012). *GEM 2011 global report*. Global Entrepreneurship Research Association (GERA).

Kelley, D., Brush, C. S., Greene, P. G., & Majbouri, M. (2017). *Global entrepreneurship monitor women's entrepreneurship 2016/17 report*. London: Global Entrepreneurship Research Association.

Klyver, K., & Terjesen, S. (2007). Entrepreneurial network composition. *Women in Management Review*, 22(8), 682–688.

Klyver, K., Grant, S., & Hindle, K. (2007). *The influence of social network structure on entrepreneurial participation: Gender differences studied across 47 countries*. Paper presented at the 3rd GEM research conference, Washington, DC.

Kwapisz, A., & Hechavarría, D. M. (2018). Women don't ask: An investigation of start-up financing and gender. *Venture Capital*, 20(2), 159–190.

Lee, J. H., Sohn, S. Y. & Ju, Y. H. (2011). How effective is government support for Korean women entrepreneurs in small and medium enterprises? *Journal of Small Business Management*, 49(4), 599–616.

Leskinen, R. (2017). Success in the female entrepreneurial networking process. *Annals of Innovation & Entrepreneurship*, 2, 7396. doi:10.3402/aie.v2i1.6000

Martinez, M. A., & Aldrich, H. E. (2011). Networking strategies for entrepreneurs: Balancing cohesion and diversity. *International Journal of Entrepreneurial Behaviour & Research*, 17(1), 7–38. doi:10.1108/13552551111107499

McAdam, M., Harrison, R. T., & Leitch, C. M. (2019). Stories from the field: Women's networking as gender capital in entrepreneurial ecosystems. *Small Business Economics*, 53(2), 459–474.

McKeever, E., Jack, S., & Anderson, A. (2015). Embedded entrepreneurship in the creative re-construction of place. *Journal of Business Venturing*, 30(1), 50–65.

Mitra, J., & Basit, A. (2019). Personal networks and growth aspirations: a case study of second-generation, muslim, female entrepreneurs. *Small Business Economics*, 1–23.

Modarresi, M., Arasti, Z., Talebi, K., & Farasatkhah, M. (2016). Women's entrepreneurship in Iran: How are women owning and managing home-based businesses motivated to grow? *International Journal of Gender and Entrepreneurship*, 8(4), 446–470. doi:10.1108/IJGE-03-2016-0006

Modarresi, M., Arasti, Z., Talebi, K., & Farasatkhah, M. (2017). Growth barriers of women-owned home-based businesses in Iran: An exploratory study. *Gender in Management*, 32(4), 244–267. doi:10.1108/GM-03-2016-0069.

Neumeyer, X., Santos, S. C., Caetano, A., & Kalbfleisch, P. (2019). Entrepreneurship ecosystems and women entrepreneurs: A social capital and network approach. *Small Business Economics*, 53(2), 475–489. doi:10.1007/s11187-018-9996-5

Nowell, L. S., Norris, J. M., White, D. E., & Moules, N. J. (2017). Thematic analysis: Striving to meet the trustworthiness criteria. *International Journal of Qualitative Methods*, 16(1), 1–13.

Parveen, M. & Junaid, M. (2019). Social networking and contextual embeddedness: An exploratory study of women entrepreneurs of Khyber. *Journal of Managerial Sciences*, 13(1), 105–115. Retrieved from http://search.ebscohost.com/login.aspx?direct=true&db=bth&AN=138289357&site=eds-live&scope=site

Renzulli, L. A., Aldrich, H., & Moody, J. (2000). Family matters: Gender, networks, and entrepreneurial outcomes. *Social forces*, 79(2), 523–546.

Rho, E., & Lee, K. (2018). Gendered networking: Gender, environment, and managerial networking. *Public Administration Review*, 78(3), 409–421. doi:10.1111/puar.12918

Rutashobya, L. K., Allan, I. S., & Nilsson, K. (2009). Gender, social networks, and entrepreneurial outcomes in Tanzania. *Journal of African Business*, 10(1), 67–83.

Roomi, M. A. (2009). Impact of social capital development and use in the growth process of women-owned firms. *Journal of Enterprising Culture*, 17(04), 473–495.

Širec, K. (2009). Gender differences in networking of Slovenian SME's. *Review of International Comparative Management*, 10(5), 1043–1059.

Stam, E. (2014). The Dutch entrepreneurial ecosystem. *SSRN Electronic Journal.* doi:10.2139/ssrn.2473475

Verheul, I., & Thurik, R. (2001). Start-up capital: "does gender matter?". *Small business economics*, 16(4), 329–346.

Welter, F. (2011). Contextualizing entrepreneurship—Conceptual challenges and ways forward. *Entrepreneurship theory and Practice*, 35(1), 165–184.

Wharton, R. F., & Brunetto, Y. (2007). Women entrepreneurs, opportunity recognition and government-sponsored business networks. *Women in Management Review*, 22(3), 187–207.

Xie, X., & Lv, J. (2016). Social networks of female tech-entrepreneurs and new venture performance: The moderating effects of entrepreneurial alertness and gender discrimination. *The International Entrepreneurship and Management Journal*. 12(4), 963–983. doi:10.1007/s11365-016-0413-8

Part 4
Early-stage Female Entrepreneurship, Drivers, and Outcomes

Chapter 18

Lessons from Global Financial Crisis: Human Capital and Business Activities among Nascent Women Entrepreneurs in China

Shayegheh Ashourizadeh and Chuqing Zhang

Abstract

This study aims to investigate the effect of the crisis on entrepreneurial activities and how it can be relieved. Specifically, we explore how the positive effects of the human capital (self-confidence, opportunity alertness, and risk willingness) on startup activities are changed after the global financial crisis. Additionally, we explore how knowing an entrepreneur boosts up these relationships. We applied data from the Global Entrepreneurship Monitor (GEM) about prospective women entrepreneurs in China in 2006–2007 (precrisis time) and 2009–2010 (postcrisis time). Results show a sharp drop in effect size of self-confidence and opportunity recognition upon women's entrepreneurial actions; however, the global financial crisis nullified the effect of fear of failure on potential women entrepreneurs' business activities. Furthermore, knowing an entrepreneur has no significant moderating effect. Theoretical and practical implications and directions for future research are discussed.

Keywords: Entrepreneurial activities; human capital; role model; women entrepreneurs; crisis; China

Introduction

Chenglei had graduated from master of computer science in London, and she decided to go back to her home country.[1] She had grown up in a small town near Xi'an. During her education, she found out that there are some opportunities to apply her knowledge and start a business in her home town. Also, she thought she can create jobs for her relatives and help them financially to have a better life.

The Emerald Handbook of Women and Entrepreneurship in Developing Economies, 355–370
Copyright © 2021 by Emerald Publishing Limited
All rights of reproduction in any form reserved
doi:10.1108/978-1-80071-326-020211018

Such thoughts excited her to go back as soon as possible and start her business. However, she was not aware of the global financial crisis that was on the way to arrive to her home country. When Chenglei arrived there in 2007, she saw a different face of the town. The central market was not crowded as before, many stalls were closed, and only a few customers wandering around the market. Many of her acquaintances and relatives had been laid off of the factories. Chenglei with the last hope in her heart went to the local bank to ask about loan, and obviously the bank denied any talk about loans. After watching such incidents, she had no more confidence to do entrepreneurial actions and thought if she takes such a risk, she will put her future more in danger.

We have observed and heard many similar stories around us in the time of crisis like the global financial crisis or the current pandemic of COVID-19. How people turn down their startup activities and depression atmosphere is disseminated. The 2008 global financial crisis transmitted from the United States to all around the world and impacted large as well as small businesses. However, the impact was more severe on small businesses that had a lack of access to loans and financial markets (DeYoung, Gron, Torna, & Winton, 2015). So, they had more difficulty in securing additional financing and gaining support from governments because they are not considered as critical players in the economy to have higher shares of loans and subsidies from the government (Boyle, 2020). Therefore, they had a higher rate of bankruptcies, layoffs, and unemployment, and a lower rate of survival in the crisis time (NĂSTASE, CREŢU, & Stanef, 2009). As an example, Martinez, Zouaghi, Marco, and Robinson (2019) have demonstrated that small Spanish firms had a higher rate of business failure during crisis. Therefore, the global finance crisis did decline not only the economic activities but also the risk willingness among economic actors and capacity to accept risk (Alcidi, Ark, Biggs, Gros, & Mayer, 2009; NĂSTASE et al., 2009).

A crisis may suppress the positive effect of such qualities on intention to start a business (Williams & Vorley, 2015) and business activities. According to Alcidi et al. (2009), the "Happiness Index" was decreased sharply in 2008 among European Union (EU) countries, which consequently caused more stress, fear, and anxiety among individuals.[2] However, such feelings can be alleviated by social networks and their companionship support (Cohen & Wills, 1985). For instance, knowing an entrepreneur may help a prospective entrepreneur to get inspired how to deal with his/her business idea (Wyrwich, Stuetzer, & Sternberg, 2016) in the time of crisis and how he/she gain a better perception about the risks of the entrepreneurial action.

Despite the few studies about the effect of crisis upon entrepreneurial activities (Devece, Peris-Ortiz, & Rueda-Armengot, 2016), women entrepreneurs, as a disadvantage group in the society, have been underrepresented in this literature. Women entrepreneurship has increased vastly through most economies. The annual report from the Global Entrepreneurship Monitor (GEM) (2017) has revealed that women's total entrepreneurship activity (TEA) rate has increased in all 74 economies and even surpassed male's TEA in some developing regions such as Asia (Philippines and Vietnam) and Latin America (Mexico and Brazil). Developing countries have a significant contribution in the global economy, and almost half of the economic actors in developing economies are women. While there are 126+ developing countries in the world, very few studies have considered women entrepreneurship in developing countries. Some examples are from India (Reutzel, Collins, & Belsito, 2018) or Bangladesh (Bhuiyan & Ivlevs, 2019).

So, the aim of this study is to investigate the changes of effects of women's self-confidence, opportunity alertness, and risk willingness upon entrepreneurial activities before and after the global financial crisis in China, and also, how knowing an entrepreneur may improve this relationship specifically after the crisis. While prior studies have investigated the direct effect of knowing an entrepreneur on entrepreneurship (Bosma, Hessels, Schutjens, Van Praag, & Verheul, 2012; Contín-Pilart & Larraza-Kintana, 2015), we attempt to disentangle the moderating effect of knowing an entrepreneur in this study.

We attempt to reach the goals of this study by applying data of prospective women entrepreneurs from GEM in China before and after global financial crisis, 2006–2007 and 2009–2010, respectively. We specifically utilize these years because it can show how the individuals' efforts to start a business were before the crisis and how it has changed aftermath. China is an emerging developing country that has a significant role in the world economy, and it is critical to investigate its specific context. The results show a sharp drop in the positive effect of self-confidence and opportunity recognition upon women's entrepreneurial actions; however, the global financial crisis nullified the effect of fear of failure on potential women entrepreneurs' business activities. And knowing an entrepreneur has no significant moderating effect which will be discussed further.

Thus, this study brings several contributions. First and foremost, it highlights the effect of institutional changes on some established effects in the entrepreneurship literature. Next, it sheds light on insignificant effect of knowing entrepreneurs for prospective Chinese women entrepreneurs. Further, we uncovered women's entrepreneurial behavior in a developing context which is in call for further investigation (Coad & Tamvada, 2012). Also, this study makes takeaways for the current pandemic which has influenced businesses and specifically women (Druckman & Sharrow, 2020).

The structure of the paper will be as follows; in the next section, we set the ground by presenting the research context and formulating the hypotheses about the entrepreneurial competencies and activities of prospective women entrepreneurs. Then, the methodology will be presented and results afterward. In the last section, we discuss and make the conclusions.

Theoretical Background and Hypothesis

Research Context

China's economic development is now entering into a new stage resource, and environmental constraints are getting factor costs higher and higher and traditional growth momentum is weakening. It is necessary to change the way of development, and mass entrepreneurship and innovation can provide new momentum for technological revolution and industrial transformation. Mass entrepreneurship and innovation can not only liberate productivity but also mobilize people's creativity. Encouraging mass entrepreneurship can effectively stimulate the vitality of the market economy, promote better social development, and increase employment rates.

However, there are still many uncertainties in China's mass entrepreneurship. The institution, market, and cultural system in China are quite different from those of Western developed economies. Nowadays, China is experiencing a profound institutional change from planned economy to market economy (Ahlstrom & Bruton, 2010). The transitional economies represented by China, on the one hand, gradually opening up and introducing competition mechanism, and the society is gradually moving toward market economy. On the other hand, the planned economic system still deeply affects the whole social economy, and the government still plays an important guiding role. These difference makes China's entrepreneurial activities face a tough entrepreneurial environment, such as the resource constraint dilemma, legitimacy dilemma, intellectual property dilemma, unethical competition behaviors, and high power distance (Lau, Chan, & Tai, 2010; Li & Zhang, 2007). The existence of these dilemmas and problems will inevitably have a profound impact on entrepreneurial intention, behavior, and strategic formulation of new enterprises. However, compared with other new economies, China has made great progress in the regulation dimension, normative dimension, and venture capital dimension. For example, China's government policies (taxation and bureaucracy), entrepreneur status, entrepreneurship, and entrepreneurship culture cultivation and promotion are all friendly toward entrepreneurship.

These characteristics have shaped the pattern of China's entrepreneurial environment, and it deserves more extensive exploration. In this chapter, we aim to open up the *black box* of China's entrepreneurship environment on female entrepreneurs' activity.

Entrepreneurial Competencies and Business Activities before and after the Global Financial Crisis

There are some universal determinants, including entrepreneurial competencies and socioeconomic institutions, on entrepreneurial behavior that have been investigated vastly in previous studies (Minniti & Nardone, 2007). There is a consensus on human capital (Ashourizadeh, Rezaei, Schøtt, & Vang, 2014) that consists of entrepreneurial competencies like self-confidence, opportunity alertness, and risk willingness which shape the entrepreneurial intention (Tsai, Chang, & Peng, 2016) and business activities (Arenius & Minniti, 2005; Ashourizadeh et al., 2014; Koellinger, Minniti, & Schade, 2004).

Self-confidence is a feeling of being assured of the individuals' own abilities and skills that are suitable for starting a business. Since entrepreneurship is an intentional action, self-confidence plays a critical role in the intention to start a business and business activities (Minniti & Nardone, 2007). Entrepreneurs are sometimes overconfident, and they overvalue the positive outcomes of their business decision (Invernizzi, Menozzi, Passarani, Patton, & Viglia, 2016; Malmendier & Tate, 2015) at the early stages of entrepreneurship. Also, self-confidence can be different from men to women, and it may change due to the situations. Women may perceive less confidence on their abilities and skills to pursue entrepreneurial actions (Minniti & Nardone, 2007). It arises from the social learning that male and female individuals may have when they are growing up. For example, Eagly (1978) describes women as considerate individuals who try to adapt themselves with opinions of their group.

Therefore, in an uncertain situation like the post crisis in a developing context that has unstable institutions, women may perceive that they are not able to forecast the future and have control on the situation as it is expected, and this may decrease the feeling of self-confidence. In the case of entrepreneurship that the process is inherently uncertain, being in unsure conditions imposes more doubts on women's abilities and skills whether it is enough to take actions. So, we hypothesize that in the crisis conditions when things get uncertain, women experience less confidence to start a business.

Hypothesis H1: The positive effect of women's self-confidence on entrepreneurial activities is decreased after the global financial crisis.

Opportunity alertness is described as an essential factor of entrepreneurial behavior in which individuals are more aware of potential benefit out of a situation. Opportunity alertness has been investigated in well-known research of Kirzner (1973, 1979) and Venkataraman (1997). It has been found that if individuals perceive that there is an opportunity to exploit, they may intend more to start a business (Minniti & Nardone, 2007). Opportunities may be created due to institutional changes. As an example, a study by Kalhor, Ashourizadeh, and Schøtt (2019) found that Iranian entrepreneurs perceive more opportunities due to the institutional change in their country. However, in the time of crisis, a developing context with unstable institutions experience more severe changes in their structures. A study by Amorós, Ciravegna, Mandakovic, and Stenholm (2019) exhibit that the state fragility in the developing context hinders entrepreneurs from opportunity recognition and pursuing opportunity entrepreneurship. For instance, the case of Greece shows that how the global financial crisis profoundly affected their society and changed the structures while it discourages entrepreneurship (Williams & Vorley, 2015). Therefore, we assume that after the global financial crisis women's opportunity perception decreases their startup activities due to the new structural conditions and existence of ambiguities.

Hypothesis H2: The positive effect of women's opportunity perception on startup activities is decreased after the global financial crisis.

While individuals with alertness seek for opportunities to exploit, they also bear the risk inherently accompanied with opportunities. Traditionally, fear of failure is regarded as a negative determinant of entrepreneurial activities (Cruz-Ros et al., 2017). It is known as a barrier to positive assessment of opportunities from psychological point of view (Bosma, Jones, Autio, & Levie, 2007; Henderson & Robertson, 2000). It is said that entrepreneurship is a risky journey (Hall & Woodward, 2010), and individuals perceive the probability of success or failure of their entrepreneurial action before starting activities. The entrepreneurship literature has demonstrated that potential entrepreneurs with less fear of failure have more willingness to take entrepreneurial actions (Ebrahim & Schøtt, 2011; Koellinger, Minniti, & Schade, 2013).

Also, previous studies have shown that there is higher amount of fear of failure among women (Dabic, Daim, Bayraktaroglu, Novak, & Basic, 2012; Kelley, Brush, Greene, & Litovsky, 2013). Previous studies have advocated the deteriorating effect of the crisis on risk willingness and pursuing risky actions (Alcidi et al., 2009; NĂSTASE et al., 2009). Therefore, a risky action in uncertain situation of post crisis may double increase the fear of failure and hinder women from taking entrepreneurial actions.

Hypothesis H3: The positive effect of women's risk willingness on startup activities is decreased after the global financial crisis.

The moderating effect of social networks on the relationship between entrepreneurial competencies and business activities before and after the global financial crisis.

There is no doubt that social networks can facilitate the entrepreneurial activities (Greve & Salaff, 2003). Having an entrepreneur as a role model in the network of individuals can inspire and motivate them to decide on starting a business (Bosma et al., 2012; Ferreto, Lafuente, & Leiva, 2018; Gibson, 2004; Lafuente & Vaillant, 2013). It also helps them to learn about the tasks and required capabilities (Minniti, 2005). Sorenson and Audia (2000) state that knowing an entrepreneur helps the organization of resources easily, and it, thus, enhances individuals' self-confidence (Wyrwich et al., 2016).

Social contacts in the form of role models can provide various support resources, including esteem, information, social companionship, and instrumental support, to the entrepreneur (Cohen & Wills, 1985). Cobb (1976) states that esteem or emotional support is a form of support in which a person feels that he/she is accepted and respected (Cohen & Wills, 1985). Through communicating with social contacts that value the person for his/her own worth and experiences, self-confidence enhances (Cohen & Wills, 1985). Consequently, knowing an entrepreneur can trigger the entrepreneurial activities (Schmutzler, Andonova, & Diaz-Serrano, 2019) specifically for women (Díaz-García & Jiménez-Moreno, 2010). Because, they are taking more dependent decision-making style (Salo & Allwood, 2011) in sensitive situations like post crisis and they consider other's opinion more (Eagly, 1978). Women need such social network (role model) and support particularly in the postcrisis time. In unstable situations, women may feel less confident on their abilities to start a business, and being in contact with accepting social network and gaining essential information may increase their confidence on their abilities and starting a business.

Hypothesis H4: Knowing entrepreneurs improves the impact of women's self-confidence on startup activities after the global financial crisis.

Role models not only provide emotional and esteem support but also grant information to individuals. Informational support assists the person to understand the situation and evaluate an existing opportunity (Cohen & Wills, 1985). According to the social learning theory, when potential entrepreneurs listen to other entrepreneurs as their role model, they can benefit from developing their entrepreneurial competencies (Gibson, 2004; Minniti & Nardone, 2007). Additionally, social networks help potential entrepreneurs in exploiting an opportunity by offering instrumental supports in form of financial aids or giving material sources and services. Thus, social network may boost the opportunity perception of the individuals, and it enhances the likelihood of taking business activities especially in the post crisis.

Hypothesis H5: Knowing entrepreneurs improves the impact of women's opportunity perception on startup activities after the global financial crisis.

Previous studies have attempted to disclose the direct impact of the role models on entrepreneurial behaviors (Bosma et al., 2012; Contín-Pilart & Larraza-Kintana, 2015); however, its moderating effect is underrepresented in the literature. Wyrwich et al. (2016) explains that knowing an entrepreneur helps prospective entrepreneurs to simulate the situation and reduce the potential risks of their entrepreneurial actions by understanding about the necessary skills and resources from their role models (Gibson, 2004). A study by Sepúlveda and Bonilla (2014) provides an evidence that having an entrepreneur as a role model potentially reduces the fear of business failure (Wyrwich et al., 2016) since they can estimate the risks and gain knowledge about the required works. This is true for women entrepreneurs as they are more conservative in taking risks (Jianakoplos & Bernasek, 1998; Schubert, Brown, Gysler, & Brachinger, 1999) and entrepreneurial activities. Knowing an entrepreneur helps them to determine the opportunity cost and consequences of exploiting that opportunity. In the crisis and postcrisis time, they can gain necessary information and capabilities to reduce the fear of business failure in uncertain situations.

Hypothesis H6: Knowing entrepreneurs improves the impact of women's risk willingness on startup activities after the global financial crisis.

Methodology

We are interested in changes of effects of entrepreneurial competencies upon entrepreneurial activities before and after the global financial crisis among potential women entrepreneurs in China. Also, how know an entrepreneur moderates the effects of entrepreneurial competencies upon entrepreneurial activities for potential women entrepreneurs in China.

We, thus, withdrew individual-level data from Adult Population Survey (APS) of GEM. GEM is a global project that is conducted by self-selected countries around the world. Annually, every GEM teams in participating countries, collects information about people's aspiration, behavior, and entrepreneurial conditions at individual and national levels. In fact, GEM data are a random sample of individuals and entrepreneurs who are nested in the participating countries. GEM methodology has been explained in details by works of Reynolds et al. (2005) and Bosma et al. (2012).

For the sake of this study, our sample comprises 6,311 prospective women entrepreneurs who were trying to start a business in China in 2006 and 2007 as a precrisis time and 2009 and 2010 as a postcrisis time.

To understand the impact of the global financial crisis, Alcidi et al. (2009) have suggested gross domestic product (GDP) growth and a combination of growth and unemployment; however, these indicators are at the macro level and cannot measure the impact of the crisis at the individual level. Here, we applied years to understand the changes in the attitudes and outcomes before and after the crisis. Such methodology has been applied in previous studies by Kalhor et al. (2019).

Measurements

Entrepreneurial activities: In this study, the entrepreneurial activity is our dependent variable. The respondents in GEM are asked to answer the following question: *Are you, alone or with others, currently trying to start a new business, including any self-employment or selling any goods or services to others?* If the respondents answer YES, it is coded as 1 otherwise 0. Thus, our dependent variable is a binary variable which requires a different treatment in the analyses.

In this study, the entrepreneurial competencies refer to people's self-confidence, opportunity alertness, fear of failure, and knowing entrepreneurs. In APS GEM, respondents answer the following questions:

Self-confidence: *Do you have the knowledge, skill, and experience required to start a new business?*
Opportunity alertness: *In the next six months, will there be good opportunities for starting a business in the area where you live?*
Risk propensity: *Would the fear of failure prevent you from starting a business?*
Knowing entrepreneurs: *Do you know someone personally who started a business in the past two years?*

Each of these entrepreneurial competencies is measured dichotomously and coded 1 for having the specific competency and 0 otherwise.

Methods of Analyses

To test the hypotheses, we applied crosstab calculations and hierarchical linear regression model. For further robust results, we applied bootstrapping to examine the relationships. Analyses with hierarchical linear modeling includes Model 1a and 1b that represent the direct effects of the research model and Model 2a and 2b that shows the interaction effects of our model.

Results

Table 18.1 presents the percentage of the responses about every variables of our interest with level of significance in the form of chi-square. Entrepreneurial action and self-confidence have slightly increased; however, it is not significant. We observe a remarkable drop in opportunity recognition from 35.8% to 30.4% with significant level of chi-square. In contrast, fear of failure has increased sharply from 29.1% to 37.8% in the postcrisis time with significant level of chi-square which confirm our hypothesis.

Table 18.1. Descriptive Analyses.

		2006–2007	2009–2010	Chi-square	No. of Cases
Entrepreneurial action	YES	15.2%	15.9%	0.43	6,311
	NO	84.8%	84.1%		
Self-confidence	YES	36.1%	35.4%	0.61	4,959
	NO	63.9%	64.6%		
Opportunity alertness	YES	35.8%	30.4%	13.28[a]	4,282
	NO	64.2%	69.6%		
Fear of failure	YES	29.1%	37.8%	37.52[a]	4,914
	NO	70.9%	62.2%		

[a]The level of significance <0.000.

Table 18.2 exhibits mean, standard deviation, and correlation of variables. Entrepreneurial activity is positively correlated by self-confidence, opportunity alertness, and knowing entrepreneurs, and they are significant at the 0.01 level. But, fear of failure has a negative correlation with entrepreneurial action as it is expected; however, it is not significant. Further analyses will show the coefficient relationships among variables.

To be ascertain about the model fit with our data (Table 18.3), we checked for R square and Hosmer and Lemeshow test. The rule of thumb for Nagelkerke R Square is to be between 0 and 1; thus, our model is in the safe side. In the Hosmer

Table 18.2. Mean, Standard Deviation, and Correlation.

	Mean	Std. Deviation	(1)	(2)	(3)	(4)	(5)	No. of Cases
(1) Entrepreneurial action	0.16	0.363	1					6,311
(2) Self-confidence	0.36	0.479	0.240[a]	1				4,959
(3) Opportunity alertness	0.32	0.468	0.168[a]	0.280[a]	1			4,282
(4) Fear of failure	0.35	0.476	−0.007	−0.07[a]	−0.001	1		4,914
(5) Knowing entrepreneurs	0.58	0.494	0.153[a]	0.258[a]	0.240[a]	0.052[a]	1	5,202

[a]Correlation is significant at the 0.01 level (2-tailed).

Table 18.3. Goodness-of-fit Model.

	2006–2007		2009–2010	
Tests Models	**Nagelkerke R Square**	**Hosmer and Lemeshow (Chi-square)**	**Nagelkerke R Square**	**Hosmer and Lemeshow (Chi-square)**
Direct effects	0.154	1.91	0.08	8.37
Interaction effects	0.171	1.02	0.089	5.24

and Lemeshow test, the chi-square reveals that our independent variables explain the dependent variable.

Table 18.4 demonstrates the direct and interaction effects of the entrepreneurial competencies on entrepreneurial actions. Model 1a and 2a are the status of the variables in precrisis time, and Model 1b and 2b express the postcrisis time.

Hypothesis 1 states that the effect of self-confidence on entrepreneurial actions will decrease in postcrisis time. In Table 18.4, Models 1a and 1b show the positive and significant effect of self-confidence on entrepreneurial activities that has changed before and after the crisis. It means that prospective women entrepreneurs experience less positive effect of self-confidence on entrepreneurial activities. So, Hypothesis 1 is supported.

We hypothesized that prospective women entrepreneurs may find opportunity recognition less significant in their entrepreneurial actions after crisis. Results show that the positive and significant effect of opportunity alertness on entrepreneurial activities has decreased for the potential women entrepreneurs in 2009–2010 compared to 2006–2007. Thus, Hypothesis 2 is supported.

Analysis reveals that the fear of failure sharply increases as a significant factor in determining entrepreneurial activities; however, it has no significant influence on entrepreneurial activities after the crisis. Hence, Hypothesis 3 is not supported.

Interestingly, knowing entrepreneurs may not accelerate the effect of entrepreneurial competencies like self-confidence, opportunity perception, and fear of failure on entrepreneurial activities among prospective women entrepreneurs in China. Therefore, Hypothesis 4, 5, and 6 are not supported.

Discussion and Conclusion

The aim of this study was to investigate the changes of entrepreneurial competencies' effects on business activities from institutional change perspective. To operationalize our ambition, we have examined the changes among prospective women entrepreneurs in China before and after the global financial crisis. Entrepreneurship literature is underrepresented in developing context, as compared to developed countries (Bruton et al., 2008; Ratten, Ferreira, & Fernandes, 2016). Also, it is far less investigated in entrepreneurship crisis literature (Kuckertz et al., 2020). It is

Table 18.4. Variables in Equation with Bootstrap.

	2006–2007		95% Confidence Interval		2009–2010		95% Confidence Interval	
	Model 1a	Model 2a	Lower	Upper	Model 1b	Model 2b	Lower	Upper
Self-confidence	1.18**	#	0.902	1.48	1.053**	#	0.821	1.305
Opportunity alertness	0.85**	#	0.575	1.12	0.35**	#	0.106	0.587
Fear of failure	0.3*	#	−0.026	0.58	−0.11	#	−0.350	0.123
Knowing entrepreneurs		0.704**	0.183	1.230		0.36	−0.015	0.764
Self-confidence × Knowing entrepreneurs		−0.18	−0.869	0.487		0.15	−0.337	0.675
Opportunity perception × Knowing entrepreneurs		−0.10	−0.787	0.668		−0.22	−0.765	0.350
Risk willingness × Knowing entrepreneurs		0.22	−0.474	1.021		0.14	−0.393	0.614
Constant	−2.38**	−2.73**			−2.13**	−2.29**		

Notes: Bootstrap results are based on 1,000 bootstrap samples. Dependent variable: Entrepreneurial Action. #. Significance not tested (is tested in preceding model). $*p < 0.05$; $**p < 0.01$; $***p < 0.001$.

necessary to study the effect of contextual factors on entrepreneurial behavior and how it shapes performance (Zahra & Wright, 2011).

Analyses of the data from GEM show that the impact of entrepreneurial competencies in the form of self-confidence, opportunity perception, and risk willingness on business activities has changed by the external changes in the environment. We had expectations that having a role model in the network of prospective entrepreneurs alleviates the adverse effect of the crisis. Interestingly, having a role model makes no significant impact on nascent women entrepreneurs' behaviors and activities. We surmise that it happens because in the time of crisis many nascent entrepreneurs would fail (Williams & Vorley, 2015). It, therefore, increases the thought that their business would fail like their role models. Additionally, in the Chinese culture, losing face (i.e. the reputation among people) is embarrassing and failing a business abashes the actor. So, knowing an entrepreneur who has failed in his/her business activities signals them that it may happen to them to lose their faces. This nullifies the positive impact of role models in context that entrepreneurship has a low status (Metzger, 2006).

Nevertheless, our study contributes in three-fold; first, it signifies the role of institutional change on entrepreneurial competencies and behavior. While our study confirms the previous findings about the positive effect of self-confidence and opportunity recognition on business activities (Minniti & Nardone, 2007; Tsai et al., 2016), it uniquely highlights decreasing of the effect size in the established relationships in entrepreneurship literature.

Further, our contribution is in examining the moderating effect of the role model on the relationship between entrepreneurial competencies and taking business actions. Previous studies have attempted to disclose the direct impact of the role models on entrepreneurial behaviors (Bosma et al., 2012; Contín-Pilart & Larraza-Kintana, 2015). Results demonstrate no significant effect of role models in a developing context. We, thus, contextualize this variable that its effect depends on the context and the time. Low approval of entrepreneurship in a society and being in the time of crisis bring incertitude and doubts. If a potential entrepreneur has a role model who has failed and lost his face, then it will be difficult for the observer entrepreneur to enjoy the benefits of having a role model. This is specifically more intense for women who are known to be more risk averse (Jianakoplos & Bernasek, 1998; Schubert et al., 1999).

Also, our study is a reply to the call about understanding of women entrepreneurs in the developing context (Coad & Tamvada, 2012). We shed light on understanding of women entrepreneurs' behavior and activities in the developing context and how they might be different from nascent women entrepreneurs in developed economies.

Further, our study has implications for policymakers in the current pandemic. We illustrated how a crisis affects dramatically the entrepreneurial perceptions and outcomes. Therefore, it is necessary to devise programs to rehabilitate the entrepreneurial qualities and spirits and turn the entrepreneurship engine on again. The support from the government and inspiration for entrepreneurship in the society is an essential movement after a crisis. It is specifically important for women and marginalized groups in the society. A study by Keller (2018) suggests that "noisy business politics" may direct the attention of government to allocate specific resources to small businesses.

The study contributes in theory and practice; however, it is not free of limitations. In the methodology, we have applied the variables from GEM data. GEM has measured the constructs in dichotomous form. Though it is understandable because GEM is a global project, and the same framework should be applied for all contexts. It provides the required knowledge about the construct; however, they do not capture all aspects of the concept yet (Lozano, Garcia-Cueto, & Muniz, 2008). So, we recommend to conduct the future studies with multiple response categories to enhance the validity of constructs.

Additionally, GEM had constrained our understanding to know the gender of the role models. Previous studies have admitted that isomorphism has a significant effect on individual's behavior (Gorman, 2005; Ibarra, 1992). Therefore, we suspect that the gender of the role model may change the effect, and we encourage prospective researchers to investigate the network homophily on the entrepreneurial activities.

Acknowledgment

Data were collected by the Global Entrepreneurship Monitor. Responsibility for interpretations rests with the authors.

Notes

1. Chenglei is an imaginary name.
2. "the growth rate of real consumption and the increase in the unemployment rate with a negative sign" (Alcidi et al., 2009, p. 7).

References

Ahlstrom, D., & Bruton, G. D. (2010). Rapid institutional shifts and the co-evolution of entrepreneurial firms in transition economies. *Entrepreneurship: Theory and Practice*, *34*(3), 531–554.

Alcidi, C., Ark, B. V., Biggs, M., Gros, D., & Mayer, T. (2009). Retrieved from https://www.intereconomics.eu/pdf-download/year/2010/number/1/article/the-impact-of-the-financial-crisis-on-the-real-economy.html

Amorós, J. E., Ciravegna, L., Mandakovic, V., & Stenholm, P. (2019). Necessity or opportunity? The effects of state fragility and economic development on entrepreneurial efforts. *Entrepreneurship: Theory and Practice*, *43*(4), 725–750.

Arenius, P., & Minniti, M. (2005). Perceptual variables and nascent entrepreneurship. *Small Business Economics*, *24*, 233–247.

Ashourizadeh, S., Rezaei, S., Schøtt, T., & Vang, J. (2014). Entrepreneurs' human and social capital: Direct and reinforcing benefits for export. *International Journal of Entrepreneurship and Small Business*, *21*(2), 246–267.

Bhuiyan, M. F., & Ivlevs, A. (2019). Micro-entrepreneurship and subjective well-being: Evidence from rural Bangladesh. *Journal of Business Venturing*, *34*(4), 625–645.

Bosma, N., Hessels, J., Schutjens, V., Van Praag, M., & Verheul, I. (2012). Entrepreneurship and role models. *Journal of Economic Psychology*, *33*(2), 410–424.

Bosma, N., Jones, K., Autio, E., & Levie, J. (2007). *Global entrepreneurship monitor: 2007 executive report*. London: London Business School.

Boyle, M. (2020). The impact of recessions on businesses. Retrieved from https://www.investopedia.com/articles/economics/08/recession-affecting-business.asp. Accessed on March 8, 2021.

Bruton, G. D., Ahlstrom, D., & Obloj, K. (2008). Entrepreneurship in emerging economies: Where are we today and where should the research go in the future. *Entrepreneurship: Theory and Practice*, *32*(1), 1–14.

Coad, A., & Tamvada, J. P. (2012). Firm growth and barriers to growth among small firms in India. *Small Business Economics*, *39*, 383. doi:10.1007/s11187-011-9318-7

Cobb, S. (1976). Social support as a moderator of life stress. *Psychomatic Medicine*, *38*, 300–314.

Cohen, S., & Wills, T. A. (1985). Stress, social support, and the buffering hypothesis. *Psychological Bulletin*, *98*(2), 310.

Contín-Pilart, I., & Larraza-Kintana, M. (2015). Do entrepreneurial role models influence the nascent entrepreneurial activity of immigrants? *Journal of Small Business Management*, *53*(4), 1146–1163.

Cruz-Ros, S., Garzon, D., & Mas-Tur, A. (2017). Entrepreneurial competencies and motivations to enhance marketing innovation in Europe. *Psychology and Marketing*, *34*(11), 1031–1038.

Dabic, M., Daim, T., Bayraktaroglu, E., Novak, I., & Basic, M. (2012). Exploring gender differences in attitudes of university students towards entrepreneurship. *International Journal of Gender and Entrepreneurship*, *4*(3), 316–336.

Devece, C., Peris-Ortiz, M., & Rueda-Armengot, C. (2016). Entrepreneurship during economic crisis: Success factors and paths to failure. *Journal of Business Research*, *69*(11), 5366–5370.

DeYoung, R., Gron, A., Torna, G., & Winton, A. (2015). Risk overhang and loan portfolio decisions: Small business loan supply before and during the financial crisis. *The Journal of Finance*, *70*(6), 2451–2488.

Díaz-García, M. C., & Jiménez-Moreno, J. (2010). Entrepreneurial intention: The role of gender. *The International Entrepreneurship and Management Journal*, *6*(3), 261–283.

Druckman, J. N., & Sharrow, J. A. (2020). Public opinion, crisis, and vulnerable populations: The case of title IX and COVID-19. *Politics & Gender*, *16*(4), 1084–1092. doi:10.1017/S1743923X20000446

Eagly, A. H. (1978). Sex differences in influenceability. *Psychological Bulletin*, *85*(1), 86–116.

Ebrahim, M., & Schøtt, T. (2011). *Entrepreneurial intention promoted by perceived capabilities, risk Emergence and Growth* (Vol. 3, pp. 119–138). Greenwich, CT: JAI Press.

Ferreto, E., Lafuente, E., & Leiva, J. C. (2018). Can entrepreneurial role models alleviate the fear of entrepreneurial failure? *International Journal of Business Environment*, *10*(2), 160–173.

Gibson, D. E. (2004). Role models in career development: New directions for theory and research. *Journal of Vocational Behavior*, *65*(1), 134–156.

Global Entrepreneurship Monitor (GEM). (2017). Retrieved from https://www.gemconsortium.org/

Gorman, E. H. (2005). Gender stereotypes, same-gender preferences, and organizational variation in the hiring of women: Evidence from law firms. *American Sociological Review*, *70*(4), 702–728.

Greve, A., & Salaff, J. W. (2003). Social networks and entrepreneurship. *Entrepreneurship: Theory and Practice*, *28*(1), 1–22.

Hall, R. E., & Woodward, S. E. (2010). The burden of the non-diversifiable risk of entrepreneurship. *The American Economic Review*, *100*(3), 1163–1194.

Henderson, R., & Robertson, M. (2000). Who wants to be an entrepreneur? Young adult attitudes to entrepreneurship as a career. *Career Development International*, *5*(6), 279–287.

Ibarra, H. (1992). Homophily and differential returns: Sex differences in network structure and access in an advertising firm. *Administrative Science Quarterly*, *37*(3), 422–447.

Invernizzi, A. C., Menozzi, A., Passarani, D. A., Patton, D., & Viglia, G. (2016). Entrepreneurial overconfidence and its impact upon performance. *International Small Business Journal*, *35*(6), 709–728.

Jianakoplos, N. A., & Bernasek, A. (1998). Are women more risk averse?. *Economic Inquiry*, *36*(4), 620–630.

Kalhor, E., Ashourizadeh, S., & Schøtt, T. (2019). An experiment of institutional change in the ecosystem of entrepreneurship: Easing sanctions against Iran. *European Journal of International Management*, *13*(4), 435–453.

Keller, E. (2018). Noisy business politics: Lobbying strategies and business influence after the financial crisis. *Journal of European Public Policy*, *25*(3), 287–306.

Kelley, D. J., Brush, C. G., Greene, P. G., & Litovsky, Y. (2013). Global Entrepreneurship Research Association (GERA). Retrieved from https://www.empowerwomen.org/en/resources/documents/2013/8/global-entrepreneurship-monitor-2012-womens-report?lang=en

Kirzner, I. M. (1973). *Competition and entrepreneurship*. Chicago, IL: University of Chicago Press.

Kirzner, I. M. (1979). *Perception, opportunity, and profit*. Chicago, IL: University of Chicago Press.

Koellinger, P., Minniti, M., & Schade, C. (2004). April). I think I can, I think I can: A cross-country study of entrepreneurial motivation. In First GEM Research Conference (pp. 1–3).

Koellinger, P., Minniti, M., & Schade, C. (2013). Gender differences in entrepreneurial propensity. *Oxford Bulletin of Economics & Statistics*, *75*(2), 213–234.

Kuckertz, A., Brändle, L., Gaudig, A., Hinderer, S., Reyes, C. A. M., Prochotta, A., & Berger, E. S. (2020). Startups in times of crisis–A rapid response to the COVID-19 pandemic. *Journal of Business Venturing Insights*, *13*, e00169.

Lafuente, E., & Vaillant, Y. (2013). Age driven influence of role-models on entrepreneurship in a transition economy. *Journal of Small Business and Enterprise Development*, *20*(1), 181–203.

Lau, T., Chan, K. F., & Tai, S. H. C. (2010). Corporate entrepreneurship of IJVs in China. *Management Research Review*, *33*(1), 6–22.

Li, H. Y., & Zhang, Y. (2007). The role of managers' political networking and functional experience in new venture performance: Evidence from China's transition economy. *Strategic Management Journal*, *28*(8), 791–804.

Lozano, L. M., Garcia-Cueto, E., & Muniz, J. (2008). Effect of the number of response categories on the reliability and validity of rating scales. *Methodology*, *4*(2), 73–79.

Malmendier, U., & Tate, G. (2015). Behavioural CEOs: The role of managerial overconfidence. *The Journal of Economic Perspectives*, *29*, 37–60.

Martinez, M. G., Zouaghi, F., Marco, T. G., & Robinson, C. (2019). What drives business failure? Exploring the role of internal and external knowledge capabilities during the global financial crisis. *Journal of Business Research*, *98*, 441–449.

Metzger, G. (2006). Afterlife—Who takes heart for restart. ZEW discussion paper no. 06-038.

Minniti, M. (2005). Entrepreneurship and network externalities. *Journal of Economic Behavior & Organization*, *57*(1), 1–27.

Minniti, M., & Nardone, C. (2007). Being in someone else's shoes: The role of gender in nascent entrepreneurship. *Small Business Economics*, *28*(2–3), 223–238.

NĂSTASE, M., CREŢU, A. Ş., & Stanef, R. (2009). Effects of global financial crisis. *Revista de Management Comparat International/Review of International Comparative Management*, *10*(4), 691–699.

Ratten, V., Ferreira, J., & Fernandes, C. (2016). Entrepreneurial and network knowledge in emerging economies. *Review of International business and Strategy*, *26*(3), 392–409.

Reutzel, C. R., Collins, J. D., & Belsito, C. A. (2018). Leader gender and firm investment in innovation. *Gender in Management*, *33*(6), 430–450.

Reynolds, P., Bosma, N., Autio, E., Hunt, S., De Bono, N., Servais, I., ... Chin, N. (2005). Global entrepreneurship monitor: Data collection design and implementation 1998–2003. *Small Business Economics*, *24*(3), 205–231.

Salo, I., & Allwood, C. M. (2011). Decision-making styles, stress and gender among investigators. *Policing: An International Journal of Police Strategies & Management*, *34*(1), 97–119.

Schmutzler, J., Andonova, V., & Diaz-Serrano, L. (2019). How context shapes entrepreneurial self-efficacy as a driver of entrepreneurial intentions: A multilevel approach. *Entrepreneurship: Theory and Practice*, *43*(5), 880–920.

Schubert, R., Brown, M., Gysler, M., & Brachinger, H. W. (1999). Gender and economic transactions – financial decision-making: Are women really more risk-adverse? *The American Economic Review*, *89*(2), 381–385.

Sepúlveda, J. P., & Bonilla, C. A. (2014). The factors affecting the risk attitude in entrepreneurship: Evidence from Latin America. *Applied Economics Letters*, *21*(8), 573–581.

Sorenson, O., & Audia, P. G. (2000). The social structure of entrepreneurial activity: Geographic concentration of footwear production in the United States, 1940–1989. *American Journal of Sociology*, *106*(2), 424–462.

Tsai, K. H., Chang, H. C., & Peng, C. Y. (2016). Refining the linkage between perceived capability and entrepreneurial intention: Roles of perceived opportunity, fear of failure, and gender. *The International Entrepreneurship and Management Journal*, *12*(4), 1127–1145.

Venkataraman, S. (1997). The distinctive domain of entrepreneurship research: An editor's perspective. In J. Katz & R. Brockhaus (Eds.), *Advances in entrepreneurship, firm emergence and growth* (Vol. 3, pp. 119–138). Greenwich, CT: JAI Press.

Williams, N., & Vorley, T. (2015). The impact of institutional change on entrepreneurship in a crisis-hit economy: The case of Greece. *Entrepreneurship & Regional Development*, *27*(1–2), 28–49.

Wyrwich, M., Stuetzer, M., & Sternberg, R. (2016). Entrepreneurial role models, fear of failure, and institutional approval of entrepreneurship: A tale of two regions. *Small Business Economics*, *46*(3), 467–492.

Zahra, S. A., & Wright, M. (2011). Entrepreneurship's next act. *Academy of Management Perspectives*, *25*(4), 67–83.

Chapter 19

Innovation Amplifies Growth Ambitions of Early-Stage Female Entrepreneurs: More in Nordics, Less in MENA Region

Mehrzad Saeedikiya, Zeynab Aeeni, Serdar Temiz and Hiroko Kawamorita

Abstract

The current research investigates the regional differences in benefiting from innovation toward growth ambitions in a sample of female entrepreneurs in the Middle East and North Africa (MENA) and Nordic region. A sample of 4,048 early-stage female entrepreneurs from these two regions who were participated in annual surveys of Global Entrepreneurship Monitor was selected for further analysis. The results of data analysis using hierarchical linear modeling (mixed models) revealed that innovation benefits growth ambitions of early-stage female entrepreneurs. Further, the regional differences affect the benefit of innovation in shaping growth ambitions, so that, in Nordic region, the early-stage female entrepreneurs expect more growth out of their innovation as compared with their counterparts in MENA region. These results have been discussed regarding to existing literature, and future research directions have been suggested based on the results.

Keywords: Innovation; growth ambition; growth aspiration; growth expectation; MENA; Nordic

Introduction

Growth of entrepreneurial firms as a measure of entrepreneurial success (Delmar & Wiklund, 2008; Hechavarria, Bullough, Brush, & Edelman, 2019; Wiktor & laguna, 2018) and economic development (Lichtenstein, 2000) has gained special research attention (Arroyo, Fuentes, & Jimenez, 2016). However, achieving a high level of growth is complicated, and studies are showing that still, a minority of businesses are responsible for creating a significant share of employment and

The Emerald Handbook of Women and Entrepreneurship in Developing Economies, 371–390
Copyright © 2021 by Emerald Publishing Limited
All rights of reproduction in any form reserved
doi:10.1108/978-1-80071-326-020211019

growth in the society (Autio, 2005). According to a study on European countries, only three to six percent of companies can be considered as high-growth businesses (Bravo-Biosca, 2011). In a similar vein, another report shows that in the Organisation for Economic Co-operation and Development (OECD) region, most of the businesses can be considered as microenterprises, i.e., the firms with less than 10 employees (OECD, 2017). These figures confirm that the growth of the firm is one of the main challenges faced by entrepreneurs, specifically, in the early stages of their entrepreneurial activity. The importance of firm growth will be magnified when it comes to the growth of the firms owned or managed by females. Some researchers have found that female-owned enterprises do not perform as well as their male counterparts in terms of sales, employment, or profit (Terjesen, Bosma, & Stam, 2016; Davis & Shaver, 2012; Fairlie & Robb, 2009). They also have shown to be less successful in acquiring the necessary resources and capitals for growing their businesses (Asiedu, Kalonda-Kanyama, Ndikumana, & Nti-Addae, 2013).

However, it is exclusively recognized that the decision to grow is a choice (Hechavarria et al., 2019; Wiklund, Davidsson, & Delmar, 2003). Hence, growth ambition is a crucial predictor of actual business growth (Davidsson, 1991; Delmar & Wiklund, 2008; Henrekson & Johansson, 2010; Hermans et al., 2015; Wiklund & Shepherd, 2003). This is because entrepreneurs with high-growth aspirations tend to allocate more effort and resources toward growing their business (Autio, 2005; Poblete, 2018; Saeedikiya & Aeeni, 2020). Previous studies show a positive relationship between growth aspiration and firm growth (Baum, Lock & Smith, 2001; Cliff, 1998; Dutta & Thornhill, 2008). However, this key indicator of firm growth has received less attention in the literature (Autio & Acs, 2010), particularly considering gender influence (Hechavarria et al., 2019). Additionally, current literature mainly focuses on studies of companies led by men, which in turn limits our understanding of the implication and application of theories of firm growth for women entrepreneurs (Jennings & Brush, 2013).

One of the main factors affecting the growth ambitions of entrepreneurs is innovation (Castaño, Méndez, & Galindo, 2016; Stenholm, 2011; Wiklund, Patzelt, & Shepherd, 2009). Nevertheless, the institutional context in which the firms operate may provide some incentives or punishments for the firms and affect the link between innovation and growth ambitions. Some recent empirical studies also highlight the importance of context for improving growth ambitions. For example, Sipola (2015) found that entrepreneurial growth aspiration differs between countries. However, most of the studies are not fully taking into account how complex institutional forces may influence growth, and the majority of the studies on entrepreneurial growth emphasizes on the individual characteristics (Wallin, Still, & Henttonen, 2016). There is still a lack of comprehensive understanding of how the broader institutional environment influences entrepreneurial growth aspiration (Wang, Li, & Long, 2019). To bridge these gaps in the literature, this research examines the institutional differences in two extremely different contexts: Nordics and the Middle East and North Africa (MENA). Since entrepreneurship in these two regions is different in terms of the level of institutional support for female entrepreneurship, support for growth-oriented entrepreneurship, and access to capitals and resources necessary for female entrepreneurship (Maxfield, 2007; Terjesen & Lloyd, 2015), the authors are interested to see if these differences can affect the expected growth of entrepreneurs from their innovation. Accordingly, our research question is whether institutional differences in Nordics and MENA affect the benefit of female entrepreneurs from their innovation toward growth aspirations?

Applying a hierarchical linear modeling (HLM) technique and analyzing the data of a representative sample of early-stage female entrepreneurs in MENA and Nordics, our study shows that innovation benefits growth aspirations of female entrepreneurs differently in the two context, so that, the benefit of innovation in shaping growth ambitions of female entrepreneurs is higher in Nordic region than in MENA region.

The chapter contributes to the entrepreneurship literature in several ways: first, it provides a comparative insight on the link between innovation and growth aspirations of entrepreneurs and shows how institutional differences play a role in explaining the growth differentials of entrepreneurs. Second, it incorporates a gender perspective into the institutional perspective about the growth ambitions of entrepreneurs and adds value to the domain of gender and entrepreneurship. Third, gendered studies in entrepreneurship are mostly focused on studying gender differences in entrepreneurship and bounded within the national boundaries of the countries (Yadav & Unni, 2016). The current chapter considers the growth ambitions of female entrepreneurs across regions that are relatively necessary, but an underexplored area.

The rest of the chapter has been organized as follows: first, the authors explain a theoretical framework arguing the interrelationship among innovation, institutional context, and female growth aspiration, which lead to hypotheses development. Then, the research method and the results of hypotheses testing for each hypothesis have been presented. After all, the chapter concludes by discussing the results, reporting the limitations, and suggesting future research agenda.

Theoretical Framework

Innovation has been linked to the growth ambitions of entrepreneurs (Castaño et al., 2016; Stenholm, 2011). However, the effect of innovation on the growth ambitions of entrepreneurs does not occur in a vacuum. According to Williamson (2000), the economic activity of the agents is embedded in the institutional context in which the firms operate. For Williamson, institutional's effects appear in four levels.

The first level is the social embeddedness level in which informal institutions affect the agent's behaviors. Culture and social norms are two important informal institutions that define roles and prescribe specific actions to the agents. Empirical evidence has supported the idea of the effect of embedded institutions such as culture and norm on a firm's entrepreneurial behavior and performance (Batjargal et al., 2019; Belchior & Liñán, 2017; Bogatyreva, Edelman, Manolova, Osiyevskyy, & Shirokova, 2019; Shirokova, Tsukanova, & Morris, 2018).

The second level is formal institutions like regulations, rules, and macrolevel social arrangements by governments or public policies. The scale, intensity, and directions of the actions in the society can be explained by these "rules of the game" (North, 1990). In the context of entrepreneurship, it has been shown that these formal arrangements can explain performance differentials of the firms regarding innovation and growth-oriented entrepreneurship. For example, a study by Jiao, Koo, and Cui (2015) found that the legal environment, government ownership, and government effectiveness have a significant effect on firms' innovation. In the same study, government ownership also found to affect negatively the link between government effectiveness and management innovation.

The third level of the hierarchy is the governance level in which institutions governing transactions matter. Instead of the rules of the game, institutions at this level target the play of the game where institutions such as firms, markets, networks, and policy instruments are important aspects of institutional effects. For example, a study by Cai, Liu, Zhu, and Deng (2015) found that entrepreneurial support policies can enhance the benefit of responsive market orientation for innovation.

The fourth level is the resource allocation (behavior) level, which is affected by the collective impact of the three other levels. This level seeks to explain the behavior based on the effects from different institutional levels. Williamson's hierarchy of the institutions and its impact on the human actions and its outcomes have been investigated in several empirical studies in which the researchers have considered a moderation effect of institutions on the link between actors' behavior and their outcomes.

Applying Williamson's framework in the context of innovation and growth ambitions of entrepreneurs, one can expect that the benefit of innovation in shaping the growth ambitions of female entrepreneurs to be context-dependent. Contextual differences in terms of female entrepreneurs' capital, institutional support for entrepreneurship, and structural developments for high-growth entrepreneurship vary in Nordic and MENA region. This idea has been the focus of this chapter to provide a contextualized understanding of the innovation-growth aspirations' link of female entrepreneurs in the Nordic and MENA region. Such a contextualized conceptualization has been recommended by the leading scholars of the field (Shepherd, Wennberg, Suddaby, & Wiklund, 2019; Welter, Baker, & Wirsching, 2019).

Accordingly, the literature review will be discussed in two parts: first, the authors discuss the effect of innovation on the growth aspirations of the female entrepreneurs. Then, we review the empirical evidence for the embeddedness of the innovation-ambition link in the institutional context to understand whether the benefit of innovation for shaping the growth aspirations of female entrepreneurs is context-dependent or not. We do the latter by comparing the innovation-ambition link for female entrepreneurs of MENA and Nordic Context.

Innovation Boosts Growth Ambitions of Female Entrepreneurs

Innovation has been argued to have a dramatic influence on business success (Bausch & Rosenbusch, 2005; Poblete, 2018; Rauch & Frese, 2007) and, subsequently, the creation of competitive advantages and performance improvement (McEvily, Eisenhardt, & Prescott, 2004). One of the lean ways to manifest this success is firm growth (Dutta & Thornhill, 2008). Hence, entrepreneurs find that doing something innovative can move them to a higher rate of expansion in their business, generates growth opportunities, and provides advantages for reaching new markets and customers (Poblete, 2018). Considering the turbulent nature of today's market competition, these positive outcomes make the pursuit of innovative activities a purposeful and proactive choice that follows a specific goal set by managers (McKelvie, Brattström, & Wennberg; 2017). Therefore, innovation through reinforcing growth aspiration will become one of the critical drivers of firm growth (Arroyo, Fuentes, & Jiménez, 2016; Autio & Sapienza, 2000; Gilbert, McDougall, & Audretsch, 2006). Further, according to resource-based theory of the firm, innovation can be considered as a resource with features such as value, rarity, nonimitability, and nonsubstitutability (Claude-gaudillat & Quélin, 2006). Such qualities make the product or service more valuable, the competition more complicated, the returns much higher, and consequently, the growth prospect clearer. Innovations also can be a source of economies of scope and scale (Saeedikiya & Aeeni, 2020), brand loyalty (Foroudi, Jin, Gupta, Melewar, & Foroudi, 2016; Leckie, Nyadzayo, & Johnson, 2018), and market performance (Aksoy, 2017). Expectancy theory also advocates that the entrepreneurs' innovation can make gestures of the firm owners about the future more optimistic and the competition more idealistic (Gaglio, 2004). Such mechanisms can explain why the firms that innovate logically are more ambitious about their growth.

In line with the above arguments, research suggests that entrepreneurs involved in innovative activities are more likely to have higher growth expectations (Stenholm, 2011; Wiklund et al., 2009). For example, Gundry and Welsch (2001) find that aspiring entrepreneurs emphasize innovative activity more than non–growth-oriented entrepreneurs. In a recent study, Castaño et al. (2016) find an indirect positive effect of innovation on growth expectations for entrepreneurs in the service sector. While prevalence of ambitious entrepreneurship has been found to be lower in female samples (Amorós, Poblete, & Mandakovic, 2019), female entrepreneurs who innovate, according to the above explanations, can shape ambitious and growth-oriented aspirations. Accordingly, it is hypothesized that:

H1. Innovation boosts the growth ambitions of female entrepreneurs.

Innovation and Growth Ambitions of Female Entrepreneurs' Contextualization in MENA and Nordics

In the previous section, the authors explained the link between innovation and growth ambitions of female entrepreneurs. In this section, we provide arguments on why the role of innovation in shaping the growth ambitions of female entrepreneurs is contingent on the context in which the firms operate. The economic agents (i.e., entrepreneurs) should be regarded as social actors. Social actors can be understood and interpreted only if we position them within an institutional framework and social networks, and not just as "atomized decision-makers maximizing their utilities" (Aeeni, Motavaseli, Sakhdari, & Saeedikiya, 2019).

Specifically, we argue that regional context can have a moderator role on the innovation-ambition link in female entrepreneurs due to two mechanisms: first, capitals necessary for females' entrepreneurial performance are context-specific. It means that female entrepreneurs in different regional contexts access to varying levels of social, human, financial, and psychological capital necessary for their entrepreneurial success. Second, the level of institutional support for growth-oriented female entrepreneurship is context-dependent, i.e., in each context, embedded institutions such as culture, institutional environment (rules of the game), and institutions governing transactions for female entrepreneurship are different. Each of the above two lines of reasoning has been further elaborated below.

Context Dependency of Females' Access to Entrepreneurial Capital

Female entrepreneurs' human, social, and financial capitals necessary for pursuing entrepreneurship are expectedly different in MENA than Nordics. *Entrepreneurial Human Capital,* i.e., entrepreneurs' skills, experience, and education, has been considered as an influential factor in innovation (Darnihamedani & Hessels, 2016; Munjal & Kundu, 2017) and growth ambitions (Capelleras, Contin-Pilart, Larraza-Kintana, & Martin-Sanchez, 2019). However, human capital and its effect can be context-specific (Krueger & Kickul, 2006). In the MENA region, the higher education systems are less productive than the Nordic region in terms of innovation and productive academic entrepreneurship. Expectedly, the productive efficiency or allocative efficiency of human capital is less than the Nordic context. Lack of managerial skills, lack of skilled workers, and limited access to training due to sociocultural and institutional contingencies are from the most critical human capital constraints affecting the growth-oriented or productive female entrepreneurship in the MENA region (Bahramitash & Esfahani, 2016; Welsh, Memili, Kaciak, & Al Sadoon, 2014; Zeidan & Bahrami, 2011). *Social Capital,* i.e., the ties and the relationships in which the entrepreneur and the firm are embedded. Entrepreneurship literature has recognized the role of social networks and connections as an essential aspect of firm success and performance (e.g., Liao & Welsch, 2003). Social networks' structure and content also play a crucial role in determining the productivity of female entrepreneurs' activities (Neumeyer, Santos, Caetano, & Kalbfleisch, 2019; Nziku & Struthers, 2018; Xie & Lv, 2016). However, it has been shown that the pattern of these networks and structures are context-dependent (Batjargal et al., 2019). It has also been shown that the benefit of innovation for growth-oriented entrepreneurial activities such as exporting is embedded in the culture and context in which the firms operate (Ashourizadeh & Schøtt, 2016; Saeedikiya, Aeeni, Motavaseli, & Farsi, 2017; Schøtt & Jensen, 2016). *Financial Capital*, i.e., the financial and monetary resources available to the entrepreneurs for enhancing their entrepreneurial performance. Access to such kinds of resources is sometimes informally embedded in the social networks and sometimes available in formal types such as bank loans or venture capitals. Research shows that financial capital and productive entrepreneurship, such as innovation, are embedded in the networks (Wang & Schøtt, 2020), and the patterns of entrepreneurial networks are different within cultures and contexts (Pellegrini, Saman, Rebhi-Tari, & Petrolo, 2020). There is some evidence showing that in the MENA region, female entrepreneurs face some structural and institutional barriers in accessing financial capital necessary for starting their businesses or boosting their firm performance. For example, in some countries of the MENA region, financial responsibility in the families mostly belongs to the men (Tansel & Kazemi, 2000), and this confines the women's ability to start or develop their businesses (Bastian, Sidani, & El Amine, 2018).

Context Dependency of Institutional Support for Female Entrepreneurship

Embedded institutions, institutional environments, and institutions governing transactions vary in different contexts (North, 1990). Formal and informal institutions interact with female entrepreneurs' agential qualities and resources to affect the scale, intensity, and success of the entrepreneurial behavior (Aeeni et al., 2019). Discussing on the Williamson's (2000) hierarchy of institutions, the effect of institutions on growth-oriented or ambitious female entrepreneurship can be addressed in terms of formal and informal institutional contingencies on entrepreneurial behavior. Accordingly, a positive regulative environment inspires entrepreneurial growth intentions by providing property rights protection (Bowen & De Clercq, 2008; Estrin, Korosteleva, & Mickiewicz, 2013), simplifying regulatory procedures for access to markets, introducing government policies to provide finance and other entrepreneurial support (Wang et al., 2019).

In the MENA region, informal institutions such as culture play a significant role in the presence of females in society and their economic activity (Tansel & Kazemi, 2000). While traditional cultural values support women's participation in traditional activities to contribute to family subsistence, it hinders their freedoms in pursuing opportunity-driven and growth-oriented entrepreneurial goals (Bastian et al., 2018). The acceptance of the status quo characterizes societies with the prevalence of such survival values. Instead, seeking a new status is an attribution of the countries with a prevalence of self-expression and secular values such as the Nordic context (Inglehart & Welzel, 2010). Another aspect of informal institutions' effects on women entrepreneurship is its effect on work–family balance. Socially constructed gender roles are rooted in the cultural system, and this assigns maternal and housework activities to women in the MENA region, rather than business activities outside the home (Tlaiss & Kauser, 2011). In other words, culture mostly recognizes the women as caregivers at home, not breadwinners at the market. They are obliged to meet their home responsibilities other than business activities, and this can discourage their growth-related decisions (Saeedikiya & Aeeni, 2020).

In addition to formal and informal institutions mentioned above, institutions such as corruption, transparency, political stability, governance of market institutions, property rights enforcement, and general level of human development are different among the two contexts. MENA region has been characterized by political instability, wars, high corruption levels (Miller, Kim, & Roberts, 2019), socialist and totalitarian regimes, and low transparency (Kandil, 2009). While the Nordics are located on the other side of the extreme, with high level of intellectual property enforcement and the rule of law (Miller et al., 2019), political stability (Swanson, 2007), innovation-driven economies, highly developed human capital and educational system (Yang & McCall, 2014), and thick institutions supporting innovation and entrepreneurship. Expectedly, such institutional arrangements boost innovation and sustain productive and growth-oriented entrepreneurship.

Accordingly, entrepreneurial activity is context-specific and significantly related to the character of the institutional environment (Hwang & Powell, 2005). These institutional differences may affect entrepreneurial attitudes and growth aspirations negatively because they operate in a weak institutional environment (Estrin et al., 2013) like the MENA region. Having a negative perception of the formal and informal institutional environment can be accounted for the lack of growth aspiration among entrepreneurs (Estrin et al., 2013), and particularly female entrepreneurs (Wang et al., 2019).

Summarizing our discussion on capital differentials in MENA and Nordics and the level of institutional support in the two regions, we argue that capital constraints in the MENA region and low institutional support for female's growth-oriented entrepreneurship (whether embedded institutions or institutional environment) expectedly leads to their underperformance in growth ambitions and causes them to expect less growth out of their innovation as compared to their Nordic counterparts. The hypotheses are formulated as follows:

H2. Female entrepreneurs in the MENA region are less ambitious to grow when compared to their Nordic counterparts.

H3. Region moderates the effect of innovation on growth ambitions, so that female entrepreneurs in the MENA region are less ambitious to grow out of their innovation when compared to their Nordic counterparts. Fig. 19.1 illustrates our hypotheses and effects.

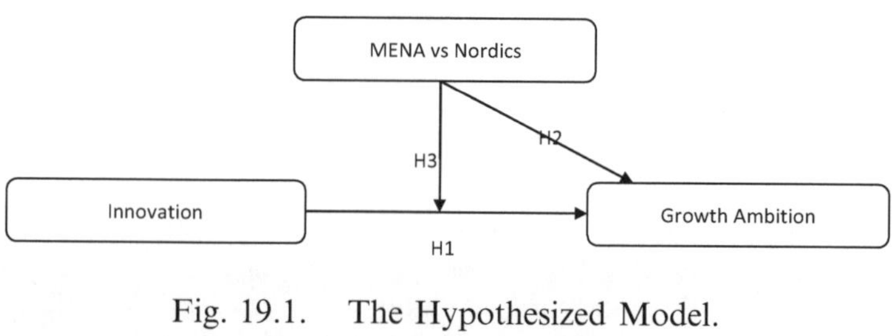

Fig. 19.1. The Hypothesized Model.

Research Method

Data

Data of the current study have been extracted from the Global Entrepreneurship Monitor (GEM). GEM annually conducts two surveys, namely, Adult Population Survey (APS) and National Expert Survey (NES). As a consortium operating in different countries, GEM members annually select to participate in the annual surveys or not. In this study, the authors have used APS survey data to investigate the interrelations between innovation, growth ambition, and institutional context.

Sample

The sample of this study has 4,048 total early-stage female (TEA) entrepreneurs (including nascent businesses and baby businesses aging less than 42 months) operating in the following countries in MENA and Nordic regions from 2001 to 2015: Algeria, Egypt, Ethiopia, Ghana, Jordan, Iran, Israel, Kuwait, Libya, Morocco, Palestine, Qatar, Saudi Arabia, Syria, Tunisia, Turkey, and Yemen. The data of the MENA region have been compared to the data of Nordic countries, including Finland, Denmark, Sweden, Norway, and Iceland.

Variables and Measurements

Innovation, growth, ambition, and the region have been operationalized as follows:

Innovation: The data of three variables, including product innovation, process innovation, and competition, have been used to make a single index of innovation. Each of these variables has been measured in the APS survey of GEM as follows:

Product innovation: *Do all, some, or none of your potential customers consider this product or service new and unfamiliar? Respondents report the level of product innovation within their company on a three-point scale from one to 3 (one denotes the lowest level).*

Process innovation: *Have the technologies or procedures required for this product or service been available for less than a year, or between one to five years, or longer than five years? Respondents report the level of process innovation within their company on a three-point scale from one to 3 (one denotes the lowest level).*

Competition: *Right now, are there many, few, or no other businesses offering the same products or services to your potential customers? Respondents report the level of competition in the market for their product or services on a three-point scale from one to 3 (3 denotes the lowest level).*

Growth Ambition: Has been operationalized using ambition in employing the staff in the next five years, considering the current number of employees. This has been done by subtracting the number of current employees of the firm from the number of expected employees in the next five years. To reduce the skewness of the data, a natural logarithm has been taken. Since the logarithm of zero has not been defined, the number 1 has been added to the current and expected number of employees. Doing so, the formula for calculating growth ambitions of entrepreneurs has been:

Growth ambition = LN (number of employees in the next five years +1) – LN (number of employees in the time of survey +1).

Region: A dummy variable was made to measure regional effects on innovation and growth ambition. The countries in the MENA region are coded 1 and in the Nordic region are coded 0.

Control Variables

To control the effect of possible intervening variables, in the current research, the impact of several variables have been controlled. Table 19.1 summarizes these variables.

Analytical Strategy

This study considers the interaction effects of the variables in different levels. Therefore, a HLM approach has been used to analyze the variables' effect. HLM is similar to multiple-regression analysis in which the impact of independent and control variables can be investigated on dependent variables. However, using

Table 19.1. Control Variables.

Variable	Description
Age	The logarithm of the age of the female entrepreneurs plus one.
Education	Education measured in years.
Self-efficacy	Dichotomous: 1 if self-efficacious, 0 if not.
Risk-willingness	Dichotomous: 1 if risk-willing, 0 if averse.
Firm age	The logarithm of the firm age plus one.
Firm size	The logarithm of the number of owner/managers plus employees.
Opportunity-alertness	Dichotomous: 1 if alert, 0 if not.
Knowing entrepreneurs	Dichotomous: 1 if she knows someone who has started his/her own business, 0 if not.
Entrepreneurs' motivation	Dichotomous: If opportunity driven = 1, necessity driven = 0.

the HLM has the advantage of using the interaction of the variables in different levels of analysis.

Results

In this section, the authors first describe the sample by reporting the mean and the standard deviation for each variable, along with a correlation analysis of the variables. Then, the results of hypotheses testing will be provided.

Sample Description

describes the sample characteristics, including mean, standard deviation of the variables, and the correlation between the study variables.

The Results of Hypotheses Testing

Hypothesis 1 predicted a significant positive effect of innovation on shaping the growth ambitions of female entrepreneurs in our sample. Data analysis indicated that as it was hypothesized, innovation plays a significant role in shaping the growth ambitions of female entrepreneurs ($\beta = 0.089$, p-value < 0.05). In other

Table 19.2. Sample Description and Correlation between Variables.

Variables	**Mean**	**Std.**	**Innovation**	**Growth Ambition**	**Region**
Innovation	1.57	0.525	1	0.133**	0.068**
Growth ambition	0.88	1.113	0.133**	1	0.057**
Region[a]	0.79	0.4050	0.068**	0.057**	1
Age	35.77	10.80	−0.044**	−0.022	−0.228**
Education	11.65	4.14	0.038*	0.126**	−0.203**
Self-Efficacy	0.85	0.361	0.029	0.001	0.016
Risk-willingness	0.74	0.441	0.044**	0.027	−0.072**
Firm age	1.13	1.54	−0.146**	−0.360**	0.020
Firm size	4.46	47.52	0.015	−0.110**	0.007
Opportunity alertness	0.67	0.471	0.101**	0.041**	−0.073
Knowing entrepreneurs	0.70	0.457	0.036**	0.018	−0.059**
Motivation[b]	0.60	0.489	0.059**	0.077**	−0.162**

Notes: [a]Middle East = 1; Nordic countries = 0. [b]Opportunity = 1; Necessity = 0. *significant at $p < 0.05$; **significant at $p < 0.01$.

Table 19.3. Growth Ambition Affected by Innovation and Region.

Variables	Model 1	Model 2	Model 3
Innovation	–	0.089*	0.451#
Region[a]	–	0.031	0.691#
Innovation*Region	–	–	−0.445**
Age	0.004*	0.004*	0.004*
Education	0.034**	0.034**	0.034**
Self-Efficacy	−0.026	−0.023	−0.018
Risk-willingness	0.045	0.044	0.046
Firm age	−0.239**	−0.235**	−0.236**
Firm size	−0.004**	−0.004**	−0.004**
Opportunity alertness	0.084*	0.079	0.079
Knowing entrepreneurs	0.0381	0.037	0.038
Motivation[b]	0.156**	0.154**	0.155**

Notes: [a]Middle East = 1, Nordic countries = 0; [b]opportunity driven = 1, necessity driven = 0, # direct effect was not tested *significant at $p < 0.05$; **significant at $p < 0.01$.

words, the more the innovation by the female entrepreneurs of our sample, the greater the growth ambition.

In Table 19.3, Hypothesis 2 predicted a significant effect of region on growth ambitions of female entrepreneurs in the way that the authors hypothesized that in the Middle East region, the women entrepreneurs are less ambitious to grow as compared with their counterparts in the Nordic region ($\beta = -0.44$, p-value < 0.05).

Hypothesis 3 predicted that the benefit of innovation for shaping the growth ambitions of female entrepreneurs is contingent on the role of context in which they operate, so that the women entrepreneurs in the Nordic context expect more growth out of their innovation as compared with their counterparts in MENA region. The results of hypothesis testing confirmed this hypothesis, indicating that as compared to MENA, in the Nordic region, female entrepreneurs are more ambitious out of their innovation and expect to employ a higher number of people in their next five years.

Discussion

Growth aspiration may significantly depend on gender, with women entrepreneurs generally pointing at lower growth ambitions than men (Autio & Acs, 2007). Hence, the literature on growth aspirations among women entrepreneurs and business growth in women-owned firms is expanding. However, there are still gaps in the knowledge base regarding this theme (Bulanova, Isaksen, & Kolvereid, 2016). We know little about the reasons why many women entrepreneurs are reluctant to business growth. Since there is a lack of knowledge concerning the key issues that determine women entrepreneurs' aspirations, we investigated the impact of the institutional environment on the growth ambition of female entrepreneurs in MENA versus Nordic regions. This study contributes to the literature as a reply to call for further studies on female entrepreneurs' growth ambitions, especially considering the institutional environment (Davis & Shaver, 2012; Wang et al., 2019). However, previous studies have revealed that female entrepreneurs experience a lower level of growth than their male counterparts, but they did not explain how this underperformance happens. Hence, we investigated the impact of institution environments, i.e., MENA region versus Nordic region, on the relationship between female entrepreneurs' innovation and their growth ambitions in the sample of GEM's data collection.

We test three related hypotheses regarding female entrepreneurs' growth ambition. First, we hypothesize that the innovative performance of female entrepreneurs influences their growth aspirations. Second, we test the proposition that female entrepreneurs in the MENA region have less growth aspirations than their counterparts in the Nordic region. And third, institutional context, i.e., MENA versus Nordic, mediates the relationship between female entrepreneurs' innovation performance and their growth aspiration.

Statistical analyses for Hypothesis 1 showed that female entrepreneurs with more innovative activities have more aspiration to grow. This finding is aligned with the literature (Amorós et al., 2019; Poblete, 2018) arguing that the entrepreneurs' expectancy from innovation outcomes, especially business growth through expanding sales, profit, or employment, may reinforce female's growth aspiration. Access to a competitive position higher than competitors and improving performance through innovation convince female entrepreneurs to pursue innovative-related activities and practices (McKelvie, Brattström, & Wennberg, 2017).

Statistical analysis for Hypothesis 2 showed that the regional environment (i.e., MENA vs. Nordic) has a significant influence on the female entrepreneurs' growth aspiration. The institutional constraints exposed by female entrepreneurs in the MENA region through influencing their access to critical capital hinder their aspiration toward growth. Lack of an entrepreneurial-oriented educational system, developed capital market, entrepreneurial-friendly regulations, and more critical, antientrepreneurship culture and norms negatively affect their entrepreneurial perception toward feasibility and desirability of growth. Culture and social norms in the MENA region have a decisive impact on female entrepreneurship by producing discrimination against women and their seeming deficiencies in entrepreneurial qualities (Chappell & Waylen, 2013). As a result, these gender stereotypes undermine women entrepreneurs' aspiration to engage in high-growth entrepreneurship (Sweida & Reichard, 2013).

Statistical analysis for Hypothesis 2 showed that institutional context moderate the influence of female entrepreneurs' innovation on growth ambition. It means that female entrepreneurs in the MENA region, influenced by institutional context, are less benefited from their innovative activities toward growth aspiration. This finding can be explained through two critical arguments. First, formal institutional inefficiencies in the MENA region, i.e., lack of property rights protection, difficulty in access to markets, labor, loans, subsidies, ineffective educational system, nonsupportive entrepreneurial policies limit female entrepreneurs from achieving critical financial (Bastian et al., 2018), human (Zeidan & Bahrami, 2011) and social capital (Saeedikiya & Aeeni, 2020). These limitations weaken the capability of innovation and its subsequent outcomes. Second, informal institutions, i.e., MENA specific culture and norms, dictate some kinds of anti-entrepreneurial beliefs to female entrepreneurs. So that female entrepreneurs in this region are more risk-averse, are less self-confident about their entrepreneurial potential, and feel less independent under the men's influence (Ahmad, 2011). Hence, female entrepreneurs feel that they do not have the necessary requirements for conducting innovative activities and utilizing their subsequent outcomes. So under such stereotypes, the aspiration to grow will not be emerged and developed.

Limitations of the Study and Suggestions for Future Studies

The findings of this study are not without limitations. First, the implications of growth ambitions were discussed solely in relation to employment growth, while in the literature, growth measures through different indicators, e.g., sale, profit, or employment (Beier & Wagner, 2017). Hence future research should apply more appropriate indicators to measure growth and growth aspiration. Second, growth aspiration is influenced by different factors in different levels of analysis. In this study, we solely focused on context, especially institutions. Considering the interactive and cocreative nature of entrepreneur and context (Aeeni et al., 2019), future research should, therefore, include individual factors as well as business environment factors simultaneously. (Bulanova et al., 2016). Third, the influence of the institutional environment is explored without separating the impact of formal and informal institutions. Hence, future scholars should explore the separate but complementary or substitutive effects of formal and informal institutions on growth aspiration, primarily through exploratory qualitative research. As a whole, women's participation in high-growth firms constitutes a recent and necessary research demand. However, to our best knowledge, research on high-growth expectation entrepreneurship from a gender perspective is scarce, and expanding this research stream would be a promising way to extend our knowledge on female growth-oriented entrepreneurship.

References

Aeeni, Z., Motavaseli, M., Sakhdari, K., & Saeedikiya, M. (2019). Extending the potential of Baumol's entrepreneurial allocation theory. *Journal of Entrepreneurship in Emerging Economies*, *11*(3), 416–435.

Ahmad, S. Z. (2011). Evidence of the characteristics of women entrepreneurs in the Kingdom of Saudi Arabia: An empirical investigation. *International Journal of Gender and Entrepreneurship*, *3*(2), 123–143.

Aksoy, H. (2017). How do innovation culture, marketing innovation and product innovation affect the market performance of small and medium-sized enterprises (SMEs). *Technology in Society*, *51*(4), 133–141.

Amorós, J. E., Poblete, C., & Mandakovic, V. (2019). R&D transfer, policy and innovative ambitious entrepreneurship: Evidence from Latin American countries. *The Journal of Technology Transfer*, *44*(5), 1396–1415.

Arroyo, M. R., Fuentes, M. D. M. F., & Jiménez, J. M. R. (2016). An international study of the factors explaining high-growth expectation in new ventures: A gender perspective. *Revista brasileira de gestão de negócios*, *18*(60), 171.

Ashourizadeh, S., & Schøtt, T. (2016). Exporting embedded in culture and transnational networks around entrepreneurs: A global study. *International Journal of Business and Globalisation*, *16*(3), 314–334.

Asiedu, E., Kalonda-Kanyama, I., Ndikumana, L., & Nti-Addae, A. (2013). Access to credit by firms in Sub-Saharan Africa: How relevant is gender?. The *American Economic Review*, *103*(3), 293–297.

Autio, E. (2005). Global entrepreneurship monitor (GEM)-2005 report on high-expectation entrepreneurship. University of Illinois at Urbana-Champaign's Academy for Entrepreneurial Leadership Historical Research Reference in Entrepreneurship.

Autio, E., & Acs, Z. J. (2007). Individual and country-level determinants of growth aspiration in new ventures. In *Proceedings of the Babson conference on entrepreneurship research madrid*, Spain.

Autio, E., & Acs, Z. (2010). Intellectual property protection and the formation of entrepreneurial growth expectations. *Strategic Entrepreneurship Journal*, *4*(3), 234–251.

Autio, E., & Sapienza, H. J. (2000). Comparing process and born global perspectives in the international growth of technology-based new firms. In P. D. Reynolds, E. Autio, C. G. Brush, W. D. Bygrave, S. Manigart, H. J. Sapienza, & K. G. Shaver (Eds.), *Frontiers of entrepreneurship research* (pp. 413–424). Babson Park, MA: Babson College.

Bahramitash, R., & Esfahani, H. S. (2016). Women's economic role in the MENA region: Growth and equality through female-Owned SMEs. In R. Bahramitash & H. S. Esfahani (Eds.), *Political and socio-economic change in the Middle East and North Africa* (pp. 155–190). New York, NY: Palgrave Macmillan.

Bastian, B. L., Sidani, Y. M., & El Amine, Y. (2018). Women entrepreneurship in the Middle East and North Africa: a review of knowledge areas and research gaps. *Gender in Management: International Journal*, *33*(1), 14–29.

Batjargal, B., Webb, J. W., Tsui, A., Arregle, J. L., Hitt, M. A., & Miller, T. (2019). The moderating influence of national culture on female and male entrepreneurs' social network size and new venture growth. *Cross Cultural & Strategic Management*, *26*(4), 490–521.

Baum, J. R., Locke, E. A., & Smith, K. G. (2001). A multidimensional model of venture growth. *Academy of Management Journal*, *44*, 292–303.

Bausch, A., & Rosenbusch, N. (2005). Does innovation really matter? A meta-analysis on the relationship between innovation and business performance. In *Babson College Kaufman Foundation Entrepreneurship Research Conference*, Babson, MA, June 9–11.

Beier, M., & Wagner, K. (2017). What determines the growth expectations of early-stage entrepreneurs? Evidence from crowdfunding. *International Journal of Entrepreneurship and Small Business*, *31*(1), 12–31.

Belchior, R. F., & Liñán, F. (2017). Individual and cultural values as psychosocial cognitive antecedents and moderators of entrepreneurial intentions. In S. C. Santos, A. Caetano, C. Mitchell, H. Landström, & A. Fayolle (Eds.), *The emergence of entrepreneurial behavior: Intention, education and orientation* (pp. 66–87). Cheltenham: Edward Elgar Publishing.

Bogatyreva, K., Edelman, L. F., Manolova, T. S., Osiyevskyy, O., & Shirokova, G. (2019). When do entrepreneurial intentions lead to actions? The role of national culture. *Journal of Business Research*, *96*, 309–321.

Bowen, H. P., & De Clercq, D. (2008). Institutional context and the allocation of entrepreneurial effort. *Journal of International Business Studies*, *39*(4), 747–767.

Bravo-Biosca, A. (2011, December). A look at business growth and contraction in Europe. In *3rd European conference on corporate R&D and innovation CONCORD-2011*, Seville.

Bulanova, O., Isaksen, E. J., & Kolvereid, L. (2016). Growth aspirations among women entrepreneurs in high growth firms. *Baltic Journal of Management*, *11*(2), 187–206.

Cai, L., Liu, Q., Zhu, X., & Deng, S. (2015). Market orientation and technological innovation: The moderating role of entrepreneurial support policies. The *International Entrepreneurship and Management Journal*, *11*(3), 645–671.

Capelleras, J. L., Contin-Pilart, I., Larraza-Kintana, M., & Martin-Sanchez, V. (2019). Entrepreneurs' human capital and growth aspirations: The moderating role of regional entrepreneurial culture. *Small Business Economics*, *52*(1), 3–25.

Castaño, M. S., Méndez, M. T., & Galindo, M. Á. (2016). Innovation, internationalization and business-growth expectations among entrepreneurs in the services sector. *Journal of Business Research*, *69*(5), 1690–1695.

Chappell, L., & Waylen, G. (2013). Gender and the hidden life of institutions. *Public Administration*, *91*(3), 599–615.

Claude-gaudillat, V., & Quélin, B. V. (2006). Innovation, new market and governance choices of entry: The internet brokerage market case. *Industry & Innovation*, *13*(2), 173–187.

Cliff, J. E. (1998). Does one size fit all? Exploring the relationship between attitudes towards growth, gender, and business size. *Journal of Business Venturing*, *13*, 523–542.

Darnihamedani, P., & Hessels, J. (2016). Human capital as a driver of Innovation among necessity-based Entrepreneurs. *International Review of Entrepreneurship*, *14*(1), 1–23.

Davidsson, P. (1991). Continued entrepreneurship: Ability, need, and opportunity as determinants of small Firm growth. *Journal of Business Venturing*, *6*(6), 405–429.

Davis, A. E., & Shaver, K. G. (2012). Understanding gendered variations in business growth intentions across the life course. *Entrepreneurship: Theory and Practice*, *36*(3), 495–512.

Delmar, F., & Wiklund, J. (2008). The effect of small business managers' growth motivation on firm growth: A longitudinal study. *Entrepreneurship: Theory and Practice*, *32*(3), 437–457.

Dutta, D. K., & Thornhill, S. (2008). The evolution of growth intentions: Toward a cognition-based model. *Journal of Business Venturing*, *23*(3), 307–332.

Estrin, S., Korosteleva, J., & Mickiewicz, T. (2013). Which institutions encourage entrepreneurial growth aspirations?. *Journal of Business Venturing*, *28*(4), 564–580.

Fairlie, R. W., & Robb, A. M. (2009). Gender differences in business performance: Evidence from the characteristics of business owners survey. *Small Business Economics*, *33*(4), 375–395.

Foroudi, P., Jin, Z., Gupta, S., Melewar, T. C., & Foroudi, M. M. (2016). Influence of innovation capability and customer experience on reputation and loyalty. *Journal of Business Research*, *69*(11), 4882–4889.

Gaglio, C. M. (2004). The role of mental simulations and counterfactual thinking in the opportunity identification process. *Entrepreneurship: Theory and Practice*, *28*(6), 533–552.

Gilbert, B. A., McDougall, P. P., & Audretsch, D. B. (2006). New venture growth: A review and extension. *Journal of Management*, *32*(6), 926–950.

Gundry, L. K., & Welsch, H. P. (2001). Te ambitious entrepreneur: High growth strategies of women-owned enterprises. *Journal of Business Venturing*, *16*(5), 453–470.

Hechavarria, D., Bullough, A., Brush, C., & Edelman, L. (2019). High-growth women's entrepreneurship: Fueling social and economic development. *Journal of Small Business Management*, *57*(1), 5–13.

Henrekson, M., & Johansson, D. (2010). Gazelles as job creators: A survey and interpretation of the evidence. *Small Business Economics*, *35*(2), 227–244. doi: 10.1007/s11187-009-9172-z

Hermans, J., Vanderstraeten, J., van Witteloostuijn, A., Dejardin, M., Ramdani, D., & Stam, E. (2015). Ambitious entrepreneurship: A review of growth aspirations, intentions, and expectations. In A. C. Corbett, J. Katz, & A. McKelvie (Eds.), *Entrepreneurial growth: Individual, firm, and region* (Vol. 17, pp. 127–160). Bingley: Emerald Group Publishing Ltd. doi:10.1108/S1074-754020150000017011

Hwang, H., & Powell, W. W. (2005). Institutions and entrepreneurship. In S. A. Alvarez, R. Agarwal, & O. Sorenson (Eds.), *Handbook of entrepreneurship research: Disciplinary perspectives* (pp. 201–232). New York, NY: Springer.

Inglehart, R., & Welzel, C. (2010). Changing mass priorities: The link between modernization and democracy. *Perspectives on Politics*, *8*, 551–567.

Jennings, J. E., & Brush, C. G. (2013). Research on women entrepreneurs: Challenges to (and from) the broader entrepreneurship literature?. *The Academy of Management Annals*, *7*(1), 663–715.

Jiao, H., Koo, C. K., & Cui, Y. (2015). Legal environment, government effectiveness and firms' innovation in China: Examining the moderating influence of government ownership. *Technological Forecasting and Social Change*, *96*, 15–24.

Kandil, M. (2009). Determinants of institutional quality and their impact on economic growth in the MENA region. *International Journal of Development Issues*, *8*(2), 134–167.

Krueger, N. F., & Kickul, J. (2006). *So you thought the intentions model was simple? Cognitive style and the specification of entrepreneurial intentions models*. Paper presented at the USASBE Conference, Tucson, AZ.

Leckie, C., Nyadzayo, M. W., & Johnson, L. W. (2018). Promoting brand engagement behaviors and loyalty through perceived service value and innovativeness. *Journal of Services Marketing*, *32*(1), 70–82.

Liao, J., & Welsch, H. (2003). Social capital and entrepreneurial growth aspiration: A comparison of technology- and non-technology-based nascent entrepreneurs. *The Journal of High Technology Management Research*, *14*(1), 149–170.

Lichtenstein, B. (2000). Self-organized transitions: A pattern amid the chaos of transformative change. The *Academy of Management Executive*, *14*(4), 128–141.

Maxfield, S. (2007). 3 The entrepreneurship gender gap in global perspective: Implications for entrepreneurship education and programming. In A. Fayolle (Ed.), *Handbook of research in entrepreneurship education* (Vol. 2, pp. 40–51). Cheltenham: Edward Elgar.

McEvily, S. K., Eisenhardt, K. M., & Prescott, J. E. (2004). Te global acquisition, leverage, and protection of technological competencies. *Strategic Management Journal*, *25*(8–9), 713–722.

McKelvie, A., Brattström, A., & Wennberg, K. (2017). How young firms achieve growth: Reconciling the roles of growth motivation and innovative activities. *Small Business Economics*, *49*(2), 273–293.

Miller, T., Kim, A. B., & Roberts, J. M. (2019). *Index of economic freedom*. Washington, DC: The Heritage Foundation.

Munjal, S., & Kundu, S. (2017). Exploring the connection between human capital and innovation in the globalising world. In S. Kundu & S. Munjal (Eds.), *Human capital and innovation* (pp. 1–11). London: Palgrave Macmillan.

Neumeyer, X., Santos, S. C., Caetano, A., & Kalbfleisch, P. (2019). Entrepreneurship ecosystems and women entrepreneurs: A social capital and network approach. *Small Business Economics*, *53*(2), 475–489.

North, D. (1990). *Institutions, institutional change and economic performance*. Cambridge: The University Press.

Nziku, D. M., & Struthers, J. J. (2018). Female entrepreneurship in Africa: Strength of weak ties in mitigating principal-agent problems. *Journal of Small Business and Enterprise Development*, *25*(3), 349–367.

OECD. (2017). *Entrepreneurship at a Glance 2017*. Paris: OECD Publishing.

Pellegrini, M. M., Saman, D., Rebhi-Tari, I., & Petrolo, D. (2020). A Contextualization study of entrepreneurial networks. *European entrepreneurship research and practice: A Multifaceted effort towards Integration of different perspectives*, *55*.

Poblete, C. (2018). Growth expectations through innovative entrepreneurship. *International Journal of Entrepreneurial Behavior & Research*, *24*(1), 191–213.

Rauch, A., & Frese, M. (2007). Let's put the person back into entrepreneurship research: A meta-analysis on the relationship between business owners' personality traits, business creation, and success". *European Journal of Work & Organizational Psychology*, *16*(4), 353–385.

Saeedikiya, M., & Aeeni, Z. (2020). Innovation and growth ambition of female entrepreneurs: A comparison between the MENA region and the rest of the world. *MENA Journal of Cross-Cultural Management*, *1*(1), 7–19. doi:10.1504/MJCCM.2020.10031020

Saeedikiya, M., Aeeni, Z., Motavaseli, M., & Farsi, J. Y. (2017). The effect of innovation on growth aspirations and internationalization in firms: Africa compared to the Protestant Europe. In *20th international scientific conference–Enterprise and competitive environment*, Brno (pp. 753–762).

Schøtt, T., & Jensen, K. W. (2016). Firms' innovation benefiting from networking and institutional support: A global analysis of national and firm effects. *Research Policy*, *45*(6), 1233–1246.

Shepherd, D. A., Wennberg, K., Suddaby, R., & Wiklund, J. (2019). What are we explaining? A review and agenda on initiating, engaging, performing, and contextualizing entrepreneurship. *Journal of Management*, *45*(1), 159–196.

Shirokova, G., Tsukanova, T., & Morris, M. H. (2018). The moderating role of national culture in the relationship between university entrepreneurship offerings and student start-up activity: An embeddedness perspective. *Journal of Small Business Management*, *56*(1), 103–130.

Sipola, S. (2015). *Understanding growth and non-growth in entrepreneurial economies. Analysis of startup industries and experimental winner generation in Finland, Israel and Silicon Valley*. Doctoral Dissertation. University of Oulu, Oulu. Retrieved from http://urn.fi/urn

Stenholm, P. (2011). Innovative behavior as a moderator of growth intentions. *Journal of Small Business Management*, *49*(2), 233–251.

Swanson, E. (2007). *World development indicators 2007* (No. 54166, pp. 1–430). Washington, DC: The World Bank.

Sweida, G. L., & Reichard, R. J. (2013). Gender stereotyping effects on entrepreneurial self-efficacy and high-growth entrepreneurial intention. *Journal of Small Business and Enterprise Development*, *20*(2), 296–313.

Tansel, A., & Kazemi, A. (2000). Educational expenditure in the Middle East and North Africa. *Middle Eastern Studies*, *36*(4), 75–98.

Terjesen, S., Bosma, N., & Stam, E. (2016). Advancing public policy for high-growth, female, and social entrepreneurs. *Public Administration Review*, *76*(2), 230–239.

Terjesen, S. A., & Lloyd, A. (2015). The 2015 female entrepreneurship index. Kelley School of Business Research Paper No. 15–51.

Tlaiss, H., & Kauser, S. (2011). The importance of wasta in the career success of Middle Eastern managers. *Journal of European Industrial Training*, *35*(5), 467–486.

Wallin, A., Still, K., & Henttonen, K. (2016). Entrepreneurial growth ambitions: The case of Finnish technology startups. *Technology Innovation Management Review*, *6*(10), 5–16.

Wang, J., Li, Y., & Long, D. (2019). Gender gap in entrepreneurial growth ambition. *International Journal of Entrepreneurial Behavior & Research*, *25*(6), 1283–1307.

Wang, D., & Schøtt, T. (2020). Coupling between financing and innovation in a startup: Embedded in networks with investors and researchers. *The International Entrepreneurship and Management Journal*. doi:10.1007/s11365-020-00681-y

Welsh, D. H., Memili, E., Kaciak, E., & Al Sadoon, A. (2014). Saudi women entrepreneurs: A growing economic segment. *Journal of Business Research*, *67*(5), 758–762.

Welter, F., Baker, T., & Wirsching, K. (2019). Three waves and counting: The rising tide of contextualization in entrepreneurship research. *Small Business Economics*, *52*(2), 319–330.

Wiklund, J., Davidsson, P., & Delmar, F. (2003). What do they think and feel about growth? An expectancy-value approach to small business Managers: Attitudes toward growth. *Entrepreneurship: Theory and Practice*, *27*(3), 247–270.

Wiklund, J., Patzelt, H., & Shepherd, D. (2009). Building an integrative model of small business growth. *Small Business Economics*, *32*(4), 351–374.

Wiklund, J., & Shepherd, D. (2003). Knowledge-based resources, entrepreneurial orientation, and the performance of small and medium-sized businesses. *Strategic Management Journal*, *24*(13), 1307–1314.

Wiktor, R., & laguna, M. (2018). Dimensions of entrepreneurial success: A multilevel study on stakeholders of micro-enterprises. *Frontiers in Psychology*, *9*, 791–802.

Williamson, O. E. (2000). The new institutional economics: Taking stock, looking ahead. *Journal of Economic Literature*, *38*(3), 595–613.

Xie, X., & Lv, J. (2016). Social networks of female tech-entrepreneurs and new venture performance: The moderating effects of entrepreneurial alertness and gender discrimination. *The International Entrepreneurship and Management Journal*, *12*(4), 963–983.

Yadav, V., & Unni, J. (2016). Women entrepreneurship: Research review and future directions. *Journal of Global Entrepreneurship Research*, *6*(1), 12.

Yang, L., & McCall, B. (2014). World education finance policies and higher education access: A statistical analysis of world development indicators for 86 countries. *International Journal of Educational Development*, *35*, 25–36.

Zeidan, S., & Bahrami, S. (2011). Women entrepreneurship in GCC: A framework to address challenges and promote participation in a regional context. *International Journal of Business and Social Science*, *2*(14), 100–107.

Chapter 20

Empowering Women through Microfinance Banks in Rural Areas of Pakistan

Salman Bashir Memon and Claire Seaman

Abstract

Women entrepreneurs are considered here as a backbone of economic growth and development. This research is conducted to explain the role of microfinance banks in women's financial, socioeconomic, and political empowerment. The sample was gathered from the customers of microfinance banks operating in the specific areas of Sukkur, Pano Aqil, and Khairpur districts of Sindh province. Women perception about the microfinance bank was found to be positive as they give positive feedback about the banks. According to the findings, limited knowledge about business and financial matters make it highly challenging for women entrepreneurs to start and run business smoothly. However, most of the women are living separate with their husbands, and due to more children, women enjoy freedom of mobility.

Keywords: Women empowerment; developing country; microfinance banks; rural areas; women/female entrepreneurship; poverty alleviation

Introduction

Women consist almost half of the population of Pakistan, and majority of them are living under the burden of poverty but contribute substantially to the development of nation. The opportunities and access to the resources among males and females differ all over the world but are more common in underprivileged developing countries. For instance, the rate of female proprietorship in Pakistan is the world's lowest percentage which is just 1% contrasted with 21% of male proprietors. According to the World Bank's survey, in Pakistan, the rate of female contribution in entrepreneurship is less than 12%, whereas this rate is above 18% in South Asia and worldwide it is 34%. Out of these, just 6% firms cover major part of female proprietorship that is almost half of the average

The Emerald Handbook of Women and Entrepreneurship in Developing Economies, 391–408
Copyright © 2021 by Emerald Publishing Limited
All rights of reproduction in any form reserved
doi:10.1108/978-1-80071-326-020211020

of South Asia, that is, 11% (https://www.thenews.com.pk/print/243346-World-Bank-says-Pakistan-positiom-most-minimal-among-nations-with-ladies-business-people).

However, the number of women entrepreneurs is increasing because of the awareness that they can do much more than taking care of their households and children. Unfortunately, women in Pakistan are still deprived of basic rights as education, freedom, authority, and due to some so-called religious and cultural values, the skilled and capable women forcefully excluded from the economic activities. The lack of financial and institutional assistance is a key factor contributing in disempowerment along with lack of mobility, education, and gender discrimination.

A large number of women are significantly engaged in economic activities, and access to financial resources to avail existing opportunities is sporadic. For instance, the women in rural areas are very skilled and hardworking, but they deprived of knowledge and funds to utilize their potential. Although the total percentage of female microfinance borrowers in Pakistan is less than 25%, the World Bank report revealed that Pakistan is most progressive in the environment of microfinance. In this regard, the microfinance institutions are considered as helping hands in terms of expanding the associate benefits, so that they can take required investment decisions. Microfinance institutions issue small loans for business, health, and education, and accept small deposits, insurance in order to reduce poverty from the country and to increase the standing of women in the society. In addition, microfinance institutions are specially backed by government for poverty alleviation, and it provides skill-based training, motivation, and helps to understand the ideas and concepts that increase the empowerment among them. It is considered that economic prosperity leads to social, political, education, and psychological welfare that leads to development.

As per the "Global Findex" published report of the World Bank, a total of 7% Pakistani females had a financial services account as compared to 77% in India, 36% in Bangladesh, and 58% in Kingdom of Saudi Arabia (KSA). South Sudan was the only country that performed more awful in this than Pakistan. For realizing maximum advantage, female entrepreneurs need to be acknowledged and be accessible to the credit facilities, insurance, reserve funds, and transfers. Likewise, it was revealed that microfinance lending facilities are mostly inaccessible to the unmarried and single female entrepreneurs because they are viewed as high risk borrowers. Moreover, strict procedures and requirements for getting loans are also enforced by the microfinance facilities that for female are much harder to complete on their own. Also, in order to meet their criteria for securing loans, around 68% female borrowers are required to have authorization of any relative male.

A research was conducted by *The British Journal of Education, Society & Behavioral Science* for investigating the gender-based obstacles that impede the female proprietors to enter in the mainstream of proprietorship in Pakistan. This study was published in the year 2012 and was conducted in the Pakistan's four major cities of Punjab province namely, Sialkot, Multan, Faisalabad, and Sargodha in the time frame of six to 8 months. The results of this research indicated that issues such as family pressure, mobility limitations, credit unavailability, absence of good mentors and exemplars, constrained decision-making, gender inequality, and male-dominated markets are the main obstructions in the path of female proprietorship in Pakistan. In the mid-1990s, Pakistan appeared on the charts of microfinance institutions, yet it did not showed much progress until 2001. In that year, the central bank of Pakistan (State Bank of Pakistan; SBP) enforced a microfinance ordinance under which it was made essential that the concerned sectors must have to be regulated as well as the institutions must be registered officially. From that time, 10 of the microfinance banks along with many nongovernmental organizations (NGOs) have been working in Pakistan all over. As indicated by the most recent statistics by the "NGO Pakistan Microfinance Network," around five million estimated individuals out of nearly 200 million populations borrow 170 billion rupees in account of microloans. But, the Pakistan Microfinance Network (PMN) reported 25% penetration rate of microfinance sector could not weigh much in comparison with the total credit arrangement of about 15 trillion rupees of commercial banking industry.

In Pakistan, the microfinance banks and institutions usually follow a model of self-sustainability, and they normally charge interest rates in between 0 and 28%. Also, only 40000 rupees is the average size of microloan, and according to the economic specials, this size is too low for making and that is the reason that this industry of our country is not really having an effect over mitigating the nation from its poverty rate of almost 40%. As per, Yasmin Zaidi, the director of Center of Gender and Policy Studies, highlighted that, "the average size of loan to women is 15,000 ($142) to 25,000 ($237) rupees." It was further added that, "Most are in the 5,000 ($47) to 10,000 ($95) category. What is a woman expected to do with that? Can you really set up a business? Seeing the fallout in both India and Bangladesh, microfinance practitioners in Pakistan say they have taken a more regulated and enterprise-focused approach".

In addition, Ghalib Nishtar, president and CEO of Khushhali Microfinance Bank, said that "Ours was, I think, a very structured and regulated model, which meant that we had to look at all aspects of the business that we were undertaking, targeting the right people, reaching out to them, looking at child protection, and other areas which are part of any mature banking industry." He also gave 30 billion rupees to its six hundred thousand borrowers. In 2012, the Central Bank of Pakistan (SBP) has also initiated an exclusive bureau for all the information regarding microfinance loans which also permitted the microfinance institutions to monitor the outstanding credits of different clients and debtors.

However, according to the financial specialists, the main concerns of the microfinance industry in Pakistan have been changed due to the intervention of SBP. It just empowered for-profit banks and commercialized the microfinance banks. Ghazal Mir, assistant professor at Lahore University of Management Sciences (LUMS), told Al Jazeera that, "The central banks are not interested in poverty alleviation or women's empowerment." She further added that, "their activity is money related arrangement – to guarantee the soundness of the monetary business of the nation and improve the effort of the establishments that they are liable for, All in all, they set an altogether different tone for the microfinance business," and she questioned, "Is microfinance enabling ladies? The ladies' monetary investment rate in Pakistan is 26%". Roshaneh Zafar, CEO and originator of Kashf Foundation, said that, "Microfinance is tied in with giving substantial answers for ladies to transform them." As indicated by a United Nations (UN) report of the year 2016, around 5% of overall microfinance credit arrangement in Pakistan goes to female borrowers, which in total construct 50% of the overall clients. Plus it was found in the World Bank report of 2012 that, ranging from 50% to 70% of these microloans given to females in our country might be really utilized by their male relatives. Also at times, female borrowers require a male guarantor to be qualified for a credit over a particular limit.

However, other than providing finance, some introductory business management courses are also offered by a few institutions that are endeavoring to embrace an overall integrated approach. Likewise beside the financial trainings, gender-based trainings are also provided by the organizations like Kashf, mostly to the villagers via theaters and TV screens to cope up with the ongoing matters such as females' education, rape, honor killings, domestic violence, and abuse. As per Zaidi, "When they [women] are told about their legal rights, are connected to organizations that work on physical education or give various skills training, that will have a higher return." Further added that, "A female's contribution to the household earnings also increases her importance in a patriarchal and conservative society like Pakistan, also the middle-class and the lower-middle class women will work because there is an economic necessity, so their household contribution must be valued." She proceeded to state that, "They [women] have to go to great lengths, and their male family members will support them in going to these great lengths." Back to grassroots, females can be the primary bread earners of the family.

Microfinance and Women Empowerment Nexus

Empowerment is related with the improvement of human being and the ways they accomplished to achieve difficult task and included themselves in the establishment of reducing the burden (Haugh & Talwar, 2016). There is a positive relationship between microfinance and female's empowerment. For example, Saha and Sangwan (2019) recognized that microfinance program positively affects female's empowerment, and the biggest part of the current studies advances a vision that microfinance contributes toward female's empowerment. Banerjee and Jackson (2017) reported that microfinance is beneficial in decreasing the helplessness of poor people through resource creation, wage utilization, and enabling females by giving them control over assets. Also expanded self-regard and learning, likewise for the most part discover optimistic effect in this association. An essential capacity of presenting women loan is to upgrade their monetary status that empowers women to procure additional pay through which they can increase more monetary independence (Rahman, 2019). The empirical studies have very different results about microfinance and women empowerment. For instance, studies report positive results measured through indicators like women access to consumption, health care, and improved decision-making, and other studies report negative results defined as male control over microfinance loan and women business, and women face heavier workload and responsibilities and confinements in low productivity business (Fernando, 2006). Therefore, the role of microfinance for female empowerment remains highly controversial (Nawaz, 2019). Because only considering outcomes, it is also necessary to examine the processes and understandings regarding the microfinance practices (Kabeer, 2017). However, the 'women empowerment' is a strategy for changing mindsets in order to allow the person to change the environment. Since, it can be done by altering the overreaching conditions faced by females in rural areas (Hinrichsen, 2018; Fig. 20.1).

Theoretically, the concept of strengthening is slightly changed from financial point of view, e.g. authority, autonomy, self-assurance, knowledge for one's authority as it has various implications from individual and group perspective. For instance, social strengthening increases level of literacy and awareness (Patel, 2019) and enhances autonomy and power in females and makes them strong female to become able to take decisions independently (World Bank, 2002a). According to Elson, 2000, women strengthening means their decision of negotiating power and creating dignity and assurance in choice making. Whereas microfinance is a source which could bring change and effect presence of middle-class females as it is a tool for female strengthening that increases the living standard and survivability (Khadka, 2015). Generally, the small businesses such

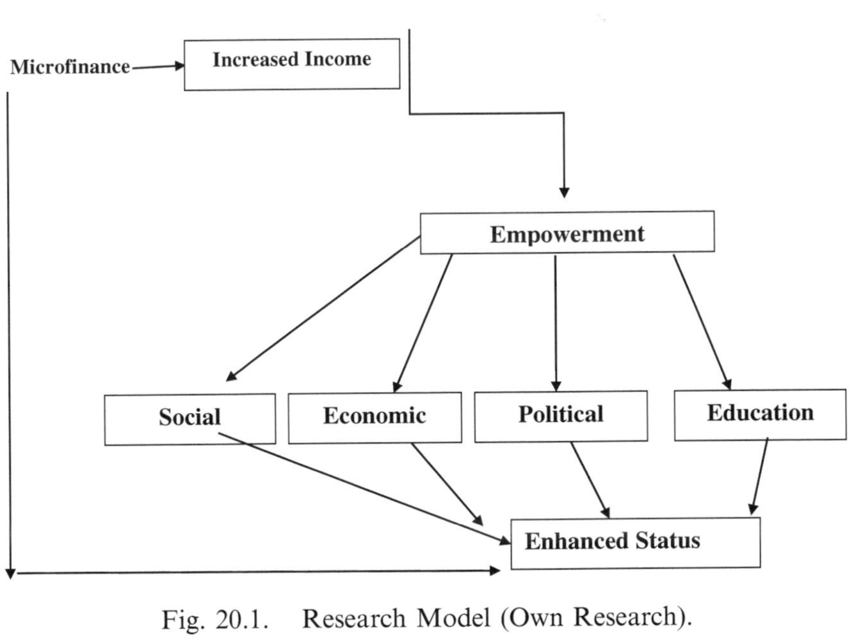

Fig. 20.1. Research Model (Own Research).

as, crafting work is common in interior Sindh started with the help of microfinance loans (Muhammad, McElwee, & Dana, 2017). Microfinance has ability to strengthen female, and then, they could develop social and economic variable microfinance programs that can reduce the poverty and strengthen the females in the society (Chaudhry, 2018).

Economic Empowerment

Women access to credit augment capability to make decisions about consumption, household welfare, and investment in economic activities improve the employment opportunities for women and strengthen females financially (Fletschner & Kenney, 2014). The ability to maintain microfinance semiannually may increase credit rating which can be used to expand commercial activity for further benefits (Akhter & Cheng, 2020). Put differently, utilization of credit for the commercial activity could "equal the initial investment" (benefit expansion). The reserved funds and benefits from its commercial work as a salary to females enabled them financially. Likewise, they utilize benefits or use funds to grow their commercial activities.

Well-Being

The microfinance accessibility to poor females is a source of economic empowerment, enables them to spend on familial well-being, and allows them to control over family decisions (Shaheen, Hussain, & Mujtaba, 2018). In addition, the access to microfinance might enhance the prosperity of the family and aiding husbands financially for the purpose of children's education and future planning (Shepherd, Parida, & Wincent, 2020). Additionally, the reserve funds or friendly loan decrease their financial weakness.

Social and Political Empowerment

Microfinance improves female's capacity to secure their individual and aggregate gender passion at families, group, and microfinance (Ajwani-Ramchandani, 2017). For example, female's engagement in economic activities results in improved skills, mobility, and access to knowledge, and supports network that leads to social and political change (Jayachandran, 2019). In addition, women financial independence is crucial for family prosperity which advances dignity and confidence. The financial autonomy is also a factor that creates an impetus to increase influence on the community and local politics during elections.

Microfinance and Women Household Financing

Microfinance helps women to start their business, and there exists a positive relationship between women's control over business and their empowerment. For instance, women's financial support to the household increases their responsibility and creates an equilibrium between workload and equality in decision-making (Jackson & Slater, 2017). The main purpose of microfinance banks is to empower females in multiple ways such as economics, sociocultural, interpersonal, legal, political, and psychological (Malhotra & Schuler, 2005).

Women Empowerment

Empowerment refers to the improvement in social and physical circumstances together with choice making capability and control over assets and method for availing these advantages (Kapoor, 2019). However, empowerment has many aspects which are linked with internal emotions than external attitude and it continuously changes. Specifically, the women empowerment approach in the less developing nations is different (Chaudhry & Nosheen, 2009). For instance, the World Bank (2002b) portrays these approaches as a quality, asset(s), autonomy, access to essential people needs, battle for privilege, and basic leadership ability. In addition, empowerment might be characterized as an expansion in female obligation that improves living standard, financial well-being on consistent premise (Katenda, 2017). Comparatively, females are socially and financially abused. This makes the females rebutted and less engaged. For instance, the inconsistency with respect to autonomy, well-being, decision-making, and socio-political support based on gender is common in various regions of developing countries (Doyle and Alfonsi, 2018). Pakistan is a men-dominated society where females are underprivileged. However, women empowerment can be expanded by helpful projects initiated by the concerned steps such as women access to knowledge and literacy (Najaf, Sultana, & Jamal, 2019; Safavian & Haq, 2013). For example, Khan and Noreen (2012) led their research in District Bahawalpur, Pakistan and found that use of microfinance in various salary generating projects enable women financially. Financial empowerment makes females effective at different levels as van Eerdewijk et al. (2017) indicated that empowerment involves an improvement in belongings, societal well-being, and change in the ideas. Put differently, a woman can be empowered if she has an autonomy of using her nonphysical and also physical assets for development of herself and closed ones. Therefore, practical awareness, suitable guidance, and primary education deemed essential for women empowerment. This is one of the most excellent techniques to address poverty issues of poor women of rural areas.

Microfinance and Women Empowerment

Over the years, lots of actions have been made by numerous nongovernment and government organizations to sustain empowerment of females. Generally, a lack of resources is one of the major constraints in the economic development and women empowerment. Specifically, microfinance strategies boost investment and add revenue creating services for the middle-class people and make sure straight returns (Bent, 2019). Majority of the females are encouraged to increase their income as a source to enhance their status within the family. As compared to male member, most of females pursued to improve status through right of mobility in terms of decision-making and earning power parity. The small and medium-sized enterprise (SME) sector usually offers a good opportunity to kick-start small-scale businesses. The economic rationale for giving money to female is that female new investor; small-scale investor is on the top. The small-scale funds provided to females by microfinance organizations enhanced the status of females in the society and also enhanced status in the family (Rahman, 2019). Microfinance is one of these options which are intended to offer credit to females in order to improve living standard and self-assurance and furtherance in nutrition. Almås, Armand, Attanasio, and Carneiro (2018) indicated that microfinance banks is a prime factor of women's empowerment as empowerment is about altering control and preferences, but its capability can be explained in the view of the social and economic environment that influence women's decision. Getting money in their hands increases women's self-worth and self-assurance within society. Microfinance is indispensable to female's nascent family earnings. Greguletz, Diehl, and Kreutzer (2019) indicate that females who successfully utilize their approved load and invest in an efficient business program eventually pay off financially sooner or later. However, a potential cultural barriers slab their ability to stretch complete concentration on revenue generation from small businesses mainly due to narrow mindedness and family commitments. Albeit, the loan approved for women to generate income usually consumed by spouse or other male member could not deliver a tangible outcome to women to change their and children's lives (Kodikara, 2018).

The finest example is Bangladesh's Grameen Bank that provides loan to the majority of female microfinance customers (Rahman, 2001). The gender difference in developing nations slows down economic development and growth. The nation with a high level of gender discrimination experiences a poor standard of livelihood. Financial help to female has, therefore, been initiated to reaffirm the confidence of females about their financial matters. Females are working to earn little amount of income to meet bread and butter. Most of Nicaragua's females are not financially strong to amplify their income. However, the research conducted in Nicaragua revealed the clearer difference in the living standard after taking microcredit (Skarlatos, 2004). The microcredit improved female's monetary power by getting loan without any security and thus enhanced their self-assurance, family, household relationship, and recognition in society. In the case of Pakistan, microfinance banks charging interest rates normally between 0 and 28% and are yet to follow a more regulated and focused methodology. Therefore, the microfinance sector, thus, needs to improve and implement reforms in the business environment of small entrepreneurs is extremely important. Although, Pakistan's microfinance segment has not been capable to build up as efficiently as other nations but the intervention of the SBP can change the institutional priorities through commercializing and reassuring for-profit banks.

Boachie (2016) revealed that microfinance banks offer loan to poor population, mainly those existing in suburb areas. This is main tool for reducing poverty from country, progress in health, education, and improvement in living standards.

Microfinance particularly focuses women by providing help, for their own small-scale business. A microfinance strategy raises talent among women customers and develops their living standard inside the households which, in turn, strengthens families. Maria & Gobbi (2005) in her study discovered the effect of microfinance on the strengthening of female in the two nations i.e. Nepal and Pakistan. She implied the variation of social change held between the females of these two nations due to microcredit. She explored that due to microfinance services in Pakistan, some females enjoy choices concerning their small business. In this manner, they gain self-assurance and create household relationship and increment in earning. Furthermore, it found that providing loans to the female is safe as compared to male, but is not riskless to provide loan to both genders, either male or female. Microfinance has clear effect on building social assets (Garikipati, 2017). Many females understand that their value and dignity is changing toward advancement due to microfinance and microenterprise improvement. Males are giving more value to female's choices. Microfinance creates them to be able to eliminate illiteracy, concerning their part in the society, and they could achieve a lot of sociological increment i.e. choice making control, learning, self-esteem health etc.

Likewise, microcredit has an important effect on the livestock, living standard, and the economic environment of suburb females. They also revealed that microcredit had a negative effect on collected amount and accommodation. It was seen that the major hindrances to female's strengthening were less income, and females have more opportunity of jobs and approach to take loan from microfinance banks. Provision of financial services made it feasible for the underprivileged people to boost their family revenue and create resources. These individuals could create planning for their future and education of their offspring (Riaz, Muhammad, Ashraf, & Zafar, 2012).

Methodology

This research concentrates on the microfinance banks and its effect on women empowerment. The survey was conducted directly from poor working women especially from the female customers who landed loan from microfinance banks in last 3 years. The data were gathered from three microfinance banks i.e. Khushhali Microfinance Bank Limited (https://khushhalibank.com.pk/), FINCA Microfinance Bank (http://pakistan.finca.org/), and U Microfinance Bank Limited (https://ubank.com.pk/) are providing loans to the poor women as a seed money to start businesses in the rural areas of Sukkur and Pano Aqil districts. The data were gathered in the field survey by directly interacting with the respondents to know the feedback of women toward microfinance banks.

Questionnaire Instrument

For the purpose of this study, questionnaire was adopted from previous research. However, some changes were made in demographic data except it, original questionnaire was used for the purpose of survey.

Empowerment

The word strengthening literally means to develop "religious, social, political and economic strength of people. It develops self-confidence of the women in her ability" (Mohammad & Mohammed, 2007). A number of researchers have defined it in different ways, "cultural, social, and political environment factors of strengthening are control over assets, autonomy, strength, independence, deserve to vote, living as per own particular desire, confidence and choice making ability" (Mohammad & Mohammed, 2007). "Strengthening can be family, societal, individual, monetary, and taking sides."

Economic Empowerment

Economic strengthening refers to increment in budgetary assets, increment in salary, investment funds, expenses, and own business females are economically strengthened when they have control over assets, consume according to their choice, and saving women work and struggle for their family and children and take financial decisions on the basis of remaining budget (Mohammad & Mohammed, 2007).

Societal and Political Empowerment

Societal strengthening refers to the knowledge among females who are misbehaved and insulted by males especially in interior Sindh, and due to the lack of education in interior Sindh, males are unequipped to speak reasonably with their wives (Mohammad & Mohammed, 2007). Political strengthening is related to the participation of individual in various political parties, choice making, motivation, and independence. Other factors included in social strengthening are increment in taking pregnancy control pills and involvement in various social and political issues.

Familial Empowerment

Familial strengthening refers to strengthening with the family, understanding between spouse and wives, less responsibility from household work, honor from spouse and in-laws, gap while giving birth to children, use of pregnancy control pills, choice-making ability within the family, and honor from the husband.

Personal Empowerment

Personal strengthening refers to women self-respect, self-actualization, life with status and dignity, choice making authority, and the ability to be strong within the family and within females. In case she strengthened, it shows that she has skills and abilities to make decision of her household and business, which she started to run up.

Data Analysis

The survey was conducted from the women who belonged to extremely poor families of rural areas. Mostly, rural women are dependent on microfinance loans for their small business activities such as stitching of cloths and quilts, embroidery work of bedsheets and Sindhi, Balouchi suits, crafting of cultural caps, and Aplic work on bedsheets and quilts, etc. The need of advance payment is the only source for purchasing of raw material. These women are expert and skillful in artwork and generate more income whatever amount they borrow from microfinance banks. In most of the cases, profit margin is double or sometimes triple of invested amount. The borrowed loan is the only source of their income for family support to survive in deprived conditions.

The primary data of this study were largely (i.e., 70.7%) taken from women respondents who belong to rural areas of Sindh province. The largest portion of respondents (i.e., 56%) are between age bracket of 39 years and above, 27.3% are between 32 and 38 years age, 14% are between 31 and 24 years age, and 2% are between 24 and 18 years age. It indicates that elder family member especially women realizes responsibility to support family by taking more loans for running business. The largest portion of rural areas women, i.e., 90.7% are married women, whereas the largest percentage, i.e., 81.3% is completely illiterate as compared to 12.7% respondents with basic primary education. The low or no literate women are coerced to borrow loan from microfinance banks to survive and manage daily bread and butter by working within the boundaries of their home. The maximum percentage (i.e., 94.7%) women in rural areas are engaged in the crafting of various handmade products for which they are taking loans for the purchase of raw material, and majority of them (i.e., 90.7%) are working like this from last 8 years.

In terms of income, the largest portion of women (i.e., 94.7%) bring in income less than 45,000 because they work in crafting which is not as expensive as compared to other work but they are compelled to do so even when they are paid low wages. In addition, the largest portion (i.e. 80.7%) are living separately because living in joint system creates problem; so, to avoid these problems, they live separate, and lowest portion of the respondent (i.e., 19.3%) prefers to live combined.

In terms of total number of children, a total of 18% women are the mother of one to two children. Whereas, a largest percentage (i.e., 34%, 3–4, and 22%, 5–6) had more children to feed, raise, and educate. However, the majority of these women respondents, i.e., 83.3% are poor, 9.3% economically active, and 7.3% very poor. Usually, the birth rate in rural women is more because they are unaware about the pregnancy control and family planning education.

The data analysis result indicates that 83.3% women are poor, 9.3% economically active, and 7.3% very poor. The only source of living is to work on borrowed money as 93.3% of the women had taken group loan from microfinance banks. The largest portion, i.e., 95.3% borrowed an enterprise loan, 2.7% new business loan, and 2% borrowed loan for agriculture to cultivate their soil. According to the results, 25.3% women took loan one time, 18.7% women took loan 2 times, 17.3% women took loan 3 times, 11.3% women took loan 4 times, and 10.7% took loan 5 times.

Family support especially attitude of in-laws is an important indicator in the rural areas which impact women's decision to take loans for business ventures. For example, 66% of the family accepted this with resistance as compared to 33.3% cases in which they approved but not happy. The spouse reaction is also not encouraging as a total of 90.7% accepted with resistance. Interestingly, 90% of the husbands accepting business mainly because of their unemployment or low income level and need support to generate more income to survive in society. This also implies that rural women usually change their husbands' mind and get their agreement to borrow loan to render services and help her family. Therefore, the majority of the husbands, i.e., 96.7% showed less quarrels with their wives because the decision of borrowing loans is taken with permission of in-laws with an agreement. However, attitude of the in-laws toward their daughter-in-law is more accepting in case of borrowing loan (i.e. 98%) because daughter-in-law in rural areas is considered as a chief member of a family. The rural areas' women are independent of making decisions. A major portion, i.e., 79.3%, indicates that they are taking decision independently and do not ask anybody when taking loan. However, the lowest portion of the respondent, i.e., 19.3%, takes decisions together with their husbands because they understand that the husband is the pillar of their family.

Results also show 64.7% of the respondents hold the view that they become central to decision-making within the family, as compared to the 27.3% of the women, who hold the view that their husband gives more respect which is the reason that makes them stronger. A total of 80.7% women become self-confident after taking loan because the financial assistance they have make them self-confident to tackle pressure of in-laws and spouse. The financial stability is also one of the reasons to gain economic independence because women are not dependent on family or spouse. Therefore, the largest portion of the women (i.e., 67.3%) gained more respect in the neighborhood due to the financial stability and receive maximum orders of crafting cloths from neighbors. Besides more respect, the largest percentage, i.e., 80%, is in gaining more freedom of mobility because they have to go market for purchase of raw material while their husbands are busy in their own work. However, the seed money obtained through microfinance loan can be used for lifesaving by managing daily bread and butter but may not be used for the improvement of the living standard. A total of 52.7% of the women respondent do not improved their living standard because women are working for the survival of their lives not for the improvement of the their living standard. In contrast, 47.3% of total respondents somehow improves their living standard and managed to buy basic amenities such as refrigerator and television etc. Likewise, 72% of women respondents yet to take decision on house repair because borrowed amount merely be used on the growth of crafting cloths. The borrowed amount from microfinance banks were also used as a saving for their daughter's marriage. Nearly, 88.7% women respondents take decision of saving borrowed money especially for their daughter's marriage because they do not have other means of saving to upkeep this expenditure. The borrowed money sometimes was used in the purchase of gold jewelry for their daughter's marriage. However, only 5.3% of the total women respondents were using this money for the purchase of gold or jewelry.

The respondents also opine that they take decision on the issues related to children's education. A total of 89.3% believed this to be true that education is an important element, and without this, children could suffer the same problems of poverty and unemployment. However, the women in the rural areas do not have authority to decide on their family size and the number of children they want to give birth.

The birth spacing related data indicate that only 28% women respondents decided the birth spacing especially due to the economic reasons. However, the majority of the respondents do not have authority to decide the spacing between the next pregnancies after giving a birth. Interestingly, 73.3% of total rural women did not use any contraceptive to prevent pregnancy and believe that children are Allah's blessing. Healths were by far an important category that needs preference. The rural women also financially support family members' when medical treatment is needed. Only 12.7% of total sample was incapable to support because of limited income. Despite having financial difficulties, rural women meet the nutritional requirements of their family. Almost, 97.3% of total respondents earnestly take care of their family's nutritional requirements.

Discussion

This research was conducted in Sukkur and Pano Aqil districts in which illiteracy rate is comparatively higher than the rest of Pakistan. The data analysis result indicates the significant relationship between microfinance banks and women empowerment. Most of the women respondents aged between 32 and 39 years. Majority of women are married as compared to widows, i.e., 91% married. Most of the women are illiterate because they belong to rural areas, but those who are primary school educated belong to the rural area (70.7%) and urban area (29.3%); the ratio of rural area is more because they need more loan to continue their "crafting work," and 95% women are rendering services, means they are doing work within the house. The basic nature of work is "crafting work." The duration of work starts from when these women were children and used to work with raw materials of their mother's finance but now they can borrow loan themselves. Income of respondent is less than 45,000 because these women are paid less wages by the market their husbands sell stock in huge quantity in a market where marketers pay them less amount. Most of the women living separate with their husbands make up 81%, while only 19% women live together with their in-laws and most of the women have two to four children or five to six children due to the fact that with more children women enjoy better freedom of mobility. As most of the women belong to a low class and are considerably poor, microfinance banks always give loans in a group, the nature of which loan is categorized as an enterprise loan, because of the services these women rendered here. A maximum of 10 times a loan can be taken by one respondent, with the minimum being once.

In-laws' reaction is positive toward their daughters-in-law because they are supporting their families. Spouses' reaction is also positive toward their wives, the same attitude as of the in-laws, being more accepting in case of taking loans from microfinance banks and there is less domestic abuse of their wives. The majority of the women take decision independently, and some of them take decision together with their husbands. Most of the women become strong after taking loans, the reason of which becomes central to their decision-making within the family and garner respect from their husbands. After taking a loan, women become more self-confident, gain more respect in the family (80%), gain economic independence in the family (80%), gain more respect in the neighborhood (67.3%), gain better understanding with their spouses (74%), and a majority of them do not reduce their household burden of work because they utilize their money for crafting work and gained freedom of mobility, but many of them do not see any improvement in their living standard while only some do. Decision to purchase any piece of land or repair home is less because it is utilized for the crafting work, Decision to work for earned income is 80% do not purchase gold and jewelry for their family 95% decision on saving and borrowing is more percent 89% this amount they utilize for their daughter's marriage husband discuss issues borrowing money with their wives, 70% women do not have their own income because they are not employed women do not spend for their family because they do not have their own income most of the women get husband's income in their hands most of the husbands discuss with their wives when spend income 75%.

Most of the women take decisions on the problems of children's education. Most of them do not decide on the number of children. They do not decide on spacing on their family members. They decide on the treatment of their family members because they care about the health of their family members. Most of the women do not use contraceptive as they think children are a blessing of the Almighty Allah. Most of the women take care of the nutritional requirements of their family. Most of the women visit their relatives and friends with permission. They do not have any association with political parties because they are uneducated women who participate in voting (83%). Husbands do not impose political ideas on women because they are not interested in political ideas and they do not participate in group meetings and social events.

Key Findings

- Husbands support their wives in borrowing loan from microfinance banks.
- Reaction of in-laws is positive toward women because they support their family to survive in the society.
- Women are playing role to literate their children.
- Women are not interested in political parties and public relation.
- Women are busy in crafting work to generate income for their family.
- Women become independent to take decision for their family.

Conclusion

The quantitative data give important outcomes to make sure the incident of women empowerment, as women become older they bring more change in their life to strengthen themselves. As past research suggested, women brought dignity to their families, and they have the skills to solve family problems a well as their own personal problems as they become more efficient with age. Married females are strong, efficient, and effective in their working ability as they have the skills to run household responsibilities and build up relationships, create pleasant family environments because their spouses are happy with them and their participation in microfinance; unmarried females are independent and are free to spend on themselves and have great choices to make decisions for themselves socially, but political strengthening is greater in married women as compared to unmarried women as self-assurance and self-esteem for married females is more as compared to unmarried females. The research explains that children are a source of strength and motivation for females, especially in interior Sindh where women avoid taking contraceptives or leaving a gap between having more children. In fact the more children one had, the more respect, more confidence, more power and authority the women possessed as they became a weapon of sorts for women. In addition, women participate in household expenses consumption according to their will and are not bounded. Practical research shows increment in salary, increment in family expenses, increment in expense on health and literacy, and microfinance bank has a positive effect on the living standard of the women of Sukkur and Pano Aqil districts where they have decision-making power for their families and where they play the role of male and female at the same time. Strengthening of women is strengthening the next generation.

Recommendation

Microfinance is a suitable instrument for strengthening females. Therefore, policy-makers ought to discover the strategies to put resources into human capital while loans should be provided to needy females. It is seen that regular customers of microfinance banks are not only satisfied with the facility of microfinance but they also utilize this loan for crafting work, Aplic work on suits and bed sheets, stitching quilt, stitching suits. The institutes that established microfinance banks should take more efforts to improve the quality of their institute and extend the area to facilitate other regions as well. It is, thus, suggested that microfinance should implement the plan according to the requirements of female customers. For example, loan should be provided to regular customers on easy terms based on their good credit rating. Female strengthening cannot be judged on any overall measuring bar, along these lines it is recommended, to build up excellent standard for improving female strengthening.

References

Ajwani-Ramchandani, R. (2017). Prelims', the role of microfinance in women's empowerment. Retrieved from https://www.aljazeera.com/indepth/features/2017/09/microfinancing-pakistans-women-entrepreneurs-170930112423093.html

Akhter, J., & Cheng, K. (2020). Sustainable empowerment initiatives among rural women through microcredit borrowings in Bangladesh. *Sustainability*, *12*(6), 2275.

Almås, I., Armand, A., Attanasio, O., & Carneiro, P. (2018). Measuring and changing control: Women's empowerment and targeted transfers. *The Economic Journal, 128*(612), F609–F639.

Banerjee, S. B., & Jackson, L. (2017). Microfinance and the business of poverty reduction: Critical perspectives from rural Bangladesh. *Human Relations, 70*(1), 63–91.

Bent, B. B. (2019). The impact of microfinance on poverty reduction and women empowerment. *Rais Collective Volume*, 72.

Boachie, C. (2016). The Effect of microfinance on poverty reduction in developing economies. *Handbook of Research on Social Entrepreneurship and Solidarity Economics*, 240.

Chaudhry, I. S. (2018). Women empowerment and micro finance programmes in Southern Punjab: An empirical study. *Pakistan Journal of History and Culture, 39*(1), 171–183.

Chaudhry, I. S., & Nosheen, F. (2009). The determinants of women empowerment in Southern Punjab (Pakistan): An empirical analysis. *European Journal of Social Sciences, 10*(2), 216–229.

Doyle, T., & Alfonsi, A. (Eds.). (2018). *Women's economic empowerment in the Indian ocean region*. New York, NY: Routledge.

van Eerdewijk, A. H. J. M., Wong, F., Vaast, C., Newton, J., Tyszler, M., & Pennington, A. (2017). *White paper: A conceptual model on women and girls' empowerment*. Amsterdam: Royal Tropical Institute.

Elson, D. (Ed.). (2000). *Progress of the world's women 2000: UNIFEM biennial report*. New York, NY: United Nations Development Fund for Women.

Fernando, J. (Ed.). (2006). *Microfinance. Perils and prospects*. Londres: Routledge.

Fletschner, D., & Kenney, L. (2014). Rural women's access to financial services: Credit, savings, and insurance. *Gender in Agriculture*, 187–208.

Garikipati, S. (2017). The impact of microfinance on poverty alleviation: Making sense of the evidence.

Greguletz, E., Diehl, M. R., & Kreutzer, K. (2019). Why women build less effective networks than men: The role of structural exclusion and personal hesitation. *Human Relations, 72*(7), 1234–1261.

Haugh, H. M., & Talwar, A. (2016). Linking social entrepreneurship and social change: The mediating role of empowerment. *Journal of Business Ethics, 133*(4), 643–658.

Hinrichsen, M. B. (2018). *Living within the narrative of microfinance: Vulnerability. Well-intentioned debt, and the individualization of social problems in quito, Ecuador* (Vol. 38, pp. 31–54). Bingley: Emerald Publishing Ltd.

Jackson, M. A., & Slater, S. (2017). Hidden biases in counseling women: Balancing work and family concerns. In M. Kopala & M. Keitel (Eds.), *Handbook of counseling women* (pp. 340–351). Thousand Oaks, CA: Sage.

Jayachandran, S. (2019). Social norms as a barrier to women's employment in developing countries. Northwestern Working Paper.

Kabeer, N. (2017). Economic pathways to women's empowerment and active citizenship: What does the evidence from Bangladesh tell us?. *Journal of Development Studies, 53*(5), 649–663.

Kapoor, S. (2019). Entrepreneurship for economic and social empowerment of women: A case study of a self help credit program in Nithari village, Noida, India. *Australasian Accounting, Business and Finance Journal*, *13*(2), 123–142.

Katenda, M. V. (2017). *The effect of microfinance institution membership in women empowerment: A case of Sumbawanga municipality*. Doctoral dissertation, The University of Dodoma, Dodoma.

Khadka, N. (2015). *Empowerment of women through microfinance in Jabdi village committee*. Master's thesis, Norwegian University of Life Sciences, Ås.

Khan, R. E. A., & Noreen, S. (2012). Microfinance and women empowerment: A case study of district Bahawalpur (Pakistan). *African Journal of Business Management*, *6*(12), 4514–4521.

Kodikara, C. (2018). Doing this and that: Self-employment and economic survival of women heads of households in Mullaitivu. *Exploring Women's Empowerment*, 380.

Malhotra, A., & Schuler, S. R. (2005). Women's empowerment as a variable in international development. *Measuring Empowerment: Cross-disciplinary Perspectives*, *1*(1), 71–88.

Maria, S., & Gobbi, D. (2005). *Nepal & Pakistan micro finance and microenterprise development: Their contribution to the economic empowerment of the women* pp. 6. 20-25 68. SEED Working Paper No. 69, International Labour Organization, Geneva.

Mohammad, A. K., & Mohammed, A. R. (2007). *Impact of microfinance on living standards, empowerment and poverty alleviation of poor people: A case study of microfinance in the Chittagong district of Bangladesh*. Umeå: Umeå School of Business (USBE).

Muhammad, N., McElwee, G., & Dana, L. P. (2017). Barriers to the development and progress of entrepreneurship in rural Pakistan. *International Journal of Entrepreneurial Behavior & Research*, *23*(2), 279–295.

Najaf, B. D. E., Sultana, H. Y., & Jamal, M. A. (2019). Women empowerment and social change through education: A brief study of Chennai city. *Handbook of research on indigenous knowledge and Bi-culturalism in a global context*, 229.

Nawaz, F. (2019). The paradox of microfinance and women's empowerment. In *Microfinance and women's empowerment in Bangladesh* (pp. 37–54). Cham: Palgrave Pivot.

Patel, M. S. (2019). Education for socio-economic development in changing competitive world. *Education*, *2*(06), 8–21.

Rahman, A. (2001). *Women and microcredit in rural Bangladesh: An anthropological study of Grameen Bank lending*. Boulder, CO: Westview Press.

Rahman, A. (2019). *Women and microcredit in rural Bangladesh: An anthropological study of Grameen Bank lending*. Abingdon: Routledge.

Riaz, A., Muhammad, S., Ashraf, I., & Zafar, M. I. (2012). Role of Punjab rural support program in improving economic conditions of rural women through micro financing. *Pakistan Journal of Agricultural Sciences*, *49*(2), 211–216.

Safavian, M., & Haq, A. (2013). *Are Pakistan's women entrepreneurs being served by the microfinance sector?*. Washington, DC: The World Bank.

Saha, B., & Sangwan, N. (2019). Credit where credit's due: The enabling effects of empowerment in Indian microfinance. *World Development*, *122*, 537–551.

Shaheen, I., Hussain, I., & Mujtaba, G. (2018). Role of microfinance in economic empowerment of women in Lahore, Pakistan: A study of Akhuwat supported women clients. *International Journal of Economics and Financial Issues*, *8*(2), 337.

Shepherd, D. A., Parida, V., & Wincent, J. (2020). Entrepreneurship and poverty alleviation: The importance of health and children's education for slum entrepreneurs. *Entrepreneurship: Theory and Practice*. doi:10.1177/1042258719900774

Skarlatos, K. (2004). Microfinance and women's economic empowerment: Bridging the gap. Wisconsin Coordinating Council of Nicaragua, Working Paper Series (1), 1–60.

World Bank. (2002a). *Empowerment and poverty reduction: A sourcebook*. Washington, DC: World Bank Group.

World Bank. (2002b). 'Social Capital' and 'Social Capital and Gender'. World Bank. Retrieved from http://worldbank.org/poverty/scapital

Index